PRAISE FOR MARK PENDERGRAST'S

For God, Country & Coca-Cola

"In *For God, Country & Coca-Cola*, Mark Pendergrast has written an encyclopedic history of Coke and its subculture, and used Coca-Cola as a metaphor for the growth of modern capitalism itself. His research and storytelling skills are prodigious."   —*Washington Post*

"A meticulously researched history. . . . [Pendergrast] aggressively sets the record straight about the birth of Coke, shattering company myths."
—*New York Times Book Review*

"A detailed and marvelously entertaining history . . . a book as substantial and satisfying as its subject is (at least in nutritional terms) inconsequential."
—*Los Angeles Times*

"Behind the glitz and fanfare, the bubbly brown beverage has had a tortured and controversy-filled history. It is meticulously chronicled in a new account, *For God, Country & Coca-Cola*."   —*The Wall Street Journal*

"A ripping good story of more than a soft drink or a company, this book is about the whole of America. It may be the greatest American story ever."
—*The New York Observer*

"In *For God, Country & Coca-Cola*, author Mark Pendergrast combines lively writing and extensive research to tell the story of the caramel-colored drink that grew into a worldwide corporation and cultural phenomenon. Like its subject, Pendergrast's entertaining book can claim to be the real thing."   —*USA Today*

"The book is full of wonderful stories and tidbits. . . . [W]hen Pendergrast reports the Cokelore he has gathered so assiduously, he is superb."
—*Washington Monthly*

"As Atlanta native Mark Pendergrast tells us in *For God, Country & Coca-Cola*, an obsession with growth has been a company hallmark for most of the past century. Pendergrast's account is a good deal more intriguing than the sanitized corporate history Coke peddles at its World of Coca-Cola museum."   —*Business Week*

"By the time we move on to Coke's globe-drenching present, we have learned to trust Pendergrast's thorough research, lively style, and sense of perspective. [His book] is an epic, unbelievably grand in scope and implication."   —*Valley News*

"It is easy to trivialize soda . . . but as Mark Pendergrast demonstrates, to the people at Coke it is a deadly serious business. . . . He succeeds admirably in demonstrating . . . how Coke conquered the world."
—*Philadelphia Inquirer*

"An excellent and entertaining book! I read this book and simply couldn't put it down! I bought 8 copies of it to give to family and friends as gifts. I'll never look at a Coca-Cola product the same way again. From a business or historical perspective, this is a great read!"
—Amazon customer review

FOR GOD, COUNTRY
&
COCA-COLA

FOR GOD, COUNTRY

&

Coca-Cola

The Definitive History
of the
Great American Soft Drink
and the
Company That Makes It

THIRD EDITION: REVISED AND EXPANDED

MARK PENDERGRAST

BASIC BOOKS
A MEMBER OF THE PERSEUS BOOKS GROUP
New York

Books published by Basic Books are available at special discounts for bulk purchases
in the United States by corporations, institutions, and other organizations. For more
information, please contact the Special Markets Department at the Perseus Books
Group, 2300 Chestnut Street, Suite 200, Philadelphia, PA 19103, or call (800) 810-4145,
ext. 5000, or e-mail special.markets@perseusbooks.com.

Library of Congress Cataloging-in-Publication Data
Pendergrast, Mark.
  For God, country and Coca-Cola : the definitive history of the great American soft
drink and the company that makes it / Mark Pendergrast. — Third Edition: Revised
and Expanded.
    pages cm
  Includes bibliographical references and index.
  ISBN 978-0-465-02917-4 (pbk. : alk. paper) — ISBN 978-0-7867-2332-4 (e-book)
1. Coca-Cola Company—History. 2. Soft drink industry—United States—History.
I. Title.
  HD9349.S634C674 2013
  338.7'663620973—dc23
                                            2012051356

10 9 8 7 6 5 4 3 2 1

~ 1916 ~

Business has its Romance. The inner history of every great business success is just as stirring and fascinating as the most imaginative story ever told. Real success never comes easy. . . . Progress has been achieved only through continual struggle and hard, patient work. It has called for ingenuity and resource of the highest order, the courage that accepted no defeat, the endurance that wore down all opposition, the confidence that overcame every jealous libel.

And such has been the history of Coca-Cola.
—"The Romance of Coca-Cola" (booklet)

~ May 21, 1942 ~

Since 1886 . . . changes have been the order of the day, the month, the year. These changes, I may add, are partly or wholly the result of the very existence of The Coca-Cola Company and its product. . . . They have created satisfactions, given pleasure, inspired imitators, intrigued crooks. . . . Coca-Cola is not an essential, as we would like it to be. It is an idea—it is a symbol—it is a mark of genius inspired.
—Letter from advertising man William C. D'Arcy

~ March 24, 1959 ~

Please, Mr. Kahn, you've written some excellent articles and profiles, but why all this effort spent on Coca-Cola? I can't conceive that it could be interesting to enough people to be worth your using all that paper, all those thousands of words, and hours of labor to write it. In addition, I consider it a most noxious drink.
—Letter to E. J. Kahn Jr. in response to a series
of articles on Coca-Cola in the *New Yorker*

~ July 10, 1985 ~

Why read fiction? Why go to movies? Soft drink industry has enough roller coaster plot-dips to make novelists drool.
—Jesse Meyers in *Beverage Digest* special edition
announcing reintroduction of original Coca-Cola

DEDICATED TO

Irene Lilienheim Angelico and Abbey Jack Neidik,
film documentarians extraordinaire, creators of The Cola Conquest

AND TO THE MEMORY OF

Roberto C. Goizueta, Coca-Cola CEO and missionary,

AND

E. J. Kahn Jr., Coca-Cola chronicler

CONTENTS

PREFACE

This book has been a kind of "roots" project for me. Since both sides of my family lived in Atlanta from the late nineteenth century on, I suppose it was inevitable that Coca-Cola would intersect our lives many times. My paternal grandfather, J. B. Pendergrast, owned a drugstore at Little Five Points, where he regularly served the soft drink to Asa Candler, the first Coca-Cola tycoon. J. B. testified amusingly about Coke's nicknames in an early, important Coca-Cola trial, then invested in the Woodruff Syndicate's takeover of the company in 1919. Unfortunately, J. B. sold the stock a few years later in order to build a house. The most intriguing family story concerns the day young Robert W. Woodruff and his friend Robert W. Schwab discussed Helen Kaiser's allure as they sat outside her home. "Well," Woodruff said, "I think I'll go propose to her right now," awaiting a protest. "Go ahead," Schwab answered, feigning lack of interest. When Woodruff returned a few minutes later, he said, "She turned me down. I guess you'll have to marry her." Schwab did, later becoming my maternal grandfather.

If Woodruff had married her, perhaps I would be a wealthy man today—or I might not be here at all, since Woodruff, who directed Coca-Cola's fortunes from 1923 until his death in 1985, had no children. It's just as well that things worked out the way they did, though, since I've enjoyed taking a more objective view of the Company and its entertaining role in world history. I hope you will, too.

—Mark Pendergrast

Prologue: A Parable (January 1, 1985)

The boss was a very old man, near death. Though his mind still ticked over a lifetime of executive decisions, it was trapped in a decaying body. All of his senses were shutting down. He could see only dimly, and his cigar, a trademark for most of his life, hung unlit from a slack mouth. His hearing, too, had nearly failed, and he seldom spoke in more than a monosyllable.

Robert Woodruff was ninety-five years old, four years younger than the soft drink he had made the world's most well-known, cherished product. For more than sixty years, Woodruff had steered the fortunes of Coca-Cola. Even in these last few years, as he and the drink approached the century mark, his approval had been sought for every major decision in the Company.

A younger man in a pinstripe suit approached the old man's bed. He had come alone to speak with the Boss, asking the attendants to leave the room. He sought the old man's blessing, looked for his benediction on the most revolutionary decision ever to be made at Coca-Cola.

Chemical engineer Roberto Goizueta, the Cuban native who had become the first foreign-born CEO of The Coca-Cola Company, planned to change the formula of the drink just a year short of its hundredth anniversary. Though the man in the pinstripes knew that tampering with the world's most closely guarded secret formula was risky, he had sound business reasons for doing so. Now, he slowly and systematically laid them out for the Boss, practically shouting to make sure that he was heard.

Motionless, Woodruff listened.

The story the younger man told was full of statistics, percentage points, market share analysis, and talk of blind taste tests. But the essential point was simple, and Goizueta repeated it loud and clear: most soft drink consumers preferred the taste of Pepsi to that of Coke. It was a slim margin, but it was there. And no matter how much Coke outspent Pepsi on ads, no matter how great their distribution system, Pepsi's market share kept creeping higher. The competition already sold more in the supermarkets, and it was advancing on Coke's superior fountain and vending sales.

The time had come to modify the taste of Coca-Cola. The drink had been good in its time, but times change, tastes change, industries change, and nothing in the business world is sacred. The chemists at Coke had devised a new formula that consistently trounced Pepsi—as well as Coke—in blind taste tests. Goizueta emphasized that the time was ripe, in fact overdue, for a New Coke. It simply had to be.

Finally, the younger man fell silent, intent on the old man's reaction. The cigar hung unmoved. The eyes glistened. Outside the window, a slight rain fell on the first day of the new year.

1

Woodruff's eyes slowly brimmed; the cigar trembled. In the silence, a grandfather clock ticked off fat, slow seconds. Finally, the Boss sighed. "Do it," he rasped, and his eyes overflowed.

Goizueta smiled. Woodruff had always liked him, had picked him as a successor. The two men used to lunch together; they had a special understanding, a bond. It was important that the Boss give his approval. People said the old man hated change, but Goizueta knew he just needed things explained in their simplest terms. This was just like Diet Coke, and look at how well *that* had done. Goizueta thanked the Boss, said he would be back to see him soon, and left.

Roberto was convincing, not so much by his facts and figures, but by his earnestness. He must be right, but that didn't mean that the Boss had to live to see his sacred formula revised. The old man stopped eating. Two months later, a month before New Coke was made public, Robert Woodruff died. He never knew the uproar that the flavor change was to create. It is not beyond imagination, however, that somewhere in his steadily ticking brain, he guessed.

For three months, the stubborn management at Coca-Cola was besieged daily by thousands of phone calls and hundreds of pounds of letters, all begging for the old drink back. The press was full of outraged reports. While Goizueta waited for the uproar to subside, it only intensified.

It became clear that the Cuban and his management team, his marketing surveys, and his advertising men had miscalculated. Taste wasn't the issue. It didn't matter whether New Coke went down more smoothly.

The letters, oddly reminiscent of those sent to the company by GIs during World War II, clearly spelled out the real issue. Coca-Cola was an old friend, a piece of everyday life, a talisman of America, a kind of icon. But unlike the wartime letters, which expressed heartfelt gratitude, these contained feelings of betrayal:

"Changing Coke is like God making the grass purple."

"I don't think I would be more upset if you were to burn the flag on our front yard."

Roberto Goizueta and his cohorts were taught a quick, incisive business lesson, and they finally capitulated, bringing back the old Coke to a grateful world.

The issue was not taste. The issue was not marketing surveys or focus groups.

The issue was God.

The issue was Country.

The issue was Coca-Cola.

Part I

In the Beginning

(1886–1899)

A hot day in August 1885.*

The tall, bearded old man hesitated before crossing Marietta Street, one of Atlanta's busy thoroughfares. Horses and buggies clattered on the cobblestone; prosperous businessmen hurried past. Elegantly dressed women with parasols strolled to Jacobs' Pharmacy on the corner for an ice cream soda. Newsboys hawked the papers, screaming, "Read all about it! Whisky Ring Fights Sin Tax! Temperance Workers Meet! Anti-Prohibition Speech at Opera House a Flop! Read all about it!"

"I'll take a paper, son." Pursing his lips, temporarily forgetting the busy street, the man read. There was the usual sensationalism. A local suicide. An attempted lynching. The birth of triplets.

Impatiently, he rifled through the paper. Ah, here was an editorial laying into the liquor license. "It is guilty, at the bar of God and humanity, of this great crime: that it creates, fosters, solicits, incites, stimulates, and multiplies intemperance. The open barroom holds the whisky glass to every man's lips at every corner." No doubt about it. Atlanta would go dry; it was only a question of time.

The street cleared momentarily. Folding his paper under his arm, the elderly man crossed the street before another buggy bounced through the intersection. As he put his key into the lock at 107 Marietta Street, a young man briskly lifted his hat on his way by. "Good day, Dr. Pemberton. Hot enough for you, sir?" The old gentleman nodded and smiled. Everyone in Atlanta knew and respected the kindly old patent medicine man, and most took one of his remedies for their cough, dyspepsia, headache, sexual debility, or whatever else ailed them.

As Pemberton entered his laboratory, he looked with satisfaction at his fresh supply of coca leaves, straight from Peru, and at the filtering system he had set up to produce coca extract. He was experimenting with a new concoction, one that he hoped he could sell as a temperance drink and medicine, because the town was in hysteria over the evils of alcohol.

---

* The mini-dramas introducing each section of the book are fictional re-creations of likely events and should be taken as such.

Suddenly Pemberton doubled over with pain. It was his stomach again—heartburn or his ulcer flaring up. His bones ached with rheumatism. Still bent, he fumbled for his secret case in a false-bottomed drawer. Shaking, he filled the hypodermic needle, turned it to his arm, and slowly pushed the plunger. With a deep sigh, he carefully put the needle and materials away and prepared for his experiments.

As he began the experiments that would lead to the invention of Coca-Cola, Dr. John Stith Pemberton was fifty-four years old. He looked at least ten years older. And he was addicted to morphine.

~ 1 ~

Time Capsule: The Golden Age of Quackery

I've been experimenting on a little preparation—a kind of decoction nine-tenths water and the other tenth drugs that don't cost more than a dollar a barrel. . . . The third year we could easily sell 1,000,000 bottles in the United States—profit at least $350,000—and then it would be time to turn our attention toward the real idea of the business. . . . Why, our headquarters would be in Constantinople and our hindquarters in Further India! . . . Annual income—well, God only knows how many millions and millions!
—Colonel Beriah Sellers, in Mark Twain's *The Gilded Age*, 1873

There's no question that The Coca-Cola Company loves its own history. As if to prove the point, in 2007 it spent $38 million on its new Atlanta museum, which indoctrinates over a million Coca-Cola-drenched tourists yearly into the company's high-tech version of its past. The press release for its predecessor called the museum a "fantasyland," and, in more ways than one, it is just that. The red-clad young guides (called "ambassadors") assure visitors, for instance, that Coca-Cola *never* had any cocaine in it.

The museum carries on a long-standing company tradition. The Coca-Cola saga has been reverentially preserved and nurtured over the years. John Pemberton, who invented Coca-Cola in 1886, has been depicted by the Company as a poor but lovable old Southern root doctor who stumbled upon the miraculous new drink. Although Coca-Cola was supposedly born in a humble three-legged kettle in Pemberton's backyard rather than in a manger, the story is treated as a kind of Virgin Birth. Coca-Cola's first archivist, Wilbur Kurtz, described the moment: "He leaned over the pot to smell the bouquet of his brew. Then he took a long wooden spoon and captured a little of the thick brown bubbling contents of the pot, allowing it to cool a moment. He lifted the spoon to his lips and tasted." Pemberton's hard work and perseverance in finding just the right taste finally paid off with a stroke of luck when the syrup was inadvertently mixed with carbonated rather than plain water. The customers loved the effervescent drink and smacked their lips in satisfaction.

From that point on, according to Company legend, the drink's future was assured. Of course, it needed a little help from Asa Candler, who purchased the formula as Pemberton was dying, advertised it widely, and quickly became the wealthiest man in Atlanta. By the early 1900s, the drink's phenomenal rise to fame was repeatedly called the "romance of Coca-Cola."

This official version of events is a myth, however. John Pemberton was not an uneducated, simple root doctor. He did not brew the drink in his backyard. More importantly, far from being a unique beverage that sprang out of nowhere, Coca-Cola was a product of its time, place, and culture. It was, like many other such nostrums, a patent medicine with a distinct cocaine kick.

One element of the myth rings true, however. The chances of Coca-Cola's success were about as remote as Colonel Sellers' "decoction." Twain's passage was an uncannily accurate prophecy of Coca-Cola's future, however. Today, Coke is the world's most widely distributed product, available in more than two hundred countries, more than the United Nations membership. "OK" excepted, "Coca-Cola" is the most universally recognized word on earth, and the drink it characterizes has become a symbol of the Western way of life. How, in a century-plus, has a fizzy soft drink, 99 percent sugar water, attained such an astonishing status? Conditions in late nineteenth-century America largely determined its future.

A NATION OF NEUROTICS

During the Gilded Age, America's metamorphosis from a land of farmers into an urbanized society of mills and factories was arguably the most wrenching in its history. With the Civil War as a catalyst and turning point, industrialization and a virtual revolution in transportation marked the emergence of a distinctively American brand of capitalism—one that idealized individual hustle and relied heavily upon advertising and newspapers to spread its gospel. The railroad became the symbol and engine of powerful change, allowing the creation of national markets for goods.

The pace was so overwhelming that it generated concern over a new disease characterized by neurotic, psychosomatic symptoms. One writer of the era diagnosed it as the fruits of "an industrial and competitive age." George Beard labeled the disease "neurasthenia" in his 1881 book, *American Nervousness, Its Causes and Consequences.** Beard attributed the new malady to the dislocations wrought, both socially and economically, by "modern civilization."

The steam engine, he noted, which was supposed to make work easier, had instead resulted in more frantic lifestyles and in overspecialization, "depressing both to body and mind." In general, Beard noted, overwork, the strain of economic booms and busts, repression of turbulent emotions, and too much freedom of thought contributed to a high state of nerves. Finally, "the rapidity with which new truths are discovered, accepted and popularized in modern times is a proof and result of the extravagance of our civilization."

Coca-Cola emerged from this turbulent, inventive, noisy, neurotic new America. It began as a "nerve tonic" like many others marketed to capitalize on the dislocations and worries of the day. After surviving an early history rife with conflict and

---

* Curiously, to be diagnosed as a neurasthenic was a sign of good breeding and high status. Only those with refined, delicate temperaments or highly charged brains were subject to the high-status disease.

controversy, this lowly nickel soft drink became so much a part of national life that by 1938 it was called "the sublimated essence of America."

The description is still apt. Coca-Cola remains emblematic of the best and worst of America and Western civilization. The history of Coca-Cola is the often funny story of a group of people obsessed with putting a trivial soft drink "within an arm's reach of desire." But at the same time, it is a microcosm of American history. Coca-Cola grew up with the country, shaping and shaped by the times. The drink helped to alter not only consumption patterns but attitudes toward leisure, work, advertising, sex, family life, and patriotism. As Coca-Cola continues to flood the world with its determinedly happy fizz, its history assumes yet more importance.

During the late 1800s, however, no one, including the inventor of Coca-Cola, had such grand visions. Coca-Cola was just one in a flood of other patent medicines foisted upon the public by hopeful marketers during the golden age of quackery.

THE PATENT MEDICINE SHOW

Clever promoters made fortunes in patent medicines.* Popular since the Declaration of Independence, these nostrums were peddled by the pioneers in the field of advertising. Patent medicine ads paid for the rapid growth of the American newspaper, whose columns, even before the Civil War, were half filled by their claims. The period after the war saw an exponential growth in the industry, due partly to wounded veterans who had acquired a self-dosing habit.

There were also other reasons for the spectacular postwar success of patent medicines. The railroad, steamship, telegraph, and other communication revolutions made a national and even international market increasingly viable. Waves of immigrants brought new consumers to the country. The American population grew from fifty million in 1880 to ninety-one million in 1910—and eighteen million of those were immigrants. The newcomers did not have much money, but they would often venture a dollar for a "cure."

Another reason for the boom in self-dosage was that the medical profession had not caught up with the industrial revolution. Many doctors killed as many patients as they cured, so cheap nostrums sometimes provided a safer alternative. Furthermore, there were few doctors in rural areas, forcing the country folk to use patent medicines. Finally, patent medicines were often taken to relieve the symptoms of overeating and poor diet, which went hand-in-hand. Remedies for upset stomachs were the most common class of medicament during the late nineteenth century, which is not surprising, given the starchy diets and heavy meat consumption. Part of Coca-Cola's appeal to Asa Candler, for instance, was that it was supposed to relieve indigestion.

---

* The term "patent medicine" was a misnomer. The more accurate term was "proprietary medicine," because a hopeful inventor would patent the label or trademark of his nostrum, but never its "secret formula." To reveal the ingredients would have ruined the mystique, opened the field for imitators, allowed the public to discover how cheaply the product was produced, and, perhaps most important, it would have revealed the amount of alcohol, narcotic, and/or poisons present.

A TORRENT OF ADS

By the 1880s and 1890s, the amount spent on advertising such tonics and concoctions reached stunning proportions. St. Jacob's Oil spent $500,000 in advertising in 1881. By 1885, some half-dozen nostrum makers were spending over $100,000 annually on ads. Ten years later, *Scientific American* announced that some drug advertisers were spending a million dollars a year, adding that the creator of Carter's Little Liver Pills "cannot spend the money he is making" and that "judicious advertising has made it possible for . . . W. T. Hanson Company [to spend] $500,000 on Pink Pills for Pale People." One promoter noted that "without advertising, I might have made a living, but it was advertising that made me rich, and advertising a very simple commodity at that."

The first national trade magazine for advertisers, *Printer's Ink*, was launched in 1888, just two years after the invention of Coca-Cola. In its fifty-year retrospective issue, the magazine credited the patent medicine industry with first recognizing the importance of trademarks and ubiquitous advertising, adding that "it was not until the twentieth century had fairly begun that manufacturers as a whole were inclined to listen to the broad proposition that advertising as such was a potentially profitable sales tool." One of the reasons that patent medicines could afford such extravagant advertising, of course, was their remarkable profitability. For a dollar, a manufacturer often sold a bottle that cost less than a dime to produce. It was easy for him to see the wisdom of spending another ten cents a gallon on advertising. He had no major capital investment, little overhead, and few employees.

Besides, he knew that, without extensive ads, few would buy his medicines, which were not essential products. He *had* to be a salesman. No wonder the nostrum peddler dominated advertising expenditures during the Gilded Age. Patent medicine makers were the first American businessmen to recognize the power of the catchphrase, the identifiable logo and trademark, the celebrity endorsement, the appeal to social status, the need to keep "everlastingly at it." Out of necessity, they were the first to sell image rather than product. At the same time, the stodgy producers of dry goods or sewing machines, with substantial capital investment and less of a margin, didn't see the need to advertise. It was beneath their dignity, a waste of good money. People needed what they had to sell, and, if they advertised at all, it was simply to list their prices. Besides, the outrageous nostrum ads were giving advertising a bad odor, as *Printer's Ink* pointed out: "Most patent medicine advertising was shamefully and flagrantly disreputable in its fake selling claims. Absolute remedial powers for cancer, consumption, yellow fever, rheumatism and other afflictions were widely claimed for preparations that had no efficacy for even the mildest ailment."

The torrent of ads was not confined to newspapers, however. The cure-all makers flooded the marketplace with all kinds of novelties in order to keep their trademarks highly visible. They specialized in items that got repeated use, such as clocks, calendars, matchbooks, blotters, pocket knives, almanacs, cookbooks, mirrors, or cards. Every time a consumer wanted to know the time or date, light a cigar, or look up a recipe, he or she was confronted with a reminder that Pale Pink Pills were good for the blood or that Coca-Cola relieved fatigue and cured headaches.

Meanwhile, outdoor advertisers strove to outdo one another. Men with sandwich signs walked stiffly by on busy sidewalks. Banners were strung across Main Street. At night, the bill poster plastered every available surface with advertisements, layering over a competitor's work of the night before.

Sign painters were dispatched to paint huge trademarks where travelers were most likely to let their eyes wander. We tend to think of the Victorian era as a gracious period in which nature was unspoiled, but it wasn't unusual for a patent medicine advertiser of the era to clear-cut an entire mountainside so that he could erect a mammoth sign for Helmholdt's Buchu, visible from a train window.

In May of 1886, the very month that Coca-Cola was invented, one writer vividly described the desecration of the landscape, saying that a traveler might admire "the undulating country, breathing Spring from every meadow and grove and orchard"—that is, "if he could see a single furlong of it, without the suggestion of disease." It was not enough, he continued, that fences and sheds were defaced. "Enormous signs are erected in the fields, not a rock is left without disfigurement, and gigantic words glare at as great [a] distance as the eye is able to read them." Viewing "sign overlapping and towering above sign," the revolted traveler "turns away, shuddering, from the sight." Consequently, the critic concluded: "We cannot complain if the intelligent stranger from foreign lands should, instead of 'the scenery,' write 'the obscenery of America.'" One enterprising nostrum maker even offered to help pay for the Statue of Liberty, which was completed in 1886, in return for using the base as a gigantic advertisement.

William James, psychologist and philosopher, reacted violently to newspaper ads when he returned to the U.S. after several years abroad: "The first sight of the Boston *Herald* . . . made me jerk back my head and catch my breath, as if a bucket of slops had suddenly been thrown into my face." In 1894, he wrote a scathing letter to the editor of the *Nation* in which he spluttered in outrage at "this truly hideous feature of our latter-day life," complaining that "this evil is increasing with formidable rapidity. . . . Now [these advertisements] literally form the principal feature of our provincial newspapers, and in many of the 'great dailies' of our cities play a part second only to the collective display of suicides, murders, seductions, fights, and rapes."

James tellingly added that "if a justification of these advertisements be sought, absolutely nothing can be alleged save the claim that every individual has a right to get rich along the lines of his own inventiveness." Most Americans were willing to put up with fraud and hype in the name of individual rights and democracy, particularly if there was money to be made. Even a scoundrel was admirable, if he was rich enough.

THE RIGHTEOUS PURSUIT OF WEALTH

The patent medicine tycoons, along with industrial titans like Andrew Carnegie and Cornelius Vanderbilt, stood at the apex of a new social order. By 1890, there were over four thousand American millionaires, and the number was growing rapidly. Their greatest problem, with no income or corporate tax, became not how to make money but how to spend it. The millionaire was the envied hero of the age, and the great new American religion had a fat dollar sign in front of it. Carnegie himself was busy spreading what he called the "Gospel of Wealth." Russell Conwell, a Philadelphia clergyman and the first president of Temple University, made a tidy living by delivering his "Acres of Diamonds" speech over three thousand times, explaining that God loves those who produce wealth. "I say that you ought to get rich," Conwell told his audiences. "To make money honestly is to preach the gospel."

At the same time, the plight of the poor was becoming increasingly desperate. While the rich industrialists raked in the money, eight-year-olds labored in their factories for ten cents a day. When confronted with the appalling gap between the haves and have-nots, men like Carnegie answered with a modified social Darwinism, piously invoking the "survival of the fittest." Such were the unfortunate but inevitable results of progress. "The contrast between the palace of the millionaire and the cottage of the laborer with us today measures the change which has come with civilization," wrote Carnegie. This situation, he asserted, was "not to be deplored, but welcomed as highly beneficial. It is . . . essential for the progress of the race." Fortunately, Carnegie said, he regarded it as his Christian duty to help lift up the lower classes through wise philanthropy.

This attitude was not limited to Yankees. Mark Twain noted a new breed of Southerner—"brisk men, energetic of movement and speech; the dollar their god, how to get it their religion." Henry Grady, editor of the *Atlanta Constitution* and spokesman of this New South, informed the New England Club in 1886 that "we have wiped out the place where Mason and Dixon's line used to be," and that the "Georgia Yankee" was the equal of the Northerner. One Georgian of the period matched Conwell in exhorting his fellow Southerners to make money their priority: "Let the young south arise in their might and compete with [Yankees] in everything. . . . Get rich! if you have to be mean! The world respects a rich scoundrel more than it does an honest poor man. Poverty may do to go to heaven with. But in these modern times. . . . Get rich!"

Asa Candler, the man who would take Pemberton's Coca-Cola and parlay it into a fortune, was not so blatant, but in his speeches he clearly equated religion, capitalism, and patriotism. Candler's drink, Coca-Cola, came to symbolize that trio. In large measure, Coca-Cola's success stemmed directly from advertising which made it an emblem of the good things in America, a kind of secular communion drink. Like his brother Warren, a Methodist bishop, Asa Candler would send out his own brand of capitalistic missionaries.

By the 1880s, however, most who attempted to make a quick buck through patent medicines were disappointed. Fortunes had indeed been made, and "the spectacle of some of the medicine kings churning about the high seas in their palatial steam yachts" (as one contemporary writer put it) caused an inordinate number of would-be entrepreneurs to test the waters of the trade. In doing so, they usually lost whatever small savings they had.

On April 25, 1886, a *New York Tribune* reporter published a long article describing the saturated market for patent medicines. The "prevailing opinion," he said, was that the nostrum racket was "lucrative above all others" and that all who ventured into the field automatically became millionaires with yachts and racehorses. On the contrary, he pointed out that only 2 percent of the latest patent medicines were even remotely successful. Thus, when Coca-Cola was first marketed two weeks after this article appeared, it faced long odds.

THE SODA FOUNTAIN DURING THE GILDED AGE

Coca-Cola became the first widely available product that was at once both a patent medicine and a popular soda fountain beverage. In retrospect, it seems a natural combination. After all, once Joseph Priestly learned to make what he called "fixed air" in 1767, artificially carbonated water was sold as a tonic and medicine, a cheaper form of naturally carbonated mineral water, which had been regarded as healthful since Roman times. An enterprising French immigrant, Eugene Roussel, first added flavors to his soda water at his Philadelphia perfume shop in 1839, and soon other soda fountains were serving orange, cherry, lemon, ginger, peach, and assorted other flavors. Because of the early medicinal legacy, the fountains formed a traditional part of drugstores, which in turn became social centers.

Soda fountains grew increasingly ornate throughout the 1870s and 1880s. They were "temples resplendent in crystal marble and silver," according to Mary Gay Humphreys, an 1891 commentator, and bore names such as Frost King, the Snow-drop, the Icicle, the Avalanche, or the Aurora Borealis to indicate the frosty nature of their beverages; the decor of others tried for a foreign flavor and were called the Persia, Ionic, Doric, Chalet, Arabia, Rialto, or France, although others, such as the Washington and Saratoga, were more patriotic. These monstrous affairs sometimes cost as much as $40,000 and offered over three hundred beverage combinations. "To supply these," wrote Humphreys, "the entire side of the wall is dedicated and made glorious with California onyx, rare marbles, and plate-glass." Sophisticated, jaded consumers demanded an ever-greater variety of beverages. Most of these new flavors were recognizable combinations of old fruit drinks. Coca-Cola, however, was one of several unique blends offering something entirely new. All survived their early years as health boosters and nerve tonics to become recognizable national soft drinks. Unlike the regular run of fountain offerings or soda pop, these concoctions appeared modern and mysterious. Their ingredients were usually secret or came from some exotic country.

Coca-Cola was by no means the first of these drinks. Charles Hires, a Philadelphia Quaker, marketed Hires Root Beer in 1876 as a solid concentrate of sixteen wild roots and berries.* It claimed to "purify the blood and make rosy cheeks." Consumers mixed the twenty-five-cent packets into five-gallon batches, making it the first drink to tap the home market. It was finally bottled in 1895.

Moxie Nerve Food was invented and bottled by Dr. Augustin Thompson of Lowell, Massachusetts, in 1885. Thompson, who had a flair for promotion and strategic untruths, claimed that the drink was made from a rare, unnamed South American plant (said to resemble asparagus, sugarcane, or milkweed and to taste like a turnip) whose therapeutic powers had been discovered by a Lieutenant Moxie, Thompson's mythical friend. Moxie allegedly cured paralysis, softening of the brain, nervousness, and insomnia.

---

* At first, Hires called his drink Hires Herb Tea, in keeping with his pacifistic religion. Russell Conwell, the capitalistic evangelist who gave the "Acres of Diamonds" speech, advised him to change the name to "root beer" in order to appeal to hard-drinking Philadelphia miners.

Charles Alderton created Dr Pepper as a Texas cherry soda fountain drink in 1885, but he soon bottled it as well. Early ads featured a naked, robust young woman cavorting in the ocean, her crotch teasingly covered by a wave, and asserted that Dr Pepper "aids digestion and restores vim, vigor, and vitality."

With so many new drinks available, the soda jerks had to become virtuosos at mixing drinks with grace and speed. One of Coca-Cola's early selling points was that it could be so quickly prepared. As a contemporary article pointed out, "time is everything to the soda water man on a hot day. With new customers crowding and jostling each other to reach the counter, it is money in his pocket to get rid of consumers as quickly as possible." The busy late nineteenth-century soda fountain first satisfied the American demand for fast food and drink.

Nowhere were soda fountains more popular than in the South, particularly in the booming, busy, hot town of Atlanta. Though still opened only seasonally, generally from March to November, they garnered a huge business. The adventurous could order a drink called "don't care," a mixture of virtually every flavor, usually with a healthy splash of hard liquor to bind it together.* In the following 1886 Atlanta ad (one of the first to mention Coca-Cola), the proprietor specified that *his* "don't care" was non-alcoholic. The incredible range of choices ran from innocent fruit drinks to more stimulating "nerve tonics":

> At the sodawater palace can be found the most cooling, delicious beverages—
> the ladies' favorite—ice-cream sodawater, any flavor that is desired.
>
> Syrups: Wine flavor—Claret, Catawba, grape, sherry, nectar, blackberry,
> ginger wine, oget, don't care, prohibition drink—great, everybody must try
> it to find out what it is—no whiskey . . . French wine of coca from Sinytis,
> coco-cola, French calisaya wine or nerve food, quiet the nervous system, ginger
> ale . . . lemons, chocolate, vanilla, cream, pine apple, raspberry, sarsaparilla,
> wild cherry, ginger, orange, blood orange, banana, coffee, ice tea, black gum,
> Beermann's egg phosphate, the most nutritious drink known, Maxey [i.e.,
> Moxie] nerve food, milk shakes. . . .

The soda fountain was a uniquely American phenomenon. In years to come, Coca-Cola would be advertised as the great national drink, a wholesome, enjoyable product that all classes of Americans could share. The seeds for that image were already germinating, as Mary Gay Humphreys (with no thought for Coca-Cola) pointed out in 1891: "Soda-water is an American drink. It is as essentially American as porter, Rhine wine, and claret are distinctively English, German, and French. . . . The crowning merit of soda-water, and that which fits it to be the national drink, is its democracy. The millionaire may drink champagne while the poor man drinks beer, but they both drink soda-water."

The fountain owner, Humphreys explained, made a tidy democratic profit from rich man and pauper alike, selling a drink for a nickel that cost a cent and a half to

---

* The "don't care" is the ancestor of the "suicide," popular at 1950s soda fountains. Using Coca-Cola as a base, a suicide called for the addition of every other flavor available.

produce. (Actually, she was overly generous to the fountain owner, because ingredients usually cost less than half a cent per glass.) Everyone was happy, because "for him who drinks it is small cost to see the 'bubbles winking on the brim,' to feel the aromatic flavors among the roots of his hair and exploring the crannies of his brain, and to realize each fragrant drop as it goes dancing down his throat."

The competition among new soda fountain drinks equaled the cutthroat patent medicine field. One writer of the era estimated that less than one percent of all new drinks ever won a following. "The summer trade in soft drinks is . . . already so loaded down with different sirups* and drinks that dealers will not take hold of a new thing unless it can be demonstrated to possess unusual virtues, or the inventor of it is willing to put a lot of money into advertising it."

John Pemberton's Coca-Cola had little chance. In 1886, the inventor did not have much money to put into advertising, but he struggled to demonstrate his drink's "unusual virtues." Pemberton, a perennial optimist despite the many disappointments in his life, clearly believed in his own product. Certainly, much of the credit for Coca-Cola's survival has to go to Asa Candler, who eventually acquired the product (in an exceedingly questionable manner) and pushed it aggressively. But an equal measure of credit must go to Pemberton and the time and place in which he found himself.

---

* All ungrammatical errors inside quotation marks are the mistakes of the original person being quoted. I make this note here rather than putting [*sic*] into so many quotations.

~ 2 ~

What Sigmund Freud, Pope Leo, and John Pemberton Had in Common

The use of the coca plant not only preserves the health of all who use it, but prolongs life to a very great old age and enables the coca eaters to perform prodigies of mental and physical labor.

—Dr. John Pemberton, 1885

John Pemberton was obsessed: he wanted to invent the ultimate medicine and the perfect drink all rolled into one. With it, he would make enough money to fund his dream laboratory, with plenty to spare for his family. He could even donate to worthy charitable organizations. After all, other inventors with far less education or dedication had made fortunes from their patent medicines, most of which cured nothing except imaginary illnesses. But the Georgia pharmacist knew that he was running out of time. By 1879, he was forty-eight years old. The average life expectancy for men was only forty-two, and Pemberton had suffered from bouts of debilitating rheumatism and a mysterious stomach ailment even before he was wounded in the War Between the States. At least he was sure now that he was on the right track, having just read about a wonderful new medicine—a plant with magical properties that grew high in the Peruvian mountains.

AN ECLECTIC EDUCATION

Pemberton's entire life had led to his pursuit of the perfect medicine. Born in 1831 in the tiny town of Knoxville, Georgia, he attended the nearby Southern Botanico Medical College of Georgia when he was just seventeen, where he discovered the wisdom of Samuel Thomson, an unlettered New Hampshire herbal practitioner whose teachings formed the basis for the college curriculum. In 1822, Thomson had published his *New Guide to Health; or Botanic Family Physician, Containing a Complete System of Practice, On a Plan Entirely New.*

Thomson's "complete system" consisted primarily of repeated steam baths and massive doses of lobelia (aptly nicknamed "screw auger" and "hell-scraper"), an herb that caused violent vomiting. Although this sounds horrific, it was actually an improvement over the "heroic" measures (as they were then known) of the period.

Doctors generally prescribed a combination of three therapies: bleeding to the point of unconsciousness with a lancet, intentionally raising and then popping huge blisters, or dosing with calomel, whose principal ingredient was mercury. Thomson called these doctors murderers who attacked patients with "their instruments of death—mercury, opium, ratsbane, nitre, and the lancet." Almost single-handedly, Thomson fomented a revolt of the masses against traditional medicine that one medical expert called "a second American revolution."

Even before Thomson died in 1843, however, splinter groups had formed. The egotistical rebel abhorred all formal education, preferring to keep himself as the sole font of wisdom. Nonetheless, various botanico colleges sprang up despite his resistance. Thomsonianism was particularly popular in the South. When the Georgia school was opened in Forsyth in December of 1839, the college president declared that "the eyes of the world are upon us" because they were ushering in "an era in the progress of civilization and a triumph for suffering humanity."

By the time Pemberton attended college, most Thomsonian schools had modified their reliance on lobelia and become more "eclectic," emphasizing other herbal remedies and some traditional medical study. At the age of nineteen, Pemberton graduated in 1850, and, after a brief stint as a traditional Thomsonian "steam doctor," he went to Philadelphia for another year of schooling as a pharmacist before beginning his real career as a druggist in Oglethorp, Georgia. There, he met Anna Eliza Clifford Lewis, called "Cliff," whose father was a prominent local plantation owner and dry-goods merchant. They were married in 1853, and the following year Cliff gave birth to their first and only child, Charles Ney Pemberton. Charley was a beautiful, precocious child, but neither of his parents could bring themselves to discipline him, and he was spoiled. For a minimal sum, Cliff's father sold two slaves to the young couple to help care for the infant.

In 1855, Pemberton moved to the larger town of Columbus, where he built a thriving practice for the next fourteen years with a number of different partners. Although primarily a druggist, he also practiced some medicine, including eye surgery. His main income, however, came from the sale of various proprietary products with names like Dr. Sanford's Great Invigorator or Eureka Oil and the occasional medicinal wine, such as Southern Cordial.

By the spring of 1861, Pemberton wrote Cliff's mother that business was booming and six-year-old Charley was "learning fast, you would be surprised to hear him spelling and I teach him his Sabbath School book every week." In urging his mother-in-law to visit, Pemberton described their "delightful home" and the twenty acres of corn, potato, sugarcane, and watermelons they had just planted. He also revealed his love of nature, referring to "the sweetest of all times below, a Sabbath Eve in the Springtime," adding that "the trees and flowers are blooming in our yard and the air is fragrant with the sweet perfume from them."

Less than a month after he described that peaceful scene, Fort Sumter was attacked, and the Civil War began. Pemberton enlisted as a first lieutenant in May of 1862 and eventually organized a home guard of the overaged and exempt into Pemberton's Cavalry. When the Yankees attacked on April 16, 1865, a week after Lee's surrender at Appomattox, Pemberton was shot and cut with a saber while defending the bridge into town in one of the final skirmishes of the war. This brush with death left him with an impressive scar across his abdomen and chest; his life was apparently saved by the money belt he wore.

SWEET SOUTHERN BOUQUET AND CARBUNCLE CURES

Pemberton must have recovered quickly. By November of 1865 he was industriously promoting his drug business again, having just returned from a buying spree in New York City, where he purchased "the largest and most complete stock of European and American drugs, medicines, and chemicals." Like many hustling Georgia business-men, he resolved to put the war behind him and didn't mind seeking the help of Yan-kees. Later, when his nephew pestered him to tell him how he got his scar, Pemberton refused, telling him he wanted to forget all about the war.

For the next five years, Pemberton's partnership with Dr. Austin Walker, a wealthy local physician, allowed him to thrive. He could never save money, however. What he didn't spend on his laboratory and research, he gave freely to family and friends. During the late 1860s, Pemberton began to experiment, creating his own proprietary items, including Globe Flower Cough Syrup, Extract of Stillingia, a "blood purifier," and Sweet Southern Bouquet, a perfume—all made from locally gathered herbs.* An 1867 visitor was so charmed by Pemberton's business, and by the inventor himself, that she wrote a long letter of praise to the local paper. "I confess I was astonished at the extent of the laboratory," she noted, "for I did not know there was such an estab-lishment in the South." Pemberton, "every inch a gentleman," had presented her with an elegant wicker-covered bottle containing what she described as "the most delightful and delicate perfume that ever regaled my olfactories."

LIFE IN THE PHOENIX CITY

In 1869, Pemberton abandoned his well-established Columbus business and moved to Atlanta to make his fortune. Atlanta had begun as a collection of shanties, whore-houses, and saloons simply called Terminus, because it happened to be the site where the railroad stopped. Although there was a prewar "Moral Party," the opposing "Free and Rowdy Party" had more attraction for the denizens of Snake Nation and Murrell's Row. Even so, there were enough banks and railroads in Atlanta before the war to give the city a "progressive" reputation.

In the wake of the Civil War, Atlanta, calling itself the Phoenix City, rose with a dynamic vengeance from the ashes to which William Tecumseh Sherman had reduced it. "The one sole idea in every man's mind is to make money," wrote one observer of the Atlanta scene just after the war. A visitor from the country wrote in 1866 that "Atlanta is a devil of a place," adding that "the men rush about like mad, and keep up

---

* Globe Flower Cough Syrup was a big seller over the next two decades, purportedly curing consumption, bronchitis, asthma, croup, bleeding of the lungs, pleurisy, and laryngitis. According to another ad, Extract of Stillingia cured "ulcers, pustules, carbuncles, scald head, salt rheum, and the 88 different varieties of skin affections."

such a bustle, worry, and chatter, that it runs me crazy. Everybody looks as if nearly worked to death." Atlanta was a whirling, self-important, frenzied vortex for Southern business after the Civil War. To this wild, wide-open city, John Pemberton brought his wife and child for a new life.

At first, he was a great success. With his partners, he established the largest drug trade in the city at the elegant Kimball House, a luxury hotel with six floors and over three hundred rooms featuring elaborate furnishings and gold ornaments, complete with steam-powered elevators, fountains surrounded by tropical plants, and its own French chef. But by 1872, Pemberton had slipped into bankruptcy. He and his partners, an R. G. Dun credit man noted, were "honorable & industrious but lack good management." Pemberton never quite recovered from this bankruptcy, though he continued to experiment with new medicines and to attract moneyed partners through the years. He suffered through two major fires, in 1874 and 1878. After the second fire, in which $20,000 worth of stock was destroyed (covered for half that amount by insurance), the Dun man described Pemberton as "a broken down merchant"— surely an unfair description, but understandable under the circumstances. In 1879, he finally paid off the bankruptcy debts and was free to devote more time to creating and manufacturing new products.

In subsequent years, he invented Indian Queen Hair Dye, a rheumatic remedy called "Prescription 47–11," Triplex Liver Pills, Gingerine, Lemon & Orange Elixir, and probably a few other now-forgotten patent medicines and drinks. In his endeavors through the last years of his life, he met with "varying success," as the newspaper politely put it in 1886.

Despite his adversities, Pemberton remained the perfect Southern gentleman, receiving customers with old-fashioned courtesy. Perhaps because his son, Charley, was a difficult child, Pemberton always found time for his sister's children. "One of my earliest memories," recalled his niece, "is of the chewing gum Uncle John always had in his pocket, but was forbidden in my home as not lady-like. . . . I enjoyed visits [there], where I received more attention than at home." Pemberton's nephew, Lewis Newman, portrayed the busy doctor as an obsessed, secretive inventor with "a laboratory in a back room to which but few were given admittance." Pemberton would forget mealtimes and work far into the night. Another visitor remembered Pemberton as having "more energy than anybody. His chemical laboratory was a very busy place; he was always getting up something."

In addition to his two degrees as a doctor and pharmacist, Pemberton was a lifelong scholar who not only kept up with the current drug journals but read widely in the increasingly international pharmaceutical literature. For years, he labored over a master reference work on drugs. In a December 1886 interview, he showed his work in progress to a reporter, who described it as containing "about 12,000 chemical tests." Though the inventor died before publishing his book, its existence attests to the breadth of his knowledge, far beyond the accomplishments of the simple country root doctor of the Coca-Cola myth. It is not surprising, then, that in creating new patent medicines, he stopped limiting himself to locally grown plants such as stillingia and globe flowers and began to experiment with more exotic substances. One of these imports, initially hailed as a cure-all—but soon to be assailed as the source of an addictive drug—particularly fascinated Pemberton.

COCA COMES INTO ITS OWN

In the late 1870s, Pemberton first read about this miraculous new substance. Chewed by native Peruvians and Bolivians for over two thousand years, coca leaves acted as a stimulant, an aid to digestion, an aphrodisiac, and a life-extender, giving the mountain-dwelling Andeans remarkable endurance during long treks with little food. The Incas had called it their "Divine Plant," and it was central to every aspect of their political, religious, and commercial life. The *cochero* was never without his *chuspa*, or coca pouch.

Around 1876, Pemberton read an article by Sir Robert Christison, seventy-eight-year-old president of the British Medical Association. Fortified by chewing coca, the elderly doctor reported that he climbed Ben Vorlich, a 3,224-foot mountain, skipped lunch, and "at the bottom I was neither weary, nor hungry, nor thirsty, and felt as if I could easily walk home four miles." Intrigued, Pemberton began reading everything available on the coca plant. And he was not the only one. By the early 1880s, doctors and pharmacists were reporting on the use of coca and its principal alkaloid, cocaine, as a possible cure for opium and morphine addiction. Cocaine had first been isolated in 1855 by the German Gaedeke, but it was Americans who pursued active experimentation.

In the cosmopolitan cross-fertilization typical of the time, a young Viennese doctor named Sigmund Freud read one of these articles in an 1880 Detroit drug journal and, like Pemberton, was excited by the possibilities. In 1884, Freud first tried cocaine himself. It seemed the perfect antidote to his periodic depressions and lethargy; he also clearly thought it increased his sexual potency, writing to Martha Bernays, his fiancee: "Woe to you, my Princess, when I come. I will kiss you quite red . . . and if you are forward you shall see who is the stronger, a gentle little girl . . . or a big wild man who has cocaine in his body."

Later that year, Freud published *Über Coca* (About Coca), "a song of praise to this magical substance," as he wrote to his fiancee. In that same year, 1884, an associate of Freud's, young Carl Koller, found that cocaine could be successfully used as an anesthetic in eye surgery. This discovery, still used, quickly made Koller famous and revolutionized surgery. It also caught the attention of John Pemberton, who had once performed painful eye surgery without benefit of painkiller.

By the mid-1880s, one drug journal described a "veritable *coca-mania*" as a result of the "crusade against the enormously increased use of alcohol and morphine." It was impossible to open a drug journal without finding numerous articles about new uses for the leaf and its principal alkaloid. In response, manufacturers produced coca tablets, ointments, sprays, hypodermic injections, wines, liqueurs, soft drinks, powders, and even coca-leaf cigarettes and cheroots. Coca-Bola, a popular masticatory that came in plugs similar to chewing tobacco, was extensively advertised in 1885.

VIN MARIANI: THE DIVINE DRINK

The coca leaf found its most famed commercial use in a now-forgotten drink called Vin Mariani, invented by Angelo Mariani, an enterprising Corsican who in 1863 began selling the Bordeaux wine with a healthy infusion of coca leaf. Pemberton's

French Wine Coca, first advertised in 1884, was a direct imitation. Because Pemberton then modified his Wine Coca to create Coca-Cola, Vin Mariani is, in effect, the "grandfather" of Coca-Cola.

Mariani's coca-laced wine became wildly successful not only throughout Europe but in the United States, where his brother-in-law, Julius Jaros, opened a New York branch. A marketing genius, Mariani specialized in testimonials from an incredible array of notables, including Thomas Edison, Emile Zola, President William McKinley, Queen Victoria, Sarah Bernhardt, Lillian Russell, Buffalo Bill Cody, and three Popes. Leo XIII went so far as to give Mariani a gold medal bearing Leo's likeness "in recognition of benefits received from the use of Mariani's tonic." The Pope apparently bore out Mariani's claims that coca extended life, because he died at ninety-three in 1903. According to an 1887 biography of Pope Leo, he took "the simplest food, a little wine and water." Looking at the Pontiff's frail body, the author wondered "how the lamp of life is fed," particularly when his face was "of alabaster whiteness," his eyes "all-radiant with the fire of piety and fatherly kindness." In fact, the Pope's lamp of life was fed by Vin Mariana, and the "all-radiant" eyes may have taken their fire as much from coca as from piety.

Mariani also collected glowing words from "kings, princes, potentates, the clergy, statesmen, artists, and from a host of people eminent in a high degree" around the globe. Only half in jest, an admirer once told Mariani he had forgotten to solicit a testimonial from God. His two major production laboratories were in Neuilly-sur-Seine in France and New York City, but Mariani had principal distribution centers in London, Strasbourg, Montreal, Brussels, Geneva, Alexandria (Egypt), and Saigon.

Just how much of a kick did Vin Mariani deliver? Fortunately, we can hazard a good guess, because a chemist studying various wine cocas reported in 1886 that Vin Mariani contained 0.12 grain cocaine per fluid ounce. The dosage on the wine's label called for a "claret-glass full" before or after every meal (a half glass for children). Assuming the wineglass to hold six fluid ounces, three daily glasses would amount to a full bottle of eighteen ounces, or 2.16 grains of cocaine per day—enough to make someone feel very good indeed.

Mariani's most important market outside Europe was the United States, and he took advantage of any opportunity for publicity there. During President Ulysses Grant's final illness in 1885, his physicians administered Vin Mariani, which soothed the pain of his throat cancer and was credited with extending his life so that he could finish his memoirs. In the midst of Grant's travail, Angelo Mariani traveled to New York City "at the request of a number of prominent physicians who desired to get from him personally a better understanding of . . . this wonderful medicine." Mariani subsequently advertised the general's use of his product before the body was cold in Grant's Tomb.

The overwhelming popularity of Vin Mariani naturally spawned imitators, particularly in the intensely competitive American patent medicine market. The drug journals of the 1880s were full of recipes for wine of coca. Most were poor copies containing straight cocaine mixed with cheap wine, resulting in a bitter taste but greater effect. By 1885, Vin Mariani ads warned against over twenty ersatz wines, and Mariani himself groused about "the many worthless, so-called Coca preparations [that are] nothing more than variable solutions of Cocaine in inferior grades of wines or other liquids, shamefully prepared by unscrupulous or ignorant persons [serving to] bring into discredit a really useful drug." In 1887, one cynical writer, describing Vin Mariani and its illegitimate spawn, referred to "the famous, expert-indorsed, world-renowned coca wine, made now by everybody and his relatives, from the skilled chemist to the mackerel and sugar handlers."

PEMBERTON'S FRENCH WINE COCA: A SUPERIOR IMITATION?

Pemberton's French Wine Coca appeared as one of the legion of imitators, though his product was probably superior to most on the market. In a March 1885 interview, it was obvious that Pemberton had read the Mariani testimonials for the "intellectual beverage." Like Mariani, he espoused his wine's beneficial effects on the educated, professional upper crust of society. The new disease, neurasthenia, had arrived as a status symbol that afflicted only the most refined, mentally active people. Pemberton not only acknowledged his debt to Mariani, but claimed somehow to have seen his formula.

"Scientists, scholars, poets, divines, lawyers, physicians, and others devoted to extreme mental exertion, are the most liberal patrons of this great invigorator of the brain," Pemberton told the reporter, explaining that "Mariani & Co., of Paris, prepare an exceedingly popular Wine of Coca. . . . I have observed very closely the most approved French formula, only deviating therefrom when assured by my own long experimentation and direct information from intelligent South American correspondents that I could improve upon [it]." Modestly, he concluded, "I believe that I am now producing a better preparation than that of Mariani."

Pemberton advertised that his wine contained "the medical virtues of the Erythroxylon Coca plant of Peru, South America—the African Cola Nuts—true Damiana, with pure Grape Wine." These two additional ingredients must have constituted the improvements he felt he had made on Mariani's drink. The kola nut quickly followed the coca leaf as a new medicinal rage. Grown in West Africa, primarily in Ghana, kola nuts were used by the natives in a manner similar to coca. Chewed for extra energy, identified with local deities, and taken as an aphrodisiac, the nuts had been a major part of the fabric of African life for centuries. Like coca leaves, kola nuts had a potent alkaloid—caffeine—in greater proportions than either tea or coffee.

By the mid-1880s, long articles on kola nuts were running in all the drug journals, praising the nuts as a hangover cure and stimulant. Many articles explicitly compared kola to coca. "Like Coca, Kola enables its partakers to undergo long fast and fatigue," read one 1884 article. "Two drugs, so closely related in their physiological properties, cannot fail to command early universal attention." In its 1883–1884 catalog, Frederick Stearns & Company featured Coca and Cola Nut on the same page in parallel columns, with a common headline running across the top: "For the Brain and Nervous System."

The second ingredient was damiana, defined by a vintage Webster's as "the dried leaf of *Turnera diffusa* of tropical America, California, and Texas, used as a tonic and aphrodisiac." An 1885 advertisement for "The Mormon Elder's Damiana Wafers" leaves little doubt that it was indeed regarded as a sexual stimulant: "The Most Powerful INVIGORANT Ever Produced. Permanently Restores those Weakened by Early Indiscretions. . . . A positive cure for Impotency and Nervous Debility." Thus, all three ingredients of Pemberton's tonic were considered aphrodisiacs.

Pemberton's ads for his coca wine featured an Americanized, supercharged version of Mariani's claims. He minimized the artistic, gentle aspects while emphasizing his drink as an aggressive cure for nervous disorders, disturbances of internal plumbing, and impotency. He also appropriated Mariani's testimonials for his own, asserting that "French Wine Coca is indorsed by over 20,000 of the most learned and scientific medical men in the world." Enthusiastic and wordy, if not completely grammatical, here is an ad Pemberton ran in 1885:

> Americans are the most nervous people in the world. . . . All who are suffering from any nervous complaints we commend to use that wonderful and delightful remedy, French Wine Coca, infallible in curing all who are afflicted with any nerve trouble, dyspepsia, mental and physical exhaustion, all chronic and wasting diseases, gastric irritability, constipation, sick headache, neuralgia, etc. is quickly cured by the Coca Wine. It has proven the greatest blessing to the human family, Nature's (God's) best gift in medicine. To clergymen, lawyers, literary men, merchants, bankers, ladies, and all whose sedentary employment causes nervous prostration, irregularities of the stomach, bowels and kidneys, who require a nerve tonic and a pure, delightful diffusable stimulant, will find Wine Coca invaluable, a sure restorer to health and happiness. Coca is a most wonderful invigorator of the sexual organs and will cure seminal weakness, impotency, etc., when all other remedies fail. To the unfortunate who are addicted to the morphine or opium habit, or the excessive use of alcoholic stimulants, the French Wine Coca has proven a great blessing, and thousands proclaim it the most remarkable invigorator that ever sustained a wasting and sinking system.

THE MORPHINE ADDICT

Pemberton had a personal reason for his interest in coca as a cure for morphine addiction: he was probably using French Wine Coca in an attempt to break his own habit. Three people associated with him in the final year of his life stated categorically that Pemberton was an addict. J. C. Mayfield recalled under oath that "Dr. Pemberton was in bad health. We did not know at the time what was the matter with him, but it developed that he was a drug fiend." Mayfield's ex-wife wrote that Pemberton was "for years addicted to the morphine habit." Finally, another partner, A. O. Murphey, said that when he discovered the doctor's addiction, he found it "distasteful."

"Morphinism," as it was then called, was increasingly prevalent, particularly among physicians and pharmacists. The importation of opium to the U.S. had increased dramatically, from almost 146,000 pounds in 1867 to over 500,000 pounds in 1880. Advertisements purporting to offer cures for the habit appeared frequently in Atlanta papers. Addiction was so common among veterans of the Civil War that it was called

"Army disease." Pemberton may have first resorted to morphine to ease the pain of his own war wounds, continuing its use throughout his periodic illnesses.*

It may seem odd that Pemberton was able to hide his habit so well, but many addicts did. "Few of those addicted to the drug for years are suspicioned even by their most intimate friends," wrote one physician in 1890. Opium, he said, allowed the habitue to "engage in his daily business pursuits with renewed energy for the time being. The opium eater's mind seems clear, his thoughts are well directed, his general appearance is above suspicion."

At least temporarily, Pemberton must have felt that he was beating his addiction, because he told a reporter in 1885 that "I am convinced from actual experiments that [coca] is the very best substitute for opium, with a person addicted to the opium habit, that has ever been discovered. It supplies the place of that drug, and the patient who will use it as a means of cure, may deliver himself from the pernicious habit without inconvenience or pain."

EARLY WARNING SIGNALS

Although patent medicine suppliers and physicians were generally euphoric about coca and cocaine, some doctors and publications were already sounding the alarm that cocaine might indeed free addicts from morphine—only to enslave them on the new drug. Freud's friend Ernst von-Fleischl Marxow, for instance, to whom he introduced cocaine as an antidote to his morphine, died horribly in 1891 after years as a cocaine addict.† A German doctor published a scathing and widely translated attack on cocaine in 1886, calling it "the third scourge of mankind," and American colleagues soon took up his cause.

As early as June 1885, Pemberton was defending himself against a short piece published in the *Atlanta Constitution*, which warned "the new drug cocaine will do almost anything . . . on the other hand, the injudicious use of cocaine will make a man more brutal and depraved than either liquor or morphine. Herein lies a new danger. Before long a remedy will be demanded for the cocaine habit." Pemberton refused to believe it. Most likely fortified with Wine Coca, in a rambling interview a few days later he dismissed the charges as predictable prejudice against anything new.

Pemberton granted that cocaine, if misused, could be dangerous, but the same could be said for any effective medicine. "I wish it were in my power to substitute the Coca and compel all who are addicted to the use of opium, morphine, alcohol, tobacco, or other narcotic stimulants to live on the coca plant or any of its true preparations," he said. "It is perfectly wonderful what coca does." Explaining that "we [Americans] are a great army of nervous invalids," he espoused coca as a universal panacea that promoted robust health, prodigious physical and mental activity, and long life.

---

* As an inventor and pharmacist, Pemberton had ready access to drugs. His formula book included recipes using not only cocaine and morphine but cannabis as well.

† "Addiction" is difficult to define; cocaine apparently is not physically addictive, because habitual users do not exhibit the classic withdrawal symptoms, but there is no question that the drug is *psychologically* addictive.

Sales of French Wine Coca were encouraging. Exactly a week after that peroration on the wonders of coca, Pemberton took out a large ad in the paper announcing that "888 BOTTLES OF PEMBERTON'S COCA WINE SOLD SATURDAY! IT SELLS AND PROVES A LIVING JOY To all who use it. Read what is said by others about this WONDERFUL TONIC AND INVIGORANT." The inevitable testimonials followed, one by a doctor in Bremen, Georgia, who cured himself of "Insomnia, Melancholia, Hypochondriasis, and all the other foul fiends that haunted my mind and body." He had also treated twenty patients successfully with Wine Coca—"all of them bona fide ladies and gentlemen of high reputation." He asserted that the tonic acted quickly on the "great Ganglionic Centers."

PROHIBITION PROBLEMS

Pemberton's fortunes were finally on the upswing. Perhaps he would join that band of patent medicine millionaires plying their steam yachts. But just when sales of French Wine Coca were booming, the Reverend Sam Jones and his temperance movement nearly ruined him.

Jones was a popular, rough-hewn, fast-talking Georgia evangelist, a reformed drinker and darling of the press because he was at the same time pious, earthy, witty, and eminently quotable. One critic dubbed him "the Cracker Evangelist." Jones made much of his rural, homespun origins, making forays from his Cartersville home to blast the sins of big-city Atlanta, while at the same time carefully flattering the city's fortunes and future. Actually, it was all an act, because the minister was quite well educated and capable of refined speech. For years, Jones had led the fight for Prohibition, slamming the "red-nosed whisky devils" and complaining that legislators were unable to pass anything—"not even a cheap bar room."

"How he did hammer the brethren!" one survivor of a Jones revival meeting recalled. "He raked us fore and aft. He gave us grape and canister and all the rest. He abused us and ridiculed us; he stormed at us and laughed at us; he called us flop-eared hounds, beer kegs, and whisky soaks. He plainly said that we were all hypocrites and liars. . . . For six weeks [work was] neglected, and Jones! Jones! Jones! was the whole thing."

The accumulation of his wit and abuse had its effect. By a slim margin, on November 25, 1885, encouraged by the local option bill recently enacted by the state legislature, Atlanta and Fulton County voted to go dry. In order to give saloonkeepers a chance to close shop, the ban on liquor would begin seven months later, on July 1, 1886, for an experimental period of two years.

Pemberton could see the handwriting on the wall, and not only in Atlanta. The national temperance movement had been gaining momentum for several years. The saloon, found on almost every street corner in America's cities, offered an all-male bastion where the lower and middle class could repair for whiskey, beer, and a free lunch. The Woman's Christian Temperance Union, founded in 1874, promoted the notion that virtually all crimes—murder, child abuse, political corruption, industrial accidents—resulted from demon rum or German beer. The emotional attacks of the WCTU polarized entire communities, so that by 1886, a Methodist minister in favor of temperance was murdered in Sioux City, Iowa, while driving his team through a pro-liquor crowd.

The days of a wine-based medicine appeared doomed, though it depended, of course, on what the law interpreted as alcohol. Pemberton frantically experimented with modifications of the Wine Coca formula. Convinced of the virtues of the coca leaf and kola nut, he removed the wine and started testing an assortment of essential oils, primarily distillations of fruit flavors. But they all tasted too bitter to him. Adding sugar masked the bitterness but made for a sickly sweet drink. To counteract that, Pemberton added citric acid. Throughout the winter of 1885, he continued to search for a satisfactory formula.

FRANK ROBINSON ARRIVES

In December, Frank Robinson and David Doe, two Yankees, appeared on Pemberton's doorstep trying to peddle a machine they called a "chromatic printing device," capable of producing two colors at one impression. Both were Maine natives but had lived for the past few years in Iowa, sprawling farm country that didn't offer much market for a slick publishing device. Touring the South, Robinson and Doe landed in Atlanta, where the booming patent medicine industry would presumably pounce on a novel advertising opportunity. Asking around for likely prospects, they were told to try old Doc Pemberton, who seemed always to be looking for new partners and ideas.

After Pemberton talked it over with his old partner, Ed Holland, the four men shook hands on a deal and agreed on a new corporate name, the Pemberton Chemical Company. Holland was the only one who had much capital to invest, but they went in as equal partners. Pemberton contributed his talents and laboratory, and Robinson and Doe put in their printing machine. The firm's letterhead soon bragged that "the great wonder of the world is printing two colors in a newspaper at one impression," but Atlanta publishers never responded favorably to the novelty.

THE COCA-COLA LABORATORY

Throughout the winter and early spring of 1886, Pemberton obsessively experimented with his new coca and kola "temperance" drink, sending it down to Venable's soda fountain at Jacobs' Pharmacy for repeated trial runs. Pemberton's nephew, Lewis Newman, visiting from college, was one of the errand boys:

> My last visit to Auntie's was when Uncle John was giving cococola a try out and he was even more glad to see me than usual. He was eager to show me through his "factory" and to tell me that he had begun selling "my temperance drink," as he called it. . . . Uncle John sent me with an order for a drink and [told me] to wait in Jacobs Pharmacy to hear comments of those who came for Coca cola when it was first introduced. [It sold about] 3 to 5 gallons per day.

Both Newman and John Turner, who apprenticed with Pemberton around the same time, remembered being sent down to the drugstore to get a drink of Coca-Cola for Pemberton, because there was no carbonated water at the laboratory. This contradicts the Company dogma that Coca-Cola was accidentally mixed with soda water about a year later.

Lewis Newman described his uncle's 1886 laboratory, revealing how the myth of the root doctor stirring his kettle probably began:

> The remodeling and equipment of the Marietta Street house absorbed all the money Uncle John had or could get. . . . The wonderful part of the equipment, to me at least, was the enormous filter made of matched flooring, wide at the top and narrowing to the base. It was built through the floor of a second story room and the ceiling of the room below. This big hamper-like receptacle was filled with "Chattahoochee River* washed sand," Uncle John explained. . . . The prepared ingredients of coca cola were poured into the top of this filter and treacled through the several wagon loads of washed sand into a metal trough.
>
> My best recollection is that this process was for the purpose of "ripening" the mixture by [letting it] filter through without access of air. There were two large kettles such as sorghum and sugar cane juices were boiled in. . . . Paddles of ash similar to those used in propelling canoes stirred the liquid while it was boiled . . . before [being] taken through the filtering and fermentation process.

This cumbersome method of making Coca-Cola was later abandoned, but Pemberton's laboratory certainly consisted of more than his kettles. Unfortunately, there is no way of knowing what this original Coca-Cola tasted like after it had been slowly "ripened" through the enormous sand filter.

A PAPER IS READ IN SAVANNAH

In April of 1886, Pemberton was scheduled to deliver a major speech to the annual convention of the Georgia Pharmaceutical Society, but he was too close to a satisfactory formula to tear himself away and travel all the way to Savannah. Instead, he sent the text of the speech to be read aloud. In the paper, he gave a detailed, scholarly account of caffeine and cocaine, including the history of both drugs' isolation and use. He noted that "caffeine, as obtained from tea and coffee in this country, is inferior to that manufactured from the kola nuts by Merck, of Darmstadt."

Pemberton's real passion, however, was obviously the coca leaf. "All of the medical journals are full of its praises and I am perplexed to know where to begin and how to end so interesting a subject," he wrote. "Never in the history of the medical world has a remedial agent, within so short a space of time, risen from comparative obscurity to such practical . . . importance. The article went up like a rocket amidst the universal plaudits of the medical profession all over the world." The veteran pharmacist then enumerated the many benefits of coca, including an account of Koller's experiments with eye surgery. Interestingly, he made the same point as Mariani—that the Peruvians did not value the coca leaf with the largest amount of cocaine, preferring a milder leaf with a better blend of alkaloids. Pemberton obviously had conducted extensive

---

* The Chattahoochee River runs near Atlanta.

experiments with the coca leaf by this time: "I must say, after considerable experience, that of many samples sent me by reputable houses, only about one out of one dozen samples proved to be of any value, many of the samples containing no Coca whatever."

A HISTORIC NAMING CONTEST

At almost the exact moment this speech was being read in Savannah, Pemberton finally pronounced himself satisfied with his new product, but he was still calling it simply "my temperance drink." He needed a good name. All four of the partners brainstormed and submitted potential titles. It would be interesting (and amusing) to hear what they were, but all we know is that Frank Robinson came up with Coca-Cola. Everyone agreed it was the best name, not only because it described the two principal drug ingredients (damiana having fallen from the formula) but because it had an alliterative ring.

Triple (and sometimes quadruple) alliterations were in vogue, particularly in Atlanta, allowing a tongue-twisting tour of the alphabet: Botanic Blood Balm, Copeland's Cholera Cure, Goff's Giant Globules, Dr Jordan's Joyous Julep, Ko-Ko Tulu, Dr Pierce's Pleasant Purgative Pellets, Radway's Ready Relief, Swift's Sure Specific. Robinson later wrote that he created the name "Coca-Cola" not only to indicate the key ingredients, but "because it was euphonious, and on account of my familiarity with such names as 'S.S.S.' and 'B.B.B.'" Robinson and The Coca-Cola Company later had good reason to emphasize the poetic rather than descriptive character of the name. For over seventy years, the fact that the name clearly stemmed from its ingredients would inspire harried Coca-Cola lawyers to write tortured legal briefs arguing just the opposite. By 1959, the president of The Coca-Cola Company was referring to it as a "meaningless but fanciful and alliterative name."

EARLY SUCCESS

At first, the new drink sold moderately well, at least in Atlanta. Pemberton, who had worked so hard on the formula, now turned the manufacture over to Robinson and took a rest. Busy brewing the stuff, Robinson soon devoted all of his time to the one drink. He made it, promoted it as best he could on a limited budget, and sold it. Further, he recognized that Coca-Cola could be marketed as a dual-purpose product. It was a stimulating medicine to cure headaches and depression, but it was also a new soda fountain drink with a unique taste. In his first ad, which ran in the *Atlanta Journal* on May 29, 1886, he emphasized its qualities as a beverage: "Coca-Cola. Delicious! Refreshing! Exhilarating! Invigorating! The new and popular soda fountain drink containing the properties of the wonderful Coca plant and the famous Cola nut." Although this first effort featured "Coca-Cola" in block letters, Robinson worked on the script logo over the winter, introducing the familiar Spencerian handwriting for the first time in a June 16, 1887, ad.

Compared with most promotions of this period, the first Coca-Cola ad was remarkably brief, pointing the way to modern advertising. It first used the adjectives, "delicious and refreshing," which would become virtually synonymous with Coca-Cola. Unlike Pemberton's tours de force of the past, Robinson avoided lengthy

Victorian perorations, nor did he mention the doctor by name. Robinson apparently wanted the drink to be set apart, not just another of Pemberton's preparations. The inventor himself used Robinson's adjectives when he wrote the label for his new syrup, but otherwise the prose was vintage Pemberton:

> COCA-COLA SYRUP AND EXTRACT For Soda Water and other Carbonated Beverages. This Intellectual Beverage and Temperance Drink contains the valuable Tonic and Nerve Stimulant properties of the Coca plant and Cola (or Kola) nuts, and makes not only a delicious, exhilarating, refreshing and invigorating Beverage (dispensed from the soda water fountain or in other carbonated beverages), but a valuable Brain Tonic and a cure for all nervous affections— Sick Head-Ache, Neuralgia, Hysteria, Melancholy, etc. The peculiar flavor of COCA-COLA delights every palate.

There was another good reason for the brevity of Robinson's original ad: it was cheaper. Because Pemberton and his partners had limited funds, their newspaper ads were sporadic. During the first year of the drink's existence, total advertising expense amounted to around $150. Although that was not a great deal of money, it bought a sizable amount of exposure for Coca-Cola. Large banner-style oilcloth signs cost a dollar apiece, streetcar signs a little over a penny, and posters about a third of a cent. A thousand coupons for sample drinks could be printed for a dollar.

Robinson soon arranged for an oilcloth sign to be pinned to the awning of Jacobs' drugstore—the drink's first point-of-purchase advertising, with red lettering on a white background ordering patrons to "DRINK COCA-COLA 5¢." Within a year, there were oilcloth signs advertising Coca-Cola at fourteen Georgia soda fountains. Thousands of Coca-Cola posters were distributed, while every streetcar in Atlanta carried an ad for the drink.

Only two days after the drink's introduction, Pemberton had written an arch note to Jacobs' Pharmacy complaining that "a certain individual, best remaining unnamed," had refused to sample Coca-Cola. "Do not give him a *free* sample," Pemberton wrote, because "profits will not permit such extravagance." He did, however, promise a refund if the drink failed to satisfy. Soon, however, Robinson convinced the doctor that he had been wrong to think that profits wouldn't permit the "extravagance" of giving away a nickel glass of Coca-Cola. On the contrary, future profits *demanded* it. Robinson had tickets printed up, to be redeemed at local soda fountains, offering free drinks and, using the Atlanta city directory, mailed them to prospective customers and gave them to traveling salesmen to distribute. Once they tasted Coca-Cola, new patrons were sure to come back for more, Robinson reasoned. He promised the soda fountain owners that he would redeem their tickets.

Meanwhile, the dreaded onset of local Prohibition arrived on July 1, 1886. In an orgy of self-congratulation, Atlanta became a pioneer as the first major city in the United States to swear off liquor. "ATLANTA DRY" the front page of the *Constitution* announced, "The First of July Marks a New Era." It is unclear, however, just how dry the city actually was. In the same paper there appeared an ad for "Duffy's Pure Malt Whiskey for Medicinal Use, Absolutely Pure and Unadulterated. In Use in Hospitals, Curative Institutions, Infirmaries. Cures Consumption, Hemorrhages, and all

Wasting Diseases." Prohibition apparently did not affect the Kimball House, whose liquor license didn't run out until October 9. The crowds there became so rowdy that the management no longer allowed drinking on the premises, forcing consumers to take their booze with them. A Kimball House ad in the October 5, 1886, *Constitution* warned buyers that they'd better stock up: "Will sell in quantities."

Not surprisingly, then, Pemberton was advertising French Wine Coca again soon afterwards, now claiming extraordinary longevity for those regular coca users: "Instances are recorded of persons who have lived over 120, 130, 140, and even over 150 years." Pemberton also began calling his Wine Coca "the Great 'EuBion' and Temperance Drink." If he could really get away with selling Wine Coca as a temperance beverage during Prohibition, sales should rise dramatically.

They did. Though Prohibition was resoundingly voted out on November 26, 1887, sales of French Wine Coca and Coca-Cola were booming long before that. On May 1, 1887, an article in the *Constitution* stated that "the daily sales are five gross for the wine coca. The sales within the last few weeks for the coca-cola syrup amounted to six hundred gallons. Both the coca-cola syrup and the wine coca are being sold throughout the United States, and everywhere are coming orders for the goods, and testimonials unsolicited pouring in on all sides." Although the paper undoubtedly exaggerated the national market for the hometown products, these figures are still impressive. "The goods manufactured by this firm," the article bragged, "are not 'nostrums' by any means but are pharmaceutical preparations and are recognized as such by the elite of the medical profession everywhere."

At 720 bottles a day, French Wine Coca sales still far outstripped those of Coca-Cola. Nonetheless, considering that the soda fountain season had only just begun, Coca-Cola's six hundred-gallon sale was a considerable achievement. Because each gallon of Coca-Cola syrup ideally yielded 128 drinks (one ounce per drink), the six hundred gallons translated to 76,800 drinks. Frank Robinson later downplayed the first year's sales, testifying under oath that "from May 1886 until May 1887 . . . he [Pemberton] sold twenty-five or thirty gallons, maybe, something like that." Either his memory was faulty or he was lying. At any rate, the twenty-five-gallon figure for that first year has become part of inaccurate Company lore.

The spring also brought changes in personnel. The shadowy Mr. Doe withdrew from the partnership, taking the printing machine with him as his share. He was replaced by M. P. Alexander, a Memphis pharmacist described in the same article as "an energetic, thorough business man [who] will reflect credit upon any business with which he is connected." Because the stock of Pemberton Chemical Company had been increased by $10,000, it is reasonable to assume that Alexander brought cash as well as energy to the partnership, which is probably why he immediately assumed the presidency. At the same time, Woolfolk Walker, "a young man of fine business tact," joined the firm as a salesman. A Columbus native, Walker had served as a private in Pemberton's Cavalry during the Civil War. Probably as a result of war wounds, Walker had a pronounced limp; he was to play a key role in the early history of Coca-Cola.

Finally, though he was not mentioned in the article, Charley Pemberton appeared on the payroll for this period and learned to make Coca-Cola, freeing Robinson for more intense promotion. Dr. Pemberton's only child was thirty-three years old and, according to all accounts, womanized and drank too much. The young Pemberton had been a gifted athlete, the champion catcher for a local baseball team back in 1872, but somehow he had gone sour (his friend Lewis Newman wrote of a failed romance). Now Charley's talents were directed at the poolroom in the local saloon. Concerned about his son's future, Dr. Pemberton hoped Charley would eventually take over his business.

Pemberton must have been optimistic and full of new schemes. As usual, he had spent the winter working on new formulae and was preparing to unveil his latest. He told the reporter that it was called Phospho Lemonade & Phospho Ironade (renaming it Lemon & Orange Elixir later); it would replace beer and wine, he asserted, comparing the new drink favorably to the finest imported champagne. The inventor appeared to be, as the paper had predicted in 1886, "on the high road to fortune." He had two best-selling drinks, with more on the way. "The success of this company has been something phenomenal," the *Constitution* reporter concluded on that May Day of 1887, and it must have seemed that nothing could go wrong.

On June 6, to assure his legal claim to the popular new drink, Pemberton applied for a Coca-Cola trademark patent. On June 28, it was granted. A week later, all hell broke loose.

~ 3 ~

The Tangled Chain of Title

It is always a relief to believe what is pleasant, but it is more important to believe what is true.

—Hilaire Belloc

All truth—and real living is the only truth—has in it elements of battle and repudiation. Nothing is wholesale.

—D. H. Lawrence

In the middle of July 1887, John Pemberton initiated a series of transactions that would lead to the most confused, convoluted genesis of a successful corporation that the world could ever have witnessed. In a little over a year, the formula for Coca-Cola would be subdivided and passed from hand to hand like the proverbial hot potato. The story resembles a Shakespearean play in which subplots weave among themselves before reaching a final resolution. None of the main characters emerged a real hero; each engaged in some form of subterfuge, deceit, or scheme.

On July 8, John Pemberton sold two-thirds of his Coca-Cola rights to Willis Venable and George Lowndes for the grand sum of one dollar, though for the time being he kept the sale a secret from his partners in Pemberton Chemical Company. Actually, Lowndes, who supplied the money, paid Pemberton $1,201, but $1,200 of it was considered a no-interest loan to be paid back out of future profits. The inventor, who retained a third interest, would also receive a third of the profits. In return, he sold Venable and Lowndes all of the necessary equipment and supplies at cost ($283.29), as well as providing a copy of Coca-Cola's formula.

Why did Pemberton sell? According to Lowndes, it was because he had fallen ill again and was worried about where money would come from—both for his family and his morphine, which he must have needed more than ever to kill pain. Pemberton and Lowndes had been close friends since sharing a boardinghouse in 1869; now the inventor wanted his old friend to buy his greatest creation. "Lowndes, I am sick," he began, "and I don't believe I will ever get out of this bed. The only thing I have is Coca-Cola." Urging Lowndes to buy it, Pemberton told him that "Coca-Cola some day will be a national drink. I want to keep a third interest in it so that my son will always have a living." Shortly before the sale, the ailing doctor confided to his nephew

32

Lewis that if only he had the proper capital, he could make a fortune from Coca-Cola: "If I could get $25,000, I would spend $24,000 advertising and the remainder in making Coca-Cola. Then we would all be rich." With the profits, he envisioned endowing "a great hospital for impecunious sons and daughters of Confederate soldiers." Now, however, he thought that he was dying and would never see the fulfillment of his dream.

The first partner to get wind of Pemberton's sale was M. P. Alexander. A small item appeared in the *Atlanta Constitution* recounting local court news of July 9, 1887, the day after the contract was signed: "Mssrs J. S. Pendleton, F. M. Robinson and C. A. Robinson [presumably Frank's brother] allege that the president of the [Pemberton Chemical Company], M. P. Alexander, has taken full possession of the books, papers, etc, and is so conducting business as to seriously prejudice their interests. They say that Alexander and other persons have formed a conspiracy to ruin the business." The judge granted a temporary restraining order and set the case for July 13, though there is no evidence that a court hearing or trial ever took place.

According to M. P. Alexander's grandson, the rebelling partner believed that he rightfully owned a quarter interest in the Coca-Cola formula. When Alexander somehow learned that Pemberton had secured the trademark patent in his own name and had sold two-thirds of the rights to Venable and Lowndes, he realized that Pemberton was an unreliable, devious partner. At that point, Alexander withdrew from the partnership, taking control of the books and what remained of his initial investment, and went back to Tennessee. Later, he migrated to Texas, where he practiced pharmacy until he retired. There is no evidence that he conspired to ruin the business, but it appears that Alexander did not tell poor Frank Robinson about Pemberton's perfidy.

FRANK ROBINSON'S SURPRISE

Two tense weeks passed. On July 21, Pemberton wrote out an inventory of materials he was selling to Venable and Lowndes and received a check for $150 with a promissory note for the balance of $133.29 to be paid in thirty days. Pemberton then calmly informed Robinson that he had obtained a patent for the Coca-Cola label as sole owner and had, in addition, sold most of the rights.

Robinson, who had named Coca-Cola, written out the Spencerian-script logo, manufactured it, and masterminded the advertising and promotion, was in shock. Because Coca-Cola was created while Pemberton was a partner in the Pemberton Chemical Company, Robinson had assumed that each partner owned a fourth interest in the formula. After all, the company letterhead specifically stated that the Pemberton Chemical Company was the "sole proprietor" of French Wine Coca, which Pemberton had invented *before* the partnership commenced. Now, however, the company was a mere shell, with Alexander (and his money) on the lam and Coca-Cola sold.

The next day, July 22, 1887, Robinson carefully reconstructed a financial statement for Coca-Cola, probably from memory, because Alexander had the books. With fitting irony, he wrote it out on Pemberton Chemical Company letterhead that proclaimed Alexander the president of the firm. The stationery listed all of Pemberton's proprietary medicines, including Coca-Cola. Robinson's figures showed that 990 gallons of Coca-Cola syrup were sold for $1,500 from March 1 to July 14, 1887. He estimated the cost of materials at a dollar per gallon, leaving a $510 profit. Then, however, he listed salaries and expenses for the same period amounting to $1,459.78. The resulting balance sheet was decidedly in the red. Still, he was sure that in time the drink would pay handsomely.

He persuaded partner Ed Holland to accompany him to consult John Candler, who had recently represented the partners against Alexander, "to see if he didn't think [we] could have [our] rights maintained." Candler, an ambitious twenty-six-year-old prosecuting attorney, agreed to look into the matter and paid a visit to Pemberton, still bedridden in what the lawyer described as "a small cheap house." Pemberton denied any wrongdoing. "They are mistaken," he said. "They have got no interest in [Coca-Cola] whatever; I have done what they say, but I never did give them any rights in it, nor their company." He sighed. "It don't make much difference, though, even if they did have any rights. I don't know how you would get anything out of me." The lawyer decided not to take the case, because neither Robinson, Holland, nor Pemberton had any money. "I laughingly told [Mr. Robinson] I didn't see much chance," Candler recalled. "I didn't care for his case on any contingent fee . . . and that was the end of it."

As far as the independently wealthy Holland was concerned, perhaps the lawyer was right. But Frank Robinson had worked hard for Coca-Cola and believed in the

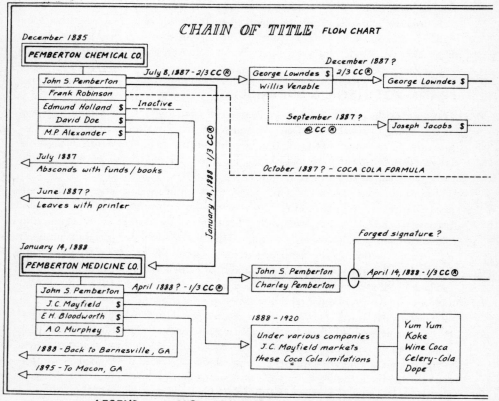

CHAIN OF TITLE FLOW CHART

LEGEND :   CC ® = Coca-Cola Rights   ? = Unsure of Date

future of the product; he wasn't about to let the matter drop, and he didn't feel it was a laughing matter. Robinson cast about for another plan. Pemberton may have sold the *rights* to the formula, but Robinson still had a *copy* of it, and he must have felt legally entitled to it. He needed to find someone to purchase the rights to Coca-Cola and promote it properly, someone with vision and capital.

VENABLE AND LOWNDES SELL OUT

Meanwhile, Willis Venable and George Lowndes had carted their inventory from 107 Marietta down the block to the corner of Marietta and Whitehall, where they dumped it in the basement of Jacobs' Pharmacy. Venable, who as the self-proclaimed "soda fountain king" of Atlanta had written a glowing testimonial to Coca-Cola in April, agreed to manufacture the product as well as market it. The first man to sell a glass of Coca-Cola, Venable was a well-respected businessman, dispensing a standard array of drinks at his twenty-five-foot soda fountain. Lowndes, who worked for another patent medicine house, simply supplied capital. Busy at the soda fountain, Venable couldn't spare the time to promote Coca-Cola, much less make it. After several months, Lowndes forced a change. "We did very little business, that's the truth," he later testified, "and it went into the concern to pay the expenses. . . . I found he wasn't handling it as a thing of that sort should be handled, and I told him we had best separate—he buy or sell to me."

According to Lowndes, Venable did indeed sell to him, but Lowndes couldn't find the time to promote the drink either. "I realized that Coca-Cola would die if it did not receive immediate attention. Consequently, I resolved to sell it." On December 13, 1887, Pemberton signed a note authorizing the sale, and the next day, Lowndes (with Venable's signature, because it had been on the original sales document) sold to Woolfolk Walker and Mrs. M. C. Dozier, for $1,200 plus the cost of the manufacturing inventory. Walker persuaded his younger sister, Margaret Dozier, to supply the $1,200 for the purchase. The ownership of Coca-Cola had become yet more fractured, with Mrs. Dozier owning two-ninths and Walker four-ninths of the total formula rights.*

JOE JACOBS MUDDIES THE WATERS

To confuse matters, however, Venable somehow disposed of his portion of Coca-Cola *twice*. At some point during the fall of 1887, he apparently gave his share of the drink to Joseph Jacobs, the owner of Jacobs' Pharmacy. As the druggist later recalled it, "thru some business deal, I acquired Mr. Venable's share [of Coca-Cola] in lieu of some money I had loaned him in completing his beautiful home in the West End." Jacobs did not sell to Walker and Dozier, keeping his share well into 1888, though his memory was frustratingly hazy and contradictory. He later testified that "at the time we bought [Coca-Cola], Moxie had a large sale and we thought we would make a big thing out of [Coca-Cola]. . . . Dr. Pemberton put this on the market and I took a part ownership and I think finally all of it."

Soon after acquiring his share in Coca-Cola, Jacobs became annoyed with both the drink and its inventor. By his own admission, he didn't know much about the soda fountain business, which he left entirely to Willis Venable. While Venable had continued to make Coca-Cola "in a small way," Pemberton kept harassing Jacobs for advances on his share of the sales. "There was a clause in the original agreement," wrote Jacobs, "in which Dr. Pemberton was to have a royalty of five cents a gallon. He seemed to be pressed for money pretty much all the time and was having money advanced constantly, based on the potential royalty. This did not please me."

PEMBERTON REVIVES

In addition to plaguing Jacobs, the ailing Pemberton was not idle. Although virtually bankrupt, he placed a misleading ad in the *Atlanta Constitution* on October 2, 1887:

> WANTED: An acceptable party with $2,000.00 to purchase one-half interest in a very profitable and well-established manufacturing business, absolutely no risk, and guaranteed a 50 per cent profit on investment, with possibilities of much larger profits and rare opportunity to right party.

---

* The contract specified that Mrs. Dozier was to get a third and Walker the balance. Because they were buying two-thirds of the entire formula, that comes out to these odd fractions.

To avoid his creditors, Pemberton's blind ad did not give his correct address, but another house on Marietta Street, presumably a friend's. With this bait, he snared three eager entrepreneurs, so he graciously allowed all three of them to pitch in $2,000, thus buying what would logically be 150 percent of his business.

J. C. Mayfield, an Alabama chemist, was reassured when Pemberton answered his response to the blind ad, because he had previously sold Pemberton's concoctions. A. O. Murphey and E. H. Bloodworth, from Barnesville, Georgia, had no experience with patent medicines but were impressed with the records Pemberton showed them. After much correspondence throughout October, November, and December, the three new partners finally moved to Atlanta in late December, ready to produce all of Pemberton's wonderful medicines, including Coca-Cola. The good doctor had neglected to tell them that he had sold off any of his formulae.

ASA CANDLER MAKES HIS ENTRANCE

With the Christmas season of 1887 about to commence, the fortunes of Coca-Cola were quite uncertain. The formula was officially owned by John Pemberton, Woolfolk Walker, and Mrs. Dozier. In fact, it is clear that several others had some interest in it, including Charley Pemberton, Joe Jacobs, Frank Robinson, J. C. Mayfield, A. O. Murphey, and E. H. Bloodworth.

One more person had almost certainly entered the picture by this point—Asa Candler, the older brother of lawyer John Candler. In his search for a savior, Frank Robinson had found his well-capitalized, industrious businessman. The epitome of the ambitious Atlanta druggist, Candler was always looking for a likely new product, but he was cautious about spending money. Robinson had a difficult time convincing Candler that Coca-Cola was a worthwhile venture, finally galvanizing him by conjuring a prophetic vision: "See that wagon going by with all those empty beer kegs? Well, we are going to push Coca-Cola until you see the wagons going by with Coca-Cola just like that."

Though Asa Candler does not appear in any Coca-Cola documents until 1888, he insisted in later testimony that he had become involved the previous year: "I had the whole control of it [Coca-Cola], as far as the business was concerned, in 1887." Curiously, however, he added, "I don't know whether I had bought it or not at that time," explaining that he acquired the drink in return for debts owed him by certain "gentlemen." Later, he "intervened into the affairs of this Pemberton Chemical Company." While vague about exactly how he became involved with Coca-Cola, Candler was positive about one thing: "Robinson had manufactured it, collected it all, and did everything else before 1888. Robinson might have been called my agent."

Candler's muddy statement becomes clearer when we compare it with his last courtroom testimony in 1924. In it, he said he *thought* he had purchased the Coca-Cola formula from Joe Jacobs, but added "I am not certain about it." What he *was* absolutely clear about was that Frank Robinson had given him the actual formula. Obviously, after Robinson brought him the directions for manufacturing Coca-Cola, Candler then had to obtain legal possession—a process that would be not only confused but highly suspicious.

With the opening of the soda fountain season in March of 1888, Candler officially began to take control of Coca-Cola. During that spring, Joe Jacobs complained to his friend Asa Candler about Pemberton's constant requests for money. Candler, without appearing too eager, offered to take the drink off his hands in return for some stock in a glass factory and "odds and ends such as bed pans, pewter syringes, wooden pill boxes, and empty bottles," according to Jacobs. The uninsured glass factory burned soon afterward. Though Jacobs kicked himself for the stupid barter in subsequent years, he remained lifelong friends with Candler.

CHARLEY PEMBERTON STAKES HIS CLAIM

Meanwhile, Mayfield, Bloodworth, and Murphey had settled in, and on January 14, 1888, they had formed a copartnership with Pemberton called the Pemberton Medicine Company, in which Pemberton specifically gave them the rights to all of his patented products, including Coca-Cola and his new Lemon and Orange Elixir. After moving to a better location on Pryor Street, the partners commenced production, naively unaware of the disintegration of the Pemberton Chemical Company or the sale of Coca-Cola. Mayfield ran the laboratory, Bloodworth took to the road as a traveling salesman, and Murphey kept the books. The only discordant note seemed to be Mayfield's rather stormy marriage—Diva Mayfield often helped her husband in the laboratory, and their arguments made Murphey and Bloodworth uncomfortable.

Within a few months, however, trouble appeared in the person of Charley Pemberton, who had returned from a drug firm in Louisville, Kentucky, to claim his birthright. He demanded that Mayfield relinquish the manufacturing job to him. Mayfield refused. Charley was "disgruntled, dissatisfied and made it up for the old man, Dr. Pemberton," Mayfield said later. "The doctor came to us and told us that he would have to give—that the son contended that he had promised him the Coca-Cola business. Of course, it was a bomb in our camps."

Charley, whom Mayfield regarded as "disagreeable, a drinking kind of boy," began throwing tantrums, boozing, wheedling, and putting his father in an awkward position. Dr. Pemberton finally told the partners he had signed the rights to Coca-Cola over to Charley some time previously but hadn't remembered it until then. He blamed his lapse of memory on his morphine habit. For a while, there was no resolution to the matter. "We ran along there quite a little while thereafter undecided just what to do," Mayfield remembered. As matters simmered, the partners were further disillusioned with Pemberton when they discovered that Asa Candler had quietly maneuvered to gain legal control of Coca-Cola, forming a new company with Charley Pemberton and Dr. Pemberton's former salesman, Woolfolk Walker. In addition, as the soda fountain season opened, Candler's company was brewing Coca-Cola faster than they were and pushing it hard.

THE UNKNOWN COCA-COLA COMPANY

On March 24, 1888, Asa Candler, Charley Pemberton, and Woolfolk Walker and his sister filed in Fulton County Superior Court for incorporation of the Coca-Cola Company. Candler soon regretted both the incorporation and the partnership with the immature Pemberton, who proved to be more a liability than a help. Although much of the wording was probably "boiler plate" for such documents, it is nonetheless instructive to see what they planned:

> The purposes of this Company . . . will be the manufacturing of Coca-Cola Syrup; the buying of ingredients and appliances necessary therefor, and the sale of the manufactured article, as a syrup in bulk, bottled, as a medicine, and as a nerve tonic; And they desire the privilege of extending such manufacturing to other specialties of like kind. . . . The Capital Stock of said Company shall be twelve thousand dollars; more than ten percent of which has already been paid in. . . . The principal office and place of business . . . shall be . . . Atlanta . . . but petitioners desire the privilege of establishing branch offices or factories elsewhere.

Like all other incorporations, this one would last for twenty years before renewal. The petition stated that over $1,200 had already been paid in. Presumably some of this was Walker/Dozier money, with the rest coming from Candler. Charley Pemberton probably paid nothing for his share.

This "first" Coca-Cola Company is not a part of the official chain of title, nor is it ever mentioned in any corporate history. Asa Candler didn't file for incorporation of *The* Coca-Cola Company (the legal basis for the current company, always spelled with a capital T) until 1892. He must have been extremely nervous about the existence of this prior company and its partners, any of whom could have caused considerable trouble for him, at least until the charter expired in 1908. The existence of this early version of the Coca-Cola Company explains some mysterious endorsement letters addressed as early as 1888 to the "Coca-Cola Company." In an 1898 pamphlet announcing the grand opening of his new Coca-Cola factory, Candler slipped, asserting that the company had begun in March 1888, a clear reference to this otherwise well-buried legality.

ASA WRITES TO WARREN

On April 10, 1888, shortly after incorporating the company, Asa Candler wrote to his younger brother Warren, a Methodist minister then editing a religious journal in Nashville. After advising Warren not to accept the presidency of Emory College because it didn't pay enough (Warren ignored him, establishing an important link between Emory and the Candlers), Asa went on:

> You know how I suffer with headaches. Well some days ago, a friend suggested that I try Coco-Cola. I did & was relieved. Some days later I again tried it & was again relieved. I determined to find out about it—investigation showed that it was owned by parties unable to put it fairly before the people. I determined to put money into it & a little influence. I put $500.00 of the first & am putting a goodly portion of what I have of the last.*

---

* It appears that although Candler claimed that he had exercised full control over Coca-Cola since late 1887, he was only now getting around to tasting it, and he still couldn't spell it correctly. Or perhaps he was only now trying it as a cure for his perennial headaches. It is likely that the $500 referred to Candler's contribution to the Coca-Cola Company capitalization.

Clearly, Candler was certain he had a winning drink, and he was prepared to promote it. In the remainder of the letter, he asked Warren to find a fountain outlet in Nashville for Coca-Cola, saying he would send two free gallons of syrup as an introductory offer. While adopting Robinson's idea of giving out free tickets, he aimed to build up a direct mail list by soliciting customers' addresses from Tennessee druggists. "I don't want to make a merchant or peddler out of you," Candler explained, as he did just that. "I enclose circulars. It is a fine thing—certain."

Just days after writing to his brother, Candler's "influence" bore fruit. Eager to dispense with Charley Pemberton, Candler arranged to buy him out. On April 14, 1888, Charley Pemberton (with his father as cosigner) sold the remaining third of the Coca-Cola title to Walker, Candler & Company for $550 ($50 to be paid down, and $500 due in thirty days). Walker, Candler & Company comprised Woolfolk Walker, Asa Candler, and Joe Jacobs, though Jacobs and Candler later insisted that it was a "dummy" corporation, because Candler supplied all of the money.*

Three days after putting $50 down on the Pembertons' third of Coca-Cola, Candler added to his legal rights, buying out half of the Walker/Dozier title for $750 on April 17, 1888. Frank Robinson witnessed the document. Around this time, Candler rented Pemberton's vacant old site at 107 Marietta Street, and the original apparatus for preparing Coca-Cola was once again trundled down Marietta Street from Jacobs' basement to its old home, where Frank Robinson began producing Coca-Cola in earnest.

THE FINAL ACT

The hot Atlanta summer arrived in full force. John Pemberton lay dying of stomach cancer (per family lore, though "enteritis" is on the death certificate). Asa Candler pushed Coca-Cola, with Woolfolk Walker on the road for him. At this point, Candler must have cursed the incorporation with Charley Pemberton, who was now marketing a competing drink and had proved anything but a stable stockholder in the Coca-Cola Company. On June 2, 1888, Asa again wrote to brother Warren in Nashville. "We are doing moderately well with Coco Cola. Its only obstacle is that [Charley] Pemberton is continually offering a very poor article at a less price & the public who pay for Coco Cola & are not benefitted erroneously decide that it is a fraud."

At about this time, Dr. Pemberton, in an attempt to make everyone happy, told his partners that although the *name* Coca-Cola belonged to Charley, they could continue to use the same formula but sell it under a different trademark. When the uninspired title of Yum Yum failed to catch on, they switched to Koke (already a nickname for Coca-Cola). Murphey, disgusted with the whole scene and his discovery

---

* If Candler really was the sole buyer, why would he bother to camouflage it? John Pemberton probably bore a grudge against Candler for buying out his entire stock of drugs and lab equipment five years earlier, when Pemberton was too sick to protect himself from predatory partners. The sick inventor had sued Candler along with everyone else involved. In a bitter affidavit, Pemberton wrote that he was "now lying perfectly helpless and utterly dependent upon the proceeds of the partnership." If allowed to proceed, the sale would be his "present and utter ruin." Nonetheless, Pemberton lost the suit and his lab.

of Pemberton's morphine addiction, withdrew from the partnership and went back to Barnesville.

Thus, as the muggy heat of Atlanta turned oppressive in July and early August, three varieties of Coca-Cola were competing to assuage thirst, cure headache and hangover, and relieve that tired feeling.

Even as he was dying, Pemberton struggled to continue his work. Several times in his final months, he staggered to his laboratory, attempting to perfect his last drink, a modified cola with celery extract. "He did not care anything about what he had already accomplished," J. C. Mayfield said. "He wanted something new." He never finished. On August 16, 1888, John Pemberton died at the age of fifty-seven, leaving behind a legacy of hard work, sound scholarship, poor business sense, shattered dreams, drug addiction, lawsuits, and a few patent medicines with quaint names that would be forgotten within a few years—Extract of Stillingia, Globe Flower Cough Syrup, Indian Queen Hair Dye, Triplex Liver Pills, French Wine Coca. His beloved and only child was an alcoholic who would die an apparent suicide six years later, and his widow would end her life a pauper. Still, Pemberton was, above all else, a gentle man, an obsessed scholar, a creative genius. He did not know it as he died, but his principal legacy was Coca-Cola, the drink that would make him famous and might have made him wealthy, had he lived long enough.

The newspaper notice of Pemberton's death called him "the oldest druggist of Atlanta and one of her best-known citizens . . . an especially popular gentleman." Asa Candler, weeping fat crocodile tears, called all the druggists of the city together at his store to suggest they close their establishments for the day of his funeral. "Mr. Candler paid Dr. Pemberton a beautiful tribute of respect, speaking of his lovable nature and many virtues," the newspaper reported. "He voiced, he said, the feelings of all present that 'our profession has lost a good and active member.'" Candler served as a pallbearer at the Atlanta funeral ceremony, before the casket was whisked to an unmarked grave in Columbus. Years later, Candler protested, "Why, I suppose Dr. Pemberton felt I was one of his best friends in this town."

Candler wasted no time consolidating his claim to Coca-Cola. Exactly two weeks after Pemberton's death, on August 30, 1888, he bought the remaining interest of Woolfolk Walker and Margaret Dozier for $1,000, payable in a series of notes. Now, except for the technicality of the Walker, Candler & Company ownership, Asa Candler had staked a solid legal claim to Coca-Cola. He had paid a total of $2,300, according to the official chain of title. By May 1, 1889, he was calling himself the drink's sole proprietor.

FORGERY AND OTHER JUICY TIDBITS

There are, however, weak links in the chain Candler forged. Even Candler's son, in the official biography of his father, noted that "this is the factual chain of title, established by attorneys and accepted by the courts, of the ownership of Coca-Cola. Behind these bare facts, there are probably others which would be interesting to know. . . ." Mrs. M. C. Dozier would have agreed.

Margaret Dozier showed up in 1914 at the age of sixty-five, insisting that she had never sold her share of the formula. A dithery witness on the stand, she nonetheless appeared quite certain about the vital issues: "I did not sign any paper at all conveying any interest to Asa G. Candler or anyone else. Most positively I never received a cent." Her brother Woolfolk had "charge of the whole thing," she said, complaining that he told her nothing; "in fact, when he got control of it he never came near me at all."

Two handwriting experts who looked at Mrs. Dozier's signatures on the questionable chain of title documents (those of April 17 and August 30, 1888) agreed that the April Dozier signature is a forgery.* The August signature may be authentic, but at least one of the experts couldn't be sure. It seems likely that Woolfolk Walker, perhaps with Asa Candler's knowledge, forged his sister's signature, at least on the April document.

Walker himself vanished immediately after signing over the rights to Candler at the end of August. His sister testified that he left town without even saying goodbye, and, though she wrote repeatedly to Hot Springs, Arkansas, where he was rumored to reside, he never answered her. His disappearance was suspiciously providential for Asa Candler.

But that's not the end of the forgery. John Pemberton's signature on the crucial April 14, 1888, sale to Walker, Candler & Company is a fake. According to handwriting expert George Pearl, the writing is "way, way out of natural variation for this signature to be genuine. The writing is not smooth and fast but rather slow and unsure, wondering where to go next. . . . This is a simulated signature and not a very good one at that."

Though there is no way to know with any certainty, Charley Pemberton is the most likely one to have forged the signature. At the same time, he tried to contrast and obscure his own handwriting by signing with a large flourish and much spilled ink. But why would Charley Pemberton have committed the forgery? Did he really need the resulting $550 that badly? It is more probable that he had made some kind of deal with Asa Candler. Candler apparently wrote the body of the contract itself in his distinctively hasty script.

Although it is difficult (and presumptuous) to play armchair detective so many years later, it seems likely that Candler was the shadowy figure behind both the Pemberton and Dozier forgeries, which occurred within three days of one another in April of 1888. Both forgeries were committed within a week of Asa Candler's admission to his brother Warren that he was exerting "a little influence" to gain full control of Coca-Cola.[†]

The other jarring note in the chain of title stems from Mrs. Pemberton's family. Her sister Elberta was convinced that Asa Candler had bought the formula, not from Pemberton or Walker, but from Mrs. Pemberton soon after the funeral. Elberta

---

* Using three genuine signatures as a standard, George Pearl of Atlanta, Georgia, stated that the April 17, 1888, signature was a forgery, though he was uncertain about the August signature. John Brullmann of Jackson Heights, New York, pronounced the April signature a forgery.

† Candler later filed a copy of the April 14 document as part of his official chain of title with the U.S. Patent Office. In doing so, he submitted a completely new document, all written in a single anonymous hand. Whoever copied it over mistook Charley Pemberton's middle initial, writing it as an "M" rather than an "N." Candler may have deliberately had the document recopied to avoid submitting the forged signature.

Newman taught her grandchildren never to drink Coca-Cola, because she did not want them to contribute even a nickel to Candler's ill-gotten fortune. "Your Auntie sold the Formula to Asa Candler in his own hand," she later wrote to her son, "and he remarked to her, he was making a risk, but if he made any thing from it he would give her a home and she would never want. He never gave her a cent. She believed to her last day that he would keep his promise."

Elberta's daughter Mary overheard Mrs. Pemberton telling her father of the transaction. When her father found that Candler had paid only $300 for the formula, he told her she should have had a lawyer. "Oh! Asa said he would give me a fine home and handsome income *if* he made anything out of it," Mrs. Pemberton said. "My aunt was a devoted Methodist," Mary explained, "and as Asa Candler taught in the Methodist Sunday school she felt sure he would keep his word."

Other versions of the family story place the blame for the sale of Coca-Cola on the dissolute Charley Pemberton, who was supposed to have sold the formula while drunk or in return for being bailed out of jail, where he was languishing for disorderly conduct. Yet another relative said that Charley had cajoled his mother into selling to Candler for $600, which he soon spent on drink. Regardless of the exact story, the entire clan was convinced, along with nephew Wilson, that "there was some crookedness about the deal."

On June 23, 1894, Charley Pemberton was discovered unconscious, lying flat on his face in a tiny bedroom above the Oriole Restaurant. A stick of crude opium was found on a chair nearby. The incident was fully reported in the sensation-loving Atlanta newspapers: "Whether the opium was taken with suicidal intent is not known, but for three hours Pemberton was walked, rubbed, beaten, and dosed." The reporter went on to comment that Charley was the son of "one of the most noted physicians Atlanta has ever had. He was the discoverer of the famous Coco-Cola and left his son in charge of the patent when he died."

After ten days of "intense suffering," Charley Pemberton died at Grady Hospital at the age of forty. His mother remained by his side during the ordeal. The notice of this death said that "Charley Pemberton was well known in Atlanta," that his father was "a physician of learning and distinction," and repeated that Charley had inherited the formula, which "he afterwards disposed of . . . for a comparatively small sum." Although Charley was an acknowledged alcoholic, this is the first indication that he took opium. His death could have resulted from an accidental overdose, suicide, or murder. A cousin later wrote that "there was something mysterious about Charley's death." Monroe King, a Pemberton expert, believed that suicide was unlikely: "Remember that Charley Pemberton had worked for years with his father and knew the drug trade intimately. He would have chosen a much more effective way to kill himself had he chosen to do so. Taking raw opium instead of a massive dose of morphine makes no sense." At any rate, Asa Candler must have been relieved that the unpredictable, unstable Pemberton was gone.

The allegations of *some* sort of questionable activities were verified by Price Gilbert, a lawyer who apparently did a good deal of work for Asa Candler. Gilbert told a friend that "if I told what I knew about the early days of Coca-Cola, what I said would be very embarrassing," adding that "I'm not going to tell the maneuvering we did to keep afloat in the early days of the company." In 1910, during one of the Company's moves to larger quarters, Asa Candler, over the objections of his nephew, ordered that the earliest records of The Coca-Cola Company be burned, leaving only the official chain of title intact. Beyond that, only circumstantial evidence and rumor remained to haunt him.

As rusty and weak as the chain of title may be, though, it is quite likely that we would view Coca-Cola Extract and Syrup as just one more quaint creation of Dr. Pemberton if Asa Candler had not taken control of it. In the end, Rob Stephens, yet another relation of Mrs. Pemberton, was probably correct when he wrote:

> Coca-Cola became a go because it was pushed and pushed by an energetic man. If the Pembertons had not sold the formula it probably would have stayed in an old drink somewhere and been lost in time. I think Cousin Cliff always thought Mr. Candler robbed her and Charley, but I doubt if it can be said he did. He paid them for something of no use to them and he made it a go by his own efforts.

~ 4 ~

Asa Candler: His Triumphs and Headaches

If people knew the good qualities of Coca-Cola as I know them, it would be necessary for us to lock the doors of our factories and have a guard with a shotgun to make the people line up to buy it.

—Asa G. Candler

I don't know a single day in my life when I have been moved by a desire to make money.

—Asa G. Candler, aged sixty-four

Asa Candler, a short bantam of a man with a high, squeaky voice, may not fit the ideal image of the Big Business Man, but even as a youth he was the quintessential capitalist. Born on December 30, 1851, the eighth of eleven children, Candler liked to paint a log-cabin portrait of his poor-but-happy rural youth. In fact, Sam Candler, his father, was a well-to-do planter and merchant who founded the town in which Asa was raised.

A gold prospector, the elder Candler named Villa Rica ("Rich Town" in Spanish) to attract others who had the gold bug. He must have passed on this spirit of enterprise and promotion. Despite his relative wealth, however, Asa Candler's father did not believe in spoiling his children—they earned every penny of their spending money. Asa soon proved that he would do almost anything for a dollar. He once chased down a wild mink, which bit him severely when he finally caught it. As Candler told the story,

> I hadn't heard of people selling mink skins, but it seemed to me it might be a good idea and I decided to try. Atlanta was thirty-six miles away and there was no railroad, but that seemed to be the best possible market, so I sent the skin in to town by wagon, and I said to myself, "Maybe I'll get twenty-five cents!" I got a dollar—the first I had ever made.

Thrilled, the young Candler soon organized other children to do the mink-trapping for him, and he established a regular Atlanta trade. On the return wagon, he purchased straight pins for resale in Villa Rica and learned a lesson he would later apply to Coca-Cola: there was good money to be made from penny and nickel sales. "Seems

45

you couldn't make anything off pins, doesn't it? But when I went away to school, I had more than $100 saved up through the sale of mink skins and speculation in pins."

Asa Candler received little formal education, because the Civil War closed schools when he was ten. After the war, he managed to complete two years of high school before quitting to apprentice as a pharmacy clerk. Candler undoubtedly received a proper Christian home education, however, from his strong-willed mother, Martha Beall Candler.

Married at the age of fourteen, the diminutive Mrs. Candler, who rose ramrod straight to less than five feet and never weighed a hundred pounds, had eleven children and dominated the family. Though her husband wasn't a churchgoer until his later years, Martha Candler belonged to the Primitive Baptist Church, whose members were more descriptively known as Hardshell Baptists. And woe unto the child who crossed her. "She tried to boss everybody in sight and came very near doing it," one of her grandchildren recalled. Martha Candler's imprint on her seven sons is quite apparent in an 1891 photograph that shows the indomitable matron surrounded by her grown male offspring. All in the picture—mother and children—display the solemn downturned mouth characteristic of the Candlers.

A YOUTH'S APPRENTICESHIP

When he abandoned his schooling in 1870, Asa Candler went to Cartersville, northwest of Atlanta, to apprentice in a drugstore run by two physicians, friends of his family. He lived in the rear of the store and studied Latin, Greek, chemistry, and medicine at night. As a child, he had dreamed of becoming a doctor—"I would concoct imaginary potions and doctor sick pigeons, hogs, dogs, and cattle"—but after two years of working in the drug business and observing the doctors' country practice, he changed his mind. He would remain a druggist, but not in small-town, small-pay Cartersville, where after two years he was earning only twenty-five dollars a month. "I think there is more money to be made as a druggist than as a physician," he wrote in the fall of 1872, "and I know it can be done with a great deal less trouble of soul and body."

At the age of twenty-one, Candler arrived in Atlanta with his trunk on January 7, 1873. In later years, he liked to tell the story of how he came to the big city looking for work, wearing homemade clothes and carrying only $1.75 in his pocket, but he told a reporter in 1909 that he had been "promised a place with a wholesale druggist." Although he had little cash, he told the journalist, he also had a note for salary due him from his old job.

Even if Asa Candler's rags-to-riches fable doesn't ring quite true, he displayed unusual fortitude once he discovered there was no job waiting for him that chilly day, applying at virtually every drugstore in Atlanta (including Pemberton's establishment) for work. Finally, at 9 p.m., he tried George J. Howard's drugstore, where he encountered a bored prescription clerk sitting on a counter. The clerk interrupted Candler's recitation of his resume to ask, "When can you go to work?" When Candler said he could start right away, the clerk led him into the back room, introduced him to Dr. Howard, and tendered his resignation, effective immediately. Asa Candler had a job. He also found a boardinghouse that was willing to wait for his first paycheck.

Howard owned stores at several Atlanta locations. In March of 1877, he took John Pemberton as a partner—an arrangement that lasted only a few months—simultaneously selling one of his stands to his two young clerks, Marcellus Hallman, twenty-eight, and Asa Candler, twenty-five. The Dun credit agent was impressed, noting that Hallman and Candler were "clever young men . . . economical & reliable." They had saved $3,000 to begin the business. "They are very energetic," wrote the credit rater. "Have no pending debts hanging over them & will no doubt be successful."

The Dun man proved to be a good prophet. Two years later, he wrote that the partners were carrying a full stock, had an active trade, paid their bills promptly, and claimed to be worth $10,000. He added that they were "correct reliable young men, close in business matters, addicted to no extravagant habits." This description was an understatement, as far as Candler was concerned. He was a workaholic, never touched liquor, and was tightfisted with his money.

THE OVERWORKED BOSS'S DAUGHTER

In the meantime, Asa Candler had gotten married. Lucy Howard, only eighteen, must have seen more in the small, determined young man than her father, who was violently opposed to her marriage to his former clerk. Grudgingly, George Howard finally wrote a curt note to his son-in-law in November of 1878: "I am disposed to 'bury the hatchet' and to be friendly in the future—if this should meet your approval you can let me know." Eight days later, Lucy gave birth to Charles Howard Candler, who was always known by his middle name. Asa and Lucy Candler appear to have had a genuinely happy marriage, eventually producing four boys and one girl. Howard later wrote, however, that "my Mother's patience was tried by household responsibilities with which she had to cope with little help from her husband, engrossed in the perplexities and problems of a growing business."

While Asa was thus engaged, Lucy was "superintendent and well-nigh slave" to a household of his relatives. Her mother-in-law, the imperious Martha Candler, moved in after her husband's death, along with Asa's mentally disabled older brother Noble and his youngest brother, John. At various points, Asa's brother Warren (with his family) and sister Jessie (who gave birth to a third child shortly after arriving) also moved in for a while. Little wonder, then, that Asa and Lucy Candler bought a home in 1879, then a larger one three years later. Lucy must have been quite relieved when her flint-willed mother-in-law finally moved to a home of her own two doors away in 1882. For the next fifteen years, until her death, Asa Candler visited his mother every day before and after work, anticipating "her every need and . . . wish," as Howard Candler recalled.

In 1881, Asa Candler bought out his partner, Marcellus Hallman, and the next year formed a partnership with his father-in-law and former boss, George Howard. Soon afterward, the pair purchased Pemberton's drug business while he lay sick in bed, then survived a disastrous fire. In 1886, Candler bought Howard's interest in the partnership, renaming the firm Asa G. Candler & Company.

ASA AND ATLANTA ARE WIRED

That spring, as Pemberton was perfecting Coca-Cola, Asa Candler cast around for a ticket to wealth. Thirty-four years old, he felt that he had served his apprenticeship in the drug trade. It was time to make some real money, and he knew that fortunes were building all over the country. As the patent medicine capital of the South and the home of major successes such as B.B.B. and S.S.S., Atlanta exceeded all cities in the country in the proportion of manufacturing income derived from questionable drugs.

The city may have been hustling to recover from Sherman's devastation when Pemberton arrived on the scene back in 1869, but by 1886 Atlanta was *booming*. It had become the capital of the state in 1877 and was, according to an observer of the 1880s, a "great, populous, and thriving metropolis . . . famous for the greatness and brilliancy of its enterprises." The Atlanta newspapers of the period were awash with boosterism and particularly delighted in quoting praise from Yankees. The city, noted a Massachusetts visitor in 1886, "has all the push and energy of the North coupled with a most delightful climate. . . . Atlanta has become one of the best advertised cities in the United States. People have come here to settle from all parts of the Union."

In their pursuit of everything they considered progressive, Atlantans naturally were fascinated by the newly invented electric generator, even though it had few practical applications. Direct current, which could travel a mile or less, was considered the only safe form of the new energy source. Still, in the mid-eighties, one innovative Atlanta druggist was advertising his electric doorbell, which rang in his residence to summon him "at all hours during the night." Another ad featured "Dr. Dye's Celebrated Voltaic Belt with Electric Suspensory Appliances" for the speedy relief of impotency. An 1885 Atlanta editorial used electricity as a metaphor for the kind of businessman the city needed. In retrospect, it appears an apt description of Asa Candler, who fairly bristled with nervous energy: "What we now need is a few electric men—men who will put their electric shoulders to the great wheel of Southern progress." Their "electric brains" would crackle with "electric ideas," which would "induce capital in abundance and immigration of an acceptable class to come southward."

In his 1886 ads, Candler described himself as "active, pushing, and reliable." His new patent medicine was appropriately called Electric Bitters, only fifty cents a bottle. Candler's ad, like many others, obviously aimed to induce the symptoms he claimed to cure:

> You are feeling depressed, your appetite is poor, you are bothered with head-ache, you are fidgetty, and nervous, and generally out of sorts, and want to *brace* up. . . . What you want is an alterative that will purify your blood, start healthy action of liver and kidneys, restore your vitality, and give renewed health and strength. Such a medicine you will find in Electric Bitters.

ASA'S AILMENTS

If Candler's copy sounds convincing, it is because he often experienced all of those symptoms himself. His son recalled that "many times when Father got home at the end of a day of hard work at the store or the office he was miserable and exhausted, suffering intense headache"—often exacerbated by eyestrain. In addition, if he were living today, Candler might be diagnosed as bipolar. Although he normally functioned at a manic, high-energy level, he was periodically morose, even at the peak of his success. He also suffered from dyspepsia, caused in part by his irregular eating pattern and his tendency to bolt his food. He often skipped lunch and came home for dinner long after the rest of his family had eaten.

This impressive list of ailments was magnified by Candler's hypochondria. His letters to family members were filled with complaints and health concerns. "Do not allow yourself to get billious or to feel in a drowsy, sleepy state," a typical message read. "Such symptoms generally indicate miasma." He sought cures for his afflictions in patent medicines (no doubt sampling the products he pushed), as his son Howard recalled: "He knew in a general way the properties of drugs and believed in and practiced self-medication, which was not only unwise but fraught with some danger," given the sometimes lethal ingredients with which he must have dosed himself.

THE ROAD TO COCA-COLA

Unlike John Pemberton, Asa Candler was no brilliant inventor. Instead, he specialized in hard-sell copy, offering a money-back guarantee if customers were not satisfied, knowing that few would take advantage of it. In addition to Electric Bitters, Candler bought the rights to a number of other proprietaries before finding Coca-Cola. These included Everlasting Cologne (presumably a perfume with an alarmingly permanent odor), Bucklen's Arnica Salve ("for cuts, bruises, sores, ulcers, salt rheum, fever sores, tetter, chapped hands, chilblains, corns, and all skin eruptions, positively cures piles"), King's New Discovery ("for consumption, colds and coughs, will surely cure any and every affection of throat, lungs, or chest"), and De-Lec-Ta-Lave ("will whiten the teeth, cleanse the mouth, harden and beautify the gums").

Even after he purchased the rights to Coca-Cola in 1888, Candler continued to look for other likely patent medicines. In 1890, he bought the venerable Botanic Blood Balm (B.B.B.), which had been a big seller for its inventor, Dr. J. P. Dromgoole. A landmark Georgia Supreme Court case in 1889 had considerably reduced the value of the company, however, when the court ruled against the Blood Balm Company in favor of a Mr. Cooper, who had taken three bottles to cure a rash on his leg. He would have been better off settling for the rash, according to the court records, because by the time he'd consumed the recommended dosage, "his head, neck and breast were covered with red spots and the inside of his mouth and throat filled with sores." Eventually, "a large part of the hair fell from his head." It is easy to see why Candler may have picked up B.B.B. at a bargain-basement price after that lawsuit.

ASA'S 1889 EMPIRE

As active and pushy as Candler may have been, there was nothing particularly unusual about him in 1888 when he finally gained complete legal control of Coca-Cola. To a casual observer of the Atlanta scene, he was just one more enterprising businessman. No one would have guessed that by the turn of the century, he would be one of the wealthiest men in Atlanta, and Coca-Cola would be the most popular soft drink in America.

In an interview, Candler later said that at the beginning of 1889, he was "in bad health, $50,000 in debt and Coca-Cola on [my] hands." But in the next months, he overcame his headaches, stomach problems, and dour outlook enough to impress an *Atlanta Journal* reporter, who described the Peachtree Street facilities of the "enterprising druggist" that May. Frank Robinson supervised the manufacturing in the basement, while Asa Candler's "private sanctum" took up the rear of the first floor, which housed the retail outlet. The shipping department, on the second floor, was "practically packed" from floor to ceiling (fourteen feet high) with $10,000 worth of various Atlanta patent medicines. Finally, on the top floor, a group of young women bottled "extracts, medicines, oils, etc."

Candler, "a continuous worker, always confined in his office," relied on Frank Robinson and one other full-time salesman to hawk his products, including Coca-Cola, identified as "one of their leading specialties."* Another salesman joined the small firm soon afterward. Sam Dobbs, who would play a key role in the company's early history, arrived as a seventeen-year-old to ask his Uncle Asa for a job. At first he was refused, but the black porter, a former Candler family slave, died the following day, and Dobbs got his position, soon proving himself as a salesman—the first of many Candler relations to find work through Coca-Cola.

Traveling salesmen in those days were known as drummers, because they drummed up trade, and the Atlanta variety already had a reputation for hustle, as an 1881 observer noted: "The trade of Atlanta is rapidly extending into wider and more distant territory. The drummers . . . for Atlanta houses swarm over Georgia and surrounding States." Candler's men must have followed the pattern, because the testimonial letters for Coca-Cola printed in the May 1889 article came from Mississippi, Alabama, and Virginia in addition to Georgia. By 1890, only 40 percent of Coca-Cola sales were made at Atlanta soda fountains, and by the following year, the figure had shrunk to 27 percent.

A few months later, veteran fountain man Foster Howell described Coca-Cola as "one of the most popular drinks ever sold in Atlanta." Howell was less circumspect than Candler in explaining Coca-Cola's popularity as a hangover cure: "Men who get on a razee the night before come up in the morning and drink . . . coca-cola . . . one of the finest nerve tonics in the world." He then recounted how one of Pemberton's employees, a "longheaded chemist," had introduced him to the new headache cure in 1886, appearing early one morning carrying a syrup bottle with "Coca-Cola scribbled on the label." Just then, a badly hung-over customer staggered in, so Howell tried the "new discovery" on him. "It worked like a charm. He came back in a few minutes and in an hour he had swallowed four glasses." Howell described another customer who drank five glasses straight, then "went away with a regretful look, seeming to feel unhappy because he could hold no more."

The combination of cocaine and caffeine must have induced repeated calls for Coca-Cola, and we have here the first indication of habitual users, soon labeled

---

* Candler told the reporter that "Coca-Cola was introduced to the public a little over a year ago in a modest way. Its inventor was unable to devote to it the means necessary to its general introduction to the public. . . ." It is interesting that Pemberton's name is carefully avoided here, though he had been dead less than a year and was well known in Atlanta. Candler was already minimizing the inventor's contribution. Note, too, that he moved the introduction of Coca-Cola to "a little over a year ago" (1888) rather than 1886.

"Coca-Cola fiends."* Nonetheless, Howell insisted that there was no danger of addiction; people would not become "soda drunkards." But he added that "if you drink it of a night you don't go to sleep."

Throughout 1889, without much advertising, Candler saw sales of Coca-Cola mushroom. He personally went back to Cartersville to ask his first employers to stock Coca-Cola. Total sales for 1889 amounted to 2,171 gallons of syrup. Because each drink called for one ounce of syrup, that meant that almost sixty-one thousand drinks were sold.

1890: YEAR OF DECISION

On January 1, 1890, Asa Candler took stock of his financial situation, writing out a personal balance sheet. He was no longer in debt, showing a net worth of $17,326, although this included his house. One of the entries shows "Coca-Cola Patent Trade Mark etc . . . $2,000," which is presumably what Candler figured he had paid for it. At the same time, he downgraded De-Lec-Ta-Lave to $1,000, though he had purchased it for almost $4,000. He did not list any other patent medicines by name.

That January, in the drab coolness of an Atlanta winter, Coca-Cola continued to sell, an unprecedented feat for a soda fountain drink, normally confined to summer sipping. By the month's end, Candler had sold 168 gallons of syrup. Inspired by these figures, he wrote a form letter that he sent to druggists in February, promoting Coca-Cola as "a delightful summer and winter soda fountain beverage." Candler asserted that "the genuine merit and deserved popularity" of the drink was proved by "a reputation that now extends all over the states of Georgia, Alabama, Florida and Tennessee, and to numerous localities in many other States."

Candler clearly had been reading Pemberton's old notes and ads, praising the "medical properties of the Coca Plant and the extract of the celebrated African Cola Nut," adding that "the best physicians unhesitatingly endorse and recommend [Coca-Cola] for mental and physical exhaustion, headache, tired feeling, mental depression, etc." Finally, Candler emphasized that "the principal customers for Coca-Cola are business and professional men, who do not generally spend their money for that which gives them nothing in return." Coca-Cola was, he implied, a practical pick-me-up for the harried man of business, a theme he would stress repeatedly in the ensuing years.

---

* The actual amount of cocaine in original Coca-Cola has been the subject of much speculation. To make fluid extract of coca leaf, Pemberton's formula for French Wine Coca (given to me by Frank Robinson's great-granddaughter) called for 10 pounds of coca leaf soaked in three gallons (twelve quarts) of water. Robinson's Coca-Cola formula, which made thirty-six gallons of syrup, called for fifteen quarts of coca extract that, if made the same way, would require 12.5 pounds of coca leaf. According to an 1887 article by E. R. Squibb (forebear of the pharmaceutical company Bristol-Meyers Squibb), coca leaf contained about 0.35 percent cocaine. One beverage used an ounce of Coca-Cola syrup, which translates to about 4.3 milligrams per drink, a small amount of the drug. Some studies, however, suggest a symbiotic relationship between cocaine and caffeine. Consequently, even the negligible amount of cocaine in original Coca-Cola could have had an effect when combined with the 80 milligrams of caffeine. A typical snorted "dose" of cocaine contains about 35 milligrams. The gentleman who drank five straight glasses of Coca-Cola at Foster Howell's soda fountain received approximately 22 milligrams of cocaine.

Although he promoted Coca-Cola as a soda fountain drink, Candler also advertised the straight syrup as a patent medicine, which he sold for twenty-five cents a bottle—about a quarter of the going rate for most medicines—in grocery and drug stores. In almanacs distributed throughout the Southern states, Candler suggested that Coca-Cola syrup "should be kept in every house to cure headache and tired feeling," as well as to "overcome depression and languor." The suggested dosage was a tablespoonful to a wineglass of water.

Sales for 1890 amounted to 8,855 gallons, over four times the previous year's record. By the end of the year, Asa Candler realized that if he could pay sufficient attention to Coca-Cola, it might well make his fortune. He finally decided to abandon the drug business and devote all of his time to Coca-Cola. Careful as always, he remained diversified for the moment, retaining the rights to B.B.B. and De-Lec-Ta-Lave. A January 1891 newspaper piece, titled "Going Out of Business," noted that Candler's trade in the three proprietary medicines had "grown to be immense and all of his time is required to look after them."

Convinced that Coca-Cola was his future, Candler decided to create a solid chain of title, and on April 22, 1891, he persuaded Joe Jacobs, the only other remaining member of Walker, Candler & Company (Woolfolk Walker having conveniently disappeared in 1888), to sign over that company's Coca-Cola rights to Candler individually. Then, on June 5, Candler deposited all of the relevant documents with the U.S. Patent Office.

Having sold his drug business, Candler sought to economize by moving that fall to 42½ Decatur Street, where he manufactured Coca-Cola above a pawnshop, secondhand clothing store, and black saloon. He was not a popular tenant, because the forty-gallon kettle of brewing syrup periodically boiled over. The sweet, sticky mixture would ooze through the floorboards and drip into the establishments below.

As the money from Coca-Cola rolled in, Candler spent more on advertising his product throughout Georgia and, to a lesser extent, the rest of the South, using the now-familiar Coca-Cola script logo originated by Frank Robinson. He soon hired a black man, George Curtright, and another nephew, Sam Willard, to make Coca-Cola, freeing Robinson to market the drink full-time.

ROBINSON: THE UNSUNG HERO

If anyone can be called the unsung hero of Coca-Cola, it is certainly Frank Robinson. A small, unassuming man—even shorter than Asa Candler—with a bushy mustache, Robinson never demanded attention or fame. Although a stark contrast, he and Candler made a complementary team. While Candler was driven, high-strung, and temperamental, always on the verge of cracking, Robinson remained calm, deliberate, and unflappable in the face of the worst controversy. Following Candler's example, Robinson taught Sunday school. But while Candler's prepubescent students made fun of him behind his back, Robinson studied the Bible with a devoted flock of young women in their twenties. One photograph of the period shows Robinson, looking quietly pleased with himself, seated on a stool surrounded by fifty of his female students.

A 1917 biographical sketch noted that "while Mr. Robinson's modesty would not permit him to make any such claim, many knowing friends do not hesitate to say that it was Frank M. Robinson who made Coca-Cola and gave it its worldwide reputation." Indeed, Robinson's behind-the-scenes creation of Coca-Cola advertising over the next twenty years would catapult the drink to fame. The mastermind of this most Southern soft drink was a native of Corinth, Maine. His father had been severely wounded in the battle of Cold Harbor during the Civil War, and Frank Robinson himself had served in the Maine Volunteers. Despite his accomplishments with Coca-Cola, one of his greatest sources of pride recalled in later years was his election as county auditor of Osceola County, Iowa, in 1872, before he came to Atlanta.

Candler, however, probably devised some early ads himself. Written in the first person, they bear his rather idiosyncratic stamp. "IT MAKES FRIENDS RAPIDLY. IT DOES WHAT IS CLAIMED FOR IT. MERIT SELLS IT," one such ad proclaimed. His statement in an early ad was, in light of Coca-Cola's subsequent history, ironic: "I challenge the world to show an article of its kind as popular as Coca-Cola, for which so little advertising has been done." In the same ad, Candler explained that he had been "a great and almost daily sufferer" of headaches before trying Coca-Cola. "In offering it to the public," he added, "I feel I am a public benefactor."

When that first year of full-time devotion to Coca-Cola, B.B.B., and De-Lec-Ta-Lave was over, Candler had sold 19,831 gallons of syrup, more than double the previous year's record, and he had done it with a relatively small promotional budget. What would happen if he *really* funneled money into advertising? Sure that there was more money to be made from Coca-Cola, a boon to suffering mankind, Candler determinedly put all of his effort behind the single product. He soon sold De-Lec-Ta-Lave to Joe Jacobs and B.B.B. to J. B. Brooks, one of his part-time traveling salesmen, and on December 29, 1891, Candler filed for incorporation of The Coca-Cola Company.

COCAINE BLUES

Even as Coca-Cola was rocketing to fame, however, rumors of its cocaine content were stirring. As they would for many years to come, patrons calling for Coca-Cola usually asked for a "dope," a practice that infuriated Candler. On June 12, 1891, just a week after depositing his chain of title with the Patent Office, Candler opened the *Atlanta Constitution* and read the headline, "WHAT'S IN COCA COLA? A Popular Drink Which Is Said to Foster the Cocaine Habit." His stomach churning and a headache rolling like a thunderclap up the base of his neck, Candler read what a "thoughtful citizen" had told a reporter.

Coca-Cola drinking was, the indignant citizen said, "a very vicious and pernicious thing," and "people are drinking it a dozen times a day." The informant asserted that "the ingredient which makes coca cola so popular is cocaine. There is evidently enough of it in the drink to affect people and it is insiduously but surely getting thousands of people into the cocaine habit." He then related the story of his friend who, in despair over his inability to shake the cocaine habit, had shot himself. The implication, of course, was that drinking a Coca-Cola was the first step on the road to self-destruction.

Candler responded by taking out an ad in which he challenged anyone to prove a case in which Coca-Cola had led to cocaine addiction. "If I thought it could possibly hurt anybody," he asserted, "I would quit the manufacture of Coca-Cola instantly."

He stated that the formula for Coca-Cola called for only a half-ounce of coca leaf per gallon of syrup and that "no sensible man would undertake to say that this quantity in a gallon would hurt a person taking a glass of the beverage." If Candler was giving accurate information, he was certainly correct that a glass of Coca-Cola had a negligible amount of cocaine in it, amounting to about 0.4 milligrams. Either Candler was lying, however, or he had substantially reduced the amount of coca leaf in the formula, because the Pemberton formula called for eleven times the amount Candler claimed to use.*

The controversy died down, and Coca-Cola drinkers indulged their nefarious habit with no visible ill effect. Nonetheless, rumors about Coca-Cola's drug content would continue to haunt Candler and the drink in the years to come. It is likely, in fact, that these rumors helped more than hindered sales. People were intrigued by the stigma associated with the drink and felt a sinful thrill when imbibing it.

THE MAGIC FORMULA

The mystique of Coca-Cola was also enhanced, of course, by its secret formula, whose blend of flavors was code-named 7X.† Soon after Frank Robinson brought him the formula, Asa Candler changed it. His son said that he did so because "the Pemberton product did not have an altogether agreeable taste; it was unstable; it contained too many things, too much of some ingredients and too little of others . . . the bouquet of several of the volatile essential oils previously used was adversely affected by some ingredients."

Candler also modified the formula to distinguish it from all of the other recipes floating around. At least ten people had access to the original Pemberton formula.‡ In addition, as Coca-Cola achieved universal popularity, versions of the formula were offered by imitators, druggists, and charlatans for varying amounts, ranging, according to Joe Jacobs, "from $1,000 down to a bottle of Whiskey."

In order to protect his valuable secret, Candler engaged in an elaborate ritual whenever he received a shipment of ingredients. Either he or Robinson would remove the labels immediately, instead adding a number code, from 1 to 9 (the essential oils for 7X were left entirely unlabeled). Candler opened all of the Company mail, so that he could intercept invoices for secret ingredients before anyone in the accounting department saw them.

---

* Drug experts, beginning with Angelo Mariani and John Pemberton, have drawn a legitimate distinction between coca and cocaine. The Peruvian Indians valued the milder forms of the leaf, disdaining the bitter variety with a higher cocaine content. As cocaine got a bad name, Mariani, Pemberton, and then Asa Candler fought to maintain a distinction between the "natural" use of coca leaves, which produced mild stimulation from a mixture of fourteen alkaloids, and the more drastic effects of the pure alkaloid, cocaine.

† For a detailed description of the formula and the ingredients in 7X, see appendix 1, "The Sacred Formula."

‡ Those with access to the formula were Willis Venable, George Lowndes, Woolfolk Walker, Charley Pemberton, Cliff Pemberton, Joe Jacobs, J. C. Mayfield, Diva Mayfield, A. O. Murphey, and E. H. Bloodworth.

At first, only Candler or Robinson mixed the precious 7X. Later, when Howard Candler joined the business, he was taught the solemn ceremony as a rite of passage. "One of the proudest moments of my life," he remembered, "came when my father . . . initiated me into the mysteries of the secret flavoring formula, inducting me as it were into the 'Holy of Holies.'" Supposedly, no formula or instructions were written down. The containers, labels removed, were identified "only by sight, smell and remembering where each was put on the shelf." Finally, either Candler or Robinson sampled each batch of syrup before it left the factory. Robinson had a particularly keen nose and palate and could detect even a trace of an off flavor.

INCORPORATION (RE-INCORPORATION)

The Coca-Cola Company was granted its corporate charter on January 29, 1892. Candler must have breathed a sigh of relief when no bureaucrat noticed that there was already a Coca-Cola Company on the books from 1888. The charter for the new company called for a capitalization of $100,000 to be divided into a thousand shares at $100 each.

In February, Candler transferred his rights in Coca-Cola to the corporation in return for 500 shares, while giving Frank Robinson only 10. Candler intended to raise money for his business in 1892 by selling the other 490 shares to investors, which explains two unfamiliar names: J. M. Berry of Virginia and F. W. Prescott of Massachusetts. Although Berry soon dropped out of the picture, Prescott, an entrepreneur "well posted in the different markets," according to one newspaper account, actively tried to market shares in the Boston area. Candler also contacted stockbrokers and venture capitalists in New York and Baltimore. Despite the demonstrated profitability of Coca-Cola, Candler located few backers for his relatively unknown proprietary medicine. Candler granted the Darby Manufacturing Company of Baltimore the exclusive Maryland territory for Coca-Cola for ten years; as an added incentive, they received a share of Coca-Cola stock for every five hundred gallons of syrup they bought (up to fifty shares). They had earned eighteen shares by 1899 when they sold back to the Candler family.

F. W. Prescott found better investors in Boston. The firm of Seth Fowle & Sons, already in the proprietary drug business, bought fifty shares and the exclusive rights to the New England trade for twenty years. The two Fowle sons became dedicated Coca-Cola men, issuing the first newsletter to boost the product. The *Coca-Cola News* of the 1890s, aimed at the retailer, emphasized the profits to be made from the soft drink, calling it a "restorative, a blessing to humanity." Recognizing the new national rage for bicycling, the Fowle brothers urged the drink upon "wheelmen" and other athletes. The ever-increasing sales of Coca-Cola soon gave Candler all the capital he needed—there were never more than 586 shares outstanding at any one time.

RUNNING AFOUL OF KENT'S COCA-COLA

As business gathered momentum, in May of 1892 Candler decided to patent the trademark Coca-Cola script. What he thought would be a routine matter threatened to destroy his business before it fairly got off the ground. He was denied the registration; incredibly, someone else had already invented and trademarked a product called Coca-Cola. This was cause for another Candler headache, a bona fide migraine.

It shouldn't have shocked Candler. By the mid-1880s, the coca leaf and kola nut were frequently mentioned in conjunction; it appeared inevitable that someone would put the two ingredients together. It is not too surprising, then, that two men not only had the same idea, but the same name.* A Paterson, New Jersey, druggist named Benjamin Kent had seen the 1883–1884 Frederick Stearns catalog with parallel columns on coca and kola and, inspired by the juxtaposition, named his new tonic Kent's Coca-Cola in late 1884, over a year before Frank Robinson named Pemberton's drink.

Like Pemberton's formula, Kent's Coca-Cola was imbibed mainly as a hangover remedy, the label, eerily similar to Pemberton's, calling the medicine "a panacea for all those tired, worn out, exhausted mental and physical conditions that require a frequent tonic." Unlike Pemberton's drink, however, Kent's contained not only caffeine and cocaine but a healthy dollop of whisky, euphemistically called "spirits of frumenty." The bitter syrup was taken with soda water and became quite popular in Paterson.

In 1888, Kent approached John Kerr, a Paterson lawyer, about registering his Coca-Cola as a trademark, which Kerr did on January 22, 1889. The application stated that Kent had used the trademark "continuously in the business since June 1, 1888." Kerr later testified that he advised Kent to use the 1888 date, because a U.S. trademark required that the article be sold outside the United States. Consequently, he had told Kent to sell his Coca-Cola through a friend in Canada, which he had accomplished in June of 1888. Due to this technicality, Atlanta's version of Coca-Cola was eventually given precedence. Pemberton had registered the Coca-Cola trademark a year earlier, on June 28, 1887, and in Interference Procedure No. 15,753, the Patent Office ruled that only the official dates given in the applications were relevant. In 1894, Candler quietly bought out Kent for $400, though the hopeful New Jersey druggist had asked for $10,000.

COCA-COLA TAKES OFF

With all major obstacles removed, properly incorporated and duly trademarked, Candler's Coca-Cola was poised for a period of phenomenal growth. From almost 20,000 gallons in 1891, sales shot up to 35,360 gallons in 1892, then (during a nationwide depression) to 48,427 in 1893, 64,333 in 1894, and 76,244 in 1895. All of this was accomplished with a tiny home office staff, never more than thirty in the first two decades of the Company. The key, as Candler and Robinson soon demonstrated, was advertising. In his first annual report, covering the ten months after incorporation in 1892, Candler reported that the firm had spent almost $22,500 on ingredients for Coca-Cola and over half of that amount ($11,400) on advertising. He commented that "we have done very considerable advertising in territory which has not as yet yielded any returns. We have reason to believe that it will show good returns during the ensuing year."

---

* Indeed, in 1885, Sigmund Freud playfully inscribed one of his papers to Carl Koller, "To my good friend, Coca Koller."

The majority of the advertising budget was spent on point-of-purchase signs, calendars, novelties, and newspaper ads, all of them prominently displaying the Coca-Cola script. Candler, who at first had misspelled his own product, became very touchy about the correct spelling of Coca-Cola—not coco-cola or cocoa-cola, it must also be capitalized and hyphenated. His concern, although sometimes petulantly expressed, was justified, because variant spellings and lower-case usage would have made it easier for the drink to become a generic term open to any competitor.

The early ads were almost universally medicinal. Although the firm letterhead did proclaim that Coca-Cola was "Delicious, Refreshing, Exhilarating, Invigorating," Candler's early ads failed to use those adjectives. Instead, Coca-Cola was "Harmless, Wonderful, Efficient, Quick . . . Relieves Headache . . . Gives Prompt Rest." It was the "Ideal Brain Tonic and Sovereign Remedy for Headache and Nervousness. It makes the sad glad and the weak strong." Clearly, Candler believed in the drink's beneficial effects, even if he denied they were due to cocaine.

Although the ads were primarily aimed at businessmen, a few addressed women: "The ladies are taking it right along. They find it relieves headaches and exhaustion, besides it's a tonic and a pleasant beverage." Another sought to attract smokers, who presumably could wash away that stale tobacco taste. Finally, Candler recognized that children, who could wheedle a nickel from their parents, were prime customers. An early trade card showed three small boys in sailor suits holding a sign proclaiming, "We drink Coca-Cola."

In 1894, free sample coupons were again issued. Over $7,000 in tickets was redeemed that year and the next, amounting to over 140,000 free drinks each year. Promising to bring in new business, a salesman would ask a dispenser for the names and addresses of a hundred regular customers. Then free tickets were mailed, along with a cover letter, timed to reach the potential consumer just as the fountain received its Coca-Cola order and a supply of point-of-purchase advertising. This system was an ingenious, effective way to build new outlets. It made it easy on the fountain owner, who could dispense free drinks and mount attractive posters to brighten his store. In addition, "premiums"—serving urns, scales, cabinets, cases, and clocks—were offered to encourage sales. All prominently displayed the Coca-Cola logo.

CANDLER AND SONS

As Candler started to make money from Coca-Cola, it was not reflected in his largess to his children. Like his father, he did not believe in spoiling his children, repeatedly stressing economy in letters to them at Emory College, then located in Oxford, Georgia. Ever the careful businessman, Candler kept a running account of every cent his son Howard spent. In 1894, apparently in response to his son's request for money, Candler wrote out a balance sheet showing Howard's expenses, including ten cents for bananas and twenty-five cents for a toothbrush. Underlining the balance of $15.40 in red, the strict father told his son that he *should* have that much money left.

At the same time, Candler exerted enormous pressure on his children to excel. "My boy, you cannot know how anxious I am about you," he wrote to Howard in 1894. "I do so greatly desire your *Success*. I hope you will *fully* appreciate . . . my efforts to aid and care for you . . . [so] as to improve your *chances*. I expect you to be first in your class." Candler made it clear that he expected Godliness to accompany Success; many of his letters resembled sermons: "Don't be religious in word only, but in your life. . . . Let your life constantly *exhibit Christ*. We live for Him."

Asa Candler was capable, however, of jumping from the most sentimental platitudes to hard-nosed business matters, in the next sentence asking Howard to help with the local Coca-Cola business: "I am sending by Express today . . . some advertising matter for your careful distribution to the fountains in Oxford." He also asked Howard to look into "empty bottle troubles" and to spy on a druggist he suspected of offering Wine Coca in place of Coca-Cola.

GOING NATIONWIDE

Although not the best child-rearing traits, Candler's obsessions with detail, frugality, and achievement worked well for Coca-Cola. So did its location in Atlanta, the center of a web of rails carrying the recycled whiskey barrels full of sweet syrup across the country. By the end of 1895, Candler could proudly report to his stockholders that "Coca-Cola is now sold and drunk in every state and territory in the United States." In the four years since incorporation, the company had achieved nationwide distribution, even though the vast majority of sales were still concentrated in the South. "The great American Eagle—that discriminating bird of freedom—is passionately fond of Coca-Cola," the *Coca-Cola News* proclaimed, "because Coca-Cola has become a National drink."

A close look at 1895 company finances reveals how money was spent and made. Candler paid $44,247 for the ingredients of the 76,244 gallons of syrup he sold—58 cents per gallon, or less than half a cent per drink. At the same time, he spent $17,744 on advertising (23.3 cents per gallon) and $12,054 on "expense, discount & interest." That last figure included salaries, which were, as Howard Candler later admitted, "moderate and in some instances inadequate."

If Candler could have effectively retailed his drink directly to consumers, his profits would have been incredible, because his total disbursements came to just under $1 for a gallon of syrup selling for $6.40 (128 drinks at a nickel apiece). Rather than expand his work and sales force, however, he chose to spread the profit among distributors and fountain owners, who would sell for him. In each territory, he sought out jobbers (usually candy or drug wholesalers) with whom he could set up a long-term, trusting relationship. He sold the syrup to them at an average cost of $1.29 per gallon in 1895, leaving himself a profit of thirty cents a gallon and allowing a whopping markup for both jobber and retailers. That smaller profit margin translated into huge influxes of cash as the total gallonage sales rose steadily. By the beginning of 1896, the Company had a surplus cash war chest of almost $50,000.

By the end of that year, the Company needed new quarters, and there was plenty of money to build them. In 1893, to the relief of the pawnshop and saloon, Coca-Cola moved to larger rented space at Ivy and Auburn Avenue, where a 100-gallon copper kettle replaced the old 40-gallon affair, and a 1,500-gallon holding tank was installed. But this space was also soon inadequate. Thus, at the December 9, 1896, annual meeting, $10,000 was allocated to buy a lot and begin construction.

The pulse of Coca-Cola beat faster with every year, as an 1896 jingle asserted: "Stronger! stronger! grow they all, / Who for Coca-Cola call. / Brighter! brighter! thinkers think, / When they Coca-Cola drink." Although others might grow stronger from the beverage, however, Asa Candler was on the verge of a complete mental and physical collapse. He had overworked himself to the point of exhaustion, and even repeated glasses of Coca-Cola were not having the desired effect. Consequently, the annual report recorded that "the President was requested to take an extended vacation during the year 1897."

"AS LONG AS SIN ABOUNDS"

Another sign of the company's coming-of-age that year was the need for lawyers. Candler had complained of "bogus substitutes" in his 1894 annual report. As Coca-Cola's success grew, so did its hangers-on. As a prelude to a century of court battles, in 1896 "the President was requested to consult an Attorney in reference to the advisability of bringing a suit, or suits, against parties who are selling substitutes for . . . COCA-COLA." It is, of course, ironic that the makers of Coca-Cola should have been so self-righteous about ersatz colas when their drink was derived from a Vin Mariani clone.

The host of imitators was led by J. C. Mayfield, who had reincorporated the Pemberton Medicine Company as the Wine Coca Company in 1894. After trying Yum Yum and Koke, he now reverted to Pemberton's well-known Wine Coca, but he modified it to copy Coca-Cola, so that Howard Candler identified it as the "deceitful" product that "cut most seriously into our business." Through the years, Mayfield would continue to be a thorn in the Company's side and would later play a crucial role in its history.

Mayfield's wife, now divorced and remarried, also made a career out of selling Coca-Cola substitutes, calling herself Diva Brown and marketing My-Coca. She too claimed to have Pemberton's recipe, though her ex-husband disputed it. In fact, he complained that she had tried to steal *his* formula. Diva Brown was "demented," according to Mayfield, although she had "rational intervals" during which she was "very grasping," demanding his copy of the Coca-Cola formula. When he refused, she threatened to kill him, unsuccessfully trying to carry out her threat on several occasions. Demented or not, Diva Brown, "the Original Coca-Cola Woman," was shrewd and determined, portraying herself on her bottle labels as a pleasant-looking woman with short, dark hair. She sniffed righteously at the numerous frauds on the market: "I have seen dozens of formulas purporting to be mine, which were not even similar."

Candler had to contend not only with these fake Coca-Cola products, but with the dilution of his own syrup. Because one universal characteristic of the imitation syrups was their lower price, it was tempting for drugstore owners to add the cheaper syrup to the real thing, hoping no one would know the difference. At the turn of the century, Candler commented on diluters and frauds: "We have them all over the country, and will have them, as long as sin abounds—where they adulterate good things." He must have been pleased when a prominent trade journal editor responded to an 1899 request for the Coca-Cola formula by protesting, "I do not know the formula, or anything near it. It has defied all attempts at imitation. Even if it could be done you could not get the result."

THE TRANSITION FROM MEDICINE TO BEVERAGE

In 1895, Frank Robinson told Asa Candler that women and other consumers frequently wrote to object to the medicinal image of Coca-Cola. They didn't want to feel guilty for taking doses of a medicine when all they wanted was a bracing soft drink. Prompted by these complaints, Robinson made a brilliant tactical move with Coca-Cola advertising. He realized that there was more future in Coca-Cola as refreshment than medicine. After all, everyone got thirsty. As Robinson put it, "We found that we were advertising to the few when we ought to advertise to the masses." By promoting Coca-Cola as a beverage, they reached thousands rather than "one man in a hundred."

Consequently, he published more ads that simply said, "Drink Coca-Cola. Delicious and Refreshing." Instinctively, Robinson understood that the older ads were too long and too negative. With a larger budget, he flooded the market with his succinct message, not only in newspaper ads, but with posters, streetcar signs, calendars, serving trays, thermometers, clocks, pencils, bookmarks for schoolchildren, and glass plates for fountains. By 1898, Robinson was distributing over a million items per year.

Since 1891, the annual Coca-Cola calendar had featured attractive young women. Appealing but suitably modest, the "Coca-Cola girls" would stir male fantasies for years to come. The Company's Philadelphia lithographer made an annual pilgrimage to Atlanta with posters displaying a new crop of young beauties. With a salacious twinkle in his eyes, Robinson would select a likely candidate, saying, "I think Mr. Asa will like this one." By the turn of the century, the Company pioneered celebrity endorsements from actress Hilda Clark, a soft-featured blonde singer, and the more imposing opera star Lillian Nordica.

The advent of the Spanish-American War indirectly gave the Company more reason to shy away from medicinal claims. In 1898, Congress passed a special war tax on proprietary medicines, but not on beverages. The commissioner of Internal Revenue ruled that Coca-Cola was a drug, not a drink, and ordered the Company to pay the tax. Furious, Candler sued the government. The case dragged on until 1902, when it was finally decided in Coca-Cola's favor, but it marked the beginning of Candler's disaffection with the U.S. government.

The Company did not abandon medicinal claims altogether, however. The 1899 Hilda Clark calendar stressed the "delicious and refreshing" qualities of the drink, but it also maintained that Coca-Cola "relieves mental and physical exhaustion" and "cures headache." About 10 percent of the ads in 1899 still talked about headache relief and benefits for brain workers, while others emphasized the use of the coca leaf by Andeans and the kola nut by Africans. But an important corner had been turned, and the future of the entire enterprise hung in the balance. If Robinson had not promoted Coca-Cola as a socially acceptable drink imbibed by the best people, it is likely that the patent medicine would not have survived the early part of the twentieth century, which saw a dramatic backlash against such nostrums.

GROWING AND BRANCHING OUT

As a new century loomed, the well-honed young company fizzed with profits and enthusiasm for the future. Despite the pending government suit and the omnipresent imitators, Candler's annual reports sounded as self-satisfied as the dour little man ever became. "Prosperity has been with the Company during the year just closed," he wrote in January of 1899. "At this rate of increase," reported the *Coca-Cola News*, "how long will it be before enough Coca-Cola will be sold in one year to make a river as large as the Mississippi?"

Candler had opened branch offices and syrup factories in Dallas (1894), Chicago (1895), Los Angeles (1895), Philadelphia (1897), and plans were under way for an office in New York (1899). Whenever possible, Candler sent nephews to assume command of these branches. Dan Candler ruled in Dallas, Sam Candler in Los Angeles, Sam Willard in Philadelphia. Yet another nephew, Sam Dobbs, had worked as a salesman since 1888 and now served as a clerk and bookkeeper in the main office. As his sons reached maturity, Candler sent them to branches as well—Asa Jr. took over in California, and Howard went to New York. At the same time, he was looking beyond U.S. borders. In his 1897 annual report, he noted that the drink was being sold in Canada and Hawaii, with an eye toward Mexico. "We are firmly convinced," he wrote, "that wherever there are people and soda fountains, Coca-Cola will, by its now universally acknowledged merit, win its way quickly to the front of popularity."

To encourage his jobbers, Candler had instituted a rebate plan in 1897, so that the more Coca-Cola a dealer sold during the year, the more he would get back as a bonus. Although the list price was $1.50 per gallon, there was a nickel rebate for every hundred gallons sold, up to a maximum of twenty-five cents for two thousand or more gallons. "At the close of his business year," Candler said, "when actual results are still somewhat in doubt, it greatly enthuses a dealer when we hand him a [rebate] check," causing him to increase his sales efforts the following year.

COCA-COLA MEN

By 1899, fifteen Coca-Cola drummers rode the country's rails, pushing the drink as early as February. Most salesmen handled cotton during the winter, because selling soft drinks was still a seasonal occupation. Nonetheless, they thought of themselves as Coca-Cola men, a distinctive breed. Before they were sent out on the road, Asa Candler fully indoctrinated them into the religion of Coca-Cola, often having them work in the manufacturing department briefly and stressing the purity of the ingredients, the sanctity of the secret formula, the extraordinary qualities of the product.

When Asa Candler believed in something, he often reacted with extreme emotion. A fundamentalist Methodist, he would get so worked up at revival meetings that, according to his son, he would become physically ill. "His eyes would shine, his body become tense, and his whole being pulse with . . . exhilaration." Candler

communicated this kind of fervor for his product to his impressionable salesmen.*
Howard commented that his father had "an almost mystical faith" in Coca-Cola. A
small man, Candler also had a bit of a Napoleon complex. He delighted in wearing
his elaborate uniform for the Georgia Horse Guard, and he continually exhorted his
children and salesmen to be *men*. Although Candler was "in no way . . . an imposing
person physically," his son wrote, "his anger and impatience could, on occasions, be
monumental." None of his employees cared to cross him.

There were many temptations for young drummers on the road, spawning the
innumerable jokes about traveling salesmen, farmers' daughters, and the like. Asa
Candler was determined that his salesmen would be enthusiastic, morally upright
representatives for Coca-Cola, and he kept tabs on them as much as possible. He
wrote to reprimand one salesman, for instance, because "you have been on *sprees* to
the detriment of The Coca-Cola Company's good name." By 1898, Candler reported
with satisfaction that "our salesmen have become known every where in this Union
as gentlemen in every respect, and have not only maintained the good name of the
Corporation, but have succeeded in making Coca-Cola a familiar and gracious name
in all the land."

Candler convinced Coca-Cola men that "theirs was the greatest product and the
greatest company on the face of the earth," as his son recalled. Because of their deep
belief, these proselytes were motivated to overcome every obstacle. Like the early
Christians, Candler's salesmen often faced hostility, rumor, and indifference—and,
like those early martyrs, they maintained their faith against all odds.

HOWARD HITS THE ROAD

One of Candler's drummers in 1899 was his twenty-year-old son Howard, on summer
vacation from medical school and armed with a letter of introduction from his Uncle
Warren, by then a Methodist bishop and president of Emory University, to the governor of Missouri, the cleric's close personal friend. Asa wrote frequently to his son on
the road; the letters paint a revealing portrait of the business as a new century loomed.
Many are concerned with petty details, worrying over "substitutes and frauds," emphasizing thrift and caution, and advising how to handle local businessmen. The
overall impression, however, is that the Coca-Cola boom nearly overwhelmed a frantic
Asa Candler, who struggled to coordinate his increasingly national enterprise.

> *April 13, 1899:* I am just as busy as it is possible for me to be. . . . God bless my
> "Wandering Boy."

> *April 19, 1899:* We are very busy here. It takes every moment of our time look-
> ing after traveling men. We now have 12 working from this office. Bradley
> leaves tomorrow. We will go into Ohio & Indiana. . . . I hope you remained

---

* Not everyone was impressed with Candler's religious devotion. Pemberton's niece, Mary Newman Sherman, called Candler a "sanctimonious pipsqueak." She and other members of his Sunday
school class ridiculed him behind his back, imitating his high-pitched voice. Another Sunday school
student made national headlines by sending Candler a series of fake blackmail threats dubbed the
Black Hand Letters.

in Wichita long enough to do business that ought to be done there and to let us catch up with you.

May 6, 1899: You are making a fine record in business. . . . We are 5000 gallons behind with orders, notwithstanding we are turning out above 3000 gallons [of] goods daily.

May 8, 1899: Demand for goods has been in excess of our ability to supply since about the 20th of April.

May 9, 1899: There is so much territory and so few of you men to work it that it seems imperative that we do a little work in a great many places.

May 12, 1899: Sales averaging 2000 gallons daily of which Atlanta does about 1000.

May 19, 1899: We are now throwing men into various large Western cities where there seems to be fine opportunity for work.

June 13, 1899: Our business this week is simply immense.

June 19, 1899: We have so much territory that must be looked after within the next 60 days that we can't give to any territory as much time even of one man as that territory seems to deserve. . . . We are inclined to furnish you with all the material, both of Coca-Cola and advertising matter that you need . . . and would prefer that you have a surplus than that you should have none.

As the summer wore on, Howard Candler proved to be the best salesman of the lot. In August, his father wrote him a thoughtful letter of praise in which he pondered the future. Could things really go on like this indefinitely? The letter also revealed Candler's inner doubts about the ultimate worthiness of his enterprise, despite the missionary zeal with which he sent out his salesmen:

August 10, 1899: I feel quite proud of your summer campaign. . . . I don't know whether I can let you be a doctor or not. If I felt sure that this business would hold out perpetually, I believe I would resign to give you the place. But my boy I can't take such risk on your future. I have no right to limit your use-fulness to the narrow compass of a 5 cent Soda Fountain Beverage. You are capable of grander achievements. . . .

Candler needn't have worried. Howard quit medical school of his own volition the following year.*

---

* Though Howard Candler joined the Company full-time, he would never be a charismatic pub-lic figure. "I really enjoy the office part of the work," he wrote his father, "but I don't like to distribute tickets and sell goods. More, I don't like to have to be sociable with the trade."

ON THE EVE OF THE TWENTIETH CENTURY

On December 28, 1899, about twenty people met at 10 a.m. in the Atlanta headquarters. For the first time, all of the salesmen, branch managers, and home office personnel assembled in one place. Other "intimate and helpful friends" were also invited to give advice. Probably half of those present were related to Asa Candler. They talked for four hours.

We do not have the minutes from that historic meeting, only days away from the new century, but we can reconstruct a scenario. First, Asa Candler outlined the firm's financial position. "Few corporations can show a more satisfactory financial condition,"* he began, pointing out that sales had exceeded 280,000 gallons of syrup for the year. "That's almost 36 million drinks of Coca-Cola that we sold this year, gentlemen. We have over $200,000 in cash, and we own real estate worth some $50,000. We have accomplished this while spending over $48,000 this past year on advertising, $38,000 in rebates, and $11,000 in extorted taxes for war revenue. I should add that we hope to get those unjustified taxes back and have gone to court to do so."

Candler expressed particular satisfaction that February volume (over eleven thousand gallons) demonstrated the drink's growing winter strength. He summarized the activity around the country, then announced that he had just hired a man in Havana, recently liberated from Spanish rule. This new Coca-Cola man would build the fountain business in Cuba and Puerto Rico. Already, over a thousand gallons had been sold on the islands. After a round of applause, Frank Robinson quietly displayed the new advertising for the year, explaining how the outside signs would be mounted, how many complimentary tickets would be disbursed, and why they were keeping Hilda Clark on the calendar for a second year.

The meeting was then thrown open to general comment. After an initial awkward silence, people began to talk about their daily concerns. The branch officers wanted more responsibility; the home office wanted the branches to be more profitable, particularly the New York and Los Angeles outlets, which were losing money. The traveling salesmen wanted better direction; Asa might tell them one thing, Frank Robinson another, and Sam Dobbs something else. Sometimes the home office was too busy, and no one told them anything. This matter was resolved when Asa declared that Sam Dobbs would be responsible for the sales force, allowing Frank Robinson to concentrate on advertising.

Then there was the cocaine issue. Everywhere they went, the salesmen were encountering more and more rumors about how Coca-Cola led to cocaine addiction. Even the temperance women, who should have been on Coca-Cola's side, were turning against the drink. Finally, someone asked the heretical questions: "Couldn't we just take out the cocaine? Does it really make that much difference?"

The room hushed as Asa Candler tapped his fingers on the desk. Finally, he spoke. "So you want me to change the formula of the country's favorite beverage because of some hysterical women? Do you really want us to change Coca-Cola, the purest,

---

* This is actually a quote from the 1899 annual report, issued on January 11, 1900. The following scene is based primarily on this annual report.

most healthful drink the world has ever seen?" His voice rose higher and cracked as he began to shout, "Never! There is *nothing* wrong with Coca-Cola." He took a deep breath and continued, more calmly. "If there was anything the matter with it, do you think we would have such a problem keeping everyone supplied with it? No, Coca-Cola has been good to me, and I will not change it. That's the end of this discussion."

When the meeting adjourned, the group enjoyed a catered dinner in the Coca-Cola building, with boxes of chocolate from Nunnally's passed out to everyone. The employees were surprised at the sumptuous spread, because it was common knowledge that Asa Candler never spent a dime he didn't have to. The company must have been doing very well, indeed.

AN OMISSION

There was one item of business that appeared too trivial to mention at this meeting. Back in July, two Tennessee lawyers had come to Atlanta to see Asa Candler about a business proposition. They wanted to bottle Coca-Cola.

~ 5 ~

Bottle It: The World's Stupidest, Smartest Contract

Yes, these early bottlers of Coca-Cola have been a hardy, a rugged, and a determined lot. . . . They had the faith, and the courage, and the dedication, and the determination to lay the road, build the bridges and weather the storms, and solve the problems that have brought this business to the position of eminence which it enjoys today.
—Lee Talley, president, The Coca-Cola Company, 1959

"Ben," he said, "I wonder how they happened to get together all the dumb sonsuvbitches in the world and put 'em in this goddam bottling business."
—*Big Beverage*, by William T. Campbell

Benjamin Franklin Thomas, a lawyer and businessman, came to Chattanooga, Tennessee, in 1887, attracted by the little town where the "drive to make money . . . almost permeated the . . . air," as one historian put it. Not content with a simple practice, Thomas had already operated a stone quarry, hosiery mill, and paving brick company, and had marketed Sofas, a patent medicine whose key ingredient was baking soda. Still, he wasn't satisfied. Sam Erwin, a friend at his boardinghouse, recalled how Thomas "used to come in every few days with a new scheme to make a million dollars."

When the U.S. went to war with Spain in 1898, Thomas became a clerk in a Cuban commissary, where he was impressed by the popularity of a carbonated pineapple drink called Piña Frio. Upon his return to Chattanooga the following year, he decided that perhaps his fortune lay in bottling the popular soda fountain drink, Coca-Cola. When Thomas told his fellow boarders his latest plan, Sam Erwin laughed at him as usual, but said that he actually might help with this one, because it happened that Asa Candler was Erwin's first cousin. He soon arranged an introduction for the eager lawyer.

Although Candler didn't appear interested, Thomas repeatedly took the short train trip to Atlanta to talk with the Coca-Cola magnate, all to no avail. Thomas decided he needed a partner to convince Candler that he was serious. Sam Erwin, his first choice, wasn't interested in his friend's cockeyed idea. Finally, after much discussion, Thomas persuaded another boardinghouse friend and fellow lawyer, Joseph Brown White-head, to join him in the tentative venture. Both men enjoyed baseball, and Thomas painted a glowing picture of the potential bottled soft drink sales at double-headers. He also noted that the soda fountain drinks they brought back to their offices went flat while they talked to clients. "Wouldn't it be great if a fellow could put this stuff in a bottle and stop it up so the gas wouldn't get away, and he could drink it whenever he wanted?"

Armed with a few samples of bottled Coca-Cola, the two men met with a harried Asa Candler in mid-July 1899. He was annoyed to find Thomas pestering him again. In addition, he wasn't particularly impressed with anyone from Chattanooga, which he considered a hick town. "I went up there once to bring back a fugitive nigger," Candler later said, "and I didn't think there was anything up there." His initial impression of Thomas and Whitehead must not have been favorable either. Thomas, thirty-eight, was a heavyset man with a florid, sweaty face. Whitehead, though a few years younger, walked with a pronounced waddle, carrying nearly two hundred pounds on his 5'4" frame.

Besides, Candler was wary of the bottling business; he remembered that Woolfolk Walker had already bottled Coca-Cola briefly back in 1888 and the product had been, to use nephew Sam Dobbs' term, "putrid." At that time, Candler had vehemently forbidden Dobbs to sell Coca-Cola in bottles. He already had enough problems defending his drink without allowing the promotion of an inferior product. Mostly, though, he was simply too busy to think about bottling Coca-Cola. As he recounted the conversation years later, Candler told them, "Gentlemen, I don't think we want to have it bottled; we can't handle it ourselves; there's too much detail about the bottling business." In summary, Candler said he had "neither the money, nor time, nor brains, to embark in the bottling business, and there are too many folks, who are not responsible, who care nothing about the reputation of what they put up, and I am afraid the name will be injured."

Although Thomas and Whitehead may not have been impressive at first, they were born salesmen, friendly and jovial. They listened to everything Candler said, nodding with understanding. Then, speaking easily and well, they described their plans, assuring Candler that they would maintain the purity and integrity of Coca-Cola, no doubt making it the best-known bottled drink in the United States, the same way that he, Candler, had so brilliantly made it the most famous soda fountain drink. Warming to their subject, the men concluded with a sincere burst worthy of their best courtroom oratory: "We promise and guarantee to you, Mr. Candler, that in all the business we do in the bottling of Coca-Cola, we will make the name better every day we conduct this business." They weren't trying to rush him, though; he should take the matter under advisement, sample their bottled product and think it over. They would be in town a few days.

Candler, his ego flattered and interest piqued, visibly softened. He had to admit that Thomas was persistent, a good trait for a Coca-Cola man. "That's a big contract you have taken on your hands; I have already spent all the money I have trying to make it respectable." He told them he would have to look into their backgrounds and would let them know his decision in a few days. In the meantime, they should prepare a suitable contract.

Candler must have been pleased that both men were lawyers; he was increasingly coming to rely on men of their profession. Thomas also had a varied entrepreneurial background, including experience with patent medicines. With satisfaction, Candler noted that Whitehead's father was a Baptist minister; hopefully, Whitehead would bring a religious fervor to the Coca-Cola business. In addition, it didn't hurt that he specialized in tax law, in light of the pending litigation over the war tax. Finally, Whitehead, too, was already involved in patent medicines as the vice president of the New Spencer Medicine Company.

GIVING AWAY THE BOTTLING RIGHTS

On July 21, 1899, Asa Candler called the men back into his office to approve their plan. Casually, the partners handed him the six hundred-word contract they had prepared and signed. After carefully reading it over, Candler also signed the document. Clearly relieved, Thomas and Whitehead assured Candler that he would not regret it and turned to go before he changed his mind. Candler called after them: "If you boys fail in this undertaking, don't come back to cry on my shoulder, because I have very little confidence in this bottling business."

Candler must have believed he had everything to gain and nothing to lose under the contract's terms. It bound the bottlers to use only Coca-Cola syrup, banning any substitutes, and it expressly excluded the soda fountain business, which would remain the sole province of The Coca-Cola Company. In addition, the contract specified that if the bottlers failed to "supply the demand in all territory embraced in this agreement," the contract would be forfeited. It is little wonder that Candler had told them they had a "big contract" on their hands. The territory included almost the entire United States, excluding only New England (held by Seth Fowle & Sons, though they never bottled there) and Texas and Mississippi, where noncontract businessmen were already putting the drink in bottles.

If Thomas and Whitehead succeeded, Candler stood to sell more syrup. If they failed, he would not have put up any capital or had to spend time on the fruitless venture. Why not let them have a go at it? He agreed to sell them syrup at a dollar a gallon and to provide their advertising needs. Candler was correct that the contract would result in his selling more syrup, though he obviously didn't realize the enormous implications. This simple contract was to revolutionize the Coca-Cola business, giving birth to one of the most innovative, dynamic franchising systems in the world.

At the same time, however, it virtually assured conflict within the Coca-Cola family of the future. Candler set no term on his contract. As long as Thomas and Whitehead fulfilled their end of the deal, it was permanent, and they could pass it along to the bottling companies they created.* In addition, the agreement did not include a provision for modifying the price of syrup, should the cost of ingredients increase. These

---

* In later years, Candler denied that he intended it to be a permanent contract. Only months earlier, when Seth A. Fowle had suggested that his twenty-year contract be made perpetual, Candler responded that "the laws of Georgia would not permit us to give you the extension of terms that you wish."

two jokers in the contract would haunt The Coca-Cola Company in the next century, resulting in numerous lawsuits.

Coca-Cola folklore relates that an anonymous tipster offered to give Candler invaluable advice in return for an unspecified sum. After Candler paid, the informant leaned over and whispered two words in his ear: "Bottle it." The story is, of course, pure fiction. In fact, no money changed hands when the contract was signed. Candler literally gave away the bottling rights. Subsequent histories say that a token dollar was exchanged, but there is no mention of it in the contract. In the years to come, The Coca-Cola Company would pay millions of dollars to buy back piecemeal what Candler so casually signed away for nothing. At the time, however, Candler did not regard the contract as worthy of note. On the same day he signed it, he wrote a letter to his son Howard, talking mostly about how to sell special fountain glasses for Coca-Cola.* He did not mention the two Chattanoogans or their bottling deal.

BOTTLING AT THE TURN OF THE CENTURY

Coca-Cola historians have treated the subsequent success of the Thomas/Whitehead venture as if it were the real genesis of bottled soft drinks. On the contrary, the bottling business was booming even as Pemberton first experimented with Coca-Cola in 1885. In that year, one bottler was interviewed at his factory, a "wilderness of bottles and machinery," revealing a snapshot of the contemporary industry. "Ten years ago I did a large business," said the bottler, "but my customers were exclusively saloons. Now my trade is five times larger, but nine-tenths of it are groceries and private families." He produced root beer, sarsaparilla, ginger ale, raspberry, pop, mead, and plain beer—in descending order of popularity. Sometimes the extracts underwent "some funny change and taste horrible," the bottler complained. "Raspberry and pop are affected by sunlight, and their flavor changes to that of turpentine."

The "raspberry" went bad because it had no raspberry in it, but cheap chemical ethers. The main reason the bottler had such trouble, however, was the uncertain seal, a problem widely recognized within the industry, resulting in a scramble to patent a better stopper. The *National Bottlers' Gazette*, a trade magazine, portrayed an amazing array of fifty stopper designs for patents issued in 1885, all purporting to solve the problem. The devices usually featured elaborate wire-and-cork contraptions, although a few elegant designs used internal balls, held in place by the pressure of the carbonation.

The industry standard throughout the late 1880s was the Hutchinson stopper, a cumbersome, unpredictable seal with an internal rubber disk pulled up into place by a wire loop. To open the bottle, a consumer knocked the loop down, releasing the pressure with a sudden "pop," which gave soda pop its name. The Hutchinson stopper was relatively inexpensive, but workers or consumers often jarred the loop accidentally, spilling the bottle's sticky contents. In addition, the Hutchinson bottles were difficult to clean because of their internal mechanism, and the acidified drinks ate away at the rubber gasket.

---

* Coca-Cola salesmen sold logo-embossed fountain glasses at low cost, in part to encourage soda jerks to mix the drink properly, a horizontal line near the bottom indicating a one-ounce level.

Nonetheless, by 1890, over three thousand American bottlers used Hutchinson stoppers. With an industry that large, the question isn't why two lawyers got the notion to bottle Coca-Cola in 1899, but why no one had thought of it sooner. In fact, they had. Sam Dobbs remembered that there were at least a dozen pre-1899 Coca-Cola bottlers in Florida, Colorado, Georgia, South Carolina, Texas, Mississippi, and New England. Two of those pre-1899 bottlers successfully continued into the twentieth century. Joe Biedenharn, a Vicksburg, Mississippi, candy manufacturer with a sideline in bottled pop, was one of the early jobbers for Coca-Cola syrup, which sold well at the city's soda fountains. Biedenharn was convinced that it would do equally well in rural areas, which had no fountains. Consequently, in 1894, he began bottling carbonated Coca-Cola for sale to the country trade. As a courtesy, he sent one of the first cases to Asa Candler, who wrote back that it was "fine" and thought no more about it. The Biedenharn brothers—all seven of them—created a Coca-Cola bottling dynasty. Similarly, the Valdosta Bottling Works of Valdosta, Georgia, started selling bottled Coca-Cola in 1897. Describing their early Coca-Cola experience, a partner said that the Hutchinson bottles caused trouble: "The rubber washer on the stopper caused a not-too-wholesome odor in the drink after it had been bottled for a period of ten days. . . ."

In April of 1892, at exactly the same time as The Coca-Cola Company, the Crown Cork and Seal Company was incorporated. Though the crimped crown bottle cap solved all of the Hutchinson problems, its acceptance was glacially slow, because it required a new stock of bottles and a special machine to attach the crown caps. By 1900, however, the change was well under way. Thomas and Whitehead were entering the business at the right time. Other innovations in the next few years made mass-produced bottled soft drinks an increasingly attractive field.

CARVING UP THE U.S.

Thomas and Whitehead wasted no time in setting up their first plant in Chattanooga. Bottling in that era was a dangerous, makeshift affair that necessitated facemasks and heavy gauntlets. The foot-powered machines allowed only one bottle to be capped at a time. Recycled bottles were hand washed, with metal shot shaken inside in a vain attempt to flush out the accumulated crud. The ten-gallon syrup keg was hoisted aloft so that syrup could flow into bottles by gravity, but the hose often came loose, with sticky results. It is little wonder that Thomas and Whitehead quickly decided to leave the actual bottling to others.

On November 12, 1899, they placed their first small ad in the *Chattanooga Times*: "Drink a *bottle* of Coca-Cola, five cents at all stands, grocers and saloons." The ad may have been short, but it spoke volumes for the future of the drink. The "stands, grocers and saloons" were revolutionary new outlets for Coca-Cola, allowing the drink to reach a completely different class of consumer. At the time, no one in Chattanooga paid much attention. An article running adjacent to that first ad carried a detailed account of business activity in town, including a section on various new companies and their products. The bottling concern wasn't even mentioned. The partners officially incorporated as the Coca-Cola Bottling Company on December 9, 1899.

Within a year, the partnership shattered. Thomas and Whitehead disagreed about almost everything except the desirability of bottling the soft drink. Thomas wanted to use brown bottles, while Whitehead favored clear or light green. Thomas thought each bottle should contain eight ounces; Whitehead opted for a little over six ounces. But the more serious conflict began when the time came to execute additional contracts with other bottlers. Thomas believed in two-year contracts so that he could replace a poor bottler if there were problems. Whitehead wanted to give permanent contracts to reinforce loyalty and enthusiasm. Finally, the two men agreed to split their territory. To assure an equitable division, Whitehead created the two territories, while Thomas chose the one he wanted. He must have enjoyed a challenge, because he picked the heavily populated Eastern seaboard and the West Coast, in addition to Chattanooga and a fifty-mile radius around it. That left Whitehead with the Coca-Cola heartland of the South, plus much of the West.

Whitehead may have had the prime territory, but he had no money. Looking for capital, he found J. T. Lupton, who had married into the wealthy Patten family, owners of the Chattanooga Medicine Company. Lupton had given up his law practice to join the family business, helping the Pattens market their two popular proprietary medicines, Wine of Cardui and Black Draught. Lupton saw the future in bottled Coca-Cola and agreed to back Whitehead in return for half interest in his territory, paying him $2,500. Whitehead relocated to Atlanta and incorporated The Coca-Cola Bottling Company, using a capital T to differentiate his company from the Chattanooga concern. Because this led to inevitable confusion, the two firms were more commonly called the Thomas Company and the Southeastern Parent Bottler.

It was obvious from the beginning that neither concern had the money or manpower to open bottling plants all over the United States. Instead, both companies began looking for prospective bottlers with a little money and a lot of hustle. In those days, it cost a bit over $2,000 to buy the necessary bottling equipment, which included a carbonator, bottling table, washing machine, settling tanks, washing tubs, bottles, and cases. In addition, a horse and wagon were recommended, as well as $2,000 working capital. Thomas and Whitehead signed contracts with these bottlers to sell them syrup and provide an expert bottler, caps, and advertising. In return, they would garner half of the plant's profits. Consequently, the Thomas and Whitehead/Lupton firms became known as the "parent bottlers," while the manufacturing plants were called the "actual" or "first-line" bottlers.*

Whitehead ran the day-to-day side of his operation, aided by his young bookkeeper, Charles Veazey Rainwater. As Whitehead's guardian angel, Lupton supplied about half of the start-up capital for most bottlers. Even with his help, however, a

---

* As time went by, and the business grew larger, other parent bottlers split off from the original two. In 1903, Texas and the Indian territories were ceded to Whitehead/Lupton, who incorporated what became known as "the 1903 Company," or the Southwestern parent bottler. In 1905, the Western parent bottler, headquartered in Chicago and covering a huge area, was split from the Whitehead/Lupton territory. In 1912, the Seth Fowle contract in New England expired, allowing bottling franchises to begin in New England, where the New England parent bottler was formed in 1916. Finally, in 1924, the Pacific Coast parent bottler was split off from the Thomas Company.

substantial number of early bottlers failed, and the partners had to find someone else to take over the territory, portraying a glorious future that, at the time, seemed highly unlikely. To induce the "right man" to tackle the business, Lupton would explain that, "while the business was new, the beverage was new, yet it was rapidly acquiring a good standing with the public, and that in the years to come there would be a large profit to be made out of it."

Lupton was right, particularly with regard to himself. Because he wound up with a substantial investment in most of the bottling plants, he raked in fantastic amounts of money in the next few years, making him the wealthiest man in Chattanooga. "His entire business life," Sam Dobbs later noted cynically, "has been spent in getting all that he could put his hands on. In a great many bottling plants, he has demanded certain interests for which he paid nothing and then as fast as they were able to make a little money he insisted on dividends." In addition, Lupton installed many of his innumerable relations as bottlers all over the Whitehead/Lupton territory. They too became wealthy, establishing the Lupton name as a fixture in the Coca-Cola bottling firmament.

Ben Thomas didn't have the Lupton resources and had more difficulty contracting bottlers, but he was also to become a wealthy man. In the process, he and Lupton transformed Chattanooga into as much of a Coca-Cola town as Atlanta. In seeking bottlers, Thomas often relied on city acquaintances, later joking that he had single-handedly depopulated Chattanooga of its young men.

Particularly in the Northern territories, Thomas had a hard time finding and keeping bottlers. His contract specified that bottlers should only use crown caps and should handle Coca-Cola exclusively, giving up other soft drinks. But he really couldn't stick to those provisions and was forced to grant contracts to veterans who kept using their Hutchinsons and pushing their old line of flavors. Many of these older bottlers were men of limited vision and capital, putting out a shoddy fruit drink on a seasonal basis for the local market. In *Big Beverage*, a thinly fictionalized narrative of the early days of Coca-Cola bottling, William T. Campbell portrayed one such bottler, Pop Butts, a Coca-Cola millionaire despite himself.* Butts resented the incursion of Coca-Cola on his own drinks. He *knew* what was in his own mix, although the mysterious syrup from Atlanta came ready-made in barrels. Besides, he objected to the higher price of Coca-Cola, which ran nearly twice what it cost him to produce his own drinks.

Describing Butts and his kind, a *Big Beverage* salesman gives one intriguing explanation for Candler's doubts about bottling:

> Those are the kind of men who got the Coca-Cola franchises—little guys that thought little, and still think little. . . . They were the only ones Thomas and Whitehead could get—*they didn't know any better!* Mr. Candler told me that he couldn't find a real business man who would even consider bottling Coca-Cola, and he was afraid the pop bottlers would ruin his product. That's why he waited over ten years before he let the bottle franchise. He knew the average druggist was sanitary and careful, but he was scared to death of the pop bottler.

Big Beverage calls the drink Solo Soda, replaced here by Coca-Cola. In the novel, Bert Simpson = Ben Thomas, Blasingame = Candler.

Although there were many who resembled Pop Butts in the early industry, there were an equal number of bright men who saw the future in Coca-Cola and fought hard for their franchise. Even for them, it was not an easy task. Take, for instance, the cases of William Heck and Arthur Pratt.

HECK AND PRATT: GERMAN TURNCOAT AND CONVERTED SINNER

Thomas had high hopes for the Nashville trade, telling Candler in 1900 that William Heck was a "sober, honest, hard-working, economical German who has had a long experience in the bottling business." Based on that experience, Heck insisted on using an eight-ounce bottle, even though Candler and Whitehead wanted a six-ounce size. Thomas supported him, pointing out that soda pop was "almost universally" sold in eight-ounce bottles. Although Whitehead might be content with a smaller bottle in Atlanta, where demand for Coca-Cola was higher, Thomas and Heck were dealing with a highly competitive situation. They were not primarily trying to sell to the "high-class" establishments where dainty sips would do. Many of their consumers were blacks, who demanded volume. "We have a customer—a firm composed of two negros who run a barber shop in a small town near here—who sold 27 cases of Coca-Cola last week," Thomas wrote. Another outlet on the road to Nashville sold eighteen cases to black factory workers. During the same period, Thomas said, the high-tone local saloon sold only three cases.

Regardless of the bottle size, Heck's main headache was Celery Cola, one of J. C. Mayfield's drinks. Thomas advised Heck that "an effectual way to kill [Celery Cola] off" was to prompt a local consumer "to talk it among the people that it was nothing but a cheap rubbish and the only reason that the dealer had for wanting to foist it off on them was that he made more off of them every time he sold a bottle." Although Thomas assured Heck that he was "absolutely certain" that he would eventually succeed, his lieutenant Henry Ewing, lacking the Thomas tact, bluntly wrote in the summer of 1901 that "we are not doing this thing for pleasure; we want some profit."

In desperation, Heck sold out, only to bottle his own ersatz version of Coca-Cola, using surplus labels he had taken with him. By the end of 1903, Thomas reported with considerable satisfaction on Heck's demise. Undaunted, Heck surfaced the next year in Indiana, marketing Heck's Cola as a suitable substitute for the real thing. Thomas wrote to the Evansville, Indiana, bottler to assure him that Heck was ultimately harmless. "Heck's Cola is not Coca-Cola and all the lying that the man who puts it up can do will not convince anyone that it is."

Although the case of William Heck was not an isolated incident, the majority of Coca-Cola bottling plants eventually flourished, although it was never an easy proposition, especially in the North. Arthur Pratt, who was to become a legendary Coca-Cola bottler, reversed the Heck pattern. Pratt began as an unsuccessful Coca-Cola imitator in Huntsville, Alabama. Failing to unseat the genuine drink, he and his brother Russ bought out the local Coca-Cola operator in 1901 and built a thriving business, operating four simultaneous bottling machines, each capable of producing fourteen cases an hour.

Reasoning that he could do "big things if we had more people," Arthur Pratt tried to persuade Ben Thomas to give him the New York City territory. Thomas told him he was reserving that "golden nugget" for whoever proved to be his most successful bottler, but he offered him Newark, New Jersey, instead, where Pratt's 1902 plant was uncomfortably wedged between a saloon and a Woman's Christian Temperance Union fanatic. "It was no easy job to start from scratch and introduce a new drink in this hard-boiled territory."

Despite some hard-earned sales, Pratt found that the Northern winters killed his trade: "Nobody thought very much of selling soft drinks during zero weather." He swung a deal with a local jam-maker to promote their products along with Coca-Cola, hoping to supplement the winter trade. It drove Pratt crazy that a ten-million-person market lay fallow in nearby New York City. He developed a single outlet there at a downtown Broadway cigar stand, delivering two dozen bottles at a time in an old suitcase. Telling the Thomas board of directors that he was already servicing the New York market (but neglecting to inform them of his single cigar store outlet), Pratt bluffed his way into the entire New York City territory, opening a plant there in 1904. Despite the enormous potential, Pratt didn't make much headway in the big city until he broke into the Italian neighborhoods, where he was at first mystified by the large turnover at vegetable stores, barbershops, undertaking establishments, and harness makers. He soon discovered that all of these stores were fronts for illegal gambling tables in the rear. The Italians had found that by mixing Coca-Cola with their Chianti wine, they could drink all night—taking longer to get drunk and keeping alert with caffeine.

EARLY STRATEGIES

With enterprising bottlers like Arthur Pratt, as well as a ready-made Southern market, the parent bottlers realized that soon they would be overseeing a huge business. In the spring of 1901, Thomas wrote to Whitehead to congratulate him on his "phenomenal" sales, at the same time reporting that the Thomas territory would soon reach three thousand cases a month. Shortly after that, the Louisville, Kentucky, plant opened with a distribution of ten thousand tickets for free drinks. It soon showed a healthy profit.

Thomas was convinced that offering free coupons was the fastest way to build trade, but to hold it he needed massive advertising, including streetcar placards, calendars, change plates, trays, posters, and steel, muslin, and oilcloth signs. Pleading with Frank Robinson for more point-of-sale advertising for Louisville, Thomas wrote that "this is the first real large city that we have operated in." The hundred signs he had were inadequate, because "we expect to have 400 or 500 places started up there within a very short time." After all, he already had two hundred stands in Chattanooga, which was less than a sixth as large as Louisville.

Thomas was equally enterprising during the slower winter months, when he urged his bottlers to infiltrate elementary schools and hand out free blotters as the children were dismissed. Thomas also advertised extensively in newspapers, after bottlers informed him which local paper had the highest circulation. Finally, the parent bottler solicited testimonials from major outlets, explaining that "an expression favorable to

Coca-Cola's selling qualities will be of great assistance in a new field." Although they did not agree on everything, Whitehead and Thomas kept in touch, sharing strategies. Both men sought out railway employees, hiring them on commission as part-time Coca-Cola salesmen. Cases of bottled Coca-Cola were thus sold on trains and at depots before the advent of the delivery truck.

AMENDING THE CONTRACT

In 1901, Thomas sold his plants in order to concentrate on administering his grow-ing bottling empire. Whitehead followed suit two years later by selling a third of his Atlanta plant to Arthur Montgomery, a railroad express agent impressed with the amount of Coca-Cola he was shipping. Montgomery took over the plant manage-ment. By that fall, the original 1899 contract was already causing problems for the bottlers as well as The Coca-Cola Company. Candler regretted his promise to provide free advertising, because Frank Robinson was deluged with requests for streetcar signs, expensive German lithography, blotters, novelties, and all the other available items. At the same time, the parent bottlers were frustrated by delayed shipments from the Company. In a testy letter to Atlanta in June of 1901, Henry Ewing complained that "we have to do business with you, certainly for this summer," adding that "I do not need to explain how a business like ours with established customers will suffer if we cannot supply them. . . . We are in a fair way to do a very large business and make you valuable customers."

The parent bottlers were also unhappy with their arrangement with the actual bottlers. It was obviously going to be impractical to hire a supervisor for every bottler. In addition, these direct employees of the parent bottlers caused bad feeling with the actual bottlers, who felt there was a spy in their midst. Or, like the Memphis bottler, they complained that this special employee was a slob who didn't show up for work on time. Finally, the parent organizations realized that by insisting on a return of half of the profits, they might well bankrupt their bottlers.

For all of these reasons, Whitehead and Thomas came to a new arrangement with The Coca-Cola Company in November of 1901. In an undated amendment, the 1899 contract was changed to allow a ten-cent-per-gallon rebate to give the bottlers respon-sibility for their own advertising. In effect, the syrup price was set at ninety cents a gallon, with the parent bottlers paying ten cents a gallon for advertising—an expense they immediately passed through to their actual bottlers. At the same time, Thomas and Whitehead abandoned their obligation to place an employee/spy with each actual bottler. Rather than taking half of the bottlers' profits, they now switched to a straight royalty of six cents per case, or a quarter cent per bottle. Given the increasing demand, this seemingly small levy would make the parent bottlers millionaires within a few years, while permitting a nice profit for the actual bottlers, jobbers, and retailers of the drink.

CHILD LABOR AND ADULTERATED SYRUP

The actual bottlers replaced the supervisor as cheaply as possible, often with child labor. Thomas helped to find responsible, inexpensive help for his bottlers, in 1902 recommending a "negro boy" who would work for four dollars a week. Although wages would rise somewhat in the future, the tedious manual labor in Coca-Cola bottling plants never commanded a decent salary. In later years, because of the noise and monotony, many plants hired deaf employees at minimum wage.

After the contract amendment, Thomas cut corners in other ways as well. He began to adulterate his own syrup, the same practice that all good Coca-Cola men professed to find so evil. In September of 1901, he rush-ordered ten pounds of saccharin (trade-named "garantose") from Merck & Company for experimentation. In January, Thomas sent a coded recipe for "simple syrup" to his bottlers. By adding caramel coloring, phosphoric acid, and saccharin in the right proportions, bottlers stretched a gallon of Coca-Cola syrup so that it would yield 144 bottles. In the ensuing months, Thomas engaged in considerable correspondence about the proportions of this saccharin mixture, because it resulted in slight variations in color, acidity, and sweetness. Writing to his Pittsburgh bottler, Thomas said, "I do not think that you can make a mistake in having your Coca-Cola too sweet. . . . I am sure that it tastes better than that which is not so sweet." He went on to say that "tastes vary" regarding the proper amount of acidity.

In Thomas' defense, he was probably adding saccharin not only because it was cheaper than sugar but because it acted as a preservative. From the outset, he had been plagued by a cloudy drink that deposited an unpleasant sediment. At first he blamed the Hutchinsons' faulty seal. When the problem continued with the crown cork, he decided that polluted water must be the cause. An amateur chemist, Thomas tinkered with pasteurization of Coca-Cola, but it killed the taste. Eventually, he devised a system of cleaning the water with alum, and recommended filtering the syrup before use as well.

PARENT BOTTLERS: PIONEERS OR PIRATES?

The efforts of Thomas have been emphasized here simply because no similar records have survived from Whitehead and Lupton. It is obvious from the correspondence between Thomas and Whitehead that both men deserve full credit for building the Coca-Cola bottling business. Whitehead, frazzled by overwork, died of pneumonia in 1906 at forty-two, and Thomas followed at fifty-two in 1914. They had seen the future far more clearly than Asa Candler, and their protean efforts paid off quickly. They were at the same time salesmen, cheerleaders, advertising agents, bottlers, lawyers, negotiators, venture capitalists, chemists, and accountants. They created the prototype of the American franchise system, and they brought Coca-Cola to the masses.

Years later, during a bitter court battle between the bottlers and The Coca-Cola Company, Company officials would denigrate the accomplishments of the parent bottlers, accurately pointing out that the parent organization never even saw the Coca-Cola syrup that was shipped directly to the actual bottlers. Why should they have a perpetual right to their royalty? In later years, there was certainly some validity to those arguments, and The Coca-Cola Company eventually bought back the parent bottlers to avoid this unnecessary tithe. But in these early years, there is no doubt that the parent bottlers performed the essential job of recruiting, coordinating, and training legions of small bottlers, all with growing capital expenditures. Without lifting a finger or investing a penny, Asa Candler and his Company saw their business mushroom and reach into untapped rural areas. Coca-Cola advertising, already extensive, gained added momentum as parent and local bottlers covered their territory with the Coca-Cola logo.

By 1902, Whitehead, even with his smaller bottle, was doing an "enormous business" of 2,400 cases a week in Atlanta alone. At the same time, Thomas observed that bottles didn't have to piggyback on an existing fountain trade. "In Charleston, where Coca-Cola had practically no [fountain] business, the bottling plant is running considerably over an average of 100 cases a day. It has been a great surprise to every one."

Some fountain operators felt threatened. "We predict the *death* of your specialty— which has had so many years of success," wrote an indignant Indiana fountain man in 1904. He complained that the bottled drink came in a motley assortment of containers, "as pleases the whim, ignorance or averice" of the local distributor, thus "throwing down the Bars for the many imitators of your drink" and "destroying Fountain trade." Although sales might initially be "immenseily increased," the angry owner predicted that the inevitable result would be that "any old thing with an amber color" would soon pass for Coca-Cola. A Company official reassured the apoplectic druggist that, far from hurting the trade, bottlers would help the fountain in the long run. "The bottled goods are as a rule so uniform and satisfactory that it stimulates the dispensers to give a better glass of Coca-Cola in order to hold their trade," wrote the Company man. "In this city the matter has been tested for years, and the dispensers are doing more business now than ever before."

By 1904, no one at The Coca-Cola Company would say anything against the bottlers. Where five years before, there had been only sporadic, informal efforts to bottle Coca-Cola, now there were over 120 manufacturing facilities covering almost every state. By the end of the year, the Company published a booklet showing the sales of the bottled drink, asking readers to consider the import of this growing branch of the business, with its "remarkable, and in many cases phenomenal" growth. Pointing out that every gallon of syrup represented about ten dozen bottles of Coca-Cola, the spokesman urged the reader to "use your pencil, make a few calculations and see what an enormous business has been done in nearly every place where a bottling plant has been established."

Although at first it had been difficult to lure anyone into the bottling business, the parent bottlers were soon turning away droves of eager entrepreneurs. In 1912, one self-promoting Texas owner had stationery printed up depicting a Coca-Cola bottle spewing dollar signs instead of a beverage. "THERE IS MONEY IN IT" the legend below bluntly stated. By 1919, there were 1,200 plants; virtually every town in America had a Coca-Cola bottler. Asa Candler was delighted but still mystified by the bottlers' success. One day in 1904, Candler ran into Veazey Rainwater, who operated the booming Athens, Georgia, plant at the time. "Veazey," Candler said, "what are you doing with all of that syrup, pouring it into the Oconee River?" Rainwater just smiled, but later, when he had taken over the Atlanta parent bottler administration following Whitehead's death, he accurately summed up the bottlers' accomplishments. Coca-Cola, he said, had been put into the hands of "thousands of merchants in the suburbs and outlying districts of every city, in the stores of every country town and village, and in the homes of thousands of people where it had not been possible to put Coca-Cola before." As a result, "an enormous field was opened up . . . and hundreds of thousands of individuals who had never before tasted or seen Coca-Cola were introduced to this product first in bottles."

THE COCAINE KICKER

The bottling business had one unfortunate, unforeseen consequence, however. No longer simply a soda fountain drink for upper-class urban white professionals, Coca-Cola was increasingly consumed by blacks. Sensational stories of "Negro coke fiends" attacking whites caused many to fear the widespread availability of Coca-Cola. As the century turned, so did public opinion, and in 1900 Candler found himself under intensified pressure to reform his "dope."

Part II

Heretics and True Believers

(1900–1922)

Asa Candler could no longer stand it. His younger brother John, the lawyer, had told him to stay away from the trial, but it was more than he could bear. He had endured enough, reading the outrageous lies every day in the Atlanta Georgian. *What possible difference could it make if he just went and sat quietly in the back?**

And so, on a rainy April morning in 1911, the president of The Coca-Cola Company snuck quietly into the back of a Chattanooga courtroom. Glancing around, he quickly found that all the Coca-Cola men, including his son Howard, sat on the left. He joined them. Putting his finger to his lips, he warned Howard not to make an issue of his father's presence. Hunching inconspicuously in his seat, he fidgeted with repressed rage, listening to government witnesses malign his drink. He recognized that great tub of lard, Harvey Wiley, nodding sagely on the other side of the courtroom.

At the noon recess, Candler had just stepped outside and was about to hurry away when a hand pulled at his elbow. "Mr. Candler, I believe." That voice! It was Kebler, the government spy he'd caught skulking around the Atlanta syrup plant two years ago. Turning around, Candler turned a shade of Coca-Cola red. "Ah, I thought it was you. Mr. Candler, I'd like to introduce Dr. Wiley." And Kebler gently pushed Candler toward the imposing chemist, who reached out a massive hand. "I'm pleased finally to meet so worthy an opponent," Wiley boomed.

"You, sir, are a hypocrite to offer your hand," Candler said. "I won't take it. You are persecuting and attempting to ruin a beneficial beverage, a boon to mankind. Well, you won't succeed." Candler was just building to one of his explosive, high-pitched climaxes when his brother John grabbed him by the arm. "Asa!" he hissed, pulling him away, "I thought you agreed not to come. You're causing a scene. Please, please, go back to Atlanta."

Asa Candler shook himself loose, straightening his tie. He took a deep breath. "Johnnie, you're right. I'd better go before I do bodily harm, sure enough. But you know that God watches over His own, and we will prevail." And reassuming his dignity, the gray-haired little man walked away.

---

*This scenario is based on fact. On March 30, 1911, Candler wrote to his son Howard, "I can't avoid wanting to be with you all, but Uncle John advises staying away. I am ready to go on a moment's notice." He then briefly attended the trial in Chattanooga sometime in April.

~ 6 ~

Success Under Siege

It is only since the rising tide of Coca-Cola's popularity has grown to the extent of attracting general public attention that this fire has been directed to it. . . . Now that everybody drinks it, a certain coterie, composed mostly of disgruntled competitors and misguided fanatics, have discovered that it is more seductive than opium, more injurious than tobacco and more pernicious than whisky.

—Judge John S. Candler, 1909

Asa Candler had a problem: by 1900, Coca-Cola was already not simply a soft drink, but a phenomenon. With success, however, came increased notoriety and controversy. The drink's cocaine content had been a source of trouble from the beginning, but it was also a major selling point. Without the benefit of the coca leaf's small kick, how could Coca-Cola survive? Also, if Candler took it out, how could he legally defend his trademark? It would be like jettisoning the first half of the name. Candler was determined not to tamper with the formula. In 1898, a zealous Oregon evangelist named Lindsay had arrived in Marietta, Georgia, near Atlanta, as the minister of the local Baptist church. From the pulpit, Reverend Lindsay had launched a hellfire attack on Coca-Cola, the ingredients of which were, he asserted, fully two-thirds cocaine; imbibing would lead to "morphine eating." His accusations made good newspaper copy, prompting a quick Candler response: "I do not propose to vend a poison or be instrumental if I know it of doing harm to anybody." By righteously denying that his magical drink had any harmful effects, Candler hoped to defuse any controversy.

The 1898 incident was a local disturbance and faded away, but cocaine was soon making national headlines, in part because racism was on the rise, in the North as well as the South. In September of 1906, a major race riot occurred in Atlanta—though it primarily involved whites attacking blacks rather than vice versa—caused by inflammatory newspaper accounts of black "brutes" attacking white women. Long before the riot, cocaine, the 1885 wonder drug, had become the 1900 scourge of humanity, and in the South it allegedly caused crazed Negroes to attack their bosses and rape white women. There may have been vestiges of truth behind the sensational headlines, since many farmers were giving cocaine to their black sharecroppers in lieu of food and cocaine in the city, where fifty cents bought a week's supply, was a cheaper high than alcohol.

Whatever the reason, the papers were filled with black cocaine fiends. A white Georgian complained to a *New York Tribune* reporter that "in Atlanta, cocaine sniffing has grown to such proportions that some of the keepers of saloons patronized by the colored people are going out of business," adding that Coca-Cola produced "similar effects to cocaine, morphine, and such like. Men become addicted to drinking it, and find it hard to release themselves from the habit." The *Atlanta Constitution* wrote in 1901 that "use of the drug among negroes is growing to an alarming extent. . . . It is stated that quite a number of the soft drinks dispensed at soda fountains contain cocaine, and that these drinks serve to unconsciously cultivate the habit."

During his testimony in the trial against the IRS, Candler admitted that there was a "very small proportion" of cocaine in Coca-Cola. With mounting frustration, he listened to physicians testify on the effects of the "Coca-Cola habit." One Atlanta doctor cited the case of a thirteen-year-old boy who usually drank ten to twelve glasses per day but lost his job and was suddenly unable to buy Coca-Cola: "He came to my office the day after in a very nervous, almost collapsed condition, stating to me that he could not get his Coca-Cola and that he knew something was the matter with him." Another doctor said that his neurasthenic partner was "very strangely affected" by drinking Coca-Cola: "If he takes a glass, he can't find his way home." Perhaps the poor man drank a double or quadruple dose, since Atlanta druggists were in the habit of using anywhere from one to four ounces of syrup per glass, according to one witness.

All of these statements come from the 1902 trial, but Candler had already heard similar testimony during the *first* IRS trial, which had ended in July of 1901 with a hung jury. At some point during the first trial, the accumulation of such testimony, combined with adverse press coverage and the spread of bottled Coca-Cola among black consumers, forced him to remove the cocaine. His first attempt was only partially successful, which explains why a chemist found four-hundredths of a grain of cocaine per ounce of syrup in 1902. It also accounts for Candler's curious, stumbling answer at one point when he was asked how much cocaine was in Coca-Cola: "If we got all of it—but we don't treat it—" The lawyer saved him by interrupting with another question. No wonder Candler was smitten with severe headaches while on the witness stand.

Soon afterward, in August of 1903, Candler contracted with the Schaefer Alkaloid Works of Maywood, New Jersey, to decocainize the coca leaves before sending "Merchandise No. 5" on to Atlanta.* The exact date of Candler's first attempt to remove cocaine cannot be pinpointed, but it was probably in 1901. That January, Coca-Cola distributed a defensive pamphlet, *What Is It? Coca-Cola, What It Is*, in which Candler admitted a small amount of cocaine. The pamphlet contained an 1891 analysis which said "it would require about thirty glasses . . . to make an ordinary dose of the drug." The text also praised the coca leaf, which "makes one active, brilliant, vigorous, and able to accomplish great tasks easily." It seems clear, then, that at the beginning of 1901, cocaine was still in the drink, but most of it had been removed by the following year.

The removal of the cocaine presented a delicate public relations problem. If the company responded to attacks by telling the truth, they would be admitting that the drink *did* once have cocaine in it. The implication would be that they had removed it

---

* The Maywood plant, renamed the Maywood Chemical Works, then purchased by Stepan Chemical Company in 1959, continues to decocainize coca leaf for Coca-Cola.

because it was harmful, which might even open the door to lawsuits. Besides, it was unthinkable to admit that Coca-Cola had ever been anything but pure and wholesome. Finally, of course, they didn't want the public to know that one of the drink's more enticing ingredients was now missing.

Consequently, Candler orchestrated a mighty revision of Coca-Cola history, perhaps convincing himself in the process. In later years, he repeatedly denied, under oath, that the drink had ever had cocaine in it. Even today, the Company feels compelled to deny it. After 1900, instead of bragging about the removal of cocaine, the Company poured on the advertising, stressing the soft drink's healthful qualities. In December of 1902, the Georgia legislature made the sale of cocaine in any form illegal. By luck, grace, or good judgment, Coca-Cola once more narrowly escaped disaster, though the controversy over the drink had only begun.

AN ADVERTISING BLITZ

When John Candler was asked during the IRS trial what sort of vehicles The Coca-Cola Company used for its advertising, he answered, "I don't know anything they *don't* advertise on." By the turn of the century, Frank Robinson was annually sending out over a million pieces of advertising in some thirty forms. In 1900, the firm spent almost $85,000 on advertising. By 1912, that figure was well over a million dollars a year, and Sam Dobbs could accurately claim that Coca-Cola was the single best-advertised product in the United States. Wherever Americans looked, they could not avoid seeing the Coca-Cola script. During 1913, the company advertised on over a hundred million items, including thermometers, cardboard cutouts, and metal signs (fifty thousand each); Japanese fans and calendars (a million each); two million soda fountain trays, ten million matchbooks, twenty million blotters, twenty-five million baseball cards, and innumerable signs made of cardboard and metal. The novelties distributed in that one year alone could have supplied every man, woman, and child who had lived in the continental United States since 1650.

It is little wonder that Coca-Cola had begun to permeate every aspect of American life. Horses were named Coca-Cola; bears at Yellowstone drank it.* Coca-Cola chewing gum, cigars, and candy were marketed to take advantage of the popular trademark.† Because of the stigma attached to the drink, Coca-Cola added a deliciously

---

* Over the years, the Company received innumerable letters and photographs testifying to the love of the animal kingdom for Coca-Cola—including horses, bees, goats, elephants, and monkeys, but mostly dogs, so that wearied Company men called them all "bow-wow letters." Those sending the photos received a stock response: "While pets drinking Coca-Cola usually make for an appealing picture, we have always thought it a sound policy to depict our product being consumed by human beings." The Company was not above taking advantage of one clever myna bird, however, who shouted at conventions: "Won't you have a Coca-Cola, huh?"

† Coca-Cola chewing gum had a long and checkered history. Like many of the early trademark spin-offs, it was never officially sponsored by the Company. In later years, when protection of the logo became a crusade, the Company was embarrassed by the gum, which had deteriorated in quality. Through an intermediary, the Company bought out the nearly bankrupt firm in 1924. According to a persistent piece of Company folklore, the Coca-Cola chewing gum trademark was then "protected" once a year when a salesman delivered a carton to a rural South Carolina store, walked around the block, bought a piece of gum, chewed it, purchased the entire carton, and left.

sinful note to lyrics of popular songs. In one ditty, a young man enjoying his first debauch in the big city wrote home to say, "Oh! mother, you wouldn't know your child / Oh! mother, I'm getting awfully wild / I am drinking Coca-Cola now / On the level, I'm a little devil." In "Follow Me, Girls, to the Fountain, and Be My Coca-Cola Girl," the drink was used as a seductive lure. The composer dedicated the song to The Coca-Cola Company, "whose delicious drink has wet the whistle of countless thousands and made 'HIGH LIFE' possible even in a dry town."

The young film industry, too, had begun its love affair with the soft drink. Asa Candler bragged that "a moving picture cannot be taken in the open air . . . , but what it is likely to catch a Coca-Cola [sign]." Buster Keaton drank it on-screen. Popular silent film stars such as Pearl White and Marion Davies appeared in Coca-Cola ads. The drink even found its way into an early Hollywood sex scandal, when comedian Fatty Arbuckle was rumored to have utilized a Coca-Cola bottle during an orgy.

Asa Candler was undoubtedly as unhappy about the Arbuckle publicity as he was with the unauthorized advertising of the Western Coca-Cola Bottling Company. In 1905, this third parent bottler, owned by J. T. Lupton, had split from the Southeastern parent bottler. Based in Chicago, it faced stiff competition from the breweries and depressed sales during Northern winters. S. L. Whitten, who ran the organization, wrote to Asa Candler at the beginning of 1907 that "not a single Coca-Cola bottling company in our territory . . . made money last year" but added that "we are working along lines somewhat differing from our work of last year."

Whitten's "somewhat differing" approach used overtly sexual advertising for Coca-Cola. One of his 1908 trays featured a bare-breasted young woman holding a Coca-Cola bottle. The surrounding text suggested trying "Coca-Cola High Balls" and "Coca-Cola Gin Rickies." Another ad showed a young woman in black lingerie reclining on a tiger-skin rug with an expression of exhausted bliss. She held an empty glass, a Coca-Cola bottle on the table beside her. The caption: "Satisfied"—obviously in more ways than one.

While the sanctimonious Candler was appalled by Western's ads, the beautiful young women used in authorized ads were suggestive in their own ways. The whole-some-but-sensuous models specialized in come-hither looks from the corner of the eye while they sipped their drinks demurely through a straw. One contemporary critic described the "bewitching sirens who lure us to Coca-Cola, with their display of charms," but were ready to flee in "innocent alarm at the possibility of spectators." Men fell in love with the millions of pictures of Betty, the 1914 calendar girl, while women made every attempt to look like her.

The most visible, widespread advertising for Coca-Cola, however, were hand-painted signs. One thirty-two-foot-high effort featured a soda jerk drawing a glass with real water flowing from the spigot. Most signs weren't so elaborate, but many were as large, taking up entire sides of buildings. The first wall turned red for Coca-Cola in Cartersville, Georgia, in 1894. By 1914, the Company had over five million square feet of painted walls, enough to give one unfortunate consumer nightmares, as a salesman reported in 1906. "Hounded almost to a state of imbecility with Coca-Cola signs," the poor man would "wake up at night with big white devils with a red mantel chasing after him screeching 'Coca-Cola! Coca-Cola!' until he made up his mind that he would have to go in somewhere and get a glass of Coca-Cola or part with his reason."

THE COCA-COLA INSTITUTE

Backed by such effective advertising, the small band of Coca-Cola men invaded the cities and towns of America in the first decade of the century. In December of 1903, the twenty-nine salesmen were summoned to Atlanta for a four-day pep rally and sales meeting grandly called the Coca-Cola Institute. As Candler noted in his annual report, "some of these men had never before been seen by the officers of the Company. They were brought into personal contact with each other and have returned to their various fields of work greatly enthused."

Sam Dobbs had taken firm charge of the sales force, traveling extensively to supervise his far-flung team. At the 1903 meeting, he praised them as "splendid men," gentlemanly and high-toned. "Never be ashamed to say you are a traveling salesman," Dobbs urged. Thoroughly aroused, the salesmen burst out with cheers of "HURRAH for Coca-Cola, the drink that strengthens but does not inebriate—Coca-Cola, the drink of the age!" Throughout the rest of the week, they shared tips with one another on how best to spread the gospel, such as rigging a "mechanical attachment" to a man in a window display so that he moved a Coca-Cola glass to his lips while rolling his eyes or putting large thermometers in a sunny window, accompanied by an offer of a free fan with every glass of Coca-Cola.

Salesmen discussed the proper distribution of free tickets, counseling one another to avoid residential neighborhoods, where most of the tickets would end up with children and to stick to the business districts, office buildings, and college campuses. "Don't cast [tickets] before swine or small boys. [But] do not be stingy. Let the public feel that The Coca-Cola Company is the most liberal Santa Claus in the world." Though one salesman noted that "female stenographers and bookkeepers are good Coca-Cola drinkers," no one identified women as a major market for Coca-Cola outside the workforce. In order to avoid counterfeits, the tickets were lithographed by a German firm in lots of two million. Even so, many soda fountain operators redeemed Coca-Cola tickets for other soft drinks. Salesmen could best prevent such practices by bribing the soda jerk with novelties such as pocketknives or watch fobs.

Frank Robinson spoke at the 1903 meeting, too, but he lacked the inspirational tone of Sam Dobbs, stressing small matters such as urging the salesmen to note the name of imitation colas. Robinson said that he ordered "high class, artistic and expensive advertising matter," which should be carefully placed: "a large lithograph costing $1.00 should not go into an obscure place or be left with a dispenser to do with as he pleases." His warnings were understandable, since the sixteen-color artwork was gorgeous. Robinson betrayed some emotion when he pointed out with pride that he had just placed 650 large lithographs in railway stations and that "in Philadelphia and Chicago the large oilcloth signs are so conspicuous and so numerous . . . as to give the impression that The Coca-Cola Company owns the town."

By the end of the week, the salesmen were well indoctrinated. Coca-Cola was "a thirst-quenching, heaven-sent drink," one employee glowed, "a blessing to this sun-parched earth." Another speaker advised salesmen to think of themselves as bearers of a secular religion. Like "the missionary going into a foreign field" to teach the "rudiments," the Coca-Cola man must be "a live one, [a] practical, hustling man." Bishop Warren Candler visited the Institute several times to open the meetings with a morning prayer. Together, Warren and Asa led the group in a rousing rendition of "Onward, Christian Soldiers" to end the week. As the printed report of the meeting stated, "the Convention . . . was carried on from beginning to end with a very unusual degree of earnestness and enthusiasm."

THE BISHOP'S BLESSING

The bishop wasn't simply doing his brother a favor. Asa's younger brother truly believed in the twin virtues of capitalism and religion. In 1888, he had helped Coca-Cola gain its first foothold in Nashville, and he owned Coca-Cola stock. Warren and Asa Candler were extremely close, sharing religious values and monetary advice throughout their lives. The bishop was the greater intellect, dominating the Southern branch of the Methodist Church for over thirty years with the force of his character, writings, and sermons. Howard Candler described his uncle as "a short, barrel-shaped man" with "quick passions and doggedly stubborn prejudices." The bishop's son compared him to a bulldog. A contentious, pompous little man, he relished good fights, and his conservative views guaranteed he would find them—often with Tom Watson, the Georgia populist-turned-demagogue who called Bishop Candler "a Coca-Cola lobbyist . . . unctuous, self-righteous, [and] self-complacent."

Warren Candler believed deeply in the superiority of what he called Anglo-Saxon culture. In his 1904 book, *Great Revivals and the Great Republic*, he asserted that the United States was destined to lead the world because of its revivalistic religion: "Romanism has made South America and Southern Europe what they are, and Protestantism has made England, Germany, Holland, and North America what they are." In other words, God was on America's side, and He smiled as Americans made money.

One of Bishop Candler's strongest arguments in favor of revivals was that they helped maintain the status quo and avert labor unrest. He pointed out that "disturbances between labor and capital have been most frequent in those industries in which the laborers have been brought from the unevangelized masses of Continental Europe." He ended by emphasizing that the efforts of ministers were essential in an industrial age: "What they [have] accomplished in the way of soothing the irritations of the social system, and of postponing if not preventing the worst industrial disorder, can scarcely be overestimated." Warren Candler's paternalistic, conservative views were echoed by his brother Asa, who set the pattern of anti-unionism at The Coca-Cola Company, whose Atlanta employees never organized.

Naturally, the bishop thought it essential for missionaries to disseminate the Protestant gospel and the virtues of industrial harmony. "The missionary enterprise must go in advance of international commerce," Bishop Candler wrote, "to secure justice in trade and safety for the merchantmen." He personally spread the Word to China, Korea, and Mexico, but his great love was Cuba. The Spanish-American War of 1898 opened the perfect target for the Methodist missionary—a country full of poor, oppressed Catholics.

The war was scarcely over* when, in late 1898, Warren Candler sailed for Cuba, the first of twenty such visits. Upon his return, he enthusiastically reported that Cuba was "our nearest, neediest, ripest missionary field." The next year, he helped to found Candler College, a Cuban Methodist mission school. Asa provided funds for the school, explaining, "We may be sure that commercial currents will follow the channels which education opens and deepens. . . . Herein our duty and our interest coincide." After hearing about this "ripe field" from Warren, Asa promptly enlisted José Parejo, a wine merchant, as a Havana wholesaler for Coca-Cola in May of 1899.

Cuba was not the first foreign country to be invaded by Coca-Cola. It had been sold in Canada, Hawaii, and Mexico by 1897. When Howard Candler went to England during the summer of 1900, he took along a gallon of Coca-Cola syrup and was delighted to find John Ralphs, an American, running one of the new London soda fountains. Ralphs used up the gallon and ordered more from Coca-Cola's Philadelphia branch.

ASA'S UPS AND DOWNS

In one of his manic moments in 1900, Asa Candler wrote to Howard in London, envisioning Coca-Cola's world dominion. While his fantasies would not come true during his tenure at the Company, Asa Candler wasn't a bad prophet. "I propose to put you and your brother in charge somewhere in some of the important places," he wrote, asking Howard to "critically observe conditions in Europe" while Buddie (Asa Jr.), presumably from his vantage point on the West Coast, would plot strategy for Asia. "Together we must map out for great conquests." The next year, Candler bragged to a reporter that "Coca-Cola is now being shipped to London and to Berlin, to Canada and to Honolulu, and it is being sold in large quantities in Cuba, Puerto Rico and Kingston, Jamaica." In fact, outside of Canada and Cuba, the amount sold was negligible. It was primarily distributed through New York and Philadelphia brokers who wouldn't even tell Coca-Cola officers who their customers were, for fear the Company would sell to them directly.

Asa Candler enjoyed picturing these "great conquests" for his children, but he was becoming increasingly morbid about his own life. In 1901, Candler wrote that "I realize with almost crushing disappointment that I can only be of importance to the interests of my generation through the good that I may bring to it in my boys. I pray constantly that my boys may be *men*." The following year, when he was only fifty-one, Candler sounded as if he were dying of old age. "Only a few years at best and I will have to sit down and wait for the *Reaper* to *carry* me off like the streetcleaner the trash," he moaned. "I have not felt well for two weeks. My head aches now."

---

*The Spanish-American War sparked military support of American businesses in Latin America—most affiliated with Coca-Cola. Major General Smedley Butler of the U.S. Marines bragged, "I helped make Haiti and Cuba a decent place for the National City Bank boys to collect revenue in. I helped purify Nicaragua for the international banking house of Brown Brothers from 1909 to 1912. I brought light to the Dominican Republic for American sugar interests in 1916. I helped make Honduras 'right' for American fruit companies in 1903." The Coca-Cola Company was to form lasting alliances with every business Butler listed.

Candler's business was outgrowing him. He was appalled at the amount of money that was being spent on advertising and labor, even though the dollars were accruing faster than he could spend them. At the beginning of 1901, he complained that "we have grown so large and so many to be paid, and with that, money goes out in great torrents." At that moment, there was a cash surplus of nearly $200,000 and the Company owned $71,000 in real estate free and clear.

Similarly, he wasn't keeping up with his drink's potential market. He continued to harbor the Victorian illusion that Coca-Cola must remain a high-class fountain drink, fighting the democratic tide that bottling had unleashed. "We must not cater to *dives* and cheap places." Nor was he eager to embrace the automobile. Complaining about mechanical difficulties plaguing the New York office's Locomobile in 1902, he expressed no confidence in "such machines," adding that "like the Bycicle I have looked upon them as a fad only."

The horseless carriage was no fad. In fact, it was a fitting symbol for the restless age that Candler himself represented. In 1901, an *Atlanta Constitution* journalist wrote that "our new friend, the automobile, [is] a striking exemplification of this queer spirit of unrest which seems to have become an heritage of our national life." Everyone in America appeared to be "incessantly searching for some new method of economizing time and condensing life into the briefest possible compass. Even our pleasures are taken in that same forceful, strenuous, nerve-straining manner."

If Candler read this editorial, he must have recognized himself in it. "I am so habituated to hurry," he wrote, "that I seem to be unable to *stay* in *one place*." When someone politely asked Candler for his ear when he next found a leisure moment, he snapped, "I am never at leisure; what will you have while I am busy?" Finding no peace in his triumph, Candler was as much a victim as a hero of his age. Coca-Cola brought him no relief, though its advertisements promised quick new energy or instant relaxation. In fact, Coca-Cola was emblematic of the modern American attempt to package pleasure. As the editorial implied, even leisure had become strenuous. Candler's nephew, J. J. Willard, who edited the *Coca-Cola Bottler*, wrote that the "fever heat" of American civilization, characterized by "rushing and striving," accounted for the growing demand for Coca-Cola, an instant pick-me-up. But for harried businessmen, including his uncle, the drink provided only temporary respite. Candler could not cope with membership in the leisure class, comprehending only the virtues of work. Years ago, he had clipped a poem which advised: "It is *hustle* that will *tell*; / It is Godlike to excel. / Have you work? Do it well." Though he had excelled, Asa Candler did not feel godlike. His stomach hurt. Searching for solace, he carefully typed out a quotation from Hawthorne: "The world owes all its onward impulses to men ill at ease."

Still, the money poured in. He created the Candler Investment Company and began to buy Atlanta real estate. In August of 1904, he watched the foundation being laid for the Candler Building, a seventeen-story skyscraper that rose above Atlanta, a monument to the New South. On January 4, 1906, elegantly gowned women and men in three-piece suits entered to admire the nearly completed showpiece, with its six elevators, artistic gargoyles, polished marble, mahogany, and brass, and glittering crystal chandeliers. On the first floor was Candler's newly formed bank, the Central Bank and Trust Corporation. Here was permanence. Here was immortality. In the building's cornerstone Candler placed a copper box containing his picture and a bottle of Coca-Cola.

The next month, as if God were mocking Asa Candler, a heavy windstorm tore a huge plate-glass window from the building and smashed it in the middle of Peachtree Street. Candler fretted. "*My friends* too often are *my enemies,*" he wrote. If that were so, even God might turn on him. "He has given me so many unmistakable evidences of His ability to carry me safely over dangerous places—yet I do not trust Him and may be lost." Still seeking immortality, he spread his name and presence across the United States, paying for skyscrapers in Kansas City, Baltimore, and New York City, all named the Candler Building. The New York effort, fronting on West Forty-Second Street near Times Square, cost $2 million and soared to twenty-five stories, with the Candler coat of arms cast into the doorknobs, elevator doors, and mailboxes. With an obsessive attention to detail and petty economy, he specified the wattage of light bulbs.

In the first twenty years of the century, Asa Candler invested in virtually every aspect of Atlanta's life. "It would literally be impossible," wrote Howard Candler, "to describe all my father's business interests." Through his railroad holdings, he traveled gratis on any line and insisted that Coca-Cola be sold in dining cars. When the bottom dropped out of the cotton market, he built a huge warehouse and bought the surplus cotton at low prices, making a tidy profit when the market improved. During the "panic of 1907," Candler bolstered real estate prices, snapping up hard-hit properties. For most of these profitable activities, he was hailed as a hero even as he raked in more money. To radicals and labor leaders, however, Candler was a villain. A 1908 political cartoon criticized the wealthy banker, showing his support of vested interests while saying "Nothin Doin" to the poor.

Indeed, Candler's money did not make him generous. When a personal friend owing him money reminded him of their longtime relationship, Candler cut him off, saying that while he appreciated all that, "we are not talking friendship now; we are talking business." An indigent missionary once begged Candler for money to support his wife and five children, explaining that it was "humiliating in the extreme" but that he would starve otherwise. Candler sent him ten dollars, along with a note: "You realize I am sure that such calls as yours are frequent on me." He wasn't even generous to Cliff Pemberton, the impoverished widow of Coca-Cola's inventor. When a group of women approached Candler to ask that he give her fifty dollars a month, he refused. In July of 1909, as Mrs. Pemberton lay dying of cancer, a relative wrote that "if someone would present her case properly to the rich man who purchased the Coca-Cola formula, his heart, if he had one, would be moved." Two months later, she was dead.

The year before Mrs. Pemberton's death, another unpleasant side of Candler was revealed. In 1908, the fourth annual convention of the National Child Labor Committee met in Atlanta, principally to protest the horrific conditions in cotton mills, where women and children worked over sixty-hour weeks, breathing cotton motes for fifty cents a day or less. Georgia would be the last Southern state to pass child labor legislation. As president of the Atlanta Chamber of Commerce, Candler gave an almost unbelievable opening speech, considering his audience. "Child labor properly conducted, properly surrounded, properly conditioned, is calculated to bring the highest measure of success to any country on the face of the earth," he began. "The most beautiful sight that we see is the child at labor." In fact, the younger the boy began work, "the more beautiful, the more useful does his life get to be." Candler ended by asserting that the proper function of the Committee was to assure that the child's work turned him into "a noble, useful, competent laboring grown person."

In commenting on this performance, a Committee official chose to interpret Candler's speech as "subtle humor," a character trait no one else ever accused Candler of possessing. He was clearly serious, perhaps recalling his own youthful entrepreneurial days but more likely defending the widespread use of child labor in Southern cotton mills—including his own in Hartwell, Georgia, which he sold two years later—and, of course, at The Coca-Cola Company and bottling franchises.

During the summer of 1913, Candler, sixty-one, took his wife on the Grand Tour of Europe, as befitted the wealthy of that era. He granted an interview just before leaving in which he was "altogether optimistic and cheerful as to the business outlook," surveying a horizon "abundantly rainbowed and promising nothing but good things." The interview was a fraud. The real motivation for Candler's trip was flight from a breakdown, as he admitted to his brother Warren: "I left home to try to recover my nerve steadiness." As usual, he hated the enforced idleness, writing that while his wife enjoyed Paris, "I do not but will tough it through."

He only parted with substantial sums of money when he felt it would add to his greater glory. While Candler was in Europe, Andrew Carnegie offered a million dollars to Vanderbilt University, which had always been a Methodist institution, on the condition that it become nondenominational. Faced with losing Methodist influence in higher education because of the godless Yankee capitalist, the religious leadership naturally turned to Asa Candler, Carnegie's Southern equivalent. Candler was embarrassed and angered by a rumor that he would give $2 million to Emory College to transform it into a fine university. He wasn't at all sure he wanted to give *any* money to Emory, which he called "a crumbling castle." Goaded by Warren, rumor, and his belief in religious education, he eventually awarded *one* million to Emory in July of 1914, noting testily in announcing the gift that "I do not possess by a vast deal what some extravagantly imagine and confidently affirm." Emory subsequently moved from Oxford, Georgia, to Atlanta. Before his death, Candler would lavish over $8 million on the college.

COCA-COLA IN COLLIER'S

While Candler spent more time caring for his other business interests and agonizing over philanthropy, Coca-Cola advertising guaranteed that he would never have to worry about poverty. Though a few years older, Frank Robinson had none of Candler's misgivings about spending money to attract new consumers. He had always bought ad space in major U.S. newspapers, but in the first years of the 1900s, the new popularity (and circulation figures) of magazines attracted him. He placed the first Coca-Cola ad in a national periodical in 1904, spending just over $4,000 for the year. The next year, however, he boosted the budget for magazines to over $56,000, hiring Atlanta's Massengale Advertising Agency to create the national spreads. Almost all Massengale ads featured long, curved arrows pointing toward a glass of Coca-Cola—clearly an early, awkward effort to induce an automatic psychological response. "Whenever, you see an Arrow," read typical copy, "think of Coca-Cola."

At the beginning of 1906, Robinson added another $25,000 to the budget, earmarked for religious and literary publications in an attempt to sway Coca-Cola's critics. Such magazines had "a powerful influence," he argued, certain that ads there would convince "the very best people in this country that Coca-Cola is not only perfectly harmless, but . . . helpful and health-giving." Robinson promised that when publications such as *Collier's Weekly*, the *Saturday Evening Post*, or the *Christian Herald* were "flooded with letters" objecting to the Coca-Cola ads, the magazines would leap to the drink's defense.

Unfortunately, the flood of such protest letters had the opposite effect on the *Wesleyan Christian Advocate*, a Methodist magazine, which in 1906 refused to accept any more Coca-Cola ads. Reluctantly, Bishop Candler sold his Coca-Cola stock to avoid controversy. Asa Candler was infuriated, particularly since the *Advocate* continued to accept advertising from obviously fraudulent patent medicines, electric belts, and weight reducers. "Cut to the quick," as son Howard put it, Candler forthwith canceled his subscription.

The defensive Coca-Cola ads of this period continued to mix messages. True, the drink was delicious and refreshing, but its medicinal, bracing qualities were also stressed. A 1905 Massengale ad in *McClure's*, for instance, portrayed a young man in a darkened room, reading a book in an armchair. The lamp threw light onto the book and the glass of Coca-Cola he was about to drink. The text, a handwritten mock prescription, read: "Rx for *Students* and *all Brain Workers*. Take one glass Coca-Cola at eight to keep the brain clear and mind active until eleven." By 1907, however, Coca-Cola spreads no longer stressed *only* brain workers. Uncle Sam himself served as a soda jerk in one ad, which depicted him drawing a glass of Coca-Cola from a spigot attached to the front of the White House. The "Great American Beverage" was for "All Classes, Ages and Sexes." While an ad in the *Saturday Evening Post* featured a businessman in the foreground, women and children drank Coca-Cola at the soda fountain behind him.

Other ads targeted specific groups, the first efforts at "market segmentation." By 1907, the advertising finally recognized that women were major consumers, calling Coca-Cola "the shoppers' panacea." Here the medicinal claims were particularly strong. In one ad, Mrs. Blue exclaims, "Oh My, how tired I am! Nothing wears me out so completely as an afternoon's shopping." Mrs. Cheerful tells her the "wonderful secret" of how she remains so bouncy: "When I start out I get a glass of Coca-Cola; that keeps my nerves quiet. On the way home I get another. This relieves that headachy feeling and I return home as fresh as when I started out." Ads in theater magazines explained that "Coca-Cola is just as enjoyable as the play itself," while the *Scientific American* ad showed a man slumped over a drafting board *before* he had a drink and explained that Coca-Cola soothed "Rattled Nerves" and restored "Wasted Energy to both Mind and Body." Other efforts simply attempted to make readers hot and bothered. "When the Sun is Red Hot, and you and your collar are limp as rags; when your mouth and throat are the only dry spots on you and you are very, very thirsty, there's just one thing to do—Drink Coca-Cola."

Many of the 1905–1907 ads contained celebrity endorsements by movie stars or athletes. Coca-Cola gave Eddie Foy "vim, vigor, and go" on stage, while Ty Cobb and many other baseball players found it put the zip back into their games. "On days when we are playing a double-header," Cobb testified in a 1906 ad, "I always find that a drink of Coca-Cola between the games refreshes me to such an extent that I can start the second game feeling as if I had not been exercising at all."

All of the advertising of the period addressed the urban consumer, calling Coca-Cola a "metropolitan beverage." Even those with a country setting stressed the sophistication of the consumers, such as two well-dressed couples served drinks in their automobile at a roadside stand. While most soda fountains were in the city, Coca-Cola had many rural customers. The Massengale men must have thought that snob appeal worked for the farmers and country folk who wished they were more cosmopolitan. Another explanation for the upscale image, of course, was the Company's effort to disassociate the drink from cheap soda pop.

It is surprising that there was no mention of bottled Coca-Cola in this ad, or those featuring baseball. After all, a bottle would be more logical for these mobile consumers in the country or for sports fans. Even though bottle sales grew enormously in the first decade of the 1900s, the Company resolutely ignored them, presumably because the bottler would advertise his own product. There was more to it than that, however. Since there was virtually no mention of the bottle in annual reports of the period, Candler must have believed that *real* Coca-Cola was served at the fountain to upper-class people, and he resisted giving credit or exposure to the bottled drink.

BOTTLING BOOM COMES OF AGE

Nonetheless, the bottling industry had come of age by 1913, when the Coca-Cola Bottlers Association was formed. By that time, technology had revolutionized the young industry. While some plants still used the horse and wagon, many had bought trucks, allowing for more efficient and widespread delivery to a growing variety of outlets, including bowling alleys, barbershops, billiard rooms, fruit stands, and cigar stores. The New Orleans bottler A. B. Freeman used the most innovative modern delivery system, servicing the bayous with his motor launch, *Josephine*. Automated bottling, soaking, and washing machines made it possible to produce a more uniform drink at higher speeds.

The Coca-Cola bottler was now one of the wealthiest men in town. He sponsored elaborate floats covered with American flags and Coca-Cola signs for the local Fourth of July parade, gave to charity, and owned a prestigious automobile—though a true Coca-Cola man wasn't too high and mighty to ride his delivery trucks to "jolly the trade" or to promote Coca-Cola through "under-the-crown" contests. The typical bottler was a true believer even more than the fountain man, since Coca-Cola had made him rich. In addition, the widespread plants meant that wherever he traveled, a Coca-Cola man could count on an instant enthusiastic friend who spoke the language of refreshment.

The quirky bottling industry soon had its share of dynamic Coca-Cola *women*, however, who proved their mettle over the years. The first was Joseph Whitehead's widow, Lettie Pate Whitehead Evans (she remarried a Colonel Evans in 1913). In 1906, when Whitehead died, she pondered selling her share of the parent bottler, which John Candler advised her to do since the business was "like a big balloon—punch a hole in it, and it is gone." Wisely, she decided to retain control, which she quietly exercised until her death in 1953. Other women took direct charge of bottling plants, usually as widows. Arthur Pratt's sister-in-law Julia didn't wait for her husband, Russell, to die, however. She despised Los Angeles (and must not have been particularly fond of her husband, who remained there), returning to Florence, Alabama, where, from 1911 on she ran an extremely profitable bottling operation.

BUGS IN THE BOTTLES

But the five hundred bottlers who formed an association in 1913 weren't banding together out of sheer love of Coca-Cola; they also needed protection from lawsuits. From the very first, the bottled soft drink had caused problems. Since a wide array of bottles and carbonation was used, the finished product sometimes exploded in the consumer's hand. Returnable bottles arrived at plants with slugs, roaches, mice, cigarette butts, slime, and other unmentionable items; frequently the rinsing machinery of the day didn't entirely remove these "foreign ingredients," and they became a part of the delicious and refreshing drink sold to the public.

One of the early "exploding bottle" cases, involving a grocer named Hudgins, made it to the Georgia Supreme Court in 1905. Hudgins lost, as did most of the plaintiffs in cases against Coca-Cola. The law put the burden on the consumer to *prove* negligence—virtually an impossibility. It couldn't have hurt, however, that Judge John Candler sat on the Georgia Supreme Court bench at the time. The "foreign ingredient" cases made for good newspaper copy, however. In one early suit, Mrs. Mattie Allen, having discovered "a large number of bugs and worms" in her bottle of Coca-Cola, couldn't return to work for a week due to "untold mental agony from fear that an untimely death might result from said poisoning drink."

Wealthy bottlers attracted fraudulent charges. Often, they preferred to settle out of court for sizable sums rather than risk the adverse publicity of a court trial. In 1913, two bottlers in adjacent states discovered that they had paid the same woman hush money. Upon further investigation, they discovered that she routinely located dead bugs in her Coca-Cola as she moved around the country. And she was not the only one. When the associated bottlers finally located an insurer, they had to write their own policy, the first liability insurance in the United States. In the ensuing years, Coca-Cola bottlers generally refused to settle out of court. In 1913, they even won a case in which a deaf-mute individual had lost one of his remaining senses when blinded by shards from an exploding bottle.

The court cases, in conjunction with the concern about newly discovered "germs," led the bottlers to emphasize Coca-Cola as a clean, pure product. "Just now a wave of sanitary ideas [is] blowing over the country," a bottler wrote in 1909. "If the boards of health and the various pure-food committees of your vicinity get on the rampage, it is a very good advertisement for you if they find your place in a first-class, spotless condition." When salmonella-tainted milk made headlines, one bottler advised, "Tell your customers to cut out the milk diet and drink Coca-Cola. They are reasonably certain to get a pure drink prepared in a sanitary way."

THE LOATHSOME FOLLOWING

While imitators had plagued the Company when it offered only a fountain drink, there were now literally hundreds of bottled drinks cashing in on Coca-Cola's fame.

Candler's nephew, J. J. Willard, contemptuously described them as "little mushroom beverages that rise up at every morning's milestone," lamenting that it was impossible to escape such a "loathsome following."

The Company's efforts in the first few years of the century to squelch imitators yielded frightening results. In 1901, the Company had sued John B. Daniel, one of Pemberton's former partners, over his Passiflora Koko-Kolo, a drink that added may-pop, or passionflower (yet another supposed aphrodisiac), to the standard coca and kola. In the suit, John Candler alleged that Daniel was "deceiving and misleading the public" by selling it in red five-gallon kegs for twenty-five cents a gallon less than Coca-Cola. Daniel's lawyers argued that he was not infringing on the name because the words "coca" and "cola" were descriptive and not subject to copyright. Coca-Cola lost the case. The next year, John Candler instituted a similar suit in New Jersey against Oscar Grenelle and Charles Schanck, who brazenly sold drinks they called Coco-Cola and Kola-Coca. Without denying their actions, Grenelle and Schanck mounted the same defense as Daniel: Coca-Cola was a purely descriptive term. Afraid to press the explosive issue, Candler dropped the prosecution.

Other Atlanta syrup manufacturers and bottlers declared open season on Coca-Cola imitation. One such firm, Afri-Kola, had the gall to open a factory just down the street on Edgewood Avenue. In 1903, John Candler arranged for a Washington law firm to send a threatening letter to the Atlanta imitators, hoping to frighten them off, and Sam Dobbs followed with a personal visit. The owner of Kola-Ade admitted to Dobbs that he had received the letter. "Why did you go so far from home to get a lawyer?" he sneered, insolently adding, "Suppose I am substituting, what are you going to do about it?"

Pemberton sold his formula to a few different people, but his ghost must have kept busy selling the secret wholesale, given the host of colas claiming to be as good as the original. Among others, these included Afri-Kola, Cafe-Coca, Candy-Cola, Carbo-Cola, Celery-Cola, Celro-Kola, Charcola, Chero-Cola, Cherry-Kola, Citra-Cola, Co-Co-Colian, Coca and Cola, Coca Beta, Coke Extract, Coke-Ola, Cola-Coke, Cola-Nip, Cold-Cola, Cream-Cola, Curo-Cola, Dope, Eli-Cola, Espo-Cola, Farri-Cola, Fig-Cola, Four-Kola, French Wine Coca, Gay-Ola, Gerst's Cola, Glee-Nol, Hayo-Kola, Heck's Cola, Jacob's Kola, Kaw-Kola ("Has the Kick"), Kaye-Ola, Kel-Kola, King-Cola, Koca-Nola, Ko-Co-Lem-A, Koke, Kola-Ade, Kola-Kola, Kola-Vena, Koloko, Kos-Kolo, Lemon-Ola, Lime-Cola, Loco-Kola, Luck-Ola, Mellow-Nip, Mexicola, Mint-Ola, Mitch-O-Cola, Nerv-Ola, Nifti-Cola, Noka-Cola, Pau-Pau Cola, Penn-Cola, Pepsi-Cola, Pepsi-Nola, Pillsbury's Coke, Prince-Cola, QuaKola, Revive-Ola, Rococola, Roxa-Kola, Sherry-Coke, Silver-Cola, Sola-Cola, Standard-Cola, Star-Cola, Taka-Kola, Tenn-Cola, Toka-Tona, True-Cola, Vani-Kola, Vine-Cola, Wine Cola, Wise-Ola. It is little wonder that one Coca-Cola man referred to the lot as "Fake-Colas."

HAROLD HIRSCH TO THE RESCUE

The situation became intolerable, but a St. George was at hand to take on the imitation dragons. Harold Hirsch, a Columbia Law School graduate, was twenty-two when he joined the Candler law firm in 1904. The next year, the Trademark Law of 1905 was passed, and Coca-Cola registered under the Ten-Year Proviso, a grandfather clause giving legal status to *any* trademark, descriptive or otherwise, that had been in continuous use since 1895. Encouraged by the trademark's secure status, Hirsch decided to do something about the imitators. In 1909, he assumed full charge of Coca-Cola legal affairs, beginning a dogged courtroom pursuit of the "loathsome following." By the beginning of 1913, John Candler could write with satisfaction that "we have brought and tried within the last twelve months at least ten infringement cases where we brought one in 1906."

Not simply a lawyer representing a client, Hirsch was a true Coca-Cola man, inspiring bottlers, company officials, and other lawyers to defend the sacred trademark. "I have known every human emotion that the soul can know in connection with The Coca-Cola Company," he once said. "I have spent my nights and my days in thinking Coca-Cola." In 1914, sounding more like a hellfire evangelist than a lawyer, he dramatically urged a convention of bottlers to use the Coca-Cola name only on the genuine product. "If you fail us, if you do not stand back of us, the trademark 'Coca-Cola' is doomed," he warned. "No one, the great God Almighty Himself could not save you from final destruction." Hirsch paused to let his words sink in. "But if you aid us with your work, this Coca-Cola becomes sacred."

In court, many defense lawyers argued that substitution was legal when customers requested a "dope" or "coke." Consequently, Coca-Cola advertisements begged consumers to "demand the genuine by full name—nicknames encourage substitution." Asa Candler offered $100,000 to anyone who could curtail the widespread habit. When one of his bank employees asked the elderly entrepreneur to join him for a dope, Candler exploded: "It is not dope! There is no dope in it! It is Co-Ca-Co-La!" It was "blasphemy and treason," one salesman recalled, to utter a nickname. "To me 'Coke' was a dirty word, just like the other four-letter words."

Hirsch hired Pinkerton detectives to go to soda fountains, ask for Coca-Cola, and take samples of bogus drinks served, which were then chemically analyzed to prove they were not the genuine product. In 1915, he persuaded the Company to form the Investigation Department and hire full-time spies. The parent bottlers agreed to pay for a portion of the detectives' salary and to share legal expenses.

By 1923, Hirsch had won enough cases setting different precedents to fill a 650-page bible of Coca-Cola law, followed in later years by two more volumes. The Company graciously distributed these volumes to lawyers and libraries, reasonably assuming that potential infringers would be intimidated. By 1926, one reporter estimated that there were more than seven thousand "burials" in the Coca-Cola "copy-cat" mausoleum.

Hirsch won his cases on various grounds. He sued any cola drink that dared to use a script logo, a diamond label like Coca-Cola's, or red barrels. If the name was too similar, such as Chero-Cola, he objected on those grounds. He even attempted to claim the dark caramel color for Coca-Cola alone. Fighting his battles in city, county, state, and district courts, Hirsch appealed adverse decisions all the way to the Supreme Court. He opposed the registration of many colas at the U.S. Patent Office, effectively nipping them in the bud. During the course of his career, spanning three decades,

Harold Hirsch virtually created modern American trademark law, filing an average of one case per week.

CREATION OF THE PERFECT PACKAGE

The Coca-Cola bottle frustrated Hirsch. Ben Thomas had tried to standardize it by blowing the logo into the glass on the bottle's shoulder. If an imitator ran its name in a similar location, Hirsch attacked it as an infringement. But he wasn't satisfied. The straight-sided bottles looked just like any other soda pop. In addition, imitators almost universally adopted the same diamond-shaped labels. Coca-Cola needed a unique bottle that required no paper label at all.

At a 1914 bottler convention, Hirsch cajoled the small bottler to look beyond the short-term expense of implementing a new bottle. "We are not building Coca-Cola alone for today. We are building Coca-Cola forever, and it is our hope that Coca-Cola will remain the National drink to the end of time." He called for a "bottle that we can adopt and call our own child." Before his death that same year, Ben Thomas had also begged for a package so distinctive that people could recognize it by feel and instantly identify even a broken bottle.

In June of the following year, the company asked several glass works to create prototypes of a distinctive bottle. Root Glass Company employees sought inspiration from the drink's ingredients. At the Terre Haute, Indiana, public library, the company auditor failed to find any pictures of the coca leaf or kola nut resembling a bottle. But the illustration of the cocoa bean pod, near the coca entry in the *Encyclopaedia Britannica*, caught his eye. He may, in fact, have mistaken cocoa for coca. If so, it was a fortuitous error. Using the cocoa bean's fluted contour as his starting point, Earl Dean, the company machinist, produced a few sample bottles only minutes before the furnace cooled for the summer season.

Dean had designed what subsequently became known as the hobbleskirt bottle, named after a dress in fashion around 1914. Understandably, the skirt didn't stay in vogue long, since it was so narrow below the knee that it "hobbled" women before spreading wider at the ankles. These first few bottles had quite a bulge in the middle, later reduced to fit standard bottling equipment. Someone looking at this bosomy first effort called it a Mae West bottle, a nickname that stuck for many years. At the 1916 Coca-Cola Bottlers Convention, a seven-man committee overwhelmingly approved the design, though it took a few years before most bottlers accepted the more expensive container.

The new bottle eventually came to symbolize Coca-Cola as much as the script logo. Solidly built, it had a nice heft in the hand, although part of its weight was added to make the consumer forget that it held only six-and-a-half ounces. Industrial designer Raymond Loewy waxed lyrical about the package, calling the "perfectly formed" bottle "aggressively female," while another authority maintained that it had "twenty cleverly concealed devices . . . to lure and satisfy the hand."

Harold Hirsch had no such grandiose ideas when he suggested the bottle, however. As the first ads made clear, the bottle was intended to stop fraud. "We've Bottled Up the Pirates of Business," one ad bragged. "They have imitated the [old] Coca-Cola bottle and label . . . but they cannot imitate the new [one]—it is patented."

DOBBS VERSUS ROBINSON

Harold Hirsch was not the only rising star in these turbulent years. Sam Dobbs, whom one observer called the "brains and beauty of the family," was eager to fill his uncle's shoes. Ever since Candler elevated his nephew to sales manager at the end of 1899, a power struggle between Sam Dobbs and Frank Robinson had been brewing. The brash, good-looking, self-assured Dobbs boasted that his sales force was "working like one great machine, without friction anywhere." As he gained power within the Company, Dobbs chafed at what he considered the old-fashioned approach to advertising that Robinson represented.

By 1906, the simmering personality conflict came to a head. Dobbs attacked one of Robinson's pet projects, a booklet showing the annual Coca-Cola gallonage of individual jobbers and bottlers. In a memo to Uncle Asa in February 1906, Dobbs, thirty-eight, wrote that "I have always opposed the publishing of inside facts of our business" and recommended that the booklet's publication cease. He explained that the widely distributed booklet furnished "*facts* and *figures* for the horde of imitators who are springing up over the country," handing them a gift-wrapped list of potential customers. In addition, he said, the impressive sales figures invited attack by hostile legislators who could manipulate the statistics to prove how widespread the "evil" of Coca-Cola really was. Dobbs certainly had a point; in 1905, sales had exceeded 1.5 million gallons, a 37 percent increase over the previous year.

Robinson, then sixty years old, countered with a dignified rebuttal pointing out that the booklet's "great mass of evidence" of the "never-ending increase" in Coca-Cola's popularity encouraged dealers to compete with one another for yet greater sales. More important, he had a fundamental philosophical objection to Dobbs' suggestion. He didn't want to scheme or hide. "We have always conducted our business in the open," he wrote. "Our flag floats from the mast head. We are far, far beyond all competitors and this fact has been established by our statements." To kill the booklet would be "equivalent to pulling down the flag, wiping out the figures on our monument, covering up our tracks and crawling into a hole and refusing to show ourselves. Clouds of doubt and distrust would be hanging over us."

Robinson lost his fight, in more ways than one. The booklet was terminated, and Dobbs took over advertising as well as sales in 1906. He moved quickly to make changes. Jealous of St. Elmo Massengale, who had been managing the Coca-Cola account, Dobbs hired his personal friend William D'Arcy and his St. Louis agency. Dobbs threw huge amounts of money into full-page magazine spreads in the summer. Robinson watched in horror while Dobbs impetuously spent most of the ad budget by the fall. In November, the older man called for a "calm, deliberate, carefully considered, conservative, continuous campaign," spreading the same amount of money over the entire year with a slight increase during the summer months, allocating $3,000 to January and $8,000 to July. He called Dobbs' approach "flash advertising" that was planned at the last minute and resulted in a flurry of telegrams and confusion.

Robinson continued to plug away in his methodical, dedicated fashion until his retirement in 1913, but he was increasingly taken for granted. Dobbs claimed full credit for Coca-Cola advertising, becoming the darling of the press. After his election as president of the Associated Advertising Clubs of America in 1909, he promoted the "Truth in Advertising" campaign, gaining public acceptance for his profession—and, of course, distinguishing Coca-Cola (truthful and good) from patent medicines (fraudulent and bad).

When Dobbs talked about his profession and its importance, his self-confidence verged on arrogance. "The advertising man of today is a schoolmaster," he asserted. "The world is his schoolroom and the people are his pupils." Some, he noted, were "unwilling pupils," but what of it? They would learn anyway. The advertiser spoke in a universal tongue that recognized "no politics, no creeds or hobbies." Dobbs compared an advertising campaign to a military action, speaking of the big guns of outdoor display and the small arms of metal signs.

For all of his braggadocio, Dobbs had a singularly limited vision. In 1908, for instance, he advised against the use of a large electric sign, which he considered too dangerous. Nor did he think it worthwhile to implement special Yiddish signs for Jewish districts. He saw no future in pushing Coca-Cola overseas, though by 1909 bottling plants were operating in Cuba, Hawaii, and Puerto Rico. Two years later, a British advertiser eloquently urged England as a market featuring "forty-five million people, with plenty of money to buy, compactly settled in a country little larger than Kansas." Dobbs wasn't interested, answering that "the old USA is keeping us fairly busy." In 1915, Dobbs wrote that "the foreign field is not a very attractive one," rejecting repeated entreaties from foreign firms.

Along with his friend D'Arcy, Dobbs stressed the beneficial qualities of Coca-Cola over the objections of parent bottler Ben Thomas. Advertised as a simple beverage, Coca-Cola attracted "every man, woman and child" as potential consumers, Thomas asserted. Calling it a tonic would create "the impression that it is a strong stimulant" and would "create a prejudice in the minds of those people who think young children at least should not be given such a drink." Dobbs reacted defensively to the criticism, noting that he and D'Arcy had met six times and had "hammered and pounded on this stuff until it looks to me like it is about just right." True, he said, Coca-Cola was a beverage, but wasn't it more than that? "If simply a beverage, we have no grounds for claiming any excellency or special merit for it." Dobbs also disagreed with Thomas about the advisability of advertising to children, saying that he had to restrain his own children from drinking too much Coca-Cola. "Children are so apt to abuse a thing like Coca-Cola."

THE HARVEY WILEY THREAT

When Dobbs wrote that sentence in April of 1907, he unwittingly echoed the thoughts of Dr. Harvey Washington Wiley, whose name would soon cause Coca-Cola men to shudder as if confronted with the Antichrist. Early that year, the pure food reformer turned his intense gaze toward the soft drink industry and its most famous beverage. Over the next decade, Wiley nearly destroyed Coca-Cola.

~ 7 ~

Dr. Wiley Weighs In

Wiley is now made chief inspector, chief examiner, instigator of the charge, prosecutor, jury and judge; and if any manufacturer dares cry out against such an unjust condition he is met with the cry from Wiley and the Wiley press: "He is an adulterator and a dopester. . . ." And all this power in the hands of a man who says: "I am the spirit and essence of the pure food law, and without me there would be no law."
—*American Food Journal*, February 15, 1912

Since his arrival in Washington in 1883, Dr. Harvey Washington Wiley, the first head of the U.S. Bureau of Chemistry, had steadfastly fought against food adulteration; but it was only in 1902 that Wiley became a household name when he inaugurated his "poison squad," a group of twelve young men who were human guinea pigs for food additives that Wiley suspected were health hazards. The "experiments" proceeded without scientific controls and ignored the fact that volunteers' expectations that their diet would make them ill could produce psychosomatic effects; but what the investigations lacked in rigor, they supplied in publicity, inspiring satirical journalistic doggerel:

> *We're on the hunt for a toxic dope that's certain to kill, sans fail,*
> *But it is a tricky, elusive thing and knows we're on its trail.*
> *For all the things that could kill we've downed in many a gruesome wad,*
> *And still we are gaining a pound a day, for we are the Pizen Squad!*

The next year, Wiley used his new public status to attack the patent medicine industry and to demand passage of a pure food and drug bill. All such proposed legislation—almost two hundred bills in the thirty previous years—had been killed by the combined lobbying efforts of the Proprietary Association of America and the whisky and food industries. "There seemed to be an understanding between the two Houses [of Congress]," Wiley recalled, "that when one passed a bill . . . the other would see that it suffered a lingering death." The tide of public opinion, however, had begun to turn, in large measure because of the press. The ads of the nineteenth-century patent-medicine maker had been largely responsible for the growth of national magazines. Now, ironically, it was those same magazines that gave men like Harvey Wiley and journalists Samuel Hopkins Adams and Mark Sullivan the platform from which to

101

blast the overblown claims and narcotic contents of the nostrums. In October of 1905, *Collier's* published the first in a series titled "The Great American Fraud"—blistering, well-researched pieces by Adams that galvanized public and legislative opinion.

In his first article, Adams exposed the "red clause" used by patent medicine men to blackmail publications into favorable editorial positions. Printed in red in advertising contracts, the paragraph voided a contract if hostile state legislation were passed. "Tyrannical masters, these heavy purchasers of advertising space," Adams remarked, commending William Allen White, editor of the *Emporia Gazette* in Emporia, Kansas, for refusing to bow to such pressure.

What made it possible for White and other editors to be so courageous was the growth of other advertising revenue from more savory products. Patent medicines had led the way, but now manufacturers of breakfast foods, sewing machines, farm implements, and other mass-produced items were finding that advertising paid. Following Adams' 1905 praise, White, using his small-town Kansas paper as a platform, became the conscience of America's heartland for the next forty years.

When William McKinley was assassinated in 1901 and an unpredictable but pugnacious Theodore Roosevelt replaced him as president, the Gilded Age gave way to the Progressive Era. Reform, a natural consequence of the rapid change and industrialization of the late 1800s, suddenly achieved a respectable status. Now members of the previously docile urban middle class demanded assurance of the safety and purity of the foods and drugs they bought. They began to suspect the worst of impersonal, powerful corporations, whose beguiling advertising often promoted adulterated products. Goaded by the muckrakers, consumers clamored for change on all fronts. Upton Sinclair's novel *The Jungle* was published in February of 1906, revealing the revolting conditions in Chicago's meat packinghouses. A socialist, Sinclair wrote his book primarily as an indictment of working conditions, but it was his graphic description of laborers falling into vats and becoming part of the lard sold at the corner store that had an effect. "I aimed at the public's heart, and by accident I hit it in the stomach," he lamented.

In the new muckraking atmosphere, Coca-Cola was the unhappy object of multiple assaults. "In the past years," J. J. Willard wrote in the *Coca-Cola Bottler*, "we have seen a great, cyclonic wave of reform sweeping over the country, pretending, upon its face, to correct all manner of evils and remedy many defects. . . . Very few of the successful industrial concerns of the country have not felt its sting." Coca-Cola, he noted, was certainly no exception, finding itself vilified by "the man who has excess zeal and little knowledge, the professional boozer, the original teetotaler, and the man with his upturned palm." Willard's list aptly summarized the drink's enemies. Reformers possessed, in his opinion, "excess zeal" and insufficient knowledge. The brewers ("boozers") were convinced that Coca-Cola was providing secret funds for the Prohibition lobby and resented the *soft* drink, which claimed to be a temperance beverage but still provided a kick reputed to be as substantial as alcohol's. Coca-Cola was also denigrated by the temperance forces ("teetotalers") because of its caffeine content and rumors of cocaine. Finally, lawmakers (with "upturned palm") saw the wealthy bottlers and The Coca-Cola Company as a convenient source of special sin taxes.

THE PURE FOOD LAW IS PASSED

In 1906, with Adams continuing his series in *Collier's* and Sinclair's book a bestseller, the time was finally ripe for passage of strong national legislation. Wiley stumped the country tirelessly, lobbying the legislatures, advising sympathetic journalists. He wrote to state chemists, talked to women's clubs, addressed trade associations. He seemed to be everywhere at once. When the Pure Food and Drug Act was passed in June of 1906, it was almost universally known as Dr. Wiley's Law.

Asa Candler and everyone else at The Coca-Cola Company were, of course, well aware of the pure food movement. Sam Dobbs archly referred to "pure food cranks," while John Candler complained of "misguided fanatics." On the state level, Coca-Cola had been fighting adverse legislation since the turn of the century, enlisting the help of local bottlers to kill bills to tax or ban Coca-Cola in virtually every Southern state. It became clear to Judge John Candler, however, that some form of national legislation was inevitable. Although appointed to the Georgia Supreme Court in 1902, he still devoted almost half of his time to Coca-Cola's legal affairs, and, as the pure food movement gained momentum, the judge realized that the Company needed a full-time lawyer. Assessing his priorities, he resigned from the bench in January of 1906. Ever politically astute, John Candler convinced his older brother Asa that the impending pure food law could actually work to the Company's benefit. By supporting it, Coca-Cola would appear virtuous and set itself apart from the "bad" patent medicines. Besides, the law could be used to Coca-Cola's advantage; it would probably put imitators with cocaine content out of business.

Consequently, John Candler traveled to Washington in the spring of 1906 to testify in favor of the Pure Food and Drug Act. When it passed, the Company ran ads prominently declaring that Coca-Cola was *pure* and wholesome, the Great National Temperance Beverage. "Refreshing as a Summer Breeze," one late 1906 ad soothingly began, "it aids digestion and is genuinely good to the taste, gives a zest for additional labor and a keener enjoyment of recreation. Guaranteed under the Pure Food and Drugs Act." Coca-Cola fountain salesmen used the new law to threaten those who were diluting or substituting, saying they would send samples to the Pure Food Commission.

As a result of the law, The Coca-Cola Company also changed the formula, apparently to take saccharin out of both bottle and fountain syrup. Wiley was known to object to saccharin as an adulterant. Exactly when and why the artificial sweetener had been added is a matter of conjecture, but it was probably after consultation with Benjamin Thomas, who convinced Candler that it would be cheaper and would act as a preservative. Since the changed formula cost more, Asa Candler attempted to raise the price of bottlers' syrup by ten cents a gallon. Thomas objected, referring pointedly to his fixed-price contract, eventually compromising at a two-cent-per-gallon hike. Though no Coca-Cola publicity called attention to the changed formula, it was soon common knowledge. In Emporia, Kansas, William Allen White reported that "a number of the drinkers of this beverage do not think the new kind is as good as the old, but the fountains have their usual run of regular customers."

WILEY TAKES ON DOPE

For a few months, it appeared that all would be well. But early in 1907, Asa Candler picked up a paper and read the headline: "Dr. Wiley Will Take Up Soda Fountain 'Dope.'" Clearly, Wiley was referring to Coca-Cola. Although its producers had *claimed* to remove the cocaine, he said, Coca-Cola's caffeine content was subject to investigation. Candler wrote to Wiley on February 25, 1907, to complain that his statement would "work vast deteriment" to his drink's sales and offered Wiley the "plain facts" that Coca-Cola was a harmless non-alcoholic beverage. "It contains *no* cocaine, nor any deleterious drug," he stressed, adding that a serving of the soft drink contained about as much caffeine as a weak cup of tea. "There can be no more objection to the consumption of caffeine in the form of Coca-Cola than there is . . . to the importation of tea and coffee and their use," Candler concluded. "We therefore ask you most respectfully to give your endorsement to the meritorious cause to which we have devoted our energy."

Candler may be forgiven for believing that this would resolve the matter, but he didn't understand how Harvey Wiley's mind worked. In many ways, Candler and Wiley had similar backgrounds. Both were imbued with a strong religious fundamentalism and grew up on antebellum country farms. Wiley was raised in Indiana, suffering through strictly observed Sundays during which, he recalled, fishing was considered a "heinous sin." Where Candler had thought of becoming a physician before turning to pharmacy, Wiley had actually earned a medical degree but never practiced, instead becoming a chemistry professor. Their most important similarity, however, was an almost fanatical belief in the righteousness and correctness of their respective causes. Wiley took his father's advice seriously: "Be sure you are right and then go ahead."

In almost every other way, Wiley and Candler were opposites. A Yankee whose father read *Uncle Tom's Cabin* aloud and made his home a station on the Underground Railroad, Wiley served in Sherman's army, though he saw limited combat. Physically, Wiley dwarfed Candler. He was a solid six-footer, "tall and massive of stature," as one journalist put it, "with a big head firmly posed above a pair of titanic shoulders." His "penetrating glance" unnerved opponents, but, unlike Asa Candler, he possessed a sense of humor and ready wit, taking robust pleasure from life. Wiley's humor left him, however, when he thundered from the pure food pulpit; he was repeatedly mistaken for a clergyman because of his dress and demeanor, earning the nickname Father Wiley. In fact, he was a professed agnostic, but all of Wiley's childhood religious training was channeled into his work. He was, as his admirers called him, a "preacher of purity," or, as his critics preferred, a "zealot." One historian has aptly described him as a "chemical fundamentalist."

Above all else, Wiley mounted a *moral* crusade against fraud and vice. "The injury to public health," he said, "is the least important question . . . [and] should be considered last of all. The real evil of food adulteration is deception of the consumer." Wiley's obsession with deceit rather than health issues was reflected in his law. The Pure Food and Drug Act of 1906 did not make poisonous substances illegal; it simply said that they had to be stated on the label.* Logically enough, Candler felt that he was safe under the new pure food law. Caffeine (unlike cocaine) was not on the list of poisonous substances and consequently did not have to be listed on the label. Candler was merely using common sense when he said that Coca-Cola was no more harmful than a cup of tea.

For Wiley, however, there was a clear difference. Everyone *knew* that tea contained caffeine, but Coca-Cola purported to be a wholesome drink and was sold to children as such. Also, caffeine was a natural constituent of tea and coffee, but not of Coca-Cola. Candler could hardly have been happy with Wiley's reply of February 28, 1907: "I have heard many complaints of the Coca-Cola habit. . . . You might as well say that hydrocyanic acid is harmless because it occurs in peaches and almonds." Ominously, Wiley ended by reassuring Candler that "the Department will not do anything that is hasty or illegal . . . and when we come to the examination of your product, you shall have full opportunity to be heard."

In July, the acting secretary of Agriculture (no doubt prompted by Wiley, whose Bureau of Chemistry was part of the Agriculture Department) wrote to The Coca-Cola Company, threatening to cancel its serial number if it did not stop claiming in ads to be "guaranteed" under the pure food law. As the Company's attorney, John Candler wrote a polite response asking how the guaranty was being abused; he was told that the Agriculture Department objected to ads claiming that Coca-Cola was "pure." The Company agreed to drop the offending word from future ads.

THE WCTU ENTERS THE FRAY

Meanwhile, Wiley plotted against Coca-Cola behind the scenes, enlisting the aid of Mrs. Martha M. Allen, chair of the Medical Temperance Department of the Woman's Christian Temperance Union and the wife of a Methodist minister. A formidable opponent, Mrs. Allen had written a book about hidden alcohol and narcotics in medicines and had been elected to membership of the American Association for the Advancement of Science. Somehow, she and Wiley found old testimony from the 1901 IRS mistrial showing that Coca-Cola contained a small amount of cocaine and 2 percent alcohol. Using the old trial testimony, Wiley and Allen elicited support from the Surgeon General of the Army, who wrote in May that "a soldier drinking a half dozen bottles of this preparation during the day would get an indefinite quantity of cocaine . . . and the same amount of alcohol [as] in an equal quantity of beer." Based on this assessment, the U.S. Army banned Coca-Cola in June of 1907—quite a blow for the Company, which was trying to position its product as the patriotic National Temperance Beverage.

Coca-Cola did, in fact, have a tiny amount of alcohol, less than one percent of the syrup, a residue from the essential oils and extracts. The 2 percent figure apparently came from an assay of adulterated syrup. To persuade the Army to remove the ban,

---

* Cocaine was made illegal by the Harrison Narcotics Act of 1914. After intensive lobbying, Coca-Cola succeeded in having a loophole written into that law, allowing the importation of coca leaves if they were decocainized under government supervision.

Coca-Cola braved the lion's den and asked Wiley's Bureau of Chemistry to analyze samples of the drink, probably hoping to convince Wiley of its harmlessness at the same time. In September of 1907, John Candler sent Wiley a chemical analysis of Coca-Cola made by an independent pharmacist, showing 1.25 grains of caffeine, compared with 2 grains in the average cup of coffee. "Tests for cocaine failed to respond," the pharmacist wrote. Wiley sent back a curt note of thanks.

Influential politicians, obviously seeking to please their powerful Coca-Cola constituents, besieged the Army with requests for reconsideration of the ban, among them Henry Cabot Lodge of Massachusetts and Georgia congressman Leonidas Livingston. At the same time, sensational newspaper coverage broke the story nationwide. "CO-CAINE IS SERVED AT SODA FOUNTAINS," blared one New Jersey headline. "War Department Bars It from Army Canteens—Concoction Asserted to Contain Not Only Cocaine and Caffeine, but Also as Much Alcohol as Beer—South Has the Habit." As a result, the Army received letters of inquiry from alarmed organizations whose executives had read the newspaper stories. The International Sunday School Association, the Illinois Board of Health, and the Chautauqua Institution wanted to know if Coca-Cola was injurious. It was a public relations disaster for the soft drink company.

Once it became clear that there was no cocaine and negligible alcohol in Coca-Cola, the Army rescinded the ban in November of 1907, but not before substantial damage had been done. Sales weren't materially affected in the United States, but the incident nearly ruined the Cuban business. The Coca-Cola Company had opened its own bottling plant in Havana in 1902 and built a thriving business based on sales to Cubans, tourists, and the U.S. Army, which had intervened a second time since the Spanish-American War to crush a revolt. When local competitors found that Coca-Cola had been banned on Army bases, they distributed handbills proclaiming that the drink was a "subtle poison." Cuban sales plummeted. "Our competitors considered us dead," the plant manager later wrote. For the first but not the last time, Coca-Cola became the symbol of American imperialism; it took years to rebuild the Cuban trade.

SAM DOBBS MEETS MRS. ALLEN

Mrs. Allen was intent on mobilizing the mothers of America against Coca-Cola. With Wiley's help, she published a pamphlet implying that the drink still contained cocaine and asserting that its caffeine, combined with the alcohol content, was a health hazard, particularly to children. In an attempt to placate the feisty WCTU leader, Sam Dobbs proceeded north where, as though taking part in a duel, he and Allen each brought a "second" to the Yates Hotel in Syracuse, New York, near Mrs. Allen's home. Dobbs opened the debate by praising his Uncle Asa. "It would be impossible for so high-minded a man to make and sell a beverage that contained the least possible danger of a drug-habit," he explained. "Why, he gives largely to missions and schools."

Mrs. Allen remained unimpressed, calmly commenting that the British tyrant Charles I had been noted for his kindness to children. "Giving to missions, Mr. Dobbs, is small atonement for years of advertising a coca beverage." At this, Dobbs lost his temper and waved the defamatory WCTU pamphlet in her face, screaming, "Do you suppose we would give *poison* to our own children? My children drink Coca-Cola; if it had *poison* in it, do you think I would let them have it?" When he sputtered into silence, Mrs. Allen replied that the pamphlet never used the word "poison," but that she believed the drink to be harmful. "I know of a lad who has become worthless in school or anywhere else because of his addiction to Coca-Cola." As a finale, Dobbs countered by invoking the patron saint of the muckrakers, Samuel Hopkins Adams, asserting that when *Collier's* had sent Adams to Georgia to investigate Coca-Cola, he had been unable to find anyone injured by the drink.

It was clear when the two parted that neither duelist had changed the other's mind, but Martha Allen subsequently wrote to Adams to ask about his trip to Georgia. "Mr. Dobbs has used my name not only without authority," Adams replied, "but in a way to produce a false impression. What I reported to *Collier's* was that I was convinced that coca cola does not contain cocaine. I do most emphatically believe that it produces a habit . . . baneful and difficult to break. There is too much smoke not to indicate some fire, and I hear from all parts of the South, both by letter and personal interview, of cases where the addict must have his fifteen or twenty [daily] glasses of 'dope.'"

Coca-Cola was the subject of an increasing amount of gossip in those years. Growing up in Asheville, North Carolina, Thomas Wolfe heard most of the rumors, but they only increased his taste for Coca-Cola. He immortalized the Great American Soft Drink in this passage from the Great American Novel, *Look Homeward, Angel*. "Drink Coca Cola. They say [Candler] stole the formula from old mountain woman. $50,000,000 now. Rats in the vats. Dope at Wood's [Drug Store] better. Too weak here. [Gene] had recently acquired a taste for the beverage and drank four or five glasses a day."

DEPUTY KEBLER TOURS THE SOUTH

Adams was not the only one who went south during the fall of 1907 to investigate Coca-Cola. Going considerably beyond the simple sample analysis requested by the Army, Wiley sent his drug deputy, Lyman F. Kebler, for an extended jaunt through Coca-Cola heartland, where he visited Army bases as well as major cities and Coca-Cola bottling facilities. Kebler's report reads, one commentator aptly observed, as if he were a "stranger in an alien and hostile land, appalled by the odd and dangerous customs of the natives."

The drug deputy characterized Atlanta as "the home of coca cola and . . . the city of fountains," observing that there was a soda fountain on almost every street corner and in all major office buildings. He noted that Coca-Cola was drunk by people "in all walks of life, but most abundantly by office workers and . . . brain workers," who, he noted with horror, took a glass before work, another at lunch, and several more in the evening. Soda jerks informed him that "Coca-Cola fiends" drank ten to twelve glasses a day. "We personally saw the beverage consumed by children of four, five and six years of age," he wrote, adding that Coca-Cola was often brought home in pitchers to be guzzled by the entire family.

Kebler inspected the Coca-Cola plant itself and was disgusted by what he observed: "The kettle in which the sirup was made appeared to boil over occasionally, and it was surrounded with filth of every description, including sticks, dirt, straw, and all sorts of debris." He noted that, although the filling area in the cellar was cleaner, the containers were not. "Dead mice and similar things have been found in the sirup barrels and kegs after they have been emptied."

Visiting bottling plants in Chattanooga, Kebler was equally offended by the "slovenly and unhygienic manner" in which Coca-Cola was bottled. "If, for example, some foreign material is present in a dark bottle," he wrote, "it is likely to be overlooked and left inside, and the bottle filled with the beverage. The cleaning, as a rule, is very superficial, and only a small portion of filth is removed." At nearby Fort Oglethorpe, Kebler learned that Coca-Cola had served primarily as a hangover cure before the ban, but a local saloon proprietor said that soldiers drank "Coca-Cola high-balls"—the soft drink mixed with whisky—which made them "wild and crazy."

Kebler finally returned to Washington late in the fall of 1907, convinced that Coca-Cola was a habit-forming menace, confirming Wiley's worst fears. At the end of October, Wiley announced that he was forming a new Poison Squad specifically for soft drinks. Newspapers reported that his twelve brave volunteers, young men in their twenties, would test one hundred different drinks "widely advertised as invigorators, nerve-restorers, and brain stimulants" and known to contain "cocaine, caffeine, chloral hydrates, or opium."

WILEY'S FRUSTRATED OFFENSIVE

When 1907 finally ended, Sam Dobbs noted in the annual report that "during the past year, we have not only had to work to get new business, but we have had to fight to keep the business we already had. Throughout the year we were constantly engaged in combating prejudice, ignorance and graft." Having weathered the multiple onslaughts of 1907, Asa Candler must have been relieved when the following year passed relatively uneventfully, with sales nearing three million gallons annually and a cash surplus of $1.2 million.

But Wiley had not retreated: he was only preparing for a massive frontal assault which he would have launched in November of 1908 except for bureaucratic interference. George McCabe, the department's solicitor and a member of the Board of Food and Drug Inspection, repeatedly refused to approve Wiley's recommended seizures, since caffeine had not been proven harmful. On February 8, a frustrated but resigned Wiley wrote to Adams to assure him that "I am going to stay by the ship until I am court-martialed and put under arrest." The next month, Wiley located an interstate shipment of Coca-Cola in New Orleans and recommended its seizure. Worn down, McCabe finally referred it to Dr. Dunlap of the board for a decision. Dunlap pointed out that "if the data are so strongly against caffeine," he would logically have to ban the importation of tea and coffee—an impossibility—and he too countermanded the chief chemist.

Infuriated, Wiley dismissed the comparison to tea and coffee, claiming that the matter did not "merit discussion." His anguished memos make it clear that his main concern was that children drank Coca-Cola. In May, he tried again, writing that a woman on a local board had objected to Coca-Cola signs erected near schools, luring students to imbibe. "If their parents knew they were drinking caffeine," Wiley asserted, "they would be horrified. I again renew my request, which has been denied on several occasions, to institute proceedings." Again, he was denied. This time, James Wilson, the Secretary of Agriculture, personally told Wiley to lay off Coca-Cola. Wiley was "surprised and grieved," he wrote later, but "as usual I could see behind it the manipulation of powerful hands." He must have reflected bitterly that while he was lionized by the public, nominated that year for the Nobel Prize in chemistry, his opinions held no weight with his superiors.

Even though Secretary Wilson had ordered him to leave the Atlanta beverage king alone, Wiley sent Inspector J. L. Lynch to look over the main factory in July, where Lynch observed a black man "cooking" the huge kettle of Coca-Cola, reporting that the cook's dirty undershirt was soaked with sweat, his feet poked through his broken shoes, and he shot wads of chewing tobacco indiscriminately onto the platform next to the mixing kettle. When sugar spilled onto the platform, the employee shoved it into the vat with his feet.

As if to taunt Wiley, Asa Candler hired a dirigible with a gigantic Coca-Cola logo to float above Washington in 1909. At the same time, Sam Dobbs and William D'Arcy were writing *The Truth About Coca-Cola*, a defensive tract that opened with the words: "This is a book of information—not of defense." During the strife of the next few years, the Company distributed millions of these pamphlets, despite Ben Thomas's objections to defensive strategies.

FINALLY GETTING THE GO-AHEAD

In August of 1909, John Candler could still boast that "not once . . . has there been a single State or Federal prosecution against . . . Coca-Cola." But two months later, that all changed. While in Washington, Fred L. Seely, editor of the *Atlanta Georgian*, asked Harvey Wiley why Coca-Cola had not been prosecuted under the pure food law. Unlike the *Constitution* and *Journal*, the *Georgian* wasn't part of the Atlanta business establishment. Seely, a New Jersey native, had founded the paper in 1906 and was considered radical for his opposition to child labor and chain gangs. The crusading editor and Asa Candler were already antagonists. In May of 1909, Seely had threatened to publish photos of the appalling conditions at the Decatur Orphans' Home, where Candler was a trustee.

Stung by Seely's question, Wiley poured out his frustrations to the editor, brandishing his file of Coca-Cola memos. Seely immediately went to Secretary Wilson and told him that unless he allowed Wiley to go ahead, he, Seely, would make trouble for him in his paper. As Wiley put it, "It is remarkable what the fear of publicity will do." The next day, Wiley was given the go-ahead.

On October 19, 1909, Drug Deputy Kebler and Inspector Lynch traced a shipment of syrup bound for Chattanooga. The next day, they made yet another unannounced inspection of the Coca-Cola factory. Howard Candler was startled to find them sneaking around in the cellar, but he remained polite and provided them with a sample of Merchandise No. 5, the coca and kola mixture. When Howard's father found out the government agents were once again snooping about, he flew at them like an enraged hornet, "very excited and very much worked up and very nervous," as Lynch recalled. "By God," Candler said, "if I had been here you would not have got [that sample]."

Lynch was baffled when Candler called Kebler "a God-damned carpenter." In fact, the Yankee inspector obviously misunderstood the epithet. In his outrage, Candler had labeled the government agent a God-damned *carpetbagger*.

Two days later, Inspector Lynch seized thirty-seven barrels and twenty kegs of Coca-Cola syrup in Chattanooga, though somehow three more barrels must have been added later. The case was officially called *The United States vs. Forty Barrels and Twenty Kegs of Coca-Cola.* Although ludicrously named, the case promised to be a fierce legal battle between formidable opponents. It was only the second case under the new pure food law to go to court. Now that Wiley finally had the Agriculture Department's support, no effort or expense was spared.

SPY/COUNTERSPY

It took almost a year and a half for Coca-Cola and the government to prepare the case for trial. After Wiley's investigators found that Coca-Cola intended to call famous scientists to testify that caffeine was not harmful, Wiley lined up his own expert witnesses. He also ordered his spies to dig up dirt on the opposition scientists, although nothing came of it. Over his strong objections, the trial was held in Chattanooga, site of the seizure, rather than Washington. As Wiley was aware, Chattanooga was a Coca-Cola town; the jury was likely to favor the defense. "It was equivalent . . . to trying the case in Atlanta," Wiley complained.

As the trial geared up in March of 1911, seven government spies infiltrated Chattanooga to keep an eye on jurors, trying to prove they were incompetent, immoral, or associated with Coca-Cola. Meanwhile, Candler hired his own counterspies to keep an eye on the government agents. The entire affair started to resemble a Keystone Kops film. One juror, it transpired, had once been arrested for horse stealing, while another frequented saloons. The agent dismissed the rest as "very low class men" who seemed "entirely incompetent to try a case of this nature." In unearthing such information, one government spy complained that they were "watched, followed and pointed out by agents of the defense. . . . This makes us almost useless now." He also noted that rooming at the downtown Hotel Patten, owned by Coca-Cola's J. T. Lupton, was a mistake.

Just before the trial commenced, Wiley, sixty-six, a lifelong bachelor, married Anna Kelton, a librarian less than half his age. Giving her a taste of what her marriage would be like, he took her on their "honeymoon" to the Coca-Cola trial, where everyone expected him to be the star witness. The Chattanooga papers and high society were thrilled to have the famous Dr. Wiley in their midst, even though he was on the wrong side, and the Wileys were treated like visiting royalty.

THE TRIAL

From opening day on March 13, 1911, the Barrels and Kegs trial attracted national attention, making daily headlines in Chattanooga and Atlanta for its nearly month-long duration. The two main charges were that Coca-Cola was adulterated and misbranded. According to the pure food law, a product was adulterated if it had a deleterious added ingredient. Consequently, the government had to prove that caffeine was both harmful and an "added" ingredient under the law. Coca-Cola was misbranded, the charge stated, because it did not in fact have the whole coca leaf in it (i.e., cocaine was removed), and it had only an infinitesimal amount of kola nut. The misbranding charge was ironic, because if the drink *had* contained cocaine, it would have been illegal as well.*

For Chattanoogans, the trial provided ample entertainment. Lynch and Kebler repeated their observations on the filthy Coca-Cola plant, appealing to racist sentiment by dwelling on the black cook's sweat and expectorations. Kebler testified that Coca-Cola was not only poisonous but had made one deceased victim's heart so hard that it was impossible to cut with a knife. At that point, Judge Edward Terry Sanford had to reprimand Coca-Cola's expert witnesses, who couldn't contain their audible amusement. Another government witness reported that he had found straw, part of a bumblebee, and other insect fragments in the seized syrup.

Well-known Methodist evangelist George Stuart took the stand briefly. Unfortunately for those eager for real sensation, he didn't get far before the prosecution had to bow to defense objections and withdraw him. Stuart had thundered against Coca-Cola from an Atlanta pulpit, then written Bishop Candler a long public letter in which he said that excessive use of Coca-Cola at a girls' school led to "wild nocturnal freaks, . . . violations of college rules and female proprieties, and even immoralities." Coca-Cola also kept boys awake, Stuart said, inevitably tempting them with the evils of masturbation.

Most of the trial, though, was taken up with expert witnesses. Whether the jurors were "low class" or not, it is doubtful they understood a fraction of the scientific jargon that the doctors and pharmacologists unleashed in the courtroom. The caliber of the witnesses was beyond reproach. All three coeditors of the 1905 edition of the *National Standard Dispensary* testified at the trial—Henry H. Rusby for the government, Charles Caspari and Hobart A. Hare for Coca-Cola. Near the end of the event, when the jurors were already dazed, Coca-Cola lawyers triumphantly unveiled a massive deposition from world-renowned German pharmacologist Oswald Schmiedeberg, delaying the trial because of the need for translation.

Despite their impressive credentials, most expert witnesses relied on flawed experiments highly colored by their own opinions. Harry and Leta Hollingworth's groundbreaking double-blind experiments on caffeine's effects on humans, still-cited classics of the literature, were the exception. Harry Hollingworth, a young psychology professor at Columbia, took the job—considered "a somewhat shady business"—only after his seniors rejected the research. Leta directed the actual experiments, which indicated that caffeine, in moderate amounts, improved motor skills while leaving sleep patterns relatively unaffected. Awaiting his turn to testify, Harry Hollingworth found the proceedings "a most interesting and often amusing conflict." Appalled by the "anecdotal and misguided testimony that appeared on both sides," Hollingworth was particularly dismayed by one scientist's conclusion that caffeine caused congestion of the cerebral blood vessels in rabbits that he had dispatched by a club to the head.

---

* During the trial, Harold Hirsch made much of Coca-Cola's *hyphen*, which, he argued, rendered the trademark a single word unrelated to the two substances, coca and kola.

Neither of the principal antagonists testified, which in Asa Candler's case was easy to understand. His lawyers didn't want the volatile owner anywhere near the courtroom. Candler stayed in Atlanta for most of the trial, firing off dyspeptic letters to Chattanooga calling Lynch a perjuring liar and expressing outrage over the *Atlanta Georgian's* sensationalistic coverage. He can scarcely be blamed. At one point, Seely's newspaper ran the headline "EIGHT COCA-COLAS CONTAIN ENOUGH CAFFEINE TO KILL." Candler concluded, "It is outrageous that our government is disposed to harass us, but I feel that right will eventually prevail." The government's scientists spent days describing the effects of Coca-Cola on various animals.* When defense attorney J. B. Sizer complained that injecting frogs with Coca-Cola hardly constituted viable evidence, Harvard professor Dr. William Boos countered, "It is a difficult thing to feed a frog. Have you ever tried it?" With relief and some contempt, Asa Candler wrote on March 21, that "U.S. has almost exhausted its rat rabbit & frog evidence."

The papers repeatedly anticipated that Wiley would take the stand, but he never did. While masterminding the prosecution, Wiley apparently preferred to let the specialists testify, telling the lawyers that he did not qualify as an expert in any specific area. Surely, however, Wiley would have testified if he had had strong evidence of Coca-Cola's negative effects on his poison squad, but apparently the young men must have thrived on the beverage.

Coca-Cola eventually won the case, though not on any scientific grounds. All of the testimony and spying on jurors proved irrelevant. Judge Sanford (who was appointed to the United States Supreme Court in 1923) issued his opinion from the bench, ordering the jury to return a verdict in favor of Coca-Cola. He ruled that the product was not misbranded, since it did contain coca and kola, even though in tiny amounts. Without deciding whether caffeine was a poison or not, Sanford said that it was *not* an added ingredient under the law, but had been an integral part of the formula since the drink was invented.

WILEY'S CRUSADE

Jubilant, Company officials publicized this victory widely. The trial did, nonetheless, cause an immediate change in Coca-Cola advertising. The most compelling case against the drink in the trial had been its consumption by children. Defense lawyers hadn't contested caffeine's bad effects on youngsters; instead, they had denied that children drank Coca-Cola at all. This assertion was somewhat awkward, since many contemporary ads showed children drinking right along with their parents. "Father likes it. Son likes it," crowed one 1907 ad that depicted a five-year-old happily imbibing. After 1911, an unwritten law stated that no one under twelve years old would be shown drinking in a Coca-Cola ad—a dictum enforced, with few exceptions, forevermore.[†]

Because of adverse publicity from the trial, two bills were introduced in the U.S. House in 1912 to amend the Pure Food and Drug Act, adding caffeine to the list of

---

* The Bureau's scientist testified that rabbits on a Coca-Cola diet had died—little wonder, since he had run the feeding tube into the rabbits' lungs instead of their stomachs, thereby drowning them.

† The trial also had another immediate effect. The decorative border of coca leaves and kola nuts gracing Coca-Cola trays and syrup barrels disappeared.

"habit-forming" and "deleterious" substances that must be listed on the label. Coca-Cola successfully fought to kill the bills, the first of many such efforts to keep its caffeine content out of the public eye.

The trial had an impact on Dr. Wiley as well. His superiors, looking for any excuse to ditch the bullheaded chemist, accused Wiley of having illegally paid Dr. Rusby too much for his testimony. A special Senate investigation was launched, and the papers were filled with cartoons and editorials about Wiley. He was finally cleared, but by 1912, he realized that he would always be frustrated in the government bureaucracy. He resigned in March of 1912, at the height of his national popularity. It is impossible to overestimate Wiley's fame and influence. The Wiley seal of approval was all-important, even after he left the Bureau, which explains why the president of Dr Pepper sent him the drink's formula (since it contained no caffeine), invited him to visit the Waco, Texas, plant, and assured the chemist that he was behind Wiley all the way. When the sixty-seven-year-old Wiley became the father of a boy in May of 1912, the infant was promptly labeled the Pure Food Baby.

If the Candlers hoped that the elderly gentleman would quietly retire, they were soon disappointed. Wiley commenced a grueling regimen of speeches all over the country. It must have galled Candler no end when Wiley delivered a speech entitled "The Advantages of Coffee as America's National Beverage," considering all his experts' recent insistence on caffeine as a poison. At the same time, Wiley joined *Good Housekeeping* as a regular columnist, using the magazine as a national platform to assail Coca-Cola. In September of 1912, he published "The Coca-Cola Controversy," in which he recounted his version of the trial. He portrayed the scientists for Coca-Cola as mercenaries whose opinions had been purchased. An accompanying cartoon showed a smiling scientist observing Coca-Cola through a magnifying glass emblazoned with a dollar sign. Another portrayed the good Dr. Wiley warning a gullible public against gremlins—labeled *nervousness*, *habit*, and *indigestion*—crawling inside a giant glass of Coca-Cola.

Even though Coca-Cola had won the case, the national publicity hurt the drink, attracting the attention of a moralistic young filmmaker named D. W. Griffith. In 1912, Griffith's enormous success with *Birth of a Nation* was three years away, and he was still working anonymously at the Biograph Studios in New York, churning out two short silent films every week. One of these was an anti-Coca-Cola epic called *For His Son* in which the inventor of "DOPO-KOKE" watches his son fall prey to the drink's cocaine. "The drink no longer satisfies," reads one caption, as the young man goes on to hypodermic injections, eventually dying of an overdose. It didn't concern Griffith that Coca-Cola no longer contained cocaine. He delighted in creating a soda fountain scene in which his nervous, addicted heroine, played by Biograph regular Blanche Sweet, pushes a young boy aside to get her Dopo-Koke, then smiles and sighs in relief. Instructed by her boyfriend, she learns to doctor her drink by pouring cocaine powder into it (a common practice then, even with dopeless Coca-Cola).

RENDERING UNTO CAESAR

The Barrels and Kegs Case was appealed to the district court level. Before a decision was handed down, though, the U.S. government struck from another direction. The first corporate tax had been passed in 1909, but it hadn't amounted to much.

Reformers cried for more: "The corporation is becoming more and more a centralized industrial power," wrote one critic in 1909. "It must therefore more and more be regulated by a centralized political power." In 1913, the reformers' prayers were answered by the accumulated earnings tax, a penalty tax imposed on corporations that hoarded cash "beyond the reasonable needs of the business." In effect, the law forced corporations to pay dividends, which were then taxable to the individual stockholders but were not deductible at the corporate level, amounting to double taxation.

The new tax law meant that harried accountants had to separate Asa Candler's personal affairs from his Company's—not an easy task. "In a very real sense," Howard Candler wrote, "The Coca-Cola Company *was* Asa G. Candler and the line between his personal property purchases and those of the company was frequently thinly defined." By the time the law went into effect at the end of 1914, The Coca-Cola Company showed a surplus of over $10 million. Candler deeply resented the tax. He had earned the money, he reasoned, and it was his to spend or keep as he pleased. Besides, he regarded a "war chest" as a necessity for any unforeseen contingencies, particularly given the hostile environment of that time. "He felt strongly on this point," his son remembered, "and often remarked that Moses . . . had tried such a [tax] system in Biblical times and saw it fail."

Nonetheless, Candler was forced to declare whopping dividends, disbursing over $10 million in cash and $6.4 million worth of real estate to shareholders in the next two years. There were about 530 shares outstanding, of which Asa Candler owned 400. Consequently, Candler's taxes must have been staggering for those years. The 1914 million-dollar gift to Emory University was undoubtedly a partial attempt to reduce his tax burden.

JUSTICE HUGHES' LAST ACT

After the government had lost its district court appeal in 1914, it took the case to the nation's highest court. Two years later, on May 22, 1916, Charles Evans Hughes reversed the decision at the Supreme Court level, in his last opinion before leaving the bench to run for president against Woodrow Wilson.* Hughes, the son of a Baptist preacher, had thought of entering the ministry himself; his decision in the Barrels Case reflected his puritanical attitude. To the government's delight and Coca-Cola's chagrin, Hughes said that the word "Coca-Cola" was not a distinctive name, but simply the conjunction of two common words. More important, he ruled that caffeine was indeed an added ingredient, and he sent the case back to Sanford in Chattanooga for a retrial to determine whether caffeine was harmful or not.

As soon as the Hughes decision was issued, Harold Hirsch commenced negotiations to avoid a new trial. Both the Company and the Bureau of Chemistry frantically experimented—Coca-Cola's scientists assessed the drink's taste and flavor with reduced caffeine, while Dr. Alsberg, the government's chemist, attempted to prove

---

* Hughes—vociferously supported by Harvey Wiley—lost the presidential election by a narrow margin.

that caffeine was harmful. Failing to come up with anything definitive, Alsberg asked for more time.

In the final event, the case was settled out of court on November 12, 1918. Coca-Cola consented to a plea of "no contest," allowing the government a technical victory. In return, the Company agreed to reduce the caffeine content by half, to no more than 0.61 grains per ounce of syrup, while doubling the amount of decocainized coca leaf and kola nut that went into Merchandise No. 5. Though Judge Sanford's notice of settlement did not specify it, there was a tacit agreement that the government would now leave Coca-Cola alone. Wiley was no longer at the Bureau to push the issue, and everyone was sick of the case by this time, eight years after the initial seizure. In later years, however, Howard Candler implied that a federal attorney had accepted a bribe in return for the settlement.

Having spent over $250,000 on the case, The Coca-Cola Company apparently got nothing out of it other than a reduced kick and the return of forty barrels and twenty kegs of very stale syrup. But all of that was beside the point. As Harold Hirsch later wrote, "It was a serious litigation and involved the possibility of the entire destruction of the company's business." In essence, Hirsch had won a major victory: Coca-Cola survived.

INTERNECINE STRIFE LOOMS

The settlement of the Barrels and Kegs Case did not, however, signal the end of Coca-Cola's troubles in the courts or tangles with government bureaucrats. The turmoil took its toll on an aging Asa Candler, who regarded it as unjust persecution. When he left the Company in the care of his children, Candler set off a chain of events that led to a graver threat to the Coca-Cola system. It did not come from a competitor, politician, or reformer. This time the trouble, like a latent virus, came from within.

~ 8 ~

The Sinister Syndicate

Complainant now shows to the Court and avers that some time in the summer of 1919 a number of promoters conceived a plan to get control of the stock of said Georgia corporation. By reason of the inflated condition of the currency growing out of the war and the willingness of the people to speculate . . . said promoters did so get control. . . .
— *Bill of Complaint,* The Coca-Cola Bottling Company vs.
The Coca-Cola Company

When Charles Evans Hughes delivered his devastating opinion in the Barrels and Kegs Case in May of 1916, it was just one more indication to sixty-four-year-old Asa Candler that the United States government was persecuting him. It would bleed him with taxes, pursue him in court, plague him with inspectors.

In addition, J. C. Mayfield, Pemberton's last partner, reappeared as a thorn in Candler's side. As much of a hustler as Candler, Mayfield never quite succeeded in his numerous ventures. Besides soft drinks, he had speculated in real estate, oil wells, and a vinegar factory. In 1909, his Celery-Cola was seized under the Pure Food and Drug Act for containing cocaine. Nothing kept the irrepressible Mayfield down for long, however. He resurrected Koke, one of the first names he had used, bought the rights to another Coca-Cola imitation called Dope, and was soon selling both drinks across much of the United States as the Koke Company of America. In 1914, as part of his crusade to protect Coca-Cola's trademark, Hirsch had sued. Unlike most imitators, however, Mayfield had enough money to hire lawyers for a rigorous, prolonged court fight.

In Koke Case testimony, many of the questionable activities during Coca-Cola's early years came to light. On the stand, Mayfield told the story of John Pemberton's morphine addiction, the reappearance of Charley Pemberton, and his own 1888 days of manufacturing Yum Yum and Koke. He asserted, with some authority, that he had the original formula for Coca-Cola, legally and directly, from its inventor. In addition, his lawyers found Mrs. Dozier, who insisted that her signatures on two crucial chain-of-title documents were forged. Asa Candler must have been extremely disturbed to have all of this material re-emerge after it had been buried for over a quarter of a century.

The Koke Case was replete with ironies. While Candler and Hirsch had fulminated for years against the use of slang terms for Coca-Cola (particularly those that implied cocaine content), now they found themselves calling pharmacists to the stand to prove that "Koke" and "Dope" were universally recognized calls for Coca-Cola, not May-field's drinks. One Atlanta druggist, J. B. Pendergrast,* testified that "when a man asks for 'dope' at my soda-fountain I understand that he means 'Coca-Cola.'" Pendergrast also served Coca-Cola in response to an amusing array of nicknames, including A-Shot-in-the-Arm and Another-Brick-in-the-Candler Building.

While the decision on the Koke Case was pending for most of 1916, Mayfield stirred up more trouble for Coca-Cola by complaining to the Federal Trade Commis-sion, created in 1914, that Coca-Cola's harassment of imitators constituted illegitimate business practice. A special agent for the Department of Justice asked pointed ques-tions of Coca-Cola bottlers and their competitors in the fall of 1915 and the follow-ing spring. That summer, Asa Candler received a letter from the chairman of the FTC officially notifying him of complaints and asking for a response. When irritated, Candler often scribbled his rebuttals on letters, and he wrote "not so" next to most of these 1916 allegations:

1. Refusing to sell Coca Cola to dealers who handle competing cola drinks.
2. Intimidating customers of competitors by threats of legal suits.
3. Maliciously instituting litigation against competitors.
4. Using rebates based on total annual purchases combined with excessive advertising, thereby, it is alleged, in practical effect compelling dealers to purchase exclusively of your company.
5. Slandering the character and business of competitors.
6. Using premiums in the sale of Coca Cola, such premiums being given only to customers who will handle no other cola drink.
7. Shutting off competitors' supplies of bottle caps by threats of litigation against bottle cap manufacturers.
8. Maintaining a system of espionage to discover names of customers and other business secrets of competitors.
9. Procuring cancellation of orders and breach of contracts secured by competitors.

Candler can hardly be blamed for feeling persecuted. He must have believed that the American government had gone mad, abusing him for being an astute business-man who employed aggressive promotion and reasonable concern to protect his prod-uct's good name and integrity.

ASA CANDLER, MAYOR

At almost the exact moment that he received the FTC's official notice, Candler was approached by a group of Atlanta businessmen and politicians, urging him to run for mayor. The city was in poor financial shape, with impoverished schools, a $150,000 debt, and streets badly in need of repair. The police chief had been fired and was suing for his job back, and the streetcar conductors were threatening a strike. At first, Candler refused to run—he was a businessman, not a politician—but his ego soon overcame his doubts, and on July 19, 1916, only four days after he received the letter

---

* J. B. Pendergrast was the author's grandfather.

from the FTC, he agreed to become a candidate. The mayoral race clearly gave him an excuse to retire—Candler had a "willingness, sometimes amounting almost to anxiety, to get out of Coca-Cola," according to his son.

Having declared his candidacy, Candler promptly departed for a mineral springs spa in Michigan, intending to remain there until the election was over, but his political advisers finally convinced him that it appeared arrogant for the multimillionaire to remain in Michigan without even pretending to mount a campaign. With only eight days left before the primary, he returned to Atlanta for a vigorous week of stump speeches. "I am not here to tell you I think so little of this office as not to want it. I do want it," he told his supporters. "If I can discharge my duty to all of you, I will get a crown that will reach far beyond the grave." His opponent, a union linotype operator, was not interested in immortality as much as appealing to the poor as "the people's candidate," calling Candler "capitalism personified."

Capitalism personified is apparently what Atlanta wanted. Easily nominated, Candler was swept into office in the December 6 election. Most citizens of Atlanta rejoiced, regarding "Uncle Asa" as the savior whose millions would solve the city's problems. When he donated his $4,000 annual salary to charity, they were heartened, but aside from that, Candler spent none of his own money during his term except for an improved waterworks. One cynic commented after the election, "Seems funny that as soon as some ordinary gink makes a fortune out of flivvers, soft drinks, liver pills or safety pins, he is always right in line for political office."

As mayor-elect, Candler served as the head of the Law and Order Committee, which helped to break the streetcar workers' strike. Atlanta's first serious labor unrest, with dynamited trolleys, gunshots, and cries of "Scab! Scab!" unsettled the status quo. The workers demanded union recognition, shorter hours, and higher pay. In the end, the remaining drivers were granted a slight pay increase, but the union was disbanded and its organizers fired. Now the man of the hour, Candler waxed eloquent in his condemnation of labor unrest: "The demagogue whose radical measures threaten the stability of the commercial system . . . is a political parasite sprung from the feculent accumulations of popular ignorance and fattened upon the purulent secretions of popular prejudice." He went on to defend the capitalist system, explaining that "commerce is not the selfish and groveling thing which many esteem it. On the contrary, it is the means of the world's progress and the instrument of boundless blessing to the race of man."

After a year of Mayor Candler, many of his supporters were disillusioned. His cabinet had suggested raising water rents, which would have hurt the poor. Others wanted to impose higher taxes on the rich, which Candler rejected out of hand. "Did the Asa boomers last fall really think that the old gentleman would furnish the money as a free gift gratis for nothing to pay the town's deficits?" asked one editorial. *Atlanta Civics*, a tract written and published by Mrs. Bessie Linn Smith, appeared briefly in the fall of 1917 and was devoted almost exclusively to Candler-bashing. "During Candler's campaign," wrote Mrs. Smith, "we were promised . . . almost that our souls would be purged of sin, our debts wiped away with a stroke of his genius hand. . . . To date, if he has accomplished a thing for the betterment of Atlanta, a single thing except Candler glory and profit, our highest powered microscope fails to see it." Mrs. Smith pointed out that while Candler urged civic-minded citizens to declare high property appraisals to swell the city's tax coffers, the mayor himself reduced his personal tax returns by $108,000. She also gleefully reported that Candler was so cheap that he had taken a paper from a newsboy, scanned the headlines, and then given it back instead of paying the three cents.

Candler's parsimonious ways did have some positive effect, however. By the time he left office, he had balanced the city's budget. On the whole, he appears to have been a conservative, decent, honest mayor, even if his priorities sometimes seemed odd. One of Mayor Candler's accomplishments was to pass an "Ice Cream and Soft Drink Ordinance" to make sure that soda fountains were "properly lighted, ventilated, and kept free from rats, flies, or other insects." He also insisted on the virtue of idle Sundays, the violation of which was "a more alarming peril," he wrote, "than the success of the German Kaiser in the pending war struggle." Of course, his critics had a ready answer for that: What about the soda jerk who dispensed Coca-Cola during the Sabbath?

A TIME OF TRANSITION

Howard Candler had officially taken over as president of The Coca-Cola Company at the January 21, 1916, board meeting, but his father still owned most of the stock. Although busy with his new political office, Asa Candler still wasn't quite ready to relinquish his power over Coca-Cola—at least not yet.

For years, going back as far as 1908, the Coca-Cola millionaire had toyed with the idea of selling out. Following the 1911 trial, he had begun to purchase the few shares held outside the family, and he had tentatively agreed to sell the Company for $8 million, but investors were too skittish. Now, in 1916, a Chicago lawyer named Max Pam, who specialized in corporate mergers, put together a deal for $25 million. His would-be buyers, a consortium of Cincinnati whiskey brewers, wanted to diversify as the prohibition movement gained momentum. On December 21, 1916, at a special meeting of Coca-Cola Company stockholders, the sale was scuttled by a single stockholder who owned five shares—probably Candler's obstreperous son, Asa Candler Jr., known as Buddie. Four days later, on Christmas Day, the elder Candler gave all but seven shares of his Coca-Cola stock to his family. Asa Candler had finally relinquished control of the Company to his children.*

Only two weeks later, a similar purchase offer was made by two New York lawyers, Bainbridge Colby and Ed Brown,† representing another syndicate that proposed to purchase Coca-Cola for $25 million. Besides netting a huge profit, the sale would have major tax benefits: the accumulated earnings tax on $25 million in invested capital would be minor compared to the huge amount then being paid, and the firm would no longer have to pay such extraordinary dividends. The details of the proposed deal were outlined in a January 15, 1917, letter. Colby and Brown would receive $1 million as their brokerage fee.

---

* Some sources say the Candler stock gift took place on Christmas Day 1917 rather than 1916, but the earlier date is probably correct.

† Ed Brown's father, Sam Brown, was Harold Hirsch's father-in-law, a cotton broker and banker from Albany, Georgia, who had been unsuccessfully negotiating to buy Coca-Cola since 1908.

A tumultuous Coca-Cola board meeting took place three days later. By the time the minutes were demanded in court in 1920, they had conveniently disappeared, along with the Colby/Brown letter. The surviving annual report contains only the cryptic statement, "Asa G. Candler made a verbal report." The *New York Times* later reported that "the deal fell through when one of the chief stockholders, a member of the Candler family, declined to sell." Again, Buddie was probably the culprit.

Although the planned recapitalization hung fire for the rest of the year, a real reorganization of the Company never took place. According to the minutes of a June 4, 1918, meeting, "it is now deemed better policy not to abandon the old corporation." Instead, "beneficial ownership certificates" for $25 million were issued in return for the stock. The move was an effort to capitalize the goodwill and trademark of the Company via an agreement among themselves, in anticipation of a future sale. Max Pam, along with Colby & Brown, threatened to sue for breach of contract. They split $1 million dollars' worth of beneficial ownership certificates as a settlement.

SUGAR AT WAR

By the summer of 1918, other major changes had been thrust upon the Company. The United States' entrance into World War I resulted in sugar rationing. Coca-Cola took out ads proclaiming that "sugar enlists for war," asking the public's patience with reduced supplies. Another patriotic spread showed a hand holding a glass of Coca-Cola with a shadow of the Statue of Liberty grasping the flame behind it. For the first time, the Company found itself actually begging its bottlers not to seek new markets, since it couldn't provide enough syrup.

Sugar was by far the most costly ingredient of Coca-Cola. For many years, its wholesale price had hovered around five cents a pound. By May of 1917, the price had gone to eight cents, which required a five-cent-per-gallon price hike. Sam Dobbs wanted to *order* the parent bottlers to pay more. Harold Hirsch disagreed, pointing out that the bottling contract called for a flat price. He advised diplomacy rather than strong-arm tactics. Consequently, Dobbs traveled to Chattanooga to discuss it with George Hunter, who had taken over the Thomas Company when his Uncle Ben died in 1914. Hunter agreed to a temporary price hike only as long as he deemed necessary because of "the abnormal conditions" of the war.

By the following January, Howard Candler decided to abandon the rebate program, partly to discourage volume and partly to dodge the FTC litigation that he knew was coming.* The same month, he issued a statement that plants would begin to shut down until the new crop of sugar came in. At government request, soft drink manufacturers had halved their output. "But we can't get the sugar just now for even half our supply," he concluded.

The effect on Coca-Cola's business wasn't as dramatic as might be expected. In 1916, sales didn't quite reach ten million gallons of syrup. In 1917, this figure jumped to over twelve million and then fell back to ten million gallons the following year. The

---

* On February 15, 1918, the FTC case finally went to trial. Even to the FTC commissioners, the evidence against Coca-Cola appeared too flimsy, and the case was dismissed on November 17, 1919.

total demand for cola drinks was rising substantially, however, and Coca-Cola clearly lost business because it couldn't obtain enough sugar. Soda fountains displayed signs such as: "COCA-COLA being unobtainable we are serving AFRI-KOLA The Next Best." Many other fountains and bottlers weren't so honest; substitution was rampant.

The war also meant more taxes. John Candler testified before the U.S. Senate Committee on Finance, arguing against a special 10 percent tax on soft drinks. "My clients," he said, "are willing to pay a tax, they expect to pay a tax, they have no desire to dodge a tax." But slim profit margins wouldn't absorb the proposed levy. "All that we ask is that we be not destroyed," Candler begged the politicians, explaining that the Company couldn't pass the tax on to the bottlers, who had perpetual contracts at fixed prices. Nor could the bottlers or soda fountains boost the price beyond the traditional nickel, or the public would rebel. In short, Candler argued, the soft drink business would shrivel, and the government would receive *less* rather than *more* revenue.

The senators passed the 10 percent tax anyway. To no one's surprise, the soft drink industry survived. The Coca-Cola Company *did* charge part of the tax to the parent bottlers, who in turn gave it to their actual bottlers, causing considerable dissatisfaction. Under intense pressure from the Candlers and parent bottlers to maintain the nickel retail price, many bottlers decided it was economic suicide and charged the wholesaler more, resulting in six-and seven-cent retail sales. One bottler wrote, "I *must* make a profit this year or I will be in bad shape. I have bought an ice machine for $3000, trucks for $6000 and have about $6000 taxes to pay on last year's profit."

Other desperate bottlers resorted to the use of sugar substitutes such as corn syrup, beet sugar, and saccharin in order to stretch their syrup supply. After the war ended in November of 1918, Coca-Cola proudly advertised that "nothing changed, cheapened, nor diluted, Coca-Cola remained 'all there' from the beginning of the war to the end," but the statement clearly bent the truth.*

With the war behind, 1919 promised to be a banner year for Coca-Cola. "Those returning soldiers will be mighty dry," one bottler anticipated, "and they will remember what it was that hit the spot." Demand for Coca-Cola syrup would soon outstrip production capacity, and at a February 12 board meeting, Howard Candler recommended the purchase of land on North Avenue for a huge new manufacturing plant, to include an office building, factory, cooperage, and sugar mill, at a cost of almost $850,000.

It must have taken a leap of faith to continue with plans for the new factory. Two weeks later, on February 24, the Court of Appeals ruled in favor of J. C. Mayfield, citing the doctrine of "unclean hands." The decision held that Coca-Cola had no rights whatsoever, since it had once contained "the deadly drug cocaine." In addition, most of the caffeine in the drink had always come from tea leaves, not from kola nuts. Thus, the court found that Coca-Cola had engaged in "such deceptive, false, fraudulent, and unconscionable conduct as precludes a court of equity from affording it any relief." As

---

* One positive outcome of the war was Howard Candler's discovery that Coca-Cola syrup did not need to be heated. Coal having been rationed as well as sugar, Candler tried dissolving sugar in cold syrup, as he did with his iced tea. Using what amounted to a giant butter churn, he eliminated the expensive, time-consuming boiling process.

a writer in the *National Bottlers' Gazette* pointed out, "under this decision the Coca-Cola Co. is utterly helpless against imitators, no matter how bold they are," adding that it put the Company in an uncomfortable and possibly "fatal" position. Coca-Cola immediately appealed the Koke Case to the Supreme Court, where the outcome was far from certain, since the same body had ruled against the Company only three years previously in the Barrels and Kegs Case.

THE WOODRUFF SYNDICATE

On July 1, 1919, with the ultimate outcome of the Koke Case looming over the Company's future, Sam Dobbs met with Ernest Woodruff at the Waldorf Hotel in New York City to continue discussions of the sale of The Coca-Cola Company. Woodruff, the president of the Trust Company of Georgia, had numerous New York contacts, and since August 1918, with inside help from Dobbs, he had been maneuvering behind the scenes to pull off the purchase that had been scuttled twice before. After the Barrels case was settled in November 1918, they proceeded with an informal understanding that the sale would indeed take place.

It was Ernest Woodruff who had masterminded the creation of the beneficial ownership certificates, a complex arrangement that would prevent any single shareholder from derailing the purchase of the Company yet again. It was due to his influence that the new factory on North Avenue was built adjacent to land owned by Woodruff and his sons, across which the Company would need a railroad easement.

Woodruff now confirmed that "certain interests" would offer the same price of $25 million. Besides the threat of the Koke Case, Dobbs realized there were powerful tax incentives favoring a sale, which would greatly reduce the accumulated earnings tax and, as important, the excess profits tax that had arrived with the war. The government taxed the company on "excess" earnings above a "reasonable" percentage of its tiny capitalization. Enthusiastically, Dobbs agreed to take the Woodruff proposition back to Atlanta.

The stocky, jut-jawed son of a wealthy flour miller, Woodruff had, like John Pemberton, come to Atlanta from Columbus, Georgia. Unlike Pemberton, he had prospered in the Gate City, putting together a string of deals that made him a much envied (and feared) power. Woodruff sought out small, struggling companies, merging them to form major corporations such as the Atlantic Ice and Coal Company, Atlantic Steel, Empire Cotton Oil Company, Pratt Laboratory, and the Continental Gin Company. But the coup of his career was the negotiation of the Coca-Cola deal, by far the biggest transaction ever to hit the South.

Careful to hide his involvement in the process, he knew that rival banker Asa Candler would prefer to sell the Southern business to anonymous New York interests rather than to Ernest Woodruff. Despite his wealth, Woodruff was so tight with money that he made Asa Candler look like a spendthrift. Notorious for his petty frugality, Woodruff saved hotel soap and strapped bulky bonds under his clothes to avoid paying freight charges on them. Once, while a porter awaited a tip, Woodruff fished unproductively through his pockets. "I have a quarter here somewhere," he muttered. "Mr. Woodruff," the porter said, "if you ever had one, you still got it." Even normally respectful newspaper columnists acknowledged Woodruff's unpleasant nature, while praising his financial wizardry. "Nobody knows just how much he is worth," a 1919 Atlanta editorial stated. "Nobody knows much about his personal business. He is a silent man, and not companionable, [with] few intimate friends. But when he calls for the dollars, they come."

Woodruff's Syndicate included Albert Wiggin, chairman of the Chase National Bank, and Charles Sabin, president of the Guaranty Trust Company of New York, though neither of the banks was officially involved. Dobbs concealed Woodruff's involvement, but he did let the Candlers know that New York bankers were interested in making an offer, and on July 8, Howard Candler went north to meet with Eugene Stetson, vice president of the Guaranty Trust Company (and a Georgia native), to negotiate the deal, while Ernest Woodruff remained in the background. After a flurry of meetings, with Dobbs acting as the go-between, Dobbs and the Candlers signed the options on July 26, giving the Syndicate until August 28 to buy all of the $25 million in beneficial ownership certificates.

At the August 2 meeting of the Trust Company's board of directors, there was "considerable discussion" about the option on Coca-Cola. Dobbs, now a member of the Trust Company board, took part. Woodruff presented his case: here was a hugely profitable enterprise run on a shoestring, essentially still a small family business. With proper management, it could explode exponentially, particularly in foreign operations. Also, with the Volstead Act just passed, Prohibition would commence on January 16, 1920, substantially boosting Coca-Cola sales.

The purchase was a gamble, dependent on a favorable ruling in the potentially disastrous Koke Case. Finally, it was resolved to exercise the option only if the bank's lawyers reported positively on Coca-Cola's odds before the Supreme Court. By August 13, the legal department must have given the green light: "Be it resolved," the minutes read, "that this company do enter into a Syndicate for the purchase of the participation certificates representing the shares of The Coca-Cola Company." Twenty thousand steeply discounted shares were voted to Ernest Woodruff personally "in consideration of the time and services given by him in connection with this transaction."

In effect, Woodruff had accomplished what would now be called a friendly leveraged buyout. The Coca-Cola Company of Georgia would be sold to a new corporation, The Coca-Cola Company of Delaware (a state famed for lenient corporate taxes). The stockholders were paid $25 million. As part of one of the agreements between the sellers and buyers, the sellers agreed to buy $10 million in preferred stock. Thus the Candlers were to receive $15 million in cash and $10 million in preferred stock yielding 7 percent interest. In addition, five hundred thousand shares of common stock would be issued. The Trust Company was to raise $4.5 million of the necessary $15 million in cash. Presumably, the rest would come from other members of the underwriting Syndicate.

The Trust Company did not have that kind of money readily available. With deposits of only $1.8 million, it was by far the smallest of Atlanta's seven banks. Nonetheless, Woodruff was confident that he could pull it off. On August 22, the day he publicized the deal, the *Atlanta Constitution* ran a banner headline across the top of the entire front page: "COCA-COLA BOUGHT BY ATLANTANS: Trust Company of Georgia Gets National Drink." The same day, the bank mailed a letter headed *Strictly Confidential* to its shareholders, who must have been contacted individually with an explanation of what was really happening, since the letter itself was quite confusing. Trust Company stockholders were given the opportunity to buy one Coca-Cola share for each of their bank shares *if* they deposited $195 per share within five days. The letter promised that when the Syndicate was dissolved, by October 1, a "distribution" would be made. The vague language veiled the behind-the-scenes reality. Those who came up with the money to help fund the buyout wound up purchasing Coca-Cola for only $5 per share, receiving a $190 refund in October. When the shares were made available to the public at 9 a.m. on August 26, they sold for $40 a share. By 3:45 p.m. that day, the stock was oversubscribed by 140,000 shares, assuring the sale. Almost half of the shares were bought by Atlantans.

Once the dust had settled, the ramifications of the completed sale became clearer. The Candlers were suddenly very wealthy indeed, and in the next few years their mansions would spring up all over Atlanta. Sam Dobbs was repaid with the presidency of the new company, while Howard Candler was kicked upstairs as chairman of the board. The real power, however, rested with a "voting trust" of three men: Woodruff, Stetson, and Dobbs. The shareholders had no voice in the running of the company, and Dobbs, the only Candler kin, could be outvoted by the bankers.

It is not at all clear how much money the mysterious Syndicate made out of the deal. Insiders bought 83,000 shares at $5 per share. The Trust Company wound up with an agreement to purchase 24,900 additional shares at $5 and would never struggle for money again. Estimates of the immediate profit ranged from $2 million to $5 million. The bottlers later complained bitterly of the backroom "manipulations" of nefarious speculators, but there is no indication that any laws were broken, other than a lingering IRS suit over taxes.*

The most important change was reflected in the bottom line of the new Delaware corporation. The beginning balance sheet showed real estate, buildings, machinery, and equipment worth less than $2 million, but the "intangible assets" were valued at $24.96 million. These intangibles formed the heart of Coca-Cola, including the formula, trademark, and "good will." Never had an accounting term been so apt. What the Woodruff Syndicate had purchased was, indeed, not primarily a syrup factory, but the good will of the American consumer. In the years to follow, it would grow considerably stronger, with tangible financial results. If the dividends from that one original 1919 share had been reinvested in Coca-Cola stock, which has split eleven times thus far, the $40 (or $5 for insiders) investment would be worth approximately $9.8 million by 2012. Using the same scale, if a forebear had purchased one of Asa's $100 shares in 1892, it would bring approximately $8.36 *billion*.

ASA'S BITTER CUP

Asa Candler learned nothing of Ernest Woodruff's involvement until he and his children had signed the option. He was, according to his biographer son, "profoundly shocked," and didn't attend the Georgia corporation's final board meeting at which the

---

* The matter was finally settled out of court in 1929 for $1 million, though the Trust Company then spent years trying to pry money out of the original sellers.

sale was approved. For the old man, the timing couldn't have been worse. Candler's wife, Lucy, had died of breast cancer in March of 1919, just after her husband's term as mayor had ended. Now, having given away his Company, the tycoon felt betrayed and powerless—King Lear at the beginning of the storm. Bereft of Coca-Cola, Candler quickly became a pathetic figure who, when most honest with himself, wrote: "I can't bring myself to a frame of mind that causes this life to be really joyous."

His accomplishments, he said, amounted to "ashes, just ashes." He began to live increasingly in a mythical past. His rural youth took on the patina of an irretrievably lost Eden. "When I think of those golden days amid these parched years of care and distraction," he said, "I sometimes think that once I lived in Heaven and, wandering, lost my way." In 1921, Candler plaintively wrote to Howard that "I was once counted with Atlanta's builders, Georgia's active sons—your advisor—now I am companion-less, not needed nor called to any service." Awash with self-pity, Candler resolved to find a new wife.

The next year, Candler, seventy, informed his family that he intended to marry a Catholic divorcee, Onezima de Bouchel of New Orleans. His brother the bishop, embarrassed and appalled, did everything in his power to stop the match. Knowing that Asa would not listen to him, Warren persuaded a mutual acquaintance to write a "friendly" letter of advice. Candler scribbled "Et tu Brute" and "Why the stab" on the letter and mailed it back. When Asa finally caved in to family pressure and called off the marriage, Ms. de Bouchel sued him for breach of promise, causing one of the bishop's friends to write that "I am more and more convinced that your brother's whole trouble comes out of a Jesuit plot to get his millions for the Catholic Church."

Only a few months later, Asa Candler married Mae Little, a thirty-seven-year-old stenographer in the Candler Building. "Tomorrow I am taking to my self a life companion," he wrote Howard, "one I believe who is interested in me and will be a comfort to me." With her ten-year-old twin daughters, the new Mrs. Candler moved into the mansion on Ponce de Leon Avenue, but eight months later, she made the *New York Times* when she was caught sharing a quart of bootleg liquor with two men. "We're just having a little party," she informed the police. In June of 1924, a year after his wedding, Candler filed for divorce, writing that "from the very first" his wife had ignored his "comfort and convenience," leaving the house early every morning to seek "the company of a man, driving out into the Country." In October of that year, weaving on the wrong side of the road, Mrs. Candler ran over and killed a five-year-old girl.

By the end of 1924, Asa Candler was a beaten man. Called to testify in court one last time (as a defense witness in a My-Coca case), he lamented that Frank Robinson was gone. "Everybody is dead but me, and I ought to be dead but I just won't die. I have lived too long. There are too many days between my cradle and my grave now." He spent Christmas Day alone in a Biltmore hotel room in New York City, writing that he would "dislike to go out of it at all," since the room was warm. "Try to think of me as I *was*," he pleaded with his children. Candler never rallied. His mental and physical health failing, he died in 1929 at the age of seventy-seven.

It is tempting to regard Asa Candler's life as a morality play, to think of him as a kind of Willy Loman, obsessed by a success that continually seemed to elude him, even as he brilliantly created its illusion. Fundamentally insecure, he desperately sought bedrock beliefs and found them in American capitalism, a Methodist God, idealized women, and Coca-Cola, the drink that was a blessing to humanity. Without Asa Candler, Coca-Cola would never have become the world's best-advertised single product; it would never even have attained national distribution. He wanted immortality, and in his drink he achieved it.

Candler had hoped to live on through the grand enterprises of his children, but they suffered from the curse of a domineering, teetotaling father, easy wealth, and fate. Asa Jr. (Buddie) became an engaging alcoholic who kept a public swimming pool, laundry, and zoo in his front yard. He named his four elephants Coca, Cola, Refreshing, and Delicious and was sued when one of his baboons climbed over the fence and ate sixty dollars out of a neighbor's purse. Walter was involved in a notorious lawsuit when he was caught attempting to rape another man's wife at 3 a.m. on a cruise ship. William, who built the elegant Atlanta Biltmore, was killed on a south Georgia road when his car ran into a stray cow. Lucy Candler Owens Heinz Leide lost her second husband in a bloody murder for which a black burglar was jailed, though rumors persisted that Henry Heinz had been done in by a relative.

Only Howard, the oldest, always seemed to live up to his father's expectations. Yet in his own way, it was Howard who resented Asa the most. It was Howard, as president of the Company, who sanctioned the secret sale to the Woodruff Syndicate (along with his brothers), knowing how much his father despised Ernest Woodruff. Driven by a mixture of guilt, love, and repressed rage, it was Howard who wrote the curious book about his father that has been quoted in these pages. On the surface, the biography is an adulatory portrait of Asa Candler. Nothing is said of his breach-of-promise suit or his failed second marriage. But Howard managed to get back at his authoritative father subtly, between the lines, and the portrait is often devastating, particularly in the story of Frank the pony:

> Many times, after harnessing and hitching this little horse to the buggy, and after taking his seat, clucking the go-ahead with a tap of the lines on the horse's back, Father would be unable to get Frank to go ahead or to do anything but spread his feet apart, squat, and tremble. At this Father would unhitch, grasp the lines in his right hand near the bridle bit, and in a towering rage administer a vigorous lashing with a long, willowy whip with his left hand, admonishing the horse in his high-pitched, excited voice to go to work—all to no avail.

In his heart of hearts, Howard Candler often must have longed to balk like Frank the pony. In the battle between man and beast, it is clear where his sympathies lay. Whatever his resentments, though, Howard kept them well buried. When Sam Dobbs was made president in 1919 after the Woodruff takeover, he did not complain. And when, the next year, the bottlers rose up against the new owners, he proved that he was a good Company man.

PREFACE TO REVOLT

The parent and actual bottlers knew almost nothing about the Syndicate maneuvers. Back in Chattanooga, George Hunter heard rumors about ominous New York meetings, however, and wired Harold Hirsch to "take a few minutes and write me what is actually coming off." Hirsch, at the heart of the negotiations, wrote back on August 8, 1919, to reassure the parent bottler. "Powerful interests are taking this proposition over and will make a big go of it," Hirsch wrote, "but the bottlers' rights will be absolutely protected without any thought of annulling the same."

Hirsch was wrong, and he was soon forced to choose sides in a bitter battle between the new management and the bottlers.

~ 9 ~

Coca-Cola's Civil War

Family quarrels are bitter things. They don't go according to any rules. They're not like aches or wounds; they're more like splits in the skin that won't heal because there's not enough material.
— F. Scott Fitzgerald, *The Crack-Up*

When you get right down to it, we all really hate each other.
— Sebert Brewer Jr., former Coca-Cola bottler

After the syndicate's triumph, Ernest Woodruff's glee soured over the contract locking him into a perpetual partnership with the bottlers. The inflexible agreement had already caused trouble in 1917, when the bottlers granted the first temporary price hike. Now, though World War I was over, the sugar situation proved even more threatening. The U.S. Sugar Equalization Board, created in July of 1918 to assure a supply at nine cents a pound, expired at the end of 1919. Even before then, the government lost control over prices, which doubled by the fall. The new president, Sam Dobbs, wrote to the parent bottlers in November, asking for permission to purchase "all the sugar [we] can at such a price as Mr. [Howard] Candler elects to pay." Dobbs stated that the Company was making no profit under the current arrangement and asked for a sliding scale on the basis of the sugar price, stressing that this was a "temporary proposition." The bottlers agreed readily enough. In December, they also acceded to the Company's request for what amounted to a temporary loan. Howard Candler wrote to George Hunter that he was "truly grateful . . . for this further evidence of your liberal policy."

What Rainwater and Hunter did *not* know, however, was that even while Dobbs and Candler acted so ingratiating, they were plotting against the bottlers. A week before Dobbs' November letter, a committee to "investigate the status of the bottling contracts" was formed, and at a December 15 board meeting, W. C. Bradley, a Columbus mill owner brought into the Syndicate and onto the board by his former neighbor Ernest Woodruff, announced a "proposed plan of readjustment" with the bottlers.

The Christmas season passed in peace. In the January 1920 issue of the *Coca-Cola Bottler*, Howard Candler sent his New Year's greetings to the bottlers: "May we join with you in hearty fellowship and accord and face the new day together: FRIENDS."

In the same issue, Harold Hirsch wrote that "the new management appreciates to the fullest extent . . . the bottlers and has the greatest confidence in this branch." Veazey Rainwater reciprocated with a message to "HAVE FAITH!" Less than two weeks later, Rainwater's faith was shattered when he discovered the Company's hypocrisy.

Hirsch requested another conference with the parent bottlers over the sugar situation, which was not particularly alarming. When Rainwater and Hunter got together to read over the meeting agenda, however, they could hardly believe it. "We saw," Rainwater said, "that it was not an amendment for relief as we had supposed it would be, owing to unusual conditions . . . but it was a proposal to change our whole method of doing business." Refusing to attend the scheduled conference, they wrote to Hirsch offering to consider another temporary price hike. After a few more days of increasingly agitated correspondence, Hirsch called Rainwater and Hunter to his office. "Boys," he said, "I have called you up here to tell you bad news." He informed them that the Coca-Cola board of directors had ruled "that your contracts are contracts at will, and can be canceled on reasonable notice." Hirsch asked the parent bottlers whether they had any suggestions to "prevent the thing from going that far." The two men were, as Rainwater recalled, "completely dumbfounded." When they recovered, they asked Hirsch what he thought of the Company position. "I think," the uncomfortable lawyer answered, "I will eliminate myself from the proposition."

HIRSCH IN A BIND

Of course, Hirsch could not "eliminate" himself, but he did find himself in an extraordinarily awkward position. For years, he had been co-counsel to the Company and the bottlers, successfully defending their joint use of the Coca-Cola trademark. The bottlers had trusted him completely, in part because Hirsch owned a bottling plant himself. Now, it seemed that Hirsch had been bought. A central figure in the Syndicate buyout, he was rewarded with a seat on the board of directors, while his annual salary jumped to an unheard-of $37,500.

Yet Hirsch actually had little choice in the matter. In vain, he argued with Ernest Woodruff that abrogating the contracts would cause irreparable damage within the Coca-Cola "family." Woodruff was appalled at the unbusinesslike situation he had inherited. From his vantage point, the parent bottlers weren't bottlers at all, but leeches. Besides, Sam Dobbs, Howard Candler, and Asa Candler agreed that the contracts were terminable at will. The elder Candler insisted that he had never intended to give away the bottling rights in perpetuity.

Rainwater and Hunter immediately sounded the battle cry among their actual bottlers who, already anxious about the changes taking place in faraway New York and Atlanta, sided with the parent bottlers, apparently their sole protection against the ruin of their "little shops," as Sam Dobbs contemptuously called them. When Hirsch reported to the board that all parties refused to attend a conference, he was authorized to commence legal proceedings. Instead, the tortured lawyer conferred with Rainwater in a final effort to reach some compromise. In a February 12 joint letter, Hirsch and Rainwater proposed a complicated sliding scale for syrup, along with the Coca-Cola formula in a sealed envelope to be opened "in case of dispute involving proportions" of ingredients. Dobbs vehemently rejected the proposal. "We will not under any consideration, or in any way, disclose or place in anybody's hands the proportion of ingredients," Dobbs wrote. "Some things must be taken upon faith."*

In the final event, both sides lost faith in the other's integrity. On March 2, 1920, Howard Candler, as chairman of the board of The Coca-Cola Company of Delaware, notified the parent bottlers that their contracts would be terminated as of May 1, 1920. In response, Rainwater and Hunter immediately insisted on the old agreed-upon price of ninety-seven cents per gallon for syrup. Forced to comply, the Company watched the price of sugar spiral over twenty cents a pound in April, by which time the Company was losing $20,000 a day.

King & Spalding, the Atlanta attorneys for the bottlers, wrote a stinging denial of the Company's right to cancel the contract. The lawyers specifically blamed the Woodruff Syndicate for the action and promised that "our clients . . . will not submit to any such outrage, but will fight in every lawful way to protect and defend their property." One last-ditch compromise proposal looked promising, but it too fell through. On April 16, the parent bottlers filed suit against the Company in Fulton County Superior Court. "The fight is on," wrote Sam Dobbs, "and we are determined to see it through." Coca-Cola's civil war had officially begun.

LOVE FEAST TURNS TO HATE ORGY

The parent bottlers won the first skirmish, obtaining a temporary injunction preventing the Company from supplying the actual bottlers with syrup after May 1. Attempting to turn this injunction to the Company's advantage, Sam Dobbs wrote to the actual bottlers, explaining that "your welfare will be materially affected" if the Company could not supply syrup. Although furious at the parent bottlers, Dobbs felt powerless, as he wrote to his friend Bill D'Arcy a few days later: "The Chattanooga crowd are moving heaven and earth to prejudice the actual bottlers against us."

Rallying the troops, Hunter and Rainwater called for a mass bottler meeting on April 22 in Chattanooga. Though Harold Hirsch was pointedly excluded, he wrote plaintively that he had always tried to encourage a "spirit of cooperation in the Coca-Cola Family" but had failed. He stressed that both sides had the same basic goal—"a continuous and ever-free flowing supply of bottlers' Coca-Cola syrup." In the bitterness of the fray, however, "this particular purpose has, to some extent, been lost in the shuffle." The angry bottlers assembled in Tennessee preferred emotional condemnations of the Company to Hirsch's plea for sanity. "If I go down," George Hunter declared, "I'm going to pull the whole business down with me."

The Company and parent bottlers backed away from their vindictive game of "chicken" before the syrup spigot was actually cut off. They compromised on a temporary solution just before the May deadline, allowing the Company to supply the actual bottlers at $1.72 a gallon with an adjustment for the volatile price of sugar (much to the relief of the Company). As the courtroom filled for what Atlantans knew would be an entertaining trial, sugar still cost over twenty cents a pound as a result

---

* By this time, the sealed envelope with the Coca-Cola formula, as modified by Asa Candler and adjusted for court settlements, rested in the Guaranty Trust's New York City bank vault as agreed upon in the 1919 Syndicate purchase.

of stockpiling by a consortium of sugar interests in Cuba, whose economy boomed along with Coca-Cola sales. In Atlanta, however, the cost of a fountain Coca-Cola rose to eight cents a glass.

COURTROOM DRAMA

The trial quickly degenerated into a literal tug-of-war. Ben Phillips, the lawyer for the bottlers, grabbed the Coca-Cola minutes book, reading the contents into the record over the opposing counsel's repeated objections. Finally, Harold Hirsch physically wrenched the minutes away from Phillips. Normally composed, Hirsch sounded more like a petulant schoolboy than a lawyer: "It is not going in the record and I demand the book back. Give me my book back." Once order was restored, Hirsch and his colleagues argued convincingly that the parent bottlers were parasites, middlemen "who serve no useful purpose, simply buying the syrup at a fixed price and reselling same at a profit—not even seeing the syrup." During Veazey Rainwater's cross-examination, he admitted that the parent bottlers took a 25 percent profit on advertising provided by the Company. With hardly any investment, the Southeastern Parent Bottler had made $2.5 million in twenty years.

The parent bottlers responded, with equal justice, that without them there would have *been* no bottling business. Hunter and Rainwater chronicled the difficult early years, the failed bottlers, the fights against imitators. The actual bottlers had invested over $20 million in real estate, plants, and equipment. The Coca-Cola Company had not had to lift a finger or spend a cent on the entire venture. Far from being leeches, the parent bottlers were constantly training and exhorting their bottlers to put out a uniform, high-quality product. They sponsored conventions and training seminars, arranged for bulk buying, secured the most modern equipment. As for the $2.5 million in profits over a twenty-year period—what about the Syndicate's one-day earnings of *twice* that figure, accomplished by financial sleight-of-hand instead of hard, prolonged work?

The truth of the matter lay somewhere in between these two positions. By 1920, the bottling territories were nearly blanketed. The number of franchises peaked at 1,263 in 1928 (the same year the volume of bottled syrup finally surpassed fountain), slowly consolidating in the following decades. While the parent bottlers had unquestionably performed a valuable service in the formative years of the bottling industry, their role had diminished by the time of the trial. They had a sweet deal and they knew it—which is why they weren't about to give up their contract.

In the midst of the testimony, the city of Atlanta exacerbated the situation by suing The Coca-Cola Company for the names of its stockholders in order to tax them. But that was nothing compared to the daring new tactic of the bottlers' lawyers. "BOTTLERS SUE FOR COCA-COLA RECIPE," headlines blared on May 15. Deliberately attacking the Company where it was most paranoid, the bottlers insisted that the original contract granted them the right to the formula. If they lost the first suit, they would at least be able to supply their own syrup if they won the second.

As a finale, the bottlers unexpectedly withdrew their Fulton County suits on May 31, simultaneously filing the same suits in Delaware federal court. "It came as a thunderbolt out of a clear sky," Dobbs wrote. "This infernal lawsuit hangs over me like the Sword of Damocles." The public explanation for this move was that "federal questions" were involved, but the lawyers probably wanted to find a more impartial judicial climate than Atlanta. The Delaware case, which got under way in June, was argued for the bottlers by John Sibley from Atlanta and J. B. Sizer from Chattanooga. Having worked effectively alongside Hirsch in the Barrels and Kegs Case, Sizer now found himself on the other side, becoming so emotionally overwrought during his opening arguments that he fainted.

The quibbling over the relative merits of the parent bottlers was really extraneous to the main question—was the 1899 contract permanent? The contract had been modified in 1915 at Hirsch's suggestion, to avoid possible prosecution under the Clayton Act for restraint of trade. One Florida bottler had refused to sign the amended contract until Hirsch specifically reassured him that it was indeed permanent. Sizer and Sibley triumphantly produced this 1916 letter. "Above all and beyond question," Hirsch had written, "the new contract is perpetual and even more binding and stronger than the original contract along that line."

On the stand, Hirsch tried to weasel his way out, asserting that "I did not write this letter as counsel for The Coca-Cola Company [but as] counsel for the bottlers." Nonetheless, he admitted that he had always considered the contracts to be permanent until he "re-examined" the subject in 1919 and decided he had been wrong. Other testimony revealed that Asa Candler, Sam Dobbs, and Howard Candler had repeatedly begged the Thomas Company to abandon its two-year contracts, pointing to the successful Whitehead/Lupton operation. The Coca-Cola Company officials had insisted, Rainwater testified, that permanent contracts with bottlers gave them "the greatest incentive to do their best at all times," and made them feel "absolutely safe" in making necessary capital improvements.

THE SUMMER OF '20

On June 23, 1920, the testimony concluded, and Judge Hugh Morris was left to mull over some 2,500 pages of transcripts before issuing his verdict, which was expected in the fall. Around this time, Howard Candler committed a terrible purchasing blunder. Unable to obtain Cuban sugar at a reasonable quantity or price, he ordered a gigantic shipment from Java at twenty cents a pound. During the summer, one of Cuba's sugar plantations broke ranks and offered to sell at a cut rate, triggering a steep drop from the artificially high price. By September, the price had fallen from its May high of twenty-seven cents a pound to fifteen cents, continuing to drift down below nine cents in December.

Candler and other Company officials prayed that the boat from Java would be caught in a tropical storm and sunk, but it arrived as scheduled on December 15 with 4,100 tons of high-priced sugar, the largest single shipment of sweetener ever received in Georgia. One unsympathetic wag said that The Coca-Cola Company had a "terrible case of diabetes." While most other soft drinks lowered their prices, Coca-Cola bottlers could not, and they were blamed for what was beyond their control. "It is very hard for the public to realize that we are NOT manufacturers of our syrup," wrote bottler Crawford Johnson. In response to pleas to lower the syrup price, the Company actually *boosted* it in November, provoking an outraged letter from Rainwater.

Tempers must have flared at the Company offices during that summer and fall of 1920. The Bottler Suit was pending, as was the Koke Case. The sugar decline spelled disaster for the next year's syrup price. Discouraged shareholders sent the price of the stock steadily down. Under these circumstances, the personality clash between Sam Dobbs and Ernest Woodruff came to a boil.

Dobbs quickly developed a distaste for the obstreperous Woodruff. At the onset of the litigation, Dobbs had written to D'Arcy that "our friend Woodruff is in no way helping by his constant butting-in and interfering. . . . He seems too disposed to tell us all what we ought to do and is very much outraged when we don't agree with him." In the midst of the trial, Woodruff further annoyed Dobbs by suggesting what might have been the tycoon's most brilliant amalgamation: "Woodruff is as busy as a mangy dog with fleas, with a great scheme of consolidating The Coca-Cola Company, the parent bottlers and all of the actual bottlers into one big corporation, with the bottlers to take Coca-Cola stock for their holdings and plants." Dobbs dismissed the idea; he would be damned if he would agree to coexist with both Woodruff *and* "Lupton and his bunch."

Now, at a July meeting of the executive board in New York, Dobbs finally blew up. Woodruff insisted on spending no more than $1.2 million for the year in advertising, despite inflated postwar prices. Wall painters, for instance, were demanding twice the previous year's wages. Dobbs had to inform the board that he had already paid $1.1 million and needed to spend considerably more by year's end (in fact, the final advertising expense for 1920 was $2.3 million). After the meeting, Dobbs took Woodruff aside and blistered him with an unaccustomed lecture. "I asked him pointedly what he knew about Advertising and Advertising costs," he recounted to D'Arcy. "I then asked him what his opinion was worth on a question of advertising about which he was densely ignorant."

From that moment on, Dobbs' fate was sealed. Harold Hirsch met the president when he returned from a Western trip, explaining that Woodruff had the board's solid support in demanding that Dobbs step down. Dobbs was blamed not only for the overspent advertising budget, but the Java sugar debacle. On October 4, he tendered his resignation, agreeing to keep silent about it until the board meeting in November, when it would become final. He complained to D'Arcy that "Woodruff, through his confidential conversations with everybody that comes into his office, will soon have it all over town." He was right. Rumors of dissension within the Company plummeted the stock five dollars in one day. To no one's satisfaction, Howard Candler was installed as president for the second time. As dividend payments were postponed, the stock dropped to a new low of twenty-five dollars a share.

Beset by management woes, loaded down with overpriced sugar, and threatened by pending lawsuits, the new Coca-Cola Company appeared to be floundering. On November 3, the Fulton County Superior Court ruled that Coca-Cola had to reveal stockholders' names to the city of Atlanta. Five days later, Judge Morris finally announced his decision. The contract, he held, was indeed permanent. "I never read a more forceful and conclusive opinion in any case," Sizer exulted. "This is a golden opportunity for The Coca-Cola Company to make a fair and reasonable settlement of this litigation." At first, he seemed to be correct. While filing an appeal, the Company asked for negotiations. W. C. Bradley and Veazey Rainwater were chosen to represent either side and commenced a protracted series of meetings.

A RAY OF LIGHT

While Bradley and Rainwater sparred, Supreme Court Justice Oliver Wendell Holmes Jr. delivered an opinion that redeemed the otherwise miserable year that had almost passed.* In his decisive ruling, Holmes reversed the Court of Appeals, favoring Coca-Cola over Mayfield's Koke Company of America. In words lovingly quoted by Company officials in years to come, he wrote that Coca-Cola was "a single thing coming from a single source, and well known to the community. It hardly would be too much to say that the drink characterizes the name as much as the name the drink." In other words, it didn't matter that the drink was originally named for its primary ingredients or that it had once contained cocaine. The judge ruled that Koke was an infringement on the trademark, but that Dope was a generic term that Mayfield was free to use.

Finally, the wrangling bottlers and Company officials could rejoice over a mutual triumph. If the opinion had gone the other way, it would have rendered their bickering meaningless, since Coca-Cola itself would have been badly damaged. "The decision is of the utmost importance," Hirsch told a reporter. "It establishes beyond all question the validity of The Coca-Cola Company's trademark and trade name, and will forever protect the company against infringement." In his temporary euphoria, Hirsch may be pardoned for overstatement. He would prosecute plenty of cases in the future, but they would be substantially easier to win.

Meanwhile, Howard Candler continued to price syrup on the inflated twenty-cent sugar in his storehouse. Bottler Crawford Johnson moaned that his consumers could not understand "why we are compelled to sell our product on a basis of 20¢ sugar when the market price today is 8¼¢." Rainwater and Bradley remained deadlocked over the Company's right to inspect bottling plants and the bottlers' demand to examine the Company's books. The new year dawned with no settlement in sight. In February, the bottlers instituted yet another suit against the Company, charging Howard Candler with using fraudulent sugar prices.

A few days later, the *Wall Street Journal* embarrassed the Company by implying that its annual report was hiding something—which, of course, it was. "The report of the Coca Cola Co. leaves plenty to the imagination. It is unlike any annual statement that has made its appearance since the first of the year." The stock took yet another dive, and Howard Candler hurriedly filed a profit and loss statement showing a 1920 loss of over $2 million from sugar. In April, in an all-out effort to woo favorable press, The Coca-Cola Company threw a bash at Atlanta's Capital City Club to unveil big new ads to editors and publishers.

On May 4, 1921, after only two days of hearings, the Court of Appeals judge in Philadelphia virtually affirmed Judge Morris' opinion from the bench. In an unusual procedure, he called the attorneys to the bar and suggested that they agree on a sliding scale for their mutual benefit. Afterward, Hirsch and Sizer agreed it would be best to leave it up to a court-appointed official, since Rainwater and Bradley were at an impasse. By the end of June, the war within the Coca-Cola family was resolved.

---

* It was only by a quirk of fate that Holmes delivered this opinion rather than Charles Evans Hughes. If the puritanical Hughes had not run for president in 1916, the Koke Case might have had a different outcome.

The contracts were permanent—even the contracts of the Thomas Company with its bottlers. Beginning on November 1, the price of syrup would be set at $1.17½ per gallon for the parent bottlers, and $1.30 to the actual bottlers, both of which included a five-cent allotment for advertising. For every cent that sugar rose above seven cents a pound, the price of syrup would increase by six cents. The bottlers dropped their other suits.

Coca-Cola had weathered its worst crisis. The overpriced sugar was almost exhausted, and sales continued to increase, despite a national economic slump. A jobber explained the drink's depression-proof status: "It is a business in innumerable articles of comparatively small cost that have a universal demand." In June, another major infringement suit against Chero-Cola—a drink that had dominated its home territory of Columbus, Georgia—came down in favor of Coca-Cola.

HARRISON JONES INTO THE BREACH

The internecine struggle may have been over, but it left deep psychic wounds that would never fully heal. The bottlers would never again truly trust the Company. Yet one man who had joined The Coca-Cola Company managed single-handedly to bridge the gap between the two parties. Harrison Jones soon achieved mythic stature among the bottlers. A solidly built 6'2", Jones was an imposing man, his curly hair boiling from an oversized head, while his booming voice dominated any conversation. A journalist, still recovering from an encounter, described him as "a very large gentleman who masks a kindly and patient disposition with a slightly ferocious exterior and a vocabulary more graphic than recordable. . . . Mr Jones appears forever to be about to hit something with an ax." Jones had joined the firm of Candler, Thomson & Hirsch in 1910 and was involved in the 1919 buyout. Perhaps recognizing that he was more suited to sales than the law, Hirsch suggested that Jones transfer to the Company to reorganize its sales force. The new employee split the country into ten sales territories, installing a manager in each, and instituted annual meetings. In 1921, Jones published the first newsletter for Coca-Cola fountain salesmen, which he called the *Friendly Hand*. He even managed to pry money out of Ernest Woodruff for thirty brand-new cars.

At the same time, he recognized that the bottlers, too, badly needed a friendly hand from the Company. As a first act of reconciliation, he planned a huge convention for all of the bottlers in 1923—a first-time event, since previous conventions had been sponsored by the separate parent bottlers. He enlisted veteran salesman Ross Treseder to assist him. According to Treseder, Jones became "all steamed up" over the need to make the convention a memorable, effective affair that would inaugurate "permanent closer cooperation" between the Company and the bottlers.

Jones wanted the bottlers to feel that it was *their* convention and traveled to solicit their suggestions. Treseder's description of the men he and Jones visited reveals the Coca-Cola bottler in his kingdom. Mobile, Alabama, bottler Walter Bellingrath was eager to talk, since Coca-Cola was "his religion morning, noon and night," punctuating his advice on Coca-Cola with biblical quotations. He used much of his wealth to create elaborately landscaped gardens. From Mobile, Jones and Treseder traveled to Memphis to see "Uncle Jim" Pidgeon, the premier U.S. bottler, who used one hundred thousand gallons of syrup annually. A white-haired dynamo, Pidgeon was another true believer. "By the time you left [him]," Treseder wrote, "any misgiving or doubt you had about Coca-Cola and its potential success would have vanished completely."* In Paducah, Kentucky, they found Luther Carson, who periodically leaped up in church to testify to Coca-Cola's wonders. Carson had good reason to praise the Lord, since he owned the best car and biggest home in town; he delighted in showing off his oriental rugs.

Armed with plenty of ideas, Jones and Treseder returned to Atlanta and prepared a complete stage set of "Typical Town," with mom and pop stores, barbershops, haberdasheries, and shoe stores. On the "wrong" side of the street, Coca-Cola displays were put in out-of-the way places or the logo was misspelled. On the "right" side, appropriately placed signs announced the drink's superiority. The 1923 spring program appealed particularly to the route salesman, who shouldn't consider himself merely a delivery man. "If a man thinks he's a salesman, he is a salesman," Jones said. "If he thinks he is a truck driver, he is a truck driver." Taking the drivers down "Brass Tacks Lane," the seminars covered every aspect of a typical day.

Harrison Jones grew positively lyrical in his grand address of reconciliation to the bottlers: "This is a great day! It is a day of reunion, a day of family unity, when the stalwart sons of Coca-Cola . . . meet together in the old homestead . . . to give inspiration and to gain it." He proceeded to give it, emphasizing the indissoluble bond between the Company and the bottlers: "You, the bottlers of Coca-Cola, and we, the manufacturers of Coca-Cola, are interlocked, interlaced and interdependent one upon the other in a way that injury cannot be done to the one without the other, and that the progress of one must inevitably be the progress of the other. Men, we are one."

Jones called the bottle and glass "the Siamese twins" of the Coca-Cola industry and summoned "men with guts . . . whole-souled, red-blooded he men" to go out and find consumers "at the crossroads country store, at the filling station, at the ball game, at the skating rink, on the trains, at the clubs—literally, anywhere and everywhere." On the bottler's heart and mind, Jones wanted the message imprinted: "Let's make it impossible for a consumer to ever escape Coca-Cola."

Treseder was awestruck. "He was the best speaker I ever listened to . . . capable of inspiring any audience." In fact, Jones spent most of his life talking nonstop, relating anecdotes liberally spiced with creative obscenities. Thomas Wolfe, in a lyrical passage about a salesman, could easily have been describing Jones: "He had . . . a wild energy, a Rabelaisian vulgarity, a sensory instinct for rapid and swingeing repartee, and a hypnotic power of speech, torrential, meaningless, mad, and evangelical. He could sell anything." Jones often called Coca-Cola "holy water"; once, however, carried away at a bottlers' convention, he declared more truthfully, "Hell, I could sell bottled horse-piss."

In his travels around the country to boost his salesmen's morale, Jones was equally enthusiastic. The Canadian business was thriving, despite the long, cold winters. One day in St. Louis, Jones launched into a vivid description of the Canadian

---

* Unlike most Coke bottlers, Pidgeon paid top wages and attracted loyal employees. Every morning as his loaded Coca-Cola trucks rolled out, he shouted after his drivers: "Give 'em hell, boys—give 'em hell!"

enterprise, explaining that in the winter the denizens of the frozen North kept their houses toasty warm and practically lived on Coca-Cola. "Wait," one of the salesmen interrupted. "Is there any chance for me to get the bottling franchise for the North Pole?" Given Jones' persuasive powers, the eager potential bottler may not have been kidding. As another Coca-Cola man noted, "Harrison Jones could sell you a snow-ball in Alaska."

ARCHIE LEE SEEKS FAME AND FORTUNE

As Harrison Jones was rejuvenating the Company, Archie Lee, the man who would revolutionize Coca-Cola's advertising, was planning his first campaigns at the D'Arcy agency. Unlike most Coca-Cola men, Lee was an introspective, quiet sort who had been seriously questioning the meaning of his life before he joined D'Arcy. Just after America had entered World War I in 1917, young Archie Lee penned a long, soul-searching letter to his parents. "The doctrines of our churches are meaningless words," he wrote. "Whither we are bound no one seems to know." Still, he said, "Ah what a loss it is when we contemplate the Garden of Eden. There is something deep in our hearts that tells us life was meant to be beautiful, peaceful and joyous. All our actions lead to turmoil and strife. Where is there a man today who is holding out a genuine and satisfying hope?" Perhaps, he wrote, "some great thinker may arise with a new religion."

Lee went on to say that he wanted to "do something really worth while. I would die happy if it should be just one recognized and lasting thing." The "great ambition" of his life was to write wonderful books. Of course, it would be nice if he earned decent money while he was at it. "Fortune and fame! They make a lot of difference." Two years later, at D'Arcy, he was indeed on the road to fame and fortune, though not as a novelist. He had, however, found something that held out a "genuine and satisfying hope." Coca-Cola, his new religion, offered a brief illusion of Eden to a world full of "turmoil and strife." Archie Lee would translate the fundamental human longings into some of Coca-Cola's most powerful ads.

"It is hard work," Archie admitted to his parents in 1920, "giving a different dress to many stories about the same thing." In Coca-Cola, however, he felt that he had found the key to his fortune as well. He borrowed $1,000 from his father to invest in Coca-Cola stock at its lowest ebb in 1920, accurately noting that "there is a big chance that it will net a good profit, perhaps leading the way to a real fortune." The next year, he wrote that he was creating "the best work I have ever done." He had designed the year's entire Coca-Cola campaign and was growing closer to Bill D'Arcy. "I feel confident that my reward will not be inconsiderable." He hadn't given up his goal of writing fiction—"at least one novel and some stories"—but he couldn't find the time. Later in 1921, he described an Atlanta presentation where they displayed over fifty pieces of ad copy, most in color. Lee basked in Howard Candler's praise of "the best material that had ever been presented." There was no more mention of writing fiction. Archie Lee had found his calling.

Lee was probably responsible for several changes in Coca-Cola's ads in his first few years. By the time he joined the agency in 1919, the D'Arcy approach had grown more sophisticated than the wordy "reason why" ads of 1907. A full-color 1916 design, for instance, featured two women, one with tennis racquet, the other with golf clubs, drinking Coca-Cola, with minimal copy and dramatic use of white space. These women were wholesome, active, full of life, as opposed to the harried, neurotic shoppers pictured a decade before. A 1917 ad stressed Coca-Cola as "a favorite friend . . . a bond of mutual enjoyment." Medicinal claims and negative advertising were nearly abandoned.

In 1920, the D'Arcy agency took the trend of minimal copy to its extreme, possibly at the suggestion of the creative Archie Lee. A *Life* ad simply depicted a busy street corner dominated by a huge wall painting that read "Drink Coca-Cola, Delicious and Refreshing." Another copyless ad featured the New York City skyline and harbor, with a hand holding a glass of Coca-Cola in the foreground. In 1921, ads showed a clean-cut young soda jerk who dispensed "with a deft, sure hand," emphasizing superb, uniform service and product.

Lee also assisted with a project to help the bottlers find new markets, sending out a packet of advertising and direct mail letters that could be tailored for varying circumstances. Aimed at retail dealers and women, the letters focused on the take-home market for the first time, urging them to request delivered cases from their local grocer. While the twenty-four-bottle case was awkward, the inventive D'Arcy approach tapped a huge potential market.

Archie Lee's real talent, however, lay with the perfect, gracious slogan, and in 1922 he devised his first big winner, "Thirst Knows No Season," which ran for several years. February and December ads using the slogan portrayed Coca-Cola in lively ski scenes. The phrase was repeated again and again at a 1922 Atlanta convention, where fountain salesmen were delighted with its message. While the Company had always pushed Coca-Cola as an all-season drink, this was the first really sustained winter campaign.

ROBERT WOODRUFF TAKES OVER

In July of 1923, Archie Lee wrote that he was busy with a major new client—the White Motor Company of Cleveland, Ohio. D'Arcy had won the account because the new president of Coca-Cola, a former White executive, had made the connection. Lee and the new Coca-Cola head were destined to become the symbiotic team that guided the company into a golden age. Lee introduced the man whose name would become synonymous with Coca-Cola:

> A fellow about my age and the son of a prominent banker in Atlanta, a fellow I met when I first went to Atlanta years ago, started selling White trucks about the time I went to work on a newspaper in Atlanta. He did remarkably well, and after the war he was taken to Cleveland and soon became General Manager of The White Company. . . . Although he was making lots of money in Cleveland, he went back in Atlanta a few months ago as president of The Coca-Cola Company. This man is Robert Woodruff.

Sculpture with inscription by E. BOISSEAU, Artiste sculpteur.

"Here's the best feeding bottle!"

Painting with inscription by G. HAQUETTE, Artiste peintre.

"It's good, my boy; it's Vin Mariani!"

Vin Mariani, the popular coca-laced Bordeaux wine (and forerunner of Coca-Cola), was unabashedly touted as a beneficial drink for everyone, from babies to the elderly.

Sketch with inscription by A. ROBIDA, Artiste illustrator.

"Vin Mariani unites all nations."

Long before Coca-Cola, Vin Mariani spanned the globe, providing a nerve tonic for people in every clime.

John Pemberton, Coca-Cola's inventor, has usually been portrayed as the scraggly-bearded inventor seen in this oil portrait (right). In his younger years (left), however, his beard was well kept, and his eyes appeared at once sorrowful and reflective.

Asa Candler in 1888, the year of Pemberton's death, when Candler solidified his claim to Coca-Cola. (*Candler Papers, Special Collections, Emory University.*)

Indomitable Ma Candler and her boys in 1891. The diminutive Martha Candler, a "hardshell Baptist," ruled her brood, passing on a grim, down-turning mouth. Asa is standing, third from left. John, the lawyer and judge, is the youngest, standing far left. Pugnacious Bishop Warren sits at the left on a stool. (*Candler Papers, Special Collections, Emory University.*)

Asa Candler with his family in 1899, the year Howard (standing at left) took to the road selling Coca-Cola. Asa put enormous pressure on his children to excel, but none of them ever lived up to their father's expectations.

Frank Robinson, the unassuming "unsung hero" of Coca-Cola, who named the drink, wrote out the graceful script logo, and manufactured the soda fountain favorite.

The Coca-Cola staff in 1899, on the cusp of a new century. Frank Robinson (first row, far left) was even shorter than Asa Candler, who stands next to him here. Candler nephew Sam Dobbs, sporting a mustache, stands in the middle of the second row. Baby-faced Howard Candler, Asa's oldest son, stands to the right of Dobbs, next to Mrs. Dobbs. In front of her, Walter Candler poses with his hands on his younger brother William's shoulders. Looking ill at ease and separate, the two black workers to the right are labeled: "Jim Reed, Porter (col.); Will Cartright, Drayman (col.)."

Three little boys proudly announce their preference for Coca-Cola in 1894, when it still contained cocaine.

As controversy swirled around the drink, the Company explicitly declared it "the Great National Drink," here served by Uncle Sam himself from a Capitol tap.

THE GREAT NATIONAL DRINK

Coca-Cola

DELICIOUS! HEALTHFUL! REFRESHING!

Relieves fatigue without undue stimulation. Is genuinely good to the taste; aids digestion. Its use after exercise is especially healthful. Recommended by such noted athletes as Napoleon Lajoie, Cy Young, Rube Waddell and Bobby Walthour.

Sold everywhere, five cents

Here, a gruff old tycoon examines the ticker tape along with his rising colleague. The 1907 text clarifies the lingering medicinal claims that Coca-Cola eases "nerve racking and physically exhausting terrors."

The Chicago Coca-Cola bottler found that overt sexual appeals helped sell his drink. Here, a 1907 beauty (above) is obviously "satisfied" in several ways. The same bottler portrayed the bare-breasted young woman holding her Coca-Cola bottle (left). The straight-laced Asa Candler was infuriated, not only by the sexual content, but also by the reference to Coca-Cola "high balls" and "gin rickies."

Even though Asa Candler professed horror at Western Coca-Cola's risqué advertising, this 1913 Company effort echoed the double-entendre prostitute portrayed five years earlier. Here, the "satisfied" female isn't quite so overtly sexual, although "it goes, straight as an arrow, to the dry spot" could be read several ways.

In a contemplative pool of light, this 1905 student enjoys a prescription to keep "the brain clear and mind active."

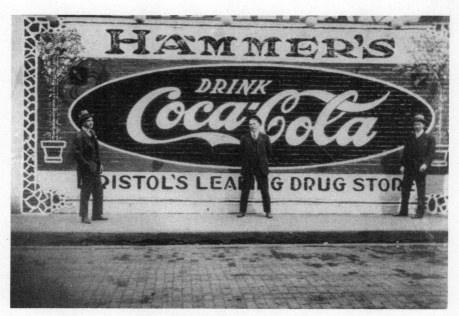

Three Coca-Cola salesmen proudly pose before one of the ubiquitous wall signs. By 1914, the Company had painted over five million square feet.

Any powerful drug, such as caffein is acknowledged to be, should not be offered indiscriminately to the public in other than its natural condition, and certainly not without the knowledge of the consumer

In this 1912 *Good Housekeeping* cartoon, Harvey Wiley warns a gullible public against the gremlins of indigestion, nervousness, and addiction lurking in Coca-Cola.

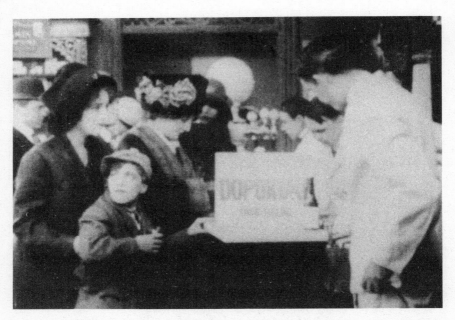

In D. W. Griffith's short 1912 film, *For His Son*, desperate heroine Blanche Sweet shoves aside a newsboy to get at her Dopokoke. Griffith's moralistic tale capitalized on anti–Coca-Cola feeling following the 1911 Barrels and Kegs trial, though the drink had contained no cocaine since 1903.

Part III

The Golden Age

(1923–1949)

Georgi Zhukov was exhausted. He still hadn't finished briefing his officers for the next day, and the sun had set hours ago. With a sigh, he asked his aide to bring him something to eat. The Russian general hadn't paused once since he had defended Moscow against Hitler's crack troops, then broken the German resistance at Stalingrad, lifted the siege of Leningrad, and championed the triumphant Russian advance from Warsaw to Berlin. Pushing his troops unmercifully to get there before the Americans, he had yearned to settle a personal score. "Soon I'll have that slimy beast Hitler locked up in a cage," he had promised his friend Khrushchev. Though Zhukov accomplished everything else, he was thwarted when Hitler shot himself.

Now, bogged down in the kind of administrative tasks he loathed, the general oversaw the Russian-occupied zone of defeated Germany. Even though he despised the enemy, he pitied the starving, pathetic Germans who begged for food. While Zhukov felt contempt for most American troops—those braggarts who had entered the war late and considered themselves the world's saviors—he had found a fellow soldier in Dwight Eisenhower, and the two had become friends at the Potsdam Conference.

Thinking about Ike reminded Zhukov of the American's favorite drink. To the Russian, it had looked evil—a dark, fizzy potion—but he couldn't offend his new acquaintance when Ike offered it to him. Smiling, he tossed off the drink as he would a shot of vodka, then felt it explode up his nose. Spluttering, he thought he'd been the victim of a practical joke until Eisenhower, laughing, told him to sip it more slowly. "It'll still give you gas," he said, "but back in Kansas they say a healthy belch is good for your digestion." Zhukov liked it the second time, subsequently developing quite a taste for the beverage.

That was what he needed to brace him for the rest of the evening. "Nikolai!" he shouted. "Bring me one of those special Red Star drinks with my food." Eager to enjoy the new drink, Zhukov had asked General Mark Clark, commandant of the American-occupied zone, if he'd arrange for a supply of Ike's drink. "But it must not look like the American product," he cautioned. "Don't put it in that funny-looking bottle. And make it a different color."

Zhukov knew that Stalin, that jealous madman, would be only too delighted to have an excuse to liquidate the people's hero. The general couldn't be caught with the capitalist soft drink.

Ah, here it was. His aide brought borscht and what looked like a bottle of mineral water. Snapping the red-starred cap, the hero of all the Russias tilted his head back and drank deeply, then emitted a small burp. "Ahh," he said under his breath. "Coca-Cola!"

~ 10 ~

Robert W. Woodruff:
The Boss Takes the Helm

*Great things are done by devotion to one idea; there is one class of geniuses,
who would never be what they are, could they grasp a second.*
                                        —John Henry Cardinal Newman

In 1923, when Ernest Woodruff's dynamic son Robert became president of The Coca-Cola Company at the tender age of thirty-three, most people assumed that the crusty old banker had willed the appointment. In fact, Robert Woodruff, the youngest executive of a major corporation at the time, was hired over the initial objections of his father, who worried that there would be criticism of installing his relatively untested son. Ernest Woodruff was consistent in his business and family activities—he was difficult in both. As Robert Woodruff's official biographer noted, his relationship with his father was "a never-ending pattern of affection, rebellion, respect, defiance, devotion, tolerance, and admiration." According to the younger Woodruff, his "dictatorial" father never approved of anything he did. "He was much harder on me than on his other sons."

If Robert Woodruff was born on December 6, 1889, with a golden spoon in his mouth, his father had promptly confiscated it and melted it down for the bullion. As the oldest of three sons, Robert received no allowance and was expected to live in the Spartan manner of his father. Though he grew up with numerous servants in a suitably ostentatious house in Atlanta's Inman Park, he was in many ways a poor little rich boy. The household's atmosphere was serious, constrained, and severe; the three boys were never allowed to roughhouse or chase one another through the echoing halls. Childhood pictures of Robert Woodruff, even at the age of two and a half, reveal a preternaturally calm, adult face—contemplative, serious, calculating, self-conscious, and deeply melancholy. His deep-set eyes seem to assess a grim world but show no sign of fear. The world had best watch out.

As one of Asa Candler's Sunday school pupils, Woodruff received a dose of Candler's fervent Methodism along with his father's Puritanical influence. While not overtly rebellious, the young Woodruff undoubtedly delighted in joining his fellow students in mocking the Coca-Cola magnate behind his back. It must have given him great pleasure to bilk both Candler and his father at the same time. Ernest Woodruff gave his son fifty cents a week to feed the pony the boy rode to school. The resourceful student befriended the groom behind the Coca-Cola factory near his school and left his pony there all day to munch on Candler's oats, allowing young Woodruff to pocket the money.

He was a uniformly poor student. At thirteen, he attended a summer school run by Mrs. W. F. Johnson, who liked the awkward, serious boy. With her encouragement, he blossomed. "I have been greatly pleased," she wrote, "to note the effort you have made since coming to my little summer school, and if you will only continue in this line, some day you will be a man to whom your parents will point with pride." Woodruff cherished this note, keeping it among his mementos. When he later became President of Coca-Cola, he sent Mrs. Johnson a small monthly stipend, explaining that "you had a great many pupils, lots of whom were much better than Robert W. Woodruff, but I had only one Mrs. Johnson."

Woodruff's response to this kind woman was probably related to his devotion to his mother, Emily Winship Woodruff, by all accounts a saint. Gentle and understanding, she served as a foil for her domineering husband and encouraged a love of music and poetry in her children. Throughout his life, along with the gruff manner inherited from his father, Robert Woodruff displayed a sentimental side, and he always sought out nurturing women in addition to his manly sporting and gambling companions.

Despite his summer school efforts, Woodruff quickly flunked out of Boys' High School and was shipped to Georgia Military Academy, where he remained a poor student but found his niche as a leader. Because of his gruesome dental braces, Woodruff couldn't take part in sports. Instead, he managed virtually everything at GMA—the football team, the school publication, the dramatic club—while putting his natural charm to good use as a salesman. Of course, it didn't hurt to be Ernest Woodruff's son. Raising money for the school band, he went straight to his father's banking cronies. Woodruff's arts of persuasion, coupled with his last name, also saved the school from bankruptcy. The brash young man visited James S. Floyd, the vice president of the Atlanta National Bank, which was about to foreclose on GMA's mortgage. The lanky sixteen-year-old fixed the bank executive with his rather intimidating stare and told Floyd to "go easy" on the school. When Floyd found the interloper was only a student at GMA, the executive started to throw him out—until Woodruff told him his name and implied that Tom Glenn, one of the Trust Company's officers, would endorse the GMA note. Suddenly Floyd was more than cooperative, and the school was saved.

Once out of GMA, Robert Woodruff caved in to his father's demands that he go to college, and in the fall of 1908 he departed for Emory College at Oxford, Georgia, where he excelled at cutting classes, spending money, and writing home with multiple complaints—his eyes bothered him, he didn't have enough ready cash, the dormitory roof leaked and he caught a cold. He paid other students to do his math homework, remaining unrepentant about it even in later life. One of his widely quoted dictums was "If you can get somebody to do something better than you can do it yourself, it's always a good idea." By the end of the semester, even Ernest Woodruff had to admit defeat when James Dickey, the president of Emory, wrote a devastatingly direct letter: "I do not think it advisable for him to return to college this term. . . . He has never learned to apply himself, which together with very frequent absences, makes it impossible for him to succeed as a student."* Furious, Woodruff's father insisted that he get a job and pay him back for the wasted tuition, room, and board.

AN INAUSPICIOUS EARLY CAREER

Robert Woodruff harbored two adolescent fantasies about his adult life—he would either make a million dollars or hunt big game like Buffalo Bill Cody, whom he had once met. He eventually achieved both goals, but they must have seemed far away to the nineteen-year-old who went to work in February of 1909 at the General Pipe and Foundry Company as a general laborer shoveling and sifting sand. That lasted only a week, after which he became a machinist's apprentice, learning to work a lathe and other machinery. After a year, he was fired for no apparent reason but was rehired by the parent corporation, the General Fire Extinguisher Company, as an assistant stock clerk, soon shining as a salesman. Or so it seemed. Again, he was inexplicably fired.

After bouncing from one manual job to the next, Robert Woodruff received a magnanimous offer from his father: a position as purchasing agent at the Atlantic Ice and Coal Company. He was about to marry Nell Hodgson, who came from a prominent Athens family, and he needed steady work. Still cocksure despite his checkered career, Woodruff soon horrified his father by purchasing a fleet of White motor trucks to replace the horses and wagons that had been delivering ice and coal. Ernest Woodruff, apparently annoyed at this extravagance, vetoed a promised pay raise.

When Robert Woodruff found, through his immediate manager, that his father was behind the decision to deny him a raise, he became suspicious and discovered that his father was also responsible for having him fired from his previous jobs. Ernest Woodruff wanted to impart a lesson in hard knocks, proving that life wouldn't automatically be easy as a rich man's offspring. The angry son promptly quit, vowing never to do business with his father again—a vow he later broke.

Walter White, impressed with the way Woodruff had negotiated for his trucks, offered the young man a job as southeastern salesman for the White Motor Company. Almost overnight, Woodruff created a sensation as a truck salesman, with his unerring way of nosing out the right contact, the "man of consequence." Unlike many salesmen, Woodruff was direct, honest, and relaxed, radiating confidence and stability. He represented a quality product that he was graciously offering to a needy public. He rose quickly through the ranks, becoming sales manager of the southeastern region. During World War I, he left White to serve in the U.S. Ordnance Department, developing a troop transport carrier that gave the White Motor Company considerable business, then rejoined the firm after the war. Ernest Woodruff, who had counseled his son against the "terrible mistake" of selling trucks, must have decided that his son was worthy after all, inviting him to join the board of the Trust Company of Georgia, where Robert participated in the Syndicate's scheme to buy The Coca-Cola Company in 1919. He purchased a substantial chunk of insider stock at five dollars a share and

---

* Robert Woodruff probably retained a feeling of defensive inferiority about his brief college stint. He eventually resumed Asa Candler's tradition of Coke philanthropy toward Emory, the "Coca-Cola School." Even the college song asserts, "We were raised on Coca-Cola, no wonder we raise hell."

also persuaded his hunting buddy, Ty Cobb, to buy Coca-Cola stock, laying the foundation for Cobb's fortune.*

As vice president of White, Woodruff was riding high, with a huge salary of $75,000 a year plus commission. He also *lived* high, much to his father's disgust, borrowing heavily to finance a luxurious lifestyle and further investments. During the recession of 1921, he narrowly avoided having his notes called in, and he watched his falling Coca-Cola stock with dismay. Although by the end of 1922 the stock had turned and sales had improved, the soft drink's future was still uncertain. The Coca-Cola board was unhappy with Howard Candler at the helm. He lacked any real drive or leadership ability and had been responsible for the disastrous sugar purchase. There was considerable discussion about bringing in a more aggressive president who would provide much-needed direction. Robert W. Woodruff was a natural choice. Initially reluctant, Ernest Woodruff finally had to admit that Robert was a gifted salesman and offered the presidency of Coca-Cola to his son at a salary of $36,000 a year.

The young executive wasn't eager to leave White for a $39,000 pay cut. Complicating his decision further, Walter Teagle had offered him a high-paying executive position at Standard Oil. Woodruff was tired of New York, however, and longed to return to Atlanta. He also saw an enormous potential for increased sales of Coca-Cola, both domestically and overseas. The 3,500 shares of Coca-Cola stock he owned ultimately motivated him: "The only reason I took that job," he later said, "was to get back the money I had invested. . . . I figured that if I ever brought the price of stock back to what I had paid for it, I'd sell and get even. Then I'd go back to selling cars and trucks."†

Woodruff made a counteroffer: he would take the presidency for a base salary and 5 percent of any annual increase in sales. His father rejected that idea. Finally, Woodruff agreed to take the job with the proviso that he be given free rein, making it clear that he would brook no opposition from his father. With the Standard Oil offer in his pocket and a promise of his old job at White if things didn't work out, Robert Woodruff assumed the presidency of Coca-Cola. For over sixty years, the charismatic leader would guide the soft drink's fortunes, making it the world's most famous product.

THE BOSS

Even to his closest associates, Robert Woodruff remained an enigma. He stood an even six feet tall, but his commanding presence made him seem much larger, as he chewed his ever-present cigar and silently assessed a room he had just entered. "You knew when the Boss had arrived," one acquaintance recalled, "even if you were facing the other way. You could feel it. He had an indescribable presence, a magnetism." Coca-Cola men would do anything to win his favor and demonstrated fanatical loyalty to

---

* When they weren't feuding, Woodruff and the volatile Cobb remained lifelong friends, which does not speak well for Woodruff's taste. Ty Cobb sharpened the spikes on his shoes to intimidate other players when he slid into a base. Even his teammates despised him. At Cobb's death in 1961, his Coca-Cola shares were worth $1.7 million.

† Robert Woodruff was actually never in danger of taking a loss on his stock, having paid almost nothing for it, thanks to his father.

him over the years. Yet, on the surface, Woodruff was a singularly uninteresting man. He didn't read. Several of his intimates swore that he never finished a book in his life, and he refused to look at any correspondence that went beyond a single page, relying on aides to digest material for him.* He didn't appreciate culture, history, or art. When stuck in traffic only minutes from St. Peter's in Rome, he impatiently ordered his driver to turn around. "But Mr. Woodruff, we're only five minutes away!" his secretary exclaimed. "That's close enough," Woodruff snapped.

Although Woodruff was a poor speaker who avoided the limelight, many of his sayings were more widely quoted by Coca-Cola men than biblical verse. Woodruff's simple pronouncements, such as the dictum that "everyone who has anything to do with Coca-Cola should make money," often cut to the heart of the obvious. Others were trite generalizations, such as "There is no limit to what a man can do or where he can go if he doesn't mind who gets the credit."

While the gregarious Harrison Jones held forth in the company cafeteria with the common man, Woodruff had a private elevator installed so that he could go directly to his office, where he ate in his private dining room with a select group. Prowling bearlike through the halls at Company headquarters, Woodruff chomped on his cigar, passing most people as if he didn't know they were there. When someone had the temerity to accost him with, "Good morning, Mr. Woodruff," he would often growl back, "What's so good about it?" The Boss could, however, suddenly turn friendly and charming, putting his arm around an ecstatic employee while he talked.

Phobic about being alone, Woodruff made sure that he was always surrounded by people. It was common for him to call at 5 p.m. and say, "Come over for dinner tonight." Regardless of what the employee or acquaintance might have planned, he would obey the summons. Likewise, if the Boss couldn't sleep, he would wake up someone for company. The groggy friend was often baffled about why he was there, however, because Woodruff had little to say. He preferred to sit in companionable silence, dismissing company when he felt sleepy again. "Being too close to Mr. Woodruff was dangerous," recalled one Company man. "It was like being a moth near a flame."

In some ways, Woodruff resembled Asa Candler. He was intensely restless, constantly on the move. He once invited a group of friends to a Florida resort for a week's relaxation. After two days, he abruptly announced he was leaving, but of course everyone else should stay and have fun. He had accomplished whatever he had come for, and he had to move on. "The world belongs to the discontented," was one of his maxims, echoing Asa Candler's Hawthorne quote. Woodruff seemed truly at home only at Ichauway, the thirty-thousand-acre plantation he bought in southwest Georgia in 1929, where the Boss was in definite command. Otherwise, he frequently moved from his home in Atlanta to his penthouse in New York or, later, the T.E. Ranch in Wyoming, where he pursued big game on Buffalo Bill's former spread.

The favorite poem of both Candler and Woodruff was Rudyard Kipling's "If," though Woodruff managed to live by the poem's injunctions better than Candler had. Through the years, Woodruff did indeed keep his head while others were losing theirs.

---

* It is possible that Woodruff was dyslexic, like many other notables such as George Patton, Woodrow Wilson, and Thomas Edison.

Woodruff also resembled Candler in never paying exorbitant salaries, though he at least understood the value of nicely timed bonuses. Finally, both men demonstrated a devotion to Coca-Cola that approached idolatry. Even in his old age, the multi-millionaire would squat next to a rural gas station's vending machine and count the number of bottle caps to see which percentage belonged to Coca-Cola.

Notoriously competitive as an outdoorsman, crack shot, and fine horseback rider, Woodruff proved mediocre at golf, which his friend Ralph McGill called his "hair shirt." Still, Woodruff never lost, even on the links. He would set a high enough handicap for himself so that he even beat his friend Bobby Jones Jr., the famed golfer. More often, he snagged Jones—who owned Coca-Cola bottling plants throughout the United States, South America, and Scotland—as his partner. Likewise, Woodruff never lost at poker, keeping the game going into the early hours of the morning if necessary. In one famous instance, he insisted that the Company plane fly in a holding pattern over the airport until he won at gin rummy.

Above all else, Robert Woodruff valued *control*, which he exercised even over himself. One acquaintance praised him for "the capacity of becoming angry and not revealing it." Instead, the Boss moved to deal with his enemies quietly but effectively, assuming natural command in virtually any situation. He rarely attended social functions. "I give parties," he said, "I don't go to them." Early on, he realized that those who wielded the greatest power often remained in the background, and so he became a master of subtle influence, of exercising velvet-gloved authority.

But Woodruff didn't use that power in a vacuum. A superb listener, he constantly questioned and asked advice. Often, he had already made up his mind about a course of action, but he asked for opinions anyway—to verify that he was right, and to make everyone feel a part of the action. His advisers ran from his top executives down to his servants. At one point, a vice president asked Woodruff's chauffeur whether the Boss had sought his input on an important matter. "No, sir," the driver answered, "but he will."

CHANGES IN THE TWENTIES

Though Robert Woodruff is usually given credit for "saving" the Company, he actually took over a well-managed business that had already weathered its most difficult period and was well on the way to recovery. The annual report for 1922 proudly noted that a whopping loan of $8.4 million (due to sugar losses) had been paid in full over the previous two years. Harrison Jones had effectively restored morale while dividing the country into more efficient sales districts. Archie Lee and Bill D'Arcy had begun to refine Coca-Cola advertising. Sales were booming. Inflation and sugar prices had moderated, assuring a nickel drink for decades to come.

More important, Woodruff inherited the corporate culture of Coca-Cola, a drink that already had a semi-mystical aura. Company men cherished a deep-seated belief in the product itself, regardless of whether Candlers or Woodruffs were shaping its future. The real protagonist of the drink's history would be Coca-Cola itself. Woodruff's genius lay in recognizing this fundamental principle and building on it, resisting all efforts to diversify. As Justice Holmes had said, Coca-Cola was a single thing coming from a single source, and Woodruff fiercely adhered to his solitary product in the six-and-a half ounce hobbleskirt bottle until he was literally forced to change it decades later.

In some ways, Coca-Cola typified major corporations in the twenties—the era of the first professional managers, who relied increasingly on lawyers, public relations experts, market researchers, psychologists, and advertisers. Woodruff, a consummate manager, brought an almost military precision to what had essentially been a family business, run in a brilliant but amateurish fashion by Asa Candler and his relations. The Boss insisted on procedure manuals for every aspect of the Company.

Like his father, Robert Woodruff understood how to manipulate corporate structure to maximize profits, privacy, and control while minimizing taxes and governmental scrutiny. Shortly before he took over as president, Woodruff helped his father create Coca-Cola International. Despite its name, this holding company had nothing to do with foreign sales; it simply replaced the awkward three-man voting trust. Its purpose was the same—to assure that Woodruff and his friends retained control of the corporation. Over 251,000 Coca-Cola voting trust certificates were traded on a one-to-one basis for International shares, although the New York Stock Exchange initially balked at listing the new issue, objecting to holding companies that conducted no actual business.

Generally, circumstances in the 1920s favored Woodruff. With economic recovery following the brief postwar recession, the United States entered the free-swinging, self-confident Jazz Age, and Coca-Cola fizzed along as a vital part of the times. The muckraking Progressive Era was essentially over, and Coca-Cola emerged from its cloud of controversy to match the image it had always sought—a wholesome family drink, a temperate alternative to bootleg liquor during Prohibition. Those who continued to attack the soft drink now appeared old-fashioned holdovers from a prior era.

Tom Watson, in his last hurrah as a U.S. senator in 1921, the year prior to his death, excoriated Coca-Cola from the floor of the Senate. "An addict who consumes from fourteen to twenty bottles of the stuff every day is no uncommon case," he thundered. "I have had the best doctors in the State of Georgia tell me that Coca-Cola destroys . . . the brain power and the digestive power and the moral fabric and that a woman who becomes an addict to it loses her divine right to bring children into the world." But no one paid attention to him any more than they did to the predictable ravings of octogenarian Harvey Wiley. Though Southerners continued to call for their "dope" with a shot of lime, cherry, or ammonia, it was just a nickname. Coca-Cola did retain a vaguely risqué mystique, but that only led to greater consumption, not persecution.

Out of the public view, however, the coca leaf content continued to plague Woodruff. In 1925, Woodruff retrieved the Coca-Cola formula from the Guarantee Trust in New York City and brought it back to Atlanta, where he placed it in a vault in the Trust Company of Georgia, his father's bank. There, no one could see that it still contained fluid extract of coca, albeit without its drug content.

That didn't stop chemists at the U.S. Food, Drug and Insecticide Administration,* protégés of Harvey Wiley, from testing a batch of Merchandise No. 5 in 1928. Alarmingly, they found a tiny amount of ecgonine, an alkaloid derived from coca leaf that could be chemically altered to make cocaine. When Coca-Cola chemist W. P. Heath

---

* In 1927 the Food, Drug and Insecticide Administration took over the Bureau of Chemistry's regulatory functions, and three years later it became the Food and Drug Administration (FDA).

tested for himself, to his horror he found not only ecgonine, but an infinitesimal amount of cocaine.

While the Maywood Chemical Works chemists scrambled to refine their decocainization process, Robert Woodruff authorized production of Merchandise No. 5 at a secret Company-leased plant in Lima, Peru, as an emergency backup measure. A few months later he was appalled when a company employee in Peru sent a $1,152 check to Atlanta, the amount he had received for selling forty pounds of cocaine, the by-product of decocainization, to a Paris broker. Fortunately, neither that sale nor the minuscule cocaine content in Coca-Cola ever became public knowledge. The Maywood chemists removed the last trace of cocaine, and the Peruvian plant stopped production.

Thus, by 1929, a WCTU campaign against Coca-Cola was ripe only for ridicule. "At the spectacle of men returning home, sodden with Coca-Cola, to beat their wives," William Allen White wrote sarcastically, "the sight of little children tugging at their fathers as they stand at the Coca-Cola bars long after midnight, . . . we remain unmoved." Another journalist commented that the WCTU might as well wage a campaign against using toothpicks in public. The same year, the *New York Times* formally announced the end of Coca-Cola's public persecution, noting that a future "studious historian" would find the assaults on the soft drink worth only an interesting paragraph. Ultimately, however, the drink "gently took its place in Big Business, where it now is."

While Woodruff may have inherited a going concern, he had a positive genius for locating the heart of its strength. He may not have saved the Company, but he unquestionably catapulted it to a higher level. Involved in all aspects of the Company from the beginning of his reign, he approved every major decision, while his own snap judgments, based on a simple philosophical framework, proved uncannily on the mark, time after time.

Part of Woodruff's ability lay in picking the right men, those he esteemed as the best in their respective fields. "He can take a man's measure so rapidly," wrote one Woodruff-watcher in 1930, "that the man does not realize he is being observed." Many of the men who would guide the destiny of the Company came on board during the twenties: Eugene Kelly, who took over the Canadian operation; Lee and John Talley, who would rise to executive levels; Al and John Staton, Georgia Tech football heroes and scholars; William "Pig Iron" Brownlee, a determined, fair, but tough manager. Many of Woodruff's recruits were Georgia natives whose soft-spoken Southern drawl charmed clients wherever they went—whether in New York, Montreal, or Paris— while their quick eyes missed no business opportunity.

If Woodruff was impressed with an opponent, he often hired him. Arthur Acklin, a Georgia-born IRS agent who tried to pry back taxes out of Coca-Cola, soon joined the Company to do battle from the other side. John Sibley, the aggressive young attorney for King & Spalding who had fought Coca-Cola in the recent Bottler Case, shortly thereafter began to work for the Company he had so bitterly opposed. Sibley became a lifelong Woodruff friend and adviser, gradually accruing power as Harold Hirsch's authority diminished.

ADVERTISING FOR THE ROARING TWENTIES

One of the reasons that Coca-Cola was no longer maligned by the end of the twenties was that Woodruff recognized that a defensive, negative posture was poor policy and forbade any further pamphlets quoting Dr. Schmiedeberg on caffeine. The Boss set a modest, gentlemanly tone that is still echoed at the Company. The drink, he said, had no earthshaking importance—a small thing, really, serving to make life a bit more relaxed and pleasant, that's all. By such "aw-shucks" false modesty, he assured Coca-Cola more importance; the stress on taking a moment for a pleasurable, sociable drink fit the hedonism and energy of the times.

Archie Lee and Robert Woodruff, who shared the same attitude toward the drink, quickly became close friends. Lee was one of the few people besides Sibley who actually dared address Woodruff as Bob. The ad man had the talent to translate Woodruff's groping thoughts into gracious, unassuming slogans—direct contrasts to most period advertising, which utilized wordy negative copy as never before, playing on consumers' fears. A hand cream featured "The Tragedy of Nan—Domestic Hands." Hoover Vacuum ads proclaimed that "Dirty Rugs Are Dangerous." Ads for Gillette Blue Blades showed a man with stubble admitting, "I was never so embarrassed in my life!" Postum depicted a boy tutored after school who was "Held Back by Coffee." The prize for the genre, however, went to a Scott Tissues ad featuring a surgeon and nurse bent over an unseen patient. The copy read, " . . . and the trouble began with harsh toilet tissue." In an era increasingly concerned with outward appearances and social status, most ads exploited a fear of appearing a misfit—unless, of course, the ad's particular product was used.

Coca-Cola advertising must have been a refreshing change for the harassed, anxious consumer of the 1920s. No longer did the ads show a tyrannical sun beating down on despondent, wilted shoppers. Instead, Archie Lee's message in 1923 was to "enjoy thirst at work or at play." Coca-Cola was "always delightful" and was found in a "cool and cheerful place." Copy was kept to a minimum, while pictures conveyed the message that active, contented, good-looking, successful young men and women enjoyed the drink.

The D'Arcy agency hired some of the best artists of the day—N. C. Wyeth, McClelland Barclay, Fred Mizen, Haddon Sundblom, Hayden Hayden, and Norman Rockwell, among others. Their oil paintings for Coca-Cola were often genuine works of art, but the illustrators were never stupid enough to put their egos above the product. "The idea in an illustration," McClelland Barclay said in 1924, "must hit [the viewer] like a shot. It ought to force the exclamation from them—What a peach of an idea! Not only that, but they must remember that it was Coca-Cola that was refreshing and good to drink." Barclay was particularly pleased with his *Ladies' Home Journal* ad of that year, a well-dressed socialite standing at a soda fountain, lifting her veil to sip a glass of Coca-Cola. Everything about the picture denoted classy restraint—the woman in white, the clean-cut soda dispenser, the understated copy that appeared underneath: "Refresh Yourself. The Charm of Coca-Cola is proclaimed at all soda fountains."

Woodruff and Lee continued the tradition of avoiding overt sexuality in ads while remaining suggestive. A 1923 effort verged unusually close to outright sex appeal, showing a pretty blonde with a low-cut white dress and an almost sultry look. "There's nothing like it when you're thirsty," the double-entendre caption proclaimed. In the ensuing years, however, more brunettes than blondes were portrayed, and while they were undoubtedly buxom, they weren't nearly so blatantly sexual. "We used to call the Coca-Cola girls the Atlanta Virgins," one ad man recalled. "They were sexy only above the hips, offering sex without sweat."

In 1923, Archie Lee first toyed with the phrase that would be his greatest creation. "Pause and Refresh Yourself," he wrote. "Our nation is the busiest on earth. From breakfast to dinner there's no end of work." This ad was actually a throwback to the negative hurry-hurry, worry-worry ads of 1905, and Lee soon abandoned it. But the idea of a magical way to stop time, to take a breather in a hectic day, was valid and useful if divorced from its negative connotations.

Already hectic at the turn of the century, the pace of life in America now appeared downright frantic. "Talk about the tempo of today!" wrote one twenties commentator, describing a typical office worker's schedule. He suffered from "speed-desire-excitement," an endless cycle that "whirs continuously in his brain, his blood, his very soul." Everything had to be accomplished in a huge hurry, according to another writer, with "quick lunches at soda fountains . . . quick cooking recipes . . . quick tabloid newspapers." In 1929, Lee first coined the phrase "The Pause that Refreshes." Over the next twenty years, this "pause" became synonymous with Coca-Cola, as harried businessmen made the luncheonette a standard part of their day.

Another interesting motif entered advertising in the 1920s: a nostalgic appeal to rural America. "Every day in every way life is getting speedier, jazzier," wrote one commentator in the twenties, calling for a return to "the simple life." In response, a 1923 Coca-Cola *Ladies' Home Journal* spread portrayed a down-home girl in sharp contrast to the upper-class models usually found in the ads. A fresh-scrubbed rural beauty with boyishly short hair and a straw hat around her neck enjoyed her drink from a bottle through a straw. "You'll like it as surely as sunshine and fresh air make you thirsty," Lee wrote. Soon, subscribers enjoyed Norman Rockwell's ads with freckle-faced boys at the old fishing hole, complete with dog and Coca-Cola bottle, just as the United States increasingly industrialized. These clever appeals to a mythical peace back on the farm have continued to produce some of Coca-Cola's best advertising.

Lee's slogans and Coca-Cola's fine new artists soon were on display along the six hundred thousand miles of new highways built in the twenties. On twenty-four-poster billboards, the first of which went up in 1925, the "Ritz boy," a white-clad bellhop, held a tray with a single bottle of Coca-Cola and a glass. The simple caption read: "6,000,000 a Day." The billboard was joined by the "Spectacular," the name Coca-Cola men applied to huge electric signs strategically placed in the heart of a city. The first neon extravaganza was created in 1929 in New York's Times Square, which one Coca-Cola man gleefully reported to be "the busiest spot in the world . . . the mammoth parade ground of the universe." Researchers estimated that over a million pairs of eyes saw the signs there every twenty-four hours. The same writer noted that Times Square was "plebeian to the core. The masses flock to the Main Stem. They eat more, talk more, see more, dress better . . . than anywhere else." Presumably, they also drank more Coca-Cola.

Finally, in an ingenious effort to attain "scientific" advertising, the Company initiated the "Six Keys to Popularity" contest. A variety of ads stressed different reasons to buy Coca-Cola: Taste, Purity, Refreshment, Sociability, Price, and Thirst-Satisfaction. Consumers could win one of 635 prizes by writing in to explain why their favorite "key" was the most important. The 1927 campaign was in reality a massive market research tool, but it also allowed consumers to participate and feel part of the advertising itself. The $10,000 grand prize was not coincidentally given to a perfect representative of middle America: Mabel Millspaugh, a stenographer in Anderson, Indiana.

DESCENT OF THE SURVEY CREWS

In 1923, Robert Woodruff had expanded the former Information Department into the Statistical Department, which soon performed what would now be called pioneering market research. During the decade's last three years, this department frenetically laid the foundation for a scientific approach to selling more Coca-Cola. By that time, there were practically no new outlets. There was a bottling plant in nearly every town. Coca-Cola was sold in each of the 115,000 soda fountains in the United States. In the title of a 1929 article, one of the few he wrote, Woodruff posed the question, "After National Distribution—What?" Could it be that the drink had reached its saturation point?

Of course, Woodruff didn't want to answer that question affirmatively. In 1927, he assigned Turner Jones,* the head of advertising, to oversee a massive survey. Over a three-year period, Coca-Cola's field workers studied fifteen thousand retail outlets to determine whether there was a relationship between traffic flow and sales volume. Sure enough, the dealers with highest sales turned out to have the largest number of potential passing customers. They also tended to pay the highest rents, since they were in desirable locations. Roughly a third of the outlets accounted for 60 percent of the sales volume, while the bottom third sold only 10 percent of the total. The survey revealed that many of the high-volume outlets had few Coca-Cola signs either outdoors or inside the store. As a result, salesmen began to visit these dispensers four times a year (twice had been the standard), offering special service, aids, and encouragement. After this initial effort, the survey crews followed up with observations of forty-two thousand drugstore customers across the country. They discovered that 62 percent of all shoppers made purchases first at the soda fountain. Of those, 36 percent asked for Coca-Cola. Twenty-two percent of customers sipping the right soda went on to a secondary purchase at some other counter.

Armed with this information, Woodruff not only directed a more intelligent distribution and sales effort but an innovative public relations campaign based on a series of soft-sell movies with names like *Soda Fountain Service*; *Come In, Customer*; and *These Changing Times*, using professional actors in the role of druggist and dispenser. The films were shown to retail dealers and chain store managers, who learned the benefits of serving the drink correctly. Coca-Cola was best served at thirty-four degrees with perfectly chipped ice in a thin-sided bell-shaped Coca-Cola glass, which had a

---

* The Coca-Cola Joneses—whether Turner, Harrison, Bobby, or others yet to come—were not related to one another.

convenient mark for the appropriate syrup level. Coca-Cola men came equipped with special thermometers to take the temperature of a possibly ailing drink. They also gave away six-pronged ice forks, explaining that the single pick was clumsy and that an ice shaver was out of the question. Finally, the carbonated water should be poured down the side of the glass to avoid losing fizz, and the drink shouldn't be over-stirred. The films also emphasized methods of maximizing profit and reducing overhead. Soda fountain items offered fast turnover, low inventory costs, and a high profit margin. As a finale, the Coca-Cola representative handed out a free manual to help individual outlets estimate a storewide departmental breakdown in gross sales and costs.

This kind of effort did not go unnoticed. Trade associations, other corporations, and the press were impressed with the quality of Coca-Cola's research and the way the Company used it. "COCA-COLA GETS UP AND GOES TO BED WITH THE CONSUMER," one headline asserted. While such behavior would probably be somewhat sticky, there's no question that the devoted soft drink man would do almost anything to get his drink down one more throat. "Follow the crowds" became the Coca-Cola battle cry, and, with the new surveys, those crowds were easy to find.

SERVICE STATIONS, SIX-BOXES, AND BLACK WIDOWS

One of Woodruff's earliest decisions was to push the bottle. Woodruff had none of the Candler defensiveness about this separate wing of the business, and it was clear to him that the future lay in the portable green bottles. As a former White salesman, he knew that Americans were more restless and mobile as paved roads and highways crisscrossed the country. It was Woodruff who insisted that Coca-Cola be available literally anywhere in the United States, and he identified the service station as a major new outlet. Company dogma asserted that the soft drink should always be "within arm's reach of desire." By 1929, 1.5 million American filling stations offered perfect outlets for soft drinks. These "elaborate, attractive oases for the motorist," a Coca-Cola journalist pointed out, provided a golden opportunity to snag the driver who has "paused for an interval and is gazing leisurely around with ready cash in hand."

In 1924, the Company publication sponsored a contest with a small cash prize for anyone who sent a picture of bottled Coca-Cola being served in a new outlet. The contest was a real challenge, given the alphabetical list of already discovered outlets: bakery, barber shop, bowling alley, cafe, cigar stand, club, college, confectioner, construction job, dairy depot, dancing academy, delicatessen, fire station, fish-game-poultry-meat store, five and dime, fraternal order, fruit stand, garage, grocery, hat cleaning and shoe parlor, home, hospital, hotel, ice cream parlor, manicure parlor, market, military organization, news agency, park, place of amusement, police station, pool room, railroad office, railroad train, restaurant, tea room, telegraph office, telephone office, wiener stand.

At many retail outlets, Coca-Cola was hidden off to the side or in the rear. Some enterprising merchants cut the red syrup barrel in half, filling one half with ice and using it as an attractive cooler. Woodruff saw the need for an inexpensive, standard cooler. In 1928, John Staton, a young Coca-Cola executive, was assigned the task. Staton disassembled all available models, testing them for durability and efficiency, then designed his own cooler and put it out for bid. After extensive negotiations, the square metal box on a stand was manufactured by the Glascock Brothers of Muncie, Indiana, for only $12.50. Within a year, thirty-two thousand had been sold.

Woodruff encouraged bottle sales in other ways as well. In 1923, Harrison Jones sponsored the development of the first six-pack (called a "six-box" until the fifties) in a self-contained cardboard box with a "handle of invitation." It really wasn't promoted until late in the twenties, however, when Coca-Cola appealed to dealers with a picture of an attractive woman holding a carton in one hand while seductively pulling her dress above her knee with the other. The caption below read, "My Six Appeal." Even so, the six-bottle carton failed to gain momentum until well into the next decade, when refrigerators became more common in the American home.

Meanwhile, nuisance suits continued to plague bottlers. In 1923, the Bottlers' Association was a nearly bankrupt shoestring operation with a part-time secretary working out of Harold Hirsch's office. When Hirsch resigned as the organization's legal counsel that year to devote full time to the Company, the bottlers hired Ralph Beach, a large, humorless, bespectacled man with close-cropped hair who injected new energy into the organization. Realizing that he needed legal grounding, Beach studied for a law degree at night. Frustrated by the increasing number of foreign-ingredient suits, he created a massive filing system to catch repeaters. To defend exploding-bottle cases, he devised a demonstration to be used in court, dropping ball bearings from varying heights onto unyielding Coca-Cola bottles.

But the real star of the foreign-ingredient cases was Perry Wilbur Fattig, an Emory biology professor who studied the results of ingesting insects thoroughly marinated in Coca-Cola. In a 1933 article, Fattig wrote majestically in the royal we, noting that "all of the most poisonous insects and small animals that we have been able to obtain have been used. We have tested the Black Widow Spider (*Latrodectus mactans*) not only upon ourselves but upon thirty-nine other people." Not surprisingly, he wrote that "it was not so easy to get volunteers."

Coca-Cola lawyers claimed, of course, that the bugs *couldn't* have gotten into the drink until after it was opened. Even if by some miracle a bug *had* invaded the bottle, however, they called Fattig for the defense. He explained that the carbonated water in soft drinks acted as a germicide, rendering any bugs harmless. He then proceeded to give a personal demonstration. Juries must have been fascinated, if appalled, by Fattig's culinary habits, as he calmly munched lizards, scorpions, blowflies, cockroaches, spiders, caterpillars, fleas, roaches, grasshoppers, beetles, snails, frogs, bees, praying mantises, centipedes, worms, and stink bugs, chased down by a black widow or two. While an undoubted phenomenon in court, Fattig was not quite so popular socially. Ralph Beach's wife, for instance, refused to attend Fattig's dinner parties, where he often spiked the drinks with roaches.

STANDARDIZING COCA-COLA

One of Robert Woodruff's bedrock tenets was that Coca-Cola should be standardized. Every bottle and fountain drink should taste exactly the same across the United States. He knew from experience that the drink's quality varied considerably from place to place, depending on the water, carbonation level, ratio of syrup to soda, and cleanliness. That, he declared, would change. In 1929, he established a Fountain Training

School, where salesmen learned exactly how to mix the perfect drink, check carbonation levels, and the like. They were to convey this information to the dispensers, along with the all-important lesson of proper temperature. Coca-Cola had to be sold ice-cold, or it didn't taste good. Lecturers coined homilies to help salesmen remember: "It's gotta be cold if it's gonna be sold."

In a brilliant psychological move, Woodruff summoned his entire fountain sales force for a special meeting in 1926. He informed them that they were all fired. Coca-Cola didn't need salesmen, since the drink was now selling itself. However, if they cared to return the next day, he was forming a new department, and they might be interested. When the shaken men came back the following day, they were rehired as "servicemen" who would no longer "sell" Coca-Cola but offer their free advice and repair service. To assure a new outlook and to emphasize change to the dealers, each man's territory was reassigned.

Woodruff also preached standardization to the bottlers, a more delicate task given their recently bruised feelings. Through Veazey Rainwater, he implemented the bottlers' Standardization Committee in 1924. At first, this group dealt primarily with appearances rather than product, issuing decrees on appropriate uniforms and truck colors. Initially, they chose a white-and-green striped cotton suit that some Coca-Cola men complained resembled jail outfits. Trucks should be yellow and red with black hoods and fenders. The real issue, of course, was whether Coca-Cola was being bottled at each of the 1,200 plants under hygienic conditions, with uniform carbonation and syrup throw. The bottlers' contract unfortunately left the matter of quality up to the individual bottler, specifying only that each drink should contain at least an ounce of syrup per eight ounces of carbonated water at more than an atmosphere of pressure.

The contract did not prevent Woodruff from exerting his considerable influence. He was horrified when visiting one bottling plant early in his presidency. Dust caked the machinery, broken bottles were piled in a corner, and spilled syrup attracted flies. The Boss summoned the owner and told him he'd better clean up his operation by the next day, or he would soon find himself in some other line of work. "But Mr. Woodruff," the bottler protested, "it don't do no good to clean up. The next day it'll just look like this again." There was a moment of tense silence as Woodruff slowly took his cigar out of his mouth, his eyes boring holes into the bottler. "You wipe your ass, don't you?" Woodruff said. With that, he replaced the cigar and left.

While this piece of Company folklore may be exaggerated, there is no question that Robert Woodruff could and did make the bottlers acutely uncomfortable, notably by manipulating the amount of advertising "cooperation" he extended beyond the minimal amount specified in their gallonage allowance. The bottlers soon got the message: if you played ball with Woodruff, if you were a good boy, you were rewarded with more advertising support, more encouragement, more perks. If you didn't, you suddenly found yourself with virtually no support, ostracized by many members of the Coca-Cola family.

Woodruff found another solution for failing bottlers during the twenties: he bought them out. By the end of the next decade, The Coca-Cola Company owned twenty-five bottling plants, most in major cities. In the ensuing years, these plants served as training grounds for new employees and future managers. Independent bottlers loved to point out that the Company-owned plants never did particularly well, largely because of management turnover.

THE SEEDS OF FOREIGN CONQUEST

As impressive as all of these changes were, none could compare to Robert Woodruff's greatest contribution to Coca-Cola's future. He applied his energy and organizational skills to opening overseas markets. It is a tribute to his independence and foresight that he did so against the express wishes of his board.

The old men on the Coca-Cola board—Ernest Woodruff and his cohorts—had initially regarded an invasion of Europe as one of their principal tasks. The last sentence in the Syndicate's official press release announcing the 1919 buyout said that the new management would "extend the operations . . . more widely than heretofore, not only in the United States, but in foreign countries." For years, Sam Dobbs had resisted every effort of eager would-be European entrepreneurs, insisting that the time was not yet ripe for real expansion beyond the United States. Under direction from the new owners, however, Howard Candler finally agreed to a European venture. "Our Sales Department is being deluged with applications to handle Coca-Cola throughout the world," Candler noted in his 1921 annual report. "We believe the foreign field should be occupied by direct representation, owning plants, manufacturing and bottling our own product." In 1922, with an expenditure of some $3 million, bottling franchises were started all over Europe, largely funded by Coca-Cola and run by locals.

The new outlets were a disaster. For six months, Coca-Cola "teaser" advertising had stimulated curiosity and anticipation for a grand introduction of the drink. Crowds assembled in cafes, restaurants, and stores to try the new bottled beverage. After they snapped the crowns, their curiosity was soon overcome by nausea. The American drink made them sick. The cafes and bars, covered with caramel-colored vomit, soon emptied.

What had happened? Although the bottlers had religiously followed instructions, putting the proper amount of syrup into each bottle and adding sufficient carbonated water at the correct pressure, no one had bothered to make sure the water was clean and nonalkaline. And no one had told them that the crown corks had to be sterilized. The bacterial Coca-Cola reacted with the germ-infested corks to produce a poisonous brew.* Only one French bottler persisted. Georges Delcroix solved his sanitation problems, then overcame a governmental ban on importation of a "medicine," but his sales, primarily to American tourists at Harry's Bar and the Eiffel Tower, remained quite small.

With the European disaster fresh in their minds, the board members responded negatively when young Robert Woodruff told them he intended to see whether only Americans could develop a taste for the soft drink. Thwarted once again by his father,

---

* Morton Hodgson related the story of the nauseating European Coca-Cola, having heard it from several industry veterans when he arrived in France in 1935. In the properly acidic environment of standard Coca-Cola, bacteria could not thrive, but fermentation due to alkaline water was common in the early foreign markets.

Woodruff took matters into his own hands, sending Colonel Hamilton Horsey to England in the fall of 1924 for a thorough survey. Long-term prospects, Horsey reported, were good. Over ten million people lived within a fifty-mile radius of Trafalgar Square, compared with only seven and a half million within a similar compass of New York City. Transportation and communication facilities were excellent. British advertising was similar in character to that in the United States. Nonetheless, Horsey noted serious obstacles. The drab year-round weather encouraged hot drinks, though mineral waters and ice cream were becoming more popular. The soda fountain was a new phenomenon in England; there were only some thousand in the entire country. The British resented any "show of pomp [or] braggadocio," Horsey observed; Coca-Cola would have to go slow, avoiding "crashing through" methods.

Horsey's final recommendation was to commence bottling in the London area, committing $500,000 to a three-year introductory period. He suggested importing syrup from Canada for political and tax purposes, since it was a member of the Commonwealth. In addition, a separate British corporation, entirely under control of The Coca-Cola Company, should be set up. Since a prospective consumer "does not become enthusiastic when he first tastes it," Horsey predicted that "the work of the English Company, in the beginning, will be similar to the pioneer work . . . done in America forty years ago."

Woodruff did not actually implement Horsey's suggestion in England until 1932, probably because he failed to secure sufficient funds from his board. Instead, in 1926 he founded the Foreign Department and sent Horsey back to the Continent to rekindle the business there on a limited budget. At the same time, he sent other emissaries to Central America and China, and the following year himself embarked on a three-month trip throughout South America.

Woodruff regarded continental Europe as a vital area, placing it directly under Gene Kelly, who ran the Canadian operation. A native Georgian and former White employee, Kelly was the only truck salesman Woodruff handpicked for work at Coca-Cola. Even more than Woodruff, he was a stickler for detail, writing trunk-filling manuals to cover every conceivable aspect of the Coca-Cola business. He had brought the per capita consumption of the soft drink in Montreal near that of New Orleans. If anyone could salvage the European trade, it was Kelly. Woodruff also put Cuba under Canadian supervision, which resulted in some overbuilt bottling plants on that tropical island—the roofs were designed to hold heavy snow.

By the end of the twenties, Coca-Cola's missionaries had installed bottlers throughout the world, and Woodruff had secured adequate advertising for the new ventures. Because the soda fountain was a uniquely American institution, sales of foreign fountain Coca-Cola were meager. Rather than ship bulky syrup containers overseas, Woodruff had his chemists develop a special powdered concentrate without sugar, which made it doubly useful for the Company. Foreign bottlers would supply their own sugar so that, if the price went up again, it wouldn't affect The Coca-Cola Company.

Woodruff did not make the mistake of locking himself into perpetual overseas contracts, leaving him free to change the price of concentrate and to replace weak bottlers. In other ways, however, he used the domestic bottlers as a model, insisting that the Company wouldn't suffer from the stigma of being an intrusive American product. Instead, the business would use local bottles (all made in the hobbleskirt shape to Coca-Cola specification), caps, machinery, trucks, and personnel. Wherever it went, Coca-Cola would benefit the economy. Everyone would make money. Everyone would be happy.

The systematic creation of a worldwide industry posed unforeseen difficulties, however. Coca-Cola had to rely either on already established local bottlers, who might not push the product properly, or on wealthy entrepreneurs who knew nothing about soft drinks. In the latter case, the Company preferred to deal with prominent locals, but it often wound up using American corporations. In Guatemala and Honduras, for instance, the United Fruit Company, which dominated the local economy, took the franchise. An Illinois flour concern owned the bottling rights for Haiti, Puerto Rico, and the Dominican Republic.

In other countries, government regulations presented major problems. In Amsterdam, health officials forced the Company to label the drink "*limonade gazeuse*," despite objections that "lemonade," the European term for soda pop, implied a cheap, common drink. In Rome, a tax was levied on all advertising signs, and the city had to approve each type of display before it was erected. That was better than Bermuda, where no large outdoor billboards were allowed at all.

In each new country, the Company hired local lawyers to handle the delicate matter of registering the trademark, a process occasionally complicated by someone who had arrived first. The American achievement of Coca-Cola had already resulted in a flurry of imitators. One British firm, Duckworth & Company, concocted an ersatz Coca-Cola syrup that it exported widely to South America and elsewhere. In 1928, The Coca-Cola Company filed its first overseas suit in Britain's Chancery Division to cut off the Duckworth syrup. As a more direct expedient, Coca-Cola simply bought out some prior registrants, such as Toni-Kola in Holland and Peru. In neighboring Mexico, the trademark situation was a complete disaster, spiced by political unrest and revolving governments. There were already four pirated registrations for the identical "Coca-Cola" name, as well as a host of registered imitators. In 1925, Harrison Jones, accompanied by company chemist W. P. Heath and a lawyer, drove to Mexico to untangle the situation. They temporarily failed, though Mexicans would in time drink more Coca-Cola per capita than any other nationality. Cuba, too, hosted innumerable imitators, but the legal system there, swayed by American intervention over the years, proved more malleable.

Different languages and cultures also caused problems. The Company developed one universal ad for distribution showing only the torso of a man in a tuxedo drinking from the trademark glass and featuring the hobbleskirt bottle. "Coca-Cola" was the only word in the ad. But even that wouldn't have worked in China. The Chinese characters which most closely reproduced the sound of "Coca-Cola" translated roughly to "bite the wax tadpole." Finally, an alternative that meant "can mouth, can happy," had to suffice.* In Dutch, the slogan "Refresh Yourself With Coca-Cola" meant "Wash Your Hands With Coca-Cola," so in Holland another phrase was devised.

---

* Coke never actually went public with its tadpole-biting title. Many years later, however, Pepsi's "Come Alive with the Pepsi Generation" was literally translated in Taiwan, where it meant "Pepsi Will Bring Your Ancestors Back from the Dead." The nearest Coke ever came to such a public faux pas was with its French version of "Have a Coke and a Smile," which, when heard as lyrics in a song, could easily be misunderstood as "Have a Coke and a Mouse."

In Cuba, an unfortunate wind blew one day as the soft drink manufacturer tested the new art of skywriting. "*Tome Coca-Cola*" (Drink Coca-Cola) was blurred so that the crowds below received the message, "*Teme Coca-Cola*" (Fear Coca-Cola). Even the Company's most earnest efforts to adapt advertising to local culture provoked trouble. An elegant lithograph showing a bullfight was prepared for Cuba, but since the sport was illegal there, it proved unusable.

Even though the overseas business didn't bring in much immediate revenue, Woodruff knew that it had great public relations value. He sent photographers around the world to take snapshots of Coca-Cola's new presence, and, apparently with the board's approval, he published them in a special edition of the *Red Barrel* at the beginning of 1929. The copy accurately pointed out that

> few Americans realize that Coca-Cola is now found within the bull fight arenas of sunny Spain and Mexico, at the Olympic Games Stadium below the Eiffel Tower above "Gay Paree," on the holy pagoda in distant Burma, and beside the Coliseum of historic Rome. For many years Coca-Cola has been a national institution of the United States with widespread popularity throughout Canada and Cuba. But during the past three years it has been extended beyond national borders and its sales are now international in scope. At present Coca-Cola is sold in seventy-eight countries.

While it was no doubt true that *some* Coca-Cola fountain syrup and special gold-foiled export bottles were shipped to seventy-eight countries, the drink was actually only bottled in twenty-seven nations—and the volume was pathetic, the drink's quality often disgraceful. Nonetheless, Woodruff legitimately considered it a remarkable achievement in a short time. A world map appeared at the end of the *Red Barrel* article, with the countries where Coca-Cola was sold shaded in black. It clearly challenged any self-respecting Coca-Cola man to fill in the empty white spaces.

AN ILL-ADVISED SHORT SALE

By the end of 1927, Robert Woodruff could look back on his first five years at Coca-Cola with satisfaction. Sales had climbed steadily from a little over seventeen million gallons a year in 1923 to nearly twenty-three million in 1927. With the money pouring in, Woodruff had retired all of the preferred stock in 1926, leaving the Company free of debt. There was a contingency reserve of $5 million in addition to a $10 million surplus. From a low of $65 in 1923, Coca-Cola stock had stormed to just under $200 in 1927, when Woodruff had declared a two-for-one stock split.

The Boss knew that the entire stock market was due for a fall, and he was sure that it would take his overvalued Coca-Cola stock with it. This run-up had been too quick, too easy. Of course, he had faith in the ultimate future of the soft drink, but no stock soared up forever. Consequently, in October 1927, Robert Woodruff quietly sold short his 4,600 shares of Coca-Cola stock. In other words, he bet half his personal fortune against his own company, planning to use the proceeds of his gamble to help his former boss and good friend, Walter White, take the troubled White Motor Company private.

As the stock market crash of October 29, 1929, demonstrated, Woodruff was absolutely right about the market in general. But he was wrong about Coca-Cola. After the stock had split in 1927, it was worth $96 a share. The day of the crash, it stood at $137. During the day, it slipped to just above $128 and by the end of the year had recovered to $134, continuing to rise steadily in the following years. By the time he actually covered all his shorts, Woodruff had lost nearly $400,000. In the future, his belief in Coca-Cola would be unshakable, but he had earned that faith the hard way.*

Even though Woodruff failed to raise the cash to take the automotive company private, he and Walter White didn't give up. They spent a great deal of time together on a thirty-thousand-acre plantation they had bought in southwestern Georgia and christened Ichauway, an Indian word meaning "where deer sleep."

Then, in late September 1929, White was killed in a car crash, and all plans to take the company private were abandoned. The Boss stepped into the breach, serving simultaneously as the president of White Motor Company and The Coca-Cola Company, an unheard-of feat that garnered much admiration and publicity. For over a year, Woodruff lived on a Pullman car, conducting business for both companies on the train between Atlanta and Cleveland. Few knew that one of his primary motivations was his "serious and critical financial condition," a phrase culled from a secret memo detailing his disastrous short sale.

Nonetheless, Robert Woodruff and Coca-Cola faced the Great Depression in remarkably good shape. Over the next decade, virtually every company in America would languish as the economy was cut in half. But the Coca-Cola cover girls smiled through it all, for good reason. The only cloud on the horizon was an imitator that had nearly died several times already. The upstart would prove a worthier opponent than anyone at Coca-Cola could have foreseen in 1929.

---

* Woodruff dreaded the negative publicity that would ensue if it became public knowledge that he had shorted his own company's stock. To hide the affair, he maneuvered funds between the Blue Ridge Investment Company (a front for his investments) and The Coca-Cola Company. The net result: the IRS refused to allow Woodruff to take the loss on his taxes.

~ 11 ~

A Euphoric Depression and Pepsi's Push

That merry symphony of nickels and dimes rolling into the myriad cash registers across the nation and eventually into the Coca-Cola Company's treasury has meant a remarkably steady income . . . both in good times and bad. You could have bought Coca-Cola stock at the top price of 154½ in 1929, carried it through a major depression and the latest business recession, sold it at the low this year and you would have had, including dividends, a profit of approximately 225%.

—*Barron's*, November 7, 1938

Pepsi-Cola hits the spot,
Twelve full ounces, that's a lot.
Twice as much for a nickel, too,
Pepsi-Cola is the drink for you.
Nickel nickel nickel nickel,
Trickle trickle trickle trickle.

—Radio jingle, 1939

"By what magic does Coca-Cola make its universal appeal? There surely must be something, for the demand grows and grows," wrote an awestruck journalist in 1932. By the beginning of the 1930s, the Coca-Cola business had become an astonishing avatar that left observers admiringly bewildered. "Regardless of depression, weather, and intense competition Coca-Cola continues in ever-increasing demand," another investment analyst wrote, adding the caveat that "Coca-Cola is after all [only] a specialty product." The "specialty," however, seemed to be everywhere. In the spring of 1931, when the Empire State Building broke through the New York skyline, it nearly did so in the form of a gigantic Coca-Cola bottle. Douglas Leigh, who had created the Spectacular billboard in Times Square, suggested the bottle's familiar contours as a fitting cap to the new skyscraper.

The same year, Coca-Cola's popularity was proved in an entirely different way in the streets below, as police finally caught up with a huge Coca-Cola counterfeiting operation in a Bronx loft, complete with a two-hundred-gallon vat, chemical laboratory, printing press, and fake labels. The elusive "bottling ring," as the *New York Times* called the five men who perpetrated the fraud, had managed to stay one jump ahead of the law in twenty-five cities over the past year. Their Bronx operation had 6,800 gallons of syrup ready to go when the police closed in.

When alcoholic beverages were finally legalized again in December of 1933, many stock analysts predicted doom for Coca-Cola. "The repeal of prohibition," a journalist wrote a year after the event, "would deal The Coca-Cola Co. a staggering blow, for who would drink 'soft stuff' when *real* beer and 'he-man's whiskey' could be obtained legally? Why, the case was an open and shut one: The Coca-Cola Co. was on the skids."* But nothing of the sort occurred. "While the advent of legal beer gave Coca-Cola a little jolt for a time, the novelty soon wore off and Coca-Cola addicts turned *en masse* to their old habits." In 1932, the soft drink company's stock had been added to the Dow Jones Industrial Average.* By 1935, selling at over $200, Coca-Cola had become the highest-priced industrial stock in the U.S. before splitting that November, four-to-one. Writing to a Company official that year, one observer commented that the stock had shot up so quickly that "you must have placed a sack of Vigero under it." As the Company approached its fiftieth anniversary in 1936, it appeared unstoppable.

THE GREAT FIFTIETH ANNIVERSARY CELEBRATION

When over two thousand Coca-Cola men assembled in Atlanta for a three-day bash to celebrate the fiftieth birthday of Pemberton's drink, they looked back from a very satisfactory promontory. The strife between the bottlers and the Company now seemed minor in light of the enormous success under Robert Woodruff's guidance. Veazey Rainwater referred to it only briefly as a "family quarrel," adding that since they were "dependent upon each other," they could "under no circumstances . . . afford to fight among ourselves."

Wealthy bottlers of the 1930s had little to worry about. They owned a simple, profitable business. As one Company veteran recalls, "The plant foreman would flip a switch and those hobbleskirt bottles would fill up, then he'd turn the switch off." Many of the Coca-Cola plants constructed during that time were monuments to their owners' wealth, stability, and vanity, complete with murals, gold inlay, sculptures, and domes. One bottler built his plant as a miniature Taj Mahal in honor of his wife.

Many of the pioneer bottlers were still active, including Joe Biedenharn, the much-celebrated Mississippian who had first bottled Coca-Cola in 1894. As a tribute to these men, a play titled *Pioneer Days* depicted the "Podunk Coca-Cola Bottling Company," with scenes of reluctant retailers finally appreciating the new drink. As good clean fun, Coca-Cola men and their wives were treated to boxing and wrestling matches in the evening. Elsewhere in the convention hall, antique machinery reminded bottlers of how far they had come, and a "Visomatic" display room illustrated the technological training of future employees. While watching filmstrips, a new soft drink man could be indoctrinated with the winning Coca-Cola attitude. By the time he had seen each of the Visomatics, he had received his first transfusion in a career-long process. In their veins, Company men laughingly acknowledged, ran not blood, but syrup.

Robert Woodruff didn't address the bottlers at the convention, but he did deliver a short speech at a special dinner for fountain men, the elite cadre he often called his

---

* Even as Coca-Cola prospered during the Depression, a nervous Harrison Jones suggested to Robert Woodruff that the Company produce Coca-Cola Beer when "near beer" became legal. The Boss nixed the idea.

Marine Corps. "We are still pioneers," he said, noting that Coca-Cola's success tended to promote "ease and financial independence" that would "soften too many of us too soon." He warned that "there are hazards in this talk of success. . . . In the long life of Coca-Cola, this half century is hardly more than a flicker; but we can use it, if we will, to light a beacon that will be a guide to us and those who follow."*

Woodruff's quiet cautions were drowned out in a wave of optimism. As the convention finale, Harrison Jones delivered a speech entitled simply "Tomorrow": "There will be trials and tribulations. Men will be sorely vexed and their souls will be tried. . . . There may be war. We can stand that. There may be revolutions. We will survive. Taxes may bear down to the breaking point. We can take it. The Four Horsemen of the Apocalypse may charge over the earth and back again—and Coca-Cola will remain!" The motto to live by, Jones concluded, was that "Coca-Cola is not *yesterday*; Coca-Cola is *tomorrow*." With a smug look backward, then, Coca-Cola men left the 1936 convention secure in their hopes for the future.

TAKING ADVANTAGE OF THE DEPRESSION

The men leaving the convention had ample reason to gloat. By 1936, it was clear that Robert Woodruff and his men had managed to turn the Depression on its head by deliberate, determined, multiple attacks on consumers. As a *Fortune* reporter observed two years later, the Statistical Department's punch cards recorded "the precise state of Coca-Cola affairs on its far-flung capillaries" and could forecast sales and profits for the following year within a 2 percent margin of error.

Increasingly, for a public prodded by the Company's calculated advertising, Coca-Cola not only quenched thirst but performed a social function, as a contemporary observer noted, "Everywhere, but in the South particularly, it seems to be taking the place of coffee—or other liquids—as the something over which men must sit to talk." Imbibing also began earlier in the day. Sam Dobbs had remarked in 1910 that Coca-Cola had found a place everywhere except the breakfast table. By 1932, there was even fizz in the a.m.: "Pay a visit to one of Schrafft's stores in New York in the early morning and note the number of people breakfasting on Coca-Cola and rolls or even Coca-Cola alone."

The soda fountain proved a magnet for all ages. Coca-Cola was the approved beverage over which teenagers mooned and spooned. In common jive parlance, the soft drink was also known as "heavenly dew," while water was called "sky juice." In the evening, working men and neighborhood women congregated under the ceiling fans to sip communally, while privileged children perched on the high stools with their own glasses, listening to the adults' idle gossip. No one was more aware of the importance of placing the soft drink at the heart of America's social activity than the Company itself. "Play up the soda fountain as an institution, a gathering place," advertising

---

* The religious overtones of Woodruff's "beacon" reference may have come from Dick Gresham, a Baptist minister known as the "Coca-Cola Bishop" because he wrote customized sermons for the Boss. In the mid-thirties, Gresham urged Woodruff to "banish forever a narrow nationalism," since Coca-Cola's saturation point was "the last man in earth's last country."

department head Turner Jones advised Archie Lee in 1934. The D'Arcy man did highlight the soda fountain, but he didn't stop there in his Depression-era efforts.

Lee was one of the first advertising men to realize that a product's image was actually more important than the product itself. During a beach vacation, Lee noticed that his four-year-old daughter lavished such attention on her Pooh bear that other children fought over it, though other toys appeared more attractive. Lee took the incident as a parable. "It isn't what a product is," he wrote to Robert Woodruff, "but what it does that interests us"—and set out to plant the proper thoughts about Coca-Cola, which he wanted to make as popular and well-loved as the Pooh bear. Extensive Depression-era advertising presented the drink as a pleasant, inexpensive time-out from an increasingly difficult reality. Everyone could find a nickel to "bounce back to normal," as Archie Lee's slogan promised. A historian looking at Coca-Cola ads of the thirties would be hard-pressed to find any evidence that the United States was suffering through hard times. Promotions for the soft drink portrayed people enjoying Coca-Cola at work and play with no hint of the Depression—exactly what people wished to see. They needed no reminders of their daily reality. Coca-Cola ads, as well as the drink, provided a temporary escape, showing happy-go-lucky tourists at the Kentucky Derby, Mardi Gras, Carlsbad Caverns, or Old Faithful enjoying themselves with the pause that refreshed.

COCA-COLA GOES TO THE MOVIES

Movies provided a similar escape, thriving along with the soft drink. Archie Lee dispatched photographers to Hollywood with expense accounts to buy Coca-Cola for movie sets. Throughout the thirties, movie stars appearing in Coca-Cola ads included Wallace Beery, Joan Blondell, Claudette Colbert, Jackie Cooper, Joan Crawford, Clark Gable, Greta Garbo, Cary Grant, Jean Harlow, Carole Lombard, Fredric March, Maureen O'Sullivan, Randolph Scott, Johnny Weissmuller, and Loretta Young. "Movies have a wider appeal than any other thing in this country," Lee wrote to Turner Jones in 1935. In the same letter, he crowed over the "free advertising that we are getting . . . in recent movies." *Imitation of Life* was "very popular," Lee said, and was "really based on Coca-Cola." *Broadway Bill* mentioned the soft drink several times, and Dizzy Dean gulped it in a film while announcing baseball games. Lee liked these movie advertisements immensely, noting that they made "many people so actively conscious of it that they subconsciously buy it."

By the end of the decade, businesses were hiring specialized agents to arrange film placements for their products. Coca-Cola's infamous Barbee brothers,* who had built their Los Angeles bottling plant in the shape of an ocean liner complete with portholes, hired J. Parker Read to hand out Coca-Cola on Hollywood back lots—two cases every month to major stars, five cases a day to all current productions. For Read,

---

* Stanley and Al Barbee, identical twins and Lupton relatives, operated the Los Angeles Coca-Cola Bottling Company with their older brother Cecil. The twins were obsessed with sex and the glitzy Hollywood lifestyle, while Cecil was all business. Stan collected expensive art (Van Gogh, for instance) while Al spent his money on world travel and yachts.

a movie mogul in the era of silent films, it was a humiliating job, but he performed it with style. In 1939, when Spencer Tracy called for "two Coca-Colas, please," in *Test Pilot*, sixty million adoring fans watched him enjoy his soft drink. "The movies," noted a *Business Week* reporter, "combining sight and sound, can boast a marked advantage over either magazines or radio when it comes to showing a product in use." This "low-pressure selling" was effective, the writer asserted, because of its "subtle suggestion."

Most of the female movie stars in Coca-Cola ads were clad in bathing suits more revealing than the modest swimming dress worn twenty years before. In fact, one series of Depression-era spreads contrasted two Coca-Cola beauties, one in the demure costume of the past, one in a skimpy modern suit. Treading the fine line between overt sexuality and wholesome allure now posed a real challenge, and, without saying so in public, some Coca-Cola men clearly came down on the side of sex. Writing to Archie Lee in 1934, Turner Jones suggested his Hollywood photographer be on the lookout: "Why shouldn't he take pictures of any stars he can get in bathing suits, in some good sexy poses?" A Portland, Oregon, bottler took the theme further. He built a huge billboard at a busy intersection, leaving a cutout section in the middle for a simulated beach scene in which Miss Oregon and another beauty queen lolled on the sand for three hours nightly, making oral love to Coca-Cola bottles. "On some nights it has been necessary to have a traffic officer present to keep the traffic moving," the local bottler gleefully reported.

AT HOME WITH IDA BAILEY ALLEN

Aside from going to the movies for escape and sexual fantasy, though, most Americans found few social outlets. With less money to spend, more families entertained and ate at home. At the same time, it was much simpler to keep soft drinks ice-cold with the new technological wonder of the refrigerator. Consequently, the Company planned major campaigns to persuade women and children to drink more Coca-Cola at home.

The Company recognized "the tremendous importance of that veritable army of women shoppers," said one journalist, noting that they bought "daily supplies for some 25,000,000 American homes." With the new carton, Coca-Cola was available for the first time in thousands of Piggly Wiggly and A&P stores. Housewives were urged to grab a six-box for the fridge, and the home market blossomed almost overnight. To ensure its growth, Woodruff sent bands of women from house to house to install the familiar Coca-Cola bottle opener and to offer coupons for free cartons.

At the same time, in 1932, the Company gave away millions of copies of a booklet, *When You Entertain: What to Do, and How*, by Ida Bailey Allen, whose cookbooks and syndicated show, *The Radio Home-Makers Club*, made her the last word on the etiquette of entertaining at home. Desperate to avoid embarrassing faux pas in front of neighbors or the husband's boss, housewives sought the advice of the redoubtable Mrs. Allen, whose matronly profile graced the frontispiece. She promised to help them craft the correct meals, right down to the doilies. Nor did she press the Coca-Cola bottle too firmly to her readers' lips, holding herself back until page 26, when she first mentioned that "Coca-Cola or tomato juice cocktails are delightful with canapés." Once having suggested the soft drink, however, she soon lost all restraint, mentioning it as an accompaniment for every meal, including "Dramatizing the Breakfast Occasion."

The recipe called for Eggs Benedict, Crisp Rolls, Crullers, and Grape Fruit Sections in Coca-Cola.*

To promote the idea of buying cartons for the home, Coca-Cola ads featured food for the first time along with the soft drink, a "natural partner of good things to eat." The hot dog or hamburger with chips, washed down by a Coca-Cola, was presented as the typical American meal.

SANTA WEARS COCA-COLA RED

Coca-Cola bottlers had always known that they had to snare the next generation of drinkers early, regardless of the taboo on direct advertising to those below twelve. Now that children could find Coca-Cola in their refrigerators, the Company went after the school-age market as well, though it took care never to show anyone of elementary age actually drinking the beverage. One approach directed at children wound up reshaping American folk culture through the art of Haddon Sundblom.

A hard-drinking Swede whose work was brilliant but usually late, "Sunny" made himself indispensable, regardless of his habits, by creating the classic Coca-Cola Santa Claus in 1931. Sundblom's Santa was the perfect Coca-Cola man—bigger than life, bright red, eternally jolly, and caught in whimsical situations involving a well-known soft drink as his reward for a hard night's work of toy delivery. Every Christmas, Sundblom delivered another eagerly awaited Coca-Cola Santa ad. When his first model, a retired Coca-Cola salesman, died, Sundblom used himself. While Coca-Cola has had a subtle, pervasive influence on our culture, it has directly shaped the way we think of Santa. Prior to the Sundblom illustrations, the Christmas saint had been variously illustrated wearing blue, yellow, green, or red. In European art, he was usually tall and gaunt, whereas Clement Moore had depicted him as an elf in "A Visit from St Nicholas." After the soft drink ads, Santa would forever more be a huge, fat, relentlessly happy man with broad belt and black hip boots—and he would wear Coca-Cola red.

The Company produced a series of miniature scenes for window displays also primarily aimed at children. The charming cardboard cutouts could be assembled to create, in successive years, a miniature circus, a tiny town, an airport, the Olympics, a corner drugstore, and the cast of Uncle Remus animals.† Millions of children took free smaller versions of each scene home, where parents helped put them together—all part of the Company's devious calculations. Similarly, a house-to-house sampling campaign made "a tremendous impression upon the younger generation," a bottler noted with pride. The kids "gathered around the truck in swarms."

The Company helped bottlers invade public schools by offering a series of Nature Study Cards along with a booklet, placing the Coca-Cola logo in classrooms across the country. Some local businessman went much further, though. In 1931, a Texas

---

* Long before Bailey's efforts, Southerners had been using Coca-Cola to baste ham, make date-nut bread, or produce a distinctive barbecue sauce.

† The Uncle Remus display caused quite a stir, though not, as it might today, because of racial stereotyping. African Americans never appeared in Coca-Cola ads of the period except as servants, though they were already a major consumer group. The 1930s flap was over copyright: Joel Chandler Harris' widow sued the Company and lost.

bottler wrote that "the kids play basketball at recess on Coca-Cola goals, use Coca-Cola blotters to blot out their troubles, consult a Coca-Cola thermometer, and write their notes on Coca-Cola tablets. Can you beat that?" Some school administrators were not so amenable to free advertising, however. One Georgia bottler found that an open house at his plant provided the "opening wedge," as he put it. "We make an appeal to the children in the form of a useful toy, forcing the parents to attend by not allowing children admission" without an adult. "Heretofore," he wrote, "it has been strictly against the rules of the school authorities" to allow the Company to pass out materials. Once he gave away the pencils, sharpeners, and tablets at his plant, however, they found their way into the schools anyway, and the financially strapped district caved in. "Due to the general economic conditions, we have received requests from practically every school in the community," the bottler concluded.

Other bottlers didn't wait until children had reached school age. N. A. Lapsley, a hustling Kansas owner, scoured local papers for birth notices, mailing a little poem in honor of the birth along with a coupon for two free bottles of Coca-Cola. "Toast your own health from the cheering bottle," Lapsley rhapsodized. "Tilt back your heads, then open the throttle." Presumably, most parents appropriated the coupons for their own use, but some undoubtedly put a feeding nipple right onto the bottle, as did James Durkin, a Rhode Island serviceman. "I have a baby boy 15 months old," he wrote, "who will drink nothing but Coca-Cola. . . . I feel so proud of my son saying Coca-Cola almost as soon as he learned to say 'Da-Da.'"

RADIO COMES OF AGE

By the end of the 1930s, families were listening on the average to over four and a half hours of radio programming daily. "No medium has ever captured the imagination— not to mention the leisure time—of the public with the speed of radio," commented one historian. Identifying the wave of the future, The Coca-Cola Company firmly committed itself to radio in 1930 with a budget of almost $400,000. Grantland Rice, one of Woodruff's buddies and a well-known sportswriter, went on the air with a sports program, beginning with interviews of Ty Cobb and Bobby Jones Jr. Leonard Joy conducted an all-string orchestra, introducing each show with a special Coca-Cola anthem he initially wrote as a tango, but Woodruff hated it. Slowed to a stately waltz time, however, the theme, played by a sweeping string section, charmed the radio generation, providing the signature for every company-sponsored show.

Coca-Cola's radio programs gave Archie Lee headaches, caught as he was between the artists, Woodruff, and the audience. Woodruff insisted that shows associated with Coca-Cola be as wholesome and upbeat as the product, employing a gracious soft sell rather than the sirens, gongs, and pistol shots that often announced commercials for other products. He vetoed any news coverage as too negative to warrant sponsorship. There would be no controversy. Lee carefully instructed a comedian to avoid not only off-color jokes but "any remarks about politics, religion, prohibition, and so forth"— anything that might even remotely "arouse antagonism."

Woodruff's favorite radio personality was "Singin' Sam," born Harry Frankel, a country smoothie from Indiana (Archie Lee called him the "homey hoosier") who crooned for the soft drink from 1937 until 1942. Lee, though, preferred the silken sounds of André Kostelanetz. Unfortunately, the conductor was a prima donna of sorts, insisting on a full orchestra of forty-five men. Kostelanetz even refused to play in a new million-dollar studio because the sound didn't suit him. By 1940, Lee looked back on the decade as his "years of struggle and grief with radio," but he felt that Coca-Cola programming had achieved a decent balance. Singin' Sam appealed to rural, blue-collar types, while the temperamental orchestra leader attracted most other adults. For the bobby-soxers, there was a new program featuring the swing and jazz bands of men such as Tommy Dorsey and Jimmy Lunceford, whom Lee referred to as a "darkey" who "shrieks and howls through his trumpet."

The great irony of the thirties was that technological innovations such as radio and refrigeration were revolutionizing American domestic life at the precise time the country suffered through its first protracted economic disaster. As technology advanced, the iced Coca-Cola cooler of the twenties evolved into an electrically chilled unit with a sliding lid. Westinghouse introduced the Standard Electric Cooler for only $76.50 in 1934. The next year, seventy-five thousand coolers, quickly dubbed "Red Devils" by competitors, were sold to dealers. Three years later, the Mills 47, a coin-operated cooler with a capacity of over a hundred bottles, hit the market.

"The Coca-Cola cooler," wrote one bottler, "is advertising manager, salesman, clerk, delivery boy, warehouseman, and sometimes even the cash register all at the same time." A Jumbo unit, introduced at the 1936 convention by a talking cooler, solemnly proclaimed, "I am the bottler's friend." Factory workers, too, soon regarded the Red Devils with affection, using their share of the soft drink profits to buy team uniforms or to fund social clubs. In 1937, eight thousand coin-operated coolers were installed in public areas.

Coca-Cola took advantage of yet another technological innovation in the 1930s, as air travel matured from the biplane into a reliable mode of transportation. Robert Woodruff's friend Eddie Rickenbacker started Eastern Airlines, whose stewardesses served the ice-cold soft drink aboard all flights on the eighteen-passenger Condors. The Biedenharn and Freeman families, both bottling dynasties, helped C. E. Woolman expand Delta Airlines from a Mississippi crop-dusting outfit to a passenger service offering free Coca-Cola. The soft drink also took to Georgia airways via a Fokker airplane named "The Voice of the Sky" whose oversized wings bore the famous logo on their underside. Citizens of Atlanta were subjected to "strange music and voices in the air" as three amplifiers blared the Coca-Cola theme song from on high. To attract airborne consumers, the Birmingham Coca-Cola Bottling Company created a hundred-foot logo in the back court of the plant, easily visible to American Airways passengers en route to and from the Alabama city.

PRESSURE ON THE D'ARCY MEN

As Coca-Cola's advertising diversified through young technologies, the D'Arcy Advertising Company involved itself in virtually every aspect of the Coca-Cola business. The agency men performed an astonishing number of tasks for The Coca-Cola Company during these years, going well beyond the creation of advertising. In 1934, for instance, the Company was frustrated by its inability to place coolers in a Chicago office building owned by a printer named Donnelly. "Why can't you get some of the magazines in which we advertise . . . to hit Donnelly?" Turner Jones inquired of Archie Lee. The agency also conducted consumer and dealer surveys for the Company. The harried advertising men even had to organize crown cap counts, a particularly unpleasant survey in which used bottle caps were collected from coolers to see what percentage belonged to Coca-Cola.*

Almost everyone, one Coca-Cola ad man once concluded in frustration, was an expert on his subject. "Even morons have ideas and opinions about advertising," he noted sourly. Archie Lee must have entertained similar thoughts when Turner Jones complained, "This is not simple and clear writing—it is most hopelessly confusing." If so, Lee kept them to himself. The Coca-Cola Company was too important a client to offend in any way. Of course, that didn't mean that ad men couldn't complain to one another. Jack Drescher, a fellow D'Arcy employee, wrote to tell Lee of an illustration that had to be changed: "[Ralph] Hayes and [Robert] Woodruff say that if the attached man had about ten years taken off of him and he was made a little more cheerful, that he would be right for the poster. I say that if you do this, you would have what we have now."

In December of 1934, Robert Woodruff wrote a letter to William D'Arcy that must have ruined Christmas for the advertising mogul. In no uncertain terms, Woodruff suggested that D'Arcy augment his staff to handle increasingly diverse Coca-Cola advertising more effectively. At the same time, Woodruff advised D'Arcy to "freshen the viewpoint of your agency . . . by throwing it more closely in contact with advertising and business thought . . . in the East." Clearly, Woodruff thought St. Louis was too isolated; he wanted a branch on Madison Avenue, emphasizing that the need was "urgent." The following year, D'Arcy opened a New York office.

By the end of the thirties, the beleaguered D'Arcy agency was almost an extension of The Coca-Cola Company, resulting in cumbersome, pedantic rules to prevent ruffled executive feathers. At the beginning of 1938, Jack Drescher wrote a memo to other D'Arcy men specifying thirty-five different commandments for Coca-Cola advertising. Among the charges were:

- Never split the trade mark "Coca-Cola" in two lines.
- The phrase "trade mark registered" must always appear in the tail of the first "C" even though it is illegible.
- When the cooler is shown *open*, the *righthand* side which shows the bottle opener should be opened if possible.
- The trade mark must never be obliterated so that it is not perfectly legible.
- The circular sign should carry the phrase "Delicious and Refreshing."
- On oil paintings or color photographs be inclined to show a brunette rather than a blond girl if one girl is in the picture.
- Adolescent girls or young women should be the wholesome type; not sophisticated looking.

---

* A greenhorn Coca-Cola rep's first "crown count" often commenced as a nasty practical joke. His supervisor handed him the bag of used bottle caps, telling him to spread them out on his motel bed, where assorted roaches and silverfish hiding in the caps darted for cover. The sidewalk was a more appropriate place for crown counts.

- Never refer to Coca-Cola as "it."
- Never use Coca-Cola in a personal sense—such as, "Coca-Cola invites you to lunch."
- Never show or imply that Coca-Cola should be drunk by very young children.

PROTECTING THE SACRED TRADEMARK

Most of those rules actually originated in the Coca-Cola Trademark Protection Department. By the late thirties, Company efforts to prevent substitution and infringement were standardized and sophisticated. The soft drink lawyers were keenly aware that they could quickly lose their trademark by letting it slip into common usage. That fate had already befallen aspirin, cellophane, and the escalator. References to "cola" drinks were anathema, as were calls for dope.

In 1938, fresh out of law school at the University of Georgia, Jasper Yeomans nervously sat through his interview for a job as a Coca-Cola investigator. "When you were a law student, how did you order a Coca-Cola at the local soda fountain?" Yeomans had not prepared for this particular question. "Dope with cherry, sir." His interviewer grimaced. "Jasper, that's the last time that you will call Coca-Cola 'dope.' Also, Coca-Cola is a product that cannot be improved upon; therefore, it needs no additives." That night, when Yeomans' girlfriend asked how the interview had gone, he answered, "You can't have any more dope with lime."

Yeomans was one of a cadre of "investigators" kept busy checking out substitution rumors. The Coca-Cola spies, mostly young lawyers trying to save money to begin a practice, were given strict orders to remain anonymous. Entering a suspect soda fountain, a hot water bottle hidden in his trench coat, the agent would order a Coca-Cola, then surreptitiously pour a sample for later analysis. Immediately after a foray, he would write detailed notes with time, place, and description of the soda jerk. The samples, sealed in small vials with hot wax, were shipped for lab analysis. "We used to call it the Gumshoe Department," one veteran Company man recalled. "Those guys were the closest thing to the FBI you ever saw."

If the fountain was indeed serving fake Coca-Cola, it received a warning letter. If two subsequent samples revealed continued substitution, *two* agents were sent at the same time—one as a witness for the impending lawsuit. Few such suits ever reached the bench, since most offenders chose to settle out of court. In the case of the minority that did go to trial, Coca-Cola never lost, but the Company sought no monetary damages, only the judge's orders that such derelict behavior cease forthwith.

WOODRUFF'S QUIET MANEUVERS

Robert Woodruff himself remained in the background, constantly maneuvering to outwit the bottlers, the government, and the competition. Woodruff bought back the parent bottling organizations one by one.* He had purchased the weak New England

---

* The parent bottlers traded their stock for Coca-Cola shares, which left Whitehead's widow, Lettie Pate Evans, with so much Coca-Cola stock that Woodruff named her to the board, making her one of the few women in the 1930s to have such a seat of power.

organization when he first took the helm in 1923. Ten years later, he absorbed the Southeastern region, followed by Western in 1935. In 1940, he purchased the Texas territory known as the 1903 Company. And, in 1942, Woodruff nearly achieved his goal of acquiring the last two parent bottlers. By that time, Arthur Pratt owned the Pacific Coast, which he had purchased from George Hunter, who still ran the original Thomas Company. Pratt sold, but Hunter backed out of the deal at the last minute, remaining loyal to his Uncle Ben's memory. As the last parent bottler, the Thomas Company continued to irritate Woodruff for another thirty years.

With Coca-Cola's continued growth came predictable attention from the tax man. In 1933, Georgia governor Eugene Talmadge announced his intention of enforcing an old tax law on intangibles. This "ad valorum" tax on stocks and bonds appeared an easy way to raise desperately needed money at the Depression's nadir. Because of the county unit voting system, poor rural areas dominated Georgia politics, and the soak-the-rich tax was passed with an even higher rate for all "foreign" corporations—firms like Coca-Cola that were technically incorporated out of state—taxing them on *all* their profits, even if they were made outside of Georgia.

Woodruff warned the governor that he would move the firm rather than submit to the tax. Each believed the other was bluffing, until Coca-Cola made good on its threat by reincorporating on January 1, 1934, as a holding company. The timing was so tight that the Coca-Cola staff finished packing and fled the tax assessor just before midnight on New Year's Eve, setting up administrative headquarters in Wilmington. While the syrup was still manufactured in Atlanta, Woodruff and his administrative staff stayed in Delaware for a decade, until the Georgia laws were amended. Harold Hirsch, however, refused to budge from Atlanta. As a result, in 1935 John Sibley replaced him as the Company's general counsel. Though Hirsch remained an important legal adviser, his domination of Coca-Cola policy was effectively ended. He died five years later.

How Woodruff maneuvered the reversal of the ad valorum tax is a telling example of his patient, unrelenting strategy. While the Boss took care to avoid any illegal activity, he used every other means of influence and persuasion at his disposal. In this case, he assigned Atlanta lawyer Hughes Spalding the task of securing a constitutional amendment to remove the ad valorum tax.* In 1937, Spalding hired journalist Frank Lawson to crank out two weekly columns arguing against a pending Georgia soft drink tax. One of these, aimed at the rural farmer, copied Tom Watson's hysterical, inflammatory style, utilizing boldface, italics, multiple exclamation points, and every conceivable propaganda tactic. The other, far less strident in tone, offered a more balanced, editorial tone. Both were printed in almost a hundred rural Georgia papers eager for filler. Copies were also sent to influential businessmen and members of the General Assembly.

As a result, the soft drink tax was voted down in December of 1937. In the early 1940s, Georgia governor Ellis Arnall asked the legislature to grant soft drink companies

---

* Hughes Spalding, the founder's son, was a partner at King & Spalding. A tight Atlanta network evolved in which King & Spalding, the Trust Company of Georgia, Emory University, and The Coca-Cola Company were virtually one vast concern.

special tax treatment, pending the passage of a constitutional amendment permitting foreign corporations exemption from the intangibles tax. By unanimous vote, it was passed. "What's good for Coke," the governor asserted, "is good for Georgia."

Another result of Woodruff's repeated tax tangles was his 1939 decision to give the Coca-Cola presidency to Arthur Acklin, the former IRS man. Acklin wasn't eager to take the job, particularly since Woodruff clearly had no intention of relinquishing any of his control, which he would exercise as chairman of the executive committee. That way, Woodruff could remain out of the public eye, which was how he liked it, letting the bureaucrat handle routine administration. Besides, Woodruff, peering over the horizon as usual, probably suspected that the United States would eventually enter World War II, and Acklin's governmental contacts would be essential.

As president himself, Woodruff had moved swiftly and secretly to assure a steady flow of Coca-Cola's most controversial ingredient. The U.S. legislature had passed a bill in 1927 to prohibit the importation of coca leaves for all but medicinal purposes. That did not necessarily incommode Coca-Cola, since the Company could take the decocainized leaf after the cocaine had been extracted. The trouble was that Coca-Cola consumption mandated more leaf than the doctors needed for cocaine. "Mr. Woodruff has been phoning us two or three times a day about what progress is being made on No. 5 [the coca and kola extract]," Harrison Jones wrote late in 1929 to Harold Hirsch. By 1930, Coca-Cola was using two hundred thousand pounds of coca leaf annually. That year, Woodruff prevailed upon New Jersey Republican Senator Walter Edge, a fellow member of the Norias Club (a Florida plantation owned by Walter Teagle), to intervene with the Hoover administration, which agreed to allow unlimited coca leaf importation for Coca-Cola, as long as the resultant cocaine was destroyed. With help from Georgia's U.S. Senator Walter George and others, both houses quickly passed the exemption legislation.

In the early 1930s, however, the United States was considering joining the Geneva Convention, which required the importation of coca leaves *only* for medicinal and scientific purposes. In addition, Harry J. Anslinger, the head of the new Federal Bureau of Narcotics, was a militant antidrug chief who was suspicious of Merchandise No. 5. The situation was too uncertain to let it rest with politicians. Robert Woodruff secretly flew to Lima, Peru, where he made arrangements to restart the plant to decocainize the leaves. The facility was ready to go by the fall of 1937, although it never proved necessary.

Woodruff had another reason, related to his overseas operation, for concern over the coca situation. In 1930, he had formed The Coca-Cola Export Corporation to replace his Foreign Department. Throughout the following decade, Coca-Cola's already established overseas outpost gradually grew, while new countries were added—small islands like Curaçao, Java, Trinidad, and Jamaica as well as major territories such as England, Scotland, Ireland, Norway, Denmark, Germany, Hong Kong, Peru, Bolivia, Chile, Switzerland, Austria, Australia, New Zealand, and South Africa. As sales increased abroad, Woodruff decided to build plants worldwide to manufacture concentrate. That way, only the secret flavoring ingredient, 7X, and Merchandise No. 5 would have to be exported. In 1935, with logic only a government bureaucrat could comprehend, the Bureau of Narcotics ruled it illegal to *export* No. 5, even though it was perfectly all right to *import* the whole coca leaves and to decocainize them under direct governmental supervision. Through delicate lobbying (including discreet monetary support for antinarcotics organizations), the Company maneuvered a reversal in 1937. Otherwise, Woodruff's Peruvian facility would have become indispensable.

In 1932, Woodruff was searching for someone with connections to help with the importation of coca leaves, negotiate with Washington officials, and advise him on the most appropriate (and useful) targets for Coca-Cola philanthropy. He found Ralph Hayes. Courteous, resourceful, and infinitely tactful, Hayes, a former aide to Secretary of War Newton Baker, was regarded as one of the few men in Washington who could keep a secret. After Baker's retirement, the accomplished young man headed the New York Community Trust, one of the first nonprofit foundations, and, by cultivating the right people, he built its coffers to over $175 million before retiring in 1967.

When Woodruff approached Hayes in 1932, the lonely, urbane bachelor was immediately attracted to the charismatic Coca-Cola boss, who replaced Newton Baker as his surrogate father. Hayes and Woodruff were an odd couple. While the Boss was taciturn and almost illiterate, Hayes was a voracious reader who wrote long, witty, insightful letters replete with Shakespearean quotations. He loved to give after-dinner speeches and enjoyed attending all of the parties that Woodruff shunned. For the next thirty-five years, Hayes would work behind the scenes as Woodruff's diplomat, lobbyist, and occasional spokesperson and speechwriter.

For decades, Hayes would bestow his obsequious charms on Harry Anslinger, the long-time commissioner of the Bureau of Narcotics. On Coca-Cola Company stationery identifying him as vice president, Hayes wrote in 1937, "I want you to know how deeply we appreciate the cooperativeness that has marked your personal attitude in this matter," after Anslinger authorized the legal export of Merchandise No. 5. "With this question now behind us, let me assure you again that our purpose, as always, will be to support every project looking to the enhancement of the prestige of the Bureau that has been so well developed under your distinguished leadership."

In return for Coca-Cola's support, Anslinger sent Hayes information about coca farmers in Latin America, along with maps of Peruvian cocaine factories, and alerted him to media inquiries and requests from potential competitors who wanted access to decocainized flavoring. Through this cozy relationship with a U.S. governmental agency, Coca-Cola maintained a steady monopoly on legally imported coca leaves.*

STUBBS AND FARLEY HIT THE ROAD

Hayes could cope with the American regulators, but fighting the same battles in every nation around the world caused massive headaches by the late thirties. The Cubans impounded a major caffeine importation, while the German health authorities protested the coca leaf content. Mexican officials demanded the formula before allowing

---

* Coke supported Anslinger during negotiations that culminated in the 1961 United Nations Single Convention on Narcotic Drugs, which made cocaine illegal worldwide but contained a provision specifically allowing Coca-Cola to use coca leaves. "The smooth and economical operation of our process demands an ample and constant supply of Coca," wrote the head of Maywood Chemical Works to Anslinger in 1959, "and I am happy to note that you realize the importance of liberal stocks of Coca for medicinal needs and for our special purpose."

the concentrate into the country. In Peru, the Coca-Soda people protested an American company attempting to monopolize the word "Coca" when the leaves themselves were actually Peruvian. The list of foreign woes appeared endless.

To help combat them, The Coca-Cola Export Corporation retained Stephen P. Ladas, a Greek native specializing in foreign patents and trademarks in New York. For the next twenty-five years, Ladas, in conjunction with Coca-Cola's legal counsel, masterminded worldwide strategy. In 1940, Coca-Cola lobbyist Ben Oehlert, who, along with Ralph Hayes, would surface repeatedly in the next three decades wherever quiet pressure and diplomacy were necessary, suggested the firm find a seasoned lawyer to travel for the Company, putting out fires where necessary. As a result, Coca-Cola hired Roy Stubbs, a small-town Georgia country lawyer.

For the next fifteen years, Stubbs crisscrossed the globe for Coca-Cola. "I became a sort of legal journeyman," he wrote, "from one trouble spot to another in Latin America, Australia, Europe and the Middle East." Already fifty-five when he started his new career, Stubbs proved to be an invaluable employee who recorded his sharp observations and research in an impressive series of bound "compilations," one for each country.

It took Stubbs a year to guide Coca-Cola's registration through the Mexican government without revealing the formula, during which time he taught himself Spanish. He then embarked on a whirlwind tour of Latin America, where he made careful observations of potential markets and interviewed local patent lawyers, seeking competent and politically well-connected retainers.

Stubbs found that he had to adapt himself to the lethargic pace of Latin life, where the lawyers customarily strolled into their offices around eleven, departed soon for long lunches at home, worked a desultory hour or two, then left for the day. Though frustrated, Stubbs, like many of Woodruff's Georgia emissaries, was remarkably sensitive to other cultures. "It takes an interminable time to get things started here," Stubbs wrote to a Coca-Cola lawyer in 1941. "Interminable red tape and delay—delay—about matters that would be wound up in our country in twenty minutes. . . . You have to catch [someone] in the right frame of mind, and catch him at the right place and at the right time, and rub him the right way—and above everything else—take your time. They have no appreciation of our notion of getting it done. And don't think anybody can change it."

Americans, Stubbs recognized, were often perceived by foreigners as arrogant and obnoxious—for good reason. "An American generally rears back on his hind legs and skids along on his ignorance," he wrote, "thinking all the time what a smart fellow he is." Stubbs did not make that mistake, and he soon came to have genuine respect for his Latin American colleagues, who valued tradition, culture, and style, finding time for "the protocol of amenities."

At the same time Stubbs was combing Latin America for legal talent, James Aloysius Farley was making *his* first goodwill trip for Coca-Cola through the same territory. "Big Jim" Farley, the imposing postmaster general who had masterminded Franklin D. Roosevelt's brilliant 1932 campaign, publicly split with FDR when the President ran in 1940 for a third term. Smelling opportunity, Robert Woodruff hired Farley as the chairman of the board of The Coca-Cola Export Corporation, a position created for the occasion, and promptly dispatched him to Latin America, where he was received as a visiting dignitary rather than a Coca-Cola executive. His daily itinerary made the pages of the *New York Times*. For the next thirty-five years, Farley, friend of every subsequent president, would represent Coca-Cola's interests around the world.

DEAR FDA

While Stubbs and Farley combated health issues in foreign countries, similar problems cropped up in the United States with a resurgent consumer movement. "The tide has turned against us," W. C. D'Arcy gloomily told his fellow ad men in 1934. The thirties and the New Deal also brought criticism of big business opportunism. The authors of *Partners in Plunder*, a 1935 book whose subtitle warned against "business dictatorship," heaped abuse on Coca-Cola, pointing out that the ingredients of the nickel drink cost a bit over one-half cent.

Members of the harassed FDA Food Control Division had to answer quite an array of letters in the FDR years. School officials and concerned parents asked whether the drink harmed children, who quaffed it with "fanatical zeal." An elderly woman inquired in a shaky hand whether Coca-Cola contained narcotics, since it increased the irritability of her grandson, a divinity school student with "a most Hypersensitive Nervous system." A Mormon wrote from Salt Lake City urging that Coca-Cola be banned and, incidentally, wondering whether FDA officials might consider a course in "the Word of Wisdom." Several writers wanted to know whether Coca-Cola was made with guano, a question that was not quite as wacky as it sounds, since caffeine could be synthesized from bird or bat dung. Others inquired about the effect of taking Coca-Cola with aspirin, which was persistently rumored to create a "high" or act as an aphrodisiac. Among the complaints about foreign ingredients was one from a North Carolina woman who found a large spider in her drink. "I have had a Poison Stomach every since," she wrote. In the end, however, one letter stated the case more accurately than any of the others: "Everybody says, 'don't drink it,' but I notice everyone does just the same. I like it."

While Coca-Cola officials had always been overly cordial to the FDA, in 1939 they became downright obsequious. The year before, during a New Deal wave of consumer consciousness, the Congress had passed a tougher Food, Drug and Cosmetic Act that required that all foods and beverages list ingredients on the label, throwing the entire soft drink industry into an uproar. Coca-Cola was particularly averse to the idea of labeling, since it would mean identifying its caffeine content, a subject tabooed by Robert Woodruff.

After a friendly visit from Ralph Hayes and Ben Oehlert failed to sway Dr. Dunbar of the FDA, the Company rallied its bottlers, who formed a well-organized local lobby. Letters poured in to the FDA from legislators and state health officials requesting that soft drinks be exempted from the new labeling requirements. In November, nine members of the American Bottlers of Carbonated Beverages (ABCB), including Harrison Jones, met with FDA officials, complaining that enforcement of the law would cost their industry some $80 million just in bottle stock replacement.

Predictably, Harrison Jones dominated the meeting. He claimed that the labeling requirement would lead to increased unfair competition and fraud, since an imitation cola could legitimately claim to have the same basic listed ingredients. Warming to his subject, Jones explained that the contour Coca-Cola bottle was practically a sacred object and must remain unchanged—and unlabeled. "It is grasped 18 million times a day," he intoned dramatically. "Even a blind man can recognize a Coca-Cola bottle."

The FDA caved in, granting a temporary exemption from labeling to allow the soft drink industry time to arrive at a suitable "standard of identity." Once such a standard was in place—specifying allowable amounts of carbonation, caffeine, acid, and sugar—labels would be unnecessary, since consumers could refer to the regulations. Loath to submit to such an iron-clad standard, the industry managed to stretch the "temporary" exemption, at first using the advent of World War II as an excuse. For years, though consumers continued to complain to the FDA about the unspecified caffeine content of Coca-Cola, they failed to get a satisfactory response. When a standard of identity was finally established in 1966, the public saw no difference, since Coca-Cola remained unlabeled.

THE RESURRECTION OF PEPSI

Bureaucratic tangles weren't the main problem Coca-Cola faced during the Depression, however. Surviving several near deaths, Pepsi-Cola emerged for the first time as a serious competitor during the 1930s. Coca-Cola, the undisputed king of soft drinks, suddenly found itself coping with an aggressive young contender. Pepsi's roots went back almost as far as Coca-Cola's, to 1894, when Caleb Bradham, a North Carolina pharmacist, developed a variant cola drink with pepsin, selling it as a tonic to relieve dyspepsia. Known merely as "Brad's Drink," its popularity grew until Bradham renamed it Pepsi-Cola in 1898. By World War I, the drink had achieved modest success, with franchised bottlers in some twenty-five states. Unfortunately, Bradham was caught in the same wildly swinging sugar market that trapped Coca-Cola. In 1920, when the price spiraled over twenty cents a pound, Bradham bought heavily. When the bottom fell out of the market, his business went bankrupt.

In 1922, Bradham tried to sell Pepsi to The Coca-Cola Company, but the Woodruff Syndicate wasn't interested in the ailing soft drink. A Wall Street speculator named Roy Megargel bought Pepsi from Bradham in 1923, only to flounder two years later. Still hoping for some return on his investment, Megargel reorganized the company and limped through until 1931, when only two bottlers remained. On the edge of a second bankruptcy, he offered Pepsi to Coca-Cola. For the second time, the Company refused to buy the nearly defunct competitor.

At this point, there is little doubt that Pepsi would have gone the way of most Coca-Cola imitators if it hadn't been for Charles Guth's temper. Guth, a New Yorker long known as the "stormy petrel" of the candy business, had taken over the Loft chain of candy stores in 1929, purchasing the Happiness and Mirror stores the following year. Through the three chains' soda fountains, Guth sold quite a bit of Coca-Cola—enough, he thought, so that he should receive a bulk discount. The Company thought otherwise. Infuriated with Coca-Cola's inflexibility, Guth called Atlanta one Friday in 1931 and left a message with a secretary. "We are not going to buy through any jobber. We are going to buy direct or not at all. Unless I hear from Mr. Judkins [in charge of fountain sales] before this evening, I will issue orders that not another drop of Coca-Cola will be served in any of the Loft stores. And once out, it will stay out." He repeated himself to make sure she wrote every word.

In the meantime, Guth swung a deal with Megargel in which he maneuvered Pepsi's third bankruptcy in return for a chunk of stock in the "new" company, which Guth would buy out of receivership. Megargel was also to receive a royalty of two and a half cents per gallon for six years. In July of 1931, the new Pepsi-Cola Company was born. Guth's chemist dropped the pepsin and tinkered with the formula to duplicate Coca-Cola as closely as possible. Guth then ordered that all of his soda fountains serve only Pepsi-Cola, which he proclaimed to be "the best 5¢ drink in America. It is a real bracer." The wily Guth was perfectly aware that Coca-Cola would be trying to prove substitution; in October, he advised his employees in writing, "Under no circumstances is Pepsi-Cola to be offered for Coca-Cola or compared with it," and offered $10,000 to anyone who found one of his outlets substituting Pepsi for another soft drink.

Coca-Cola's diligent investigators soon descended on Loft stores and found at least some employees who gave them a Pepsi in response to a call for Coca-Cola. In the spring of 1932, Coca-Cola sued. At the same time, Harrison Jones wrote to Guth claiming $30,000 as Coca-Cola's prize for having proved substitution in Loft, Happiness, and Mirror stores. Guth responded with a barrage of seven countersuits. Four, filed individually by Pepsi-Cola and the three candy stores, claimed that Coca-Cola had interfered with sales and harassed their staff. The other three suits were for libel, claiming that the Harrison Jones letter was "defamatory."

Guth soon sent The Coca-Cola Company a defamatory letter of his own. In July of 1932, he mailed a cartoon to the Company's Atlanta headquarters, depicting a Pepsi bottle overturning a cart containing "Coke" and "Dope" apples, which were being eaten by "Coke" pigs. Underneath, Guth had written: "Pepsi-Cola will soon be the largest selling 5¢ drink in your city both in bottles and at the soda fountain." While Coca-Cola executives must have been outraged at Guth's gall, they had no evidence that he posed a serious threat in Atlanta or anywhere else. Pepsi's sales were dismal, even with a guaranteed outlet at the candy stores. When Guth approached Coca-Cola the following year offering to sell Pepsi for $50,000, the soft drink behemoth refused for the third and final time.

Desperate now, Guth took an unexpected tack: he decided he had nothing to lose by promoting a twelve-ounce bottled drink for the same nickel Coca-Cola got for its six-and-a-half ounce container. In 1934, he test-marketed the oversized drink in Baltimore, putting it up in used beer bottles. It immediately scored in blue-collar neighborhoods where a Depression-era nickel buying twice the drink made Pepsi the obvious choice, regardless of Coca-Cola's ubiquitous advertising. Soon, Pepsi was selling nationwide in a motley assortment of recycled beer bottles, and Guth was turning a profit, with net earnings in 1934 of $90,000 on gross sales of $450,000. The additional cost of the actual twelve-ounce drink was minimal, since most of the expense involved bottling machinery, bottles, distribution, and advertising. By 1935, Guth realized that there was more future in Pepsi than in Loft, and he resigned from Loft to devote full-time to the Pepsi-Cola Company, where his field was clear, since Megargel had died two years earlier.

The Loft directors, led by new president James W. Carkner, realized they were left holding an almost bankrupt candy bag and decided to sue Guth for using Loft funds and personnel to develop the soft drink. They knew, however, that without a quick infusion of capital, they might well lose a proxy fight with Guth at their 1936 meeting. Phoenix Securities Corporation, which specialized in saving troubled companies, jumped in with the necessary funds at the last minute. Phoenix head Walter Mack, who had an unerring way of diagnosing a firm's critical problem, usually assumed management responsibilities.* In Loft's case, he decided that going after the upscale market was a mistake, redirecting sales efforts at five-cent candy. He knew that the real future of the company, however, lay in winning the court case with Guth. As Loft struggled, Phoenix continued to lend the candy firm money. In September of 1938, the case was decided almost completely in Loft's favor. Guth had to turn over his 91 percent share of Pepsi.

WALTER MACK INHERITS WORLDWIDE LITIGATION

For six uncomfortable months, as the case remained on appeal, Walter Mack served as the president of Pepsi while Guth, as general manager, made Mack's life as unpleasant as possible, locking him out of the men's room and sticking him in a cubbyhole office above the boiler room. Finally, in April of 1939, Guth lost his appeal and Mack assumed full charge of the soft drink's future. He found himself knee-deep in litigation with The Coca-Cola Company in twenty-four countries, the result of John Sibley's master strategy.

When Sibley officially replaced Harold Hirsch as general counsel in 1935, he conducted an intensive, year-long study and decided that Coca-Cola was in jeopardy from "an organized and insidious effort . . . to seriously impair or ultimately destroy this company's trade-mark." Half of the logo, he said, was in peril. "Cola" was well on its way toward becoming a generic part of the language. In the past, Hirsch had attacked only those imitators that most closely resembled Coca-Cola—usually, like Chero-Cola, beginning with "C" and mimicking the familiar script. Sibley felt that such a lax attitude was a huge and perhaps fatal error. He believed in "the ultimate . . . assertion" that "Coca-Cola" was "an aggregate word consisting of two inseparable parts, and that each part is so linked and riveted to the other part in the public mind that when one is used the other is drawn to it." In other words, said Sibley, *all* other soft drinks using the word "Cola" should be regarded as infringers. He was particularly alarmed that a judge had ruled Roxa-Cola a valid trade-name in 1930. Also, Nehi had recently come out with the twelve-ounce Royal Crown Cola and was doing very

---

* While Walter Mack was the titular head of Phoenix Securities, financier Wallace Groves, known as the "silent man of Wall Street," owned most of it. Ironically, Groves was a *protégé* of Ernest Woodruff, who had dated Groves' mother. In October 1938, Groves wrote Woodruff that he planned to take a "very active interest in the Pepsi-Cola Company," and in December 1939 he wrote again, hoping to see Woodruff, "provided we will not discuss any business, that is Pepsi-Cola/Coca-Cola." By that time, Groves was under indictment for mail fraud, for which he was convicted and briefly imprisoned in 1942. He then moved to the Bahamas, where he developed Freeport as a major resort and gambling area.

well with it. As his final recommendation, Sibley, regarding it as too dangerous to sue Pepsi in the U.S., proposed aggressive litigation in foreign countries while instituting domestic suits against RC Cola and "the most flagrant infringers" with similar names such as Cleo-Cola.

In 1938, The Coca-Cola Company simultaneously brought suit against Pepsi all over the world, with the most conspicuous case right across the border in Canada. In July, the Canadian Exchequer Court found in favor of Coca-Cola. Still in charge at that point, the embattled Guth immediately appealed and launched a two-pronged counterattack in the United States. In a bold stab at the heart, Guth filed an interference suit in the Patent Office, claiming that "coca" and "cola" were descriptive terms and could not be trademarked. At the same time, he sued in Queens, New York (Pepsi headquarters), charging that Coca-Cola had resorted to "illegal and fraudulent" methods, including intimidations, threats, and "trap orders" to deter Pepsi sales in New York City and elsewhere.

Goaded into action, Sibley took the Queens bait and countersued Pepsi for trademark infringement. The circle of worldwide litigation was complete. With so many lawsuits hanging fire, it is little wonder that one of Sibley's colleagues, considering the coming year, wrote that "1939 may well be the most critical year to date in the history of the Legal Department." Sparing no expense, Sibley sought the best trademark lawyers in the country, including Edward S. Rogers and Harry D. Nims, to defend the sacred name of Coca-Cola. He also hired Judge Hugh Morris, who had ruled in the Bottler Case and had now returned to private practice. Such was the volatile legal situation that Walter Mack inherited.

Described by a contemporary journalist as "a long-limbed, sad-eyed man who in looks, zeal, and tenacity bears a . . . resemblance to a bloodhound," Mack immediately set about mastering the far-flung court cases, as well as plotting the further sales of his soft drink. He forced himself to attend the pretrial hearings every day at the Queens courthouse when they started in 1941. "Every morning," he remembered, "a big Coca-Cola truck would pull up in front of the courthouse and all these Coca-Cola men in livery would march in carrying volumes of books showing all the court cases they had won. It seemed overwhelming."

One morning, Mack received a phone call from Mrs. Herman Smith, a Coca-Cola imitator widow. She wanted to commiserate. "Coca-Cola is going to put you out of business. . . . My husband thought he was right too, but they still put him out of business. And I still have a photograph of the check they gave him." His bloodhound pulse quickening, Mack asked if he could borrow the picture, which indicated that Coca-Cola had bribed its way to victory to the tune of $35,000. Confronted with this evidence in court, Coca-Cola's lawyers hastily requested a three-day recess.

The next day, Robert Woodruff phoned Mack, asking him to lunch at Woodruff's apartment in the Waldorf Towers. The two had become friendly acquaintances in 1934, before Mack had ever heard of Pepsi, when they happened to share the same transatlantic ocean liner. Now, after a few drinks, the Coca-Cola magnate said, "You know, Walter, I've been thinking. This lawsuit between us isn't doing anybody any good. . . . Don't you think we ought to settle it?" On a piece of Waldorf stationery, Mack penned an agreement stipulating that Coca-Cola would henceforth agree to acknowledge Pepsi's trademark in the United States, and Woodruff signed it. When

Sibley found that Woodruff had agreed to settle, he felt betrayed and attempted to quit the Queens case. Woodruff refused to hear of it. At the end of 1941, Sibley wrote a bitter memo outlining his "fundamental disagreement" with Woodruff. "The responsibility of the position I occupy is heavy and the work is very taxing. Under the existing situation, I am unwilling to continue except on a temporary basis." In 1943, he finally relinquished his position as general counsel to Pope Brock, a fellow King & Spalding lawyer, but Sibley remained concerned with Coca-Cola matters for the rest of his life.

Sibley was even more unhappy when the British Privy Council ruled in favor of Pepsi-Cola in March of 1942 (the Canadian trademark case had ended there after the Canadian Supreme Court reversed the Exchequer's ruling of 1939). The poor Coca-Cola lawyer must have been nearly suicidal two months later, when Woodruff and Mack settled *all* litigation over the trademark forever. Coca-Cola promised never to assail Pepsi's trademark rights again, dropping suits worldwide. Coca-Cola had irrevocably lost the exclusive right to "cola."* Afraid of this possibility, Sibley had decided in 1941 to protect the *first* part of the name. In the Koke Case decision, Oliver Wendell Holmes had virtually ruled that "Coke" belonged to the Company. Now, in a deliberate campaign, Coca-Cola reversed its long-held policy and actually encouraged the use of the nickname "Coke," intending to patent that trademark after establishing use.

While the court battles raged, Walter Mack arranged for the Pepsi-Cola Company to swallow Loft. In order to spread Pepsi bottling franchises, he hit upon an ingenious system. "In my travels around the country," he wrote, "I found that there was always a wealthy bottler in each area, and that was the Coca-Cola bottler. . . . So I went out and found the best of the little bottlers and tried to seduce them into taking Pepsi-Cola." Mack bought a huge quantity of secondhand beer bottles and sold them to franchise owners for a quarter cent per bottle. Filled with Pepsi, the bottles brought a two-cent deposit, providing instant start-up capital. Later, when his franchises were established, Mack designed standard bottles that cost four cents each but could be amortized over many refills. Baked onto the new bottles, the Pepsi logo was red, white, and blue, making blue the distinctive color in contrast to Coca-Cola's red and white.

With a minuscule advertising budget, Mack achieved maximum impact. While Coca-Cola had been permanently soured on skywriting by the Cuban fiasco of the twenties, Mack had no such reservations. He sent pilot Sid Pike up and down the Eastern Seaboard, starting in Florida in the winter and slowly moving north. With a patented mechanism, Pike scripted the Pepsi logo over city skies, prompting one cartoonist to draw Coca-Cola antiaircraft gunners trying to shoot the skywriter out of his Pepsi cloud.

Mack's real triumph, however, was the jingle. Two offbeat writers named Alan Bradley Kent and Austen Herbert Croom Johnson played a phonograph record for Mack one day in 1939. To the tune of "Do Ye Ken John Peel," they had written lilting doggerel. "Pepsi-Cola hits the spot," Mack heard, and began to tap his toes. "Twelve full ounces, that's a lot. / Twice as much for a nickel, too, / Pepsi-Cola is the drink for you." Mack liked the jingle so much that he ordered his advertising agency to

---

* As a result of the settlement, Coca-Cola cases around the world were reassessed, and only those with a "phonetic similarity" to Coca-Cola were continued.

cut the surrounding hard-sell verbiage and run it alone as a thirty-second radio spot. Although no major radio station would accept his jingle—too short in an era when ads lasted at least five minutes—Mack found small New Jersey stations that needed money badly enough to run anything. The jingle, the first of its kind, was an immediate hit. Soon the big stations were begging for it. When Mack pressed an orchestrated version, it sold a hundred thousand copies. The music was adapted as a march, waltz, rumba, and country song, becoming "the scourge of the continent," according to one disgusted commentator. In 1941, the jingle played nearly three hundred thousand times over the airwaves. Mack had started a trend.

THE DIE IS CAST

While Robert Woodruff constantly warned against becoming too rigid to shift with the times, he refused to abandon his single-size drink in the face of the twelve-ounce colas. In public, Harrison Jones loudly defended this official viewpoint, but in private, he urgently confronted Woodruff with the need to act. "Every day's delay . . . aggravates the situation and makes the fort harder to hold," he wrote in an August 1941 seven-page memo reviewing the situation. Although Coca-Cola retained 46 percent of the entire soft drink market, other colas, which he designated "X drinks,"* had climbed to 14 percent, while ginger ale, grape, orange, root beer, and the rest had the last 40 percent. "The bed has been erected by us," Jones said, "and the bed-bugs just crawl in." The solution, according to Jones, was to give the bottlers "a definite revelation . . . of the true picture," which "should have been done long ago instead of now, and it is not being done now." He recommended a daring diversification in which the Company and the bottlers would set up a separate corporation to produce a twelve-ounce cola, under a completely different trade name, and to experiment with other flavors as well. Ultimately, Jones hoped, the competition would be "snuffed out or eliminated."

Woodruff ignored the warning. Instead, he tried in vain to bribe Walter Mack away from Pepsi by offering him the White Motors presidency at $250,000 a year. But it was too late to buy off Pepsi, setting the pattern for what Mack termed "a fundamental American struggle." The competition ultimately benefited Coke, however, as one prophetic journalist observed in 1938: "Pepsi, if it survives the courts, may prove to be a good thing for Coca-Cola; the latter's sales have surged ahead in the places where Pepsi's campaigns have been the hottest."

Pepsi posed as the brash upstart, willing to indulge in questionable taste in order to grab attention. As if to prove the point, Walter Mack attempted to buy the rights to *Popeye* so that he could replace that hero's magic spinach with magic Pepsi. Failing that, he created *Pepsi and Pete*, two cops who careened through adventures in a comic strip, always overcoming evil by drinking the right stuff at the last moment. Implicit

---

* Even as Harrison Jones issued a clarion call to face reality, he refused to designate Pepsi or Royal Crown by name, a practice common to Coca-Cola men for years. In a form of magical thinking, the Company men apparently thought on some level that if they didn't name Pepsi, it would go away and leave them alone.

in all Pepsi advertising was a competitive jab at Coca-Cola; otherwise, "twice as much" would mean nothing. Coke remained the measure of success.

As proof of the soft drink giant's central place in American culture, Coca-Cola was the first firm awarded a contract for the 1939 New York World's Fair, where the public could view a real bottling operation, a huge mural, and a color version of the film *Refreshment Through the Years*. The next year, a bottle of Coke was interred in a Georgia "crypt of civilization" to be exhumed (and presumably drunk) in the year 8113. Even a woman complaining about the drink's health effects to the FDA wrote that "'Coke' nowadays is synonimous with a 'Date.'" When veteran editor William Allen White, the voice of middle America, was featured in *Life* on his seventieth birthday in 1938, he insisted on having his picture taken sipping a Coke at a soda fountain in Emporia, Kansas. "Coca-Cola," he wrote soon afterward, "is . . . a sublimated essence of all that America stands for, a decent thing honestly made, universally distributed, conscientiously improved with the years."

Coca-Cola men might display a sense of humor about other things, but never about their sacred drink. On the brink of World War II, Robert Woodruff addressed his own troops just before Pearl Harbor. "We have the greatest product in the world," he said. "I can never divorce myself, my affections, my life from Coca-Cola, and neither can any of the rest of you." He warned against complacency, reminding the men of Sapolio, once a household word as a cleaner and now forgotten. "Whom the gods would destroy they first make fat. . . . Never let it be said of our business, 'This is a Nice Highclass Old Business.'" The Boss called for "young, virile, ambitious men" to spread the Coca-Cola gospel.

Woodruff couldn't have known it at the time, but the Japanese were about to give his virile young men the chance for the Coca-Cola adventure of their lives.

~ 12 ~

The $4,000 Bottle: Coca-Cola Goes to War

> *Today was such a big day that I had to write and tell you about it. Everyone in the company got a Coca-Cola. That might not seem like much to you, but I wish you could see some of these guys who have been overseas for twenty months. They clutch their Coke to their chest, run to their tent and just look at it. No one has drunk theirs yet, for after you drink it, it's gone; so they don't know what to do.*
> —Private Dave Edwards, 1944, in a letter to his brother from Italy

By the time America entered World War II, Coca-Cola was over fifty years old, so well-entrenched in the nation's culture that a 1942 ad for the U.S. Rubber Company asserted that among "the homely fragments of daily life" American soldiers fought for were "the bottles of Coke they'll soon be sipping in the corner drug store." Outside the United States, however, was a different story. True, Woodruff had tried to spread the drink worldwide, but in most places it was quite *thinly* spread. While Coca-Cola had established a strong presence in Canada, Cuba, and Germany, it barely had a toe-hold elsewhere. The Japanese didn't realize that by bombing Pearl Harbor they were indirectly giving The Coca-Cola Company a worldwide boost that would ensure the soft drink company's unquestioned global dominance of the industry. It's unlikely that the Japanese were thinking about soft drinks at all, though four Hawaiian Coke coolers were martyred that day at Hickam Field. Nonetheless, the war would be a pivotal point for Coca-Cola, validating the wartime claims for the drink as "the Global High-Sign." Already sacred to Coke men, the fizzy drink would assume an almost religious significance to the American soldier as well.

ESSENTIAL MORALE-BUILDING FOR THE BOYS

Shortly after Pearl Harbor, Robert Woodruff issued an extraordinary order: "We will see that every man in uniform gets a bottle of Coca-Cola for five cents, wherever he is and whatever it costs our company." Woodruff's gesture was undoubtedly a genuine act of patriotism, but his shrewd business sense and eye for publicity also prompted his magnanimity. Certainly he was aware that young soldiers had an unquenchable thirst for beer and Coke. Well before Pearl Harbor, he had assigned George Downing (later to set up bottling plants in Europe behind the lines) to supply Coca-Cola to troops in the United States during war games. Late in that summer before Pearl Harbor, during sweltering Army maneuvers in Louisiana, Coca-Cola proved predictably popular. "One military unit came right into a small local bottling plant to get some Coke," Downing recalled. "Their supply was gone, so the soldiers literally bought the bottles off the line before they were capped." Requests for Coca-Cola from the military were urgent, even before America's entry into World War II, as demonstrated by rafts of letters in the Coca-Cola archives. In September of 1941, for instance, a base surgeon begged for adequate provisions, explaining that "I cannot conceive of any greater calamity than a loss of the base supply of Coke."*

After Pearl Harbor, the trickle of letters swelled to a deluge, pouring into Coca-Cola's mailroom in response to sugar rationing. In January of 1942, an exchange officer wrote to his local bottler:

> Very few people ever stopped to consider the great part Coca-Cola plays in the building and the maintenance of morale among military personnel. Frankly speaking, we would be at a loss to find as satisfying and as refreshing a beverage to replace Coca-Cola. Accordingly, we sincerely hope that your Company will be able to continue supplying us during this emergency. In our opinion, Coca-Cola could be classified as one of the essential morale-building products for the boys in the Service.

Ben Oehlert shifted into high gear as Coca-Cola's Washington lobbyist. Already sophisticated in weaving his way through the halls of Congress and the FDA, Oehlert now moved effortlessly through the political jungle, unctuously and persistently presenting the case for Coca-Cola. He urged the Company to sell its twenty-three thousand bags of stockpiled sugar to the military as a goodwill gesture that would put the Company in "a better psychological and public relations position." At the same time, Oehlert offered to "aid the policymaking" of the War Production Board's Sugar Section, helping it to "formulate the proper orders" in administering the available supply. He forwarded market surveys showing the flood of Coca-Cola drunk on military bases, following up with a hundred sample letters from Army and Navy units, USO branches, Red Cross chapters, and defense industries, all "stressing the importance to them of our product." Oehlert added that "there may be a thoughtless tendency . . . to regard the soft drink industry as being somewhat non-essential in a period such as this." Nothing could be further from the truth!

To prove it, Oehlert and the D'Arcy agency created a 1942 masterpiece of pseudo-science entitled "Importance of the Rest-Pause in Maximum War Effort." The first eight pages, simply quoting various authorities to show that factory workers and military men performed better if given periodic breaks, didn't mention Coca-Cola. Then the ninth page revealed a huge illustration of a tilted Coke bottle with a pointed text: "Men work better refreshed. Time rules the present as never before. A nation at war

---

* Shortly before Pearl Harbor, the U.S. Army contacted the Bureau of Narcotics to ask about research on chewing coca leaves or making coca tea. "I suppose the future will find each soldier chewing a wad of coca leaves as he repulses the attack of the invading hordes," joked a narcotics bureaucrat, but soldiers got Coca-Cola instead.

strains forward in productive effort in a new tempo. . . . In times like these Coca-Cola is doing a necessary job for workers."

As part of his "aid," Oehlert managed to get Coca-Cola executive Ed Forio appointed to the sugar rationing board; the Company granted the soft drink executive an extended leave so that he could serve his country's sweet tooth. Meanwhile, James Farley, new head of The Coca-Cola Export Corporation, engaged in his special variety of quiet back-room politicking, along with Washington tax lawyer Max Gardner, who was urged to render the bureaucrats "docile, receptive, tractable, malleable."*

All of the lobbying paid off. By the beginning of 1942, Coca-Cola was exempted from sugar rationing when sold to the military or retailers serving soldiers. Finally, in June, Brehon Somervell, the Army's quartermaster general, asked the head of the Sugar Board for an extension of the exemption, specifically naming Coca-Cola. The Army's attitude toward the soft drink had dramatically shifted since it banned Coca-Cola on its bases thirty-five years before. Harrison Jones, who had burst into creative obscenities when sugar rationing commenced, was ecstatic. While the rest of the soft drink industry suffered from an 80 percent quota (based on prewar figures), Coca-Cola readied for an all-out effort to send its sweet beverage fizzing down as many GI throats as possible. At its worst, U.S. sugar rationing dipped to 50 percent, but only domestic Coca-Cola bottlers unfortunate enough not to have any military base nearby were ever seriously affected.

COCA-COLA COLONELS

At first, the Company attempted to ship already-bottled Coca-Cola abroad. But, despite its privileged status, Coca-Cola ran afoul of military shipping priorities. In a 1942 NBC radio broadcast, Martin Agronsky criticized a massive Coke transport to Australia when there was a critical need for guns and planes. With logistics and the media against them, Company officials devised another plan, copying the Army's use of dehydrated food. Why not ship only Coca-Cola concentrate and bottle the stuff overseas? And where a bottling plant wasn't feasible, why not import portable soda fountains to the front lines?

The Company began experimenting with these ideas only a month or so after Pearl Harbor, sending Albert "Red" Davis to Reykjavik, Iceland, to bottle Coke for the air base under construction. Using sign language, Davis demonstrated the clunky mysteries of an antiquated Dixie unit, and the local bottler sold his first carbonated drinks to the military in May of 1942, the same month Agronsky's complaint aired on NBC. Nazi sympathizers and locals were initially skeptical of the American drink, since they resented the sexual exploits of the occupying GIs, but Coca-Cola quickly demonstrated its universal appeal. Previously unknown in Iceland, the drink achieved such

---

* At the same time, former Coca-Cola advertising director Price Gilbert joined the Office of War Information (OWI) along with a swarm of other ad men who were soon "happily painting the war in glowing terms," according to Henry Pringle, whose parting shot upon his departure from the OWI was a mock poster of a Coca-Cola bottle wrapped in the American flag, with the legend: "Step right up and get your four delicious freedoms. It's a refreshing war." Another jaded journalist inquired, "What do they think this war is—the cause that refreshes?"

popularity that the prime minister demanded that half of the sugar ration sweeten beverages for civilians, who agreed that Coke was "*Heilnaemt og Hressandi*" (delicious and refreshing).

Davis was the first of 248 Coca-Cola employees who followed the soldiers, serving them ten billion Cokes in the process, from the jungles of New Guinea to officers' clubs on the Riviera. During the war, sixty-four bottling plants were established on every continent except Antarctica—largely at government expense. The adventures of the overseas Coca-Cola men would become legendary within the Company, while the fruits of their labor would yield a postwar Coke marketing explosion.

In a remarkably cozy arrangement, the U.S. Army gave the Coca-Cola representatives the pseudo-military status of "technical observers," a designation invented during World War I for civilians needed in the war effort—those servicing military machinery, for instance. Charles Lindbergh for a time served as a technical observer during World War II for United Aircraft Corporation. Incredibly, it appears that technicians who installed Coca-Cola plants behind the front lines were deemed as vital as those who fixed tanks or airplanes. The Coke representatives wore Army uniforms with "T.O." as a shoulder patch. Each Coke man received military rank commensurate with his Company salary, leading some wags to nickname them "Coca-Cola Colonels."

Though the Coca-Cola Technical Observers were exempt from the draft, rarely were in any real physical danger, and often led soft lives compared with the common soldier, no one resented them or the profits they garnered from a captive market. Rather, the soldiers were grateful that The Coca-Cola Company cared enough to send representatives to bring them a taste of home in the midst of the hell of war. An anecdote related by T.O. Quint Adams illustrates how they were treated. North of Naples, Adams and an officer were stopped by a guard who demanded to see a Fifth Army pass, which they hadn't brought. The guard was insistent. The officer obediently backed up, telling Adams that the bottling plant would have to wait. "Why the hell didn't you say he was a Coca-Cola man?" the guard complained, stepping aside to let them proceed.

A GENERAL FONDNESS

It was not only common soldiers who liked Coca-Cola: generals seemed particularly fond of the drink. Patton reputedly regarded a cache of Coke as a necessity, making sure the T.O.s transported a bottling plant wherever he went, perhaps because of his well-known thirst for rum and Coke. He once suggested, not altogether facetiously, a way to end the war more quickly: "Hell, we ought to send the Coke in first, then we wouldn't have to fight the bastards." MacArthur autographed the first bottle of Coke produced in the Philippines after his famous return. General Wainwright, the hero of Bataan, combined three American symbols when photographed after the war at Yankee Stadium: baseball, a half-eaten hot dog, and an uplifted bottle of Coke.

General Omar Bradley suffered from a double weakness: ice cream and Coca-Cola. "Even in Britain, where the climate encourages the drinking of more warming beverages, the general keeps a case of Coca-Cola in his office," a journalist reported. Even Filipino General Carlos Romulo wrote "with trembling hands" of the important day during the Battle of the Philippines when he had a Coke. He added, apparently without a trace of irony: "That day I had seen men blown to shreds; I had seen white-faced nurses drag themselves from the bloody debris of a bombed hospital. All this paled and was forgotten before the miracle of a five-cent drink any American can buy at his corner store."

But the real Coca-Cola addict was Eisenhower, who would become a close personal friend and golfing buddy of Robert Woodruff after the war. "MILLIONS CHEER IKE AT PARADE HERE," a Washington, D.C., paper headlined its front page of June 19, 1945, while commenting on the hero's taste in beverages:

> After feasting copiously at the Statler luncheon yesterday, Gen. Eisenhower was asked if he wished anything else.
> "Could somebody get me a Coke?" he asked.
> After polishing off the soft drink, the General said he had one more request. Asked what he wanted, he answered:
> "Another Coke."

It is not surprising, then, that Eisenhower sent an urgent cablegram from North Africa on June 29, 1943, which threw the T.O. program into high gear:

> On early convoy request shipment three million bottled Coca-Cola (filled) and complete equipment for bottling, washing, capping same quantity twice monthly.
> Preference as to equipment is 10 separate machines for installation in different localities, each complete for bottling twenty thousand bottles per day. Also sufficient syrup and caps for 6 million refills. Syrup, caps and sixty thousand bottles monthly should be an automatic supply. Monthly shipment bottles is to cover estimated breakage and losses. Estimate ship tons initial shipment 5 thousand. Ship without displacing other military cargo. Data available here very meager as to these installations and operations. Request they be checked by fully qualified sources and this Headquarters advised promptly recommended installation to meet the two hundred thousand bottle daily demand and when same can be shipped.

Eisenhower's request that the plants arrive "without displacing other military cargo" was clearly intended to placate anyone who might object, though certainly no one was going to countermand the general. And so the man who years later was to warn the American public of the dangers of the "military-industrial complex" implemented an openly cooperative arrangement between the U.S. Army and The Coca-Cola Company.

Army Chief of Staff George C. Marshall quickly validated the Eisenhower telegram in an innocuously worded War Department order: "Articles of necessity and convenience will be made available to troops overseas in adequate quantities." Early in 1944, after Company lobbying for stronger language, Marshall issued Circular No. 51, specifically allowing commanders to requisition Coca-Cola plants by name, along with the Technical Observers to install and operate them.

RIDING THE RED BALL EXPRESS

Woodruff hurriedly dispatched T.O. Albert Thomforde to Africa by high-priority military air transport to satisfy Ike's troops. Thomforde arrived ahead of his supplies and encountered the same difficulties that most T.O.s would confront: antiquated native bottling plants, polluted water, and a frustrating relationship with the Army Exchange Service. Nonetheless, by Christmas of 1943, the first Coke was rolling off the line in Oran. Once Coke had established a beachhead, the Company quickly mobilized its bottling forces for every available front. Thomforde flew to Italy to commence bottling there, followed by other Observers shadowing the U.S. military up the Italian boot. From England, they crossed the Channel just after D-Day.* T.O. Paul Bacon rode in the first "red ball express" (an open Army jeep) that jounced into Paris after its liberation. As the Allied forces pushed the Germans back toward Berlin, the Coca-Cola men surged into Germany along with their bottling plants, refurbishing European mineral water operations and continuing to serve the troops their favorite beverage.

Meanwhile, T.O.s were also flooding into the Pacific theater, but because of the war's geography and the quickly shifting front, bottling was not nearly as feasible as in Africa or Europe. Consequently, thirsty Pacific troops drank cups of Coke dispensed from portable "jungle fountain units." In the wilds of New Guinea, black and white soldiers were at least temporarily integrated, drinking from the same Coke fountain, unlike the segregated soft drink spigots on American bases.

"THE TECHNICAL OBSERVERS ARE WINNING THE WAR"

By and large, the Technical Observers took their jobs seriously, attempting to produce an adequate supply of their drink under difficult circumstances. Some of their exploits were truly Herculean, such as John Talley's retrieval of a filler dropped into the Le-Havre harbor, or Fred Cooke's 1,300-mile trip "over the Hump" of the Himalayas to bring a bottling plant to China. The day-to-day life of the T.O. involved more prosaic battles with Rube Goldberg contraptions. "It will long be a mystery to me," wrote one Coke man of another, "how Bill Musselman keeps that hunk of junk he calls a bottling machine in continuous operation a full seventeen hours a day. Bailing wire seems to be his main support plus weld upon weld for practically every moving part."

Military personnel supplied most of those welds, as well as other repairs. The line between private industry and government forces was, to say the least, blurred during the war, so that T.O. Gene Braendle could write from New Guinea that "the

---

* Coke didn't actually hit the beaches with the boys, though shortly after the Normandy invasion, GI Mike Barry wrote a humorous letter to his sister about "the most important question in amphibious landings: Does the Coke machine go ashore in the first or second wave? I've told you before what a problem this is. If you send the Coke machine in with the first wave, future waves come pouring in without enough nickels. Obviously, getting change for a dime or a quarter on an enemy beach is quite difficult. On the other hand, if you hold the Coke machine up until the second wave, the men of the first wave wait on the beach for it to come in, instead of driving forward to attack the enemy."

one most important thing in our favor is the fact that everyone from the Base Commander down to the lowly private are vitally concerned in the Coke situation and go all out to help us all they possibly can." Another Observer happily remembered that "the first thing we did [at a new location] was make friends with either a port construction battalion or the Seabees. You could get anything done with those fellows. They would forge a new piece of machinery or do anything else." GIs also worked in bottling plants, presumably on Army rather than Coke pay. One T.O. bragged of his eighteen-hour work days, explaining that "both the Quartermaster and the Army Exchange Service were kind enough to furnish the night labor gang for this work. All of the Army personnel assigned to the plant have been very cooperative."

If they *hadn't* been cooperative, they would have been in deep trouble, according to war correspondent Howard Fast, who nearly died as a result of a pilot's fear of offending Coca-Cola. At first, Fast couldn't fathom why his transport plane landed at a remote Saudi Arabian Army outpost where the thermometer read 157 degrees Fahrenheit. They were there to pick up thousands of empty Coca-Cola bottles. When the overloaded C46 lumbered off the desert runway, it failed to gain altitude, barely clearing the sand dunes. The writer logically suggested jettisoning bottles. That, he was told, was impossible. "Guns they could dump, jeeps, ammo, even a howitzer . . . but Coca-Cola bottles? No way. Not if you wanted to keep your points and not become a PFC again." The pilot summarized the well-learned moral: "You don't fuck with Cola-Cola."

Prisoners of war were also assigned to work in Coke plants. The Coca-Cola men preferred diligent Germans and Japanese POWs to locals whose work ethic was not so strong. One Observer complained that French workers had "very little conception of what is meant by the words cleanliness and sanitation. They are not too much concerned whether they work or not, and when they work they are indifferent, to put it mildly, toward the kind of work they do." On the other hand, the German POWs "make very good labor and are easy to handle. When you show them what you want done, they go ahead and do it, and do it well."

Just as the soldier's life consisted of danger, fear of death, long periods of boredom, and occasional binges, the Coca-Cola T.O. led a roller-coaster existence, a mixture of harsh conditions and a life of ease. In the unpublished Company history of the period, James Kahn waxed poetic about the hard life of the T.O., who often suffered from poor, inadequate rations and uncomfortable sleeping arrangements. "They got malaria and frostbite and jungle rot," he wrote, "and came home yellow from the endless capsules of atabrine they took." Three of them, he concluded, never returned, "killed in plane crashes as they made their determined rounds."

While Kahn's account may be overdramatized, it is essentially true, as far as it goes. He neglected, however, to mention the soft side of the Coca-Cola men's overseas life. T.O.s reported game hunting, sitting around in officers' clubs drinking and playing poker, buying sailboats, and spending weekends in the Alps with Red Cross nurses. "You express solicitations for my personal comfort," one Observer wrote from Italy. "In this regard I am almost ashamed to report." He went on to describe his luxurious Mediterranean villa, complete with servants' quarters.

Though the Coca-Cola men often lived the good life in the midst of war, poverty, and starvation, they could console themselves with the knowledge that their jobs were actually important and meaningful. They saw ample daily evidence that many soldiers regarded the drink as a miracle. Though The Coca-Cola Company had abandoned its medicinal claims long ago, the drink's placebo effect was revitalized during the war. An Observer commented on "one poor devil with one leg and one arm gone" who had given up on life until he was offered a Coca-Cola. "He told the nurse not to kid him. When he really did get a drink he cried like a baby because it reminded him so much of home." Another Observer from New Guinea, recounting how wounded soldiers limped to obtain their drinks, could have been describing a scene with a faith healer: "Men on crutches, in wheelchairs, men with bandaged hands, some who cannot see—all lined up by the hundreds to get their Cokes. It makes you feel all tied up inside and long for just one more carbonator. . . ." At such moments, the T.O.s must have felt that they really *were* dispensing a morale-boosting beverage, rendering "The T.O. Theme Song" somewhat more understandable:

> *The Technical Observers are winning the war, Parley Vous.*
> *The Technical Observers are winning the war, Parley Vous.*
> *The Technical Observers are winning the war, so what do*
> *The Heinies keep fighting for? Hinkey, Dinkey, Parley Vous.*

THE HOME FRONT AND THE HIGH SIGN

Back in the United States, Coke's ad campaigns exploited the drink's patriotic presence abroad. To avoid paying more excess profits taxes, the Company poured money into wartime promotions. One showed sailors bellying up to a ship's bar for the soft drink, with the caption: "Wherever a U.S. battleship may be, the American way of life goes along. . . . So, naturally, Coca-Cola is there, too." Set in exotic locales such as Hawaii, Great Britain, Russia, Scotland, Newfoundland, and New Guinea, Coke's ads carried the new catchphrase, "the global high-sign," and introduced American readers to a few foreign phrases. The Russians, for instance, reacted to Coke by saying "*Eto Zdorovo*," translated as "How grand!" The ad men continually touted the soft drink's status as an American icon: "Yes, around the globe, Coca-Cola stands for **the pause that refreshes**—it has become a symbol of our way of living."

These international ads were balanced by scenes from the home front, where Coca-Cola was shown assuaging the thirst of busy Victory gardeners, war bond salesmen, and returning soldiers whose doting wives and children plied them with soft drinks while listening wide-eyed to their war stories. As with Depression-era efforts, the wartime ads avoided unpleasant reality. There were no gory scenes, just good-looking WACs and whole-bodied veterans. According to a 1943 survey, these ads were effective with both men *and* women: "Feminine readership went up when personalized copy of people on the battle line and home front replaced the story of gleaming planes, tanks, and jeeps."

Other products also sounded patriotic themes but were roundly condemned for their efforts. One soldier penned a "Memorial to the Great Big Beautiful Self-Sacrificing Advertisers" in which he pilloried "four-color-process hypocrisy" that portrayed "not so much blood and filth, of course, as to offend good taste. . . . Some day somebody will fracture an arm thus publicly waving a flag." Although Coke's ads were guilty of just such "hypocrisy," no GI criticized them. Coca-Cola was such an imbedded part of the American Dream that its advertising *couldn't* be offensive. The most popular, widely quoted ad during the war, "The Kid in Upper 4," was produced by a railroad company and featured a soldier lying in his berth "wide awake . . . staring into the blackness," thinking about "the taste of hamburgers and pop, [and] a dog named Shucks, or Spot."

Consequently, the Company feverishly boosted its patriotic image during World War II. For a dime, the Company sold thousands of copies of a "Know Your War Planes" booklet—an ingenious appeal to war-happy kids. The "Our America" pamphlet series, designed for junior high students, told the story of the U.S. steel, lumber, coal, or agricultural industries with minimal advertising. Coca-Cola distributed cribbage boards, playing cards, Chinese checkers, dominoes, dartboards, Bingo, table tennis sets, and comic postcards illustrated with military themes. As sponsor of the popular radio series *Victory Parade of Spotlight Bands*, Coca-Cola hired over a hundred name bands to play concerts and drink Cokes at bases around the country. Irish tenor Morton Downey, destined to play a postwar role in the Company's affairs, sang on his own Coca-Cola-sponsored radio show.*

Despite Oehlert's attempts to persuade the War Production Board that Coca-Cola was essential for civilian morale, too, the general public's supply was severely rationed. A Kansas editor wrote that the Coke shortage really brought home the *seriousness* of the war, while Texas Coca-Cola addicts were particularly upset by rationing, according to one journalist, who feared protestors "swinging a six-shooter in one hand and a Coke bottle filled with TNT in the other." One customer, rushing to pull a warm bottle of Coke out of a cooler just after it was stocked, explained it all: "Those people have spent twenty years making a drinker out of me and [they] can't shut me off this easy."

ACKLIN'S AGONIZING WAR

The tall, frail, gentle man responsible for the daily management of the Company during World War II, Arthur Acklin, assumed the Coca-Cola presidency just before the war began, apparently because Robert Woodruff no longer wanted to be in the spotlight or to deal with mundane matters. Acklin hated pressure; he had already broken down once in 1934, and he begged Woodruff not to make him president in 1939 but to no avail. As he put it himself, Acklin possessed a "temperament that takes seriously any problem with which I am confronted." He found it difficult to cope with day-to-day decisions—and there were enough during the war to rattle any executive. He worried over buying Peruvian sugar for the domestic business at inflated prices. He had to negotiate with Monsanto Chemical Company, encouraging them to build special plants to manufacture caffeine in Brazil and Mexico. He contracted for recycled bottle caps because of metal shortages. Monthly, Coke consumed twenty-five

---

* When Downey was considering the $3,500-a-week offer from Coca-Cola, his friend Joe Kennedy advised him to take $500 in cash and $3,000 in Coca-Cola stock options. As a result, when Downey stopped singing for Coke ten years later, he was a major shareholder and held bottling interests in Australia, Chile, Uruguay, Argentina, Brazil, and Connecticut.

thousand gallons of vanilla extract; annually, the drink needed a million pounds of Merchandise No. 5, the coca leaf and kola nut extract. Shortages loomed for both ingredients.

The pressure started to tell on Acklin, who grew gaunter by the day. He asked Woodruff to form a "working policy committee" to help him, but the Boss refused. Coca-Cola's mismanaged baseball team, the Atlanta Crackers, lost money. The government froze wages and prices. The Thomas Company wanted everything for nothing. Over half of the Company personnel were drafted. Three weeks after the Germans surrendered, Acklin cracked. "Naturally you cannot be conscious of the multitude of problems with which I have been confronted," Acklin wrote plaintively. "The strain has taken a rather heavy toll." Woodruff had to assume the presidency again as an interim measure. Acklin managed to steer domestic Coca-Cola through the war in good shape, but he himself was a casualty.

WALTER MACK MAKES HIS MOVES

In the meantime, Pepsi president Walter Mack thrived on the same pressure that undid Acklin. Complaining that Coke had "an inordinate amount of political influence," Mack attacked Ed Forio's position on the Sugar Rationing Board, telling the head of the War Production Board that Forio was a "phony" and threatening to cause a public stink unless he was replaced within a week. Three days later, the Coca-Cola man resigned.*

Regardless of who was in charge of sugar rationing, however, Pepsi was in trouble. Desperate for sweetener, Mack pursued every conceivable avenue. Initially, he bought a Cuban plantation but was unable to export anything until after the war because of Cuban regulations. Mack then went to Mexico and cemented a deal with the government to purchase forty thousand tons of sugar a year at slightly above the top asking price. That didn't really help, though, since Mexican law prohibited the export of sugar and U.S. law forbade its importation. Undaunted, Mack incorporated the Mexican-American Flavors Company in Monterrey, where he converted the sugar into a syrup he called "El Masquo" and legally transported it over the border to his Pepsi bottlers. Coca-Cola dubbed Mack's syrup "El Sneako" and eventually pressured the government into closing the loophole in 1944. The unstoppable Mack then turned to a New Jersey condiment maker and bought a million and a half gallons of sugarcane juice, which he clarified into twelve million pounds of sweetener before the government again foiled his strategy.

Although his aggressive style didn't help when he protested Coca-Cola's virtual monopoly on bases, Mack was determined to attract military business anyway, opening three huge Pepsi-Cola Servicemen's Centers in Washington, San Francisco, and New York, where soldiers could find free Pepsi, nickel hamburgers, and a shave, shower,

---

* Walter Mack tried to exert his own political influence by persuading the president's son, Jimmy Roosevelt, to become a Pepsi bottler. In the meantime, Joseph Kennedy negotiated with Woodruff to spend $5 million on Coke bottling plants. "He has a number of sons," Archie Lee explained in 1942. The elder Kennedy wanted to lay the "foundation for jobs for them." The deal fell through, however, and the boys had to go into politics instead.

and free pants pressing. And in 1942 Pepsi invaded military installations to offer another free service. GIs could record greetings and send them anywhere they chose. For tongue-tied soldiers, Mack even provided sixteen boiler-plate messages addressed to Mom, Dad, or the girl back home. "Let me tell you," thousands of these ghostwritten messages sincerely commenced, "Uncle Sam is doing a good job keeping me in the pink of condition for you, honey, so don't be worrying about me." By the end of the war three million personalized Pepsi recordings had been delivered to loved ones. To further cheer the lowly private, Mack dispatched professional wrestling troops to perform in Army camps.

Nor did Mack neglect the civilian population. Taking advantage of Coca-Cola's scarcity at the soda fountain, Mack pushed into this traditional Coke stronghold with syrup for a ten-ounce fountain drink selling for the same nickel as Coke's six-ounce glass. Pepsi sponsored national softball tournaments, huge square dances, and clubhouses for teenagers. While Pepsi couldn't match Coke's presence in Hollywood, it did garner a plug on Broadway. In 1943's *Something for the Boys*, Ethel Merman, playing a woman whose tooth fillings brought in radio broadcasts, tuned in her incisors to the famous jingle. As the orchestra played the opening bars, Merman loudly announced: "Pepsi-Cola!"

Through such shenanigans, Walter Mack made inroads on Coca-Cola's American empire during World War II, securing a place in the postwar market. Nonetheless, despite his showman's flair, Mack could do nothing about Coca-Cola's monopoly overseas, where sipping a Coke in his foxhole was a minor miracle to the war-weary GI.

WARTIME TESTIMONIALS

The triumph of Coca-Cola during the war was in many ways due to its relative scarcity, which enhanced its value and desirability. One young soldier, writing from New Guinea to his parents, described his home-brewed Coke. "The syrup is old and the [carbonated] gas low, but it's still our greatest luxury. The syrup is dipped with a tin spoon into an aluminum canteen cup and stirred with a stick and we still love it." He concluded that American ingenuity could accomplish wonders. "This war should be a cinch now." His attitude was echoed by many other letters from homesick young Americans for whom Coca-Cola assumed an astonishing significance:

> It's the little things, not the big, that the individual soldier fights for or wants so badly when away. It's the girl friend back home in a drug store over a Coke, or the juke box and the summer weather.

> I always thought it was a wonderful drink, but on an island where few white men have set foot, it is a Godsend. I can truthfully say that I haven't seen smiles spread over a bunch of boys' faces as they did when they saw Coca-Cola in this God-forsaken place.

> . . . one real bottle of Coca-Cola, the first one I have seen here. It was pulled out from under the shirt of a pilot. . . . He caressed it, his eyes rolled over it, he smacked his lips at the prospect of tasting it. I offered him one dollar for half of it, then two, three, and five dollars.

You will probably think your son has had his head exposed to the sun too long. But the other day, three of us guys walked ten miles to buy a case of Coca-Cola, then carried it back. You will never know how good it tasted.

The crowning touch to your Christmas packages was the bottled Coca-Cola. How did you ever think of sending them? To have it here and turn up the bottle and see "Ronceverte, W. Va.," on the bottom was an added thrill.

This week, Coca-Cola came to Italy. Seemingly everyone had heard the rumor, but no one put much faith in it. How could it be true? Coca-Cola is some vaguely familiar nectar, reminiscent of some far-off paradise land. Italy is a land of C-rations and Spam and dehydrated food.

To have this drink is just like having home brought nearer to you; it's one of the little things of life that really counts. I can remember being at Ponce de Leon Park, watching the [Atlanta] Crackers play baseball as I filled up on Coca-Cola and peanuts. It's things such as this that all of us are fighting for.

One soldier summarized the sentiments: "If anyone were to ask us what we are fighting for, we think half of us would answer, the right to buy Coca-Cola again." Letters such as these poured into Company offices, though they were publicized only to Company employees. Consequently, the Company was delighted when Colonel Robert L. Scott, in his best-seller *God Is My Co-Pilot*, explained that his motivation to "shoot down my first Jap" stemmed from thoughts of "America, Democracy, Coca-Colas." Before World War II, Coca-Cola men had been taught to have faith in their drink, to hustle and sell every day, to proclaim the virtues of their product everywhere they went. Certainly, here was the proof that Coca-Cola *was* America, at least by 1945. George Brennan, a corporal, wrote back to his old boss at Coca-Cola that his wartime experience had given him a new appreciation for the drink: "In civilian life, when there is an abundance of Coca-Cola, you feel convinced that it is good and more or less let it go at that. But you have to experience the scarcity of Coca-Cola or suffer its absence to acquire a full appreciation of what it means to us as Americans."

OPENING CEREMONIES, CARBONATED RAFFLES, SACRAMENTAL WINE

Given the depth of the feelings expressed in those letters home, it is understandable that the downing of a Coke overseas often became a matter of considerable ceremony. One soldier wrote: "I have seen four high-ranking officers opening a bottle of Coca-Cola as if it were a magnum of Cordon Rouge 1929." Another soldier, with tongue somewhat in cheek, wrote:

The pop, as you open it; with some pomp and a good deal of ceremony you bring open bottle to within 3 inches of your nose. No mistaking now, it is; it is Coke. The urge now is to quaff the whole thing in one gulp, but if you have the least bit of the esthetic in you, you don't. One more sniff, and, deftly holding the bottle between thumb and two middle fingers, small finger slightly raised,

you bring bottle to eager lips and straining, impatient tongue. Then—this takes
a lot of will-power and self-control—you don't take a full swig, but just a wee
bit of a sip, and smartly roll the liquid on your tongue. A fraction of a fraction
of a moment you hesitate and pause. By golly! Coke, all right! Finally, what the
hell, down goes the entire contents of the bottle in one gulp.

Given the popularity and symbolic weight Coca-Cola achieved during the war
(and the lack of GI spending outlets), it was predictable that Coca-Cola would bring
a considerable amount of money on the black market and the informal commerce
common to soldiers. One bottle was reported to sell for anything from $5 to $40. In
an auction in Iran, a bottle went for $1,000. The most famous (and expensive) bottle
was sold on Italian auction for $4,000.

Coca-Cola developed a psychological significance akin to an icon or rare religious
relic; many bottles remained unopened after the war, kept hidden away as sacred mementos. It seemed fitting that Mary Churchill, Winston's daughter, should christen
a new destroyer with a bottle of Coke. During the war years, explicit treatment of
Coke-as-religion cropped up. Since the notion of a soft drink being worshiped was
disconcerting, these references were often humorous. Corporal Frank Hardie, for instance, wrote a parody of Jesus' parable of the foolish and wise virgins: "But the wise
converted their quarters into nickels when he who filleth the Coca-Cola machine
passed through. And lo, there came a time when the red light disappeared from the
face of the machine, and the machine was filled. . . ."

T.O. Maurice Duttera recalled dining at the officers' club in Cannes with two
Catholic priests, who frequently kidded him about the soldiers' attitude to Coca-
Cola, urging him to requisition a plane, fly to Rome, and obtain the Pope's blessing
on Coke as holy water. Those clerics were joking, but during the Battle of the Bulge,
Ken Hogan, an Observer, really did supply a priest with Coca-Cola in lieu of sacra-
mental wine.

INSULATORS, SHANDIES, AND URINALS

The near-religious awe with which many soldiers regarded Coca-Cola did not prevent
others from putting the ubiquitous bottle to other uses. Coke bottles were drafted as
emergency electrical insulators in the Pacific, dropped on Japanese airfields in "Coke
runs" to puncture tires, wielded by sailors in life rafts to kill sea turtles for food. The
British scandalized GIs by mixing Cokes with beer and calling the result "shandies,"
while another groggy soldier brushed his teeth with the soft drink every morning.
Coca-Cola cases were much in demand as portable mailboxes and stools. "Coca-Cola"
was the battle password while crossing the Rhine.

Other alternative utilizations were more risqué. Like the boys back home, many
soldiers advised their girlfriends to douche with the fizzy drink. Perhaps the most inventive recycling of bottles, though, combining nostalgia with irreverence, concerned
a Navy officers' club men's room in the New Hebrides. Hundreds of Coke bottles
embossed with local franchises' locations were embedded, bottom out, in the concrete
urinal wall, with varicolored lights behind them providing an eerie glow to a continual
wash of water. "It was something to see," one nostalgic veteran recalled. "People came
from long distances 'just to piss on the old home town.'"

THE GERMS OF THE DISEASE

Coca-Cola's symbolism and its insidious infiltration were not lost on the Axis powers. Otto Dietrich, the Nazis' press chief, declared in 1942 that "America never contributed anything to world civilization but chewing gum and Coca-Cola." Japanese radio proclaimed that "with Coca-Cola we imported the germs of the disease of American society. These germs, however, were introduced in such a pleasant way that we failed to realize it." The "pleasant way" worked all too well, despite the propaganda. German, Japanese, and Italian soldiers all knew and enjoyed the taste of Coca-Cola. A photo of a U.S. captive aboard a German sub showed him drinking—of course—a Coke. Nor were the Japanese immune. When a luxurious Japanese "jungle city" was captured in western New Britain, it disgorged cases of captured Coca-Cola. And on one hot summer day, Italian prisoners of war refused to continue working until they had been given the pause that refreshes. The Technical Observers were well aware of the possible markets they were opening. "I'm sure that many of the smaller children had never tasted Coca-Cola before," wrote one T.O. from New Guinea, "but they'll certainly be steady customers from now on."

Coca-Cola men also discovered a potential market in more primitive cultures, joyfully reporting that Zulus, Bushmen, and Fijians relished the drink. Even making allowances for the time, their attitude was often racist, condescending, and ethnocentric, such as a New Guinea T.O.'s description of a native's first encounter with a Coke, which he downed too quickly. "Then the fun began. He belched, the gas went up his nose and brought tears to his eyes. He was a scared native for a few minutes. So now it can be said that we have sampled and opened up a new outlet—the Fuzzy Wuzzy market." Another Coke man snapped a photo of a Polynesian king sitting on a wheelbarrow throne, prophesying that he would soon be sitting "on one of those famous Red Barrels and surrounded by full and ice-cold Coca-Cola bottles, and be wearing crowncorks with the 'trademark registered' in his ears." One soldier, writing home from India to say he was getting Coke at his PX, went on to describe Kayo, a six-year-old Indian boy who had learned the American way—soft drinks, popular tunes, and obsessive hygiene—all too well. "He brushes his teeth three or four times a day and takes showers regularly. They told him that if he washes frequently he will become white like us, and he certainly tries hard."

PROFITABLE PATRIOTISM

As the war wound to a close, the fervor of the Coca-Cola Technical Observers in selling their product only increased. The T.O. program continued for another three years before a graceful transition to a civilian operation, symbolized by the death in 1948 of one publication, *T.O. Digest*, and the birth of another, *Coca-Cola Overseas*. The pseudo-military Coke men were in a delicate position. While they were acutely aware of the potential profits and future markets they were creating, they had to moderate their sales pitch. With selling, sampling techniques, and catchy slogans drilled into their heads, however, they found it difficult to be circumspect about pushing the product. In a series of unpublished notes written while he served as a Technical Observer in Germany in 1946, George Downing explained that "the T.O.'s only merchandising tool was a friendly spoken word. No profit, no increased sales, no rapid turnover, no small investment could be stressed. Ours was to be a giving of service in making Coca-Cola available to GIs wherever they might be." Then, in two columns, Downing listed the way Coca-Cola language had to be translated for the patriotic war effort:

Regular Coca-Cola Language (accustomed to)	Lingo Due to Military Necessity
"If we are gonna make sales rise, boys, we gotta merchandise."	"Fellows, as representatives of the Army Exchange Service in charge of soft drink production and distribution, we would like to help you with any problems that you have."
"If they are gonna be sold, they gotta be cold."	"We have learned that people prefer their Cokes below 40 degrees and we would like to show you how it can best be done."
"Mr. Dealer, in order for you to capitalize on advertising, we would like to place this attractive custom built sign to identify your business as one having Coke for sale."	"Fellows, we can make lithography available to you that would add a touch of home to your soda fountain, Coke bar, etc."

Because Downing and his cohorts had virtually a captive market, the euphemisms and appeals to the "fellows" worked—so much so that, when Jim Farley and other Coke executives came for a tour of inspection, they were embarrassed by the extent of blatant advertising at the PX and urged the T.O.s to "soft pedal it a bit." Despite Company protestations that the war effort was a purely philanthropic gesture, it was, on the contrary, clearly a profitable operation in the postwar environment. As their wives and children flew over to join them, American servicemen brought home cases of Coke, much to the delight of the T.O.s, who competed fiercely for the highest sales figures.

WHITE COKE FOR A RED RUSSIAN

One of those Technical Observers was Mladin Zarubica, sent to Austria in 1946 to install a gigantic bottling plant. He went at the direct request of President Truman, who was concerned by the number of green troops who were drinking poisonous schnapps and going blind. Zarubica, a wartime PT boat commander, all-American football player from UCLA, and son of a Yugoslav immigrant, threw himself into his new job with exuberance, helping to construct thirty-eight Coke plants in southern Europe within two years. He also purchased as much warehouse space as possible, in part to keep Pepsi out, in part to stockpile materials while the Army was still paying for transportation. His largest plant, in Lambach, Austria, was four city blocks long and ran continuously, bottling twenty-four thousand cases of Coca-Cola every twenty-four hours. "I had a railroad siding that I had midnight requisitioned [i.e., stolen] out of the Russian Zone," Zarubica recalled. "I even built my own CO_2 plant because I couldn't count on the purity of the local gas." To protect shipments from black market bandits, five hundred American soldiers guarded his sugar train on its way to Austria.

Zarubica was flying high, with a huge expense account. At James Farley's suggestion, he refurbished a villa near Berchtesgaden into a hunting lodge for influential visitors from Paris, London, and New York, who were met at the airport and escorted to the beautiful lodge overlooking a mountain lake. "We had waiting lists to come there—senators, potentates, you name it."

The White Coke episode was, however, the most astonishing coup Mladin Zarubica pulled off. When Dwight Eisenhower introduced the American drink to his new friend General Georgi Konstantinovich Zhukov, head of his country's occupied zone, the Russian liked it. He asked General Mark Clark, in charge of the American zone, for more, with one proviso: it couldn't look anything like Coke. As the central Russian war hero, Zhukov knew he couldn't be seen drinking an American imperialist symbol. Clark passed the request up the line to President Truman, who summoned Jim Farley, and soon the word filtered back to Zarubica, who found a chemist to take out the caramel coloring. Then the Coca-Cola man had the Crown Cork and Seal Company in Brussels make a special straight, clear bottle and a white cap with a red star in the middle. "My first shipment to Zhukov was fifty cases," Zarubica said. "White Coke for Red Russians. That was a deep, dark secret." The subterfuge was worthwhile, though. The regular Coke supply from Lambach had to pass through the Russian zone to reach its Vienna warehouse. While others often waited weeks for the Russian bureaucracy to allow them through, the Coke shipment was never stopped.

SWASHBUCKLERS, SAMPLING, AND SEX

Zarubica called the T.O. program "the greatest sampling program in the history of the world," during which the drink practically sold itself, not only to Americans (and the occasional Russian general), but Germans and Austrians.* The order forbidding GIs to fraternize with frauleins was impossible to enforce. "So every time a soldier would take two cases home, the girl and her kids drank it all up, and they transferred to drinking Coca-Cola without even a blink."

The soldiers weren't the only ones fraternizing with frauleins. Some T.O.s took advantage of their position to trade Coca-Cola for sex or money. "Anything with sugar in it was currency on the black market," recalled one Observer. "It was a joke that you could give a woman a Hershey bar and she was yours. And Coca-Cola was a close second."

Another T.O., a lover of literature who felt out of place in the world of gung-ho Coke men in postwar Germany, recalled one of his cohorts as "the horniest individual" he ever knew. "I never did understand why they sent over the shabby people they did. The black market was just rampant. The opportunity was almost laid out in front of

---

* The Japanese also presented a gigantic potential market. "We are casting covetous eyes towards the civilian population out here—some 18 million potential Coca-Cola customers on Kyushu alone," wrote one T.O. "The transition period from a Military to a Civilian market will be very interesting." In this instance, however, Coke would be frustrated by governmental regulations that effectively prevented the sale of the drink to the Japanese until the early 1960s.

you." Zarubica verified that there were some bad apples, hired as friends of friends with little training. "We had a lot of alcoholism there," he acknowledged. There were also the swashbucklers and soldiers of fortune, as T.O. Don Sisler called them. "I'd say these adventurers made up about 20% of us," he recalled. "They liked the excitement of being in an unusual place at an unusual time. They had no intention of taking this whole thing seriously. They were great womanizers, but that was just part of the whole stew and added a little spice."

UNIVERSAL ACCEPTANCE

Swashbucklers and serious Coke men alike could read the writing on the wall by 1947, when the military presence in the occupied zones was dwindling, along with soft drink sales. By the end of the following year, the Technical Observers would hang up their military uniforms, but the plants and goodwill they had established remained. Everyone wanted to try the American soldiers' soft drink. The GIs were heroes, liberators with seemingly endless supplies of chocolate bars, cigarettes, and Cokes in the midst of a bombed-out world. Admiration was often mixed with envy, but even envy was easily converted to emulation. The world was primed for Coca-Cola. As a postwar Coca-Cola official acknowledged, World War II resulted in "the almost universal acceptance of the goodness of Coca-Cola. . . . Anything the American fighting man wanted and enjoyed was something [others] wanted too."

And Coca-Cola was even more popular on the home front, where the returning veterans brought a decided preference for the drink that had meant so much to them overseas. This result was anticipated by at least one soldier. "Personally, I think that The Coca-Cola Company's cooperation with the Army in getting Coca-Cola to the men in the field is the best advertisement that Coca-Cola has ever had," he wrote to his former Company boss. "The things that are happening to these men now will stick with them for the rest of their life."

He was right. In a 1948 poll of veterans conducted by *American Legion Magazine*, 63.67 percent specified Coca-Cola as their preferred soft drink, with Pepsi receiving a lame 7.78 percent of the vote.* In the same year, Coke's gross profit on sales reached a whopping $126 million, as opposed to Pepsi's $25 million; the contrast in net after-tax income was even more telling, with Coke's $35.6 million towering over Pepsi's pathetic $3.2 million. As the Company's unpublished history stated, the wartime program "made friends and customers for home consumption of 11,000,000 GIs [and] did [a] sampling and expansion job abroad which would [otherwise] have taken 25 years and millions of dollars." The war was over, and it appeared, at least for the moment, that Coca-Cola had won it.

---

* Soon after the war, when the Army quizzed 650 recruits, 21 had never drunk milk, but only 1 soldier had never sampled a Coke.

~ 13 ~

Coca-Cola Über Alles

Ein Führer [ist] ein Mann, der Anhänger hat. Ein Führer verdient, dass er Anhänger hat. Er hat sich Anerkennung erworben. . . . Ein Führer vervielfacht sich in anderen. Er ist ein Menschenbildner. . . . Er ist ein Mann des Geistes und der Tat—Sinnender und Schaffender zugleich.

[Translation] *A leader is a man who has followers. The leader deserves to have followers; he has earned recognition. . . . The leader duplicates himself in others. He is a manbuilder. . . . He is a man of thought and a man of action—both dreamer and doer.*

—1963 Tribute to Max Keith

One man must step forward in order to form, with apodictic force, out of the wavering world of imagination of the great masses, granite principles, and to take up the fight for their sole correctness.

—Adolf Hitler, *Mein Kampf*

In early 1945, a group of German prisoners of war debarked in Hoboken, New Jersey, apprehensive and lonely in a foreign land. When one of them pointed to a Coca-Cola sign on a nearby building, the prisoners began excitedly gesticulating and talking among themselves. Taken aback, the guard yelled for order, demanding an explanation from a prisoner who spoke English. "We are surprised," he answered, "that you have Coca-Cola here too."

Coca-Cola executives loved to retell this anecdote as proof that Coke is a native product wherever it goes, but the story's real significance can only be understood in the context of Hitler's Third Reich. In order to thrive inside Nazi Germany, its Coca-Cola franchises had waged a rigorous campaign to disassociate themselves from their American roots. While the soft drink came to symbolize American freedom—all of the good things back home the GI was fighting for—the same Coca-Cola logo rested comfortably next to the swastika. The drama of German Coke's survival before, during, and after World War II swirls around one central figure—Max Keith, at once the quintessential Coca-Cola man and Nazi collaborator.

In 1933, the same year that Hitler came to power, thirty-year-old Keith (pronounced "Kite") went to work for Coca-Cola GmbH. Like many Germans, Keith desperately sought financial security as well as something to believe in. Whereas others embraced the Fatherland and Aryan supremacy, Max Keith found Coca-Cola. "I was full of activity and enthusiasm," he recalled thirty years later, "and the thing which then took possession of all that was in me and which . . . has never lost its hold on me, was Coca-Cola. From then on, and to all eternity, I was tied to this product for better or for worse."

The German soft drink business was in its infancy. Ray Rivington Powers, an American expatriate, had started bottling German Coca-Cola in 1929 after a colorful, if shady, career in post–World War I Europe. A huge man—almost six and a half feet tall and nearly as wide, with a personality to match—he enjoyed playing the part of the American buffoon, speaking tortured German mixed with English, even though he was perfectly fluent in German. But Ray Powers had the gift of creating believers through his hyperbole. "One day," he would tell prospective Coca-Cola men, "you will have a villa in Florida and you will be one of the richest men in the world."* During the first four years of the business, he boosted Coca-Cola sales from just under six thousand cases to over one hundred thousand in 1933.

A great salesman but a terrible manager who couldn't be bothered with financial details, Powers had just persuaded Woodruff to give him the franchise for the entire country when his German partner pulled out, demanding his money back late in 1929. Frantic, the American fled to New York in a vain attempt to raise capital, then tapped Woodruff for over $100,000. There ensued a tangle of incorporations and mergers in an attempt to replicate the structure of the American business. The auditors sent to examine the Essen books found them "in a state of chaos," according to an internal memo by Hamilton Horsey. The auditors and lawyers, wrote Horsey, "advised us to have nothing to do with Mr. Powers' company in Essen," so an entirely new corporation was formed to purchase its assets.

In the final event, two primary entities emerged from the mess. Coca-Cola GmbH would manufacture the syrup and own the trademark, while the Deutsch Vertriebs GmbH für Naturgetränke, commonly known as Deverna, would act as the parent bottler. Powers, running Deverna, was supposed to live off the royalties of the bottlers he found. Unfortunately, he couldn't find anyone to risk bottling, which required too much cash. Instead, he sold through "concessionaires," distributors who picked up cases of the soft drink and sold them in exclusive territories near Essen.

When Keith opened Powers' desk drawer and found unpaid bills and unopened bank statements, the former bookkeeper recognized a satisfying challenge. He soon put Coca-Cola GmbH's finances in order and turned his formidable organizational skills to promoting the business. While he lacked the American's winning personality, he more than made up for it with a forceful style. Men laughed with Ray Powers, but they trembled before Max Keith.

Keith was an imposing man, over six feet, with high Teutonic cheekbones rarely dimpled by a smile and a little whisk-broom mustache that, like the Führer's, quivered alarmingly when he was enraged. In several other ways, Keith's mannerisms and

---

* Not surprisingly, Powers admired a fellow propagandist: Adolf Hitler. In 1930, Powers defended Hitler to Robert Woodruff, and in the spring of 1936 the American closed a letter to the Boss with the salutation, "Heil Hitler."

leadership style resembled the dictator's. His high-pitched voice proved hypnotic when raised in anger. "Max Keith could chew you out like you've never been chewed out before," one of his aides recalled, "but he could also build you up again." He could be charming, gentle, and conciliatory when it suited him. Once he decided something, Keith never changed his mind, and he brooked no opposition in public. It was suicidal to espouse a conflicting point of view in a staff meeting. "He was a born leader, a very charismatic figure," according to Klaus Pütter, a longtime employee. "You liked to work for him although he was almost a slave driver. . . . Oh, yes, I was scared of him. We *all* were, even aides who were older." Still, Pütter said, most of his followers "would have died for this man."

Keith's tactics could be brilliant. Against enormous odds, including near disaster at the hands of both the Nazis and the American conquerors, he built the Coca-Cola business into a thriving enterprise. Through cunning, bluff, intimidation, wheedling, influence, marketing, and sheer willpower, Max Keith survived along with his beloved drink. For Keith, as one aide put it, the ruling thought was not "Deutschland Über Alles," but "Coca-Cola Über Alles."

BOOM YEARS WITH MAX AND ADOLF

As Hitler had collected ragtag malcontents to form his Brown Shirts, Keith too looked for lost souls who would become true believers. "They were mostly people who had almost tried everything in their life and failed," Keith remembered in an interview near the end of his life. "They thought that by taking Coca-Cola, what could they lose more?" The Coca-Cola manager had little choice in employees, since there was virtually no German soft drink business. Nonalcoholic beverages were considered syrupy concoctions for children, not for robust beer-drinking adults. It was also widely believed that cold beverages (with the exception of beer) caused stomachaches.

Determined to alter that attitude, Keith forced himself and his men to work twelve-hour days and more, sometimes collapsing at 2 a.m. before rising early to start all over again. On foot, bicycles, pushcarts, three-wheeled motor scooters, and one old Chevrolet truck, Keith's concessionaires delivered the goods. In 1934, he added a bottling plant in Frankfurt, with warehouses in Cologne and Koblenz. He forged ahead despite the stingy Canadian supervision of Gene Kelly, who refused to buy a second truck until Keith had accrued over six hundred retail accounts.

At least Kelly provided as many small point-of-purchase signs as the Germans could nail up, and he allowed Keith to print millions of leaflets titled *Was Ist Coca-Cola?* (What Is Coca-Cola?), which his men would distribute at sporting events and restaurants. "We went to restaurants on weekends [and] put this prospectus on every table," Keith remembered, and when distraught proprietors threw them out, the Coke men doggedly replaced them. Many who picked up the folder expected to find an analysis of the ingredients and were angered when it simply said that Coke was a refreshing drink, but the endless repetition of the product name had its intended effect.*

---

* Hitler himself learned valuable lessons from Western advertising techniques. "All effective propaganda has to limit itself only to a very few points and to use them like slogans," Hitler wrote. "It has to confine itself to little and to repeat this eternally."

To encourage his distributors, Keith initially hired three field men to demonstrate proper sales technique and open new outlets. These overworked salesmen had to lug around a large briefcase dubbed the *Seufzertasche*, or the "case of sighs." It contained a tin lining, ten Coca-Cola bottles, and ice. Entering a tavern, early field men such as Joe Knipp opened markets by persistent sampling, offering ice-cold (*eiskalt*) drinks. "Ja, Blah! I've had it before, I would not touch it," the owners would say, but once they tasted a cold drink, they would often exclaim that it was an altogether different taste when properly chilled.

Once a retailer was convinced that Coca-Cola might make money for him, he often had to hide the bottles under beer in the ice, since over half the pubs and restaurants were owned by local breweries that forbade the sale of another drink. At times, Keith's personal presence alone solved the problem; ten minutes of Keith was enough to cow most brewers. Other times, Keith brought in Walter Oppenhoff, the attorney who had incorporated the Company in 1930 and who took an almost daily part in the business. The lawyer usually procured a satisfactory out-of-court settlement. With Keith's guidance and Powers' continued sales efforts, Coca-Cola sales grew quickly throughout the decade. In 1934, they doubled to 243,000 cases and, two years later, broached 1,000,000 cases for the first time. By the time war broke out in 1939, the Coca-Cola men were selling almost 4.5 million cases inside Germany.

While Keith deserves much of the credit for this phenomenal growth, he himself recognized that "the time marched with us." As in America, refrigeration invaded the home during the 1930s, while automobile travel was facilitated by the Autobahn system, dotted with its Coke-supplied filling stations. Even as the first concentration camps were opened by the Nazis in 1933, Germany was experiencing the onset of relative prosperity. By 1937, the German national income had doubled. "Germany in the mid-Thirties," wrote William L. Shirer in *The Rise and Fall of the Third Reich*, "seemed like one vast beehive." The busy workers needed the pause that refreshed. "The requirements of the people were much higher than in the past," Keith said. "They had to work harder, had to work faster, the technical equipment they had to handle required soberness."

Of course, the "technical equipment" was part of the vast military machine that created new jobs. And while unemployment shrank to almost nothing, workers were little more than serfs, forbidden not only to strike but to change jobs. The employer became a kind of mini-dictator, a *Geschäftsführer*, or "leader of the enterprise." Wages were deliberately set quite low, but most workers were happy just to have jobs and to believe Hitler's propaganda that the Teutonic "Volk" would overcome all obstacles. Far from being resentful of a brutal dictatorship, most workers, Shirer noted, were imbued with "a new hope and a new confidence and an astonishing faith in the future of their country." No wonder Max Keith's faithful workers labored so diligently. By 1939, forty-three German plants bottled Coca-Cola, with nine more under construction. Over six hundred concessionaires, independent franchisees making considerably more money than most German workers, distributed the drinks. Each was his own mini-Führer, though bowing ultimately to Max Keith, who had made it all possible for them.

COKE AT THE BERLIN OLYMPICS

The 1936 Summer Olympics in Berlin marked a moment of triumph for Max Keith, who provided enormous quantities of Coca-Cola for athletes and visitors. That August in Berlin was equally satisfactory for Hitler, proud host to the nations of the world, showing off his blond Aryan athletes and his revitalized Germany. Just before the Olympics, Max Schmeling had proved that a white German could beat a supposedly inferior black American when he knocked out Joe Louis in the twelfth round at Madison Square Garden. Arriving in Germany, Schmeling was welcomed by a huge crowd as he stepped off the zeppelin *Hindenburg*, then whisked to lunch with Hitler, who slapped his thigh in appreciation every time he saw Schmeling hit Louis in the film of the fight. A prominent Nazi publication gloated that "Schmeling's victory was not only sport. It was a question of prestige for our race. With his hard fists he has won the respect of the world for the German nation."*

German athletes dominated the Olympics, winning thirty-six gold medals while America took home only twenty-five first-place finishes. Although Hitler seethed over black superstar Jesse Owens' four gold medals, on the whole he was smug about his Berlin charade. Signs such as *Juden Unerwünscht* (Jews Unwelcome) had been quietly removed for the duration while the country put on its best behavior. Max Schmeling, viewing the games with Hitler in his private box, summarized the feelings of most Germans when he told a U.S. reporter, "We have no strikes in Germany. Most everybody has a job. Times are good. We have only one union. We have only one party. Everyone agreeable. Everybody happy."

Göring and Goebbels hosted elaborate parties for foreign guests, most of whom were suitably impressed by what they saw. One of those guests was Robert Woodruff, who had brought over an entire Coca-Cola entourage. Woodruff, however, was not taken in by Hitler's facade. His finely tuned antennae felt the rumbles that could destroy a business. True, Woodruff approved of the modern Berlin bottling plant with its forty-spout filler. But while pleased to see Coca-Cola prominently on sale at the Olympics, he was most unhappy with the wrapper around the neck of every bottle, which read *Kaffeinhaltung* (Caffeine-Containing). The Nazi Health Ministry, perhaps prodded by the Führer's food faddism, insisted that the caveat be placed on the bottles. For many German consumers, however, the wrapper served more as an advertisement than a deterrent, since coffee was a rare commodity.

Nonetheless, the label violated one of Woodruff's sacred tenets, and he ordered his high-powered chemists and lawyers to write affidavits in an attempt to undo the damage. Referring to this incident, John Sibley wrote to Woodruff in November of 1936, "That country is feeding itself on prejudice and this is just another evidence of this fact. I hope that we get through without getting scarred up." In his meeting with Max Keith and Walter Oppenhoff, Woodruff refused to allow them to combat the rumors about caffeine. When Keith pressed the issue, Woodruff dramatically banished

---

* Two years later, however, the Brown Bomber knocked out the German in the first round.

the visiting Americans from the room so that he could be alone with the Germans. "I am not accustomed to giving my American people explanations," he said, "but I will break the rule for you. You must *never* engage in defensive advertising. It simply gives dignity to your opponents and prolongs the issue."

For once, Keith had met his match. Without ever raising his voice or displaying irritation, Woodruff had exercised steely command. "When Max Keith met Robert Woodruff," one of his aides remembered, "he was overwhelmed. That was the man he worked for, the only man in the world he really deeply respected." For his part, Woodruff recognized in Keith a potent personality who could build the German business. The two men remained lifelong friends.

While in Berlin, Woodruff also dealt with the Ray Powers situation. Deverna as a parent bottling company hadn't worked out, and Powers had failed to make any money from his contract arrangement. After a lengthy meeting, company lawyers agreed to dissolve Deverna, to make Keith the official *Geschäftsführer* of Coca-Cola GmbH, and to give Powers a flat royalty fee for all the drinks sold in Germany until 1950.

In September of 1936, a month after the Olympics, Hermann Göring, Hitler's designated successor and head of the Luftwaffe, took charge of a new Four-Year Plan that stressed German self-sufficiency in preparation for war. The Nazi leader cut imports to a bare minimum and discouraged foreign businesses. In a letter to the German Revenue Office, Oppenhoff had taken pains to present Coca-Cola GmbH as a *German* business, despite the fact that The Coca-Cola Company owned most of it. (Oppenhoff called the foreign capital a "loan.") Under Göring's iron rule, such prevarication was useless, and the supply of U.S. concentrate appeared doomed until Woodruff pulled his magic strings.

Woodruff belonged to a network of corporate executives, many of whom were worried about their German subsidiaries and interests. With war clouds darkening, these titans of American industry quietly maneuvered to protect themselves against all contingencies. Some, like Henry Ford, were in fact Nazi sympathizers, while others, such as Walter Teagle of Standard Oil, avoided taking sides but saw nothing wrong with doing business with the Nazis. Like his friend and hunting companion Teagle, Woodruff practiced expediency. His politics were Coca-Cola, pure and simple.

Through his New York banking connections, Woodruff moved behind the scenes to influence Göring. In 1936, he enlisted the aid of Henry Mann, a German agent for several American banks, who convinced Göring to permit the importation of Coca-Cola concentrate. "He accepts gifts," one acquaintance had murmured helpfully to a favor seeker early in Göring's career. In order to reduce the imports to a minimum, Keith began making his own concentrate so that he needed only Merchandise No. 5 and 7X from America. Woodruff toyed with the idea of producing even these ingredients inside Nazi Germany if war broke out. "Some consideration should probably be given to the . . . possibility of having Number 5 manufactured in Germany in case developments should make that desirable," he wrote to Sibley, but he finally abandoned the plan as impractical.

The correspondence between Robert Woodruff and John Sibley during this crucial 1936 European trip reveals that Woodruff, while outwardly calm in the face of any adversity, was actually high-strung and restless. Writing from London before his

German visit, Woodruff said that he was "nervous and lonesome" but that he was at least sleeping well for a change.* Despite the problems facing him in Germany, he wrote that his five-day visit would "pass fairly quickly (I hope)." Recognizing Woodruff's tension, Sibley expressed the hope that his friend would get a "complete rest" while playing golf in Scotland.

FIGHTING THE "JEWISH SLANDER"

Woodruff may have helped Max Keith by interceding with Göring, but he was unable to control other looming problems. The caffeine rumors were only the beginning of controversy. As Coca-Cola became a big seller in Germany, the mineral water interests, breweries, and cola imitators used every smear tactic available. Phosphoric acid, they claimed, ate the lining of the stomach, demonstrating that a piece of veal left overnight in Coke was leached white. Some competitors complained that Coca-Cola was misnamed because it had no cocaine; others spread the rumor that it *did* contain the "poison," which had a "stimulating effect on the brain." As an "artificial coloring," even the caramel coloring caused problems. The sacred hobbleskirt bottle itself was maligned because it held 0.192 liters rather than the German standard of 0.2.

But the most devastating threat to Coca-Cola's future in Germany came from one Herr Flach, who manufactured an imitation drink called Afri-Cola. Flach belonged to the so-called Labor Front, the Nazi organization that had replaced unions in 1934. In 1936, Flach and other Labor Front representatives visited the United States on a goodwill tour of American industries. Ray Powers arranged for a visit to a New York Coca-Cola bottling plant, where Flach scooped up a handful of bottle caps with Hebrew inscriptions indicating that Coca-Cola was kosher—not a big surprise, since the huge New York Jewish population comprised a ready market.[†] Back in Germany, Flach distributed thousands of flyers featuring photographs of the bottle cap. Coca-Cola, he claimed, was a Jewish American company, run by Harold Hirsch, a prominent Atlanta Jew.

Sales plummeted. Nazi Party headquarters hastily canceled their orders. The entire business was in jeopardy, and Keith, forbidden to print defensive literature, could do little about it. Walter Oppenhoff fought for a preliminary injunction in Cologne against the "Jewish slander," but F. A. S. Gwatkin, Coke's London counsel, and Sibley prevented further court proceedings, fearing the consequent publicity. The independent bottlers and concessionaires felt betrayed and instituted their own lawsuits, sometimes defiantly naming Coca-Cola GmbH as coplaintiff. Oppenhoff wrote to

---

* Woodruff was traveling with his wife, Nell, but though a devoted husband, he apparently derived little comfort from her company. He rather plaintively asked Sibley to sail across the Atlantic, spend less than a week with him in Germany, then accompany him back on the cruise ship. Sibley politely declined. Woodruff apparently preferred the company of close male friends to the somewhat rarified company of "Miss Nell," who frowned on cigar smoke and poker games.

† The Jewish market was so important to Coca-Cola that it apparently revealed its ingredients (though not the precise formula) to Atlanta rabbi Tobias Geffen in 1935. The minute amounts of glycerin (from animal fat) and alcohol (from grains) were problematical, so, for its kosher Coca-Cola, the Company used glycerin made from vegetable oil and its alcohol from molasses.

Gwatkin, explaining that no one living outside Germany "could have any conception" of the scope of the problem. Desperate for relief, Keith begged Woodruff to
remove Harold Hirsch from the Coca-Cola board or at least to clarify that he did not
own the company. Woodruff stood by Hirsch, but he did ask the legal department to
draft a notice verifying the large number of shareholders, proving that no one person
"owned" the Company. In the face of Flach's jubilant defamations, however, the list
of shareholders was a blunt weapon.

INTO THE HEART OF NAZISM

Ultimately, Coca-Cola weathered even this fiasco, though pictures of the kosher bottle
cap kept surfacing for years. As Woodruff had done in America, Keith zeroed in on
"special events," such as patriotic mass meetings, realizing that sampling was the best
way to build the business. Coca-Cola appeared at bicycle races, emphasizing its wholesome refreshment for athletes. As young men goose-stepped in formation at Hitler
Youth rallies, Coca-Cola trucks accompanied the marchers, hoping to capture the
next generation.

In 1937, the year after Flach's initial accusations, Keith placed Coca-Cola at the
heart of the Nazi industrial renaissance. That year, the Reich *Schaffendes Volk* (Working
People) exhibit opened in Düsseldorf, displaying the accomplishments of the German
worker during the first five years of Hitler's rule. A functioning bottling plant, with a
miniature train carting *Kinder* beneath it, bottled Coca-Cola at the very center of the
fair, adjacent to the Propaganda Office. Touring the Düsseldorf fair, Hermann Göring
paused for a Coke, and an alert Company photographer snapped a picture. Though
no such picture documented the Führer's tastes, Hitler reputedly enjoyed Coca-Cola,
too, sipping the Atlanta drink as he watched *Gone with the Wind* in his private theater.

In March of 1938, as Hitler's troops stormed across the Austrian border in the
Anschluss, Max Keith convened the ninth annual concessionaire convention, with
1,500 people in attendance. Behind the main table, a huge banner proclaimed, in
German, "Coca-Cola is the world-famous trademark for the unique product of Coca-
Cola GmbH." Directly below, three gigantic swastikas stood out, black on red. At
the main table, Keith sat surrounded by his deputies, another swastika draped in
front of him.

Although acknowledging glorious past efforts, Keith urged his workers to forge
onward into the future, never to be content until every German citizen was a Coke
consumer. "We know we will reach our goal only if we muster all our powers in a total
effort," he said. "Our marvelous drink has the power of endurance to continue this
march to success." If he sounded like Hitler, it was probably deliberate. The meeting
closed with a "ceremonial pledge" to Coca-Cola and a ringing, three-fold *Sieg-Heil*
to Hitler.

Far from expressing horror at Nazi aggression, Keith and his men swiftly followed
the troops into Austria, establishing a Vienna branch in September. Keith registered
no protest a month later when, on November 10, 1938, Kristallnacht, the "Night of
Broken Glass," heralded a new level of terror for Jews, whose Austrian businesses
were demolished and synagogues set on fire. Nor were Woodruff or Powers disturbed,
though the Anschluss did cause friction between the two men. Powers felt that his

royalty should cover all Coca-Cola sold within German borders, wherever they might extend because of Hitler. Woodruff demurred, saying the contract specified the borders as they existed when it was signed. Shortly after the argument was settled, Powers was killed in an automobile accident, and Keith was left the undisputed leader of the German Coca-Cola business.

Keith presided over the tenth anniversary of the German Coca-Cola business in April of 1939, lavishing praise on the recently deceased Ray Powers, though Keith's joy at achieving control could scarcely be concealed. The past year, he gloated, had been historic because Hitler had annexed Austria and the Sudetenland, bringing those lands back into the German fold. The phenomenal spread of Coca-Cola during 1938 was a close second, however. Then Keith ordered a mass *Sieg-Heil* for Hitler's recent fiftieth birthday "to commemorate our deepest admiration and gratitude for our Führer who has led our nation into a brilliant higher sphere."

BOMBED-OUT BOTTLING PLANTS

On September 1, 1939, when Hitler's troops rolled into Poland, and England and France finally declared war, Max Keith realized he was in trouble. While Göring may have previously permitted the flow of 7X, it was only a matter of time before the supply was severely curtailed or cut off altogether by the exigencies of war.* Not only that, Keith feared that as a "foreign" business, Coca-Cola GmbH might be nationalized and its leaders imprisoned. Quickly, he moved on two fronts to forestall disaster.

First, he maneuvered to become a part of the vast German bureaucracy. Hitler may have had ultimate power, but he was bored with the details of governing, leaving much of it to old-line civil service men, many of whom were quite sympathetic to the plight of businessmen. Fortunately for Keith, Walter Oppenhoff was good friends with the head of the Ministry of Justice. Oppenhoff managed to get himself and Keith appointed to the Office of Enemy Property to supervise all soft drink plants, both in Germany and captured territory. As German troops overran Europe, Keith and Oppenhoff followed, assisting and taking over the Coca-Cola businesses in Italy, France, Holland, Luxembourg, Belgium, and Norway.

Keith's second move was to find another product. While rationing Coca-Cola carefully to the different plants, he asked his chemists to invent an alternative drink that would see the Company through the war. They created a fruit-flavored drink. Like Coca-Cola, it was a unique caffeinated blend not readily identifiable as orange, grape, or lemon. Relying on available ingredients—often the leavings from other food industries—the new drink used whey, a cheese by-product, as well as apple fiber from cider presses. Keith later commented that the drink was made of "left-overs from left-overs." The mix of fruit ingredients shifted, depending on the availability of Italian produce. At first, the drink had to be sweetened with saccharin, but in 1941 it was exempted from sugar rationing and allowed to use 3.5 percent beet sugar, resulting in a beverage far better than any wartime competitor's.

---

* Even after the war's 1939 commencement, Atlanta continued to ship Coca-Cola syrup to Keith. With the U.S. entry into the war, however, the syrup spigot was shut off.

In a christening contest, Keith asked his assembled employees to let their fantasy—*Fantasie* in German—run wild, and veteran salesman Joe Knipp immediately blurted the winning name, Fanta. Walter Oppenhoff registered the new trademark in Germany as well as all occupied countries, though in Belgium manager Carl West opted for the name Cappy, thinking that Fanta sounded too Germanic for angry Belgians. A new, distinctive bottle was created, and Fanta sold well enough to keep the business alive during the war, even after the U.S. entered late in 1941 and all Coca-Cola supplies ceased. In 1943, Keith sold nearly three million cases of Fanta. Many bottles weren't drunk but were used to add sweetness and flavor to soups and stews, since wartime sugar was severely rationed.

At the same time, Max Keith did everything possible to keep the name Coca-Cola before the German public. The Nazis outlawed "reminiscent advertising" for products no longer available. Still, in all Fanta advertising, he included the phrase, "a product of Coca-Cola GmbH." Before the supply of Coca-Cola itself ran out at the end of 1942, he reserved his German supply only for hospitals with wounded Nazi soldiers, though branches of the German military also managed to snag a few cases.

When the army requisitioned his best trucks, Keith's mechanics nursed the old ones with constant repairs. Ford Motor Company also continued to do business inside Nazi Germany, supplying the *Geschäftsführer* with special coal-fueled trucks. To ensure that his remaining trucks weren't confiscated, Keith (like Woodruff) rendered his business "essential" to the war effort by capping carbonated water in his now-idle Coca-Cola bottles and storing them in mine shafts, safe from air raids. His trucks then became emergency vehicles to distribute free "catastrophe water"—and to maintain goodwill.

Keith could hide his bottles from the bombs, but not his plants. All forty-three Coca-Cola plants were bombed at some point during the war—a few on several occasions. The Company's Essen headquarters and plant were hit more times than any other. Located in Germany's industrial heartland, the town was completely demolished by the end of the war, not one building left whole. Nonetheless, Keith continued to bottle both Fanta and water, even at the height of the bombing. "I arranged for so-called siding plants on the outskirts of the cities where we had our bottling plants," he explained. Housed in old farmhouses or dairies, the makeshift operations kept the Fanta supply steady while the main plant in the city was repaired.

When his employees were drafted, Keith replaced them with ex-convicts unacceptable to the army. "One of our best salesmen in Essen," Keith proudly remembered, "had killed his father and was imprisoned for twenty years." Later in the war, Keith used Chinese labor and "people who would come from anywhere in Europe—the war brought them from everywhere." For Keith to say blandly that "the war brought them" implies that they were willing refugees, which is somewhat misleading. In fact, the wartime railroads carried not only Jews, Gypsies, and others to concentration camps but some nine million *Fremdarbeiter*, or foreign forced labor, who accounted for a fifth of the German labor force by 1944.

Clearly, Max Keith was willing to do almost anything to keep the Coca-Cola business going, including collaborating with the Nazi government. His associates later excused his behavior, asserting that he had no other alternative. "Yes, Max Keith tried not to offend those in power," Klaus Pütter admitted. "He was a very skilled negotiator, a cautious man. You know, when you live in a country governed by a dictatorship, you have to watch your tongue and be very careful. If your neighbor heard you say anything against Hitler, they came at night and fetched you and off you went. It's impossible for you here in the United States to understand." As a result, Keith honed a fine-tuned diplomacy while representing a foreign company. "One false step, one false remark would have been fatal."

When his loyalty to Coca-Cola came under fire, Keith proved himself willing to die for his drink rather than submit to the Nazis. By the beginning of 1945, it was clear to everyone except Hitler and his fanatical followers that the war was lost. In reaction, devoted Nazis turned paranoid, looking for an enemy within to blame. Keith and Oppenhoff were summoned that January to report to the general in charge of the Ministry of Commerce and told to nationalize their company. "Change the name to anything else," the general ordered. "Call it Max Keith GmbH if you want, but change it within two days, or you will be placed in a concentration camp."

Keith remained obdurate. He and Oppenhoff went to see their old friend at the Ministry of Justice, who was afraid that if he interfered he too might be imprisoned. Unsure what would happen, the two Coca-Cola men prepared for the showdown the next day, but it never came. The general was providentially killed in an air raid, saving the business. Three months later, in a Berlin bunker, Hitler shot himself through the mouth. The war was over.

INVASION OF THE TECHNICAL OBSERVERS

Max Keith had prevailed. "Coca-Cola GmbH still functioning," he telegraphed to Woodruff. "Send auditors." Astonished, Woodruff promptly dispatched Stephen Ladas, the New York lawyer for Coca-Cola Export, to try to locate Walter Oppenhoff in his home city of Cologne, whose bombed-out population of a million people had been reduced to only thirty-five thousand. Ladas couldn't find Oppenhoff, but he did learn from neighbors that he was alive. Leaving an encouraging note, Ladas returned to America.

In the meantime, the Technical Observers poured into Germany just behind the liberating American troops, quickly commandeering a mineral water plant at Niedermendig and bottling Coke there by April, just before the German surrender. The three top T.O.s hopped in a jeep and set out to find Max Keith and "whatever remnants of our pre-war German company we could," as one later remembered. When they found Keith, he was busily bottling Fanta in a half-destroyed plant.

To the Company executives back home, Max Keith was a hero. Harrison Jones, in his 1946 speech to the newest batch of Technical Observers headed for Germany, told them that Max Keith was "a grea-a-t, grea-a-t man" who had united the bottlers during the war. At the time, however, such praise rang hollow for Keith, who felt betrayed and angry. He had survived the war, keeping his little bottling kingdom intact, only to have it usurped by the American T.O.s. Later, he called this postwar period an "even worse breakdown" for him than he had suffered under the Nazis.

Keith's distress was understandable, but so was the attitude of the Technical Observers in their U.S. military uniforms, ordered not to fraternize with Germans. Eisenhower had ordered that industry be "de-Nazified." Together with Walter Oppenhoff (who had surfaced intact), Keith attempted to negotiate with Army officers and the American Coke men. "We had quite some discussions," Oppenhoff remembered later. T.O. George Downing, who flatly called Keith "a second Hitler," was appalled at his effrontery. "Could you imagine a German in a defeated Germany coming and telling Americans how to do something?" Downing was sure that Keith planned to take over Coca-Cola's worldwide operations if Germany had won the war. Those might well have been Keith's aspirations, but he was well schooled in patient diplomacy, and he now tried to ingratiate himself with the victors. At first, the Americans not only refused to give Keith any Coke syrup but curtailed his Fanta production. They eventually compromised, allowing Coca-Cola GmbH to bottle Fanta while the T.O.s monopolized the American drink for GI consumption.

In the uneasy truce, the Technical Observers bottled Coke on one side of the Frankfurt plant, while Keith capped Fanta in the other half. But in the devastated postwar economy, he couldn't scrounge enough sugar or fruit—nor could most Germans afford to buy his drink. Sales fell from over two million cases in 1944 to a half million in 1945, even though he also started bottling soda water and a new flavor called Rosalta.

Keith was determined to take over the business when the American soldiers eventually left. He instructed his men to infiltrate the T.O. operations, and the Americans were more than happy to find experienced help. "As life around this plant took shape," reported the T.O. in Stuttgart in August of 1945, "native Coca-Cola men became once again part of a great business. From the fields and prison camps old employees returned to the business. Good machinists and diligent effort have made what first appeared to be a hopeless mess a shining success." No wonder one T.O. said, "I couldn't teach myself to hate the Germans—they were so *industrious*." No one seemed unduly concerned that these "native Coca-Cola men" were ex-Nazis or collaborators, partly because a magical transformation had taken place overnight with the Allied victory. "It was amazing," one Technical Observer noted sarcastically, "but not one member of the populace was a Nazi, all were anti-party members and were definitely against Hitler and his objectives."

Despite his precarious position, Max Keith tried to keep in touch with these former employees while offering his "help" to the T.O. operations. In Augsburg, Cliff Johnson explained to his assistant Don Sisler that "this Kraut, Max Keith, is coming to visit, and we've got orders to be nice to him." When Keith arrived, clad in a huge fur coat, his former employees, now working at Augsburg, were "practically fainting with ecstasy," as Sisler recalled the scene. "Elsie was swooning because Herr Keith was there, and Herr Kohler was bowing all over the place." Sisler himself was impressed with Keith's "regal presence."

Finally, Keith seized an opportunity to outwit the Americans in 1949, when he discovered that a large supply of stale Coke syrup, shunted around the world during the war by the military bureaucracy, had arrived in Germany. He persuaded Paul Lesko, then in charge of the German Technical Observer operation, to sell him the syrup so that he could extract sugar from it for Fanta. To guard against its being reused, Lesko nearly dyed the syrup green, but Keith convinced him that such precautions were unnecessary. Putting his chemists to work, Keith clandestinely filtered and reworked the syrup, then hastily bottled his first Coca-Cola since 1942. Lee Talley, head of Coke's operations in Europe, happened to call Keith to say he was planning to visit Frankfurt. "That's wonderful," Keith said, "because I want you to cut a ribbon tomorrow morning. We are starting with the Coca-Cola business again." On October 3, Talley, who was quite surprised that Keith had all that syrup, nevertheless snipped the ribbon, and Keith's trucks ventured forth with huge signs proclaiming "*Coca-Cola ist wieder da!*" (Coca-Cola is back again!). Lesko was infuriated at being hoodwinked, but with Talley tacitly approving the operation, he was powerless to do anything about it.

Keith's timing was perfect. As the American military presence and T.O. operation dwindled, Woodruff decreed that the bottling should be returned to natives, and Lesko suddenly found himself having to answer to Keith, who was once again in command. To make peace with the American, Keith allowed him the Bremen bottling rights. It didn't take Keith long to rebuild the German industry, now that he had free access to Coca-Cola concentrate. It was impossible to find Germans who had the capital requirements set down by the Export company—one dollar for every person in the franchise territory. Keith arbitrarily reduced that amount, demanding one deutsch mark per capita, the equivalent of a quarter. Still, few had such resources, so Keith had to cosign loans for many of them, extorting oaths of lifelong fealty. "I pick you," he told his bottlers, "and I will make you rich, but you do what I tell you."

Keith was true to his word. When former T.O. Don Sisler returned to Germany many years later, he found that Elsie and Herr Kohler owned the Augsburg bottling plant and were "rolling in wealth." They treated him at the town's best restaurant and laughed tolerantly at memories of those difficult days just after the war. One thing had not changed, however: they still groveled before Max Keith, now Coca-Cola commander throughout Europe. Braver bottlers, in hushed tones, called him "Super-Führer."

THE GREAT WHITE ARYAN HOPE BECOMES A COCA-COLA MAN

Even Max Schmeling showed proper obeisance to Keith when Schmeling became a Coca-Cola bottler in 1957. The German hero contacted James Farley, New York's boxing commissioner in the prewar years, when the Coke executive came to Essen in 1954 to celebrate the twenty-fifth anniversary of Coca-Cola in Germany. Farley immediately recognized that Schmeling would be a real catch. Down on his luck, the boxer jumped at the chance to bottle Coke in Hamburg and would serve as a goodwill ambassador for the drink in Germany for years to come. Once the personification of Nazi superiority, the man who kept a signed autograph of Hitler in his study joined the *gemütlich* Coca-Cola family.*

---

* It is only fair to note that Schmeling was always uncomfortable as a symbol of Nazism, insisting that he was only a professional boxer—with a Jewish manager for a while. After World War II, Schmeling made a point of befriending Joe Louis and escorting him on a tour of his Coca-Cola bottling plant.

Part IV

Trouble in the Promised Land

(1950–1979)

"Into the Eighties with Coke!" The flashing red signs in the great empty hall, once so comfortably familiar, appeared bizarre and disorienting to Paul Austin. Why were they so bright, so much like an incandescent bloodletting? His heart pounded irregularly; he felt dizzy.

Stumbling toward the bar at the side of the amphitheater, Austin confronted a huge photograph of a beautiful woman's head, her gigantic teeth bared in a ferocious grin. "Have a Coke and a Smile!" she ordered. He leaned against the counter, steadying himself. "I'll have a Scotch on the rocks," he heard himself say, his voice sounding unreal and distant to his ears, as if it echoed from a corner of the hall. The technicians scurried purposefully around the room while a few bottlers and their wives strolled among the displays. Mumbling his thanks, Austin gulped his drink.

A man hurried toward him, deferentially nodding his head and holding out a hand. "Oh, there you are, Mr. Austin," he said. "Would you mind coming up on the podium for a sound check, sir?" Refilling his glass quickly, the tall Coca-Cola executive moved toward the stage. Perhaps another drink would calm him, ease the confusion. Deliberately, heavily, he ascended the steps and stood behind the microphone. His hand quivering slightly, he carefully placed his glass on the table beside him, as he had done countless times in the past. He leaned over the podium, grasping both sides.

Paul Austin stared into the pulsing red space before him. Sucking in a deep breath, he leaned further forward, and, his speech slightly slurred, asked a question which reverberated throughout the hall. "Excuse me, but could anyone tell me why I'm here?"

~ 14 ~

Coca-Colonization and the Communists

Apparently some of our friends overseas have difficulty distinguishing between the United States and Coca-Cola. Perhaps we should not complain too much about this.

—One Coca-Cola executive to another, 1950

In April of 1945, representatives of fifty countries converged on San Francisco for a conference with the idealistic mission of creating the United Nations, a postwar organization to maintain the peace. Sensing a pivotal moment in history, Robert Woodruff dispatched James Farley to San Francisco with an unlimited entertainment budget to wine, Coca-Cola, and dine the powerful delegates so conveniently assembled in one town. "The relationships I established," Farley later wrote with characteristic understatement, "might be helpful in our efforts to establish Coca-Cola bottling companies" around the world.

Farley was the consummate politician, famous for his prodigious memory for names and his paper flood of polite correspondence signed in green ink. He once explained that "it's the little things that cause trouble, it's the little sores that cause bitter feelings." Consequently, he vowed early in his life to be a consistent friend to everyone; no detail was too minor, no gift too small to be acknowledged. During the 1932 Democratic Convention, a journalist wrote that wherever Farley appeared, "rainbows flashed and quivered," perhaps reflected from his enormous bald pate, a beacon at the top of his burly 6'2" frame. "Give him time," noted the reporter, "and he will call everybody in the United States by his Christian name."

As a Democrat, Farley stressed loyalty above policy. Naturally gregarious, he neither drank nor smoked and needed only six hours' sleep a night. He loved to travel, meet new people, and exert subtle influence—in short, he was the perfect Coca-Cola man. In 1941, Ralph McGill, the famed Atlanta journalist and friend of Robert Woodruff, wrote solemnly that Farley's new job with Coca-Cola "entirely divorced him from politics." Far from being divorced from the process, Farley's diplomatic missions for his soft drink in the postwar world required every ounce of his skill. Increasingly, Coca-Cola *was* politics, particularly to the Communists.

For a brief moment near the war's end, it appeared that the traditionally antagonistic relationship between the USSR and the United States would give way to the friendship of victorious allies. But Stalin's purges, power hunger, and rebuffs to tentative American feelers soon led to the Cold War's first chill.

That spring of 1945, while Farley hobnobbed with Faisal of Saudi Arabia, Lord Halifax of Great Britain, and representatives from Egypt, Mexico, Brazil, and many other countries, he pointedly avoided Andrei Gromyko, the Russian delegate. Within a few years, American hostility to the Soviets would turn to paranoia, as Richard Nixon prosecuted Alger Hiss, the State Department member accused of being a Communist. Ironically, Hiss arranged Farley's San Francisco meetings with foreign delegates.*

Farley proved as loyal to Coca-Cola as he had been to the Democratic Party. Indeed, he delighted in the product that made him a nonpartisan goodwill ambassador and gave him entree to the rich and powerful. After a three-month trip around the world in 1946, Farley confidently told the press that the countries of the world "look to the American nation to lead them out of their difficulties," adding that "there isn't any doubt of the affection" these foreigners felt for Americans. The Coca-Cola ambassador was equally certain that the Chinese, torn by a civil war between Chiang Kai-shek and Mao Tse-tung, could "work out a solution to their problems."

Building on the goodwill fostered by the American soldier and his soft drink, The Coca-Cola Company swiftly licensed bottling plants in new countries and held its first international convention in Atlantic City in 1948, clearly intending to impress its newfound overseas bottlers. "When we think of Communists, we think of the Iron Curtain," a placard at the convention read. "BUT when THEY think of democracy, they think of Coca-Cola." At the convention, an executive prayed fervently: "May Providence give us the faith . . . to serve those two billion customers who are only waiting for us to bring our product to them." By the end of 1950, the business had started in Egypt, Morocco, Barbados, Liberia, Rhodesia, Guadeloupe, Algeria, Gibraltar, Kenya, Thailand, Tunisia, India, Congo, Iraq, Lebanon, Cyprus, and Saudi Arabia. Meanwhile, additional plants and aggressive marketing in countries where the industry was already established—primarily Europe and South America—substantially increased per capita consumption around the world.

The first step when entering a country was to locate a wealthy, socially prominent, politically influential bottler. Key employees were then brought to the United States for an extensive eight-month indoctrination—working in plants, riding the trucks, putting up advertising, properly icing coolers, enduring endless Visomatics in the appropriate language. By the time they went home, the new Coca-Cola men had received multiple syrup transfusions. "They are linked," wrote one Company man, "by a common faith in Coca-Cola, their belief in the honesty of the product and its value to mankind."

Giovanni Pretti, a thirty-year-old Italian salesman, was typical of the new international Coke man in 1950. Bounding from bed, he confronted a bathroom mirror whose signs inquired: "Hair Combed? Shaved? Uniform Clean and Neat? Shoes Shined? Friendly Smile?" Properly clothed and brimming with enthusiasm, he lovingly polished his shiny red and yellow truck and drove through Milan, explaining to a journalist that because of his "responsible position," he was now known as *Signor* Pretti.

---

* While Coke officials could rely on powerful politicians, Pepsi had to woo more unsavory types such as Senator Joe McCarthy, dubbed the "Pepsi-Cola Kid" for his blatant lobbying.

As part of morale-building continuing education, Coca-Cola Export field men staged skits for bottling plant workers. In Cairo, for instance, the assembled employees watched a morality play about Barsoum, a mustachioed Egyptian bottler who, failing to apply proper ice to his Coke, lost sales. Taking advantage of this lapse, a nefarious salesman for a competing drink convinced Barsoum to push the inferior product. Fortunately, the wise Coca-Cola salesmen arrived just at the crucial moment, booted the imitator, and restored refrigeration and the proper soft drink.

As an epilogue, one of the Coke field men, extolling the virtues of the Coca-Cola cooler, was interrupted by a loud voice. "Stop talking! I can speak for myself," the machine shouted. "I'm a twenty-four-hour salesman," it explained to the rapt Cairo audience. "I advertise the product, I cool the product, I present your product attractively." In another overseas presentation, a giant Coke bottle proclaimed: "I am Coca-Cola, vigorous with life and more than a mere shape," immodestly calling itself "a royal bottle . . . the object of your strivings." This sort of hokey presentation, standard since the 1930s in America, created a sensation abroad. By 1950, sales in the six Egyptian bottling plants, owned by the four Pathy brothers, mushroomed, reaching 350 million drinks annually only five years after the first Coke rolled off the line there.

The growth of the business overseas fascinated American media. Henry Luce, the anti-Communist publisher of *Time* and a Woodruff hunting companion, featured the Company in his May 15, 1950, issue. When Robert Woodruff refused to allow his portrait on the cover, Luce commissioned a classic painting in which a smiling red Coca-Cola disk with a skinny arm held a Coke bottle to the mouth of a thirsty globe. The legend underneath read, "WORLD & FRIEND—Love that piaster, that lira, that tickey, and that American way of life." The article pointed out that the "gentle burps" evoked by the drink could be heard amid "the bustle of Parisian sidewalk cafes" and "the tinkling of Siamese temple bells." By that time, a third of the Company's profits came from abroad. The *Time* reporter noted that "to find something as thoroughly native American hawked in half a hundred languages on all the world's crossroads from Arequipa to Zwolle" was strange—"like reading Dick Tracy in French." Nonetheless, he concluded, it was rather reassuring.

James Farley agreed. In a speech to the American Trademark Association, Farley pointed out that the American flag itself was "the most glorious of all trademarks," representing the "greatest tide of products and services in the history of mankind." As an example of America's contribution to global progress, Farley cited the Philippines, where at first he had been disturbed by the primitive conditions—homes of bamboo and grass raised on stilts, with shabbily dressed natives and naked children wandering along mud streets. "But you turn a corner in all this poverty," Farley said, smiling at the memory, "and suddenly you catch sight of a beautiful Coca-Cola bottling plant." In the midst of the squalor, here was a well-constructed, sparkling white factory equipped with "the latest and most modern bottle fillers, bottle cleaners and water treating equipment." The floors, Farley noted, were meticulously clean. The local employees, despite their unsanitary regular lives, showered at the plant daily and wore freshly laundered uniforms. If they were sick, there was a plant doctor. In conclusion, Farley bragged that Coca-Cola plants had "raised the standard of living in each of these islands."

Naive and thoroughly ethnocentric, Farley accepted the poverty he saw around him, easily condemning native culture and assuming that the American way of life, represented by Coca-Cola, was the *only* way of life. He added that the soft drink was effective in "influencing" favorable attitudes toward America and would eventually embrace all nations in "a brotherhood of peace and progress." It was true, however, that Coke often brought much-needed technology for cleaning water, that Coca-Cola employees were paid decent wages by local standards, and that the bottling plant was usually owned and run by natives. In 1950, only 1 percent of Coca-Cola Export employees were Americans. As one Coke executive pointed out, "in Germany it is a German business; in France, it is a French business; in Italy, it is an Italian business." Local industries to produce glass, carton, crown, and bottling equipment started in each new country. The Coca-Cola Company even supplied specifications, blueprints, and economic advisers.

NOT EVERYBODY LOVES US

Nevertheless, the result of Coca-Cola's postwar onslaught was not a "brotherhood of peace and progress." The fate of China proved symbolic of Coca-Cola's new woes. Farley's optimistic prediction that the opposing factions would "work out a solution" amicably was dead wrong, and in 1949 Mao Tse-tung founded Communist China, while Chiang Kai-shek fled to Taiwan. All of Coca-Cola's Chinese bottling plants were nationalized except for the British outpost in Hong Kong.*

Traveling a barren road next to the barbed wire fence separating Hong Kong from Communist China in 1950, a Company man braked impulsively before a huge, bright red billboard with the single word "Coca-Cola" in English and Chinese characters. Only feet from the Bamboo Curtain, it faced Mao's regimented realm. Inspired, the Coke executive reflected that the sign painter had been "a man with a soul" who created the sign "to breathe its defiance of communistic doctrine." The Communists, too, viewed Coca-Cola as the fitting symbol of "degenerate capitalism." In countries around the world, they defamed the American soft drink in the press, lobbied against it in legislatures, and whispered of its vile effects in back alleys.

The Communists were not the only ones concerned about Coca-Cola's postwar expansion, however. While the native Coke bottlers may have been happy, many of their countrymen were not, particularly if they sold competing beverages such as wine, beer, mineral water, or soft drinks. Many citizens across the Atlantic also resented the brash, aggressive Americans and their powerful new position in the world. This was particularly true of Europeans, whose love/hate attitude toward Americans was easily transferred to Coca-Cola.

Under the Marshall Plan, named for Coke's old friend George C. Marshall, Europe was rebuilt with massive infusions of American capital. The aid was not altogether

---

* When China disappeared behind the Bamboo Curtain, it caused a panic at Coca-Cola, since one of the key ingredients of 7X was cassia, otherwise known as Chinese cinnamon. Through a London intermediary, however, Coke continued to do business with the Chinese, who willingly sold the secret ingredient of the capitalist beverage.

altruistic, however, but intentionally gave American multinational corporations such as Coca-Cola a mighty boost. A bitter Englishman observed in the 1950s that "victory brought an intensification of the state of siege" for his country, while it triggered "a paradise of consumption" in the United States. The lavish spending and infantile behavior of American soldiers who remained on huge bases (sneeringly called "Coca-Cola towns" by locals) didn't alleviate this resentment. Thrifty Germans were appalled by GIs who left lights on all night, opened windows in winter, and never turned off the radio.

In 1949 and 1950, the French and several other nationalities, afraid of the imminent "Americanization" of their cultures, blindly fought back at the most convenient, blatant symbol of American hustle, a product that threatened to alter consumption patterns and attitudes of the next generation—Coca-Cola, the drink with the singsong name, the alluring poster girls, and the low cost. "There are many Europeans," commented one journalist, "who genuinely believe that the object held aloft by the Statue of Liberty is a Coke bottle."

THE UNHOLY FRENCH ALLIANCE

In planning for Coca-Cola's return to the French civilian market, Company executives made a valiant effort at cultural harmony, worrying over issues such as the gender of their drink. The French-Canadian ads were masculine, but in all other Latin languages, such as Spanish, Italian, and Portuguese, it was a less aggressive female. After considerable discussion, they decided to skirt the issue with simple "Buvez Coca-Cola" signs, dropping "le" or "la." The ploy backfired when grammatically punctilious Frenchmen complained about the lack of the proper definite article. The American company, they said, tortured their language.

Such niceties were lost on the French Communists, who howled in 1948 when Coca-Cola applied to the authorities for permission to bottle in France. Forced out of the governing coalition in 1947, the Communists still remained the largest party in the French National Assembly, where they raged against "American imperialism" and the Marshall Plan. Throughout 1949, using smear tactics and whipping up the wine and mineral water interests, the Communists warned against the "Coca-Colonization" of Europe. When the first bottles were sold in Paris in December of 1949, their propaganda intensified, insisting that the Coca-Cola distribution organization doubled as a spy network. Skull and crossbones appeared overnight on Parisian Coke signs. In the Assembly, the Communists pressed unsuccessfully for a bill to ban Coca-Cola as a poison.

Coke's man on the scene was Prince Alexander Makinsky, a suave, multilingual White Russian émigré. The French-educated anti-Communist had worked for the Rockefeller Foundation in Paris before joining Coke in 1945. He now quietly conferred with the U.S. ambassador and French officials to calm the waters and prevent revelation of Coke's ingredients. He diplomatically pointed out the "innocent error" of a French analytical laboratory that had found cocaine in the drink, but he couldn't prevent a furor over the phosphoric acid and caffeine. The matter reached a head at the end of February in 1950, when the Communists formed what Farley called "a strange alliance" with the wine and mineral water interests, supporting a bill introduced by

Paul Boulet, the deputy mayor of Montpellier and spokesman for many winegrowers. Boulet proposed a general measure against all non-alcoholic beverages with vegetable extracts—a thinly veiled assault on Coca-Cola. On February 28, it passed one house of the French legislature. Soon afterward, a suit was filed charging Coca-Cola with violation of a 1905 law prohibiting the sale of pharmaceuticals without ingredients on the label.

There was actually no immediate cause for concern, since the bill, even if passed by both houses, only made it *possible* for the Health Ministry to ban Coca-Cola. The lawsuit, which took years to drag through the courts, would at worst change the labeling. The moderate coalition government, led by Premier Georges Bidault, wasn't eager to offend the Americans, who might cut off the financial spigot. Secretary of State Dean Acheson fired off a memo to David Bruce, the U.S. ambassador to France, asking him to inform Bidault that the State Department was "disturbed" by legislation that was "prejudicial to legitimate American interests," asking Bruce to "emphasize unfavorable . . . U.S. public opinion" which would inevitably result. Bidault, anxious and conciliatory, assured the American ambassador that he wouldn't stand for "discrimination against the product" and would prevent the Health Ministry from taking any adverse action. He was powerless, however, to control the Communist propaganda, which he described as "widespread and effective."

Acheson's prediction of American outrage was accurate. Billy Rose banned French champagne from his New York nightclub. The *New York Daily News* suggested that "France would be smart to watch her chic little step. Should worse come to worst, we could lop off Marshall Plan aid." The *Philadelphia Inquirer* commented that "this is worse than Marie Antoinette. The Commies won't even let 'em drink Coke." A Denver paper complained of the French habit of "snooting our beverages, soft and hard, as so much dishwater."

Atlanta's mayor William B. Hartsfield, preparing for a European tour, declared his intention of bringing two cases of Coke along. "I'm going to offer myself as a living example of what happens to a lifetime drinker of Coca-Cola," Hartsfield told reporters, though the dumpy, bespectacled politician may not have helped his cause once the French saw him. Georgia legislator Prince Preston read his concern into the *Congressional Record*, suggesting retaliatory laws again French wine, champagne, and perfume. It was ridiculous to pretend that Coca-Cola was a health hazard, since "doctors prescribe it for babies." Besides, Preston said, the French were entirely too prissy. Drinking Coke would give them a much-needed "good belch." James Farley described the French legislation as "the weirdest bit of political shenanigan I have ever encountered," pointing out that "Coca-Cola was not injurious to the health of the American soldiers who liberated France from the Nazis. . . . Benevolent Uncle Sam, after his usual pause to refresh, may think this is one straw too much."

The French press jumped to the defense. *Le Monde* denounced "dangers that Coca-Cola represents for the health and civilization of France," comparing the Company's advertising with Nazi propaganda—both "intoxicated" the masses. "The moral landscape of France is at stake," the paper concluded. French intellectual Raymond Aron foresaw the destruction of his culture, with "Coca-Cola substituted for the noblest product of the soil (I mean, of course, wine)." Some of the anti-American French statements were classic for their hyperbole: "The Yankee, more arrogant than the Nazi iconoclast, substitutes the machine for the poet, Coca-Cola for poetry." A Frenchman at the zoo, watching a panther having diarrhea, told his son, "*Voilà la production de Coca-Cola!*" Encouraged, Communist deputy Gerard Duprat led a spontaneous seven-hour filibuster in the French Assembly, breaking out into impassioned oratory, waving his hands and decrying warmongers and Coca-Cola.

Mobs overturned Coke trucks, the bottles broken and trampled as a brown stream fizzed into the gutters. At a French bicycle race sponsored by Coca-Cola, angry spectators protested by throwing debris on the track. The level of hysteria reached such a pitch that Alexander Makinsky's wife feared the Communists might bomb their home. It was, Makinsky said, "McCarthyism in reverse," philosophically commenting that "the best barometer of the relationship of the U.S. and any country is the way Coca-Cola is treated." Time and patience, as Woodruff and his cronies knew, would ultimately solve their problems. In the meantime, they rushed to establish new bottlers throughout France as quickly as possible.

Stephen Ladas, the Export Corporation's trademark lawyer, writing in July of 1950, noted that "when Frenchmen place their millions into plants and factories and trucks, etc., they will see to it through their deputies and friends that any interference with their business is avoided." The lawyer suggested signing bottling contracts with wine, beer, fruit juice, and soft drink interests. That way, he said, "we will bore into the enemy from within." Ladas was correct. Through bottling contracts with Pernod and other French concerns, Coca-Cola won a few friends inside the country. In addition, a Parisian temperance leader favored the American drink, claiming that half of his countrymen were alcoholics. The Health Ministry never enforced the Boulet law, and the lawsuit was finally dropped in 1953.

The French controversy may have helped rather than hindered Coca-Cola sales. "Probably no other product in the world," observed one Company executive, "has received such an extensive amount of gratuitous editorial mention." It was, as Milton Bellis, an American living in Paris, noted, "a press agent's dream." The Communists' claim that Coca-Cola would poison innocent French men, women, and children with its mysterious 7X formula only piqued the native curiosity, rendering Coke "an enchanting, exotic temptation: THE FORBIDDEN DRINK!" Watching a belly dancer in a French dive redolent with hashish smoke, Bellis noticed that Coca-Cola constituted a third of the drinks. Makinsky, too, realized that the younger generation viewed Coke as an "emancipation" from parental authority.

Nonetheless, the French fears of Coca-Cola's domination of their country proved, at least in the short term, ill founded. For decades, the Gallic per capita consumption would lag behind most other countries. As one American journalist observed in 1950, "The Frenchman replace wine with a soft drink? Fantastic!" Not even Coca-Cola, he wrote, could "wean the Frenchman away from the grape."

AGITATION AROUND THE WORLD

While the French uproar captured all the headlines, Coca-Cola faced similar threats and rumors at midcentury around the world, particularly in neighboring European nations.* In Italy, the Communists asserted that Coca-Cola turned hair white and caused the dread disease, Coca-colitis. "Tremble!" advised an Austrian newspaper. "Coca-Cola is on the march!" Alarmed Viennese were informed that the American soft drink company intended to market cuckoo clocks whose birds announced the hour by chirping, "Coca-Cola! Coca-Cola!" Another Communist-inspired story claimed that the huge Lambach bottling plant was actually manufacturing atomic bombs. Soviet guards in Austria clutched their stomachs, exclaiming "Coke nix gut, make kaput." Belgian brewers urged their association to buy Coca-Cola franchises and then refuse to bottle the soft drink, which their Health Ministry declared a harmful laxative. In Morocco, Pepsi-wielding Francophiles attacked Coke drinkers, and vice versa, since Coca-Cola represented the independence movement. In Cyprus, vandals defaced Coca-Cola signs with the hammer and sickle. Even the British became concerned when a female Labour Party member vilified Coca-Cola in the House of Commons, asserting that her countrymen shouldn't waste money on the American drink.

In Switzerland, Company men waged a bitter battle against health legislation that would have prohibited the drink because of its phosphoric acid. As in other countries, the mineral water, fruit juice, and beer industries lobbied hard against Coca-Cola. Burke Nicholson Jr., the Coke executive sent to Switzerland to douse the flames, found that "we had some people who had talked rather big," bragging of the advertising avalanche about to descend on the Alpine valleys. In reality, he said, the Coke business was a tiny infant. "It was like people climbing up on furniture and yelling 'Snake! Snake!' and a tiny little worm would come out." The Defense Center Against Coca-Cola, which printed its own magazine and placed defamatory articles in other local media, initiated a well-coordinated Swiss campaign against Coca-Cola. While the Communist press was predictably rabid, the Defense Center material complained only of Coca-Cola's "loud propaganda and the free distribution of products," aggressive American tactics "unknown in the Swiss sector of beverages." Unless such promotions were stopped, Switzerland would become Americanized by Coca-Cola, ballpoint pens, and nylon stockings.

Eventually, by maintaining a low profile, remaining patient, and promoting the drink more subtly, the Company prevailed. Coke's public relations firm, Hill & Knowlton, arranged an "educational" tour of bottling plants for Swiss hairdressers and barbers, assuming that they gossiped with their customers. The Company sponsored a contest, consisting of carefully tailored queries about Coca-Cola—for example, Question: "For every Swiss franc spent on Coca-Cola, what percentage stays in the country?" Answer: "94.2%." The winner, who just happened to be the son of a prominent Swiss brewer, received a free trip to the United States.

---

* In her 1951 novel, *The Blessing*, British satirist Nancy Mitford drew a nasty portrait of Hector Dexter, the quintessential American blowhard. In order to spread the "American way of living," he said, "I should like to see a bottle of Coca-Cola on every table in England, on every table in France, on every—" He was interrupted by his British hostess. "But isn't it terribly nasty?" Not at all, Dexter said. It tasted good. But that wasn't the point. "When I say a bottle of Coca-Cola, I mean it metaphorically speaking. I mean it as an outward and visible sign of something inward and spiritual, I mean it as if each Coca-Cola bottle contained a djinn, and as if that djinn was our great American civilization ready to spring out of each bottle and cover the whole global universe with its great wide wings."

In Germany, the brewers, winegrowers, and soft drink manufacturers formed the Coordination Office for German Beverages, which the Coca-Cola men saw as a "mastermind of conspiracy." All of the familiar stories surfaced, along with a defamatory pamphlet entitled "Coca-Cola, Karl Marx, and the Imbecility of the Masses," asserting that Coke, not religion, was the opiate of the people. Walter Oppenhoff finally convinced Pope Brock, the Company's Atlanta general counsel, that he should sue for libel, and the German court ordered the campaign stopped.

Coca-Cola's battles against slanderous stories weren't limited to Europe, however. Around the world, wherever the new drink appeared, so did outrageous rumors. In Egypt, Coke sales temporarily plummeted when a Muslim demagogue asserted that the drink was made with pig's blood—not only disgusting but against his religion's prohibition against pork. In the Philippines, word spread that Coca-Cola made teeth fall out and that a San Miguel Coke employee had fallen into a vat of syrup, the dissolved body adding flavor to the drink. Company men quickly started a counter-rumor: the story was true, but it was a *Pepsi* vat.

In Japan, where Coke was only available to the U.S. military, the drink reputedly sterilized women. In Brazil, on the other hand, Coca-Cola supposedly caused cancer and rendered macho Latin men impotent—such a serious charge that Coke men, winking knowledgeably, whispered that the drink was an aphrodisiac. In fact, the negative stories often backfired on the drink's opponents. An inadvertent message conveyed that the mysterious drink had strange and magical powers. Spontaneous myths surfaced in Barbados that Coke would turn copper to silver. In Haiti, an old woman was reportedly revived by the drink—long enough to rewrite her will to include her grandson, at any rate—and in Russia, women used smuggled syrup to smooth wrinkles.

In Trinidad, however, the association of Coca-Cola with the American soldier hurt more than helped. Before World War II, native sentiment had favored an American takeover from the hated British, but, by the end of the war, locals were infuriated by American racism and conspicuous consumption. The song "Rum and Coca-Cola" originated in Trinidad and, with its bouncy Calypso beat, achieved enormous popularity in the United States. The lyrics, however, indicated the islanders' bitterness. While the men got drunk on rum and Coca-Cola, "both mother and daughter" were "working for the Yankee dollar."

Coca-Cola, the overseas men soon learned, generally required repeated sampling before people found it palatable. Predisposed by Communist propaganda, first timers vied to outdo one another with disgusting similes to describe the taste. A Tokyo shoeshine boy commented that it resembled dog medicine, while a Brazilian maintained it had the bouquet of a burnt comb. A poetic Irishman, thoughtfully swirling the liquid in his mouth, described the flavor as "foot's asleep." More graphically, Italians asserted that drinking Coca-Cola was like "sucking the leg of a recently massaged athlete." One sentimental Japanese waitress, however, described it as "the sweet-and-bitter taste of first love."

Philosophical about the Communist antagonism, Woodruff said that it was natural for the Reds to resent Coca-Cola, since it was "the essence of capitalism." Another executive explained that "with Coca-Cola, every shopkeeper makes a profit and becomes a member of the bourgeoisie. That's why the Commies are anti-Coke." In America,

the Reds recognized a losing battle, advising fellow travelers that they shouldn't antagonize the American proletariat by disparaging the workers' drink. After a leftist
meeting filled with valiant speeches against the imperialistic American beverage, Italian Communists retired to a cafe, where they all quaffed Coca-Cola. Even in France,
one of the Communist deputies, holding up a half-empty Coke bottle, complained,
"Isn't it a tragedy? I drink it and I have to vote against it."

BLESS THIS BOTTLE, OH LORD

Company men prudently adapted themselves to local cultures, particularly where
religious leaders acknowledged the sacred nature of the drink. When Jim Farley attended the Cork, Ireland, plant opening, he prayed right along with the Catholic
priest who blessed the plant. Similarly, nine orange-robed Hindu priests walking bare-
foot through the new Bangkok bottling plant sanctified it by dabbing gold paint on
the equipment and workers' foreheads. Coke officials made sure that governmental
muftis officially announcing the month-long fast of Ramadan all held Coke bottles
and that there were plenty of bottles to quench thirst after dark.

Since "everybody is a customer for Coca-Cola," explained a Company executive,
"we just can't be offensive and stay in business. We can't offer a measure of hospitality
with a drink and be inhospitable ourselves." Consequently, Coca-Cola representatives
were determinedly good-natured and malleable as long as people imbibed their brown
liquid. They hoped to make Coca-Cola an "integral part of every community . . .
woven into the pattern and customs of every land."

Devout Company men who had been trained never to dilute their drink with
any other substance soon learned that, in the overseas business, it was best to look
the other way. Signor Pretti told skeptical Italians, "Ah, but you must try Coca-Cola
in the wine." In the Caribbean, rum and Coca-Cola was known as a Cuba libre. In
Bolivia, locals mixed the American soft drink with *pisco*, a native brandy, to produce
a poncho negro. The Austrians liked it with schnapps, while the British diluted their
beer with the soft drink. Filipinos mixed their Coke with a potent native corn liquor,
selling the concoction in jelly jars. Finally, as the Cold War thawed somewhat at the
Geneva Summit conference in 1955, some Soviets suggested mixing a "coexistence
cocktail" of vodka and Coke.

Once past initial resistance, Coca-Cola representatives pushed their product in
every conceivable way, including Tasmanian car trials, Brazilian waiter races with open
bottles, Peruvian home delivery, and a white South African anniversary celebration of
the Zulu defeat. In some well-established overseas businesses, bottlers could act out
what remained tantalizing fantasies for their American counterparts. In the Philippines, for instance, where the United States had dominated since military intervention
at the turn of the century, refreshment stands and Coca-Cola coolers were routinely
installed in schools, while Company men blanketed Manila with neon Coca-Cola
signs and twenty-four-sheet posters. The worldwide signs looked nearly identical,
since the Company inaugurated "pattern advertising," using the same illustrations and
message—all portraying middle-class white Americans.

To combat allegations that the drink was a health hazard, the Company sponsored
numerous sporting events, identifying Coke with robust bikers, soccer players, and

boxers. At the 1952 Helsinki Olympics, Coca-Cola donated a cooler to the Russian compound, snapping photos of the Soviet athletes drinking the imperialistic American soda. Four years later, at the Melbourne Olympics, Russian and Czech participants downed 10,776 bottles of Coke—Company representatives, of course, keeping careful records of each Communist gulp.

OUR LATIN AMERICAN NEIGHBORS

During World War II, Coca-Cola had made substantial strides in South America, a major untapped market in the Western Hemisphere unaffected by the war overseas. After the war, business south of the border boomed, despite the widespread rumors about Coca-Cola's health effects. As a counterpart to the European Marshall Plan, the World Bank, which emerged in the postwar world as another American-dominated institution, promoted projects in Latin America and worked sympathetically with Coca-Cola. Mladin Zarubica's continuing saga illustrates the tight military/government/business network. Eugene Black, new head of the World Bank, was the former chief disbursement officer for the Army in Italy. Impressed with Zarubica's handling of the huge Austrian Coke plant, Black asked Export president James Curtis if he could "borrow" the Coke man. Curtis was only too glad to comply, since Zarubica could perform double duty. While on salary from Citibank in Montevideo, he conducted surveys of potential bottling franchises, with the full knowledge of the bank. "Don't forget that Coke was a major customer for Citibank," Zarubica recalled years later. The detailed surveys covered every aspect of a territory, including age and sex distribution, natural resources, the water situation, cultural prejudices, available refrigeration, and weather.

As a result of Zarubica's surveys, Robert Woodruff's nephew Morton Hodgson opened and operated a chain of South American bottling plants in Uruguay, Argentina, and Chile. These plants were partially owned by the Joroberts Corporation, a syndicate of forty Augusta National Golf Club members put together by golfer/investor Bobby Jones and Cliff Roberts, a New York investment banker. Most members of the Georgia club were well-connected corporate giants who flew from New York for a few rounds of golf and business. Joroberts investors thus included the heads of U.S. Steel and General Motors.

At the same time, Bill Bekker, a Dutchman who had pioneered the Italian and Spanish bottling industries, was establishing a Coca-Cola kingdom in Argentina, where he ruled with the same iron will exercised by Max Keith in Germany. An astute but stingy businessman, Bekker resented intrusion or advice from the New York Export office, simply throwing directives in the trash if he considered them nonsense. All who worked for Bekker lived in fear of his tread. Sweltering in cubbyhole offices above the bottling plant's din, they worried about Bekker sneaking around to catch them goofing off. The great man himself had a red light outside his door that, when lit, indicated that he was deep in thought and not to be disturbed. He drove himself as hard as he did his employees, often working late into the night.

Despite his tyrannical ways—or perhaps *because* of them—Bekker effectively fostered the business in a difficult territory. For years, the profit margin for Coke in South America was quite thin, due not only to the poverty of the people but to government-imposed price controls. At the same time, Bekker had to contend with a well-entrenched trucking union. He solved that problem by abolishing regular Coca-Cola vehicles and hiring *fleteros*, independent truckers who would work for less money and make multiple daily trips without complaint. The main offices in New York demanded that Bekker send his profits back north, but he refused, plowing the money back into his Argentine trade.

While the South American business may not have been terribly profitable, it overcame most prejudice against Coca-Cola. By 1953, a Brazilian intellectual identified the drink as a symbol of the "complete overthrow of the gloomy concepts of a dark, moldy past." On the contrary, he said, Coca-Cola was emblematic of "light, health, air, frankness, simplicity, strength and hope for a better future for Brazil." Coca-Cola, he asserted, meant progress and was opposed to diverse ills such as corrupt politicians, bad roads, gangsters, malaria, yellow fever, and bare feet.

THE ROYAL SOFT DRINK

To promote Coca-Cola as a high-status product, Company photographers loved to catch snapshots of the rich and famous drinking it. King Farouk reportedly had such a love for Coke that every restaurant in Egypt kept an iced supply in case the monarch should arrive unexpectedly. Two boy kings, Hussein of Jordan and Faisal of Iraq, sipped Coke together, as did four Dutch princesses. Batista drank it in Cuba, while Nixon and Eisenhower upended bottles in the United States. The sultan of Morocco kept his palace supply well chilled, while all elegant foreigners with fine sensibilities treated Coca-Cola as if it were the rarest champagne—or so Company executives claimed.

Many of the potentates who drank their Coke so religiously had an economic incentive. "The leading commercial, social and government leaders in all countries of the world wish to become associated with our product," one Coca-Cola man bragged, and he wasn't far off the mark. Like the American government, The Coca-Cola Company was perfectly happy to conduct business with dictators, as long as they were professed anti-Communists. Several ministers serving Franco, Spain's fascist ruler, doubled as Coca-Cola bottlers. James Farley met and befriended Getulio Vargas, the Brazilian dictator; while in Nicaragua, he solicited Anastasio Somoza's autograph for his daughter. Big Jim was always lavishly entertained in Taiwan by Chiang Kai-shek and his wife. He even unsuccessfully wooed Portugal's autocratic ruler, Antonio de Oliveira Salazar, undeterred by the fact that Salazar ran a police state. In 1954, the United Fruit Company, Coke's Guatemalan bottler, helped overthrow the democratic leftist government, replacing President Jacobo Arbenz with a series of strong-arm dictators. In a *Coca-Cola Overseas* feature three years later, the Company blandly ignored the overthrow, praising United Fruit for supplying workers on its banana plantations with Coca-Cola, their favorite soft drink.

In India, the maharaja of Patiala oversaw his Coca-Cola holdings from his huge, ornate palace, complete with golf course, tennis courts, four swimming pools, gardens, and lakes—all maintained in manicured splendor by hundreds of servants. Coca-Cola Export representative Frank Harrold, who traveled the world to encourage local bottle sales, was awed by the maharaja's opulent lifestyle. "His jewels have been estimated at one hundred million dollars," he wrote, casually adding that "outside the palace walls and so on for three thousand miles is the worst squalor and filth and poverty in the world."

THE ADVENTURES OF FRANK HARROLD

Harrold kept a diary of his world travels in the early 1950s that paints a fascinating portrait of the business. Riding the Coca-Cola trucks for two days in Bombay, he saw "a seething, boiling mass of humanity striving to survive from one day to the next." Despite their wretched lives, they still managed to purchase a miraculous amount of Coca-Cola. By the end of the day, Harrold had an overwhelming desire to lock himself into the Taj Mahal Hotel to "shut away all the misery." The next day, with no apparent sense of irony, Harrold described the "perfectly gorgeous" Coca-Cola bottling plant, surrounded by five acres of grounds. "There is nothing else like it in Bombay, so I am told," he noted with pride. At a party one night, he met several Indian movie stars. "Coca-Cola has a marvelous tie-up with the moving picture industry here," he wrote, explaining that the actors felt a part of the Coca-Cola family. This was fortunate, since the movie industry in India was second in size only to that of the United States.

Wherever he went, Frank Harrold found that "the best way to feel a city is to put on a Coca-Cola uniform" and follow the local route salesmen for a day. "A Coca-Cola truck goes anywhere and everywhere," he wrote, "to the finest cafes and hotels as well as to the lowliest dumps in the slums." His uniform gave him entrée where no other white men dared go, such as Algiers' infamous Casbah, a "criss-cross puzzle of crooked alleys" where desperate hands grabbed at anything.

In Hong Kong, Harrold saw rickshaws, tattoo artists, and little Buddhist shrines in local groceries. He later marveled at the Filipino women and children who carried Coca-Cola on their heads in "buckets, cases, baskets, chamber pots." In Marrakech, he met Malika, a renowned high-class prostitute, "the most beautiful creature of color" he'd ever seen. He was taken by "the flickering flames, the tinkling bells, the shouting showmen, the smell of smoke" of Casablanca. He posed for a photograph with Iola the Coca-Cola lion, who rode as a mascot on a Kenyan delivery truck. In Cairo, Harrold socialized with King Farouk, who told him dirty jokes.

"How did you ever get here?" the man from Americus, Georgia, frequently asked himself. The answer, of course, was Coca-Cola, the former patent medicine, now seasoned world traveler. Spurred by foreign growth, sales volume soared. While it took until 1944 to sell the first billion gallons of Coca-Cola syrup, the second billion had gurgled down thirsty throats by 1953.

THE LIMITS OF CIVILIZATION

Coca-Cola men loved to point out that, wherever they went, they boosted the beverage market for everyone. Once local competitors were faced with Coke's sampling and advertising campaigns, they usually rose to the challenge, resulting in a more competitive but larger market. People drank less water and milk, lured by sugary drinks. In fact, one Coca-Cola president bragged in the 1950s that Coke was often imbibed by people who had never drunk milk.

Unfortunately for the Coke men, Pepsi representatives could attest that Coca-Cola did indeed open up attractive new markets. Following on the leader's heels, Pepsi salesmen soon claimed an alarming share of the market, particularly in poor areas such as Egypt, Thailand, Mexico, and the Philippines, where the sweeter, bigger drink made heavy inroads. Nonetheless, in 1950, Coca-Cola enjoyed a five-to-one worldwide dominion over Pepsi. As in the United States, Pepsi suffered from a downscale image. It was, according to one Coca-Cola representative, "like the difference between an orchid and a bunch of wild daisies."

By the early fifties, travelers couldn't avoid the cheery red Coke signs, which appeared, as one British writer put it, "like a measles rash over scores of countries." While Coke men might not like the analogy, they appreciated the thought. "No matter where one goes, cool, refreshing Coca-Cola is near at hand," a Company publication crowed. "No other soft drink has ever enjoyed such world-wide popularity. None has been so enthusiastically accepted by so many different races in so many different climes." As proof, Company officials loved to tell the story of the Mexican Indian who had never heard of World War II but broke into a grin at the mention of the soft drink. "*Sí, sí, Cola-Cola es perfecto, es magnifico!*" he exclaimed.

Halfway around the world, an American traveling across the Sahara asked his driver when they would leave civilization behind. The native asked for a definition of the term. "Well, when will we reach the point where there won't be any Coca-Cola?" The driver shrugged. "Never," he answered, pointing to a billboard emerging from behind the next sand dune.

~ 15 ~

Breaking the Commandments

Any change, even a change for the better, is always accompanied by drawbacks and discomforts.

—Arnold Bennett

It may be mere sentimentalism, but there are some of us who can never see an old way of doing things passing without regret.

—Robert Lynd

At the onset of the fifties, Robert Woodruff exercised unprecedented power on the local, state, and national level. Known affectionately by employees as the Old Man, he was a vigorous sixty years old in 1950, reveling in his established lifestyle. Woodruff's tenure as president had lasted only briefly after Arthur Acklin fell apart in 1945. The next year, the Boss appointed Bill Hobbs, a former government functionary, as his chief executive. Freed of day-to-day responsibility, Woodruff resumed his comfortable nomadic existence, hunting quail at Ichauway in the fall and winter and stalking big game at his Wyoming ranch during the summer. He visited Europe once a year, usually finding time to golf at Scotland's Gleneagles. In between, he nested briefly at his Atlanta and New York homes. Woodruff often hit New York bars with singer Morton Downey, who served as a kind of court jester there and at Ichauway. The Boss put away an astonishing amount of Scotch without any apparent effect on his athletic constitution.

Everywhere he went, Woodruff conducted business, facilitated by an eager staff who jumped at his every command. His man Friday from 1943 until the end of Woodruff's life was Joseph W. Jones, a quiet, tactful Delaware native who arranged the Woodruff itinerary, bought his custom-made clothing and cigars, handled correspondence, and served as gatekeeper to the Boss. Joe Jones' work was unremittingly demanding, a twenty-four-hour-a-day, seven-day-a-week project without vacation. As Woodruff's virtual slave, Jones lost two wives, but he remained the faithful retainer to the end.

Woodruff's power base unquestionably lay in Atlanta, where the Coca-Cola magnate's influence was subtly omnipotent. When Woodruff got an idea, "you can depend upon it, others will get the idea," lawyer Hughes Spalding explained in 1950, because the Boss would summon a few of the inner circle and tersely introduce it, sometimes at 3 a.m., when the restless Woodruff often had his brainstorms. "We do not engage in loose talk about ideals and all that other stuff. We get right down to the problem. All of us are assigned tasks to carry out." Spalding amiably admitted that, like many others, he was a "stooge" for The Coca-Cola Company. "I guess I'm a *top* stooge," he said. "When Mr. Woodruff wants something done, and if I can possibly do it, I do it!"*

Similarly, Mayor Bill Hartsfield told an interviewer that "I never made a major decision, that I didn't consult Bob Woodruff." The mayor periodically hunted as an Ichauway guest and kept a prominently framed picture of Woodruff in his office. He invariably offered visitors a Coke as his first gesture of Southern hospitality. Without any apparent anxiety over conflict of interest, Hartsfield accepted a $6,000 annual retainer from The Coca-Cola Company while he served as mayor.

In *Community Power Structure*, which featured sociologist Floyd Hunter's classic 1950 "sociogram" of the Atlanta power structure, Hartsfield and Spalding nested obviously in the center, while Woodruff, hovering to the side, was attached by strategic lines to important points, like a spider monitoring its web from the fringes. "The actions of the top leaders who may attend meetings of the lower echelons are watched with acute attention," Hunter wrote. "Even grunts of disapproval are carefully recorded." In fact, as Woodruff grew older, he seldom spoke, and his minions became adept at deciphering his rumblings, which could either indicate approval, indecision, or absolute disagreement, depending on their inflection.

By this time, Woodruff had added two other soubriquets. At meetings, he was sometimes called "the Consensus," ever since one memorable moment when the Coca-Cola board had convened, only to find that Woodruff was absent. The chairman had banged his gavel and declared, "This meeting is cancelled for lack of a quorum." In Georgia, Woodruff was also known as "Mr. Anonymous," since his enormous gifts to Emory University, cancer research, and other charities[†] were never attributed to him—partly because Woodruff was genuinely reclusive, but mostly to avoid beggars. In 1941, Ralph McGill wrote an article on his friend Woodruff for the *Saturday Evening Post* entitled "The Multimillionaire Nobody Knows." The Boss was annoyed, since it prompted an onslaught of requests for money.

The Atlanta realm over which Woodruff ruled in 1950 featured a meticulously balanced, graciously administered, smoothly functioning "old boy" network. Nonetheless, there were signs of friction. Floyd Hunter was dismayed to find that no African Americans were part of the official Atlanta power structure, though he could construct

---

* Robert Woodruff sometimes abused his extraordinary power. When he was annoyed with one of his managers, he might summon him to Atlanta, keep him waiting for a week, then summarily fire him. When Woodruff decided that Bill Hobbs was not an effective president, he let him know in the rudest possible manner—one Monday morning, Hobbs found his office door locked and was informed that his possessions would be sent to his home. Woodruff could be, as one source put it, "ruthless as hell."

† Woodruff's interest in medical research kindled in the 1930s when he discovered the prevalence of malaria at Ichauway. Because of his concern, the disease was eliminated in southwest Georgia within a few years. When his mother later died of cancer, Woodruff turned his money to fighting that malady, and in 1947 the Boss donated land for the CDC near Emory University.

a separate (but unequal) sociogram for them. When Hunter interviewed Benjamin Mays, the distinguished black president of Morehouse College, the educator told him that "the first thing I can remember is a white mob looking for a Negro to lynch." Significantly, Hughes Spalding called segregation *the* major issue facing Atlanta. Many of the two thousand annual Atlanta black college applicants were shunted North. "Maybe it is not what the Negroes want," Spalding said, "but it is what they are going to get!"

Woodruff wasn't involved with such petty details of Atlanta life, however, but rather devoted his energy to a national and international vision, informing Hunter that he wanted to "put Atlanta in the center of the world." In reality, the Boss himself resided at the hub of the action. "How is policy really developed?" Hunter asked him. "Is it made in board rooms, or where?" Unblinkingly, Woodruff told him, "It's made wherever I am. I may be at Ichauway, on a boat, anyplace I call it." Alexander Makinsky once compared Woodruff to a Russian czar who, when asked to identify the important people in his court, replied that "they're the people to whom I talk—and only while I'm talking to them."

THE BOSS LIKES IKE

One indication of Woodruff's awesome power, which reached well beyond Georgia, was a casual remark he made to Floyd Hunter in 1950 when the sociologist asked why General Eisenhower's picture hung on the wall. "Some of us want to see him made president," Woodruff said. "We sent him overseas to give him an international flair, then we made him the president of Columbia so the eggheads would like him."* No one had decided just yet, Woodruff concluded, whether Eisenhower should run as a Democrat or a Republican.

The popular general had resisted a movement to draft him as a candidate in 1948, but by 1952 he had been thoroughly prepared by his "gang," as he called them—a group of calculating, high-powered businessmen, all of whom played golf with Ike at Augusta National.† Aside from his demonstrated wartime fondness for Coca-Cola, Eisenhower had other qualities that endeared him to Woodruff and his cronies. For one thing, he wasn't a business-bashing New Dealer. Instead, Ike genuinely believed in the partnership of free enterprise and moderate government. He was also the perfect leader to calm the country's postwar anti-Communist jitters and usher in a decade of good feeling and conspicuous consumption.

An astute investor as well as military man, Eisenhower kept close tabs on his portfolio. In October of 1951, for instance, he wrote from Paris to Cliff Roberts, his (and Woodruff's) financial adviser, asking whether he should consider moving some bonds into stocks because of increased inflation. By that time, the general and his son had invested in the Joroberts Corporation, which owned Coca-Coca bottling plants in

---

* In 1948, Eisenhower became president of Columbia University. Three years later, he moved to Paris as supreme leader of NATO troops. While there, he lunched with James Farley and Alexander Makinsky.

† Eisenhower and Woodruff were close enough friends for Ike to twit the Boss about his golf game. When the two were playing as partners one day, someone asked Eisenhower what his handicap was. "Woodruff," he promptly responded.

South America. Morton Hodgson, who managed the plants from his Montevideo office, invited Eisenhower to Uruguay to see the Coke operations in person, and though Ike never ventured there, as president he routinely sent aides to assess the progress of his South American Coca-Cola plants.

For the Coca-Cola executives, Eisenhower was the perfect antidote to Franklin Roosevelt's legacy. Ike believed in "reasonable protection for American industry," declaring that an explicit purpose of foreign policy should be the encouragement of a hospitable climate for U.S. investment abroad. Not only that, he emerged from World War II as a popular symbol on a par with Coca-Cola, with a boyish grin that was a public relations man's dream. "Ike, with that puss you can't miss being President," one of his friends told him. With Woodruff and his gang behind the popular candidate, his election was assured. Eisenhower's presentation to the public was as carefully packaged as a bottle of Coca-Cola. Ike appeared as a somewhat naive, straightforward guy, not really a politician, but representing all of the American virtues. In reality, Eisenhower carefully calculated every move he made. "Frankly," he wrote to Cliff Roberts, "my discard of manuscript at Detroit was on the unanimous advice of everybody around me" in order to produce "an atmosphere of complete spontaneity."

In 1952, Eisenhower was elected in a landslide, and Robert Woodruff had placed an intimate friend in the White House. As a benign, ironic gesture, Woodruff now prefaced letters to the president with "Dear Boss," but there was never much question about who was really the dominant character. During the fifties, Eisenhower hunted with Woodruff several times at Ichauway, as well as joining him for lunch or golf elsewhere. In 1959, Woodruff scolded Eisenhower for a photo in which the president sipped from a Coke bottle through a straw—a sissy way to imbibe. Ike responded that "when I tip up a bottle of Coca-Cola for a good drink it lasts only seconds—with a straw, a lot of talk and more walking, I was able to contact more photographers and newspaper correspondents."

FIGHTING FOR THE NICKEL COKE

Despite Woodruff's immense influence and a Coca-Cola investor in the White House, the fifties brought a maze of woes for the soft drink company and its bottlers, starting with postwar inflation. The United States had spent its way out of the Depression during World War II, and many economists expected a postwar recession once the war ended. They were wrong. Instead, Americans released their pent-up savings in an orgy of spending. Besides, the war never really ended, since the Korean conflict soon flared. Even when that war was over, the arms race with the Soviet Union resulted in an ever-increasing defense budget. In 1945, America began a steady inflationary spiral that would cut the value of the dollar in half by 1970.

At first, increased costs worked in favor of the Coca-Cola bottler, since they played with a bigger profit margin than their Pepsi and Royal Crown counterparts, who were trying to eke out a living while selling their twelve-ounce drinks for a nickel. Within two years of the war's end, Walter Mack had to modify his popular jingle to "twice as much for a penny more," since Pepsi bottlers could no longer afford to sell their drink for a nickel. Some bottlers raised the price to six cents, seven cents, or a dime, while others reduced the bottle size to ten or eight ounces. Chaos reigned. A new slogan promising "more bounce to the ounce" didn't help. Pepsi's profits plunged from over

$6 million in 1946 to just over $2 million in 1949. During the same period, its stock dived from $40 to $8 a share.

Meanwhile, Robert Woodruff was determined to hold the traditional five-cent price, even when exorbitant sugar costs triggered the 1921 Consent Decree's automatic jump in syrup cost to the parent and actual bottlers. The five-cent Coke had become, as Woodruff's crony Ralph Hayes put it, "a national expectation and an American institution," and neither he nor the Boss sanctioned deviation from the sacred price. Hayes noted that, with the proper "evangelical zeal," any potential backsliders might be held in check.

Company men could easily toe the line, since it was the bottler who actually felt the low retail price's squeeze. In 1950, Coca-Cola accounted for half of all U.S. soft drink sales, and those associated with the drink were accustomed to the good life. "Coke bottlers," commented a financial journalist, "have had two Cadillacs in their own and their children's garages for so long that they think their rights are being trifled with when the profits don't just roll in." By 1950, inflationary pressures had intensified, and many Coca-Cola bottlers nudged their wholesale prices above the traditional eighty cents per carton. In turn, most retailers in the area then bumped prices above a nickel for a bottle.

While the situation was merely uncomfortable for Coke bottlers, it was killing the opposition. The soft drink trade journals clamored for Coca-Cola to let go of the nickel price, hailing every defection with loud hurrahs. An executive for Bireley's Bottling Company plaintively begged Coca-Cola for "some relief" for "those who would like to stay in business." The situation grew so desperate that some competing brands actually lobbied in favor of state soft drink taxes, which would force even Coke bottlers to abandon the nickel.

Dr Pepper tried a different tactic, suing Coca-Cola in 1951 for $750,000 damages for "restraint of trade," accusing the soft drink giant of monopolizing the market. The rival drink company claimed that Coke threatened to cut off supply to retailers who sold for over a nickel. At the same time, a Senate committee investigating the "Crisis in the Soft Drink Bottling Industry" accused Coca-Cola of the same ploy, asserting that Company officials should "release their stranglehold on the industry and let bottlers set their own price on a competitive basis." The media and general public rallied to the nickel drink's support, however. "It is true that the price of nearly everything has gone up," wrote an editor for the *Pittsburgh Post-Gazette*, "but should this company be penalized if its bottlers can still undersell their competitors?" Coca-Cola deserved "a medal instead of a lawsuit," he concluded.

The abandonment of the nickel price was inevitable, however, as the Chicago sales representative recognized when he beseeched the Company not to add a huge neon "5¢" to the local Spectacular. As costs of labor, transportation, energy, bottles, and ingredients rose steadily throughout the fifties, even the die-hard bottlers were forced to disregard the Boss. By the beginning of 1951, the Company ceased mentioning the five-cent price in national ads, and by mid-decade, the nickel drink was all but dead.*

As Woodruff attempted to hold the line on price, Coke stock fell for the first time in years, and a few disgruntled bottlers felt that the Boss had lost his leadership ability.

---

* In 1951, Woodruff lobbied Congress for a new coin worth seven and a half cents so that Coke's vending machines could accept it, but for once the Boss could not prevail.

Veazey Rainwater Jr. planned a daring insurrection in April of 1951. Renting a huge hall in Florida, he invited major bottlers and other stockholders to a banquet to plot strategy. His father, getting wind of Junior's efforts, sent telegrams urgently advising bottlers *not* to go. The next day, only one curious stockholder appeared, and Veazey Jr.'s abortive coup attempt flopped.

PARABLE OF THE NEW SHOES

The price debacle was the first in a string of unwanted changes forced on Woodruff. The Coca-Cola magnate had led the Company with uncanny brilliance through the Roaring Twenties, the depths of the Depression, and a tumultuous world war by adhering to several simple iron-clad principles. Coca-Cola was the greatest soft drink in the world. No human market should remain untapped. The 6.5-ounce hobbleskirt bottle for five cents offered the drink in the perfect container at the optimal price. With quality control, efficient distribution, and massive advertising, everyone associated with the drink would make more and more money. There was no need to market any other drink. There was no need to diversify into other businesses.

Although he guarded against it, Woodruff was a victim of his own success. "Flattery is like chewing tobacco," Woodruff liked to say. "It tastes sweet, is very satisfying, and does no harm unless you swallow it." Inevitably, however, the Boss was surrounded by toadies who, as Ralph Hayes put it, chanted "an everlasting litany" of "yessir, yessir, thatsrightsir, yousaiditsir." Lawyer Hughes Spalding, for instance, told Woodruff that "more depends on you than any other man in the Southeast." Woodruff naturally assumed that he was infallible. In addition, the sentimental Coca-Cola man hated change. He saved knickknacks to such an extent that his office resembled a rummage sale. Once Woodruff found the right way to do something, he stuck to it unless absolutely compelled to do otherwise. Joe Jones illustrated the point with the story of Woodruff's hand-tooled British shoes. The Boss complained that a new pair didn't fit as well as the old ones, which he had worn for twenty-five years. "Well, Mr. Woodruff," Jones said, "you wear these new ones for twenty-five years and then we'll return them if you don't like them."

While Woodruff may have been forced to admit defeat over the drink's price, that seemed a small matter compared with the beloved little bottle that fit the hand so neatly. In 1948, Cecil Barbee, the oldest of the California bottling brothers, shocked his fellow Coca-Cola men at a convention by directly defying Woodruff. "Men," he said, holding up a brown parcel, "I have here the answer to all our troubles." As he spoke, he removed layer after layer of paper, finally holding up a specially made carton of twelve-ounce hobbleskirt bottles. It took more than a renegade bottler to change Woodruff's mind, though. In the end, that job fell to a traitorous Coca-Cola executive named Alfred N. Steele.

PALLY STEELE'S CIRCUS

Steele, a D'Arcy advertising man, joined The Coca-Cola Company in 1945 at the age of forty-three as vice president in charge of bottler sales. A large man with tortoise-shell glasses and wavy iron-gray hair—a younger, less profane version of Harrison

Jones—Steele brimmed with energy and big ideas. "Call me Al," he bountifully ordered subordinates, whom he routinely accosted with "Hey, Handsome," or "Let's try this out, Pally," accompanied by a robust slap on the back. Consequently, he himself soon earned the nickname of Pally Steele.

The new Coca-Cola salesman had once run a circus, where his favorite act had not been the trapeze artists or lion tamers but the sideshow barkers. Like them, he could "talk the horns off a brass bull," as Delony Sledge, Coke's advertising director, put it. He could also outspend anyone else at the Company. In 1948, Steele went all out to create the most elaborate pep skit ever seen at a bottlers' convention. Unfortunately, the sound system failed, and the drama flopped as actors flailed and jumped about without being heard, while bottlers tittered nervously.

Steele's personality irritated Woodruff, but the Boss could have tolerated the flamboyant salesman's excesses if they had yielded results. Unfortunately, this disastrous convention was soon followed by an unforgivable incident at the Atlanta Biltmore. Steele, unhappily married for the second time, brought a call girl with him to Atlanta and had her publicly paged as Mrs. Steele. Word of this behavior reached the Boss. Typically Southern, the Coca-Cola moral code forgave adultery but punished anyone stupid enough to get caught, and Steele soon found himself in a new office, Woodruff's version of Siberia—no mail, no phone calls, no meetings, no responsibilities. The Boss disliked firing his people, but he didn't mind humiliating and boring them into quitting. For a man like Steele, who could never sit still behind a desk anyway, such treatment was torture. In 1949, he joined Pepsi as a vice president under Walter Mack. Along with him, he took a group of daring Coke men who believed Steele when he told them that at Pepsi they wouldn't be stifled by tradition—and it didn't hurt that he doubled their Coca-Cola salary.

But Walter Mack wasn't ready to relinquish power to Steele, and he had his own traditions—promoting square dances, sky-writing, and art exhibits while his demoralized bottlers were bailing out in droves. Steele informed the Pepsi board that he would quit unless he was given complete control of the company. Consequently, at a dramatic March 1, 1950, board meeting Mack was booted upstairs as board chairman, and Al Steele became president of the Pepsi-Cola Company. Mack quit a few months later.

Pepsi, Steele recognized, was plagued by its past image as a lot of drink for little money—oversweet bellywash for kids and poor people. In the South, racist whites considered it a "nigger drink," and even in the rest of the country people preferred to pour Pepsi into glasses and serve it as Coke. Steele recognized the need, as he put it, to get Pepsi out of the kitchen and into the living room. To revitalize the drink's advertising, he lured his old friend John Toigo away from D'Arcy and installed him at Pepsi's agency, the Biow Company. At the same time, Steele's chemists reformulated the drink, lowering the sugar content to approach Coca-Cola's tartness.

In the calorie-conscious fifties, Toigo touted Pepsi as "the Light Refreshment" which would "refresh without filling." Svelte socialites drank from the bottle, redesigned with elegant swirls. On television, the new American craze, classy Faye Emerson hosted a fifteen-minute Pepsi show, leaning in her low-cut dress over iced bottles. When Al Steele saw that the studio was using a plain container, he rushed to Tiffany's, bought an ornate silver champagne cooler, and placed it in the shot. "Pepsi-Cola's up to date / With modern folks who watch their weight," perky Polly Bergen sang in TV spots.

At the same time, Steele penetrated the vending market, which Mack had abandoned to Coke because the twelve-ounce bottle wouldn't fit the standard machine. It was clearly impossible to hold the line on a five-cent drink in the big container anyway, so he created an eight-ounce bottle (still offering more for the money than the tiny Coke) that fit vending machines. He then arranged low-interest loans for the machines with payment to begin six months after purchase. That way, poorer bottlers could buy the $1,000 units on credit and pay for them out of profits. He also spearheaded paper cup vendors, correctly surmising that Coke bottlers, trapped by their own history and contract, wouldn't compete, since the bottlers had no access to fountain syrup.

The flamboyant Steele knew that none of his innovations would matter unless he could instill new confidence and pride in his bottlers. Undeterred by his disastrous experience at the 1948 Coke convention, he threw huge bashes for Pepsi franchisees, urging them to plow money back into their businesses and local advertising. "You can conserve yourself into bankruptcy," he told them, "or you can spend your way into prosperity." Steele demonstrated his belief in this maxim by plunking down a cool $6 million for 1952 advertising. He assigned his right-hand man, Herb Barnet, to copy Coca-Cola tactics—insisting on quality control, standardized blue uniforms, shelves of procedural manuals, and military organization. Steele built a coterie of managers in his own image. "The whole trick in hiring executives," he told a subordinate, "is to find a good man and turn him into a prick. A good man will be able to stand the course, but if the guy was a prick to begin with, he'll crumble along the way."

Steele's charismatic exhortations also inspired his syrup salesmen. "I don't care if the consumer wants carbonated sweat in a goatskin pouch," he told them. "If so, this side of the room go looking for goats and this side start running fiercely in place." Pepsi men targeted twenty-five metropolitan areas for particularly heavy sales efforts. Spending $13 million, Steele bought out key Pepsi bottlers who were failing to push the product and installed his own men. Unlike Coca-Cola, which had sold most of its ailing Company-owned plants after World War II, Pepsi's directly managed plants turned a profit quickly. Steele even dared to invade the fortress of Coca-Cola's virtual monopoly on the fountain trade. For $30,000, he placed Pepsi in six hundred Fox Theater outlets on the West Coast. Finally, leaving the domestic business in Barnet's hands, Steele commenced globe-hopping to jump-start the Pepsi trade overseas.

The radical Pepsi overhaul proved incredibly effective. As Coke's Delony Sledge put it, Pepsi's sales jumped "like a scalded cat." In less than five years, Coke's worldwide lead dwindled from five-to-one to three-to-one, with Pepsi's share of the domestic cola market rising from 21 percent to 35 percent. Even in Atlanta, the mecca of Coca-Cola, Pepsi's sales increased 30 percent a year. Al Steele, back in his competitor's hometown to open a new Pepsi bottling plant, had the gall to inform Atlanta journalists that Coca-Cola was not Pepsi's biggest competitor—tea and coffee were. Rubbing salt in the wound, he added, "It's a tribute to The Coca-Cola Company that a number of its former employees are on the management team that is helping Pepsi-Cola move up."

COCA-COLA ENTERS THE TELEVISION AGE

While Pepsi roared to life under the direction of Al Steele, a Coca-Cola shareholder wrote that the Company "slumbers peacefully, self-satisfied with all of its past progress." Coke's public relations consultant compared Coke to a frumpish housewife, "modest, sedate, pretty for a long time," while Pepsi was the Marilyn Monroe of the business. "Lots of people think she's too common. But they look—and a lot who won't even admit it want to feel." Momentarily rising above his "stooge" role, Hughes Spalding was also alarmed, writing to Woodruff that his executive board was aging. "Pardon me for saying so," he wrote, "but I just have a hunch that when a fellow has his prostate removed he has lost his ambition, certainly in some respects." Coca-Cola was, in some ways, growing old and fat, just as Woodruff had feared. Bottling plants were celebrating their fiftieth anniversaries; many of the third-generation bottlers took profits for granted. They lacked the fire in the belly that characterized their hungry Pepsi counterparts, and they hated change as much as Woodruff.

During the early fifties, The Coca-Cola Company could hardly be accused of standing still, however. Aware that television was revolutionizing home entertainment even more than radio had in the thirties, Coca-Cola sponsored a 1950 Thanksgiving special in which the Company's radio stars, Edgar Bergen and his dummy, Charlie McCarthy, debuted on TV. The dummy amused audiences by complaining about the wooden nickels he received as pay, demanding real money so he could buy Coca-Cola. A month later, Bergen also starred in a Christmas Day special, *One Hour in Wonderland*, which marked the first association of Coke with Walt Disney's animated characters. Later in the decade, Coca-Cola sponsored *The Mickey Mouse Club*.

The advent of television steadily changed America's leisure habits, along with other trends of the 1950s. Soda fountains at the local drugstore went into a long, slow decline, as people clustered around the TV set instead of gathering in public places. The take-home market, where Pepsi was scoring its greatest gains, now accounted for two-thirds of all soft drink sales. To worsen matters, the corner grocery stores where Coca-Cola was so well entrenched folded as chain supermarkets sprouted in the young suburbs.

While the Company had always targeted children, they now had an added incentive because of the postwar baby boom. *The Adventures of Kit Carson*, starring clean-cut, well-spoken Bill Williams—the star never uttered "He went that-a-way"—lit the TV screen in 1951. Delony Sledge, the Company's in-house advertising chief, studied demographic figures closely, though his attitude toward life and death was somewhat skewed by his devotion to Coca-Cola. "In 1951," Sledge told one audience, "1,535,406 people died in the United States. In spite of our best efforts, this large group has been eliminated as consumers of our product." Fortunately, he observed, almost four million potential Coke guzzlers had been born during the same year.

Sledge recognized that Coca-Cola advertising had to reach virtually every consumer group. "Our product appeals to the entire population without consideration for race, color, economic status, geographical location or religious preference," he said. "We believe to the depths of our collective hearts that Coca-Cola is the best beverage buy in the world. Our work is a religion rather than a business." Consequently, "anybody, anytime, anywhere, is a fruitful prospect for Coca-Cola." The trouble with such a messianic, universal approach, Sledge noted ruefully, was that it made specific campaigns aimed at particular consumer groups impossible. The Company continually searched for a spokesperson to appeal to all age groups. In 1953, with Eddie Fisher, they thought they had found him.

Twice a week, the twenty-four-year-old Fisher sang hits such as "Oh! My Papa" and "I'm Walking Behind You" to adoring living room audiences whose members ranged from toddlers to grandparents. The boyish crooner had "the sort of face that middle-aged ladies want to put through college," according to one critic, but his artfully tousled hair appealed to the bobby-soxers, who were "swooning for Eddie, not Frankie"—and who were an increasingly distinct market for soft drinks and other consumer products. On *Coke Time*, Fisher personally praised Coca-Cola in soft-sell commercials. His handsome likeness appeared in life-size cardboard cutouts, holding out the hobbleskirt bottle and coaxing shoppers to "Have a Coke." In drugstores across America, teenagers began to order "Eddie Fishers" when they wanted a Coke. No one knew that Fisher's effervescent personality was fueled not only by Coca-Cola—he really did drink twenty Cokes a day—but also by hypodermic shots of vitamins and amphetamines, administered by Dr. Max Jacobson, otherwise known as Miracle Max, Dr. Needles, or Dr. Feelgood.*

Like Morton Downey, the Irish tenor who had just retired from his professional career in order to devote the rest of his life to Coca-Cola, Fisher and his new wife, Debbie Reynolds, attended Company conventions as part of the Coca-Cola family. In 1955, they spent their honeymoon at an Atlanta bottlers' convention, where fresh-faced Debbie Reynolds, holding her new husband's hand, stepped to the microphone and announced, "I don't drink Coke. It's bad for your teeth. I drink milk." And she smiled beatifically. After a moment of stunned silence, the bottlers burst into laughter. They thought Reynolds was just being funny. It was inconceivable to them that anyone would seriously make such a statement in such a place. (She was serious, and she didn't like Fisher's amphetamine addiction either. They divorced a few years later, after Fisher's Coke contract ran out and in the wake of his affair with Elizabeth Taylor.)

Nor did Coca-Cola's Hollywood agents neglect the movies, though it was no longer simply a matter of supplying the back lots with soft drinks. Now a "buried plug," as it was called, cost $250 per mention for most companies. To avoid such expense, Coca-Cola arranged for payment through "reciprocal publicity," as with the 1950 film, *Destination Moon*, which featured four astronauts drinking Coca-Cola in their spaceship.

Such efforts were augmented with all of the traditional point-of-purchase advertising, blanket distribution, local bottler under-the-crown promotions, and the numerous other ploys familiar by that time. Nonetheless, Coca-Cola's share of the market slowly eroded in the early 1950s, while the share price tumbled from a high of $200 in 1946 to $109 in 1952. That year, Woodruff fired Bill Hobbs, a sort of Millard Fillmore president who never made much of a mark. Rumor had it that he tried to assert his

---

* Jacobson turned many celebrities and politicians into speed freaks, including Alan Jay Lerner, Tennessee Williams, Yul Brynner, Zero Mostel, Nelson Rockefeller, and Marlene Dietrich. Eddie Fisher later met President John Kennedy, another Jacobson addict. Kennedy didn't question what was in the shots. "I don't care if there's panther piss in there," he said, "as long as it makes me feel good."

independence of Woodruff, which was a cardinal sin.* In his place, Woodruff placed Burke Nicholson, a dedicated, lifelong Coca-Cola executive who had overseen the Export Corporation. Woodruff never took Nicholson seriously as a president, however, regarding him as an interim caretaker.

KING-SIZE HEADACHES CALL FOR KING-SIZE SOLUTIONS

"Coca-Cola can hardly be said to be foundering," reported one Wall Street analyst in 1955. "Yet it is faltering." It seemed obvious to almost everyone except Robert Woodruff that "the only thing wrong with Coca-Cola is Pepsi-Cola," as a veteran observer pointedly remarked. For the first time, Coca-Cola's primacy as the leading soft drink was challenged, and until Coke matched Pepsi ounce for ounce and penny for penny, the gap between the two would continue to narrow. Lee Talley, the short, freckle-faced Alabama boy who had joined the Company in 1923 and now ran the Export company, confronted the Boss in the fall of 1954. "Mr. Woodruff," he said, "I've never been on the losing side of a business in my life, and I'm not going to start now. Unless you allow me to increase the bottle size, you'll have to accept my resignation." The next day, Woodruff succumbed to the inevitable. While he wouldn't officially grant his permission, he didn't withhold it.

News of Coke's plans to test-market larger sizes in the United States rocked the industry. While the soft drink giant had troubles, it still dominated, accounting for 40 percent of domestic soft drink consumption. Digesting the "awesome scope and ramifications" of Coke's decision, a trade journal editor noted, competitors registered "a maximum of interest, anxiety, speculation, and . . . trepidation," and they were not alone. Although many Coke bottlers had been howling for a larger container, others resisted the change, which meant massive capital investment in new equipment. Besides, the emotional attachment to the diminutive standard bottle was overwhelming. "Bringing out another bottle," Ed Forio noted, "was like being unfaithful to your wife."

The plans for test-marketing couldn't come soon enough for Lee Talley, who desperately wanted a bigger bottle overseas, too. At the beginning of 1955, the Export head spelled out his troubles around the world in a long memo to the board of directors. In the Philippines, where Coke bottlers were "very aggressive," sales had still declined by 40 percent over the previous year. The same was true in Thailand, while Egypt was experiencing a "long downward trend." The only real bright spot was Europe. The fault, Talley said, lay in "our dark, scuffed little bottle," which made "a miserably bad showing" alongside the bigger, brighter Pepsi bottles on shelves around the world. Coke needed an applied color label like its competitor, he said. And most important, it must have a twelve-ounce bottle.

---

* One night at dinner in New York, a top executive told Woodruff that the only job that might attract him would be the presidency of The Coca-Cola Company. "You're hired," the Boss said. Later in the evening, Woodruff asked him how he planned to run the Company. "With an iron hand," his friend answered. "I'll take the burden off your shoulders. I'll make the decisions and call all the shots." Deadpan, Woodruff said, "You're fired."

In February, Coke test-marketed a twenty-six-ounce Family Size and two nearly identical King Size bottles of ten and twelve ounces, all in the familiar hobbleskirt design. The package suited the times, as Americans reveled in oversized cars and consumption. Coca-Cola executives insisted that research indicated "the majority of the public prefer the standard size bottle"; they were offering alternative sizes only for "group refreshment in the home." Pepsi knew better, jubilantly taking out ads declaring, "It's fun to be followed—to be recognized as the leader." While the 6.5-ounce bottle indeed constituted the majority of sales for a few years, the shift to larger sizes was inexorable.* By 1958, King Size Coke was available to 81 percent of the U.S. population, though the traditional small bottle still accounted for 80 percent of Coke sales.

Pepsi responded to Coke's King Size drink by attacking with a 6.5-ounce size, but they had little chance in such familiar Coca-Cola territory. Now on the offensive, Coke men got wind of competitive launches, flooding the markets to prevent the new Pepsi size from gaining cooler space. In the United States as well as in foreign markets, the cola wars became intense by the late fifties. Coca-Cola men obsessively spied on Pepsi and its plans; the Coke archives are filled with reports on the Imitator's conventions, telephone polls, and Nielsen market ratings of the period.

The decision to change the bottle size opened the floodgates of change. In his message to the Export board, Lee Talley recommended a "second line of products" because his bottlers were "finding it difficult to keep their businesses going on Coca-Cola alone." Consequently, he sought permission to resurrect the Fanta trademark, which Max Keith had providentially registered in several Nazi-controlled countries during World War II. In April of 1955, Fanta Orange was introduced in Italy, but Woodruff resisted offering "rainbow flavors" in the United States. "Competition has successfully used the multi-flavor approach to take exclusive accounts from us," wrote a harried Coke executive to the Boss in 1957, "and the trend is increasing." The next year, Woodruff authorized the test-marketing of a whole new line of Fanta flavors for the United States, finally providing other Company drinks for vending machines.

At the same time, "pre-mix" Coca-Cola was introduced, precipitating a crisis between the Company and bottlers. In large stainless-steel containers, Coke syrup was mixed with carbonated water. The pre-mix machines were useful at small fountain outlets, baseball games, and other special events, where salesmen with modified backpacks could dispense individual drinks. Recognizing the bottlers' superior distribution system, the Company allowed them to handle pre-mix, but created a special "B-X" syrup and charged ten cents a gallon more for it than regular bottlers' syrup. Company officials admitted that the B-X cost them exactly the same to produce. The price differential resulted, Lee Talley wrote, because they were "free to negotiate on this" and could finally escape the dead weight of the old contract. Minneapolis bottler Tom Moore sued the Company over the pre-mix issue, claiming with some justice that the original contract applied to all bottled, carbonated Coca-Cola, regardless of its size.

---

* In 1955, faced with new sizes, bottle manufacturers complained about the massive inventory needed to service different plants, their locations blown into the bottle base. When bottles were left anonymous, however, consumers complained that they couldn't play "Far Away," a game in which the bottle from the most distant point won.

The large stainless steel container was, in effect, a huge bottle. Afraid that he would lose his suit, Moore finally settled out of court. Al Steele and his Pepsi men were, of course, delighted with the internecine strife, thankful that they were not saddled with the cumbersome contract that continued to plague Coca-Cola.

The rise of national supermarket chains also caused friction between the Company and bottlers. In order to combat Pepsi, the Company's national sales representatives often offered price incentives to a store without first consulting the local bottler. "Every man that called on national accounts wasn't an angel," one Coke man recalled, "and they did whatever they had to do." As a result, the autonomous franchise owners fumed, chafing under Atlanta's high-handed supervision. At the same time, Coke abolished the antiquated parent bottler organization—at least the portion under Company control. Woodruff had already bought all but the Thomas Company, and now he eliminated the extra layer of bureaucracy, replacing it with the "Bottle Sales" department.

Unfortunately, the Thomas Company, which covered 40 percent of the United States population, remained stubbornly independent. When Woodruff encouraged his executive and friend DeSales Harrison to assume control of the parent bottler in 1941, the Boss had expected his troubles to be over. After George Hunter, the long-time head of the Thomas Company, died in 1950, however, Harrison refused to sell; he had come to enjoy his kingdom, and Company representatives who set foot in Thomas territory without permission were in dire trouble.

THE ROBINSON REGIME

During the same February of 1955 that King Size Coke was introduced, Robert Woodruff announced the appointment of Eisenhower's friend Bill Robinson as the new president of The Coca-Cola Company. Loyal Company men were shocked. A rank outsider, a marketing and public relations man, Robinson had very limited experience with Coca-Cola and was—God forbid—a Yankee. Not only that, but Woodruff apparently intended to give Robinson real power. Just turned sixty-five, Woodruff officially retired, assuming the chair of the newly created Finance Committee.* Later in the year, Woodruff also brought in Curt Gager from General Foods as first lieutenant. Robinson and Gager, working primarily from Coke's New York offices, made a formidable team. The new president at least conformed to the Coca-Cola mold: a big, bluff, red-faced promoter, he valiantly tried to adjust himself to the prevailing culture, touring the country to meet skeptical bottlers. Gager, on the other hand, was a small ferret-like man who spoke a strange new bottom-line language. Worse, he was rumored to have been a hatchet man at General Foods.

About the same time Gager came on board, Robinson switched ad agencies, curtailing the long-standing D'Arcy relationship in favor of McCann-Erickson, a bigger, more sophisticated New York outfit with worldwide offices—in fact, McCann had already produced Coke's South American programs. The agency switch symbolized

---

* Woodruff never really gave up ultimate authority at the Company. "Don't take this retirement business too seriously," he wrote to Max Keith thirteen years later. "However official it is, you'll learn that it doesn't mean much. I've been through it half a dozen times."

the formal end of the gracious golden age of Coca-Cola advertising. Its poet, Archie Lee, had died in 1950, and now the new agency abruptly abandoned the classic oil paintings of Haddon Sundblom and Norman Rockwell in favor of color photography highlighting socialites and glistening King Size Coke bottles. A "devil-ridden" workaholic and fierce devotee of social science research, McCann's Marion Harper Jr. brought a contemporary "scientific" bent to Coca-Cola commercials. Harper assigned Murray Hillman to work with Curt Gager, jettisoning old dogma in an all-out effort to reverse the Pepsi gains.

The $15 million ad campaign actually bore a noticeable resemblance to Steele's efforts, relying on the same upper-crust appeal to young moderns. Layouts showing sophisticated couples drinking Coke in front on the Taj Mahal and the Great Pyramids flopped with the folks back home, however. "You can sell all the Coke you want in Pakistan," Delony Sledge complained of the McCann efforts, "but we want to sell it in Punkin Center." Even though it took a while for the new ad agency to produce a winning approach, however, Harper's willingness to butt heads with competition stimulated the stodgy soft drink firm. The first campaign slogan, "Almost Everyone Appreciates the Best," marked a clear revolution, since it was a competitive ad, at least implicitly acknowledging Pepsi's existence.

Up until that moment, Coke men had haughtily ignored Pepsi. Inside the Company, the "P-word" was never mentioned. Instead, memos referred to the Competition, the Imitator, or the Enemy. Drinking a Pepsi constituted a capital crime. If a Coca-Cola man and his family pulled into a motel and saw a Competitor's vending machine, they righteously moved on. One Coke bottler, enraged at encountering a Pepsi vending machine in his territory, hauled out his hunting rifle and shot it. In the fifties, a Coke bottler's son hid in the attic with friends on his seventh birthday to smoke cigarettes and clandestinely drink Pepsi. When his father discovered this perfidy, he lectured him sternly, not on the evils of smoking, but on drinking the wrong soda.

Morton Downey, the crooner who appeared everywhere for Coke in the fifties—at druggists' meetings, bottlers' conventions, American Legion affairs—was one of Robert Woodruff's best friends. "Every week the Coke man would drop off six or seven cases," his son remembered, "and whenever we went out we were all required to have a Coca-Cola bottle in front of us for a picture. My father was the best PR they ever had." Such pressure on children could backfire, however. Years later, Morton Downey Jr. would exact revenge on his father. As "Mortification Mort," he consciously developed an obnoxious, obscene talk-show persona in direct contrast to this father's schmaltz. "My father wanted me to run one of his bottling plants," the son recalled. "The last thing I wanted to do was work for Coke. To this day I only drink Pepsi."

In the fifties, however, there were no such rebels. The immense pride and loyalty to Coca-Cola occasionally stood in the way of necessary business decisions. Gager and Hillman agreed that simply offering a larger bottle wasn't sufficient. There wasn't enough of a difference between Pepsi and Coke to warrant charging more for Coca-Cola. In fact, to their horror, they discovered in blind taste tests that Pepsi had a slight edge, and they unsuccessfully petitioned Woodruff to increase the syrup throw to produce a sweeter drink. The reaction to the secret taste tests at Coke headquarters was swift: "Don't *ever* do that again." In general, the Boss resisted *any* change in advertising and marketing.

Setting the price for the King Size was problematical, since bottlers tended to boost it considerably beyond the standard size drink, putting it above the equivalent Pepsi price. McCann man Murray Hillman persuaded bottlers to *cut* the King Size price while *raising* the price of the traditional bottle. "The regular bottle sales were on a steady downhill trend anyway," he said. "People who drank it were loyal regardless of price." The maneuver worked. At the same time, Hillman suggested charging a premium for the twenty-six-ounce Family Size bottle in the New York City area, where the huge Jewish population accounted for most sales. "Typically, Jewish consumers wanted a big bottle to put on the table and pour at mealtimes," Hillman remembered. "They appreciated quality and demanded a brand name product." Consequently, rather than playing up the savings in price—which would have been difficult, since it cost more per ounce than the smaller sizes—ads for the large bottle bragged: "There's a giant in my house."

Elsewhere, however, King Size purchases fell inexplicably after an initial surge. Sample consumers complained that their Coke didn't taste as good in the big bottle. "You must have diluted it," they reasoned. "How can you afford to offer it at such a low price otherwise?" In response, the McGuire Sisters saturated TV and radio with a lilting jingle in the late fifties: "King Size Coke has more for you, / King Size Coke has more for you, / King Size Coke has more for you: / Flavor, Lift, and Value too."*

PROBING THE SUBCONSCIOUS WITH THE DEPTH BOYS

Hillman wasn't alone in discovering that consumer behavior is often irrational, based on subconscious psychological motives. By mid-decade, "the depth boys," as they were known, had brought motivational research (MR) into the mainstream. Suddenly, sociologists, psychologists, and anthropologists were jumping out of their ivory towers to tender expert advice to businesses like The Coca-Cola Company. For the first time, the Company attempted to plumb the depths of the subconscious mind. In long tape-recorded interviews, as Delony Sledge explained, the psychologists "probe long enough and deep enough to find out (almost, in some instances, against the will of the interviewee)" what motivated representative consumers to choose either Coke or Pepsi. The unrelenting question, according to Sledge, was "Why? Why? Why?"

While Coca-Cola men may have welcomed the depth boys, many critics were alarmed at this manipulative approach, which turned social scientists into "super hucksters" advising on how to write copy with "sell appeal." In *The Hidden Persuaders*, Vance Packard sounded the alarm about this exotic new approach in which

---

* Poet James Dickey helped write such glorious lines in the late fifties as a McCann-Erickson employee. "I didn't mind writing for Coke," he recalled. "It was the easiest thing in the world. My wrestling match was with my poetry. I sold my soul to the devil all day and tried to buy it back at night." In 1959, the head of the Atlanta agency introduced Dickey to a bank executive, adding: "And Jim's hobby is writing poetry." Dickey thought, "That ties it. Hobby, my ass! This *job* is my hobby; the poetry is my real work." He quit soon afterward.

people were swayed subconsciously. Typically, he said, the MR men "see us as bundles of daydreams, misty hidden yearnings, guilt complexes." People were "image lovers given to impulsive and compulsive acts." To a large degree, however, the jargon-ridden academics were simply recognizing what Coca-Cola men had known for years. The Color Research Institute discovered that red was "hypnotic" and particularly attractive to female shoppers. Without articulating it in the same way, Archie Lee had long ago realized that image was more important than substance. Nonetheless, for the first time Coca-Cola men moved beyond mere "nose-counting" surveys to a more sophisticated positioning of the drink.

In the late 1950s, sensational reports on "subliminal advertising" inflamed public fears of nefarious subconscious manipulation. For six weeks, on alternate nights, a New Jersey movie theater projected "Coca-Cola" and "Eat Popcorn" on the screen every five seconds for three-thousandths of a second—too fast to register on the conscious mind. The directors of the Subliminal Projection Company claimed that Coke sales went up 18.1 percent as a result. At special screenings, journalists then viewed a short film about underwater life in which 169 hidden Coca-Cola messages swam amongst the fish. One *New York Times* reporter wasn't impressed, since he had no urge to drink a Coke after watching the groupers and mackerel. Nor, he reported, did he have any "visions, dreams, drives, images, trances, inclinations or hangovers that were not directly attributable to conscious guzzling of something else than Coke the night before." While Coca-Cola men may have been initially intrigued by subliminal advertising, it turned out to be a hoax, and the impressive increase in Coke sales in the lobby a fiction.

A BLAND NEW WORLD

The eager motivational researchers were symptomatic of fifties America during the "age of affluence," as John Kenneth Galbraith dubbed it, in which a sales executive exulted that "Capitalism is dead—consumerism is king!" The question was no longer how to produce enough goods to satisfy needs, but rather, how could consumers be induced to absorb the flood of products? By the mid-fifties, the gross national product had increased over 400 percent in just fifteen years. "We must consume more and more," wrote one commentator, "whether we want to or not, for the good of our economy."

On the surface, at least, Americans appeared to be a complacent, conformist lot, nestling into identical little houses in Levittowns across the country, compliantly purchasing ever-increasing numbers of cars, TV dinners, and soft drinks. To Mochtar Lubis, a visitor from Indonesia, the United States was a garish hell: "Mass advertisements in newspapers, radio, TV, billboards, for twenty-four hours a day, seven days a week, fifty-two weeks a year, year after year, telling people to go to the same places, buy the same cars, gadgets, dresses, build the same house, read the same pulp literature, to feel the same, think the same." This resulted in a leveling of taste, a uniformity in food and politics. "Everybody liked Eisenhower," Lubis noted, because "he's a nice guy." It was, as Vance Packard wrote, a "bland new world" in which the American per capita soft drink consumption swelled from 177 in 1950 to 235 drinks per year by decade's end.

"Bland" is the only word to describe McCann-Erickson's early TV spots featuring Johnny, a chunky fourteen-year-old with slickly combed hair and a double chin—a dork even by 1958 standards. "Hi, Mom. Hi, Sis," he exclaimed as he burst through the door with his schoolbooks. "Got any ice-cold Coke?" Looking up from her ironing, Mom answered, "Why, Johnny King, you know we have. Only this morning you brought in a whole case of Coca-Cola," and the charming family scene closed on the bliss of simultaneous Coke consumption, as the announcer affirmed that "everyone likes Coke."

Nowhere was the uniformity of the age more obvious than at "the new jungle called the supermarket," as one critic put it, where housewives, children in tow, dutifully filled their shopping carts. Coca-Cola and Pepsi fought over optimal locations at eye-catching levels with ingeniously designed portable display racks. The battle for supermarket shelf space called for heroic measures from devoted Coca-Cola salesmen like Charlie Bottoms. Wearing his Coke uniform, he entered a store with a big Pepsi display, telling the manager he was compiling a merchandising survey. "The smartass said, 'Let me buy you a Pepsi, they've got this new sixteen-ounce size.' I told him I'd like that, since I'd never tasted Pepsi." Bottoms upended the bottle and guzzled it until he gagged. "I threw up all over the damn display and kept saying, 'I didn't know it tasted so *bad*.' The women with their carts all scattered, and the store manager was just mortified. He didn't know what to do. He took the Pepsi out to the dumpster and bought enough product from us to make a beautiful Coca-Cola display." Out in the car, Bottoms' companion turned to him and said, "Can you do that again?"

The housewife, who typically ruled her nuclear household roost with an iron hand while her husband wore his gray flannel suit to the office, busied herself at the heart of American consumption. Ozzie and Harriet Nelson provided role models for millions of fifties' families on their Coke-sponsored television show. Like Eisenhower, Ozzie was a nice guy, but he was endearingly fuzzy-headed and lost without his efficient wife. In a typical commercial, Ozzie got hopelessly confused over which hamburgers were rare or well-done while presiding over the backyard grill. Harriet saved the day by bringing on the Coke.

Advertisers approached this newly powerful woman with some trepidation. As Coca-Cola's adviser Charlotte Montgomery warned, "Mrs. 1956" was a new consumer who could be "wooed away by a more convenient package, a big promotion, a slightly more interesting presentation." The insecure young homemaker, anxious for excitement in her circumscribed round of shopping and child-rearing, also yearned to impress the neighbors. Mrs. Montgomery advised Coke men to "jump on the bandwagon," depicting the soft drink as an integral part of TV parties and barbecues. When Mrs. 1956 went to the supermarket, she might *think* she was "a completely independent agent," but with good promotions, Mrs. Montgomery assured the Coke men, "you hold her in the hollow of your hand."

The housewife was really only a conduit to the fastest-growing market of the decade—children. During the fifties, the total population jumped by almost 30 million, the largest increase in American history. Significantly, 83 percent of that growth occurred in the suburbs, nicknamed "Fertile Acres." As one historian of the period put it, "never in American history had a generation of children been so much the center of attention and so catered to." If children were spoiled anyway, why not spoil them with Coca-Cola?

One new way to reach the kids arrived in the fifties. In 1954, Ray Kroc bought a small chain of California hamburger stands from the McDonald brothers. By the end of the decade, his fast-food golden-arched franchises were sprouting across the country. Kroc offered his customers Coca-Cola, a relationship the Company has jealously guarded ever since. The McDonald's beckoned motorists from nearby interstate highways, the dazzling new arteries where chrome-polishing, car-happy Americans found high-speed travel addictive. Always aware that filling stations provided perfect "use occasions"—McCann-Erickson jargon—Coke revved up promotions for fifties dealers. Murray Hillman's booklet, entitled *Automobilus Americanus*, conveyed a basic message: "Get the guy out of his car, and he'd spend money," Hillman recalled. "It was a great cycle. He'd stop to fill 'er up and go to the bathroom, have a Coke, and drive on. Then he'd have to find a rest room again." Company researchers, spying on over twenty thousand gas station customers, concluded that Coca-Cola accounted for 14 percent of all transactions.

Presiding over the materialistic era was a benign consumer-oriented God who blessed the enormous outpouring of American goods, toasting it with a Coke. In the mid-fifties, Congress passed legislation to include the phrase "under God" in the Pledge of Allegiance. "Religious emphasis weeks" sprang up on college and high school campuses. Billy Graham, Bishop Fulton Sheen, and Norman Vincent Peale prayed their way into American homes through the print media and the TV screen.

By far the most popular religious figure of the period, Peale preached an easy gospel of success based on "the power of positive thinking," the title of his best-selling book. Named one of the "Twelve Best U.S. Salesmen" in 1954, Peale agreed with Billy Graham that "I am selling the greatest product in the world; why shouldn't it be promoted as well as soap?" Peale told his audiences that they could overcome any obstacle and obtain peace of mind, social acceptance, and wealth by simply believing in themselves and avoiding negative, unpleasant thoughts. In the words of one critic, he "turned God into a friend and business partner." Robert Woodruff concurred. Stirred by Peale's comforting message, the Boss provided major funding for the evangelist's *Guideposts* magazine and urged Eisenhower not only to invite him to one of Ike's famous stag dinners for influential men but to publicly endorse the publication.

FLAWS IN THE FABRICS

Still, devils lurked in God's country. Armageddon was only the push of a button away, so that the typical upper-middle-class home not only had two cars but a bomb shelter. Children routinely drilled for nuclear war by crouching under their school desks. In the 1959 movie *On the Beach*, an American submarine commander, hearing a persistent but random Morse code message, searched for its source in a post-holocaust world. He discovered that a windblown Coke bottle, tangled in a curtain cord, was the sole "survivor," tapping out its feeble message. Under the placid surface of American consumption, then, lay a constant dread so awful it had to be ignored.

Perhaps in part as a sublimated response, other anxieties emerged. While the indulged children gorged themselves on candy, Coke, and Frosted Flakes, their teeth were riddled with cavities. Coca-Cola, always vulnerable to attack from health fad-dists, received an inordinate share of the blame. Clive M. McCay, a Cornell professor, led the charge against the soft drink. Testifying before James J. Delaney's Congres-sional committee on food additives, McCay made headlines with his allegations that Coke would eat away the marble steps of the Capitol Building and soften teeth placed in a glass of the beverage. "The molar teeth of rats were dissolved down to the gum line," McCay told the politicians, when "given nothing to drink except cola beverage for a period of six months."

In response, Coca-Cola's head chemist, Orville May, testified that McCay offered a "distorted picture" intended to frighten unsuspecting consumers. May pointed out that the .055 percent level of phosphoric acid was far below the 1.09 percent acid content of an orange and that McCay's studies ignored the neutralizing effect of saliva. Finally, he noted that orange juice or lemonade would also dissolve ten-penny nails and eat holes in the Capitol steps. Bill Robinson was more forceful. "The only way our product could harm children," he said, "would be for a case of Coke to fall out a window and hit them."*

RESTIVE HOUSEWIVES, REBELLIOUS TEENS, UNHAPPY BLACKS

Company officials expected health issues to crop up periodically. Other signs of social unrest were more confusing, however. Women, for instance, were restless and bored in their suburban kitchens. In fact, increasing numbers of them bolted the confines of the home and went to work. By 1960, women constituted a third of the American work force, although they were underpaid and underemployed as secretaries, teachers, nurses, and assembly-line laborers. As in the home, the women often actually ran the office and made executive decisions without receiving credit. At The Coca-Cola Com-pany, this pattern was particularly common, as bright young secretaries like Claire Sims and Mary Gresham ran important sales campaigns.

The docile, spoiled children of the fifties also displayed signs of discontent. Social commentators labeled these inexplicably violent youths "juvenile delinquents." Mys-tified and alarmed by critical adolescents, Robert Woodruff unsuccessfully sought a solution to a problem that was transforming some of his best consumers into hood-lums. In 1955, Bill Haley and the Comets performed "Rock Around the Clock" in the movie *Blackboard Jungle*, sparking the new reign of rock 'n' roll. Parents were appalled by Elvis Presley's suggestively grinding hips and the driving rhythms of their teenagers' music. Even Ozzie and Harriet's cute son Ricky grew a ducktail and became a rock star. While Woodruff insisted on the satiny sounds of the McGuire Sisters for his Coca-Cola ads, Chuck Berry and Ray Charles introduced a generation to black soul and funk.

---

* Coke went to great lengths to secure scientific support. With Coke funding, Dr. Frederick J. Stare, a Harvard nutritionist, wrote articles in *McCall's* and *Ladies' Home Journal* in 1954, suggest-ing Coke as an appropriate part of a teen diet. Dr. Glenville Giddings of Emory conducted research indicating Coke's harmlessness to teeth and health until his retirement in 1957, when he was put on a $12,000 annual retainer by the Company.

African Americans themselves were causing trouble. On their television screens, they viewed a beckoning middle-class world of white affluence. In the aftermath of the 1954 *Brown v. the Board of Education* decision, smoldering racial tensions flared in the South. Several conservative Coca-Cola bottlers served as prominent members of newly formed White Citizens Councils, vowing to close public schools rather than submit to integration. In response, local blacks staged Coca-Cola boycotts. At a black service station in South Carolina, an ominous sign on a Coke cooler read: "This machine has economic pressure. It is dangerous to insert money."

For the first time, The Coca-Cola Company grasped the need to address African American consumers. In 1955, before a group of eager black business students, Export chairman James Farley described opportunities in the "15 billion dollar Negro Market," explaining that "American business has of late discovered a vast, unexploited market-within-a-market." By the time of Farley's speech, Coke had initiated advertising efforts aimed at the African American market, featuring prominent black athletes such as Jesse Owens, Satchel Paige, Floyd Patterson, Sugar Ray Robinson, and the Harlem Globetrotters. Ads in *Ebony* portrayed wholesome black models in exactly the same poses as their white counterparts. "There's nothing like a Coke," both ads proclaimed. The messages were equal, but strictly separate.

The Company also hired Washington, D.C., public relations man Moss Kendrix, a light-skinned, articulate African American, as a kind of roving ambassador who appeared at an incredible number of black functions during the fifties—giving away prizes for guessing the correct number of Coke bottle caps at a National Negro Insurance Association meeting, hosting a career conference at Howard University, applauding the Tuskegee Institute Choir on Eddie Fisher's *Coke Time* show, patting black children on the head at the National Baptist Sunday School Convention and meetings of Negro Scouts. Kendrix attended a hundred or more conventions a year for Coca-Cola. The Company encouraged its Southern bottlers to enlist special black representatives. Reluctantly, older white bottlers like Uncle Jim Pidgeon in Memphis and Dick Freeman in New Orleans hired their first executives of color. Given the explosive racial situation, Company officials had to walk "a very fine line where we're friends with everybody," Delony Sledge told an interviewer, adding that he had taped evidence of Pepsi men spreading rumors that Coke financed White Citizens Councils, while an opposing story claimed that the company had contributed $150,000 to the NAACP.

Everyone kept demanding the adoption of a firm moral stance, Sledge complained. "Sure, we'll stand up and be counted, but we're on both sides of the fence," the advertising man said, noting that African Americans constituted 30 percent of the Southern market. "For God's sake, just let us go on selling Coca-Cola to anybody who's got a gullet we can pour it down." With care, the Company managed to avoid any major disasters, its public position determined by the bottom line, as always. Under pressure from Woodruff, Mayor Hartsfield, a staunch segregationist, modified his position, calling Atlanta "a city too busy to hate." Nonetheless, he changed slowly: instead of removing the "white" and "colored" signs from airport rest rooms, the mayor reduced their size.

Woodruff himself had no love for the civil rights movement. In 1956, he betrayed his longtime ally, Senator Walter George, dumping him at the age of seventy-eight in favor of white supremacist Herman Talmadge. At Ichauway, he maintained what aide

Joe Jones called "a traditional master-slave relationship." Blacks were valued servants to Woodruff, and he treated them—as he treated most whites—with grace, kindness, and condescension. Ichauway field hands sang moving spirituals so beloved by Eisenhower that he called from the White House to hear them. In an unguarded moment, however, Woodruff revealed his resistance to black equality in a note to Ralph Hayes, sarcastically urging passage of "appropriate civil rights laws" that would protect "the right of a chimpanzee to vote."

Finally, as if the trouble with women, juveniles, and blacks weren't enough, the 1950s brought labor troubles. While no one at the paternalistic headquarters would consider joining a union, many of the Company-owned and independent bottlers faced severe agitation and strikes. In Tennessee, militant Teamsters took out ads in local papers saying: "Coca-Cola is being delivered by scab laborers." Union men slashed and shot out Coke truck tires and dynamited local groceries that still dared to stock Coca-Cola. In Houston, on the other hand, the bottler hired union-busting Texas Rangers to ride the delivery trucks with directions to "shoot for the belly" if labor agitators appeared.

BLACK FRIDAY AND BLOODY CHAIRS

Such unrest was unthinkable at the comfortable red brick building on North Avenue, where loyal employees enjoyed a lifelong sinecure, eating thirty-five-cent lunches and drinking all the free Coke they wanted. Jobs at the Company might not yield the highest pay in town, but they did mean prestige and security. Or so everyone thought until the fall of 1957, when Curt Gager, the former hatchet man for General Foods, moved to Atlanta and conducted a series of mysterious meetings with department heads.

On Friday, November 8, one out of ten employees reported to work at 9 a.m. as usual and were summarily fired, given severance pay, and ordered to clean their desks and leave by 9:30 a.m.* Some managers found their offices locked, belongings stacked in the hallway. Black Friday, as the day was quickly labeled, came as a complete shock to almost everyone. Nor did there seem to be any logic to the dismissals. "We had some people that weren't worth a shit, but they stayed," Charlie Bottoms remembered. Others, longtime employees doing "a fantastic job," were dismissed. In the advertising department, Troy Neighbors, a popular twenty-seven-year veteran, was a victim. The young man reassigned to Neighbors' desk shuddered. "I'm not going to sit in that chair," he said. "The blood's not dry yet."

The event shattered lives. One man drowned himself in nearby Lake Spivey. At the end of the day, after everyone had left the office, a guilt-stricken woman in the personnel office shot herself in the head. Because their identity as Coca-Cola men or women was so all-important, those suddenly shut out of the soft drink family panicked. "For most people," Bottoms said, "the loss of face in leaving here was so great that they would stay even if they had to wipe the bathroom out."

---

* The actual number of people who were fired is unclear, since no one at the Company officially talked about it. Some sources insisted that one out of three were dismissed.

No trace of Black Friday exists in the Company archives, nor did anything about the layoffs or suicides appear in the Atlanta papers. "At that time, Coca-Cola could have kept anything out of the paper," one employee recalled. "Robert Woodruff could have run naked across the top of the building with flood lights on him without any news reports." It is almost inconceivable that the Boss didn't sanction the mass firings, but he certainly took pains to disassociate himself from the event. A few months later, in the spring of 1958, Bill Robinson found himself kicked upstairs to board chairman, with Curt Gager pushed out of the fold soon after. The two outsiders had done the dirty work, shaking up the tradition-bound Company, and employees were relieved when Lee Talley, an old Coca-Cola man who had come up through the ranks, was named the new president. The son of a Methodist minister, Talley wore red suspenders and spoke with a soft drawl, but underneath his country-boy grin, he was a steel-edged, tough-minded manager.

THE END OF A FRANTIC DECADE

As the noisy, materialistic, conformist Eisenhower era raced toward the turbulent sixties, Coca-Cola and Pepsi were locked in a grim struggle for world domination. Coke's lead had been cut to two-to-one and "an era of aloof grandeur had ended," as one commentator noted. The older soft drink would never stand alone again, though Company executives consoled themselves with the knowledge that intense competition spelled increased sales for both colas at other beverages' expense. Coca-Cola stock had resumed its steady upward trend, splitting three-for-one in 1960.

The McCann-Erickson men had begun to find more effective themes after the disastrous around-the-world campaign. The McGuire Sisters sang on radio and TV, urging consumers to be "*really* refreshed" with Coke, implying that Pepsi just wouldn't do. For the first time, photographers sought real-life scenes involving Coke for the "America Pauses" series. Coke was the "sign of good taste," a slogan that performed triple duty in reference to the ubiquitous signs, the supposedly refined sensibilities of Coke consumers, and the literal good taste of the product. The "Party From Your Pantry" series depicted Coke as a fitting complement to tempting cold cuts, fruit salads, and barbecued chicken—a direct appeal to supermarket sales. Special displays featured Coke with Ritz crackers and Triscuits, while the Company sent food editors packets of menus, photographs, and party game ideas.

The most innovative program of the late fifties was Coca-Cola's Hi-Fi Club, aimed at teenagers. Playing on the enormous popularity of local disc jockeys on top-40 radio stations, the Company's public relations agency, Hill & Knowlton, collaborated with McCann men to create instant teen "clubs" built around pop music and the proper soft drink. "The D.J. would run out of things to say," McCann man Neal Gilliatt recalled. "We gave him something to talk about and got good placement. We'd conduct taped interview of hot celebrities and he could put his own voice into them. It worked like gangbusters." By the end of 1959, there were clubs in 325 cities, with over two million members. The local Coca-Cola bottler hosted weekly dance parties at which the radio show provided the music and entertainment. The bottler and his wife often chaperoned the affair, ensuring that the lights remained undimmed and that nothing stronger than Coke was served. The $1.5 million invested in the Hi-Fi Clubs was well spent, as Coke edged up on Pepsi's lead in the teen market.

Faced with these Coca-Cola tactics, Al Steele redoubled his efforts to fire up his Pepsi bottlers. More than any other man, Steele epitomized the hustling fifties. In 1955, he had married actress Joan Crawford—ironically, a Coca-Cola girl in 1930s ads. Together, the two embarked on a nonstop life of travel, logging over a hundred thousand miles a year and opening new Pepsi plants in country after country. In 1957, they visited twenty foreign lands, where the actress, always holding a Pepsi bottle, was greeted by ecstatic fans. As Crawford's daughter Christina recalled, "she had bottles of Pepsi next to her at press conferences, cases of Pepsi backstage when she went on talk shows, and she learned to mention the company name whenever she was interviewed for any purpose whatsoever."

In public, Joan Crawford was the perfect wife to her fourth husband, but she did not come cheap, and the Pepsi executive went deeply into debt, which only fueled his frenzied need to boost soft drink sales. In 1959, he conducted a six-week whirlwind tour of the United States he dubbed "Adarama," a $200,000 extravaganza to whip up bottler enthusiasm. On April 18, the night after the grueling tour's end, Steele died suddenly of a heart attack, days short of his fifty-eighth birthday. His widow soon joined the board, where she proved to be, as a Pepsi man said, "one of the company's most treasured and highly valued assets." Ultimately, she logged over three million miles for Pepsi.

A few months later, halfway around the world in Moscow, Vice President Richard Nixon loudly argued with Russian premier Nikita Khrushchev over America's capitalistic virtues, as exemplified by a model kitchen at the American National Exhibition. Despite the tension, Nixon fulfilled his pledge to Don Kendall, head of Pepsi's international sales efforts. Leading the belligerent Russian leader to the soft drink stand—Coca-Cola had refused to participate in the Communist fair—he cajoled Khrushchev into sampling Pepsi while the photographers' light bulbs flashed. "KHRUSHCHEV LEARNS TO BE SOCIABLE," declared headlines around the world.

Although Nixon returned home a hero for standing his ground during the kitchen debate, this conniving friend of Pepsi was about to engage in a bitter presidential campaign that he would lose to John F. Kennedy, a Coke drinker. As the sixties ushered in the New Frontier, Coca-Cola led the way.

~ 16 ~

Paul Austin's Turbulent Sixties

Things Go Better With Coca-Cola,
Things Go Better With Coke.

—Advertising slogan, 1963–1968

Do your own thing.

—Unofficial slogan of the counterculture

In his inaugural address, John F. Kennedy, asserting that he represented "a new genera-tion," spoke of renewal, change, energy, faith, devotion, and sacrifice. With his inspi-rational words, the complacency of the fifties gave way to the adrenal rush of youth, though no one stopped to question exactly what the President's men had in mind. Eisenhower, writing to Robert Woodruff, complained bitterly that Kennedy's cabinet choices lacked experience. One was a "crackpot," the other indecisive, and the third "famous only for his ability to break the treasury of a great state." Why, Ike wanted to know, did Atlanta journalist Ralph McGill praise Kennedy?

Woodruff, however, attracted by the potency of Kennedy's charisma, had already arranged Coca-Cola liaisons with the new President. Boisfeuillet (pronounced BO-full-ay) Jones, an Emory University administrator and Woodruff associate, accepted a top post under Abe Ribicoff in the Department of Health, Education, and Welfare (HEW). Ben Oehlert, the perennial Washington insider, befriended Vice President Johnson, calling him Lyndon and posing with him and a beauty contest winner. Morton Downey, already an intimate of the Kennedy clan, and traditional Democrat James Farley quickly established warm ties with the White House, with Farley of-fering to be "available at any time" to talk "about anything" with JFK. After a 1961 South American foray, Farley conveyed his lengthy impressions to the president. In 1963, Kennedy scrawled "from a consumer" on an autographed photograph of himself drinking a Coke and dispatched it to Big Jim. "It was kind indeed of you," the Coke ambassador responded, to "publicly give proof of the fact that you find the product—to use the advertising term—'Delicious and Refreshing.'" According to one source, Kennedy offered Robert Woodruff the U.S. ambassadorship to England—a post Ken-nedy's father had held—but the Boss declined.

Kennedy's plans for a manned moon mission, introduced during his first State of the Union address, inspired a number of eager entrepreneurs. "I just heard President Kennedy," one Michigan man wrote to The Coca-Cola Company in May of 1961. "I hereby make formal application for the exclusive Coca-Cola franchise on the Moon." He also modestly requested sole distributorship for all bodies and planets in space, adding that he could "think of nothing that is more symbolic of our way of life than a Coca-Cola sign." Apparently astronaut Gus Grissom agreed, assuring his son that "when you're my age they'll have Coke machines on the moon."

While requests for Coke franchises in outer space were merely amusing, Coca-Cola jumped aggressively into the sixties under Lee Talley's direction, introducing Fanta flavors nationally and offering Sprite as a lemon/lime alternative to the market leader, 7-Up. The first nonreturnable bottles were implemented to meet the demand for "convenience" packaging. At the same time, Talley delved into Coke's huge cash hoard, buying Minute Maid for $72.5 million.* With the orange juice giant, Coke also acquired Tenco, a coffee and tea manufacturer. "THIS IS COCA-COLA?" queried a 1960 *Business Week* headline. The traditionally single-minded Company was in an "expansionist mood" along with the country, the journalist noted. Coca-Cola was even available in cans.

A traditional Coca-Cola loyalist, Talley brought a determinedly objective managerial style to the Company. In 1961, the Company hardly paused to celebrate its silver anniversary, afraid that Pepsi might advance against a self-congratulatory Company. Similarly, Talley had no patience with tension between fountain, bottle, and pre-mix sale of Coca-Cola. No one, he noted sternly in a 1961 memo, "should ever disparage the product Coca-Cola in any of its accepted forms of distribution, or draw unfavorable comparisons of one form against another." As a token of its aggressive new stance, the Company sponsored a Tour of the World Sweepstakes, with $25,000 in traveler's checks as a first prize. The Post Office complained when a flood of envelopes containing bottle caps jammed their new electronic machines.

STRUGGLING FOR A THEME

Though such promotions temporarily boosted sales, the Company's resolve alone wasn't enough to build and sustain marketing momentum. It sorely needed another Archie Lee. With the baby boomers hitting their teens, the Coke advertising team struggled for a campaign to match the crackling energy of youth in the air. They hired singer Anita Bryant, a fresh-scrubbed born-again Christian who, as a former Miss Oklahoma, combined piety and sex appeal in the traditional Coca-Cola manner. As a fitting farewell to the fifties, Coke canceled its sponsorship of *Ozzie and Harriet* while purchasing TV airtime for Bryant to sing the new jingle. "Only Coca-Cola gives you that refreshing new feeling," she chirruped. "Zing! What a feeling with a Coke." The ad men dropped the word "pause" from their copy, since it seemed too staid

---

* Minute Maid, established in 1946, owned twenty thousand acres of Florida citrus groves, making Coca-Cola one of the world's largest orange growers.

for the times. Unfortunately, "Zing!" too had an artificial fifties ring to it, while the Imitator's ads were proclaiming "Now it's Pepsi for those who think young," lilted by sassy-voiced Joanie Sommers—the debut Pepsi campaign by Batten, Barton, Durstine & Osborn (BBDO). While both Coke and Pepsi ads featured young people disporting themselves with soft drinks, Coca-Cola's direct pitch to any one segment of its vast market was limited by its strategic appeal to every possible consumer—though the Hi-Fi Club still attracted teens to Coke. Pepsi, on the other hand, was better positioned to target one market, since it had less to lose. While Coca-Cola advertising floundered, searching for a unifying theme, Pepsi's efforts to identify with the dynamic youth market appeared more effective.

In 1962, an unhappy Lee Talley called for an "agonizing reappraisal" of Coca-Cola's program. In trying to make commercials "scientifically and mathematically defensible," he observed, the McCann ads had lost direction. In the past year, they had presented Coca-Cola as light refreshment at a ski lift, the contents of a Coke Float with ice cream, or a drink by a swimming pool. "We have been garnishing it with a slice of lemon or lime," Talley complained, or selling Coke as the chief ingredient of a wassail bowl of Lemon Grog. "We are losing sight of WHAT WE ARE," he wrote, "in trying to be all things to all people, and in doing so we are blurring and confusing our image." Talley suggested a new concept for 1963 advertising that would "ELEVATE THE PRODUCT and PUT IT ON A PEDESTAL."

The McCann men had been conducting intensive research for almost three years in search of the right campaign, swimming through "pretty deep motivational research waters," as a *Business Week* writer put it. They discovered that Coke acted primarily as a social catalyst. McCann hired a slim, soft-spoken young copywriter and lyricist named Bill Backer to transpose the research findings into song. Backer, who hailed from a wealthy Charleston family and always wore trademark bowties, turned out to be the new Archie Lee; he demonstrated an uncanny knack for probing the heart of America during the next two decades. The resulting 1963 campaign, "Things Go Better With Coke," introduced the "one-sight, one-sound, one-sell" approach with a slogan that dominated the sixties. The vaguely promising "things" that went better with the soft drink fit Coke's traditional universal thrust. As the Limelighters, a popular folk group, sang in Backer's upbeat jingle, "Food goes better with, / Fun goes better with, / You go better with Coke." The umbrella ad covered the disparate approaches that had bothered Talley, allowing a Coke Float or ski-slope refreshment. As one McCann man put it, the ad attempted to be "'in' enough to win the young adults without being so 'way out' as to alienate people of other age groups."*

The Coke campaign drove Pepsi's advertising men crazy. "'Things Go Better' was killing us," one Pepsi veteran recalls. "No matter what we said, they'd say, 'Yeah, but things go better with Coke.'" In addition, an important subtheme highlighted the product's magical qualities. A Coca-Cola suddenly transformed an unhappy boy in

---

* Coke's notion of "way out" flabbergasted cinematographer Ed Vorkapich. "There's a girl in there that doesn't have Coca-Cola–length hair," a Company man complained at a screening. Such hair should just brush the shoulder, and the pert blonde in question had a shorter bob. Such strictures soon drove Vorkapich to desert Coke for Pepsi, where he had a freer hand.

one spot, for instance, while sharing a Coke guaranteed a couple's mutual devotion in another. The McCann ads had indeed succeeded in putting the drink on a pedestal.

Pepsi countered with devastatingly effective advertisements that completely contrasted with their drab old Sociables commercials. In the new TV spots, created by John Bergin of BBDO, a brief, tranquil interlude was broken by the dramatic burst of a motorcycle coming around a bend or a roller coaster cresting a height. After a brass fanfare, Joanie Sommers' insinuating voice beckoned consumers to "Come Alive! Come Alive! You're in the Pepsi Generation." Using innovative techniques—handheld cameras, "real" California kids instead of actors, spontaneous use of a helicopter flying with a Pepsi vending machine—the new Pepsi commercials effectively identified the drink with the baby boomers and Kennedy's inaugural invocation of a "new generation."

With these two seminal campaigns, the future thrust of both Pepsi and Coke ads was set. Pepsi ads were brash, loud, overtly sexy, centering not on the product but on the consumer. If you drank Pepsi, you could become popular, a part of a new generation. Through lifestyle advertising, Pepsi sought to woo the seventy-five million baby boomers. Coca-Cola ads always focused on the product itself. True, they mixed lifestyle with product attribute themes, but at the heart of the commercial lay a bottle of Coca-Cola. *It* was the star, not the actors.

"Things Go Better" debuted through all of the traditional modes, including point-of-purchase signs, novelties, and radio, but by 1963, television dominated promotions, eating 80 percent of the $53 million ad budget. The nickel gallonage allowance of the bottlers' old contract now amounted to an inadequate pittance. The Company had to persuade bottlers to match TV ad expenditures dollar for dollar, a task complicated by local TV station reception cutting across franchise borders. Cooperative television advertising agreements solved the problem, though they resulted in constant bickering and readjustments.

PAUL AUSTIN'S BEST AND BRIGHTEST

In 1962, Hughes Spalding once again wrote to Robert Woodruff, worried over the grooming of new management. Lee Talley was approaching the mandatory retirement age of sixty-five; the Company needed younger men—"intelligent, sophisticated, cautious, and slightly suspicious. They must know the score." He had penned a perfect description of J. Paul Austin, who became the tenth president of The Coca-Cola Company in May of 1962.

Austin, though a native Georgian, formed part of the new breed of Ivy League managers. A graduate of Harvard Law School who spoke Spanish, French, and Japanese, he could easily have served as one of Kennedy's "best and brightest" advisers. In fact, Austin shared several characteristics with the president. Like Kennedy, Austin, forty-seven, had commanded a PT boat during World War II. A tall man with a riveting presence, the new Coca-Cola president had a thick shock of reddish-brown hair that fell on his forehead like JFK's. There the resemblance ended, however. While Kennedy specialized in charm and wit, flashing his ready smile for the cameras, Austin's mouth was usually set in a determined thin line. At Harvard, Austin had rowed for the United States team in the 1936 Berlin Olympics. "If you wanted to beat Paul Austin," his coach once observed, "you'd have to kill him."

Austin's austere managerial style led one journalist to comment on his "seemingly imperious demeanor." Even though he was the youngest president since Woodruff, Austin terrified his employees. "A certain degree of anxiety and tension has to exist," he insisted, "for people to function at the highest level of their potential," likening this "nervous quickness" to a well-tuned violin string. Normally self-contained, Austin occasionally unleashed a ferocious, quick-flash temper that rendered him still more formidable. Even his metaphors proved alarming. "We really zero in on a problem," he once told a journalist, "pull all the legs off the centipede and see what he's like."

PROJECT ALAKEA

In October 1962, Austin directed insiders Ralph Hayes and Ben Oehlert to zero in on the perennial irritant of having to import Peruvian coca leaves and decocainize them. Hayes approached Henry Giordano, who had just replaced Harry Anslinger, the long-time head of the Bureau of Narcotics, about growing experimental coca in the U.S. Virgin Islands in order to develop plants that were "high in flavor elements and, hopefully, low in alkaloidal content."

Giordano proved as friendly to Coca-Cola as his predecessor and greased the skids for the experiment, though Coke eventually settled on the island of Kauai in Hawaii as the growing site. "You may be assured that we will do what we can to let the appropriate Hawaiian authorities know that your proposed project has the Bureau's approval," Giordano wrote to Hayes. The Coke men called the top-secret effort Project Alakea (a Hawaiian word meaning "white path," implying a righteous road). For twenty years, from 1964 to 1984, University of Hawaii researchers tried to grow coca plants, but they kept dying from a mysterious infection eventually identified as the fungus *Fusarium oxysporum*.* Coke never succeeded in developing a coca hybrid with minimal cocaine content.

THE COLD WAR TURNS FRIGID

Like Paul Austin, Jack Kennedy relished a sense of tension, and in 1961 the new President faced his first challenge just ninety miles off the coast of Florida. Clearly aligned with the Russians, Fidel Castro had begun nationalizing American companies, including Coca-Cola bottling plants worth over $2 million. A thriving market for Coca-Cola since 1899, the well-developed business disappeared overnight. Austin reacted to Castro with typical Coca-Cola restraint, but Kennedy jumped into the ill-planned Bay of Pigs fiasco, followed the next year by the terrifying Cuban missile crisis, when the world teetered on the brink of nuclear war.

---

* In a 2011 book, *Feasibility of Using Mycoherbicides for Controlling Drug Crops*, the National Research Council advised against using the fungus to eradicate illegal coca in Latin America, concluding that "the available data are insufficient to determine the effectiveness of the specific fungi [*Fusarium oxysporum*] proposed as mycoherbicides to combat illicit drug crops or to determine their potential effects on non-target plants, microorganisms, animals, humans, or the environment."

Although Coca-Cola men were not engaged in such weighty decisions, they, too, suffered from a Cold War mentality at odds with their usual habit of supplying Coke to every human being on the planet. Stung by the Communist propaganda against the soft drink in the early fifties, Company policy righteously ignored the potentially huge market behind the Iron Curtain. Pepsi had no such compunctions, which accounted for Nixon's 1959 public relations coup with Khrushchev in Moscow. After his 1962 defeat for the California governorship, Nixon joined Pepsi's law firm at a comfortable $250,000 yearly salary. Don Kendall, who had recently assumed the Pepsi presidency, sent the former vice president globe-hopping as Pepsi's ambassador abroad.* While opening doors for Pepsi, Nixon also gained international experience and stature. Kendall, a savvy executive who was to guide Pepsi for over twenty years, was consciously grooming Nixon for a political comeback.

In 1962, Billy Wilder directed *One, Two, Three*, a satire about Coca-Cola's Communist phobia. James Cagney starred as C. R. MacNamara, a hard-driving, ambitious Coca-Cola executive in postwar Berlin, where his staff included several ex-Nazis who snapped their Prussian heels whenever the American executive spoke to them. After MacNamara opened negotiations with Soviet bureaucrats to sell Coke to Russia, he gloated over "all this virgin territory—300 million thirsty comrades, Volga boatmen and Cossacks, Ukrainians and Outer Mongolians, panting for the Pause That Refreshes." He told his Atlanta superior that "Napoleon blew it, Hitler blew it, but Coca-Cola's gonna pull it off." MacNamara was baffled and frustrated when the Boss nixed the deal: "I wouldn't touch the Russians with a ten-foot pole. And I don't want anything to do with the Poles either."

THE JAPANESE COMPRESS HISTORY

Austin probably agreed with the Cagney character's expansionist attitude. Like many of Woodruff's favorites, he had extensive overseas experience, primarily in South Africa, where he had built the business during the fifties before assuming the presidency of Coca-Cola Export in 1959. Austin's international outlook meant continued growth overseas, particularly in Japan. In 1957, Japanese strict import quotas had been eased, but Coke could still be sold in that country only at selected outlets serving American tourists. There were no such restrictions on Fanta, which sold extremely well, since it lacked carbonated fruit drink competition.

Paul Austin's optimistic 1959 survey of the ripe market was confirmed two years later by Murray Hillman, the McCann-Erickson man, who sensed an "almost fanatical desire to change every fiber of Japanese life." In his 1961 memo to Austin, Hillman described "a set of economic growth forces second to none in the world." Daring teenagers wore blue jeans and danced the twist. "Today," Hillman wrote, "the Japanese are emulating everything American which they can possibly copy and improve upon. It would appear that they are trying to compress the American experience of the last twenty years into twenty months."

By year's end, thanks to heavy lobbying by Coke executives and Japanese bottler Nisaburo Takanashi, controls were finally lifted so that Coca-Cola could be sold

---

* Nixon circled the globe six times for Pepsi between 1962 and 1968, plus numerous shorter trips.

directly to Japanese consumers. The American soft drink, widely visible in the hands of the occupying forces since World War II, was an immediate sensation. Pacific Export director Hal Roberts (known as "the Emperor" by Japanese bottlers) divided Japan into sixteen bottling territories, larger and more efficient than those in the United States. Coke wisely chose well-connected Japanese business partners as bottlers, including Mitsubishi, Kirin Brewery, Fuji, Sanyo, Kikkoman, and Mitsui. Coca-Cola's direct distribution system, which avoided the traditional Japanese layers of wholesalers, threw the soft drink industry into an uproar, while Coke's insistence on cash upon delivery appalled dealers. This was the American way, though, so it must be good. Soon, other businesses were emulating the revolutionary new methods.

Coke men introduced the Japanese to their first vending machines, placing them in schools, factories, and hospitals. The concept of leisure found its way into Japanese thought, and convenience foods achieved enormous popularity. Coca-Cola signs sprouted everywhere in lighted plastic and garish neon. The Japanese Coke jingle, even more insipid than the American version, was a hit record. "Let's have some Coca-Cola, cold Coca-Cola, Coca-Cola, Coca-Cola, we are all friends, Coca-Cola, *Skatto sawayaka* Coca-Cola." The phrase *skatto sawayaka*, translated roughly as "bubbly refreshment," became a popular slogan as instantly identifiable as "the pause that refreshes."

At the 1964 Tokyo Olympic Games, Coca-Cola flowed everywhere, while bottlers paid for Japanese TV coverage. The following year, Coke sponsored the Grand Sumo Championship, presenting a gigantic Coke bottle trophy commensurate with the size of the wrestlers. Sales boomed, nearly doubling every year—2.62 million cases in 1962, 6 million in 1963, almost 20 million in 1965. That surge of gallonage, together with some forty new bottling plants opening overseas annually, swelled foreign sales until they accounted for 45 percent of the Company's volume by 1966. Under Austin, Coca-Cola's overseas operations became increasingly standardized. In addition to English, German, French, and the like, Coke was now advertised in over sixty languages, including Ashante, Ewe, Ga, Ibo, Lingala, Sindebele, Swahili, Tagalog, Urdu, Xhosa, and Zulu. Regardless of the dialect, advertising was, as Austin commented in 1963, "a world language—the Esperanto of world business," adding, "We used to be an American company with branches abroad. Today we're a multi-national business." To facilitate decision-making, Coke's worldwide Export managers exercised increased autonomy in Austin's decentralized management system.

At the same time, the new Coca-Cola president instituted management courses for his executives and bottlers. Using the "case study" method, Harvard professors taught the latest business concepts to sometimes unwilling Coca-Cola men. "There are an increasing number of management techniques," Austin said, "that are spun off from new and different areas—like organizing to put a man on the moon." A great believer in committees, Austin divided problems into component parts and assigned small teams to work on them.

KEEPING TAB ON BULGING WAISTLINES

One of the first tasks Austin oversaw as president in 1962 was the creation of a new diet drink. Until then, Coke had ignored the diet market, since it threatened its sweet, quick-energy drinks. American women had become more calorie conscious in the fifties, however, and now they frantically sought to emulate Jackie Kennedy's slim elegance. "The bulging waistline and middle-age spread," wrote one commentator, had taken on "the proportions of a national calamity." In 1961, Royal Crown had taken its Diet Rite Cola out of the medicine section and promoted it nationally as a soft drink, impacting the traditional cola market. Coke and Pepsi scrambled to catch up, particularly after market research revealed that 28 percent of the population were watching their weight.

Austin code-named Coke's diet drink research Project Alpha, lavishing on it the same manpower and attention more appropriately devoted to a moon shot. Fred Dickson, head of Coke's new marketing division, spearheaded the effort, while Dr. Cliff Shillinglaw tinkered with the traditional Coca-Cola formula, trying to discover a saccharin and cyclamate-flavored cola that would have the proper "mouth feel" and wouldn't leave a kerosene aftertaste. Even more effort was spent on finding the proper package and name. Tom Law, head of the subsidiary Fanta Beverage Company that would sell the drink, argued that it should be called Diet Coke. Even for a progressive leader like Paul Austin, however, such a suggestion was heresy. As a flip McCann man put it, "If God had wanted Coca-Cola to have saccharin in it, he would have made it that way in the first place." Instead, Austin sought a suitable name through his huge mainframe computer, which generated over 250,000 random three-and four-letter words, ranging from ABZU, ACHU, and ACK to ZAP, ZORG, and ZUFF. Company personnel also made suggestions. This elephantine labor finally produced TAB. Short, easy to remember, and completely different from Coke, it could also suggest keeping *tab* on weight problems.

Coca-Cola introduced TaB (perhaps the small "a" stood for the waistline) in magazine ads asking "How can just one calorie taste so good?" Almost apologetically, the Company explained to bottlers that it had no desire "to injure its existing Coca-Cola bottle business," but it was forced to offer a diet drink to prevent competitors from appropriating "this important segment of the market by default." In addition, the memo asserted that since TaB was *not* Coca-Cola, it wasn't subject to the restrictive bottlers' contract.* Because of the Company's ambiguous attitude toward the new diet drink, TaB failed to command a large part of the diet market—which comprised over a tenth of total U.S. soft drink consumption. By 1964, TaB held only a 10 percent share of the weight-watcher market. When Pepsi, less tradition-bound than Coke, debuted Diet Pepsi that year, it grabbed even more of the segment.

BLACK WASN'T BEAUTIFUL

John Kennedy and Paul Austin both faced more ominous problems than a newly weight-conscious America, however. Kennedy had wooed African Americans during the presidential campaign, but, for most of his term, he ignored the pleas of civil rights leaders for federal support, as the aggressive movement, encountering staunch

---

* The Thomas Company insisted that because the new drink was a dietetic form of Coca-Cola, the old contract should apply. Without granting the validity of the claim, Paul Austin agreed to pay a "tribute" to the Thomas Company to assure its advertising cooperation.

Southern racism, led to confrontation and bloodshed inevitably involving Coca-Cola. The passive bus boycotts of the fifties gave way to a more alarming activism when, on February 1, 1960, four black college freshmen sat down at the Woolworth's lunch counter in Greensboro, North Carolina, where they were refused hamburgers and Cokes. Stoically, they simply sat there, and the next day they returned with twenty-three classmates. The sit-in had been born, and the violence and furor that followed in the next three years jarred America's complacency. By demanding equal rights to Coca-Cola, the civil rights activists were striking at the heart of Southern and American culture. They were also announcing a desire to *join*, not to destroy, middle-class Americans. Coca-Cola men like Delony Sledge who could see through the smoke must have realized that, were it not for the emotionally entrenched racism, the South would have embraced blacks as equal consumers. In fact, the Greensboro sit-in eventually succeeded because of economics. The Woolworth's owner, seeing his business slowly erode, finally capitulated.

The next year, as Freedom Riders were clubbed in Alabama and Mississippi, the atmosphere at the traditional Ichauway Fourth of July barbecue seemed tranquil. Woodruff always threw a huge free party for his black tenants and their families. That year, three thousand guests enjoyed the Boss's largess, while the Coca-Cola and beer flowed, but racial tensions were lurking there as well. For years, Guy Touchtone, the white Ichauway manager/overseer, had bullied, robbed, and threatened his African American workers, sleeping with any black woman he fancied. Woodruff aide Joe Jones, aware that this behavior was demoralizing Ichauway—and angry that Touchtone was stealing timber and beef from the farm—had repeatedly attempted to persuade the Boss to fire him, but to no avail.

During the festivities, Charlie Ware, an African American, made the mistake of flirting with one of Touchtone's mistresses. The overseer complained to his friend "Gator" Johnson, the local sheriff, who had a reputation for brutality. That night, Sheriff Johnson went to Charlie Ware's house, intermittently beating his wife until Ware came home. Then, with the black man handcuffed in the front seat of his car, the sheriff picked up his radio transmitter and said, "This nigger's coming on me with a knife! I'm gonna have to shoot him." Wounding Ware twice in the neck, he said, "He's still coming on!" and shot him a third time.* Miraculously, Ware survived, and the incident sparked what became known as the Albany Movement. Charged with felonious assault, the wounded black man languished in jail for over a year because Woodruff didn't come forward to meet his bail bond. In fact, Woodruff apparently ignored the entire incident, though he forcibly "retired" Touchtone the next year by giving him a three-hundred-acre farm adjacent to the plantation and constructing a house for him.

By 1963, neither Kennedy nor Austin could ignore increasingly militant African Americans. In August, Martin Luther King Jr., standing in front of the Lincoln

---

* This was by no means the first racial incident at Ichauway. In 1932, Woodruff had hired a Pinkerton agent to investigate a series of lynchings on the plantation. The detective discovered that a white employee was the ringleader, but Woodruff didn't fire him for fear of his possible return to do damage. The blacks didn't blame Woodruff for the lynchings, but they, along with local whites, did resent the rich Atlantan for buying the property and preventing the free range of their hogs and cattle. At least the Boss provided work, however—for fifty cents a day.

Memorial, declared "I have a dream!" The following month, the Congress of Racial Equality (CORE) demanded that African Americans appear in Coca-Cola's television and print advertising. "We are appealing to you on a moral basis," program director Clarence Funnye wrote to Paul Austin, but he added a thinly veiled threat that "selective purchasing committees" would "aid us in our bargaining position." In other words, there would be a Coke boycott if the Company failed to respond.

Paul Austin could not afford to antagonize CORE, but at the same time, if he aired integrated commercials in the South, he stood to lose white consumers. In a long memo, Austin bitterly blamed Harvey Russell, Pepsi's black vice president, for the CORE attack.* In addition, he noted, Coca-Cola, "being a Southern institution," provided a satisfactory emotional target. "We are the largest advertiser of a single product; the nature of our product makes it vulnerable to an organized boycott." As a solution, Austin suggested creating a TV commercial at a beach "with a white attendant serving alternatively white and Negro customers." The Company could also agree to produce an integrated print ad, but "we might run it only in a Negro publication, such as EBONY, *if we should decide to run it at all*." Basically, Austin advocated stall tactics, hoping the furor would die down, and he hoped that others would soon be running integrated ads so that "we will not stand out."

At the same time, Operation Breadbasket, an Atlanta organization of ministers, pushed the Company to hire African Americans on the production lines of bottling companies. A local white activist found the Coca-Cola men polite and seemingly cooperative, "doing their best under the circumstances." Black workers were already common in Northern bottling plants. Southerners, however, were still convinced that syphilis was transmitted by drinking fountains and toilets, and they didn't want blacks bottling their Coke. When a boycott loomed, however, the Atlanta bottler promised to hire blacks and remove signs designating "Colored" and "White" bathrooms.

Ivan Allen Jr., who replaced William Hartsfield as Atlanta's mayor in 1962, bore the brunt of civil rights demands. Coming to power at the same time, Allen and Austin were friends, part of a tight group of WASPs Allen later described as "business-oriented, nonpolitical, moderate, well-bred, well-educated, pragmatic." It was, he recalled, "not a particularly colorful group," in all of that phrase's meanings. When these young leaders were confronted with angry African American men and women, they had no idea how to proceed. In 1963, President Kennedy personally begged Mayor Allen to testify before Congress in favor of his civil rights bill on public accommodations, since the mayor was the only moderate Southern politician who might have the guts to do it. Allen agonized over the decision, finally baring his soul to Robert Woodruff. He told the Boss that he felt compelled to testify in favor of the bill, on both moral and practical grounds. The civil rights movement appeared unstoppable, and Atlanta business would suffer from more violence if some accommodation weren't made.

Woodruff considered what the mayor had said. He hated change of any kind, particularly if it meant upsetting a well-oiled social order. Only three years ago, he had

---

* The Ku Klux Klan circulated a picture of Harvey Russell and his wife, a light-skinned African American, urging a white boycott of Pepsi because its "nigger vice-president" was married to a white woman. Local Coke bottlers were rumored to have funded the brochures, but there was never any proof.

written scathingly about voting rights for chimpanzees. "You are probably right," he told Allen, but suggested that the mayor ask Congress to allow a reasonable delay for rural communities. Similarly, Austin convinced Woodruff to hire Charles Boone, the company's first black bottle sales representative. After all, research demonstrated that while African Americans comprised 11 percent of the population, they consumed 17 percent of all soft drinks.

When white Coke veteran Charlie Bottoms learned he would train Boone during a six-month partnership, he resented grooming the black man for a higher-paying position. The odd couple soon closed ranks under duress, however. For the white Bottoms, the experience proved illuminating. "When we pulled into a filling station, they'd see Charles and say their rest rooms were out of order," Bottoms remembered. "When we stayed in a hotel in Greenville, they called my room all night long every fifteen minutes to tell me I was going to be dead by morning." At bottling plants, Boone and Bottoms had to enter through the back door. Willie Barron, the Rome, Georgia, bottler, told Bottoms not to drive his car on a service visit "because it will be full of blood when you leave."

Gradually, however, the bottlers accepted the black Coca-Cola man, who performed his job extraordinarily well. A big man with a deep, booming voice and a startling resemblance to Martin Luther King Jr., Boone had been a college football star, held a master's degree, and announced radio shows before joining a South Carolina bottler to boost sales to local African Americans. A classically dedicated Coca-Cola man, Boone eventually rose to vice president of Special Markets before dying of a heart attack one Saturday morning, at work in his office.

FROM CAMELOT TO THE GREAT SOCIETY

Just as President Kennedy was maturing in office, taking a strong stand on civil rights and making peace overtures to the Russians, he was assassinated in Dallas. His successor, Lyndon Johnson, strove for the Great Society, hoping to unite whites and blacks, rich and poor. As the consummate politician and compromiser, Johnson found a friend and kindred spirit in Robert Woodruff. LBJ imagined the same kind of ideal America—founded, as he put it, on "the desire for beauty and hunger for community"—that Coca-Cola advertising portrayed.

Furthermore, Johnson deeply needed a stable father figure. During his White House years, Johnson often sought out Woodruff as a drinking companion and counselor. On the surface, the two men were quite different—Woodruff the quiet, reserved gentleman, Johnson the loud, raw buffoon—but they shared similar philosophies and Southern backgrounds. When Johnson won a landslide victory over Barry Goldwater in 1964, Woodruff wrote to LBJ that "I'm sorry the vote was not unanimous." The president scrawled an undated message for Woodruff: "Tell Bob to come see me whenever he's in town." Johnson's motorcade once screeched to a stop when he spotted Ovid Davis, the Coca-Cola lobbyist, on the sidewalk. "Hey, there's Bob's boy!" the president yelled. "You tell Bob I said hey, you heah?"

Only a few years earlier, neither Woodruff nor Johnson had espoused black equality, but they were changing. Whether out of pragmatism or ethics, the two white leaders became significant voices for moderation and the end of racism. When Martin

Luther King Jr. won the Nobel Peace Prize in 1964, Ivan Allen's biracial banquet in his honor nearly foundered, since the Atlanta white establishment at first refused to attend any event featuring "Martin Luther Coon," as they privately called the black leader. Realizing that the national media would embarrass Atlanta and, by extension, Coca-Cola, Woodruff let it be known through Paul Austin that *he* favored the dinner, and the rest of Southern society promptly fell in line.*

At the same time, Woodruff finally permitted Coke advertising to showcase African Americans. In 1965, Barbara McNair appeared in the first "main thrust" TV commercial for Coca-Cola to use a black celebrity. The cheerful folky sound of the Limelighters gave way to Ray Charles, the Supremes, the Fifth Dimension, Aretha Franklin, Gladys Knight & the Pips, and Marvin Gaye soulfully conveying the message that "Things Go Better With Coke." Each artist created a distinctive version of the song. The Supremes' effort, for instance, sounded almost exactly like their hit, "Baby Love." The Ray Charles blues style featured powerful, emotion-laden visuals of a concert. "In between the sad songs that I sing all night long," Charles wailed, "it's so nice to leave the show / let my throat have a Coke, don't you know."

The new advertising was not simply an accommodation to more militant African Americans, though. The entire mood of America was shifting. The docile baby boomers of the fifties had transformed into rebellious teenagers who sought meaning in the revolutionary new music of the Beatles, with their long hair, driving beat, and suggestive lyrics. Coca-Cola couldn't afford to let Pepsi own the new generation. In addition to black performers, Coke hired white pop stars such as Leslie Gore, the Moody Blues, Petula Clark, Neil Diamond, the Everly Brothers, and Jan & Dean to sing upbeat, youthful versions of the jingle. The McCann men even negotiated with the Beatles, who often posed with Coke, but they proved too expensive for Woodruff's taste.

The mid-sixties retained many vestiges of normal middle-class life from the previous decade, however, despite the whiff of change in the air. *Pause for Living*, an extraordinarily popular Coca-Cola publication since 1953, covered "flower arranging, table settings and decorations, food preparation, teen-age entertaining and various handicrafts." The flower arrangements, "enhanced" by bottles of Coca-Cola, continued to mesmerize garden clubs and home economics classes across America, pulling some five hundred weekly letters to the editor. Similarly, a 1966 television commercial portrayed a "typical" housewife rushing through her day as mother, wife, and student, with no hint that she sought any liberation other than an occasional drink of Coke. Outside each office at The Coca-Cola Company, one journalist wrote, "sits an engaging, competent secretary who guards her man pleasantly but firmly." Sexism thrived in the America of the mid-sixties. Coca-Cola's "Smile Girl" promotion offered prizes to the most toothsome beauties, while "curvaceous misses" added sex appeal to bottler convention skits.

---

* It is difficult to know what Robert Woodruff's real feelings about civil rights were by 1964. He remained good friends with J. Edgar Hoover, who had placed Martin Luther King Jr. at the head of his "enemies list" and delighted in replaying tapes of the black leader's illicit sexual encounters. In August of 1963, the same month in which King made his famous "I Have a Dream" speech, Hoover wrote to Woodruff, assuring him that "all of us at the FBI will strive to continue to merit the support you have given us."

Unconcerned by sweeping societal changes, Coca-Cola's legal department fussed and fretted over the proper use of the trademark. One should never relegate the product to the status of a "common adjective," for instance, as in "Coke party." Nor should the sacred product ever be pluralized—one drank several bottles of Coke, never several Cokes. Advising disc jockeys in 1965, the Company men gave them a list of appropriate "happy words you may use," such as "Coca-Cola lifts your spirits," or "Any meal goes better with Coke."

Soft drink sales in 1965 were bubbling along, rising to an annual American per capita of 260 drinks. Coca-Cola commanded 41 percent of the market, with Pepsi trailing at 23.5 percent. Nor was the Company resting on its laurels under Paul Austin's management. In 1964, it acquired a coffee business with Houston-based Duncan Foods in exchange for $30 million worth of Coke stock. Many Company men surmised that Woodruff had pursued the merger primarily in order to bring dynamic young Charles Duncan Jr. into the Coca-Cola fold. On another front, Coke was offending orange juice competitors by advertising Minute Maid as if it were a soft drink. Ben Oehlert, now the president of the subsidiary, pointed out that traditional ads urged mothers "to see to it the kiddies take a four-ounce dose of the stuff at breakfast." Abandoning such medicinal claims, Coke stressed the "natural sweetness, natural freshness" of orange juice, selling it in vending machines. Along with Hi-C, the Company's diluted fruit drink, Oehlert pushed orange juice as a fine refreshment any time of the day.

Meanwhile, the Company was developing other flavors. In Texas, it introduced Chime, a cherry-flavored cola designed to compete with Dr Pepper. That was a flop, but Fresca, a carbonated grapefruit-lemon diet drink, proved an overnight sensation, surprising even Coca-Cola men. The drink's cool refreshment was emphasized rather than its lack of calories. As an announcer recounted Fresca's virtues, snow drifted down, gradually building to a windblown storm. "It's a blizzard!" he yelled through chattering teeth. Providentially, the worst snowstorm in years hit New York City on February 7, 1967, the day of the local Fresca roll-out. An inspired ad man had his picture taken holding a bottle of Fresca in the white swirls. "New York, We Are Sorry," read the caption.

Pepsi-Cola's Don Kendall matched Coke step-for-step in the creation of other drinks with Teem, Mountain Dew, and others. In 1965, Pepsi joined Frito-Lay to become PepsiCo. "Potato chips make you thirsty," Kendall offered as explanation of the merger. "Pepsi satisfies thirst." With the addition of snack foods, Pepsi relied much more heavily than Coke on nondrink income, a trend that would increase with the years. In 1968, Pepsi acquired Trailer Convoy, American Van Lines, and Chandler Leasing.

The Coca-Cola phenomenon garnered most of the attention, though. The Company "gyrates with new products, new packaging, new acquisitions," wrote an awed commentator. Not since Robert Woodruff assumed command in the twenties had the Company been so supercharged. "Growth is essential," Paul Austin said. "We must grow as individuals, as a Company, as a nation." As a sign of change, Austin authorized construction of a multistory edifice on North Avenue to complement the old red-brick building. New marketing head Fred Dickson stressed that "we sell Coca-Cola to a vast, fickle, forgetful public. Right now some new trend may be starting that will change the whole contemporary scene."

Coke was well aware of one clear trend. Fast-food chains were "mushrooming," a Company publication noted, mentioning McDonald's, Carrols, Burger Chef, Burger King, Henry's, Biff-Burger, Jiffy's, Chip's, and Braziers. While these new outlets dispensed a flood of Coca-Cola, the Company was convinced they could sell more. "Whaddayahave, whaddayahave?" was the impatient query at the Varsity in Atlanta, the world's largest fast-food outlet. In the training film *Walk-Up Hospitality*, Coca-Cola urged counter personnel to smile brightly and suggest a large ice-cold Coke along with that order of fries. McDonald's and Jiffy's were viewed as battlegrounds in a deadly serious contest. Veteran Lee Talley reveled in the challenge, issuing a call to arms in the cola wars, taking "joy in the fray, asking no quarter and giving none." Coca-Cola skits, elaborately staged by Jam Handy Productions with professional actors, whipped Company men into a frenzy. "We'll fight 'em in the streets, in the drive-ins, in the skating rinks," an actor playing a district manager promised in 1965.

THE ARAB BOYCOTT BLUES

That same year, Paul Austin convinced Woodruff that things could go better for Coke behind the Iron Curtain as well as in the drive-ins and skating rinks of America. The Bulgarian government signed on as a Coca-Cola bottler, importing concentrate from the Company, since the local imitation, Bulgar Cola, failed to find a market. Romania, Czechoslovakia, and Yugoslavia soon followed suit.

Austin initiated contacts with the Soviet government, but he was afraid that selling Coke in the USSR might prompt an American backlash. Testing the waters, he dispatched Boisfeuillet Jones, who now worked for Robert Woodruff's philanthropic endeavors, to meet secretly with Averell Harriman, LBJ's Ambassador at Large, in Washington. When Jones asked whether the State Department would object to the sale of Coca-Cola in Russia, Harriman responded that the venture would be "in the national interest." After a favorable consensus from other advisers—even cold warrior Jim Farley approved, writing that if Coca-Cola didn't "get in there," Pepsi undoubtedly would—Austin sent Alex Makinsky and another Russian-speaking Coke man to the Kremlin to work out the details. Coca-Cola would be bottled in Moscow for sale only to outlets operated by Intourist, the Russian travel bureau, as part of an overall Soviet plan to attract foreign money. When word leaked of the impending deal, however, the Company received negative press. The profits from Russian Coke, one paper complained, would "help the Kremlin's pals—in Red China and Viet Nam—pals whose troops and Viet Cong puppets are killing, wounding and capturing good U.S. fighting men." Concluding that Americans probably weren't yet prepared for a rapprochement with the Communists, Austin—possibly at Woodruff's behest—postponed the project.

In 1966, despite Austin's best efforts, Coca-Cola became a hot political topic anyway. The Company refused to grant a franchise to an Israeli bottler, and the Anti-Defamation League accused Coca-Cola of compliance with the Arab League boycott of Israel. Within a week, the American Jewish community was calling for a boycott of its own. Manhattan's Mount Sinai Hospital stopped serving Coke in its cafeteria, and Nathan's Famous Hot Dog emporium on Coney Island threatened to turn off the spigot as well. Offended Jews threw Coke coolers out of second-story windows in

Chicago and Los Angeles. Coca-Cola had to act quickly if it didn't want to lose the lucrative American Jewish market. James Farley defended the Company by pointing out that Coca-Cola had attempted to enter Israel back in 1949 but had been denied because of rampant anti-American feeling. Furthermore, market research had revealed that conditions in Israel weren't conducive to profitable sales. No one bought Farley's explanations, and boycott plans progressed.

Swiftly, The Coca-Cola Company moved to find a bottler, announcing within days that New York banker Abraham Feinberg, one of the original applicants back in 1949, was interested in funding an Israeli franchise, and the Company had signed a letter of intent with him. The hubbub in the United States died down, but the war drums began beating in the Arab countries, where Coca-Cola sold a hundred thousand cases a year through thirty locally owned bottling plants. The hot, dry Middle Eastern countries provided ideal customers for Coke, since Muslims were not allowed to touch alcohol. "From Morocco to Pakistan," one journalist noted, "the modern oasis is the soft-drink stand." Now, the Arabs gave Coca-Cola until August 15 to cancel its commitment to Feinberg. The Company stood to lose some $20 million in profits per year, in addition to handing over the huge territory to Pepsi, which was avoiding Israel without fanfare.

Coke's customary lobbyists shifted into high gear. Ben Oehlert brought a personal plea from President Johnson to Mostafa Kamel, the United Arab Republic's ambassador to the United States. His Excellency Kamel was terribly sympathetic, writing that "nothing is closer to my heart than participating through my modest efforts in promoting cooperation between our two countries," but he was powerless on "this delicate issue." Feinberg, he suggested, should proceed as slowly as possible to gain time. Meanwhile, Alexander Makinsky rushed around the Middle East taking stock of the grim situation. Egypt, whose lead other Arab countries would follow, was looking for an excuse to jettison Coke anyway, since it needed to save on foreign exchange. Makinsky hoped that his friend Angel Sagaz, the Spanish ambassador to Cairo, who had once served as the Coke lobbyist's intermediary with Franco, could help. Since the Spanish were firm friends of the Arabs and refused to do business with Israel, perhaps Sagaz could intercede for the soft drink in Cairo.

Coke's only real hope, Makinsky believed, lay in immediate negotiations to construct a concentrate plant in Egypt, which would result in most of the capital remaining in the country. The Egyptians, he pointed out, were realists; money spoke louder than anti-Semitism. Makinsky also stressed that all of the bottling plants were owned by Arabs and that the boycott would put some twenty-five thousand natives out of work. In addition, Coca-Cola men emphasized that they were not investing one cent inside Israel—like Hilton Hotels and other international companies that had franchises in Israel without actually owning the business there themselves.

Nothing worked. Coca-Cola fell victim to its own symbolism as *the* typical American product, and the Arab demagogues whipped up such an emotional climate that the soft drink company could find no middle road. Refusing to renege on the promise to Feinberg, Coca-Cola watched helplessly as the Arab boycott against the product finally commenced in August of 1968. Coca-Cola men like John Brinton, who watched the Middle Eastern business collapse after nearly twenty years of hard work, insisted that it was ultimately a business rather than a moral decision: "They would have lost a lot more if they hadn't given the franchise to Israel because of the Jewish boycott in the United States."

UNRAVELING AT HOME

By the time the Arab boycott officially went into effect late in 1968, America itself was coming unglued, primarily because of protests over the escalating conflict in Vietnam. Regarding the civil strife in Vietnam as a fight to the death with Communism, Lyndon Johnson was determined to win at any cost. As the war heated up, Coca-Cola men first saw it as one more patriotic opportunity to sell soft drinks to GIs, as with World War II and Korea. They sent Anita Bryant to Southeast Asia to sing for the boys in 1965, tagging a photo with the caption, "Our Anita Cheers Troops With Bob Hope." The same year, the Company built bottling plants in Danang and Qui-Nhon to supplement the overworked Saigon operation. As American troops poured into Vietnam, where returnable bottles presented quite a problem, the Company also shipped over nearly four hundred thousand cartons of canned Coca-Cola. In the John Wayne movie *The Green Berets*, an entire pallet of Coca-Cola parachuted to thirsty jungle troops.

Writer Tom Wolfe suggested that, rather than saturation bombing, the United States should "seduce its way to victory" by showering North Vietnam with Coca-Cola. A Japanese philosopher urged the same tactic for a different reason. "That will destroy them faster than bombs," he said. The war in Vietnam starkly contrasted with World War II, however, and the Company soon realized it. While wartime advertising in the forties highlighted Coca-Cola's vital presence in the foxholes, no ads proclaimed that things went better with Coke in Vietnam. James Farley, the aging Coca-Cola cold warrior, couldn't understand the escalating antiwar protests, offering his "unhesitating support" to the president. Similarly, Robert Woodruff wrote to LBJ that the "American people are supporting your position. I am with you."

Johnson's earnest appeals to "my fellow Americans" fell on increasingly deaf ears, however, as television ushered bloody jungle scenes into American living rooms. The Tet Offensive early in 1968 nailed the final peg in the coffin of a presidency devoted to unifying America, eliminating poverty, and promoting peace throughout the world. Instead, Johnson faced race riots, burning inner cities, massive antiwar demonstrations, and a growing counterculture that rejected all the American virtues of hard work, cleanliness, respect for authority, and restraint. By the end of March, Johnson was completely demoralized and announced that he would not run for another term.

The dismal year of 1968 also heralded personal tragedy for Robert Woodruff. In January, his wife, Nell, suffered a stroke at Ichauway and died soon after. Though Woodruff was often away from his wife, she had provided his emotional anchor. At the age of seventy-eight, with the America he had known in shambles, Woodruff, always a heavy drinker, now increasingly turned to alcohol rather than Coca-Cola. When news of Martin Luther King Jr.'s assassination reached the White House, President Johnson and Robert Woodruff were there together, drinking away their mutual sorrows. Aware that the country, and particularly the South, could explode with racial violence, the Boss called Atlanta's mayor Ivan Allen. "Ivan," he said, "the minute they bring King's body back tomorrow—between then and the time of the funeral—Atlanta, Georgia, is going to be the center of the universe. I want you to do whatever is right and necessary, and whatever the city can't pay for will be taken care of. Do you understand what I'm saying?" The mayor understood that he could dip into the deep pockets of Woodruff and Coca-Cola, and he promptly dispatched the *Windship*, Coca-Cola's Lear jet, to bring Coretta Scott King back to Atlanta. As African Americans rioted in over a hundred American cities, Atlanta avoided major bloodshed, thanks largely to the collaboration of Allen and Woodruff.*

Richard Nixon, resuscitated and scripted by Pepsi men and their ad agency, BBDO, won the presidency at year's end, after a campaign appealing to the "silent majority" of Americans who recoiled in horror from the discord tearing the country apart. Nixon's election, however, only signaled more trouble ahead for a deeply divided country. Coca-Cola's vintage advertising appeared more and more out of synch with the times. In an attempt to stay hip and cool, the company hired Bruce Brown, creator of the film *Endless Summer*, to narrate a 1968 "Things Go Better" commercial in which California surfers swigged Coke. "Someone's always makin' waves in this world," Brown philosophized on the voice-over. "Maybe that's why Coca-Cola is the world's most popular drink." The implication of this non sequitur was that people who "made waves" drank Coke, but the young people who were shaking up America had advanced beyond the Beach Boy mentality. Johnny the Dork of the fifties Coke commercial had grown into Johnny the Hippie.

By 1968, in other words, things weren't going better anywhere in America, and the six-year-old campaign was showing its age. In an attempt at relevance, the Company ran an ad that was an elaborate takeoff on the Statue of Liberty inscription. "America," it read, "give me your hot, your thirsty, your weary, . . . your sons, your daughters, your surfers, your skiers, your football players, . . . your sun worshipers, your moon worshipers, your potato chip nuts, your pretzel eaters, . . . your vacuum cleaner salesmen, your ushers, your hippies, your high school students yearning to pass math. Things go better with Coke." The message, of course, was that Coca-Cola stood for America and appealed to everyone, but the Coke ad seemed flat, forced, and unbelievable.

Looking toward the seventies, Coke men searched desperately for a new unifying theme. Again, lyricist Bill Backer came through with the perfect vehicle. McCann's psychological researchers reported that young people despised hypocrites and phonies and valued genuine, spontaneous feelings. With these findings, Backer resurrected an old 1942 slogan and created "The Real Thing" campaign. Coca-Cola was "real," not phony. It was part of the authentic, natural goodness that the counterculture was seeking. At the same time, the phrase was a subtle dig at Pepsi, which by implication was a fraud. The new slogan echoed the hippies' catch-all invocation to "do your own thing." Sure, the song implied—but do it with the Real Thing in hand.

The visuals to accompany the sincere new lyric utilized still documentary style photography, with the movie camera performing the action by zooming and tilting to

---

* It is ironic that on the day before his assassination, Martin Luther King Jr. called for a local boycott of Coca-Cola in Memphis because "they haven't been fair in their hiring practices" and to demonstrate "the power of economic withdrawal" while calling attention to the plight of the striking garbage collectors.

highlight each shot. One of the first "Real Thing" television commercials, launched in October of 1969, opened in Manhattan with a group of white and black teenagers playing basketball—the first real integrated Coke TV spot. It then traveled across America showing peaceful dirt roads, farms with windmills, log cabins, pretty young women, the American flag, and a California beach scene. The ad implied that *this* was the real America, not the violence and dissonance seen on the evening news.

Coca-Cola had miraculously implemented a slogan and campaign that appealed to both hawk and dove, National Guard and hippie, parent and child. While the commercials were innovative, however, they remained firmly grounded in the Coca-Cola tradition. Although the ads were oriented to lifestyle and emotional issues, the drink itself remained the star of the show. Somewhat illogically, Paul Austin observed that the new ads would "reflect Coke's awareness of minority and other social sensitivities by stressing the product rather than people."

Pepsi changed campaigns the same year, returning to the social implications of the earlier Pepsi Generation. "You've got a lot to live," the jingle asserted, "and Pepsi's got a lot to give." The emphasis was on people, however, not Pepsi. Unlike Coke's tranquil, almost elegiac commercials, the Pepsi efforts showcased strenuous group activity. These young cola drinkers were "coming at you, growing strong," bursting with energy and good times. As Coca-Cola men smugly noted, Pepsi people had to try harder in an effort to catch the leader.

As Coke's "Real Thing" commercials flooded the airwaves late in 1969, the Company performed a simultaneous face-lift. Coca-Cola men concluded that the Company had done its work *too* well with its ubiquitous signs. Ike Herbert, Coke's new advertising chief, enjoyed pointing toward downtown Atlanta from his office window. "There are eleven signs down there," he said, "but most people can find only two or three, and they know what they are looking for." The innumerable Coke signs had vanished into the landscape. Particularly concerned about the battered old red disks and multi-colored signs in the nation's urban ghettos and rural outbacks, the Company hired a New York firm, Lippincott & Margulies, to design a "mod" look for Coke. Code-named Project Arden as a reference to the famed cosmetic line, the assignment, as a Company memo put it, was to "take Coca-Cola, shorten her skirt, lift her face, give her a new hairdo, a whole 'now' style and catapult her back into the awareness of the consumer." The resulting square sign sported a white "Dynamic Ribbon"—echoing the hobbleskirt bottle contour—running under the traditional script logo. At the same time, the simple phrase "Drink Coca-Cola" was altered to "Enjoy Coca-Cola"—a more fitting command from the image-conscious Company.

In a burst of self-important pizzazz, the Company introduced the new look and the "Real Thing" campaign simultaneously at its national bottlers convention in October of 1969 with a sound-and-light show that was the biggest thing to hit Atlanta since *Gone with the Wind* premiered there in 1939. Some journalists weren't impressed with the hype, comparing it to "a flourish of trumpets and a roll of drums—followed by two Coke bottles clinking weakly together."

The new look and campaign were, however, more than window dressing: the Company really *had* changed, and many longtime employees didn't like it. In 1965, when the brand manager system commenced, different groups were scattered around Atlanta in satellite locations, pending the completion of a new eleven-story complex on

North Avenue. During the remainder of the decade, the separate departments swelled, often duplicating functions. "Whenever you needed something done," Charlie Bottoms recalled, "you just created a new position." Within a few years, a staff below 500 mushroomed to 1,500 people. When the Company moved into its new quarters in 1969, secretary Mary Gresham found her surroundings drab and depressing as she sat behind her coffin-like black desk in the hall, staring at the modern wallpaper which, she thought, resembled aluminum foil. The thirty-five-cent lunch served by waiters had ceased. Instead, employees filed through a cafeteria to buy blander, more expensive food. "For so many years," Gresham lamented, "it had been like living in a small town where everyone knew everyone else and their business. That closeness just wasn't there anymore."

POTENT NUTRITION AND THE GREAT CYCLAMATE SCARE

With a new decade only two months away, Paul Austin had navigated Coca-Cola through the turbulent sixties in remarkably good shape. The stock had split two-for-one twice, in 1965 and 1968. In 1969, gross sales for the Company topped $1.3 billion, with its $121 million profit more than double that of Pepsi. True, Coke was spending nearly that amount with its $100 million annual advertising campaign, but thinner profit margins were simply a fact of life in a competitive market. Coca-Cola was now sold in 135 countries, and the overseas opportunities appeared limitless.

Nonetheless, the Company could hardly rest easy with its new campaign and logo, particularly in its home market, which still produced 50 percent of its sales volume. The Vietnam War had artificially stimulated the U.S. economy, now tottering from accumulated debt. Meanwhile, the protesters were shifting their attention from the war to pollution, poverty, malnutrition, racism, sexism, poor education, and chemical additives. Sensitive to increasing criticism about Coca-Cola's lack of vitamins or nutritional value, Paul Austin authorized the development of Saci (pronounced "SAH-see"), a protein-rich soft drink—equivalent to a glass of milk—that would also taste good. The previous year, test marketing had begun in Brazil, but kids apparently didn't like the taste.* In 1969, Ralph Nader, fresh from his victory over General Motors, attacked Coca-Cola in a hearing before the Select Committee on Nutrition and Human Needs. "While The Coca-Cola Company is distributing a high protein chocolate drink . . . to developing countries," the crusader complained, "it supplies the United States with cola—a massive affliction that someday may be characterized as a disease."

On short notice, Austin rushed to testify before the committee, exercising damage control. "The Coca-Cola Company is keenly mindful of its responsibility as a member of society wherever it does business," he informed the senators. Nonetheless, it couldn't just give away the new drink but must create a sound business venture, making Saci "equally attractive to the consumer and producer." Austin promised that the Company intended to market Saci to America's undernourished children as soon as the kinks were finessed. The Coca-Cola executive admitted that "we are twisting

---

* Advertising for Saci emphasized that it made consumers "powerful" and healthy. Brazilian men interpreted this to mean that the drink would render them more virile. Consequently, Saci never reached many malnourished children.

and turning" and that the taste had been modified twice and was still unsatisfactory. One senator who had brought two Saci bottles home to his Coke-loving children told Austin they hated the protein drink. "I thank you for your candor," Austin replied between gritted teeth.

The beleaguered Coke executive would find plenty of reasons to grind his molars in the years to come. Only a week after the flashy bottlers' convention unveiling the Real Thing and the Dynamic Ribbon, the Food and Drug Administration sounded another theme of the approaching seventies by revealing alarming test results on cyclamates, the sweetener in most diet drinks. The experiments, funded in part by the sugar industry, showed that laboratory rats on a cyclamate diet developed malignant bladder tumors. The FDA had no choice but to remove the chemical from the Generally Recognized as Safe (GRAS) list and to ban it under the 1958 Delaney Amendment.

It didn't matter that the rats had ingested fifty times the amount a human was likely to absorb. Coke's Fred Dickson pointed out that an adult would have to drink 550 Frescas a day for the equivalent dosage. "You'd drown before you'd get cancer," he told a reporter. Another soft drink executive noted bitterly that "under that law, you can ban sunshine." With sensational coverage in all the media, however, the country panicked. Cyclamates, virtually unheard of the week before, were suddenly the equivalent to poison. Even before the drinks were banned, The Coca-Cola Company started pulling TaB and Fresca from the shelves.

The Company quickly produced alternative versions of the drinks, converting Fresca completely to saccharin, while adding sugar to TaB's saccharin. Trying to mask the new calories, the Company obtained FDA approval to advertise TaB as "six calories per fluid ounce" rather than revealing the total amount per drink as it had before. Coke men worked feverishly around the clock on new formulae and labels. The cyclamate ban didn't hurt the Company too much domestically (a mere $2.5 million loss in the fourth quarter of 1969), since its diet drinks accounted for only 10 percent of sales. Royal Crown, whose Diet Rite dominated the market, was badly shaken. Oddly enough, Coca-Cola experienced its worst problems in Japan, where the Company didn't even market drinks with cyclamates. Rumors spread that Coca-Cola itself contained the alarming sweetener, and Japanese consumers, even more finicky and quick to panic than their American counterparts, stopped buying the American soft drink. It took a determined public relations campaign to build sales volume again.

Another American problem spilled overseas to South Africa, where Coca-Cola's thirty-seven bottling plants dominated the soft drink industry. Because of America's heightened racial awareness, in 1968 Congress passed sanctions on the apartheid regime for the first time—a particular blow to Paul Austin, who had managed the South African business in the fifties. The newly imposed restrictions would "force us to milk our European business," Austin complained.

As the year drew to a close, Paul Austin outlined his concern over "anti-establishmentarianism" in a detailed memo to Robert Woodruff. The under-thirty generation had literally forced LBJ out of office and was now focusing on other concerns. Because of its dominant position, Austin noted, The Coca-Cola Company "epitomizes the Establishment" and needed to implement programs to deflect criticism. "Following withdrawal from Vietnam," he predicted, "the Group's target will become pollution." Austin observed that "we participate in the litter to a significant degree" with throw-away bottles and cans, not to mention billboards. The nutritionally empty drink also lay open for criticism. Its highly visible truck fleet made Coke an "ideal target." Coca-Cola, the star of the show, desperately needed supporting products and programs to appeal to idealistic youth. Austin urged prompt action on several fronts. Perhaps more important than any profit, however, he sought what he called "the halo effect." Coke must appear to be doing good in the world.

Austin's words proved prophetic, if too late to avert trouble. Coca-Cola, the "ideal target," had already caught the eye of politicians and government bureaucrats. Worse, the Company had attracted the ferocious attention of Cesar Chavez, a hero of the baby boomers. For Coca-Cola, the seventies would commence on a sour note.

The 1915 prototype of the classic hobbleskirt bottle was a buxom affair, which may have inspired the nickname "Mae West bottle." It proved too bulky for bottling machines, however.

Here are a chronological procession of six-and-a-half-ounce Coca-Cola bottles, beginning with the unsatisfactory Hutchinson stopper, then the straight-sided bottle with diamond-shaped labels, and finally the classic hobbleskirt bottle, adopted in 1916.

Benjamin Thomas (left) and Joseph Whitehead (right), the two portly lawyers who finally convinced Asa Candler to let them bottle Coca-Cola, made a fortune while democratizing the soft drink, though both died relatively young.

Even at the age of two and a half, Robert Woodruff observed the world from a calm, adult face—contemplative, serious, calculating, and melancholy. (*Woodruff Papers, Special Collections, Emory University*)

Robert Woodruff jauntily steps onto a running board in 1923, the year he assumed the helm at Coca-Cola.

In 1929, Archie Lee introduced "the pause that refreshes" as the appropriate social role for Coca-Cola. He also coined a phrase to take advantage of its huge sales volume: "It had to be good to get where it is."

Coca-Cola advertising always matched the times. In the 1920s, this flirtatious flapper espoused the drink. Note the line on the special Coca-Cola glass, indicating the proper syrup level before mixing with carbonated water.

During the thirties and forties, Coca-Cola commissioned artists like Norman Rockwell and N. C. Wyeth to paint bucolic ads, such as this country boy with his dog, fishing pole, and Coke.

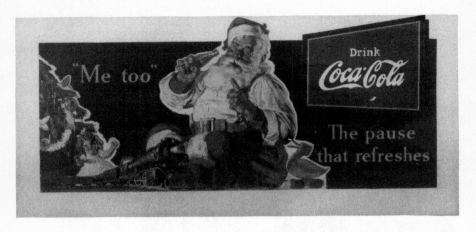

For years, Haddon Sundbloom's Christmas ads depicted a jolly, red-clad Santa Claus who paused for a Coca-Cola while making his rounds. As a result, Sundbloom shaped the American version of St. Nick.

Actress Joan Crawford smiled for Coca-Cola in 1933, but when she married Pepsi president Al Steele in the fifties, she became a roving ambassador for the rival soft drink.

During World War II, Coca-Cola "Technical Observers" flew overseas to bottle the drink behind the lines for homesick GIs such as these, for whom the drink assumed an almost mystical significance.

"Congratulations. You're the 100th soldier who has posed with that bottle of Coca-Cola. You can drink it."

Cartoonist Bill Mauldin took a somewhat jaundiced (but probably realistic) view of Coca-Cola's superhuman efforts to reach soldiers during World War II.

Max Keith, who developed a thriving German business during the Nazi era against great odds, bore a physical resemblance to Adolf Hitler and led chants of "Sieg Heil!" during Coca-Cola conventions.

In 1939, Coca-Cola trucks massed in Essen's Adolf-Hitler-Platz in a show of strength.

Max Schmeling, former heavyweight champion and the symbol of Aryan supremacy during Hitler's reign, became a born-again Coke bottler in Hamburg, Germany.

When Robert Woodruff refused to allow his portrait on this May 15, 1950, *Time* cover, the magazine commissioned a classic painting depicting the worldwide flood of the soft drink. (*Copyright 1950 Time Warner Inc. Reprinted by permission.*)

In 1950, the French Communists led the fight against Coca-Cola, depicted here as a seductress luring France away from his legitimate Beaujolais wife. (*Cartoonists & Writers Syndicate*)

Coca-Cola welcomed the post-war world with the 1946 "Yes" girl. Before the Freudian "depth boys" discovered phallic symbols in advertising, the Coke men were using them.

In the mid-fifties, Coca-Cola targeted the burgeoning black middle class for the first time in publications like *Ebony*. It would be years, however, before minorities appeared in mainstream ads designed for general audiences.

~ 17 ~

Big Red's Uneasy Slumber

We used to say, "Be careful not to wake up Big Red. Be aggressive, but don't wake up Big Red."

—Deke DeLoach, retired Pepsi lobbyist

IN 1979, a Coca-Cola executive reviewed a dismal decade. "Had we stood in Atlanta in 1969 on the threshold of the seventies," he told assembled bottlers, "and were endowed with some Gypsy ability to see into the future, I think that we would have quailed at the prospect that lay before us." Paul Austin had no such "Gypsy ability" in 1969, but he sensed trouble when Cesar Chavez, fresh from his victory over the California grape growers, toured Florida. "His next target," Austin lamented in a memo to Woodruff, "will be Citrus. He mentioned our Company by name." Austin knew that Chavez couldn't be lightly dismissed. "He has adopted the role and general mien of a Messiah," he wrote gloomily. The situation in Florida's Minute Maid groves was vulnerable, since the Company hired some six thousand migrant workers during the picking season. Most were black. Pay was minimal. Men, women, and children lived in "barrack-like structures" without bathrooms or recreation facilities. "If we were the subject of a pictorial news report," Austin concluded, "we would come off badly."

In 1960, the same year in which Coke acquired Minute Maid, Edward R. Murrow had first spotlighted the horrendous conditions in Florida's orange groves in the CBS documentary *Harvest of Shame*. No one at the soft drink company had shown much concern. Ten years later, just months after the alarmed Austin memo, Chet Huntley narrated an NBC update called *Migrant*, showing that nothing had changed in a decade. Coca-Cola's groves were highlighted, with an irate Minute Maid overseer caught on camera, belligerently ordering the TV crew to leave. Although Paul Austin and Luke Smith, the president of Coca-Cola Foods, had explained Coke's strategies to improve conditions to Martin Carr, the show's producer, the documentary did not mention them.

Only days before *Migrant* was aired, Smith and Austin sat in on a closed-circuit pre-screening for Houston NBC affiliates. They were not happy with what they saw. Enraged, Austin called NBC president Julian Goodman, screaming that the station was doing "a bitch job on Coke." The television executive listened politely, since Coca-Cola had already purchased over $2 million worth of TV spots on NBC for the 1970 season. In the end, NBC agreed to add one sentence about Coke's "major plan which it claims will correct . . . failings," and to delete a statement that Coke set the standards for the entire industry.

The cosmetic changes failed to deflect bad publicity. When Martin Carr told the press of the "enormous pressure" applied by the Coke men to modify his documentary, the Company came across as a corporate censor. Less than a week after the documentary aired on July 15, Senator Walter Mondale chaired a subcommittee to explore the migrants' plight. "Nothing will change," Mondale said in his opening statement, "until this rotten system is exposed and held accountable." Philip Moore, the head of the Project on Corporate Responsibility, told the senators that while the migrants worked for slave wages, Paul Austin earned $150,000 a year and owned fifty-five thousand shares of Coke stock paying annual dividends of $79,200. "I would like to ask Mr. Austin," Moore said, "why is it that when it comes to profit, corporations work fast, but when it comes to human conditions, corporations at best plod along?" Moore concluded with a scathing forecast. "I just know that Austin and other Coke officials are going to come breezing into these hearings and they are going to say, 'Boys, we're sorry. We're sorry for raping these people. We're sorry that we don't pay them enough to live a month, much less a year. We're sorry that migrant workers die at the age of forty-nine. . . . But now we're going to be better.'"

Several days later, when Austin, accompanied by lawyer Joseph Califano, appeared before Mondale's committee, he fulfilled Moore's expectations.* He admitted that conditions for the Minute Maid workers were "deplorable," but the Company now planned to hire many migrants as regular employees with full benefits. Coca-Cola would properly house and feed them, provide adequate child and health care, and offer recreational opportunities. Finally, Austin called for a National Alliance of Agri-Businessmen, modeled on the National Alliance of Businessmen.

Austin's performance was nearly flawless under the senators' hard questioning. He observed that, in addition to problems of malnutrition and poor housing, the migrants suffered from "a profound sense of futility." He proposed giving them "human dignity" and a chance "to rise not only in our citrus operations but throughout the whole structure of our organization." The Coca-Cola executive slipped only once, betraying a condescending racism. "These people," he explained, "do not have a philosophy of work discipline."

Combined with tangible results of the subsequent Agriculture Labor Project (ALP), Austin turned the initially adverse media reaction into a public relations bonanza. *Time* headlined Austin's Senate speech as "The Candor That Refreshes." African American orange picker Willy Reynolds became a star interviewee after moving into his own home in Frostproof, Florida. "It's like bein' born again," he said. "I'd been in houses like this but I was always a visitor. I never thought I'd own one." *Business Week* gave Coke its 1970 Award for Business Citizenship. Even Ralph Nader was impressed by Austin's sincerity when Joe Califano arranged a dinner for the two men. After listening politely to the Coca-Cola executive's description of his horror at conditions in

---

* Califano recalled that "it was the most hostile hearing room I've ever walked into, jammed with interns and angry students." A young, dark-haired woman with glasses came up to him and said, "You shit, you've sold out." It was Hillary Clinton.

the orange groves, Nader asked, "What's a sensitive man like you, with a degree from Harvard Law School, doing pumping syrupy brown drinks into people's stomachs?" Looking the consumer crusader straight in the eye, Austin answered, "I don't think there's anything wrong with selling a refreshing drink."

LITTER, POLLUTION, AND OTHER IRRITANTS

Even as the Company narrowly escaped accusations of cold-hearted neglect of migrant workers, however, it faced angry environmentalists. By the beginning of the seventies, 40 percent of all soft drinks were packaged in "one-way" containers, and the figure was steadily rising. Just after the first Earth Day in April 1970, protesters dumped mounds of nonreturnable Coke bottles in front of the North Avenue headquarters. At the same time, bottle deposit bills cropped up in state legislatures. One 1971 survey claimed that 5 percent of the country's solid waste litter consisted of containers manufactured by The Coca-Cola Company. Company men explained, with some justification, that if Coke went back to returnable bottles and Pepsi didn't, they would invite disaster in the marketplace. Consumers demanded an end to litter in the abstract, but at home they wanted the convenience of a throw-away container.

Hoping to defuse criticism, Coca-Cola urged recycling, stressing that most of the Company-owned bottling plants were returning glass and paper to vendors for reuse. Company advertising teams introduced billboards with a clever wordplay on the hawkish chant of Vietnam hard-liners to either love America or leave it. "If you love me," exhorted the sign displaying Coke cans and bottles, "don't leave me." To catch the public's attention, the Company willingly broke its rule about overt sexuality in the interest of litter prevention. "Bend a little," one ad teased, showing a pretty girl's behind as she leaned over to pick up a bottle.

While Austin had clearly approached the migrant uproar as a pragmatic business problem, he appeared to be genuinely concerned about environmental issues. In the tropical serenity of the Bahamas, Coca-Cola managers engaged in a series of Harvard-run seminars with high-power academics from across the United States. Unlike the standard management meetings, these humanistic sessions emphasized broad, sweeping visions, self-actualization, and environmental awareness. They had an enormous impact on Austin and his associates. In the world of the future, they learned, clean water would prove more valuable than gold. Austin asked Bob Broadwater, already in charge of subsidiary acquisitions, to hire a cadre of eager young Harvard Business School graduates and devise practical ways to apply the seminar's lesson. Reporting directly to Austin outside of the run-of-the mill Coke bureaucracy, the group soon earned its nickname as "Austin's Orphans."

Broadwater and his Orphans delighted in their freedom to explore new areas. Their first find was Aqua-Chem, a leading company in the field of desalinization and water purification that might also provide leverage for ending the Arab boycott, since the arid countries of the Middle East badly needed desalinization plants. The Orphans purchased a natural-water bottler in Massachusetts, raised hydroponic fruits and vegetables under plastic on Kharg Island in Iran, bought a Wisconsin plastics company to experiment with biodegradable garbage bags and bottles, and shrimp farmed in

Mexico. After an all-day session with Sterling Livingston, a former Harvard professor who had founded his own management-teaching complex in Boston and Washington, D.C., the educator suggested the enterprising Coke men buy his Sterling Institute outright. "Hell, it was only a million dollars," Broadwater recalled. "We spilled that much before breakfast in those days."

With the exception of the natural-water company, none of Broadwater's acquisitions paid handsome returns. Clearly, Paul Austin was willing to forgo immediate profits to pursue his "halo effect." After all, in 1970 the Company sat on $150 million in cash, and the money kept pouring in from soft drink sales, mounting to $300 million by 1974. Why not let the idealistic young managers have a go? Austin took a fatherly interest in them. "It's fascinating," he said. "In three years you watch a boy grow into a businessman."

Not merely a paternalistic executive treating new businesses as toys, Austin was a born-again ecologist, lecturing the Georgia Bankers Association in an apocalyptic 1970 address grandly titled "Environmental Renewal or Oblivion . . . Quo Vadis?" The Coca-Cola president passionately reviewed "the stark evidence of environmental homicide," warning of "an oblivion comprised of undrinkable water and air that can't be breathed." The complacent Southern bankers must have been astonished to hear the head of Coca-Cola sounding like Ralph Nader on amphetamines. "We're firing rockets at the moon—while standing knee deep in our own garbage," he continued. "Unless *all* of us begin *immediately* to reverse the processes of impending self-destruction which *we* have set in motion—this green land of ours will become a *graveyard!*"

Not only that, but Austin was alarmed over the population explosion. "Within the lifetime of a child born *this* year, there will be some *fifteen billion* inhabitants on this incredibly delicate Earth." Austin called these "vast hordes of humanity" a frightening prospect, but his fellow Coke men must have thought he had lost his mind. What had happened to the traditional value system which held that a human being's primary function on earth was to serve as a conduit for Coca-Cola? On one level Paul Austin sincerely believed what he told the bankers; however, he never lost sight of his ultimate goal of selling more soft drinks. As one commentator observed a few years later, The Coca-Cola Company and its men "seem to function simultaneously on two levels: one lofty, even Platonic, the other unrelentingly practical." After all of Austin's fulminations, his concrete proposals for Coca-Cola were rather tame. As soon as some "efficient device" came along to eliminate hydrocarbon emissions, he promised to convert the enormous fleet of Coke trucks to it. In the meantime, they would continue to go their polluting rounds. He noted that 70 percent of Coke's containers were still returnables, and he hoped to find a one-way plastic bottle that could be incinerated without releasing hydrocarbons.

THE FTC ATTACKS

Sincere or not, Austin's speeches and Coke's ecological efforts failed to avert renewed governmental attention. Any Coca-Cola man with a sense of history must have foreseen it, since the Federal Trade Commission had sued Asa Candler more than fifty years before. Now, led by crusading commissioner Robert Pitofsky and encouraged by the strong consumer movement, the FTC again attacked Coca-Cola.

The first brush concerned Big Name Bingo, an under-the-crown promotion. TaB and Coke consumers could win $100 by attaching appropriate bottle-cap liners, on which twenty famous people were portrayed, as answers to ten questions on the Bingo card. The FTC objected to the contest, since the rules didn't clarify that the trick questions demanded multiple answers. Most entrants, for instance, correctly identified Admiral Byrd as having gone on an Arctic expedition. To win a prize, however, they also had to glue Horatio Nelson's bottle-cap liner to that question. Similarly, both Woodrow Wilson and Guglielmo Marconi attended the Paris Peace Conference. Not surprisingly, there were only 831 winners out of 1.5 million entries. Shortly after the FTC lodged its complaint, two class-action suits, totaling $425 million, were lodged against Coca-Cola and the Glendinning Company, which actually administered the contest for the soft drink company.

While the Bingo farce garnered unfavorable headlines, it cost the Company little money. Undaunted, the FTC promptly opened a second front. In 1971, it brought suit against Coca-Cola for Hi-C advertisements in which a hapless father allowed his children to consume potato chips, cookies, and other junk food. "Some lunch!" the narrator said. "But Dad knows the only sensible thing about it is ice-cold Hi-C." The drink was, he continued, "made with real fruit and it's high in Vitamin C." FTC prosecutors observed that there was little real fruit juice in Hi-C and that it contained less vitamin C than orange juice, while the ads implied otherwise. The commercials also conveyed the notion that it didn't matter whether kids ate junk food or not, as long as they drank Hi-C. The FTC men were particularly upset by a joint promotion with Kellogg in which a little girl ate a Pop Tart and drank Hi-C for breakfast. The Company defended itself by declaring that the complaint was based on "personal and unscientific dietary notions." Just because the commission preferred the consumption of natural fruit juices was no reason to penalize Hi-C and "discourage the American public from exercising its free choice of refreshment beverages." In 1972, the commissioners agreed with Coke's lawyers and dismissed the case.

The same year, however, the FTC struck at the heart of the soft drink industry, alleging that the exclusive franchise system violated the Sherman Antitrust Act, since a bottler's monopoly over particular territory prevented fair competition. A mighty howl of protest rose over the United States, while Coke and Pepsi banded together to fight the common enemy. The FTC suit would drag on for years, casting a pall over the entire decade. The Coca-Cola Company and its bottlers pursued two strategies simultaneously, seeking vindication through the courts while lobbying hard for specific legislation to exempt soft drinks from prosecution. The legal twists and turns would profoundly affect the traditional relationship between the bottlers and the Company, but no one could have foreseen that in 1972.

TRICKY DICK WORKS HIS MAGIC

By the time of the third FTC suit, some frustrated Coca-Cola men smelled a rat, feeling that the many-pronged assaults could not be coincidental. President Nixon, deeply indebted to Pepsi's Don Kendall, must have decided a few dirty tricks were in order. "It's just my humble feeling," wrote one longtime fountain man, "but I think someone was sure trying to please the boss." Of course, the FTC case impacted Pepsi too, but the paranoid Coke men reasoned that the destruction of the exclusive franchise system would harm the leader far more. Concerned about the situation, Coke lobbyist Ovid Davis suggested the need for a high-level Washington retainer who would be "wired to the Nixon Administration."

Whether Nixon gave the word to the FTC or not, he clearly facilitated Pepsi's entry into the Soviet Union. Paul Austin had directed Export president John Talley to reopen negotiations with the USSR, and in September of 1972, Talley reported to Robert Woodruff that "it would seem that we have carried our 'holier than thou' attitude towards Russia far beyond the limits of good business judgment." What Talley didn't know was that Don Kendall had already cemented a deal with Soviet premier Kosygin nearly a year before, during Kendall's Moscow visit as chair of an American delegation on U.S.-Soviet trade. Eager to buy U.S. wheat, Kosygin surmised that working a deal with Nixon's friend from Pepsi would be politically expedient. It took ten more months to iron out the details, but in November of 1972, just after Talley wrote his memo, Pepsi announced a ten-year exclusive contract with the Soviet Union.

Infuriated, Austin berated himself for backing out of his opportunity in the late sixties. Determined to gain a Russian foothold, he assured Coca-Cola executives of his confidence that "Coca-Cola as the world's most popular soft drink in due course will be available in the Soviet Union," delegating the project to Bob Broadwater, who made over twenty trips to Russia during the next few years.

Nixon may have succeeded through back-door diplomacy with the Chinese and Russians, but he failed in many other presidential endeavors. As campus antiwar protests erupted, he sent National Guardsmen to Ohio to suppress dissent at Kent State University, where they opened fire, killing four students. The war had come home to roost. Incredible as it seemed, now Americans were killing their own children.

TEACHING THE WORLD TO SING

In the stunned aftermath, the antiwar movement lost its momentum, as many counterculture baby boomers abandoned the political struggle for a more personal peace. They clustered at love-ins, rock festivals, communes, and cults, seeking meaning in a society that seemed bent on destroying itself. Popular music reflected this yearning for serenity and security. In 1970, Simon & Garfunkel's "Bridge over Troubled Waters" went platinum, while the Beatles' "Let It Be" was a gold record. In the meantime, Coca-Cola's "Real Thing" campaign still clung to the theme song introduced in 1969, together with quick vignettes of American life. The ads showed their age, though, and the frenetic style—a picture every second—didn't match the shattered country's search for tranquility.

In response, Bill Backer modified the "Real Thing" song as a quiet folk ballad that spoke of "Friendly feelings, friendly feelings, / Hope they're happenin' to you." The new lyric glided over visuals of happy, clean-cut young hippies—a boy and girl, guitar slung over her shoulder, dancing in a rural field, an outdoor wedding ceremony, a teen couple with white stars on their shirts, along with a suitable mixture of African Americans—all laughing and enjoying a Coke. As the song ended, a warm-toned announcer informed audiences that "a bottle of Coke has brought more people together than any other soft drink in the world." In the final shot, one bottle of Coca-Cola leaned for comfort against another.

Backer's timing was impeccable. A few months after "Friendly Feelings" aired in February of 1971, James Taylor's version of "You've Got a Friend" debuted with similar sentiments. Meanwhile, Backer was working on another variant of the "Real Thing" that would extend this yearning for friendship and brotherhood beyond the borders of the United States, uniting the entire world in a fantasy of togetherness. Billy Davis, a black Motown producer and former member of the Four Tops, had joined the ad team, composing the music for one of the most popular commercials ever made.

On a hilltop in Italy, Coca-Cola assembled some 200 fresh-faced young adults from every corner of the world, clad appropriately in their national costumes. Standing in ordered ranks in an inverted pyramid and clutching bottles of Coke, they looked straight ahead as they earnestly sang, "I'd like to buy the world a home and furnish it with love, / Grow apple trees and honey bees and snow white turtle doves." The vision of the idealistic youths crooning to a weary world soothed like a hymn in an outdoor church, and their firmly clasped bottles of Coca-Cola were hopeful peace talismans. Just as Coke was building homes for its migrant workers, it meant to house the world in some ambiguous way. As hippies were retreating to hill farms, Backer's song spoke lyrically of growing apples and tending bees.*

"I'd like to teach the world to sing in perfect harmony," the sweet voices continued. "I'd like to buy the world a Coke and keep it company. That's the real thing. . . ." Released in July of 1971, the commercial created a sensation. It didn't strike anyone as preposterous that a soft drink was somehow supposed to save the world, that the lyrics were oozing with stereotypical sentiment, or that the young people in the ad were only lip-synching to the voices of the New Seekers, a British pop group. The Company and bottlers were deluged with over a hundred thousand letters and requests for sheet music. Coke granted them, along with 45 rpm records of the song. When radio stations balked at giving a commercial free airtime, Backer rewrote the ballad to eliminate any reference to Coca-Cola, and the New Seekers recorded it. When their record hit the top of the charts, a hastily assembled group called the Hillside Singers issued a country-and-western version. By the beginning of 1972, the two recordings had sold a combined total of a million copies. It was, as *Newsweek* wryly observed, "a sure-fire form of subliminal advertising." Although Coca-Cola wasn't mentioned in the lyrics, everyone automatically thought of the soft drink every time they heard the song.

THE GOOD OLD DAYS AND TRAYS

As Americans struggled to fathom their troubled times, they not only sought the solace of a world singing in harmony but looked back fondly to a time that now

---

* The famed "Hilltop" commercial was nearly a disaster. During the first take, 1,200 Italian orphans waited in steaming buses in the rain for their appearance. Eventually, they rioted, threw Coke bottles at the director, and began to rock a Coke truck, trying to overturn it. As Bill Backer recalled, it demonstrated the exact opposite of what was intended—"lack of harmony and understanding between diverse peoples."

appeared sweetly innocent, when Americans believed in a benevolent God, rebellious kids did nothing worse than wear ducktails, the economy boomed, and America and its products dominated the world. In 1972, with the advent of *Grease* on Broadway, nostalgia for the fifties swept the country. Along with it, somewhat to the Company's surprise, a Coke memorabilia craze boomed.

In that same year, Cecil Munsey wrote the *Illustrated Guide to the Collectibles of Coca-Cola*, complete with early Hilda Clark and Lillian Nordica serving trays, twenties' flappers, Norman Rockwell's freckle-faced boys of the thirties, Haddon Sundblom's Santas, World War II flyboys sipping their soft drinks, and wholesome fifties' beauties announcing Coke time. Across the country, collectors discovered one another through antiques publications, chance meetings at flea markets, and word of mouth. By 1975, the Cola Clan had been born. Kentucky architect Thom Thompson, still an active collector decades later, was one of the charter members. "When Munsey's book came out, we treated it like the Bible," he recalled. The book was dedicated to Wilbur Kurtz Jr., the Company archivist, pictured among the trays and old bottles. At the club's first convention in Atlanta, Kurtz escorted the Coke devotees to his sanctum at North Avenue. "Wilbur was like a god to us," Thompson remembered. "We'd seen him in Munsey's book, and here he was in person. He was a great storyteller, even though a lot of his lore was probably fiction."

Suddenly, old calendars and trays swelled in value, selling for tens, then hundreds of dollars. Kurtz was at first startled by the flurry of interest, then delighted to find himself the center of attention, especially since various Company officials had tried to fire him in the past. "They thought I wasn't making any real contribution to the Company," Kurtz reminisced in an interview shortly before his death. "These were businessmen. They didn't think in terms of history and preservation." The nostalgia boom elevated the lowly archivist's status within the Company, as Coke marketing men, eager to cash in on the memorabilia, came to Kurtz for old items. Reproducing them, they resurrected early models like Hilda Clark on trays sold as premiums and given as prizes through the bottler system.

As riots and smog clouded once-vital cities, Coke's ad men mined America's mythic rural past. In 1972, country singer Dottie West wrote and performed another classic Coke commercial. "I was raised on country sunshine," she twanged, "I'm happy with the simple things: / A Saturday night dance, a bottle of Coke, and the joy that the bluebird brings." Shifting away from the quick vignette, this commercial told a sentimental homecoming story. As the young woman's taxi drove down the farm's dirt road, her brother jumped from the hayloft, little sister left the tire swing, Grandma beamed joyfully, and Dad abandoned his tractor. The final scene showed the prodigal daughter rocking on the front porch swing with her handsome hometown boy, talking quietly and drinking Coke as the music concluded that this was the Real Thing. This and other carefully crafted sixty-second short-short stories were minor gems that consumed thousands of feet of film, multiple takes, and thousands of dollars for each second of finished product. The apparent bliss and spontaneity resulted from monumental labor. "You in the striped shirt," yelled a McCann director in 1972, "hold the bottle lower down so we can see the label. Blonde girl in the back, lie on your stomach!" Every gesture in the commercials was scripted to achieve the maximum effect.

CHARLES DUNCAN'S MOMENT IN THE SUN

As McCann's creative geniuses were filming inspired commercials, The Coca-Cola Company itself was slowly changing and evolving. In 1970, Robert Woodruff had recalled Charles Duncan from London, where he had gained valuable international experience as head of Coca-Cola Export's European office. At the end of the following year, the Boss installed Duncan as president of the entire Company, leaving Paul Austin as chair of the board. While Austin's elitist philosophy had steered Coca-Cola throughout the sixties, Duncan supplied much-needed hands-on management. Together, the two men composed a potentially complementary team, though Austin continued to call the shots.*

Duncan still pulled enough weight to change the way Coca-Cola Export was run. As the overseas business exploded during the fifties and sixties, Export men operated independently as rough-and-ready adventurers, ready to improvise and make split-second decisions, displaying a macho disdain for deskbound Atlanta executives. By the early seventies, however, labor unrest, socialist governments, and anti-corporate backlash around the world spelled trouble for the autonomous Export leaders. In Uruguay, when two Coke employees were arrested for their involvement in a liberation movement, their fellow workers revolted and took possession of the bottling plant. Salvador Allende's Marxist government "bought" all the Chilean Coca-Cola operations, installing its own personnel. A series of Argentinian Coke officials were kidnapped and held for ransom. In Italy, when a Company-owned bottling plant declared bankruptcy rather than submit to a strong union, the workers occupied the facility. Back in Atlanta, just before Charles Duncan's arrival as president, a Company spokesman shrugged off the Italian situation. "It may be serious; it may not," he said. "These things have a tendency to lose something in the translation."

That kind of attitude, coupled with worldwide unrest, persuaded Duncan to bring the Coca-Cola Export offices from New York City to Atlanta in 1972. Also, by that time foreign earnings far exceeded domestic income. "There was a real danger that the tail would start wagging the dog," one Export man remembered. The move to the still-parochial heart of the South provoked tremendous resentment among the overseas Coke men. They opted for cross-town offices, as far away from North Avenue as possible. Nonetheless, Austin's decentralized system had begun to pull back toward Atlanta.

Taking advantage of Duncan's day-to-day attention to operations, Austin traveled more extensively, spending over half his time globe-hopping. To his dismay, he often encountered hostile attitudes toward his Company. As colonialism dwindled, nationalism grew, along with a tendency to vilify powerful multinational corporations. Coca-Cola, as the most ubiquitous product on earth, provided a tempting target. The authors of *Global Reach*, a book published in 1974, blamed Coke for "commerciogenic

---

* At Coca-Cola, power was where you found it. Robert Woodruff, "retired" since 1955, continued to rule from his perch on the Finance Committee. When Paul Austin was appointed president of the company, he maintained real control, although Lee Talley chaired the board. Austin retained his authority when he became chairman.

malnutrition," claiming that Mexican families commonly sold their eggs and chickens to buy Coke for the father, "while the children waste away for lack of protein." African health officials called a local form of malnutrition "the Fanta syndrome" because they thought it was related to overconsumption of sugary soft drinks. The following year, in *Sugar Blues*, William Dufty blamed most of man's ills on overindulgence in white sugar, Coke's primary ingredient. "The sugar pushers are our predators," he wrote, "leading us into temptation, peddling a kind of sweet, sweet human pesticide." Only the strongest would survive, the author claimed, "while the rest go down in another biblical flood—not water this time, but Coke."

While coping with such allegations, Austin and Duncan also strove to accommodate themselves to the women's liberation movement. Throughout the early seventies, women gradually struggled into lower and middle level positions previously occupied only by men at The Coca-Cola Company. In 1973, the *Refresher* profiled Carol Hinkey, the first female field representative. While she "lives and works in a man's world," the article assured any threatened males that she was "amply feminine."* In the same year, the Company conducted an internal "social audit" to determine how well it was coping with affirmative action and women's issues. The consultant's report specified that "considerable progress" had been made but there was "still some distance to go."

For the first time, Coca-Cola employees convened in small groups to discuss something beside the wonders of the soft drink. In "normative sessions," they spoke freely in a kind of business-sponsored encounter group. Mary Gresham, who had started working in the mailroom in 1943 and had slowly wended her way up to a managerial position in the advertising department, found herself in an all-women's seminar. The young secretaries complained that men addressed them by their first names, while expecting a "Mister" in return. Gresham finally broke in: "They can call me anything they want, if they would only pay me the same salary as the man whose job I took." The meetings resulted only in men cracking jokes. "I hear you'll be calling me by my first name now," one told Gresham with an edge in his voice. Diane McKaig, hired away from HEW to advise Coca-Cola on how to deflect threats from the consumer movement, was one of the few women who commanded a decent salary.

Even powerful men weren't always safe, however. With Austin in Africa on an extended 1974 trip, Robert Woodruff decided that the time was ripe for a power shift. He prompted an independent consultant to suggest that the president of the Company needed to receive more authority—that is, Duncan should really guide Coke. Woodruff had acted prematurely, however, before Duncan had sufficient support at the board level. When Austin returned from overseas and found what had happened, he angrily went straight to the board, demanding Duncan's resignation. In a thunderous session, he won his point, the first man ever to stand up to Woodruff and survive.

The relationship between Paul Austin and Robert Woodruff had always been a peculiar love/hate affair. "One minute they were as close as son and father," an associate recalled. "The next, they were spitting at each other like two cats." Now the younger man had seemingly asserted his independence of the aging company patriarch once

---

* The Company's residual sexism wasn't hard to find. A 1972 *Refresher* article on Company women received the headline "Girls Girls Girls"—including an older woman who had joined Coke in 1963 after fifteen years with a trucking firm.

and for all. Woodruff recovered from two successive strokes early in 1972, but his health gradually declined throughout the decade. In the ousted Duncan's place, Austin promoted J. Lucian "Luke" Smith, a popular traditional Coca-Cola man who had joined the Company in 1940. Although a bright man, Smith was no dynamic leader, looking to Austin for ultimate guidance. Most important, from Austin's viewpoint, Luke Smith had a fine relationship with the all-powerful bottlers—a relationship soon to become crucial.

THE THOMAS COMPANY AND THE FTC TANGO

By the beginning of the seventies, Coca-Cola clearly had too many bottlers. From a peak of 1,200 in the twenties, the number of American Coke franchises had dwindled to 800 by 1970, but almost two-thirds of them carbonated their syrup in cities with populations of fifty thousand or fewer. While the small-town bottler remained a Company tradition, he simply wasn't terribly efficient in the modern marketplace. The Company facilitated mergers and sales with a new Bottler Consolidation Department. In the century's early decades, the independent franchise system had effectively disseminated the soft drink throughout the United States. Now, however, the fifty-mile-radius territories, appropriate for the horse and buggy, proved minuscule to tractor trailers thundering down American superhighways with full loads. High-speed bottling and canning lines could spurt enough product to cover whole states. Supermarket chains such as Winn-Dixie or Safeway didn't want to negotiate with multiple local bottlers offering different services and prices. Coca-Cola faced stiff competition not only from Pepsi but generic colas mass-produced for private-label sale in the chains.

Because of the perpetual bottling contract, however, the Company had limited power to enforce change—unlike Pepsi, where Walter Mack had commenced with larger territories, fewer bottlers, and more flexibility. Consequently, Pepsi could easily offer lower prices to large national outlets. When Coca-Cola Company national sales representatives negotiated cut-rate deals with supermarkets, bottlers who hadn't been consulted resented the intrusion, since they were forced to sell for a narrow profit margin. An intolerable tension built inside the Thomas Company territories, where silver-haired DeSales Harrison still held absolute sway, collecting a 12.5-cent tithe on each gallon of Coca-Cola syrup sold to his bottlers, making it almost impossible to match Pepsi's prices.

In 1973, Harrison died, and Company men immediately negotiated to acquire the Thomas Company, whose territory contained over a third of the U.S. population. Even though past offers had failed, Paul Austin was more optimistic this time around, for several reasons. First, the inflation of the early seventies was gnawing away at the 12.5-cent fixed income of the Thomas Company. Second, "allied brands" such as Sprite, Fanta, Fresca, and TaB were steadily eroding Thomas Company profits, since the perpetual contract applied only to Coca-Cola with an added pittance for TaB. As more products came on line—such as Mr. Pibb, a 1973 creation designed to challenge Dr Pepper—the Thomas bargaining position would weaken.

The real pressure, however, stemmed from the pending FTC case against the exclusive franchise system. While ostensibly The Coca-Cola Company fought valiantly against the FTC, there were strong hints that it *wanted* to lose the case in order to weasel out of the perpetual bottling contract. When a Taft, California, bottler sued the Company for permission to sell product in an adjoining territory, Coca-Cola responded with an ingenious argument. If the Taft businessman or the FTC won, Luke Smith served notice, the Company intended to use the ruling as an excuse to abrogate the sacred perpetual contract. Without the exclusive territory clause, the Coke lawyers argued, the entire contract could be declared null and void.

Smith's threat panicked the Thomas Company managers. Through the grapevine, they learned that Austin believed further negotiations were unnecessary, since he thought that, given time, the contract would be worthless anyway. Soon thereafter, Thomas Company representatives agreed to a price of $35 million, and in 1975 the sale was consummated. Viewed by most standards, the price seemed absurdly high for rights that had been given away by Asa Candler in 1899. By the seventies, the parent bottling company performed no major useful function. From the Company's point of view, however, it was a bargain, since it was paying over $8.5 million annually under the old Thomas contract, and the price rose each year. Within four years, the purchase would pay for itself.

A FORCED LOOK UPWARD

The shorter duration of ad campaigns provided another indication of the Company's concern over its bottlers. As soon as they launched a slogan and song, the McCann men began brainstorming a new one, since the bottlers and their wives tired of whatever they saw on TV long before anyone else. And the bottlers had to be appeased, since they were paying for half of the enormous television budget. Consequently, in the summer of 1974, the Company introduced a new twist on the "Real Thing" theme, even though the McCann men had been generating powerful commercials. Ike Herbert, the normally placid Coke director of marketing, grabbed Bill Backer by his bow tie. "Give me a campaign that'll make the bottlers come to their feet," he told him, "or I'll have your balls."

By that time, the country's gloom had deepened. Nixon remained in the White House under a state of siege as the Watergate hearings revealed the underside of American politics. The OPEC countries, in retaliation against U.S. support of Israel, imposed an oil embargo, and the energy crisis worsened. With the dollar devalued, inflation hit double digits. The unemployment figures swelled. The Vietnam War was clearly lost. Since Coca-Cola symbolized America more than any other product, Company executives perceived the country's faltering self-image as a direct threat. Pulling back from messages of worldwide brotherhood, they directed the McCann men to implement an ad campaign that would renew American pride.

In response, Bill Backer created "Look Up, America" in march time, orchestrated with plenty of brass. Unabashedly patriotic, the first commercial portrayed the Liberty Bell, Niagara Falls, the Empire State Building, cowboys, pounding surf, a farm family dining on roast beef, amusement parks, the Rocky Mountains, a bald eagle, a county fair, buffalo stampeding, a square dance, a corn harvest, a softball game, a football player, and a marching band—all in sixty seconds. "We've got more of the *good* things in this country than anywhere else in the world," a narrator informed viewers. "Have a Coke and start looking up!" The soft drink men actually believed that they could swing the nation from despair to joy. "It's up to people like us," an executive told employees, "to dispel the nation's mood of gloom." A month after the campaign debuted, word circulated that Nixon would announce his resignation in a televised speech on August 8, so Coca-Cola bought prime-time slots on all three stations just prior to the speech, repeating the maneuver the next day before Gerald Ford was sworn in as President. "Let in the sunny side of living," Backer's lyrics entreated. Regardless of who was in the White House, Americans should remember their priorities and keep on drinking Coke.

The ads weren't nearly as effective as their predecessors. They seemed forced. The march tempo and voice-over announcer weren't as memorable or singable as Backer's best efforts. "Look Up, America" did, however, match the country's frantic desire to deny its faltering economy and loss of world power. As the bicentennial of 1976 approached, Americans whipped up an artificial patriotic fervor, and the Company announced that it was sinking $800,000 into sponsoring *1600 Pennsylvania Avenue*, a Broadway show written by Alan Jay Lerner and Leonard Bernstein, intended as an upbeat American history lesson.

THE INITIATION OF A CUBAN REFUGEE

Worldwide sales for the first quarter of 1975 reached all-time highs, but the figures hid an alarming trend. In the United States, gross sales had actually fallen below those of the previous year. Despite the bravura of Coke's ads, Pepsi was slowly gaining in the domestic market, causing Paul Austin to value the international business even more. To keep tabs on the far-flung Coke empire, Austin went outside the normal Export hierarchy, relying instead on high-level technical men such as Cliff Shillinglaw, mixer of the top-secret 7X formula, who traveled the globe to monitor ingredients. Since only two or three men in the Company knew the formula at any one time, they never flew on the same airplane. In 1974, Shillinglaw, in the Far East to retrieve some cassia leaves, felt chest pains as he boarded his plane for London, where he intended to replenish the European 7X supply. Once in England, he suffered a serious heart attack.

In Atlanta, news of Shillinglaw's critical condition provoked a frantic transfer of power and knowledge. Asa Candler had passed the secret to his son Howard, who in turn had taught the company's first chemist, W. P. Heath. In 1948, Dr. Heath had given the 7X formula to his successor, Orville May, who had initiated Cliff Shillinglaw in 1966. Now, in February of 1974, Dr. May came out of retirement to instruct a young Cuban chemist named Roberto Goizueta (pronounced Goh-SWET-a), who had fled his native land in October 1960 when Castro was poised to nationalize the business.* Aide Joe Jones informed Robert Woodruff that Dr. May had also shown Goizueta "the system for purchasing the highly sensitive ingredients. Roberto is now

---

* In the 1940s, when Roberto Goizueta attended Colegio de Belen as a teenager, he must have known Fidel Castro, four years ahead of him. Castro was an exceptional athlete and a brilliant, if erratic, scholar, in contrast to Goizueta, a studious, quiet boy. The two Cubans were destined to find their place in history as virtual monarchs of their respective realms. Goizueta's kingdom, the worldwide Coke empire, was the more impressive. Yet in a way, he owed it all to Castro for nationalizing American companies.

our full-fledged No. 2 man in this area." On March 15, May and Goizueta, on separate planes, flew to London to rebuild the 7X inventory.

In the meantime, Bob Broadwater, returning from a negotiation session in Moscow, picked up Shillinglaw's cassia leaves in order to smuggle them to Atlanta. "I was afraid I'd get caught," Broadwater recalled, "so I stuffed them into the Russian fur hat I was wearing."* Despite the anxiety at the top echelon, the situation was soon resolved. Broadwater arrived at headquarters with the cassia. Mild-mannered Goizueta, who had been brought to Atlanta and groomed by Shillinglaw, quietly assumed much of his ailing boss's authority. Although Shillinglaw recovered in due time, he never regained his former stature, and he died in 1979. Most significantly for the Company's future, Roberto Goizueta had entered the inner circles of power.

PURPLE PROBLEMS IN JAPAN

By the early seventies, the Japanese business had blossomed into the largest Coke market outside the United States. In 1973, Japan contributed 18 percent of Coca-Cola's entire corporate profit, despite an increasingly militant consumer movement and administrative mishandling. When "Emperor" Hal Roberts, the head of Coca-Cola there, died of cancer in 1971, Paul Austin named Masaomi Iwamura as president of the Japanese Export business, making him the first native manager of an American company in Japan. A brilliant chemist, Iwamura turned out to be a miserable administrator. "He had a complex mind that saw 27 alternative plans of action," a colleague remembered, "but he couldn't get himself to take any of them." Iwamura, a member of the prestigious Samurai class, also refused to speak to Nisaburo Takanashi, the Tokyo bottler descended from lowly merchant stock.

To make matters worse, the huge twenty-six-ounce Home-Size bottles received an inordinate amount of attention from the Japanese media when a few of them exploded and the American area manager failed to offer the traditional Japanese apology. "The Coca-Cola Company wasn't about to say, 'Oh, we're sorry this lady got her eye put out,'" a Coke veteran explained. "We were afraid she was going to sue." Even as Austin directed that the big bottles be encased in protective plastic, regardless of the extra cost, an even greater disaster struck in Japan. An active consumer movement spurred a crisis by objecting to the artificial coal-tar coloring in Fanta Grape. Protesters smashed vending machines, and sales plummeted. In response, the Company developed a new version tinted with real grape skins. It tested well in the winter, but by the summer of 1974, Fanta Grape on shelves all over the country fermented, leaving an unpleasant though harmless precipitate in the drink. "It looked like a snowstorm in the bottle," a Coke man recalled. Millions of recalled cases, poured into the ocean, literally turned Tokyo Bay purple for several days.

In 1975, a desperate Austin placed a telephone call to Morton Hodgson, enjoying his poolside retirement in the Virgin Islands. "I'm in big trouble out in Japan," Austin told him. "We've lost half of our net profit in less than eighteen months, and that's

---

* The normal cassia importation process was legal, but Broadwater knew that individuals were forbidden to bring plant material into the United States. He could picture the scene: "Oh, so you're a Coca-Cola official, and this is part of the secret formula?"

big enough to jolt the entire Company's balance sheet." At first, Hodgson demurred when Austin asked for help. "Why don't you send out some of your young tigers?" Austin explained that he needed someone with plenty of experience in converting bottling plants from mismanaged jokes into money-making outfits. "The real reason I want you to go," Austin admitted, "is that the Japanese revere ancient things, and you are an old bastard." Knowing Hodgson's sensitivity to accusations of nepotism, Austin didn't mention one other crucial element in his scheme—Hodgson was Robert Woodruff's nephew.

When the impressive Coca-Cola veteran, then sixty-six, emerged from retirement to head the Japanese business, the bottlers were suitably humble. The legendary Old Man was sending his own beloved kin to save them. Unlike Iwamura, who was kicked upstairs to supervise a worldwide technical project, Hodgson immediately established cordial relations with the Japanese bottlers. He apologized profusely to the media for the Fanta fiasco, promising to restore goodwill and harmony. With a battle cry of "Back to the Basics," Hodgson applied time-honored marketing techniques, concentrating on better service to dealers and consumers. He arranged "Sawayaka Tours"—weeklong sightseeing tours to Paris and other European cities—for Coca-Cola bottlers and prominent *sake* store owners. A "Big Sky and Big Sound" sweepstakes attracted twenty million entries. A new ad campaign, "Come On In, Coke," featured American, Italian, and British youth joyously imbibing. The Company introduced Georgia Coffee, a canned sweetened coffee product, with a commercial spoof on *Gone with the Wind* in which the Rhett Butler character chose the drink over Scarlett O'Hara. When Hodgson left Japan three years later, sales for Coca-Cola products had surged to record highs.

"A MASTER AT FAKING IT"

By the time Hodgson retired for the second time in 1978, it was clear to everyone close to Paul Austin that something was wrong. He kept inexplicably forgetting things. Bob Broadwater first noticed trouble late in 1975: "I knew Paul was drinking a little, and I just put it down to that. We all did." At the age of fifty-nine, Austin had begun the slow, terrifying descent into Alzheimer's disease. Throughout the latter part of the decade, as his condition gradually worsened, Austin reacted defensively. "He was a master at faking it," Broadwater remembered. Always an austere, aloof figure, Austin now withdrew from all but his closest associates.

His charade was effective, in large measure because his memory lapses were temporary. Despite his persistent drinking and increased irritability, Austin remained a commanding presence who functioned not just as a figurehead but as a real leader. In 1975, he unveiled plans for a new multimillion-dollar tower to soar twenty-six stories above the dwarfish old brick building next to it. The next year, reacting to the complexity of the worldwide industry, he reorganized the Company into three operating groups, nominally reporting to President Luke Smith. At that time, Coca-Cola Export finally transferred to North Avenue, firmly tucked under the corporate wing.

Based in Atlanta, all three group leaders were strong managers, any of whom might reasonably replace Austin instead of Smith. German Claus Halle, president of the Export Corporation until 1976, had survived the autocratic rule of Max Keith and brought an urbane, meticulous approach to his sector. South African Ian Wilson, who had learned under Austin during the fifties, emerged as an aggressive, cultured, hardheaded manager who had recently turned the ailing Canadian business around. Don Keough, an Iowa native, had arrived as part of the Duncan Foods purchase in 1964. A masterful speaker and marketer, Keough quickly sounded more like a traditional Coke man than anyone else.

THE CARTER CONNECTION

Austin's control of the Company was highlighted by his much-publicized friendship with Democratic presidential nominee Jimmy Carter. When the peanut farmer had run for governor of Georgia in 1970 against Carl Sanders, a longtime friend of Coke, Austin had naturally supported Sanders, particularly since Carter publicly castigated "big business." When it became clear that the man from Plains would win, however, Austin and his forces contributed $6,200 to his campaign. As it routinely did for Georgia governors, Coca-Cola flew the Company plane for Carter trips to conferences and paid for limousine service to and from airports. Like his predecessors, Carter reciprocated with almost obsequious gratitude, frequently requesting Austin's counsel. Normally, businesses seek to influence local politicians, but in Georgia, that scenario was reversed. As one commentator noted, public officials received with an ice-cold Coke at North Avenue felt "honored, like the commoner invited to take tea with the Queen."

In 1972, Carter revealed that he had ambitions beyond Georgia, asking Austin for Coca-Cola's support if he ran for president. Austin laughed and said, "Sure," never dreaming that the nationally unknown Carter would actually pull it off. Nonetheless, when the Georgia governor groomed himself by traveling overseas to Tokyo and Brussels—ostensibly to boost the state's trade, but also garnering international experience and exposure—local Coca-Cola men squired him around the country, providing background information on the local politics, culture, and economy. With Austin's sponsorship, Carter joined the prestigious Trilateral Commission as a fellow member.

In 1974, Carter bragged, "We have our own built-in State Department in The Coca-Cola Company. They provide me ahead of time with . . . penetrating analyses of what the country is, what its problems are, who its leaders are, and when I arrive there, provide me with an introduction to the leaders of that country." Two years later, during the 1976 presidential campaign, Austin hosted a luncheon at New York's swanky 21 restaurant, where Carter reassured nervous businessmen that his speeches about the "unholy, self-perpetuating alliances" between money and politics was just talk. "I will be a friend of business," Carter told the assembled economic elite. "I would not do anything to subvert or minimize foreign investment." When the Federal Election Commission ruled that the $500-a-plate dinner constituted an illegal campaign contribution, Austin, embarrassed, began to downplay his friendship with the Democratic candidate.

Nonetheless, in the closing days of the campaign, when Carter's ambiguous positions on issues were pulling down his popularity ratings, he hired Tony Schwartz, a New York media consultant who had developed hundreds of Coca-Cola commercials. "Whether it's Coca-Cola or Jimmy Carter," Schwartz explained, "we don't try to convey a point of view, but a montage of images and sounds that leaves the viewer with a positive attitude." The commercial puffery worked. Carter assumed the mantle of leadership as a humble born-again Christian peanut farmer, an outsider who stood for justice and righteousness. He tapped quite an array of Coca-Cola figures—Charles Duncan became the deputy secretary of Defense (before graduating to secretary of Energy), Joseph Califano snagged HEW, Griffin Bell of King & Spalding served as attorney general, and law partners Charles Kirbo and Jack Watson remained close advisers. The "Georgia Mafia" was securely in power. Unfortunately, Carter and his cronies brought none of Coca-Cola's good-old-boy political savoir faire with them to Washington. The hype had apparently gone to the new President's head, and he really behaved as an outsider, disdaining normal protocol and alienating important Democratic figures such as Tip O'Neill and, almost as important, the press.

As a consequence, the media pounced on any morsel suggesting Carter's favoritism, such as the President's banishment of Pepsi from the White House and its replacement by Coke vending machines. When Bert Lance caught a secretary drinking Pepsi, a journalist overheard him ribbing her and reported it verbatim: "You know, ma'am, our crowd drinks a good old Democratic drink, Coke." The president couldn't even attend a National Gallery of Art exhibit of antique masks without newspapers noting that it was cosponsored by Coca-Cola and its Japanese bottlers. And when Jimmy and Rosalynn journeyed down the Mississippi on the *Delta Queen*, syndicated reporter Jack Anderson pointed out that the free publicity was a lifesaver for the failing tourist boat—which happened to be owned by the New York Coca-Cola Bottling Company.

Some reports had more substance, though. In 1977, when sugar prices dropped, a U.S. Trade Commission study recommended a two-cent duty on imported sugar to help protect domestic growers. Coca-Cola used a million tons annually, making it the world's largest consumer. Lobbying through the Sugar Users Group (run by Coke man John Mount), the Company prevailed on Carter to approve a plan *paying* two cents a pound to the domestic industry, effectively keeping prices down. Indirectly, then, the taxpayers were subsidizing Coca-Cola. When Mount maladroitly commented that Coke would have to "call in a few chits" to ensure that things went their way, some congressmen labeled the piece of legislation the Coca-Cola bill.

In 1977, Paul Austin quietly flew to Cuba, where he held secret meetings with Fidel Castro—presumably to negotiate the Company's return to the country, even though Coca-Cola officially held a $27.5 million claim against Cuba for confiscating its plants in 1961. His mission failed, except for some Havana cigars that Castro sent to Robert Woodruff by way of Austin. Having promised President Carter that he would report on his trip, Austin met with him briefly in the White House. When acid-penned William Safire learned of the episode, he concluded that it was a nefarious scheme to obtain Cuban cane. "The Carter-Coke-Castro sugar diplomacy is not merely a potential conflict of interest," wrote Safire. "It's the real thing."

OPENING DOORS AROUND THE WORLD

Austin was more successful in negotiating for Coca-Cola's entry into Portugal, Egypt, Yemen, Sudan, the Soviet Union, and China. Though none of these coups could be attributed directly to Carter's intervention, the American president's well-publicized bias toward the soft drink undoubtedly provided essential leverage. It just happened, for instance, that the long-awaited Portuguese permission coincided with the U.S. Treasury Department's approval of a badly needed $300 million loan. Likewise, when Austin met with Anwar Sadat, delicately preparing to ease back into Egypt despite the Arab boycott, the Coke executive asked Sadat whether he should keep their wide-ranging discussion confidential or report it to his government. "I'd like very much if you would report it," the unruffled Egyptian answered. "That's the reason for our conversation."

With the implicit Carter clout behind them, the Coca-Cola men triumphed in country after country—with the exception of India, where Coke departed in 1977 rather than reveal its formula to the government.* Their achievements, however, came only after years of patient negotiations that predated any presidential aid, as with Bob Broadwater's Moscow efforts. Although Pepsi's exclusive Soviet cola contract ran through 1984, Kosygin's men decided Coca-Cola could be served at special events. In 1978, Broadwater signed a contract to supply Coca-Cola to the Spartakiada, the Eastern Bloc sports festival, the following year. But that would only serve as a warm-up for the 1980 Moscow Olympics, where Coke paid $10 million for exclusive rights. Fanta Orange would fizz not only during the sporting events, but on a long-term basis throughout the Soviet Union. The real Austin plum, however, fell into his lap late in 1978, when Coke executive Ian Wilson, holed up in a Beijing suite, hammered out an arrangement with the Chinese Communists only days before the U.S. State Department normalized relations. Now, despite Mao Tse-tung's pronouncement in his *Little Red Book* that Coca-Cola was "the opiate of the running dogs of revanchist capitalism," the symbolic beverage found a home on the Chinese mainland.

PEPSI'S UNGENTLEMANLY CHALLENGE

While Coca-Cola grabbed headlines around the world, however, the business back home was stagnating, as Pepsi made inroads on the valuable take-home market, scoop-ing Coke with one-and-a-half-and two-liter plastic bottles. As a symbol of Coke's loss of direction, *1600 Pennsylvania Avenue*, the Broadway production that had cost the company $800,000, folded after seven performances, as *New York Times* critic Clive Barnes pronounced it "tedious and simplistic." While Coca-Cola switched to the lackluster "Coke Adds Life" campaign in 1976, Pepsi bounced back with its new invocation to "Have a Pepsi Day." As usual, Coca-Cola maintained a product focus while its rival concentrated on lifestyles.

Almost by accident, however, Pepsi launched a simultaneous strategy in direct con-trast to its traditional approach. Pepsi man Dick Alven had been sent to Dallas with the seemingly hopeless mission of injecting life into the business there, where Pepsi claimed a miserable 4 percent of the soft drink market. Alven convinced his boss that they needed drastic measures, so they petitioned Pepsi headquarters to allow them to use the local Stanford Agency instead of BBDO. Bob Stanford, who had discovered

---

* In 1977 the nationalistic Indian government demanded that *all* of the soft drink must be manu-factured inside India, which meant turning over the secret formula. Coke balked, and the Company reluctantly withdrew, abandoning twenty-two bottling plants.

that Pepsi beat Coke in taste tests while promoting a 7-Eleven generic cola, suggested a daring assault on Coca-Cola. In 1975, Dallas TV stations aired commercials urging viewers to "Take the Pepsi Challenge," showing candid shots of die-hard Coke consumers astonished to discover that they preferred Pepsi in blind taste tests. Only Pepsi would have stooped to such an outrageous, virtually taboo approach, since comparative ads were considered unsportsmanlike. Nonetheless, the results were indisputable: within two years, Pepsi's Dallas market share jumped 14 percent.

At first, the local Coca-Cola franchise ignored the scurrilous new ads, pretending that their effect was temporary and unworthy of response. Then, however, Coke slashed prices, initiating a price war. In Project Mordecai, named after the Biblical figure who saved the chosen people from a plot to destroy them, Coke purchased huge chunks of airtime on all three networks to block Pepsi commercials. "One sip is not enough," Coke spots asserted. Another featured a grizzled Texan complaining about the New York Pepsi types with their "little bitty sips, . . . skinny britches and pointy lizard shoes." Echoing a racist line, he ended, "You've got to watch what you do down heah, boy," and swigged a Coke. Other commercials tried to reduce the Challenge to absurdity, showing chimpanzees taking the taste test, or actors deciding which of two tennis balls was fuzzier. By mocking the Challenge, though, the Coke ads backfired. Pepsi men and viewers sensed their panic. Back in Atlanta, Coke's technical men conducted their own secret tests, and, to their horror, they discovered that consumers actually did prefer Pepsi by a 58–42 split. Encouraged by the results, other Pepsi bottlers in the Southern Coke heartland adopted the Challenge, along with the aggressive Los Angeles franchise. By decade's end, the Challenge commercials were airing in a quarter of the U.S. markets.

While Coca-Cola's domestic market share remained relatively flat, Pepsi's steadily rose throughout the latter seventies. In 1977, Pepsi's advertising budget actually surpassed Coca-Cola's for the first time, with each firm spending just over $24 million a year on their main brands. By the following summer, Nielsen market figures demonstrated that Pepsi had finally overtaken Coke in supermarket sales, which Pepsi dubbed the "free choice" arena. Defensive Coke men asserted that their drink still held an edge in the total retail outlets. "They must use some strange numbers," speculated John Sculley, the combative young Pepsi-Cola president.

Because Coca-Cola still dominated the vending machine and fountain outlets, it maintained a considerable overall lead, but corporate pride and self-confidence suffered. The trends, too, were disheartening. In 1978, Coke products' U.S. market share fell from 26.6 percent to 26.3 percent while Pepsi's rose from 17.2 percent to 17.6 percent. At a time when every fraction of a percent amounted to millions of dollars, such shifts would have alarmed any company. For Coca-Cola, steeped in a corporate culture that rendered its primary product a religious artifact, the numbers were horrifying.

MULTIPLE HEADACHES

Coca-Cola men were equally paranoid about issues affecting the entire industry. The FDA ruled that saccharin, like cyclamates, caused cancer in laboratory rats and must therefore be prohibited under the Delaney Amendment. Responding to heavy lobbying from the diet industry, Congress voted a "moratorium" on the saccharin ban, but that had expired in May of 1978, and no one knew what lay ahead for all-saccharin TaB. Zero population growth represented a more ominous, long-range threat, however. Ever since a 1977 *Business Week* cover article had warned of "The Graying of the Soft-Drink Industry," demographers had forecast a gloomy future. The baby boom was over, the domestic market seemed saturated, price wars raged, and future advances would be carved inch by inch.

In addition, colas, while still comprising over 60 percent of U.S. soft drink consumption, were challenged by a welter of new beverages aimed at more specific audiences. The segmentation of the soft drink market, gaining momentum during the 1960s, was a well-researched and financed war by the end of the seventies. Pepsi's Mountain Dew, only a regional phenomenon as a hillbilly drink, surged ahead by "going into John Denver country," as one wry analyst put it, with an ad campaign of "Hello sunshine, hello Mountain Dew." Coke responded with Mello Yello.

Rather than setting the pace within the industry, The Coca-Cola Company had become reactive and fragmented. Although still a massive money machine, it seemed to meander aimlessly, without any particular sense of purpose. By the late seventies, only 70 percent of Coke's business stemmed from soft drinks, as the increasingly confused Austin insisted on his shrimp farming, water projects, and the like, despite their slim or negative profit margins. Bottler consolidation had shrunk the number of U.S. franchises to 550, but that was still far too many. In 1977, Coke diversified into the wine business, but viniculture, unlike Coke syrup, required major capital expenditure and time for proper aging. Coke's Wine Spectrum (created by combining several labels) never earned much money, while angry Southern Baptist stockholders complained that their pure Company should not promote alcohol.* Coca-Cola responded to its multiple problems by pouring unprecedented amounts of money into ad campaigns.

COKE AND THE DEATH SQUADS

Meanwhile, smoldering foreign crises exploded, as Coca-Cola's cozy relationship with dictators blew up one after the other. In 1978, after the shah of Iran was deposed, the Ayatollah Khomeini handed over the nation's Coca-Cola plants to the Association of the Oppressed, but the formerly downtrodden did not make good bottlers, and the business soon died. The following year, the Sandinistas threw Somoza out of Nicaragua. Adolfo Calero, the Coke bottler there, had opposed Somoza, who had jailed him (Jimmy Carter, friend of Coke, secured his release). Although Calero continued bottling as the eighties loomed, his strident criticism of the Sandinista leadership jeopardized the business.

---

* In the meantime, Pepsi had become much more diversified than Coke, with its Frito-Lay division performing well. In 1978, Pepsi purchased Pizza Hut and Taco Bell, which guaranteed exclusive national soft drink outlets. Coke men consoled themselves: PepsiCo had become more of a conglomerate than a soft drink company, with over half of its sales coming from nonbeverage enterprises after 1975.

The worst problem, however, loomed in neighboring Guatemala, where workers in a Guatemala City bottling plant had unionized in 1975, sparking a chain of intimidations and violence that became very public news at The Coca-Cola Company's annual Delaware meeting in May of 1979. The Company had always prided itself on its brief, untroubled yearly business affair, which usually lasted only fifteen minutes. In 1979, however, Sister Dorothy Gartland, a diminutive but strong-willed nun representing the two hundred shares of Coca-Cola stock owned by the Sisters of Providence, submitted a resolution calling for the development of minimal labor-relations standards in its worldwide franchises. Sister Gartland lamented a South African Coke franchise that employed black prisoners on work release, paying them only twenty-five cents a day. In Laredo, Texas, she continued, the Coca-Cola manager paid a $2.40 hourly wage to Mexicans, informing them that they were disposable. But the nun was most urgently concerned over the Guatemalan situation. To explain why, she introduced Israel Marquez, former general secretary of the Guatemalan Coca-Cola union, who had traveled from Central America to tell his story in person.

As the uneasy Coke executives listened to a translator, the Guatemalan delivered an emotional speech. A cooler repairman at the Guatemala City Coke bottling plant, Marquez spoke scathingly of John Clayton Trotter Sr., the Houston lawyer who managed the franchise for Texas widow Mary Fleming. Trotter, a tall, lanky right-winger with a fondness for polyester suits, perceived his workers' unionization as a conspiracy fomented on the one hand by Communists and on the other by the competitive Pepsi franchise. According to Marquez, Trotter had at first unsuccessfully resorted to bribes, bullying, and legal maneuvers to quell the nascent union.

In 1978, when repressive General Romeo Lucas Garcia stormed to power in Guatemala, sporadic violence escalated into a bloodbath, as the notorious Secret Anti-Communist Army (ESA) and its death squads terrorized the country. A few days after Marquez narrowly avoided death from gunfire at his Jeep, union leader Pedro Quevedo was murdered, shot twelve times while delivering Coca-Cola. Soon afterward, Marquez' tenant, mistaken for the union man, fell in a machine gun barrage. After a third attempt on his life, Israel Marquez reluctantly fled Guatemala, seeking refuge in nearby Costa Rica. Although he could not prove it, Marquez was absolutely certain that Trotter had collaborated with the death squads in plotting the violence directed at the union, although there was no evidence linking him with any specific incident.

As the flood of Spanish was haltingly translated into stories of atrocities in some faraway banana republic, the executives in the Delaware boardroom stirred uneasily. Marquez told them that after he left Guatemala, Manuel Lopez Balam replaced him as union secretary. Just a month before the board meeting, Balam's throat was slit as he retrieved a case of empty Coke bottles from a grocery store. "Besides being inhuman," Marquez concluded, "the situation is also one of poor economics. Coca-Cola's image in Guatemala could not be worse. There, *murder is called 'Coca-Cola.'*"

For a moment, there was a stunned silence. Then Paul Austin swiftly concluded the meeting. The nun's labor resolution, he said, would mean an "unnecessary intrusion into the internal activities of . . . affiliates" and would be difficult to foist upon independent bottlers. "While lamenting the problems in Guatemala," he said, "we also must respect the laws and processes of other nations." The board meeting ended in a chaos of loud protests from the minority stockholders, while Austin slammed his gavel.

Austin's performance was uncharacteristic of the man who had displayed such concern for migrant workers when testifying before the Senate nine years before; that spring he was often confused and belligerent, as he entered the serious second stage of Alzheimer's. Nonetheless, his statement accurately reflected the Company policy of denying responsibility for independent bottling franchises. Since Coke affiliates now bottled in 135 countries, the implications of the proposed resolution were mind-boggling. If the Company really assumed responsibility for the welfare of workers in every plant, it could easily devolve into a nightmare for the personnel department—not to mention the public relations team.

The Guatemalan situation refused to go away, however, and Marquez' dramatic recitation caused headlines across the country, including the *Wall Street Journal*. During the summer of 1979, as the killings, kidnappings, and beatings proliferated, Amnesty International and the Swiss-based International Union of Food and Allied Workers' Associations (IUF) joined the chorus of voices demanding that The Coca-Cola Company replace Trotter and his management. Although the Company dispatched security chief Leo Conroy to Guatemala for a week-long investigation, the ex-FBI man failed to uncover evidence directly linking Trotter to the killings, which was hardly surprising, since Conroy spoke no Spanish, didn't meet Trotter, and never even entered the bottling plant. Confidentially, Conroy told another Company man that he wouldn't return to Guatemala. "It's not safe there," he said. "I value my life!"

Brandishing Conroy's report, Coke executive Don Keough told critics that the Company couldn't proceed without proof. "We have revulsion and are embarrassed by the kind of shenanigans Mr. Trotter is doing," Keough said, "but we haven't got the luxury to operate in any environment but the legal one." In fact, the Company would have loved to dump Trotter, but they didn't want to look as if they were yielding to external pressure. Under Trotter's mismanagement, Coke's market share in Guatemala City had dwindled to 30 percent. He also bottled Dr Pepper, 7-Up, and other flavors, despite Coca-Cola's protests, and there were allegations that he had charged the Company for import taxes he never had to pay.

Unfortunately, the wily Texan knew that he could now charge an outrageous amount for the troubled bottling plant, since the Company yearned so desperately for him to disappear. Consequently, Company men decided to wait until 1981, when the franchise contract was due to expire. With more blood than syrup flowing at the Guatemalan bottling plant, however, Coca-Cola's critics grew more shrill. Congressman Donald Pease escalated pressure on the Company by writing a letter to President Carter about Coke's "callous disregard" of the "wave of murder, torture, kidnapping, and intimidation." Citing Carter's close ties to the soft drink concern, Pease demanded action. The "confidential" letter was leaked to the press and widely publicized.

AMENDING THE SACRED CONTRACT

While Don Keough realized that the situation in Guatemala was spiraling out of control, a battle much closer to home diverted his attention. Company executives had decided that many of their domestic troubles were attributable to the ancient bottling contract, which did not allow for increased labor costs, advertising, overhead, or ingredients besides sugar. In late 1977, with inflation raging, Paul Austin directed President Luke Smith to secure a contract amendment at all costs, now that the Thomas Company no longer stood in the way.

If anyone could pull off such a seemingly impossible task, it was Smith, a traditional, warm Southerner whom the bottlers loved and trusted. Although a nucleus of faithful franchises agreed that the Company needed some relief in order to advertise more effectively, Smith's proposed contract amendment, allowing the Company unlimited flexibility in pricing syrup, proved a hard sell. In May of 1978, Smith and Keough took what derisive bottlers called their "dog-and-pony show" to six meetings around the country to persuade hesitant bottlers to sign.

Bill Schmidt, whose grandfather first bottled Coke in 1901, exemplified the devout Coca-Cola man, having just opened a museum full of memorabilia and artifacts inside his Elizabethtown, Kentucky, bottling plant. At first, he listened with an open mind to the Company presentation, but he was disgusted by the Company's high-handed amendment. Finally, as he recalled later, "it just boiled up in me," and he penned a series of protests sent to a growing list of fellow bottlers. Unintentionally, Schmidt found himself the unofficial leader of the opposition. The most divisive issue to hit Coca-Cola since its great internecine battle of the early twenties, the amendment split men whose forebears had pioneered the business.

Both sides argued that the still-pending FTC assault on the exclusive territorial provision supported their position. Schmidt's contingent, the "unamended bottlers," argued that it was unwise to tamper with the contract until the FTC matter was settled, since it might rouse the bureaucrats to greater efforts. Luke Smith wielded the potential dissolution of territories as a club, as he had with the Thomas Company—just in case the FTC case went against them, the bottlers should sign the amendment to ensure they had a contract.

Into this maelstrom stepped Brian Dyson, an Argentinean brought in to assume control of the U.S. division of the Company. When his friend Don Keough begged him to leave his position as head of the South Latin America Division, Dyson initially demurred. "Why don't you get an American?" He knew that the American system was in chaos, and if he failed to turn it around, it could signal the end of his career. Keough remained convinced, however, that Dyson could salvage the situation. After all, the Argentinean had cut his teeth on the business in Venezuela, one of the few places where Pepsi utterly dominated the market. As a consequence, Dyson was accustomed to scrapping for every sale. In addition, the Argentinean, a grandson of British immigrants, was tall, lean, athletic, and urbane. Moving to Atlanta in August of 1978, he immediately tangled with the bottlers in the amendment dispute.

The next month, the Company finally yielded to criticism, modifying the amendment to put a ceiling on the amount the syrup price could be raised. Now there would be two sliding scales—one for sugar and one for the "base element" of all other ingredients, tied to the Consumer Price Index. As a bonus, the Company agreed to eliminate the awkward BX pre-mix syrup, with its artificially inflated price, and to allow amended bottlers to purchase concentrate instead of bulky syrup. Schmidt still objected, since the CPI rose more quickly than inexpensive ingredients. Nonetheless, after hard lobbying, the Company finally succeeded in signing more than half the bottlers by April of 1979, when two huge outfits, New York and United, capitulated.

THE GREAT GET-TOGETHER

The agreement arrived just in time for Brian Dyson's June Great Get-Together, a gigantic San Francisco convention—the first bottlers' assemblage since the "Real Thing" campaign, launched in Atlanta ten years before. Still battered and divided over the amendment issue and discouraged by Pepsi's advances, the bottlers warily gathered to see what this South American would say. Hardly any of them had seen him in person, much less heard him speak. After the customary Broadway-style song-and-dance number, the tall, angular Dyson somewhat nervously approached the podium, clutching the traditional six-and-a-half-ounce bottle. As he spoke, his image was projected onto a huge video screen.

"In recent times," Dyson told the bottlers, "we have all been through a period of self-appraisal." Ears pricked up. Perhaps he would actually acknowledge some of their problems instead of making the expected rah-rah speech. After mentioning the amendment debate, he ticked off the decade's disasters—the FTC, energy crunch, sugar crisis, saccharin attack, refund legislation, consumer movement, inflation, wage and price controls. He admitted that Coke's corporate share had grown a mere three-tenths of one percent in ten years. "In the same period, Pepsi's [Cola] corporate share has grown from 21.4% to 24.2%." The bottlers collectively gasped. Dyson had broken all precedent and uttered the "P" word in front of most of America's Coca-Cola men. Pepsi, Dyson continued, had labeled Coca-Cola "the nostalgia company, an enterprise that is wholly preoccupied with its past glories." If so, the Company was doomed. But, Dyson promised, "we are willing to do *whatever is necessary* for as long as is necessary to turn this business around. . . . Together, we must *fix the problem*, however long it may take."

Dyson clearly meant business, but could Big Coke really deliver? As a first step, the bottlers knew they needed a spectacular ad campaign. Could McCann pull it off? On the big video screen, the new commercials took over. "Have a Coke and a smile," sang effervescent young people. "It makes me feel goo-oo-ood, / it makes me feel *nice*, have a Coke and a smile." They danced energetically about. Coke fizzed and gurgled. In the audience, feet tapped. This was all right. It sounded like something Bill Backer might have written, though he had recently left McCann to form his own agency. "That's the way it should be, / and I'd like to see / the whole world smiling with me."

In between screenings of the new ads, deadly serious marketing man Bill Van Loan explained that just as the macho cowboy was associated with Marlboro cigarettes, "the world of smiling Americans can be literally owned by Coca-Cola." But it couldn't be just any smile. "It must always come out of the product itself." Unlike Pepsi's ads, which urged people to join some mythical group, the new Coke commercials featured the product as hero. "*Coke* causes the smile."

In most of the ads, though, the rehearsed smiles were too obviously forced, with one extraordinary exception. While others flashed vignettes, this one conveyed a heartwarming story. As wounded black Pittsburgh Steeler "Mean" Joe Greene limped down a stadium tunnel toward the locker rooms, a shy, moonfaced boy holding a sixteen-ounce Coke timidly called after him: "Mr. Greene, Mr. Greene." The defeated football player half turned. "Yeah?" he snarled. The kid stammered, "I just want you to know I think, I think you're the best ever." Unmoved by this praise, Greene grunted, "Yeah, sure," and started to leave. In desperation, unable to think of anything else, the boy offered his Coke but was rebuffed. "Really," he persisted, "you can have it." With resignation, Greene relented, upending the bottle and draining it in one long, glorious chug. The music swelled while joyful voices harmonized, "Have a Coke and a smile." As the boy turned away dejectedly, the player, now thoroughly refreshed, shouted "Hey, kid!" and threw him his jersey. Flashing an incredible smile that made all right with the world, he headed for the lockers.

The Mean Joe Greene drama created an instant sensation. Though it wasn't planned for airing until a year after the campaign's introduction, bottlers mobbed Bill Van Loan after the presentation, demanding its immediate release. Thousands of viewers wrote to thank the Company for the greatest commercial they had ever seen. The media liked it just as much, running articles on Mean Joe's performance in *Newsweek, People, Sports Illustrated,* and the *New York Times,* while the Steelers' lineman/actor appeared on *Good Morning America* and *Today* television shows. The ad even inspired a made-for-TV movie. Greene revealed that the effort had consumed three grueling days, in part because Tommy Oken, the ten-year-old actor, kept muffing his lines on account of his genuine awe for Greene. The final day, the football player guzzled eighteen 16-ounce bottles of Coca-Cola, and still managed to smile.* "When Joe turns around at the end," one literate Coke executive said, "he looks like he's playing Othello." It was, former Pepsi ad-maker John Bergin noted ruefully, "the perfect commercial."

A STAB IN THE BACK

The Coke bottlers felt encouraged as they left the great convention hall that June of 1979. Shortly afterward, however, they received a Mailgram from Paul Austin that radiated shock waves throughout the system. The beloved Luke Smith, only sixty years old, was "retiring for personal reasons," Austin announced. "The board has not named a successor. I will assume the additional duties of the presidency." Rumors flew within the Coca-Cola family as to what had really happened. Everyone in the Company understood that Luke Smith had almost single-handedly secured the amendment signatures of the majority of the bottlers. He had cajoled, charmed, threatened, pled; had crisscrossed the country, spent hours on the telephone. To relax, he took two weeks in August to putter around Lake Lanier, just north of Atlanta, on his houseboat. On a Friday, he got a call over the radiophone from Fil Eisenberg, Coca-Cola's chief financial officer. "Paul wants you out," Eisenberg told Smith.

No one ever knew exactly why Austin had suddenly fired Smith, though Austin's rapidly progressing Alzheimer's certainly contributed. At the Great Get-Together in

---

* Greene threw up after the sixth Coke, but he manfully continued to chug drink after drink—all for nothing, since the directors eventually used the first take. One bootleg clip became a famous TV blooper in which Greene was supposed to say "Hey, kid! Catch!" Instead, he said "Hey, kid!" and emitted a gigantic belch.

June, Austin had fumbled through brief comments, refusing to allow the video cameras to project him onto the big screen, which would have shown his quivering facial expression. Later that year, he flew to New Orleans to deliver a speech and forgot why he was there. Even without a diagnosis, Austin realized that something was terribly wrong with him, and his reaction was to cling desperately to power.

A *Business Week* headline blared, "SUCCESSION AT COKE IS A HORSE RACE AGAIN." Austin created the new position of vice chairman and named six men to the post, any of whom might assume control. Within the Company, the arrangement was soon dubbed the "vice squad," or "beauty contest," with bets on the winner. *Business Week* picked Don Keough, though insiders thought South African Ian Wilson a more likely candidate. In fact, Wilson himself was quite sure he would be chosen, since both Woodruff and Austin had privately told him he was the one. At any rate, as one journalist noted, "Austin does not look like a man thinking of retirement." Though he was approaching his sixty-fifth birthday, the board could extend his mandatory retirement year by year.

As Austin failed, his wife grabbled power within the Company. The former Jeane Weed, a Mississippi native, was a secretary at the Chicago bottling company when Austin met her in 1950. Now, as her husband grew more confused, she tried to help, taking particular interest in plans for the nearly completed Tower. Mrs. Austin raised the hackles of traditional employees with her approach to interior decorating, replacing classic Norman Rockwell Coca-Cola paintings with avant-garde artists. Disaffected employees called her Mrs. Vice Chairman, while others placed grades such as D-plus or F on her paintings.

STUMBLING INTO THE EIGHTIES

Late in 1979, when the huge old Coca-Cola Spectacular, which had blinked the time and temperature in Atlanta's Margaret Mitchell Square for thirty years, crumbled to make way for a park, the demolition was emblematic of Company morale, which had never dipped so low. The approaching eighties found Coca-Cola in disarray, except for one brilliant new commercial.

The bottlers remained divided and angry. The courts had ruled against the Company in the FTC case, with overriding legislation still pending. Market share was slipping, and the Company had severed communication with the financial press. Nuns and labor leaders protested death squad killings in Guatemala. Anita Bryant, "the voice that refreshes," shrilly crusaded against homosexuals. In 1979, Coca-Cola stock was worth less than its value at the beginning of the decade, despite a two-for-one split in 1977 that was supposed to encourage the small investor. While reported annual growth for the decade registered 12.5 percent, the 7.1 percent inflation rate reduced that to an unimpressive 5.4 percent.

Even Coke's much-publicized friendship with Jimmy Carter didn't prevent the president from declaring a U.S. boycott on the 1980 Moscow Olympics to protest the invasion of Afghanistan, rendering Coke's exclusive contract with the Soviets meaningless. Besides, association with Carter was becoming a liability, with the peanut farmer appearing powerless and indecisive in the face of spiraling inflation and the

Iranian hostage crisis. Paul Austin, wandering the top floors of the North Avenue Tower, screamed, "Get out of my office!" in the wrong executive suite, while his wife antagonized everyone. The six vice chairmen jockeyed for position, and Robert Woodruff, nearing his ninetieth birthday, was reportedly near death from pneumonia.

No one would have guessed that a hopeful new era was about to commence, sparked by a frustrated secretary's letter.

Part V

The Go-Go Goizueta Era

(1980–1997)

If any father had a right to feel proud of his son, it was Crispulo Goizueta. When Roberto graduated from Yale, his father had wanted him to settle down in the family's Cuban sugar empire. After a year, however, the young man became restless, eager to strike out on his own. In 1954, thirty-one years ago, Roberto answered a blind ad and went to work as a chemical engineer for Coca-Cola.

So much had happened since then, Crispulo reflected. Castro had stolen his land, his heritage, and most of his wealth, and now he lived in Mexico City as an expatriate. In the meantime, Roberto had risen within the Company, achieving more than he or his father could ever have dreamed. As CEO, he had galvanized the staid old soft drink company in just a few years, transforming it into an aggressive dynamo.

Yet Crispulo's pride was tempered with anxiety. Mexicans were saying that his son had committed a grave error: he had changed the formula of Coca-Cola, and the entire world seemed in tumult over it. The change hadn't even come to Mexico yet, but it seemed that people spoke of little else. The troubled former plantation owner looked at Roberto now and saw a handsome man in his mid-fifties, a slight bulge beginning around the belt. Roberto, attending his own son's marriage on this hot May day in Florida, appeared typically unruffled and in command, yet Crispulo sensed a hesitancy he had never noticed before.

When the two men were alone, they spoke in Spanish, making polite conversation about the weather, the joyful occasion, and other small talk. Finally, Crispulo could bear it no longer. He had to know why his son had alienated so many people. "Roberto," he burst out, "this is awful, terrible! People are calling you names. What have you done?"

~ 18 ~

Roberto Goizueta's Bottom Line

Two vultures [are] sitting on a branch of a dead tree in the middle of the desert where, frustrated, they have been waiting for days on end for something to eat. One vulture finally turns to the other and says, "Patience, hell. Let's go kill something!"

—Roberto Goizueta

Her jaw clinched, Dianne Smith stormed back to her office. The blonde secretary had worked at The Coca-Cola Company for ten years and, like most employees, she was fiercely loyal, proud to work for Atlanta's best company. In 1972, she had won the Miss Refreshing contest. On this particular May morning in 1980, however, with the dogwood in bloom, something inside the secretary snapped. The Company used to feel like one big gracious Southern family, but, in the last two years, ridiculous corporate strictures had descended from on high. And today, when Smith walked across North Avenue to the little park for her lunch, security guards informed her that no one was allowed to eat there anymore. Mrs. Austin didn't want anyone to attract pigeons and their droppings, which would sully the manicured grounds. The frustrated secretary defied the guards and grimly, determinedly ate her sandwich on a bench anyway.

Back in her office, Smith rolled a fresh sheet into her typewriter, banging the keys with a letter of complaint to Paul Austin. "I am speaking for 'the little people,'" she wrote, "who do not have releases from the daily pressures, and the park affords us the opportunity of a wonderful outlet." It had always been "a major source of pride for me to say that I am employed with this fine company," she typed, "but as of late, I have reason to doubt my source of pride." Smith wrote that she had never seen morale lower. With a flourish, she ended the letter with her full name, Constance Dianne Smith. "That ought to get some attention," she said to herself. Just to make sure, though, she sent a blind copy to Robert Woodruff. After all, the pigeon-plagued park was named after him.

The secretary's letter galvanized the Boss. Just the week before, Woodruff's chauffeur had returned empty-handed from an errand to North Avenue, when a security guard told him he couldn't park in front of the building—sorry, no exceptions, orders of Mrs. Austin. Shortly afterward, Grumman Aircraft had called Woodruff's office to iron out some details on the new jet that Mrs. Austin had just ordered to facilitate her search for works of art. Then came the crowning blow. On May 28, the Company announced a $100 million debt offering to pay for the new tower. Woodruff, who prided himself on steering the Company out of debt in the twenties, was livid. The ninety-year-old patriarch now summoned Paul Austin to his office and demanded his resignation, effective the following year, and he insisted that Austin appoint his successor immediately as the Company president.* A shaken, confused Austin drafted a letter nominating his friend Ian Wilson, who was traveling in Asia on a month-long business trip. When word of the recommendation spread through the North Avenue Tower, concerned executives—none ever willing to admit their role—convinced the Old Man that Ian Wilson, an autocratic Austin acolyte, would simply be more of the same. The Company needed a new direction. Besides, the appointment of a white South African would be foolhardy and might alienate black consumers.

THE RISE OF ROBERTO

At a special meeting of the board on May 30, 1980, Roberto Goizueta was appointed president of The Coca-Cola Company. Virtually everyone was surprised, since Don Keough seemed the obvious choice after Wilson. A skillful politician, tough marketer, and the best speaker and motivator since Harrison Jones, Keough could "read from the phone book and make you cry," as one admirer put it. Goizueta, on the other hand, a technical man with no operating experience, spoke in a halting accent, a curious amalgam of Cuba and Dixie. It seemed strange that a Latin chemical engineer should run the Company that produced the most American of products. Insiders like Joe Jones weren't so surprised, however. Only forty-eight, Goizueta, the consummate corporate politician, had risen quickly within the Company since his arrival in Atlanta in 1964. Most important, he had grown very close to Woodruff in the last year, joining him every day in his private dining room for lunch. Goizueta flattered Woodruff's vanity, seeking his opinion, deferring to his wisdom. The Boss in turn called Goizueta his "partner," perceiving something in the Cuban that reminded him of himself when he first took over the Company.

Like Woodruff, Goizueta, the son of a very wealthy man, had established his own career outside the family business. Raised in his grandfather's baronial mansion paid for by sugarcane, he grew up in a culture that valued tradition and older people. Goizueta enjoyed the attention of his grandfather, and his conversation was still sprinkled with the Cuban proverbs he learned from him. In Woodruff, Goizueta found another wise old man. While his devotion to the Boss was politically expedient, it was also probably genuine. Woodruff's simplistic aphorisms reminded him of his grandfather's, and Southern culture resonated with the same social graces Goizueta had acquired in Cuba.

As journalists dug into Goizueta's past, trying to assess the dark-horse winner, they discovered a remarkably intelligent man. In 1948, when eighteen-year-old Roberto Goizueta attended the prestigious Cheshire Academy in Connecticut for his senior year, he knew little English. He learned the new language by going to the same movies

---

* In the meantime, word of the defiant secretary's letter spread through the efficient Company grapevine, and Dianne Smith won folk hero status. One clever employee posted a sign in the foyer. "Why worry about pigeons in the park," read the query, "when there are turkeys in the tower?"

over and over again, absorbing American values along with the lingo. His discipline, combined with a photographic memory, helped him to excel. "My professor said that my sentence structure was textbook-perfect," Goizueta recalled. "It should have been; it came right out of the textbook! The only way I could accurately convey a thought was to memorize, word by word, entire passages." Incredibly, by the end of the year he delivered the valedictory address. Later, he graduated tenth in his class at Yale.

Coca-Cola associates knew Goizueta as a dedicated, impeccably dressed employee who left a bare desk every night. Never a brilliant researcher, he was an able administrator, a notorious perfectionist with an eye for detail. "He knew where every grain of sand was in the office," a fellow worker recalled. Goizueta's courtly, affable manner and Latin good looks hid what some called ruthlessness, but he rewarded results, and he never assumed an absolute position, quoting one of his grandfather's proverbs: "The quality of one's compromises is much more important than the correctness of one's position." Intensely pragmatic and somewhat cynical, he once observed, "It's a pretty good bet that human beings will act in their own self-interest most of the time." Although Goizueta kept his emotions under a steely, logical control—"his mind is like a piece of crystal," an associate said—the surface tranquility was belied by his chain-smoking and slight hand tremor. Outside of work and family, he had few interests aside from swimming laps and reading everything in sight. Somewhat incongruously, the Cuban blue blood also developed a fondness for country music.

Asked what he would do if he weren't the head of Coca-Cola, Goizueta gave a wholly unexpected answer: "I'd probably be a good teacher in a business school." What would he assign? Not *In Search of Excellence* or other popular management tomes but *The Brothers Karamazov* and the Gospel of St. Luke. His answer revealed not only his eclectic reading but deep philosophical and religious concerns. Nonetheless, the Coca-Cola executive's brand of religion did not call for turning the other cheek. When asked for his best characteristic, Goizueta did not speak of his devotion to God, incisive mind, intuitive grasp, or managerial expertise. "I'm very persistent." His greatest fault, he said, was impatience. These two traits together produced a man who, like the vultures in his parable, favored well-planned aggression over passivity.

SETTING THE SLEEPY GIANT IN MOTION

Before assuming the chairmanship from Paul Austin in March of 1981, Goizueta spent an uneasy year as a president without full powers. He used the time well, making alliances with key executives and solidifying his power base. Recognizing that Don Keough's interpersonal skills would complement his more private analytical bent, Goizueta told the Iowan that he wanted him as his chief operating officer. Goizueta and Keough began to appear everywhere together. In their speeches, each talked about what Don or Roberto had said about this or that.

In the meantime, Goizueta made certain that Ian Wilson's star did not rise again within the Company. "There was never any doubt that it was Keough or me," he informed journalists. "I do not think Wilson had a chance." He noted that Wilson's territory of Canada and the Far East contributed only 15 percent of the Company's sales and hadn't maintained a high profit margin. And when Wilson's name came up in a scandal, Goizueta did nothing to clear it. The South African couldn't secure his

U.S. citizenship, since a black Atlanta immigration official took pleasure in blocking his application. Anxious to obtain his green card before his anointment as CEO, Wilson had contacted Washington "fixer" Irving Davidson. Now, when word leaked of Davidson's imminent indictment in conjunction with an alleged Mafia don, Wilson splashed onto the papers and national TV for his involvement with the shady character, and the official Coke spokesman left the South African twisting in the wind with a "no comment" response.

Similarly, Wilson suddenly found himself implicated within the Company for illegal shipments of concentrate to Rhodesia in the late sixties, in violation of U.S. sanctions. Although in charge of the southern African territory at the time, Wilson denied any knowledge of the shipments, claiming he was framed. One anonymous source hypothesized that for Goizueta, "the stakes were enormous. What would you do if you were a displaced Cuban whose only recognized expertise was engineering and quality control for soft drinks, and you were confronted with someone who might do you in? On one side, there was the power and glory; on the other, the absolute abyss." Symbolically, after Wilson's departure, Goizueta appropriated his locker at the Peachtree Golf Club, where Woodruff had long controlled the sought-after membership.

At the same time, Goizueta worked on a major strategy statement that would, he hoped, revolutionize the way the Company did business. Grasping that an eighties' CEO would have to become a financial wizard, the new president determinedly taught himself about accounting, currency fluctuation, and economics, applying the same persistent curiosity and sponge-like memory to the task as he had to acquiring English. "He used to come into my office fifteen or twenty times a day," remembered Sam Ayoub, who was then the assistant financial officer. "He didn't know a word about accounting or finance, but he just asked questions and questions and questions."

The more Goizueta learned, the more uneasy he felt about management decisions within the Company. The fountain business, for instance, which Coke had always dominated, was considered the financial backbone of the Company, since the syrup price was flexible, unlike the bottler contract, which hamstrung the Company. Goizueta noted, however, that capital expenditures on fountain had gone up substantially since the introduction of the five-gallon (known as figal) aluminum fountain dispenser in the late sixties. The figures showed that while the fountain business returned 12.5 percent, the cost of capital was 16 percent. In theory, at least, the business was liquidating itself. Goizueta's technical men quickly solved the problem for their old boss by inventing inexpensive disposable bag-in-a-box containers.

Similarly, Goizueta concluded that the corporate obsession with market-share figures meant neglect of the bottom line. The Pepsi paranoia had blinded everyone to the ultimate goal of a good return on investment. Goizueta had, in fact, already demonstrated his ability to merge his technical background with concern for a cost-effective business when, in January of 1980, he persuaded Robert Woodruff to let him use high-fructose corn syrup (HFCS) in Coca-Cola in lieu of cane sugar.*

---

* Initially, Coca-Cola was sweetened with 50 percent HFCS, 50 percent sugar. Beginning in November 1984, Coke in the United States was sweetened completely by HFCS, although cane and beet sugar remained in the formula elsewhere.

CORN SYRUP AND ANGRY NON-AMENDERS

Luke Smith and Paul Austin had insisted that corn syrup lent an "off-taste" to Coca-Cola, but now a taste panel found no discernible difference. Although cane sugar would have been cheaper in a free market, HFCS offered a 20 percent savings over prices imposed by the traditional U.S. protective tariffs on sugar. At first, Goizueta had a difficult time convincing Woodruff to substitute HFCS, because it would, after all, change the sacred formula. Before the Finance Committee, the Cuban chemist elaborately explained the technical aspects, muddling Woodruff. John Sibley, even older than Woodruff but just as sharp, intervened, giving Goizueta his cue. "Remember when we approved of beet sugar back in the thirties, Bob? Well, this is just another kind of sugar, that's all." Once the decision was couched in such fundamental, simple terms, Woodruff quickly agreed.

In his war against Pepsi, Coca-Cola USA head Brian Dyson locked up almost the entire fructose supply with long-term contracts, then boosted the Company's share of advertising. While holding out such carrots to most bottlers, though, Dyson used HFCS as a stick to beat the non-amended renegades. The 1978 amendment specified that any savings in the cost of sweetener would flow through to the amended bottlers. But for the minority who had refused to sign, the Company held firmly to the old syrup price.

Bill Schmidt, already angry at Big Coke's cavalier attitude, became apoplectic at this financial blackmail. Didn't his perpetual contract call for 5.32 pounds of cane sugar per gallon of Coca-Cola syrup? They couldn't just foist off this corn syrup without permission. Schmidt ventured forth from tiny Elizabethtown, Kentucky, in search of an Atlanta lawyer to pursue his case, though he had little hope of finding anyone willing to risk collision with the monolithic Coke/King & Spalding business establishment.

Providentially, the disaffected bottler located Emmet Bondurant, who had already established a reputation for championing unpopular causes. Representing the ACLU, for instance, Bondurant had destroyed Georgia's loyalty oath. In February of 1980, only months before Schmidt appeared, Bondurant had gone beyond the bounds of Atlanta propriety, however, when he took on King & Spalding in a sex discrimination suit. "You've lost your damn mind!" a fellow lawyer told him. "Suing King & Spalding—Good God Almighty—in Atlanta!" Now, Bondurant agreed that Schmidt did indeed have a case, and in 1981 he brought a class-action suit for Schmidt and seventy other disgruntled bottlers. Bondurant, who professed admiration for Atticus Finch, the courageous Southern lawyer in Harper Lee's *To Kill a Mockingbird*, saw himself as a moral crusader, the underdog's last hope. He began to amass material for the case.

THE SPARKLE OF DEATH

As a new Coca-Cola civil war brewed, however, Goizueta was relieved to resolve two other menaces he had inherited from the seventies. The IUF had ushered in the new year with a Coke boycott because of the Guatemalan atrocities. On January 2, 1980, the IUF mailed a gory picture of Pedro Quevedo, a slain Coca-Cola union organizer, to its affiliates. The international union flexed its muscles as Coca-Cola bottling lines clattered to a halt in Finland, New Zealand, and Sweden, with threatened stoppages in six other countries. The relatively brief pause in Coca-Cola's production delivered its intended message to the Company. Hastily, Latin American Coke chief Ted Circuit assured the union, the nuns, and other critics that John Trotter's contract would be canceled in September of 1981.

Unfortunately, the assurance failed to prevent more bloodshed. In May of 1980, four more Coke union members were killed, including Marion Mendizabal, the third murdered union secretary. Letters from Amnesty International members poured into Guatemala. Throughout Latin America, angry protesters ripped down point-of-purchase signs and, by changing one word, converted them to placards with the chilling legend, "Coca-Cola: La Chispa de la Muerte"—"Coca-Cola: The Sparkle of Death." IUF head Dan Gallin insisted that The Coca-Cola Company act immediately to get rid of Trotter. In July, as the situation deteriorated, Goizueta, now president, directed Ted Circuit and Company lawyers to fly to Geneva to confer with Gallin. As a result, Circuit arranged for Antonio Zash, a Mexican McCann-Erickson executive with operating experience, and Roberto Mendez, a Mexican Coke plant manager, to buy out Trotter. The Company, however, supplied most of the purchase price and retained some managerial control over the franchise. In December, Zash and Mendez signed a union contract, and the Guatemalan crisis was over for the time being.*

The quick, bold action to halt the boycott was characteristic of Goizueta, who understood that Coke men couldn't simply sit in Atlanta and wait for the world to come to their door. By flying directly to Geneva, they had signaled their willingness to compromise. Goizueta was also ready to risk criticism from hard-line industrialists who would never negotiate with an international union. While Coke men denied that they had done any such thing, they were clearly playing with semantics. "If this isn't a negotiating situation," Gallin crowed, "I don't know what is. Our objectives were exactly what we got."

GETTING AGGRESSIVE WITH BOTTLERS

The month before Circuit flew to Switzerland, another seventies headache was laid to rest. In June of 1980, the Soft Drink Interbrand Competition Act passed both houses of Congress. Finally assured of exclusive territorial rights, bottlers could thumb their collective noses at the FTC. Without the grassroots clout of the small-town bottler, the bill would never have become law. Ironically, though, the law's passage cleared the way for Brian Dyson and his aggressive team to hasten the demise of the small bottler.

Free of the FTC threat, which had discouraged potential franchise buyers, a flurry of mergers and acquisitions commenced, and the price of bottling territories, held down artificially for many years, spiraled dizzily. Many longtime family names sold out, retiring on the proceeds. Big Coke not only encouraged sales of weak bottlers, it

---

* Four years later, Zash and Mendez declared bankruptcy, but the union workers occupied the plant, claiming that the owners had milked the franchise before closing its doors to defeat the union. Again, the IUF called for a boycott and Coca-Cola once more forced a solution, locating Carlos Porras Gonzalez, a Salvadoran economist, to restart the bottling plant.

actively promoted consolidation, sometimes buying an interim equity position while looking for a new owner. Still, Dyson, Keough, and Goizueta repeatedly vowed that they had no intention of assuming permanent ownership. In fact, the Company jettisoned its Baltimore plant and Dyson promised to unload other Company-owned bottlers unless they performed well.

In 1980, Pepsi's John Sculley, who sensed a worthy opponent in Dyson, decided to push the Pepsi Challenge nationally, hoping to maintain the momentum of the late seventies and retain leadership in the supermarkets. Sculley faced unexpectedly violent opposition from within his own ranks; terrified Pepsi bottlers begged him to "stop this madness," convinced that in *their* territory, Pepsi would lose the Challenge, or that Coke would initiate vicious price wars. Their apprehension was justified. Dyson reacted by funneling Company money into areas where the taste tests ran. At one Challenge campaign kickoff, Coca-Cola trucks surrounded the Pepsi plant in an attempt at pure intimidation. The Company hired Mean Joe Greene to wield a sledgehammer against Pepsi vending machines at Coke rallies. Dyson's blunt message to Pepsi bottlers, as Sculley interpreted it, was "if you're in the Challenge program, we're going to go out and kill you." Nonetheless, the taste test continued to plague Coca-Cola.

FINDING A BETTER DIET DRINK

As early as 1979, Goizueta had directed Mauricio Gianturco and his technical people to launch work on Project David, an ultimately unsuccessful attempt at a cola formula to trounce Pepsi in taste tests. Frustrated in the sugar cola arena, he now focused on a drink that would outperform *Diet* Pepsi, since the fast-growing diet segment would soon account for 20 percent of the entire soft drink market. Goizueta and Dyson agreed that Sergio Zyman should head the diet project. The brilliant, aggressive, multilingual young Mexican had been lured from Pepsi along with a raft of other key employees active in the Challenge campaign—a reversal of the Coke defections led by Al Steele thirty years earlier. In February of 1980, Zyman initiated Project Harvard. Zyman fashioned a number of code names for the new product he was working on—Fresca Plus, Lucy, Shrimp, and BPS, which stood alternatively for "Bottler Productivity Study," "Best Product Under the Sun," or "Beat Pepsi Soundly." If the Mexican had really proposed any of these silly names, Austin and other Coke executives wouldn't have been disturbed. The whole point of the project, however, was to utilize the "brand equity" of the Coca-Cola name. The new product, Diet Coke, would constitute a "line extension."

To lend the magical Coke name to any other soft drink was heretical. When a few daring Company men suggested the idea in 1963 when TaB was invented, Austin had condemned them for it. Now, TaB held a commanding lead over all other diet drinks. Why would the Company want to cannibalize its venerable drink with another diet entry? Furthermore, wouldn't another product with the Coke name simply dilute the brand, confuse consumers, and contribute to already poor bottler morale?

Zyman, Dyson, Keough, and Goizueta were convinced, however, that the introduction of Diet Coke would energize the business. As Zyman put it in a February 1980 memo to Brian Dyson, "Over the last few years, the Company has drifted . . . to a perceived image of a traditional, sedentary, conservative company." The bold

introduction of Diet Coke would have a "tremendous impact" on this image, revitalize the bottlers, and capitalize on the Coca-Cola name. It would also be profitable,
since a saccharin-sweetened drink wouldn't cost as much to produce. The timing was
demographically perfect as well: the aging baby boomers weren't drinking fewer cola
drinks, as doomsayers had warned, but were switching to diet drinks as part of the
emerging fitness craze. Zyman concluded that "*competition cannot duplicate this effort,*"
simply because there already *was* a Diet Pepsi. Because Coke had held back so long,
this late bloomer would have an enormous catalytic effect, motivating bottlers to "go
out and *really* get aggressive." In short, concluded the Mexican marketer, "this could
be the silver bullet."

Then Paul Austin abruptly and inexplicably pulled the plug on Project Harvard in
a cryptic April telegram to Don Keough, who was plotting strategy with Zyman and
Dyson in Buenos Aires. Convinced of the project's wisdom and urgency, Goizueta
sought Woodruff's support. He had learned his lesson from the corn syrup presentation—to win approval from the Old Man, it was necessary to argue the case in
its simplest terms. Besides, Woodruff displayed limited patience and attention span.
Goizueta explained that the market share for sugar colas had been declining for years,
while diet drinks were steadily growing. "In a few years, Mr. Woodruff, we might
have to rename this operation The TaB Company if we don't do something." When
his trusted "partner" described it that way, Robert Woodruff readily agreed to Diet
Coke, but Austin still stood in the way. The Boss took care of that, too. When the
board convened on August 6, Goizueta was elected chairman of the board and chief
executive officer to replace Austin upon his retirement, which would occur on March
1, 1981. Posing for pictures after the board meeting, Goizueta looked like a movie star,
while Austin, looming beside him like a great disheveled bear, grimaced a thin-lipped
imitation of a smile. Immediately afterward, Goizueta gave Zyman the go-ahead.

THE AUSTIN LEGACY

Following his retirement, Austin was finally diagnosed with Alzheimer's disease, and,
after a swift decline, he died in 1985 at seventy. Although his troubled final years tend
to obscure his achievements at Coca-Cola, his overall record reveals the astonishing
growth he fostered. In 1962, when he assumed the presidency, the Company was still
essentially a one-drink outfit with bland, old-fashioned advertising and deep-seated
corporate racism. Profits amounted to $46.7 million on sales of $567.5 million, with
the overseas branches accounting for 30 percent. Austin provided visionary, professional management, deftly guiding the Company through the difficult sixties and
seventies. Under his supervision, the Company introduced a rainbow of drinks for
a segmented market, developed a social conscience—albeit under considerable pressure—and aired some of the most powerful commercials ever made.

Austin's greatest legacy, however, was his globe-girdling zeal in spreading the business to country after country. By the end of 1980, Coke earned $422 million on
revenues of nearly $6 billion—a tenfold increase over 1962—and 65 percent of the
profit flowed from outside the United States. Even Austin's pet projects—his ill-fated
shrimp farming, desalinization plants, and whey-based nutritional drinks—reflected

a curiosity and daring that the Company had never seen. "Paul was too big for Coca-Cola," mused his friend Ian Wilson, who quit the same day Austin retired. "His vision was too broad to be satisfied selling colored carbonated sugar-water."

UPENDING SACRED COWS

Soon after the Coca-Cola board announced that Goizueta would succeed Austin, Company managers from around the world convened in Atlanta for their annual October meeting, where they usually presented a five-year plan for their sectors. Goizueta, assuming that no one could see ahead that far, requested three-year plans instead. Once again, Goizueta asked "questions and questions and questions" of his ill-prepared executives, who dubbed the collective two-week grilling the "Spanish Inquisition." Frustrated that Coke men were simply reacting to competition in setting their goals—with some going after increased sales, some market share, and only a few concerned over return on capital—Goizueta felt that something had to be done.

Determined to shake up the staid, stuffy Company, Goizueta labored over an aggressive strategy statement. Within a month of his official investiture as CEO in March of 1981, he summoned the top fifty Coca-Cola managers from around the world to a five-day conference in Palm Springs, California. "A company starts to worry about holding on to success when it's decided it has more to lose than it has to gain," he told them. "At that point, it gets timid and overly concerned with appearances." Goizueta promised that the days of Coca-Cola's passivity were over. "Those who don't adapt will be left behind or out—no matter what level they are." He flatly stated that "there are no sacred cows." To prevent competition from winning, Goizueta stressed, he would consider "the reformulation of any or all of our products."

Goizueta's carefully crafted *Strategy for the 1980s* was passed out at Palm Springs and reprinted for widespread distribution to financial analysts, the media, and Coca-Cola employees. At the heart of the innocuously worded statement lay the profit target—"a rate substantially in excess of inflation, in order to give our shareholders an above average total return on their investment." In order to accomplish that, the document warned that the Company would probably diversify. Ruling out heavy industry, Goizueta promised to search instead for "services that complement our product lines and that are compatible with our consumer image."

Although few people, including the media, took Goizueta terribly seriously, his managers soon discovered that he followed through. Those who bucked Goizueta's authority or failed to address the bottom line effectively were ruthlessly weeded. "Roberto was a tyrant," Sam Ayoub recalled. "Fire him!" was often the peremptory order, but Ayoub usually arranged for a gentler exit with an early retirement package.

On the surface, though, it was business as usual at Coca-Cola for the rest of 1981. Brian Dyson strove for further bottler consolidation and rejuvenation of the domestic system, producing a motivational film in which Coca-Cola men shot it out in a Western-style gunfight against Pepsi's "Big Blue Gang." As a climax, a tank clanked over a hill and blew a Pepsi vending machine to bits. Dyson also attempted to placate disaffected bottlers by allowing them to choose from alternative seasonal commercials and by responding more promptly to local problems. Most bottlers were pleased when

Goizueta announced his intention of boosting the Company's domestic earnings, since they felt that their importance had diminished with increasing income from abroad. Goizueta wanted to achieve a 50–50 balance by the end of the decade. With the dollar strengthening against most other currencies, it made sense to look for more profits at home. In addition, foreign sales had flattened in 1980, due partially to record rainfall in Japan.

IN THE PHILIPPINES: #/&$ PEPSI!

The dismal performance of Coke's business in the Philippines also contributed to the poor showing overseas. Where Coca-Cola had once ruled the market, Pepsi now dominated with a 70 percent share. Andres Soriano Jr., the heir of an enormously influential, wealthy family, had neglected his Coke franchise in order to push his beer business. In the meantime, Pepsi dumped huge amounts of money into its company-owned Philippines plant. The haughty Soriano refused to listen to the bright young men Coca-Cola sent to him, dismissing them as "pipsqueaks."

Clearly, drastic measures were necessary. Breaking precedent, the Company bought a $13 million 30 percent equity position in the business in return for managerial control. Neville Isdell, an impressive 6'5" Irishman summoned from a Coke post in Australia, quickly assessed the situation in June of 1981. Although a basic infrastructure—over a thousand delivery trucks and 7,500 employees—was already in place, dispirited workers perfunctorily bottled in filthy plants. Isdell set out to instill pride and aggression into the employees. While the Sorianos had worn a traditional upper-class *barong tagalog*, Isdell deliberately fostered an informal, gutsy image, sporting a T-shirt with the Coca-Cola logo. He inspected every toilet, not only to promote cleaner hands on the bottling line, but to deliver the message that he cared about plant conditions.

With twelve-ounce and liter packages, as well as new flavors such as Mello Yello, Isdell sought to rejuvenate the market, holding a spirited rally for each product introduction. For Mello Yello, advertised as "the world's fastest soft drink," he wore running shorts and led the workers in push-ups and a sprint around the bottling plant. To dramatize the liter, Isdell proved he was *literally* willing to work in the trenches with his employees. Wearing Army fatigues, he led a military-style rally, hurling a Pepsi bottle against a wall.*

The new approach galvanized the workers. Within a year, Coke's Philippine share grew by 30 percent even as the local economy took a 4 percent dive, and within two years Coke had overtaken Pepsi. By decade's end, Coca-Cola would command 71 percent of the business, neatly reversing the market-share figures at the beginning of 1981. Lauded as a hero, Isdell rose quickly in the Company. More important, a long-standing taboo had been broken. Big Coke clearly could take an equity position in its own bottlers with impressive results. The lesson was not lost on Goizueta, who would soon lead the Company into many such ventures.

---

* As he threw the bottle, the Coke commando screamed an epithet in Filipino. Relating this incident, Isdell paused. "I won't say what I said." When urged to supply a paraphrase, he responded, "Beat Pepsi," and laughed.

JESSE JACKSON PUSHES COKE

In 1981, Goizueta and Keough, while searching for ways to show the world that Coke had revived, encountered the exact type of publicity they did not need. Reverend Jesse Jackson, the outspoken, politically ambitious civil rights activist, turned his attention to Coca-Cola. To some degree, his call for more jobs for African Americans repeated CORE demands twenty years previously, but neither Coca-Cola nor the South were overtly racist anymore. In fact, the soft drink company supported local black colleges and the NAACP and other civil rights groups; 24 percent of the Company's workforce was African American. Like others before him, Jackson chose Coke not so much because of any glaring corporate abuse but because the firm was so temptingly vulnerable because of its cherished image. In July, he and his Chicago-based People United to Save Humanity (PUSH) threatened to launch a boycott—euphemistically termed a "withdrawal of enthusiasm"—if Coke did not bow to their demands. Jackson complained that there were no black-owned bottling plants or syrup wholesalers nor was there an African American on the board of directors. While Coke spent over $500,000 on ethnic ad agencies, that wasn't enough, considering the $169 million budget for annual advertising.

Don Keough and Carl Ware, an impressive black Coke executive who had once headed the Atlanta City Council, were negotiating with Jackson when he abruptly escalated publicity. Declaring an impasse, he called for a boycott and told the press that Atlanta's black ministers would denounce Coca-Cola from the pulpit that Sunday. Though nothing of the sort occurred, Keough and Ware didn't want to tangle with PUSH, and on August 11, with a triumphant Jesse Jackson standing at his side, Keough held a press conference heralding Coca-Cola's new "moral covenant," promising African Americans a package worth $34 million. In the audience were Atlanta mayor Maynard Jackson, Coretta Scott King, Andrew Young, and other prominent black leaders. Coca-Cola gave Jackson everything he had asked for, promising to spend more on minority advertising, increase the number of black managers, and find suitable ethnic owners for a bottling franchise. Fooling no one, Keough insisted that the new program had nothing to do with the PUSH boycott, but rather represented Coca-Cola's sincere effort to obey President Ronald Reagan's recent summons for private industry to intervene as government affirmative-action programs were trimmed.

Neither Keough nor Goizueta anticipated the reaction to their well-intended plans, though the election of the archconservative Reagan should have given them a hint. Many white Americans were sick of civil rights agitation. Even the name of Jackson's organization was offensive—they were tired of being pushed around by loud-mouthed blacks. A severe white backlash whipped the soft drink firm. Lewis Grizzard, the *Atlanta Constitution*'s syndicated professional redneck, complained of Coca-Cola's "show of spinelessness," comparing PUSH activists to Chicago mobsters and suggesting that Jesse Jackson be granted the bottling franchise on the moon. Even *Barron's*, the well-respected financial weekly, chided Coca-Cola for agreeing to find black entrepreneurs to bottle or wholesale the drink, since it would "injure meritorious whites." Similar letters of protest deluged the Company, such as one Tennessee businessman who wrote to protest "blackmail pressures of one minority organization." Keough painstakingly responded to these concerned white Southerners, tactfully refuting the presumed "cave-in." Finally, the Coca-Cola president was forced to admit publicly that he had made a mistake—he should never have called a press conference with Jackson at his side.

COKE IS IT

Soon, however, Goizueta and Keough forgot all about the uproar over Jackson, when a new advertising campaign, "Coke Is It," was unveiled in February of 1982, after over a year of unprecedented research and consumer testing. The man behind the commercials was John Bergin, who had created the Pepsi Generation and "You've Got a Lot to Live, and Pepsi's Got a Lot to Give" at BBDO. Now at McCann-Erickson, the advertiser inherited "Have a Coke and a Smile," with its pretty tune and feel-good approach, which he considered "limp-wristed," without real punch. Bergin yearned for a feistier battle cry to reassert the leading cola's confidence. He discovered it in a Canadian campaign that Ken Schulman, another McCann man, had cobbled together with New York songwriter Ginny Redington. Bergin was immediately taken by the compelling music: after a gradual buildup, it punched a brassy climax with three quick blasts in succession: "Coke is it!"

Bergin modified the lyrics to eliminate references to Canada, and Goizueta and Keough loved it. Just before the launch, however, Ginny Redington made a startling admission. She had originally written the music for a network news show promotion. The three beats were initially intended for "N-B-C!" The studio heads had rejected the music, however, judging that it was too flashy for a simple station identification theme. Bergin, aware of the touchy Coca-Cola pride, was outraged. "We had egg all over us, not just our faces," he recalled. Fortunately, Coke executives were understanding, since they sensed a winner.

On February 4, Coca-Cola unveiled the commercials on all three TV networks at 9:15 p.m. in a "roadblock." Simultaneously, two thousand bottlers gathered at the Atlanta Civic Center to watch the ads. By midnight, more than 150 million Americans had heard "Coke Is It," which Don Keough dubbed the Company's new marching song. On-screen, as the song's momentum developed, students, parents, and toddlers threw crates and scrap wood onto a large pile. "The most refreshing way / To make the most of every day," sang eager voices. "And wherever you go and whatever you do, / There's something big waiting for me and you." Then, just as the pile was torched into a huge bonfire, the message slammed through: "Coke is it! / The biggest taste you've ever found. / Coke is it! / The one that never lets you down." The fire turned out to be the centerpiece for an all-American pep rally before a football game. Of course, it wasn't altogether clear whether the cheerleaders, appropriately garbed in Coca-Cola red, were leading the crowd in joyous celebration of the home team or Coca-Cola, which was displayed in fifteen separate scenes of the sixty-second commercial. In all the "Coke Is It!" spots—whether a farmer's surprise birthday party or a break for energetic young dancers—consumers pulled glistening Coke bottles from ice chests. After gulping, they conveyed their overwhelming joy, holding the bottle up to admire and sighing with relief.

Roberto Goizueta hailed the new campaign as a fitting introduction to his reign. "This strong, assertive message," he told his bottlers, "mirrors the nature of Americans today. We say what we mean and we tell it like it is." Actually, the lyrics intentionally *didn't* say exactly what "it" was. As Brian Dyson admonished, "We should not be too precise, too descriptive or too literal." That way, each consumer could fantasize appropriately. "Whatever the feeling, whatever the need," Dyson concluded, "Coke is it. *Period.*"

At the same time, Coke unveiled its secret weapon against the Pepsi Challenge: Bill Cosby. The black comic's love affair with Coke dated to his childhood, when he sometimes drank fifteen Cokes by 2 p.m. during his "periods of addiction," as he put it. "It helped me to burp very good and clear the area." In the late sixties, the Company had sponsored Cosby's radio show. More recently, he had made commercials for the "Coke and a Smile" campaign, appearing in person at the Great Get-Together in 1979. John Bergin now directed Cosby in "Coke Is It" commercials that mocked the Pepsi Challenge. Directly addressing the audience, mugging with his well-rehearsed charm, Cosby simply drank a Coke and talked. "This is real refreshment, real big taste," he said. "Now see, if you were another cola, number 2 or number 29, you'd do taste tests and challenges and stuff and try to compare yourself to this, wouldn't you? Sure, don't shake your head, you would too, you sneaky devil." Other Cosby commercials did the previously unthinkable, showing a Pepsi vending machine, but only in order to knock it. "If you're number two," he said, "you know what you want to be when you grow up. Yes, Coke is it. You're nodding, yes?" In one ad, Cosby spied on a Pepsi taste test with binoculars, pointing out that the Challenge commercials never depicted *anyone* choosing Coke, which was misleading.

Bergin credited Cosby with killing the Challenge, which was halted in 1983. "He was brilliantly entertaining in his ridicule." As the comedian immodestly informed bottlers at the Great Get-Together, "I don't think there is anyone who, when they believe in the product, can sell it as well as I, as a projectionist." Bergin found Cosby "inconceivably arrogant," but he had to admit that "magic happens when the camera starts. That man is the greatest thing I've seen in terms of making his face work." Despite blow-ups on the set, the ad man acknowledged that "our greatest weapon has been Bill Cosby when we have used him." In 1983, Cosby invested more personally in Coke's future when he bought part ownership of the Philadelphia bottling plant along with black entrepreneur James Bruce Llewellyn. The sale fulfilled Coke's promise to PUSH to give African Americans management of a bottling plant, though Cosby was hardly an underprivileged minority member.

THE IMAGE MASTERS DIVERSIFY

Although pleased with the universal acclaim given "Coke Is It," Goizueta was smarting from the adverse reaction to his acquisition of Columbia Pictures only two weeks earlier. The field of entertainment was alluring, particularly to Goizueta, who had been seduced by Hollywood in his schoolboy days. Coca-Cola commercials were, after all, mini-movies. Furthermore, the eighties were transforming into a decade of glitz, image, and instant replay. The "Gimme Generation," as some journalists dubbed eighties consumers, was obsessed with video, so Columbia's library of 1,800 classic films promised to be a gold mine. Consequently, Coca-Cola surprised even Columbia's management team of Herb Allen and Fay Vincent by paying $750 million for the studio, the equivalent of nearly twice its stock market value at the time.

Financial analysts dumped on the deal. Coke had paid too much, they said, and besides, what did a soft drink company know about making movies? Coca-Cola stock lost 10 percent of its value within a few days. Goizueta was angry and puzzled, since he had served notice that he wanted to diversify and to increase the Company's U.S. prof-its until they contributed half of the revenue, and, with domestic soft drink growth slowing, Columbia offered a solution. "We're doing absolutely the only thing we could have done to maintain our growth into the future," Goizueta told reporters.

During the rest of the year, the critics had to admit that Coke hadn't been so stupid after all. Columbia churned out three smash hits in a row with *Tootsie*, *Gandhi*, and *The Toy*. More important, the Company signed a sweet deal with Home Box Office, Time Inc.'s pay-cable movie channel. HBO agreed to pay for a quarter of the produc-tion cost for all Columbia movies, as well as forking over whopping rental fees. At the same time, Columbia, HBO, and CBS formed a new studio called Tri-Star. Goizueta and Keough had no direct hand in the deals, but they soon befriended Allen and Vincent, who had pulled off a real coup. Soon thereafter, Allen joined the Coca-Cola board.

Although Goizueta and Keough repeatedly denied meddling with Columbia's cre-ative output, they did install Peter Sealey, one of Coke's top marketers, as the studio's new researcher. Sealey started asking questions never before addressed, using the jar-gon of the soft drink industry. Who were the movies' "heavy users," and what did they really want? How effective was Columbia's advertising campaign? How badly did home video "cannibalize" movie attendance? Sealey even discussed "pretesting" script concepts. By combining ad budgets with its new owner, Columbia immediately benefited from the Coke tie-in, getting discounts on bulk advertising.

While Goizueta and Keough did not overtly fiddle with the creative content at Co-lumbia, they made sure that certain products never appeared in their films, sending a memo to studio executives forbidding the use of any PepsiCo or Philip Morris (owner of 7-Up) items. As expected, under its new ownership Columbia's celluloid featured a goodly amount of Coca-Cola, particularly in feel-good, happy-ending efforts such as *Murphy's Romance*, a James Garner/Sally Field film that premiered three years later. Pepsi appeared, too, but only in a negative context, as Field's son was denied a job in an inhuman supermarket where, as film critic Mark Crispin Miller wrote, "two blue Pepsi signs loom[ed] coldly on the wall like a couple of swastikas."

Of course, it wasn't necessary for Coke to buy a studio to ensure product place-ment. In 1982 the movie *E.T.* galvanized marketers' attention when Reese's Pieces experienced a 70 percent sales jump the month after the cute alien munched them on-screen. The message was not lost on Coke, also plugged in *E.T.* Soon, all man-ner of consumer goods prominently paraded on movie screens. Ken Manson, Coke's full-time film agent, suddenly found his job more difficult and competitive. While other firms paid thousands of dollars for product placement, Manson offered vintage Coca-Cola soda fountains or trucks as "authentic" period props. Almost unbelievably, he continued to place Coke in films without paying for the privilege.

DIET COKE ROCKETTES AWAY

In July of 1982, when Brian Dyson held a press conference to trumpet the pending debut of Diet Coke, Goizueta discovered that the Columbia deal wasn't the *only* thing he could do to boost domestic growth. News of the project hadn't leaked, despite a widening circle of people aware of it. The can alone had gone through 150 possible designs. Over ten thousand consumers had participated in extended home-use and purchase-simulation tests. It was, in Dyson's words, "the most carefully developed and researched product in the history of The Coca-Cola Company." As a show of the Company's confidence, Diet Coke would roll out in the tough New York territory, which accounted for 10 percent of the country's volume. In August, Charles Millard of the New York Coca-Cola Bottling Company, with support from Big Coke, rented Radio City Music Hall, complete with the dancing Rockettes, to launch the drink. Then SSC&B/Lintas (hereafter called Lintas), McCann's sister organization responsible for the Diet Coke account, rented an auditorium in Los Angeles for a day, filled the theater with extras, and hired scores of stars to appear as if they had been at the New York premiere. Altogether, the resulting sixty-second commercial cost some $2.5 million, making it the most expensive spot ever.

The gamble was worth it, though. An instant phenomenon, Diet Coke surpassed all Company expectations. Much of the drink's impact undoubtedly stemmed from its clever positioning as the drink for the eighties' lifestyle. In contrast to TaB, using "perfumy and lacy imagery" to appeal exclusively to women, Diet Coke's theme song proclaimed that "you're gonna drink it just for the taste of it." Men, increasingly worried about their weight, health, and appearance, already bought 30 percent of diet beverages. Coca-Cola research indicated that Diet Coke could grab the majority of the newly named Yuppies—those young urban professionals who did aerobics and worked out on their Nautilus machines. As Roy Stout's research had shown, however, many of the new consumers were attracted simply because of the magical brand name—Coke. In labeled taste tests, consumers preferred TaB to Pepsi by a slim margin, but when Stout dispensed TaB from a can marked "Diet Coke," the name alone swung the results twelve more points in Coca-Cola's favor. In essence, the consumers were tasting the world's best-known trademark, with goodwill built over a ninety-six-year history. Whatever the reason, Diet Coke took off. By the end of 1983, it had captured 17 percent of the diet soda market, making it the fourth-best-selling American soft drink, and it was already available in twenty-eight overseas markets.

Not all Coke men delighted in Diet Coke's unprecedented surge, however, since the Company charged more for the new syrup than it did for Coca-Cola, even though the saccharin-sweetened drink cost considerably less to produce. Big Coke's proposed bottling contract for Diet Coke awarded the parent company total control of pricing, in addition to numerous other restrictions. When many bottlers balked, the Company dragged out negotiations while the rollout and national advertising sparked an intense public clamor for Diet Coke, forcing reluctant franchisees to sign a temporary contract. At that point, renegade bottler Bill Schmidt and thirty cohorts, already suing the Company over the HFCS issue, instructed lawyer Emmet Bondurant to file suit over Diet Coke for the non-amended bottlers. A few weeks later, Bondurant also filed a separate case for selected amended bottlers.

Though legally complex, the basic Diet Coke Case issues boiled down to an existential question: What was Coca-Cola? Bondurant and the disaffected bottlers argued that Diet Coke constituted an alternatively sweetened form of the old soft drink. After all, the Company called it Coke, and the advertising claimed similarity to the "real thing." If so, the Company had to abide by its original contract with the non-amended bottlers, rendering Diet Coke technically illegal, because it didn't contain 5.32 pounds of sugar. For amended bottlers, the case seemed clear cut, since their 1978 contract called for the Company to pass through any savings on alternative sweeteners.

All of the cases—E-Town, the nickname for the argument over corn syrup, and the Diet Coke suits—would be decided by Murray Schwartz, a district court judge in Wilmington, Delaware. Over the course of the decade, Schwartz, an unusually meticulous and attentive jurist, would develop an unwanted expertise in the history and nuances of the soft drink industry. Publicly, Big Coke pooh-poohed the lawsuits, dismissing the angry bottlers as a disgruntled minority with little effect on the Company's bottom line. Coke's lawyers regarded the cases as simple contract disputes over incremental profits. Nonetheless, the outcomes remained crucial, since they tested the Company's right to bend bottlers to its will. For Schmidt and Bondurant, the battle assumed the dimensions of a moral crusade. With neither side interested in an out-of-court settlement, a bitter legal war commenced.

GLORY DAYS

By the end of 1983, Goizueta felt vindicated in the eyes of the world. Columbia, a money machine, earned $91 million in its first full year as a Coca-Cola subsidiary. In 1983, following hard on the heels of Diet Coke's unparalleled achievement, the company introduced caffeine-free versions of Coca-Cola, Diet Coke, and TaB. As usual, Big Coke lagged behind the rest of the market in terms of innovation. Philip Morris was already trumpeting that 7-Up "never had it, never will," while Royal Crown had pioneered the previous year with the first cola to lack a stimulant. The day before the Diet Coke announcement, Pepsi unveiled Pepsi Free. At first, Coca-Cola resisted any movement that implied that caffeine constituted a health hazard, since the ingredient provided the drink's famous "lift." Goizueta proved that Coke could adapt, however, and once the giant finally stirred, it usually dominated a market segment.*

Later in the year, Brian Dyson revealed that Diet Coke's taste would be improved with NutraSweet, the brand name for aspartame, a revolutionary new alternative sweetener just approved by the FDA. The only drawback to aspartame—aside from serious unanswered questions about its effects on the human body—was its instability, which would limit shelf life. Consequently, Diet Coke initially derived its sweetness from a half-and-half blend of saccharin and NutraSweet. Soon afterward, the Company opted for 100 percent of the better-tasting sweetener, despite its limits and exorbitant expense. The diet drink market share, 24 percent and still climbing, convinced Coke to guarantee that its new drink measured up to the boasts about taste.

As if to symbolize the dramatic changes, the wrecking ball smashed into the sixty-three-year-old red-brick building on North Avenue to make way for a fancy new entrance rotunda. The squat, solidly built veteran of the cola wars resisted demolition as nostalgic older employees looked on, but the job was completed by the fall. Memorial bricks, distributed to every Coke employee as souvenirs, served as the only link

---

* By the eighties, Coke and Pepsi didn't crawl out on unnecessary limbs. If a trend manifested itself, they figured they could use their enormous advertising budgets and distribution systems to dominate with the brands.

to the past. Goizueta, suddenly the media's darling, dominated a spring 1983 issue of *Business Week* in a cover story on "Coke's Big Market Blitz." At a press conference for one hundred market analysts late in 1983, the confident CEO declared that the Company intended to double its size by the end of the eighties. To emphasize his determination, he held the meeting in a Boston bottling plant with a backdrop of three million cans stacked twenty-five feet high that would, he told the audience, land in vending machines and on grocery shelves within forty-eight hours. Emanuel Goldman, a longtime follower of the Company, proclaimed that "the giant has awakened." *Adweek* named Goizueta the Marketer of the Year, while *Dun's Business Month* praised him for running one of America's five best-managed companies.

1984

The next year only intensified Goizueta's triumph. The Cuban had established a dynamic eighties management style while capitalizing on the nearly century-old asset of Coca-Cola's identification with American culture. Naturally, Coke became the official soft drink of the 1984 Summer Olympics in Los Angeles, where everything coalesced for the soft drink concern—projecting an active, healthy, athletic worldwide image, with competitors drinking gallons of Coca-Cola and Diet Coke right there next to Hollywood, where Columbia slaked the country's thirst for entertainment. Even the nation's "Teflon" president, a former movie star, signaled the triumph of image over substance, the apotheosis of the soft drink mentality. As a conservative Republican, Reagan was primarily a Pepsi man, but what did it matter?*

Increasingly, the two cola giants were squeezing competition out of vending machines, fountain spigots, and grocery shelves. The much-publicized "cola wars," while real enough on one level, actually benefited both brands. There was no more essential difference between Coke and Pepsi than the line separating most Democrats and Republicans. When Reagan hired Pepsi advertising guru Phil Dusenberry to produce his 1984 campaign commercials, it was not so much an endorsement of a particular brand of soft drink as an indication that, in America, politics had been reduced to the art of master image manipulators. Even Walter Mondale's most cutting criticism of Reagan during the campaign—"Where's the beef?"—derived from a fast-food commercial.

"I'm always going to be searching for emotion," Dusenberry told reporters. "In an age when most products aren't very different, the difference is often in the way people feel about [them]." In his Reagan spots, Dusenberry highlighted elderly couples smiling and holding hands, children playing, and important officials meeting in the Oval Office. What they were discussing seemed immaterial—the fact that they conveyed a serious, competent atmosphere sufficed.

It was so evident that Reagan would win by a landslide that the Coke PAC contributed no money at all to Walter Mondale, even though the Southern soft drink company traditionally supported Democrats. Instead, $5,000 went to Reagan, while Jesse

---

* Reagan cabinet member Casper Weinberger was on the Pepsi board, but Reagan also had Coke ties. From 1954 to 1962, he had hosted TV's General Electric Theater, and Robert Woodruff was a long-time GE board member. Reagan's older brother, Neil "Moon" Reagan, worked for McCann-Erickson in Los Angeles, where he cultivated the Hollywood crowd for Coke.

Jackson got $1,500, since Coke wanted to avoid accusations of racism. At the same time, the Company contributed $1,000 to archconservative Jesse Helms for balance.

Researchers of the eighties, whether working for political campaigns or soft drinks, honed sophisticated techniques for identifying target groups to an extent that would have alarmed cola drinkers had they been privy to insider documents. At the end of 1984, the depth researchers at Lintas developed a profile of the "typical" Coca-Cola and Diet Coke user. According to the study, Coca-Cola drinkers possessed rigid personalities; a drink should taste a particular way. They lived in a "traditional reality based on early experiences, stereotypes and cultural generalizations." To a Coke drinker, the world should remain immutable, ruled by "certain self-evident truths." The researchers also identified a feeling of resignation and "lack of personal control." Consequently, Coca-Cola drinkers demanded immediate gratification and didn't really worry about putting on weight.

Diet Coke consumers, on the other hand, felt that "the world is changeable" and that they could exercise personal control and a degree of choice. Capable of long-range planning, they could delay gratification. While Diet Coke drinkers, like their Coca-Cola counterparts, often valued family relations, they sometimes assumed alternative family roles with greater flexibility. "Both the husband and wife could work, the husband can go shopping and prepare a dinner while the wife comes home late from the office." More critical, Diet Coke drinkers cared deeply about personal appearance.

Though the Lintas researchers didn't mention it, 1984 Diet Coke consumers might snort a line of cocaine or two while seeking self-fulfillment. The Peruvian drug, popular with the upper crust in 1885 and 1925, once more enjoyed a vogue with hedonistic Yuppies. T-shirts with "Cocaine" written in Coca-Cola script caused consternation at North Avenue, where no one discussed the soft drink's coca leaf content, decocainized or not. As a defensive measure, the legal department reversed its long-standing taboo against the logo's use on anything except the soft drink. Now, the Company licensed script Coca-Cola for clothes, furniture, toys, clocks, art objects, and innumerable other items. By selling the rights to quality manufacturers, the lawyers hoped to ensure easy prosecution of violators.

Aside from the embarrassing cocaine connection, the Goizueta regime seemed charmed, an energized juggernaut that couldn't fail. By then, Coca-Cola had jettisoned low-margined Aqua-Chem, Wine Spectrum, and shrimp farming. *Ghostbusters*, the highest-grossing Columbia film ever produced, provided ideal tie-in opportunities for local bottlers. A new Coca-Cola USA tower rose steadily over North Avenue. A toll-free 800 line allowed instant feedback from consumers, while the just-established Coca-Cola Foundation provided a high profile for corporate donations. Diet Coke leapfrogged past 7-Up to become the third-best-selling soft drink in America. The Company signed Julio Iglesias, the popular Spanish crooner whose records trailed only Elvis Presley and the Beatles in global popularity, to woo swooning older women, foreign consumers, and thirty million Hispanics in the United States.

By the time Brian Dyson summoned his bottlers for another "Get-Together" in Atlanta five years after his promise to shake things up in 1979, he was bursting with self-confidence, having overseen the refranchisement of over 50 percent of Coca-Cola's bottling territory. Coke commanded a 37 percent share of the U.S. market. Despite Burger King's defection to Pepsi in 1983, the Atlanta firm controlled a whopping 63 percent of the fountain business. "We believe in two eyes for an eye and two teeth for a tooth," Dyson boasted, "and if our competitor swats us in the face, we will turn around and knock the hell out of him." He promised the assembled bottlers, "We will go for it. Ready, Fire! Aim."

Roberto Goizueta had every reason for self-congratulation. Since he had assumed the presidency in the spring of 1981, Coca-Cola stock had appreciated 95 percent, including dividends, more than doubling the performance of the S&P 500 index. The Company had recently demonstrated confidence in its own future by repurchasing six million shares of common stock. Still, Goizueta felt uneasy. When someone told him that he looked nervous, the Cuban replied, "We live nervous." Now he uttered a prophetic warning: "There is a danger when a company is doing as well as we are. And that is, to think that we can do no wrong. I keep telling the organization: We can do wrong and we can do wrong big." In April of 1985, a shocked nation learned just how right he was.

~ *19* ~

The Marketing Blunder of the Century

To the Master Dodo this concerns: What ignoramus decided to change the formula of Coke?!?! The new formula is gross, disgusting, unexciting, and WORSE THAN PEPSI!!
            —Coke Consumer, Anniston, Alabama, May 12, 1985

As the company coasted triumphantly into mid-decade, one nagging problem refused to go away. For twenty years, the market share of the world's most famous drink had steadily declined. In 1984, Coca-Cola lost one percent of its market share, while Pepsi-Cola gained one and a half points. The Company had tried everything—massive, effective advertising; aggressive marketing; price promotions; almost universal distribution—and nothing had halted the slide. It was difficult to avoid the conclusion that, just as the Pepsi Challenge had asserted, the real problem was the product's taste. People no longer appreciated the Coca-Cola bite. They wanted a sweeter drink.

Late in 1983, Goizueta had authorized the Mexican *wunderkind* Sergio Zyman to spearhead a supersecret new project and ordered Mauricio Gianturco to speed up his search for a cola flavor that would trounce Pepsi in taste tests. The ultrasuspicious Zyman wrote his own reports and shredded all memos. As with the Diet Coke project, he kept changing the code name from Zeus to Tampa, then Eton, and finally Project Kansas, in honor of Kansas editor William Allen White, who would have hated the idea of changing Coca-Cola if he'd still been alive. After all, White had called the drink "the sublimated essence of all that America stands for." While the technical department rushed to concoct a winning formula, Roy Stout's market researchers asked sample consumers a long list of questions, based on the supposition that the Company had "added a new ingredient" that rendered Coca-Cola "smoother." The results indicated that 11 percent of the exclusive Coke drinkers would be upset, but Stout figured half of them would get over it. The remaining 5 percent probably would remain angry.

No one dared to say explicitly that Coke was planning to alter its formula. Even John Bergin of McCann-Erickson remained unaware of the Company's plans, though he might have guessed. In 1982 and 1983, he and Zyman toured the country for "focus groups" composed of local consumers, primarily to test potential commercials. At the end of each session, however, the moderator presented an unrelated scenario. Pretend, he told them, that a great new formula for Product X had already been introduced in a nearby city, where everyone loved it. Now it was coming to *this* town. Would you be in favor of it? No one objected to a new, improved Budweiser or Hershey

328

Bar, but Bergin was astonished at the outburst over Coca-Cola. "Goddam it, don't tell *me* you're taking my fucking Coke away!" The focus groups also revealed another disturbing fact. Although many interviewees forcefully asserted that Coca-Cola was their favorite drink, when asked what cola they actually drank, they wavered—Coke, sure, but sometimes Pepsi or even the generic store brand if it was on sale. Stout thus discovered that while Coca-Cola had a place in the heart, it wasn't necessarily in the refrigerator.

In the fall of 1984, Gianturco finally devised a new cola that, he assured Zyman and Stout, would beat Pepsi. Sure enough, Stout's blind taste tests showed that consumers preferred the new formula by a six-point margin. Enormously excited, Zyman convinced Dyson that the time for action had arrived. The "ready, fire! aim" philosophy had worked so far, and this audacious, bold move would prove Coca-Cola's flexibility and leadership to any doubters. At almost the same moment, Scott Ellsworth was interviewing Pepsi's Dick Alven for a Smithsonian Institution oral history of Pepsi. Alven told Ellsworth that the Pepsi Challenge had been completely halted, but that "it's a nice thing to have in your arsenal. See, for them to put that thing to rest totally, they would have to do something to their formula—I mean *dramatically*—and I don't think they're going to do that. It's too risky." Alven noted that Coca-Cola was, after all, a good product that sold a lot of drinks. "It's kind of dangerous for them to play with it."

Goizueta, who had promised in 1981 that he was willing to reformulate "any or all of our products," didn't question the new recipe, but he wasn't sure it should replace the standard drink. Why not call it Coke Two or some other name? There were multiple objections to that idea, though. The product called "Coca-Cola" had to be the best, number one. It just wasn't conceivable to market a better-tasting drink as a competitor. Such a move would also probably split Coke drinkers into two smaller shares of the market, allowing Pepsi to emerge as the undisputed leader. Nor could the Coke men alter the formula quietly. Consumers would notice an entirely different flavor complex, and then the Company would have to lie to the public or admit tampering with the world's most famous secret formula. Clearly, they must introduce the new flavor with great fanfare.

Aside from these considerations, the Company never publicly acknowledged another underlying motivation to replace the old formula. New Coke would contain no decocainized coca leaf, and the never-ending rumors about the drink's supposed drug content could finally be put to rest. Furthermore, Reagan's announced determination to eradicate the South American coca plantations made Company officials nervous, even though their supply grew in fields owned by the Peruvian government. As head of the technical division in the late seventies, Roberto Goizueta had encouraged Dr. Andrew Weil, who planned to market a coca-based medicinal chewing gum, because a legitimized coca leaf might "take the heat off of Coca-Cola," as Weil put it. Weil even persuaded Goizueta to pay $10,000 for an Ecuadoran conference on coca, but nothing ever came of the project.

ROBERT WOODRUFF'S WILL

Over the Christmas holidays of 1984, Roberto Goizueta, Don Keough, Brian Dyson, and Ike Herbert decided unanimously to change the world's best-known product just short of its hundredth anniversary. First, however, they needed the Boss's blessing. Robert Woodruff had celebrated his ninety-fifth birthday a few weeks earlier. Despite his failing hearing and sight, he had lost none of his mental acuity. On New Year's Day, Goizueta made the pilgrimage down to Ichauway. Alone with the old man, the Cuban CEO kept his story short and simple, reviewing the rationale for the formula modification—dwindling market share coupled with a superior new taste. In the end, Woodruff agreed, convinced that Goizueta was right and that tastes had shifted.* It was more important that Coca-Cola be the best-tasting drink in the world than to cling to an outmoded formula. Strangely, though, the Boss couldn't eat his dinner that night. The next morning, he refused his customary huge breakfast. An era was ending, and Robert Woodruff would end his life with it. The Boss demonstrated the remarkable power of his will one last time. He simply stopped eating.

As Woodruff literally shrank from life, Edith Honeycutt, his father's old nurse, cared for him. Connected to intravenous tubes in his private suite at Emory Hospital, Woodruff held her hand and asked, "Honey, where am I?" When she told him, he whispered, "Don't you ever leave me." She recited his favorite poem, Rudyard Kipling's "If," as she had many times before, and, as always, he cried at the last line: "And—which is more—you'll be a man, my son!"

Honeycutt knew why he cried. No matter what Robert Woodruff did, it had never been enough for his father. When Ernest Woodruff visited Ichauway in his final years, for instance, he had been horrified by the number of servants and guests and had predicted his son's imminent bankruptcy. Now, as Robert Woodruff lay dying, the man everyone called Boss, one of the world's most brilliant entrepreneurs, reverted once more to his unhappy childhood. Despite a lifetime of achievement, he would never be a real man in his father's eyes.

In a rare moment of public introspection, Woodruff once recalled his youth, when he sought answers not from his disapproving father, but from Samuel Jones, a neighboring parent who understood his "boyish and immature searching after the realities of life." As they were talking one day, Jones asked the boy to jot down the greatest things life had to offer. Woodruff wrote "wealth, power, influence, genius." The older man nodded and said those were fine goals, but that he had left out the greatest of all—peace of mind. "I'm not sure I have [ever] achieved what he suggested," Woodruff said. "Some drive has always impelled me to keep reaching—struggling."

On March 7, 1985, at the age of ninety-five, Robert Woodruff finally stopped struggling, a little over a month before the world learned that The Coca-Cola Company was transforming the flavor of its most famous soft drink. While making Coca-Cola a global drink, he had dismissed those who praised him as a visionary. "I was just curious," he would say, "to see if people in other countries would like it, too." Though he lived almost a century, he remained an enigma even to his closest associates. "I'm not sure anyone really knew him," Joe Jones reflected. Woodruff left Jones,

---

* Since Goizueta and Woodruff were alone during this crucial meeting, we have only Goizueta's word for what took place. While no one has accused Goizueta of telling an untruth, many old-time Coca-Cola men adamantly refuse to believe that Woodruff would ever have sanctioned a changed formula. Others question whether he could hear well enough to understand what Goizueta was saying or speak clearly enough for a real assent to be understood.

his long-suffering secretary, a million dollars in his will. "And he earned *every penny of it*," Wilbur Kurtz emphasized.*

To the end, Woodruff embodied contradictions. A sentimental, loyal, gentle man who gave his friends a single rose on their birthdays, he could also be harsh, vindictive, autocratic—a real bastard who sometimes barked obscenities. He had donated untold anonymous millions to worthy causes, including $230 million to Emory University, but he failed to provide bail for Charlie Ware, the black man shot as a result of conflict with the white Ichauway overseer. Woodruff could be a gruff, manly hunter, lord of the plantation, a huge cigar clamped between his teeth. Beneath his macho image, however, lay a fundamental insecurity and a phobia about being alone, leading to 3 a.m. vigils with his doctor or friends when he couldn't sleep.

Whatever the truth may be, the inscrutable tycoon carried his secrets to the grave, leaving his "partner," Roberto Goizueta, to face an incensed American public. Perhaps, having granted his permission to change the formula, Woodruff viewed his successor's summer of agony with a wry smile from his vantage point in heaven, toasting Goizueta's future health with a six-and-a-half-ounce bottle of good old-fashioned Coca-Cola.

THE BUNKER MENTALITY

Only days after Goizueta's fateful January meeting with Woodruff, five McCann employees filed into an isolated fourth-floor room. With a paper shredder and Pinkerton guard posted at the door, Ike Herbert and Sergio Zyman informed them that they must produce an exciting set of introductory commercials in less than four months while maintaining strict secrecy. Although John Bergin and the other creative talent were flabbergasted, the decision appeared irrevocable. At first, Herbert forbade the word "new," an indication of drastic alteration, but focus groups showed that a "new" product provoked the most immediate response, and Goizueta, afraid the introduction would be greeted with a gigantic American yawn, authorized the use of the word in bold black type on the label. The harried, claustrophobic McCann men quickly dubbed the tiny New York City U-shaped office "the Bunker." Any new footage had to be shot with actors unaware they were pitching a new formula.

The meetings in the Bunker were disastrous. Gradually, more McCann men joined the secret team, but no one could brainstorm a campaign that would really resonate. Partly, they were handicapped by Zyman's insistence on eschewing "reason why" advertising that described the new flavor or explained its replacement of the old formula. In desperation, they amended the recently modified "Coke Is It" campaign, which proclaimed the drink a "kick" and a "hit." In London's "Bunker II," Marcio Moreira, the Brazilian who headed McCann's international ad efforts, oversaw high-tech product shots featuring the new can. Later, these would be incorporated into commercial footage filmed in the United States. To the British production crews, a transformed Coca-Cola formula didn't mean much. When the film director asked why "new" appeared on the Coke can, Moreira answered, "It's a new tin," eliciting a disinterested

---

* Liberated by Woodruff's death, Jones soon became absorbed in administering Ichauway, which he converted to an environmental preserve, where biologist identified over nine hundred species of plants among the longleaf pines—the largest single tract still in existence anywhere in the world.

shrug. "We shot the whole fucking thing without anyone saying anything," Moreira recalled. By this time, with barely a month left before the scheduled public introduction, an impatient Sergio Zyman assumed direct creative control, reducing McCann men to flunky status. In this nerve-racking atmosphere, the premier commercials lurched into final edit.

A DISASTROUS PRESS CONFERENCE

As the feverish ad men labored in their bunkers on both sides of the Atlantic, the media love-fest with Coke persisted in the early months of 1985. In January, Don Keough revealed a contract to bring Coca-Cola to Soviet citizens for the first time. Then, in March, the Company rolled out Cherry Coke, violating yet another old commandment never to add other flavors to the drink. Consequently, on Friday, April 19, 1985, when Goizueta invited the media to a press conference the following Tuesday for news on "the most significant soft-drink marketing development in the company's nearly 100-year history," he was confident of a friendly reception. The three-day lag virtually guaranteed a leak, allowing stunned Pepsi executives time to prepare their rebuttal. On Tuesday, the day of the big announcement, readers of the nation's major newspapers saw a full-page ad in which Pepsi president Roger Enrico's open letter to his employees crowed that "the other guy just blinked" and was "reformulating brand Coke to be more like Pepsi," obviously because "Pepsi tastes better than Coke." He concluded by declaring a companywide holiday that Friday.

In New York City on Tuesday morning, Keough and Goizueta were exhausted, not fully recovered from the previous day's bottler convention in Atlanta. They walked onto a stage at Lincoln Center for a press conference before seven hundred journalists and film crews, along with satellite hookups to media in Los Angeles, Atlanta, and Houston. The lights dimmed, leaving only three huge red screens with the logo. "We are, we always will be. . . ." swelled a chorus. "Coca-Cola, All-American history." The screens filled with shots of the Grand Canyon, wheat fields, cowboys, athletes, the Statue of Liberty, and old Coke commercials. Even for a gullible public, this effort would have been too much. For a jaded press, it was insulting. No one saluted or dabbed away a tear.

Then Goizueta declared that "the best soft drink, Coca-Cola, is now going to be even better." He explained that the new flavor had been discovered as a result of experimentation on Diet Coke and that the Company would now "buy the world a new Coke." It was, he asserted, "the boldest single marketing move in the history of the packaged consumer goods business," adding that it was also the "surest move ever made." Keough emphasized that while the new formula beat old Coke 55–45 in 190,000 blind taste tests, it *increased* the margin by 61–39 when both drinks were identified. Coke had always provided a "mirror of the times," Keough explained, sometimes even shaping them, and now the new formula would "propel Coca-Cola into this second century." He promised that the superior taste would flow globally by the centennial celebration in May of 1986.

As soon as the floor was thrown open, however, the media lobbed unfriendly questions. "Are you one-hundred-percent certain that this won't bomb?" a St. Louis reporter inquired. Another journalist asked Goizueta to describe the new taste. At first, he demurred, saying that "it's a matter better left to poets or copywriters." When pressed, he stumbled through a chemist's reply: "I would say it is smoother, uh, uh, rounder yet, uh, yet bolder . . . a more harmonious flavor." Keough added that "the taste kind of surrounds you."

Even though Keough and Goizueta had carefully rehearsed every answer, their attempts at humorous deflection fell flat. Had they changed the product in response to the Pepsi Challenge? "Oh, gosh, no," Goizueta answered. "The Pepsi Challenge? When did that happen?" Would the old formula remain in the Trust Company vault? High-strung and miserable without his cigarettes, Goizueta slowly lost his composure. "It stays there," he snapped. A hostile reporter, phoning from the traditional Coca-Cola heartland of Houston, began to ask a question but turned it into a protest: "Are you tell—I mean, if we wanted Pepsi, we'd buy Pepsi," prompting a big laugh from her fellow journalists. "Well, honey," Keough replied patronizingly before correcting himself and calling her ma'am, "this new product is Coca-Cola, even better." Goizueta interjected: "It's not even close to Pepsi. Not at all. Not at all." Unaccountably, when asked if they had tested the new Coke against Pepsi in taste tests, the executives refused to divulge that in fact it *did* beat Pepsi by a small margin. Instead, Goizueta arrogantly responded: "Surely, we did. But we don't have to show them and we don't want to."

In response to the final question, asking whether Diet Coke might be reformulated "assuming that this is a success," Goizueta answered testily. "No. And I didn't *assume* that this is a success. It *is* a success." Moderator Carlton Curtis, the Company's top public spokesman, quickly cut off further questions, and the ordeal was over. It had not been a shining moment for the executives. Even the normally unflappable Keough admitted at one point during the grilling, "There's a lot of things I'd rather be doing than being here right now."

COKE WAS IT

Despite the ordeal, Goizueta and Keough remained certain that their bold move would succeed. They had told the simple truth—New Coke, as it was inevitably called, tasted better than the old version. It was only a matter of time before Coca-Cola would sweep past Pepsi and reclaim the coveted Nielsen rating lead in supermarket sales. With great pageantry, the Company launched its sampling campaign, literally transforming downtown Atlanta into a three-ring circus. "Step right up to the greatest taste on earth," the barker cried. In New York, the first cans off the line were ceremoniously delivered to workers renovating the Statue of Liberty. Red and white balloons, fireworks, and banner-waving airplanes filled the skies. "We're using every glitzy thing you can imagine," one spokesman confided to the press.

No amount of hoopla could mask the shocked misery of loyal Coke drinkers, however. All of the taste tests had missed one crucial point. Roy Stout's researchers had never informed their respondents that the hypothetical new formula would *replace* the old. Incredibly, no one had examined the psychological ramifications of withdrawing the old formula. In the rush to unveil the great new flavor, a kind of corporate hypnosis had occurred. "No one would have listened if someone had said we were going to catch unholy hell," Sergio Zyman admitted later. "Everybody just said, 'This can't go wrong.'"

For Coke loyalists such as Dan Lauck, a San Antonio television news reporter, New Coke couldn't go right, however, and taste tests were irrelevant. Lauck drank nothing but six-and-a-half-ounce bottles of ice-cold Coca-Cola at the rate of fifteen a day. The thirty-six-year-old was so fond of Coke that he skipped breakfast and lunch to keep his weight down so he could drink more. When he heard about the flavor change, Lauck rushed out and bought 110 cases. He had no intention of conducting taste tests; he would never switch.

If Zyman had taken the 1984 Lintas report on the personality of Coca-Cola drinkers more seriously, he wouldn't have been so surprised at the reaction of devoted consumers like Lauck. "The world is immutable, it doesn't change, there are certain self-evident truths," the report had stated.* Bill Backer had crawled directly into their minds back in 1969 when he had written, "That's the way it is, / And the way it will stay, / What the world wants today / Is the real thing."

That truth was quickly and forcibly brought to the Company's attention. Within a week, over a thousand calls a day were jamming the company's 800 line, almost all of them expressing shock and outrage at New Coke. The media loved the hot story, which pierced the American heart. "Next week, they'll be chiseling Teddy Roosevelt off the side of Mount Rushmore," a *Washington Post* columnist groaned. The *Detroit Free Press* mocked Goizueta's "smoother, rounder, bolder" taste, wondering in print if that made the old drink "lumpy, square, and bashful." Bob Greene of the *Chicago Tribune* mourned the passing of his old friend. "Every part of my life is associated with Coke," he wrote, chiding the Company for "a sort of smugness—that if you don't like New Coke, you will." *Newsweek*'s headline declared, "Coke Tampers with Success," identifying the old soft drink as "the American character in a can." At the press conference, Keough had promised that "you're just flat going to enjoy it," but many consumers modified his remark, complaining that it was difficult to enjoy a drink that was so flat. One elderly woman, interviewed at an Atlanta supermarket, sipped New Coke and gave her verdict: "To use the vernacular of the teenagers, it sucks." George Pickard, a Nashville songwriter, quickly cashed in on the publicity with a recording entitled "Coke *Was* It."

At first, Goizueta and Keough reveled in the avalanche of free publicity, negative or otherwise. Within days, 96 percent of all Americans knew about the flavor change. The Company proceeded with the national roll-out, along with a new Cosby campaign and modified "Coke Is It" spots. Even granting the rushed and secretive conditions under which the commercials were spawned, they seemed inexplicably clumsy, all too literally interpreting the singsong lyrics, often with negative or violent implications. As the singer bragged of "a style, a groove," a little girl watched her wobbly bowling ball drift toward the gutter. "It is Saturday night" showed an ugly professional wrestler twirling an opponent before a body slam, the spinning feet catching the referee in the head. A teen shook up her New Coke and sprayed it in her

---

* In September 1979, Coke marketer Peter Sealey wrote a memo about then-tentative plans for New Coke. "The brand cannot be made new or improved," he observed, "for to do so would destroy the mystique, mystery, and lore that surround the brand and constitute its heritage. In the minds of our consumers, the brand cannot be improved." Obviously, no one paid attention to his memo.

boyfriend's face; a master sergeant screamed at a private; a Brahma bull rider ended a commercial rolling helplessly on the ground with his legs splayed in front of a huge Coke sign. Coca-Cola had always promoted romance. In *these* commercials, a girl jumped up, threw her napkin in the boy's face, and stormed off. As a fitting capper for the stumbling campaign, several commercials ended with the line "it's more than a taste, it's the smile on your face," as a hockey goalie lifted his face mask to reveal a smiling teenager—only he was missing four or five teeth.

The Cosby ads weren't much better, even though the comedian's new television show achieved enormous popularity. In the TVQ (Television Quotient) ratings of celebrity endorsers, Cosby dominated the number one spot for "most persuasive" and "most familiar." It didn't help, however, that the overexposed Coke sponsor had stressed the tart taste of old Coke just before the sweeter version replaced it. Now, he switched gears. Dressed in a silly-looking toga, Cosby intoned: "The words I'm about to say will change the course of history. Here they are. Coca-Cola has a new taste." His words weren't terribly convincing. "Now, more than ever, Coke is it!" he finished, but his fatuous smile looked pasted on.

A LONG, DRY JUNE

At first, Roy Stout's weekly surveys indicated a positive response to the new flavor; as delivery trucks roared into U.S. cities throughout May, millions of curious consumers tried the notorious taste. But the furor refused to die. By the middle of the month, five thousand calls a day were assaulting the ears of the poor employees manning the consumer hot line. Roberto Goizueta was shaken when his father, who lived in Mexico City, told him that everyone there was in an uproar, even though New Coke hadn't arrived yet. Even Goizueta's nemesis, Fidel Castro, took potshots at Coke, directing Radio Havana to pronounce that the death of the Real Thing was symptomatic of American decay.

By the beginning of June, eight thousand calls a day were coming in. The media still hyped the story, particularly when a fifty-seven-year-old Seattle opportunist named Gay Mullins saw New Coke as his ticket to fame and fortune, founding the Old Cola Drinkers of America. The chubby, white-bearded Mullins, wearing a protest T-shirt, publicly dumped bottles of New Coke into the city sewers. The self-appointed spokesman became the media's favorite gadfly, even though he repeatedly failed to identify Coke in blind taste tests. After one suit was thrown out of court, Mullins filed a second class-action attempt to force the Company to return to the old formula. New Coke became, according to one journalist, "a universal conversation topic, like the weather or money or love."* Houston Astrodome crowds booed New Coke commercials on the stadium's giant video screen. One Beverly Hills wineshop owner obtained a limited supply of the rare old formula, selling bottles for three times their

---

* During the New Coke debacle, Ronald Reagan endured a cancer operation, death squads terrorized Guatemala, ten thousand died in a Bangladesh cyclone, and Lebanese Shiites hijacked an airliner, but apparently none of these events compared to the tragedy of the altered Coca-Cola formula in the eyes of the media or Coke consumers.

list price. As Roberto Goizueta noted with annoyance, it was chic to dump on New Coke. "We could have introduced the elixir of the gods," one bitter Coke man said, "and it wouldn't have made any difference."

In addition to phone calls, the Company fielded over forty thousand letters of protest. Each unhappy consumer received a form letter from Lynn Henkel, an assistant manager at Coca-Cola USA, assuring them that "our latest research shows that . . . consumers overwhelmingly like our great new taste." This official response was cold comfort to most consumers, who either mailed back the enclosed coupon or tore it up. The letters, like the phone calls, were cries from the heart, making it clear that much more than a soft drink was involved. A bewildered consulting psychologist told Company officials that the emotions he heard were similar to those of grief-stricken parents mourning the death of a favorite child. Most letters came from people who had never written to a company—young and old; upper, middle, and lower class; literate and unlettered. The message, however, was essentially the same—The Coca-Cola Company had betrayed them:

> I'm 61 and have been a confirmed "Coke" drinker since that memorable day my Dad took me on a little excursion up Mill Mountain in Roanoke, Va., and bought me my first Coke with a package of Planter's Salted Peanuts. . . . I was five years old. . . . "Old" Coke is sensual, it has pizzazz. God! On a hot day you wish you could jump into a tub of it and gulp down a 16 oz. bottle all at the same time.

> My littele sisther is cring because coke changed and she sayed that shed is not going to stop cring every day unitl you chang back. . . . I am geting tryer of hearing her now if you don't chang I'll sue evne if I'm just 11.

> I am a very heavy coke drinker. I do not drink coffee, tea, milk, water, nothing but coke. I drink coke all day long. I always have a glass or can of coke. Always. I have now to try and find something to drink that I can tolerate. It will not be new coke. Never.

> Changing Coke is just like breaking the American dream, like not selling hot dogs at a ball game.

> We want the old and wonderful Coke back *PLEASE*. Keep the "New" Coke if you want and call it Cokesi if you like. . . .

> For years, I have been what every company strives for: a brand-loyal consumer. I have purchased at least two cartons of Coke a week for as long as I can remember. . . . My "reward" for this loyalty is having the rug pulled out from under me. New Coke is absolutely AWFUL. . . . Don't send me any coupons or any other inducements. You guys really blew it.

> Millions of dollars worth of advertising cannot overcome years of conditioning. Or in my case, generations. The old Coke is in the blood. Until you bring the old Coke back, I'm going to drink RC.

Where's the Fizz-zz-zz? What happened to the fizz? *I MISS THE FIZZ!!!*

I do not drink alcoholic beverages, I don't smoke, and I don't chase other women, my only vice has been Coke. Now you have taken that pleasure from me.

Who is this Roberto Goizueta and where did he come from that is Chairman? Who is Sergio? They don't sound mainstream American. . . . *OLD COKE IS IT AND THERE WILL NEVER BE ANYTHING TO TAKE ITS PLACE.*

Your bright marketing people will figure out that instead of converting Pepsi drinkers, you're losing us Cokaholics to indifference if not suicide. . . . You're just kidding, right? You did this as a stunt, to teach us all a lesson in humility and gratitude. . . . Well, OK, I get the point. You can stop any time now.

Would it be right to rewrite the Constitution? The Bible? To me, changing the Coke formula is of such a serious nature.

There are only two things in my life: God and Coca Cola. Now you have taken one of those things away from me.

You Fucked Up! What you inherited *WAS* the real thing.

Can you imagine anyone ordering Rum and Pepsi? I've been hearing such blasphemy.

My dearest Coke: You have betrayed me. We went out just last week, as we had so often, and when we kissed I knew our love affair was over. . . . I remember walks across campus with you discussing life and love and all that matters. . . . I remember the southern summer nights we shared with breezes leaving beads of water hanging delicately from your body. . . . But, last week, I tasted betrayal on your lips: you had the smooth, seductive sweet taste of a lie. . . . You have become a prostitute, corrupted by money, denying your ideals.

One retired Air Force officer, explaining how much Coca-Cola had meant to him, revealed that his will called for his cremated ashes to be sealed in a Coke can for interment in Arlington National Cemetery, but he was rethinking the matter. A more pragmatic writer said that Coca-Cola used to make an excellent douche. "Does the 'New Formula' Coke pack the same wallop?"* One enterprising correspondent included a blank signed check for up to $10 million, with a note: "Since you are no longer making Coca-Cola, perhaps you would like to sell me the recipe?"

---

* Although the Company did not respond to the New Coke douche query, the answer was "No," according to a scientific study conducted by a group of Harvard Medical School researchers who found that Coca-Cola Classic killed five times as many sperm as New Coke. The researchers didn't recommend any form of post-coital douche, however, since "sperm can make it into the fallopian tubes in minutes."

All along, the standard Coke response remained that New Coke, the better-tasting soft drink, had replaced the old formula. Period. The self-confident assertions masked anxiety bordering on panic by the end of June. Bottlers begged for the old drink back, since they were becoming social pariahs. In rural Alabama, a minister led his congregation in prayer for the local bottler's soul, which was undoubtedly destined for hell. In Marietta, Georgia, a woman assaulted a Coke delivery man with her umbrella as he tried to stock a supermarket shelf with New Coke. "You bastard," she screamed, "you ruined it, it tastes like shit!" When a nearby Pepsi driver laughed, she spun around. "You stay out of it! This is family business. Yours is *worse* than shit." Clearly, something had to be done. "I'm sleeping like a baby," Roberto Goizueta told his friends. "I wake up crying every hour." Sergio Zyman, already quite thin, lost ten pounds during the month. Monitoring the consumer hot line, he staggered away in disbelief, muttering, "They talk as if Coca-Cola had just killed God." In desperation, the chemists increased the acidity level in New Coke to give it more "bite," but nothing helped. June's sales plummeted, and Roy Stout's surveys underscored that Coke's image was slipping badly.

THE SECOND COMING

On Friday, July 5, the *MacNeil/Lehrer NewsHour* devoted twenty minutes to the New Coke disaster, showing Mullins and his cronies pouring the drink out on the street. The protests were not subsiding, nor was the media's negative coverage. Over the next week, the only real argument involved what to call the old formula when it returned. Dyson favored "original," but the Company lawyers objected, since they suddenly saw a way to benefit from the situation. If they called it "classic," as Goizueta ultimately determined, they could argue that it was an entirely new drink, not covered by the original contract. Schmidt and Bondurant would be outfoxed.

Plans for Coca-Cola Classic leaked, and the Company had to issue a terse acknowledgment on July 10, a day before the scheduled press conference. Peter Jennings interrupted an ABC soap opera to bring America the news, while Arkansas senator David Pryor, in a speech sandwiched between debate over South African disinvestment and action on the Safe Drinking Water Act, solemnly declared that the return of the original formula was "a meaningful moment in American history." Within the Company, employees rejoiced over what they termed the Second Coming. Thursday morning, virtually every newspaper in the country carried a front-page story on Classic Coke, bumping reports on President Reagan's cancer operation out of the spotlight.

The same day, the chastened Goizueta, Keough, and Dyson faced the press in Atlanta, less than three months after the glitzy New Coke debut at Lincoln Center. While Goizueta curtly told Americans, "We have heard you," Keough stole the show by eloquently confessing just how badly the Company had miscalculated, speaking of the "passion" that had taken them by surprise and calling it "a lovely American enigma" which was no more measurable than "love, pride or patriotism." Some, Keough said, portrayed this moment as a Company retreat, a victory of the little man over a giant corporation. "How I love that!" he said. "We love any retreat which has us rushing toward our best customers with the product they love most." He concluded with an accurate prediction. "Some critics will say Coca-Cola made a marketing mistake. Some cynics will say that we planned the whole thing. The truth is we are not that dumb and we are not that smart." At the close of the press conference, a reporter asked Goizueta, "If you knew in April what you know now, would you have gone ahead with the reformulation?" The CEO deflected the question with a Spanish proverb from his grandfather: "*Si mi abuela tuviera ruedas seria bicicleta*," which translated, "If my grandmother had wheels, she would be a bicycle."

The euphoria following the return of old Coke surpassed the despair of the past three months. Supporters deluged Gay Mullins with celebratory bottles of Coke as he sprawled in a bathtub. A small airplane circled North Avenue headquarters with a banner reading, "THANK YOU, ROBERTO!" Dan Lauck heaved a sigh of relief, since he was down to a mere sixty-five cases. Eighteen thousand calls of gratitude jammed the toll-free line on the day of the announcement. Now the mail inundating the Company read like love letters. "Thank you for bringing old Coke back," wrote one sixty-eight-year-old woman. "The only thing better is sex!" Astonished Coke marketer Ike Herbert remarked, "You would have thought we had invented a cure for cancer."

> We love you for caring! You have given us back our dream! We are grateful. . . . You have made our hard lives easier to bear and have given us confidence in ourselves to change things for the better.

> I drank Coke the morning of my wedding to calm me. . . . My first request after the births of my two children was for a Coke on ice. I drank a Coke on the way to my father's funeral. . . . You've made my day and I appreciate that.

> With the return of "Coca-Cola Classic," you might say that the old coke has been "reincarbonated."

> I feel like a lost friend is returning home.

> Thank God for Coca-Cola! We DO Have It GREAT in America!

> God does work in mysterious ways and I thank him for answering my prayers to bring back the "real" Coke.

> The old Coke recipe reflects the love of every good American today. There is only one Holy Bible, one Elvis Presley, others have tried to copie them, but never quit make it.

> How can you say the old Coke is only liked by the older generation? I'm 13, the now generation. I happen to like old Coke the best!

> I am most pleased that you announced today that I will again be able to obtain the Coca-Cola I have been drinking since 1909. I am now 91½ years of age.

Keough's brilliant one-liner, asserting that the Company was neither that dumb nor that smart, was only half true. While a few analysts and consumers were certai that the Company had staged the entire fiasco simply to grab publicity and rem their loyal consumers how much Coca-Cola meant to them, the Company clearly did no such thing. Goizueta and colleagues *had* been "that dumb," however, committing what *Business Week* termed "the marketing blunder of the decade." Oddly enough, pride still blinded the executives. Despite the return of Coca-Cola Classic, they steadfastly maintained that New Coke would surge ahead.

In his letter to shareholders confirming the original formula's return, Goizueta insisted that New Coke (a term he despised) was "the best-tasting Coca-Cola we have ever made," condescendingly referring to a group of older consumers who demanded "a taste of nostalgia." Consequently, Coca-Cola Classic would appear "alongside our flagship brand, [New] Coca-Cola." In an obvious attempt to minimize embarrassment, Goizueta illogically called the reintroduced Classic "the newest addition to the lineup of Coca-Cola branded products," which he termed "the most formidable megabrand in the soft drink industry." The Coke executives were so certain that New Coke would flourish that they cooperated with Thomas Oliver, the *Atlanta Constitution* business reporter who planned to knock out a quick book on the flavor change. Now, in the fall of 1985, he conducted lengthy interviews with Stout, Herbert, Zyman, Dyson, Keough, and Goizueta.

A DRAMATIC COURTROOM TWIST AND OTHER DISASTERS

Meanwhile, the legal battle between Bill Schmidt's group of disaffected bottlers and the Company heated up. Under oath, Roberto Goizueta insisted that Coca-Cola was whatever he and the Company *said* it was. On April 22, 1985, it had been one formula, and the next day, it was something completely different. Now, the Company insisted that Coke Classic constituted a completely "new" drink with a different name, reserving the right for flexible pricing in the future. Emmet Bondurant dubbed this mentality "Alice in Wonderland thinking," and quoted Lewis Carroll's officious Humpty Dumpty, much to the amusement of Judge Murray Schwartz:

> "When I use a word," Humpty Dumpty said, in rather a scornful tone, "it means just what I choose it to mean—neither more nor less."
>
> "The question is," said Alice, "whether you *can* make words mean so many different things."
>
> "The question is," said Humpty Dumpty, "which is to be master—that's all."

An August ruling from the bench stunned Goizueta and his lawyers. Judge Schwartz ordered the Company to reveal the secret formula for virtually every cola drink it made, including Coca-Cola Classic, New Coke, Diet Coke, and all the decaffeinated versions. He could thus determine whether Diet Coke was, in fact, similar to Classic or New Coke, which would help legitimize the litigious bottlers' claims. To no ~'s surprise, Big Coke categorically refused. "The Company has never disclosed its ~ to its own General Counsel," wrote a Company lawyer, and it was not ʃnch of bottlers see them now. The media loved the drama. *U.S. News ʃ* printed a story about the Company's "brazen defiance" along with a ʃst Company guard inside the vault containing the famous formula. For the next eight months, the matter lay unresolved, since Judge Schwartz was reportedly incapacitated by a mysterious illness.

At the same time, the embattled Company found itself mired in more controversy from an unexpected quarter—the result of the recent licensing program. The new line of Coca-Cola clothes, manufactured by Hong Kong's Murjani International, caused a fashion sensation with their July debut. "Suddenly," a Company trademark lawyer mused, "people are like walking billboards for the product." Not only that, Murjani was *paying* Coca-Cola for the privilege. There was, however, a downside to Coca-Cola's magical, symbolic name. Even as Americans proudly donned their hip clothing, Southern textile plants cried foul. How could the Company have allowed a foreign company to make these sweatshirts and pullovers, advertised as "All-American"? Coca-Cola officials quickly admitted their mistake and promised that Murjani would find domestic sources for its garments soon.

Even a supposed coup turned sour. Coca-Cola had arranged for its new taste to travel aboard the space shuttle in a special can that permitted carbonation under zero-gravity conditions. It would be the first soft drink in space. NASA reneged on the promise, however, allowing Pepsi to go along for the ride as well. Furthermore, the astronauts complained that lukewarm cola wasn't terribly satisfying.

Roberto Goizueta smarted under the glee with which journalists jumped upon any negative news about Coca-Cola. At the *Atlanta Constitution* offices, the CEO had earned a reputation for thin skin, since he often sent reporters handwritten, pedantic corrections for the most minor inaccuracies. Company men recognized this trait as perfectionism, not petulance. Thin-skinned or not, Goizueta's precise engineering mind did not understand feature writers and their penchant for human interest hooks. In October of 1985, addressing a national group of editors, he vented some of his frustration, beginning with a sarcastic reference to the publicity over New Coke. "How boring this past summer would have been for you," he said, without the tumult over the changed formula. "Just picture those reporters on your staffs with little to do all summer long!" He proceeded to chide the media for "pandering to what is provocative," preferring stylistic cuteness to objective investigation. "Journalists need to remember," Goizueta lectured, that "they are entering quickly into other persons' minds. They must understand this power they possess." It didn't seem to occur to the Coke executive that Coca-Cola commercials were subject to precisely the same criticism and had given the cue to newsmen by emphasizing image and the quick gloss.

COKE ARE IT

The return of the original formula as Coca-Cola Classic posed a major conundrum for Coke advertising. The New Coke disaster effectively killed the "Coke Is It" campaign, since it wasn't quite clear *which* Coke was it. *Newsweek*'s headline declared, "Hey America, Coke Are It!" Nor could the Company rely on Cosby again. "May we now expect to see a commercial featuring Bill Cosby speaking from both sides of his mouth simultaneously?" a snide consumer inquired. During the fall of 1985, the ad men floundered with two weak "megabrand" slogans—"We've Got a Taste for You" and "Coke Belongs to You." The commercials tried to push *both* colas at once, displaying New Coke and Classic together. Sergio Zyman lamely explained that both drinks shared "the same affection for and identification with the brand." Ed Mellett, recently hired away from Pepsi as Coke's new marketing chief, admitted that "we don't know the relative role and importance of each sugared cola."

By year's end, however, Classic was clearly surging while New Coke's market share shrank. Worse, Pepsi-Cola had snagged the lead as the best-selling single sugar cola in America. The combined sales of Classic and New Coke still fell slightly *below* Coca-Cola's comparable 1984 figures. As he hurried to finish his book, Thomas Oliver suddenly sensed a distinct chill at the Company. His calls weren't returned, and several appointments were broken. "The Coca-Cola executives had been giving me a lot of information about why they had changed the formula," Oliver recalled, "and I think they realized that they were supplying me with ammunition which could shoot their number one brand in the foot again." In February of 1986, the McCann men abandoned their attempt to promote both colas at once. For New Coke, they exhorted consumers to "Catch the Wave," a reference to the logo's dynamic ribbon. The curvy line was supposed to lead to New Coke, the "wave" of the future. "The advertising addresses the visionary," Brian Dyson insisted, "those consumers who are peering into tomorrow." To position New Coke as the "in" taste, he promoted commercials that united "high-tech promotion with highly contemporary imagery."

The new ads couldn't find a center. Some showed people doodling or globbing catsup in the shape of the curve. In "Horizontal Pour," an enormously expensive, slick production, a rugged hunk served a bikini-clad woman basking in a recliner—only he poured the Coke *sideways* through the house, and she caught the liquid in her empty glass. While the ad was a technical masterpiece, accomplished by turning a house on its side, it was practically devoid of content, a perfect New Wave product. Other ads for the new formula broke every rule, overtly comparing Coca-Cola with Pepsi. In one, a castaway on an island found a bottle of the rival soft drink. While Italian opera inexplicably blared in the background, the desperate man opened the bottle, dumped the drink onto the sand, and tossed the bottle with an SOS note into the surf. The tide, of course, returned a six-pack of Coke.

As a final assault on viewers' intelligence and sanity, the Company launched a series of New Coke commercials aimed primarily at teenagers, who were depicted as mindless zombies playing video games. On the screen, Max Headroom would suddenly appear—a smiling, simpering, narcissistic, computer fad with a dazzling smile, dark glasses, airbrushed hair, and an annoying stutter. The ads proved enormously popular with adoring teens, who imitated Headroom's admonition to "C-C-Catch the Wave," followed by a sigh or growl. At a mass meeting of "Cokeologists," Headroom asked, "So what I want to know is, if you're drinking Coke, who's drinking Pepsi?" The commercials debuted on MTV and on David Letterman's hip late-night show, testing extraordinarily well with high recall and brand association.

In the meantime, Lintas's Coca-Cola Classic advertising remained closer to traditional Coca-Cola values, overplaying the all-American nature of the drink with the slogan "Red, White & You." Instead of celebrating Coca-Cola Classic as an integral part of everyday life, these ads, aired during soap operas and the Cosby Show, harkened back to the overpatriotic "Look Up, America" campaign of 1974, replete with the Statue of Liberty, the Grand Canyon, rural folk, and celebrities sprinkled throughout for good measure. Although the Company spent far more on New Coke ads than on efforts for Classic, the new formula's share continued to slip as Classic climbed. The kids loved Max Headroom, but they failed to translate their affection to the vending machines, or they misunderstood which Coke he was touting. By the end of April, two weeks before the centennial bash, New Coke had fallen below a 3 percent market share, while Classic had fizzed past Pepsi to regain the overall sugar cola lead. The final blow came when McDonald's switched its huge account to Classic. Since one out of every twelve Americans passed through the Golden Arches daily, that amounted to a gigantic vote against New Coke.

AN EXPENSIVE HISTORY LESSON

It cost The Coca-Cola Company $4 million to research and develop New Coke. The masses of data, the taste tests, the well-honed strategy had failed to reveal just how well Asa Candler and Robert Woodruff had done their jobs. Coca-Cola, as much icon as soft drink, stood for traditional values. In the shifting kaleidoscope of the late twentieth century, Americans felt rootless and ill at ease. Computers seemed to know more than people. Avuncular Walter Cronkite had retired and no longer calmed the national psyche every night. The Latin mass no longer soothed with its sonorities. The full-service filling station was a rarity, and the old-fashioned soda fountain lingered in just a few anachronistic small Southern towns.

Only Coca-Cola stayed the same—the perky, fizzy, social drink that made instant friends of strangers, gave a little jolt of energy, rewarded hot work on a summer day. In the stampede to assign blame for the New Coke debacle, many American consumers and veteran bottlers sneered at the "Latin mafia" of Goizueta, Zyman, and Dyson. Since they weren't "real" Americans, how could they comprehend the nation's passion for good old Coke? This racist scenario didn't factor in Keough, who jokingly referred to himself as the "token American" at the Company, and who was just as sure as Goizueta about New Coke's ultimate triumph. The corporate blindness stemmed not so much from geography or cultural background as from the eighties mentality. Aggressive, ruthless, and cocky, the new team wanted to repeat the blockbuster breakthrough of Diet Coke. In the process, they overlooked the most vital emotion of all—love.

The American public loudly and clearly taught the corporate strategists a history lesson. Like William Allen White, they revered a drink that symbolized America, that was associated with almost every aspect of their lives—first dates, moments of victory and defeat, joyous group celebrations, pensive solitude. As a poetic Texas consumer had written in his June 1985 love letter to the drink, "Whenever things began to look too bleak, I'd come over and pick you up, we'd share a few minutes together, and I would be comforted. And do you remember the times I and our friends shared concerns when you were around? It seems as if the richest hours of my life have been shared with you." As a result of the New Coke disaster, original Coca-Cola garnered much more than $4 million worth of publicity, rendering the Company's horrendous advertising irrelevant. The venerable cola roared back to claim its lead as the premier American soft drink. Unintentionally, Goizueta and Keough had converted the gigantic marketing blunder into a commercial coup.

~ 20 ~

The Big Red Machine

Can Big Red make its soda as ubiquitous as water? . . . One gets the feeling there's a recurring nightmare in the marketing department of Coca-Cola USA. A plane goes down in the desert. Everyone is safe, everyone is sound. They make their way to an oasis. Plenty of food. Plenty of water. Plenty of shelter. But no Coke machines.

—Jeffrey Scott, *Adweek*, Dec. 12, 1988

For four days, Coca-Cola literally painted Atlanta red for its $23 million centennial bash. John Pemberton would have retreated hastily to his laboratory if he had stumbled into the Omni on the evening of May 7, 1986, where laser beams blazed, miniature Coke trucks zipped up and down the aisles, a Coca-Cola blimp floated overhead, and scantily clad dancers twirled to loud music—all to honor the moment when the kindly pharmacist and morphine addict perfected the formula.

The Company outdid itself to impress the 12,500 bottlers who came from all over the world. First, 650,000 dominoes toppled across six continents, brought live by satellite to the audience. The Nairobi segment nearly stopped the chain reaction, since gigantic African moths kept knocking over the carefully stacked pieces ahead of time. It wasn't terribly clear what the point of the topple was—perhaps it was a play on "Catch the Wave" or a demonstration of the Company's global connections—but it was great fun, particularly since the final domino in London triggered a bomb that blew a huge Pepsi bottle to smithereens. Celebrities galore studded the festivities. Dick Cavett hosted the domino topple, for instance, wryly inquiring of a Swahili-speaking spokesman via satellite, "So, do you have any hobbies?" Merv Griffin was there, since Coca-Cola had just purchased his television production interests, including *Jeopardy!* and *Wheel of Fortune.* Chuck Berry twanged his guitar and one-footed it across the stage, Kool and the Gang electrified, Marilyn McCoo crooned, Lionel Hampton and his orchestra swung.

The multimedia show, narrated by Ike Herbert, covered all of Coca-Cola's history in typical Company fashion, presenting it as a seamless success saga, the rise of a humble drink to deserved greatness. Herbert, the quintessential marketing man, noted that "people in remote corners of the world who don't even know the names of their own capital cities know the name Coca-Cola," because "we've been able to infiltrate Coca-Cola into the minds and hearts and lives of everyone everywhere." Throughout the audience, bottlers cheered and stomped as singers chanted the refrain, "Take it to the people."

The assembled throng was, as Herbert said, "one family with one mighty voice raised in bold self-congratulation." Just before midnight, a seven-and-a-half-ton birthday cake was wheeled onto center stage, where, instead of a gigantic party girl, a fourteen-foot Coke bottle rose from the middle of the cake as loyalists sang "Happy Birthday." On Saturday, almost everyone in Atlanta turned out for a parade down Peachtree Street with over a hundred floats and five hundred thousand balloons wafting the Coca-Cola logo skyward. Two members of the Coca-Cola Collectors Club (who had met and fallen in love amidst the memorabilia) exchanged marriage vows on a float. Mickey Mouse and Goofy cavorted for Coke, along with Uncle Sam and a tinsel-haired Statue of Liberty, also celebrating her hundredth anniversary. Thirty marching bands blared, while Miss Universe and America's Junior Miss waved to the crowd. Although the colossal event went off without a hitch, some demonstrators carried anti-apartheid placards admonishing the Company to "Get Coke out of South Africa."

Underlying the celebration was an uneasy, unspoken awareness of the recent New Coke debacle. While Company officials had promised that the new formula would be available around the world by the centennial, it had never traveled beyond Canada and the United States. The formula change's failure in America shook the confidence of Coke men around the world, however. In private interviews, Goizueta continued to describe New Coke as "the product of the future," but its highest market share was already receding into the past. In one of the few minor crises during the big parade, a walking can of New Coke symbolically deflated in midstride.

ASSESSMENT AT MID-DECADE

Well aware of their awkward situation, Roberto Goizueta and Don Keough emphasized to the assembled bottlers that the Company was in excellent shape. In fact, it really was. Despite—or because of—the New Coke fiasco, the Company's soft drink market share in the United States had swelled to 39 percent versus 28 percent for Pepsi. Between them, the two giants were squeezing out other players. "Coke and Pepsi Stomp on the Little Guys," a 1985 *Fortune* headline had bluntly stated. Just before the centennial, Pepsi announced it was buying 7-Up, and Coke countered by attempting to gobble Dr Pepper. The FTC intervened to prevent both deals, which was pretty much what Coke had anticipated, but the Company didn't really care. Not only had Coke Classic surpassed other sugar colas, Sprite had surged past 7-Up in the lemon/lime category.

The Company's entertainment sector also raked in money from videocassette sales and TV show syndication, but Columbia's creative endeavors proved embarrassing flops—and there were a great many of them, since Coke pushed the movie company to disgorge a glut of films such as *Perfect*, *Crossroads*, and *The Slugger's Wife*. One forgettable effort, *Fast Forward*, cost $17 million, netting only $500,000 at the box office. Nor did Columbia's television shows fare any better, despite Peter Sealey's focus groups and surveys. All five of the Company's productions that season were canceled, killing any future syndication possibilities. To Goizueta's chagrin, the media paid no attention to the overall health of the bottom line, instead gloating over the box of-fice failures. "Coke: Flat in Hollywood," *Newsweek*'s headline read, while *Business Week* asked, "Columbia Pictures: Are Things Really Better with Coke?" Stung by the criticism, Goizueta hoped that the forthcoming *Ishtar*, the expensive comedy starring Dustin Hoffman and Warren Beatty, would reverse the studio's public fortunes.

By that spring of 1986, Goizueta had accomplished his every goal. Earnings per share averaged 10 percent per year, and the stock had shot up from $35 in 1980 to $120, which spelled a compounded annual return of 24 percent compared to 13 percent for the S&P 500. As he had predicted, the domestic operations were now accounting for about half of the Company's profits. What difference did it make whether New Coke and Columbia were causing bad publicity? "My job is not to be right," Goizueta philosophized. "It is to produce results."

IVESTER THE FINANCIAL WIZARD

Goizueta owed many of those results to a bright young Georgian named Doug Ivester, who was promoted to chief financial officer when Sam Ayoub retired at the end of 1984. Despite his folksy accent, Ivester, a shrewd businessman, perceived that strate-gic debt could boost the bottom line, particularly if he recycled the borrowed money for a sizable return. By the time of the centennial celebration, Coke maintained a 20 percent debt-to-equity ratio, up from virtually nothing five years before. Besides, the new debt load reduced the corporate tax rate from 45 percent to 39 percent because of deductible interest payments. Ivester also brought financial innovation to the film industry when he sold Columbia's accounts receivable for cash. This process, known as "factoring" in the garment industry, had never been applied to Hollywood. TV stations didn't have to pay for syndication rights until shows aired, which could entail a delay of several years. By selling the receivables, Ivester gained immediate access to the money.

By increased debt offerings, lowered percentages of dividend payouts, and inven-tive financing, Coca-Cola found itself sitting on enormous piles of cash, amounting to some $1.5 billion by its centennial year. Goizueta, Keough, and Ivester faced the pleasant though difficult task of allocating the funds. In the past, excess cash had been used for more subsidiary acquisitions and repurchase of the Company's stock. Now, Goizueta clearly wanted to refocus the Company on its primary mission of worldwide soft drink saturation.

LOOKING OVERSEAS

He had good reason. Late in February of 1985, the dollar peaked. Concentrating on U.S. investments during the decade's first half made sense because of the muscular dollar. During the latter part of the eighties, however, the massive U.S. trade and bud-get deficits drove the dollar to 70 percent of its top value by the end of 1990. Against specific currencies, such as the Japanese yen, it lost nearly half of its buying power. Although the dollar's demise spelled disaster for most American firms, it furnished a wonderful opportunity for the multinational Coca-Cola. Sales in Germany or Japan yielded fatter profits due to favorable exchange rates. As Goizueta and Keough hastened to point out, Americans accounted for less than 5 percent of the world's population. The other 95 percent remained a largely untapped market. Goizueta thus decided to pursue the same hard-driving strategies in countries around the world as he had already in the United States.

The possibilities were tantalizing. If the rest of the world's human beings drank anywhere *near* the same amount of Coca-Cola as the typical American, the Company would experience more than exponential growth. By 1986, every man, woman, and child in the United States drank an average of 660 eight-ounce soft drinks every year. The steady growth of American soft drinks per capita had overtaken beer in the early sixties and swept past coffee and milk in the late seventies. By 1986, it had surged beyond imagination. "Right now," Roberto Goizueta informed the assembled bottlers at the centennial, "in the United States, people consume more soft drinks than any other liquid—including ordinary tap water." The Coke CEO then painted a glorious scenario. "If we take full advantage of our opportunities," he said, "someday, not too many years into our second century, we will see the same wave catching on in market after market, until, eventually, the number one beverage on earth will not be tea or coffee or wine or beer. It will be soft drinks—*our* soft drinks."

Internationally, Coke led Pepsi 3-to-1, and the gap between American and foreign consumption beckoned the eager Coca-Cola men. In Africa, per capita amounted to only 4 percent of the U.S., while the economically surging Pacific Rim stood at 8 percent. In Western Europe, where Coca-Cola dominated competition, the per capita remained 23 percent of that in America, while Latin America held at 29 percent.* The future for soft drinks, as Don Keough told *Beverage Digest*, appeared rosy. "As population centers become more complex, potable tap water is very difficult to find, and there is an anti-alcohol phenomenon here and abroad." Fizzy, enjoyable, tasty soft drinks could jump into the thirst gap.

Keough, the Company motivator, concluded the centennial celebration with a magnificent proof of the Coke system's power and unity, asking everyone present— over twelve thousand people—to stand and hold hands. "This is the world of Coca-Cola," he told them. "What other international group in the world could do this right now? From every continent, from every culture, over 125 countries in this room. The United Nations can't do it. We're not mad at anybody. We love each other. Can you feel the energy—can you feel the love—can you feel the affection?" The bottlers left Atlanta with Keough's words ringing in their ears, returning to their corners of the world with renewed inspiration. "You are the Michelangelo of Coca-Cola in your territory," Keough had told them. "And tomorrow the canvas for Coca-Cola as we begin that second century is blank, is bare. You are the artist."

THE TRIPLE A'S

While the bottlers may have been the "artists," Keough and Goizueta, exceedingly aggressive tutors, often grabbed the paintbrush right out of the bottlers' hands. By the

---

* Brand Coca-Cola accounted for nearly 70 percent of the Company's overseas volume, followed by 14 percent for Fanta Orange, making Fanta, a virtually ignored name in America, the world's third most popular soft drink.

time of the centennial, the Company had already taken a 49 percent equity position in the ailing Taiwanese bottler and had divulged a partnership with Cadbury-Schweppes in Great Britain to take effect in 1987. Inspired by the results in the Philippines, Coca-Cola went on to form joint ventures in country after country throughout the remainder of the decade. In the past, the Company had assiduously avoided the "vertical integration" that buying bottlers implied. Consequently, the quality of the market depended on how motivated or competent the bottlers were. In addition, a certain cultural fatalism had hampered growth in selected countries. In Great Britain, for instance, Coke men always blamed their lackluster showing on the drizzly weather, along with the British penchant for quaffing warm beer; they simply weren't used to ice-cold drinks. Similarly, the reasoning went, the French would never accept Coca-Cola because they loved their wine too much and objected to the Americanization of their culture.

Goizueta refused to accept these excuses. While cultural deterrents existed, they were not insurmountable. The same traditional methods that had prevailed in the United States would work anywhere in the world, with appropriate modifications. The Cuban CEO coined an alliterative slogan—*availability, affordability, acceptability*. Before the drink could be sold, it must be *available*, or, as Woodruff always put it, "within arm's reach of desire." Coca-Cola should elbow its way into every conceivable retail outlet, while vending machines dotted roadsides and invaded sports arenas, factories, offices, shopping malls. Because soda fountains had always remained a strictly American phenomenon, convincing small cafes and bistros to dispense "post-mix" Coke posed problems, though as McDonald's franchises spread throughout the world, fountain Coke tagged along.

Second, Coca-Cola must be *affordable* even to those living below the poverty line. While maintaining a hefty profit margin, the soft drink shouldn't ascend to luxury status. Increasingly, the Company pushed larger containers of two and three liters, resulting in bulk sales at lower cost. Keeping Coke cheap enough for cash-poor African consumers proved particularly challenging. In Latin America, where governmental controls checked price and packaging, the Company had little choice but to offer the drink at low cost.

Third, and perhaps most important, Coca-Cola had to be *accepted* by consumers as a refreshing, healthy, sparkling beverage associated with good times, friends, achievement, athletics, and patriotism. Massive advertising and promotion were essential to that acceptance. Attractive, smiling girls must carry trays with free samples at Company-sponsored sporting events, overwhelming any negative rumors with a wave of good feeling.

In each country, Keough and Goizueta understood, implementation would vary somewhat, depending on the culture, economy, and stage of industrial development. They coined another Company slogan: "Think globally, but act locally." In China and Indonesia, for instance, the first task involved building a strong infrastructure—concentrate factories, glass manufacturers, bottling plants, trucks, point-of-purchase signs, and the like—in American terms, time-warping back to 1905. In Germany, on the other hand, the Company already had a well-established business, but, as in the United States, too many bottlers vied in small territories. In 1985, Neville Isdell left a thriving Philippine business to supervise Germany, where he undertook the delicate task of consolidating the country's ninety-six bottlers.

THE 49 PERCENT SOLUTION

Shortly after the centennial celebration, The Coca-Cola Company fortuitously found itself in possession of two gigantic bottling concerns. Jack Lupton, the grandson of the original Whitehead partner, elected to sell the JTL Corporation for $1.4 billion just before the California bottling concerns owned by Beatrice Foods went on the block for $1 billion. Coke snapped them up and, together with the bottling plants it already owned, wound up controlling a third of American Coke production. The purchases matched Company strategy, but they added unwieldy debt to the bottom line. In addition, they threatened the Company's profit margins, since selling syrup and concentrate was far more profitable than bottling, and less capital intensive.

Doug Ivester solved the problem by creating an entirely new corporate entity called Coca-Cola Enterprises. As with other joint ventures, The Coca-Cola Company would retain a minority interest—in this case, 49 percent, guaranteeing control while shoving the huge bottling operation's debts off of Big Coke's balance sheet. Goizueta tapped Brian Dyson, a fine guerrilla fighter in the cola wars, as the new head of CCE, removing him from the main Company, where he was too closely linked to the New Coke disaster. The week before Dyson's appointment, Sergio Zyman resigned, providing another convenient fall guy for New Coke in the public mind, though Zyman continued to serve as a well-paid consultant for the Company.

In the next two years, Big Coke gobbled stray bottling concerns and added them to CCE, consolidating the world's largest single bottler. Despite its mammoth size and Dyson's best efforts, the new corporation stumbled from the start. First, CCE was embarrassed when reluctant capitalists twice forced its initial stock offering—the largest in history—down from $24 a share. By the time it finally hit Wall Street, CCE stock sold for $16.50 and promptly lost another $2 a share within a few days of going public. Investors remained unimpressed by the much-touted cash flow, which would supposedly boost the stock price. While huge amounts of money did wash in and out of the bottling concern, its profits remained razor thin because of price wars with Pepsi.

For Big Coke, however, CCE fulfilled its purpose. Because the parent company could call the shots, it sold concentrate to CCE at relatively high prices, leaving the bottler to scrape out narrow margins. Emmet Bondurant scornfully called CCE "a syrup pump for Big Coke, pure and simple." Ivester didn't care what it was called. The "49 percent solution," as insiders dubbed the arrangement, made financial sense. Quickly, he employed the same trick with Company-owned Canadian bottling plants, spinning them off as TCC Beverages Ltd., with the Company maintaining a 49 percent interest.

Shortly afterward, Ivester again performed his "financial alchemy," as a *Fortune* writer put it. He packaged all of the Company's entertainment holdings as publicly held Columbia Pictures Entertainment Inc., merging with Tri-Star in a stock swap leaving Coke with an 80 percent stake. He avoided an awkward initial stock offering by issuing 31 percent of the stock as a "dividend" to Coke shareholders. When the smoke cleared, The Coca-Cola Company owned just less than half of the new movie conglomerate, while netting $1.5 billion—about the same amount it had paid for everything in the sector. Goizueta was delighted with the new arrangements, which swept $3 billion in debt off the Company books, reducing the debt-to-equity level to a modest 12 percent and disassociating Big Coke somewhat from Columbia flops. Finally, it constituted what the *Wall Street Journal* termed "a potent takeover defense," with "layer upon layer of poison pills." Goizueta declared that Coca-Cola led the vanguard of "the emerging post-conglomerate era," comparing unwieldy traditional corporations to fifties cars with gratuitous tail fins.

PLACATING THE DO-GOODERS

Only months after the anti-apartheid activists picketed the centennial celebration, The Coca-Cola Company revealed that it planned to disinvest in South Africa, following a boycott threat from the Reverend Joseph Lowery and his Atlanta-based Southern Christian Leadership Conference. Furthermore, it would try to sell its bottling plants to qualified black owners. The Company set up an Equal Opportunity Fund (EOF) with a $10 million endowment, to be administered by Nobel Peace Prize winner Desmond Tutu and the Reverend Allan Boesak, among others. Finally, the Company's concentrate plant relocated from Durban to black-controlled Swaziland, instantly doubling the tax revenue of that tiny country.

Most apartheid critics lavished praise on Coca-Cola for "making a strong moral statement," as the Reverend Lowery said, while Mayor Andrew Young proclaimed it "a bold and significant step in the battle against apartheid." In fact, Coca-Cola had reduced its actual ownership of bottling plants in South Africa since 1976 because of the politically unstable situation, and its divestment involved less than $50 million in assets. The Company had no intention of relinquishing its domination of the South African soft drink market, continuing to supply its independent bottlers with syrup and marketing advice.

A few hard-line anti-apartheid activists challenged Coke's "disinvestment." Tandi Gcabashe, the daughter of former African National Congress leader Albert Luthuli, lived in Atlanta and persistently agitated for a boycott. She argued that for every eighty-cent bottle of Coke sold in South Africa, ten cents went as tax revenue to the government and that Coke therefore still supported the racist regime. She dismissed the $10 million EOF as "an insult, a drop in the bucket." When critics pointed out that other American companies offered more logical targets, Gcabashe shrugged them off, pragmatically asserting that Coke was the ideal scapegoat because of its worldwide presence and image. "They are so visible and so *good* with their advertisements," she explained, "that it works to our advantage. We can say, 'What company profits from apartheid? Coke is it!'" College students, ever eager for noble causes, fervently responded to Gcabashe's anti-Coca-Cola pamphlets, forcing the Company to counter with its own literature. Suave Carl Ware, Coke's highest-ranking black executive, traveled to reassure students personally of the Company's exemplary position. Desmond Tutu, visiting Atlanta to deliver the commencement speech at Emory, posed with Keough, Goizueta, and the Atlanta archbishop for a photograph in which all four smiled broadly. The boycott sputtered, though Gcabashe refused to let it die completely.

In the meantime, Coca-Cola Foods provoked an international uproar as well. Late in 1985, frustrated by repeated freezes that had decimated Florida orange groves, the Houston-based subsidiary purchased 196,000 acres of Belizean forest and grasslands, intending to clear 25,000 acres to guarantee a supply for Minute Maid. Paying only $6 million, Coca-Cola suddenly owned an eighth of the entire landmass of tiny Belize, formerly British Honduras. The deal, helped along by a new probusiness Belizean regime, quickly translated into a cause célèbre for environmentalists, nationalists, and angry native fruit growers.

Unfounded rumors flew that Coca-Cola had bought the land for use as a resupply base for Nicaraguan Contra rebels, since Contra chief Adolfo Calero was, after all, a Coca-Cola bottler. Calero's Coke plant had been seized by the Sandinista government in 1983 when he was out of the country. When other growers discovered that Prime Minister Manuel Esquivel had sweetened the deal by granting Coke a fifteen-year tax holiday, they were livid. Nor were the U.S. grove owners pleased with the situation, since the Coke move directly threatened their profits. The American citrus lobby blocked the issuance of essential "political-risk insurance." Without it, the Company couldn't reasonably proceed.

The greatest agitation, however, developed from environmental groups such as the International Audubon Society, Rainforest Action Network, and Friends of the Earth, which screamed that the contested forest nurtured unique wildlife such as ocelots, pumas, howler monkeys, harpy eagles, and the world's largest jaguar population. By 1987, the protests were garnering international headlines, with demonstrations in Stockholm and the occupation of a German bottling plant by Green Party activists. In September, Coke finally relented, placing the Belize citrus project on "indefinite hold." In addition, the Company donated forty thousand acres as a nature preserve and declared its intention of selling most of the balance. The Company managed to transform a public relations disaster into a bonanza. Coca-Cola, a Sierra Club publication declared, had "joined the rainforest generation."

THE "APRIL MASSACRE"

Meanwhile, Judge Murray Schwartz had recovered from his mysterious ailment and delivered two 1986 interim judgments, apparently decisive victories for the upstart bottlers led by Bill Schmidt. First, Schwartz issued a "preclusion order" in the Diet Coke Case because of the Company's refusal to divulge its secret formulae. In doing so, he allowed Emmet Bondurant to assert that the difference between Diet Coke and Coca-Cola was "as narrow as the width of a piece of paper," varying only in type of sweetener used. Unfortunately for Bondurant, Schwartz stopped short of saying that Diet Coke was *exactly* equivalent to Coca-Cola and therefore covered by the same contract.

Later in the year, Schwartz ruled in the E-Town Case that high-fructose corn syrup did *not* equal cane sugar according to the wording in the original bottling contract. The Company did not, therefore, have the right to switch to HFCS without the bottlers' permission. In his summary, the judge wrote that "this case was a pleasure to try because of the outstanding ability of both teams of lawyers," but suggested that their talents were misdirected. What was the use of the protracted, bitter dispute, since it was clearly in the best interests of both parties to compromise? Surely, these superb lawyers could convince their clients to negotiate a more reasonable contract with the object of "increasing the bottom line rather than incurring horrendous litigation expenses."

The judge's gentle admonition fell on deaf ears. Bondurant and Schmidt, jubilant over their apparent victories, were not about to relent. Nor, it soon appeared, would Big Coke. In an unexpected move the following March, the Company reacted to Schwartz's sugar judgment by *insisting* on supplying the non-amended bottlers with cane-sweetened syrup, even though that would cost the Company a projected $7 million annually. At the same time, the Company cut off all cooperative funds to non-amended bottlers. "We underestimated the vindictiveness of The Coca-Cola Company," Bondurant lamented, switching tactics to insist that the corn syrup had become the standard and must therefore be supplied under the contract. "The Company," he wrote, "is attempting to win through unfair and coercive tactics a victory it has lost to the bottlers in court." The Company responded by declaring that non-amended bottlers had until May 1 to sign the 1978 amendment. After that, the window of opportunity would stay closed forever.

Many of the non-amended bottlers panicked, particularly the smaller outfits that relied on other bottlers for cans and large plastic containers. They knew that the bigger amended supplier would cut them off rather than arrange for a separate cane syrup flow through their lines. Bill Schmidt, a medium-sized bottler who supplied nearby plants with canned Coke, wasn't in such dire straits, though he would now have to run two separate lines—one for amended, another for non-amended bottlers. He assured his fellow plaintiffs that he would ship them canned goods, but that failed to stem a flood of defections that Schmidt lamented as the "April Massacre." Many bottlers called in tears to apologize. "I believe in what you're doing," they said, "but I'm scared. This could ruin my whole business." Within a month and a half, the number of non-amended bottlers fell from sixty-four to twenty-nine. As the lawyers jockeyed, however, the final outcome of both trials remained uncertain.

NOT FUN ANYMORE

The dwindling renegades were the last holdouts against the dramatic changes the entire Coca-Cola system had undergone in the prior ten years. The small-town bottler, king of his countywide domain, had been replaced by a warehouse. In 1937, for example, Bill Carson built his gorgeous plant in Paducah, Kentucky, with select maple, stained glass, and a thirty-foot round dome. Its gilded splendor now held only a few offices; no one actually bottled Coke in Paducah anymore. Instead, in an impersonal process known as "double-bottoming," two loaded semitrailers pulled into the parking lot. In the old days, the bottler called each of his customers by first name, and each route driver developed a personal relationship with even the smallest account. For forty years, for instance, Charlie Schifilliti serviced Vermont. Because his name was difficult to pronounce, customers often called asking for "the Coca-Cola man," and the operator would give out Schifilliti's home phone number. If Pepsi dared to place a cooler, the typical Coke bottler would simply express disappointment in his old friend, who would remove the interloping machine. Now, the gigantic modern bottler shipped product hundreds of miles away, primarily to chain accounts: Kmart, 7-Eleven, Piggly Wiggly. Because of mergers and consolidations in almost every industry, including supermarkets, convenience stores, and service stations, the most important customers were bigger and bigger chains, which expected commensurately large, efficient service.

By 1988, the top ten U.S. Coke bottlers accounted for 78 percent of the brand's volume, and Big Coke owned equity positions in half of them. The raging price wars between Coke and Pepsi steadily narrowed profit margins. As industry commentator Jesse Meyers put it, discounting had become "not just a way of life, but . . . life itself," resulting in prices that were actually lower per ounce than in 1970, when adjusted for inflation. Inevitably, the squeeze on profits prompted a private cease-fire among some competing Coke and Pepsi bottlers—an illegal practice known as price-fixing.

Even though the Reagan administration's trustbusters had been notably lenient, Tony Nanni, the litigation chief appointed under Carter, was relentless once he smelled soft-drink blood. In a speech before bottlers, he spoke of his job as a "mission," and the shudder running through the room testified to his sincerity and power. After filing his first price-fixing case in 1986, he rapidly uncovered other cases of collusion. In 1987, CBS's *60 Minutes*, in a report called "Cola Payola," revealed that Coke and Pepsi bottlers had conspired in hotel bathrooms, parking lots, fast-food booths, and airport coffee shops to forge price agreements. By the end of 1988, Nanni had filed twenty-nine separate legal actions against bottlers and was investigating many others. Jim Harford, president of a major Coke bottling plant, was jailed in 1987 for collusion in price-fixing and admitted that he had created "an environment where people got hurt. Frankly, we were street-fighters. We were cocky, really cocky, competitively boastful that we could do anything because we were winning the war."

In this cutthroat world, only bullies won. Royal Crown and other smaller competitors were slowly being crushed between Coke and Pepsi, who literally left them no room through calendar marketing agreements (CMAs) in which the bigger bottlers paid supermarkets huge fees for the rights to exclusive end-of-aisle promotion space, dividing the year between them. Complaining that these CMAs were more properly termed "lock-out agreements," Royal Crown unsuccessfully sued.

The frantic effort to reap profits in such a volatile market forced most Coca-Cola bottlers to apply severe pressure on their employees. Traditionally, the Coke deliveryman took immense pride in his work, since he represented a worthy, gracious product and company. Now, for a driver at Coke Consolidated (in which Big Coke held a 20 percent equity position), the job became "psychologically devastating," to quote former route salesman Allen Peacock. During his fifty-four weeks with the Company, he routinely worked from 5:30 a.m. until 11 p.m. "They threatened termination if you didn't finish your route," he recalled. If the product didn't sell before its ninety-day shelf life expired, the salesman had to buy it out of his salary. That sort of pressure led to a 260 percent annual turnover rate at Consolidated in Nashville, where Peacock worked. Working strictly on commission, he pulled down $35,000 a year, but the stress and abuse weren't worth it. When his car broke down, he was told to appear anyway or face dismissal. The following day, his boss told him he could have one more chance. "I told him to kiss my ass," Peacock said. "I had never been written up or missed a day of work. I walked out, and I'll never go back."

Life at The Coca-Cola Company didn't become that vicious or harried, but the eighties brought unwanted change there as well. Coca-Cola men had always worked like hell, but in the corporate, computerized, buttoned-down world of the North Avenue Tower, there was less room for creative flair. Coca-Cola USA men chafed under increased bureaucratization, paperwork, and a top-down system of orders. The new, impersonal world at headquarters disheartened Company veterans. "At one time," Charlie Bottoms recalled, "I could have walked through the building and I would have been glad to give you a million dollars for anybody we passed that didn't know who I was and I couldn't at least call their first name. I can't call their names anymore." Bottoms complained of a "different breed" of employee who had never known the passionate loyalty to the Boss or the Company and regarded his or her job merely as a rung on a career ladder. "Some of them don't even drink our products. That's a sin. They work for money. They don't work for Coca-Cola." One day in 1988, Bottoms discovered one of his coworkers cleaning his desk in preparation for early retirement. "Why?" Bottoms asked him. "You've still got so much left in you." The man sighed. "Charlie," he answered, "I always promised myself that when it wasn't fun anymore, I would go. Well, it isn't fun anymore." Bottoms, who chose early retirement himself a few years later, could not find a rebuttal.

WITHIN WRIST'S LENGTH OF DESIRE

The same sort of centralization also destroyed the fun in the Fountain Division, Woodruff's old "Marine Corps," though Coke continued to dominate Pepsi in the post-mix wars. Income from fountain constituted a third of the Company's domestic profits. The most important accounts by far were fast-food outlets—all 122,000 of them. Dual-income families, too hassled to cook, grabbed more and more quick meals at the franchises, along with recently divorced singles. McDonald's, of course, topped the list. Although the Golden Arches had always served only Coca-Cola beverages, there was no written contract, and nervous Coke men knew that McDonald's could walk away without notice, taking the firm's largest single account with them. By the late eighties, McDonald's sold three billion drinks annually. To keep the big fountain accounts happy, Coke had to be satisfied with nearly invisible profit margins and offer superb, quick service.

In 1986, PepsiCo acquired Kentucky Fried Chicken, making the soft drink concern the world's second-largest restaurateur and providing one more exclusive outlet for Pepsi-Cola. Clever Coke salesmen exploited the KFC purchase to woo Wendy's, however, noting that Pepsi now competed for the fast-food dollar at Pizza Hut, Taco Bell, and Kentucky Fried Chicken. Wendy's switched to Coke. "Pepsi was subsidizing its expansion with *our* soft drink dollars," a Wendy's spokesman complained. "We were supporting a competitor." Similar thinking caused Domino's Pizza to dump Pepsi soon afterward. To Coca-Cola's delight, Pepsi was metamorphosing into a fast-food conglomerate more than a beverage company, and Coke men fervently hoped that Pepsi's attention would be diverted from the cola wars.

Determined to fill every niche of American society, in 1988 the Coca-Cola fountain men introduced the BreakMate, a miniature dispenser that could fit on a countertop in any office.* "Now we're targeting one of the last remaining dry channels in the United States—the workplace," a Coke executive exulted, though industry observer Jesse Meyers opined that the unit was really the prototype for a home soft-drink dispenser. Whatever the ultimate goal of the newest dispensing gadget, Coke was attempting to place its soft drinks not just within *arm's* length of desire, but within *wrist's* length, as Meyers put it. People could even buy a Coke on some intercity buses. "Perhaps coming years will see a time," Goizueta mused dreamily, "when consumers will have Coca-Cola taps in their homes."

BEATING THE FEELING TO DEATH

By the beginning of 1987, it was clear that the "Red, White & You" campaign was more black and blue than effective and that New Coke had fizzled, despite Max Headroom's popularity. Consequently, McCann-Erickson compromised on a "megabrand umbrella" approach intended to advertise all products with the Coca-Cola name. "When Coca-Cola is a part of your life," the new song promised, "you can't beat the feeling." This rather vague concept was supposed to claim consumers with a "special relationship" to Coke. At the end of each spot, a tagline for Classic, New Coke, Diet Coke, and Cherry Coke materialized, but the ads emphasized the "flagship brand," Classic. Roberto Goizueta stubbornly refused to abandon New Coke, however, and during 1987 the Company spent over $21 million on commercials for the controversial cola while allocating only $36 million to Classic—slightly more than half of Pepsi's main-thrust budget.

In the meantime, Pepsi was lavishing big money on celebrity campaigns, once again turning to Michael Jackson, whose *Bad* album reaffirmed his hold on young consumers. Michael J. Fox performed in funny, innovative Diet Pepsi ads created by Roger Mosconi (director of the Mean Joe Greene spot), who had quarreled with John Bergin and shifted from McCann-Erickson to BBDO. Phil Dusenberry continued to mastermind Pepsi attack spots, such as one in which an archeologist of the future could not identify a Coke bottle. Finally, Pepsi resuscitated a modified Challenge, once again airing taste tests touting Pepsi as "America's Choice" over Classic by a wide margin.

No one cared anymore. American consumers were sick of taste tests, and they kept drinking more Classic despite "evidence" of their ignorance. Throughout 1987 and 1988, Pepsi regained a slight edge in the take-home market, however, while most analysts agreed that Pepsi ads were more effective than Coke's diffuse efforts. As head of Coca-Cola USA, Ed Mellett had antagonized almost everyone, and when he fired two hundred people because of the reorganized bottling system, morale bottomed. At the end of 1988, Ike Herbert replaced Mellett, promising to revitalize the ad campaigns and restore good feeling to the American division.

Herbert's first change was, as Jesse Meyers noted, an "elegant marketing maneuver." Since third-place Diet Coke gained market share faster than any other soft drink,

---

* The BreakMate failed to find a major market, primarily because of technical malfunctions and cost.

Herbert decided to position *Diet Coke* against sugar Pepsi-Cola, asserting that the aspartame-sweetened drink would eventually surpass the Imitator to become number two—a doubtful claim in the short term, since Diet Coke claimed 8.5 percent of the soft drink market compared to Pepsi's 17.7 percent. Still, the Diet Coke attack ads, featuring singer Whitney Houston, hunk actor Pierce Brosnan, and sexy actress Demi Moore, helped to reposition the rivalry in Coke's favor. Don Johnson of *Miami Vice*, a previous shill for Pepsi, now confessed the error of his ways in Diet Coke spots. The surprise assault was called Project Manhattan—an obvious reference to the development of the atomic bomb. Making the military analogy explicit, Herbert explained that he had carefully defined a battlefield of his own choosing.

Simultaneously, Herbert virtually abandoned New Coke advertising. Within a year, McCann men improved "Can't Beat the Feeling" by a simple inversion of the lyrics. Research indicated that no one remembered or cared about the ethereal "feeling." As a Pepsi man queried, "What is the feeling? Why can't you beat it? It just doesn't express anything." Now, instead of mentioning the "real thing" in the penultimate position, the song crooned: "Can't Beat the Feeling, Can't Beat the Real Thing." With the minor change, warmth and effectiveness flowed back into the commercials, and the recall rate jumped.

Meanwhile, Pepsi embroiled itself in an unwanted controversy precisely because of its chosen image—hip, wild, creative, and slightly risqué. The pop superstar Madonna agreed to shoot a Pepsi spot in the spring of 1989, a video to her new song, "Like a Prayer." Roger Mosconi loved working with Madonna, who was professional, savvy, and took direction beautifully. The $5 million ad campaign, in which the singer touchingly encountered her eight-year-old self, debuted in the U.S. and forty other countries. Without telling Mosconi, however, Madonna had filmed a rock video of the same song to premier simultaneously on MTV. In the sacrilegious video, Madonna cavorted in front of burning crosses, displayed Christ's stigmata on her hands, and made love with a black saint on a church pew, instantly provoking a public furor. Pepsi had to pull its ads.

THE POWER OF PRESENCE

Despite an improved campaign, by the late eighties Coke men appreciated that traditional television, radio, and print ads were not the only effective forms of advertising. Coke's sheer presence in public venues, or "prestige" locations, provided enormous exposure. Don Keough emphasized "the power of presence" in a 1987 internal memo. "It is at the play, at the game, at the sorority and at the drugstore," Keough wrote. "The name, Coca-Cola, is in front of every pair of eyes, every day, everywhere." That, he pointed out, was what separated Coke from Pepsi. Through its exclusive presence at the Houston Astrodome, the San Diego Zoo, Madison Square Garden, Yankee Stadium, Disney World, and four hundred other prestige U.S. locations, Coca-Cola encountered over 280 million patrons a year. "We reach into the soul of America through these accounts," a Coke man observed.

The Disney account was by far the most important avenue into America's soul, and not just because of presence at the entertainment parks in California, Florida, and Japan. Coke's association with the beloved animated characters dated back to the fifties and sponsorship of *The Mickey Mouse Club*. In 1985, Coke signed an exclusive global marketing agreement. As a Company publication observed, "even a fairy godmother or sorcerer would be hard-pressed to match the wizardry of Mickey Mouse and Coca-Cola," since they were both "family-oriented" and "stand for good things." In 1987, to help celebrate Disney World's fifteenth birthday, Coke sponsored a tie-in contest with the April Disney Sunday Movie. "We've always wanted to lock up Easter as a major sales period," a Coke executive glowed. Forget celebrating the resurrection—a "Watch & Win" sweepstakes with free vacations to Disney World provided infinitely better advertising.

By the late eighties, advancing beyond mere product placement in movies, Coke paid for advertisements on rental videos. In addition, at thousands of theaters around the country, Coke ads introduced the main feature. Theater managers were delighted, since the ads boosted Coke sales at the concession stand, with its standard 80 percent markup. And more than ever Coke relied on the films themselves for product placement and co-promotions. To offset *Ishtar's* dismal performance earlier in the year, Coca-Cola turned to Bill Cosby, hoping for a blockbuster comedy for the 1987 Christmas season with his *Leonard Part 6*, a spy spoof that Cosby himself had written. Coke men could hardly contain their joy over the co-promotional opportunities. "The synergies between soft drinks and entertainment are endless and growing," a Coke marketer crowed. "We want to capitalize on these opportunities to the fullest."

He wasn't kidding. Coca-Cola soft drink divisions were prepared to spend over $12 million for *Leonard*, including tiny promotional spy cameras, supermarket displays with Cosby's smug smile presiding over stacked six-packs, Porsches as sweepstake prizes, and a deluge of cups, posters, pullover shirts, and buttons featuring Cosby and Coke. The movie seemed a surefire winner, with the comedian's TV show at the top of the charts and his book on parenting the world's fastest-selling hardback thus far. Cosby himself assured everyone that his film was "flat-out comedy, with punch lines that people will be able to laugh at over and over. I've been in this business for a long time, and I know this is really funny stuff." Unfortunately, he was wrong. "The audience *hated* it," the film's editor noted. "Jesus Christ, a rainbow trout got a bigger laugh than the great God Cosby!" The film failed utterly, pulling in only $5 million at the box office and incurring a net loss of $33 million.

Undeterred, Coca-Cola cut a deal for the ultimate product-placement film the following year. *MAC and Me*, an unabashed *E.T.* rip-off, made Coca-Cola the alien's only source of sustenance. "This must be like what they drink on their own planet," young Eric informed his brother as MAC slurped his Coke. Near the movie's end, sips of magical Coke revived the alien's nearly dead family members. In the final scene, the visitors from another planet drove into the sunset in a Chevy convertible, chewing bubble gum and drinking Coke. Though the movie was predictable, with a pedestrian script and poor acting, it undoubtedly helped to sell a lot of Coke and grossed over $34 million at the box office in just over a month.

WE'LL BUILD A BETTER WORLD FOR YOU

While Coke was engaged in a bitter struggle for supremacy in the United States—often looking somewhat silly in the process—the real action had shifted overseas, where Coke totally dominated Pepsi. Embarrassed by the New Coke debacle, Coca-Cola ordered Marcio Moreira to make a new commercial to restore worldwide Company pride. Once more, freelancer Ginny Redington devised a winner in which over a thousand eager, fresh-faced youngsters of every ethnic and geographical origin intoned an uplifting message reminiscent of the "Hilltop" commercial.

"I am the future of the world," sang a fifteen-year-old blonde girl with sweet sincerity, sitting alone at a table. "I am the hope of my nation. / I am tomorrow's people, I am the new inspiration," she continued, rising as hordes of other teenagers streamed into the imposing assembly hall and joined the song. "Please let there be for you and for me a tomorrow," they begged, each clutching a bottle of Coke. "If we all can agree, there'll be sweet harmony tomorrow." A girl laid her head on her boyfriend's shoulder. "Promise us tomorrow, and we'll build a better world for you." After panning the throng, the camera once more focused on the original soloist, while across the bottom scrolled, "A message of hope from the people who make Coca-Cola."

The song was beautiful, touching, stirring, and, as always with Coke's best efforts, not terribly specific. The emotional rush sufficed, particularly if all these young people kept drinking Coca-Cola. McCann men filmed "General Assembly," the perfect pattern commercial, in St. George's Hall in Liverpool, a harbor town where they could easily gather kids from around the world. The creative team shot the mob scene for the first two days, then filmed various soloists in nineteen different languages for as many versions of the commercial.

First released early in 1987, "General Assembly" effectively reasserted Coca-Cola's global image of peace, brotherhood, and all-encompassing goodwill. Over the next few years, it was broadcast again for appropriate events such as a Gorbachev-Reagan summit and the 1992 Olympics. In the Philippines, it served as the entire campaign for two years, with new versions filmed locally. In Peru, an entirely new Spanish cast assembled at Machu Picchu for a dramatic restaging. Where the Inca had once grown terraced fields of coca atop the world, singers now claimed the future for Coca-Cola. The wheel had come full circle.

Outside the United States, the Company maintained "Coke Is It" well beyond the introduction of "Can't Beat the Feeling" domestically—a normal procedure to see how well the American campaign was progressing and to allow time for testing it in foreign venues. Finally approved for overseas ads late in 1988, it didn't translate well in several markets, where "beating a feeling" meant something nonsensical or obscene. In Chile, the new slogan was transmogrified into "The Feeling of Life," in Italy "Unique Sensation," and in Japan, with its fractured English, "I Feel Coke."

Marcio Moreira, constantly frustrated by Coca-Cola's prudish standards, traveled the world in the early eighties policing women's nipples, which were taped over for swimsuit ads. "Sexiness and sensuality are a more acceptable part of many foreign lifestyles," the Brazilian ad man knew. By late in the decade, Moreira's international ads, extremely racy by American standards, featured lingering shots of swaying behinds, suggestive kissing and embracing, and commercials such as "First Time," which implicitly associated the excitement of an initial sexual encounter with drinking Coke. Rerecorded without reference to Coke, the song dominated the top rock spot in England for several weeks.

Under Moreira's direction, Coke's pattern advertising became more "universal," as he put it. In previous years, international commercials featured a careful blend of blacks, Asians, and whites. Now, research revealed that actors with dark Latin looks—a kind of middle ground—played well everywhere except Japan and a few other countries. "Anything that is too topical or local or ethnic won't work," Moreira explained. Likewise, wardrobe, locations, and props were carefully screened to avoid "contravening any major cultural streams."

ROCKIN' AND SOCKIN' WITH COKE

Around the world, ads and promotions strengthened Coke's ties with two universals—music and sports. Any singers used for international ads—such as George Michael, Cyndi Lauper, Whitney Houston, or Sting—had to appeal worldwide, particularly to teens. While America was graying, the world population as a whole grew younger, and satellites and cable TV rendered rock videos universal fare. In Brazil (average age: seventeen), Coke sponsored "Rock in Rio," a gigantic nine-day concert attended by over a million people. Lulu Santos, a Brazilian pop star, indicated his appreciation for Company support by mentioning Coke frequently in his song lyrics. In the Philippines, Coca-Cola actually recruited and groomed local rock groups, carefully fostering their popularity through concerts, tours, and TV commercials. Thailand's fans started wearing Coca-Cola clothes to Carabao concerts because of the singers' close identification with the soft drink, while in France, the Company sponsored a daily radio/TV show, the *Coca-Cola Top 50*.

Similarly, Company athletic sponsorship spanned the globe. Taking advantage of the Japanese fascination with American football, the Company flew two U.S. college teams to Tokyo for the "Coca-Cola Bowl," in which Oklahoma State beat Texas Tech 45–42. Since 1982, the Company had sponsored Sawayaka (Refreshing) Baseball Clinics in Japan. When the Brazilian soccer league nearly went bankrupt in 1987, Coke stepped in to sponsor it—but only if every player on every team sported a gigantic bright-red Coca-Cola logo. "The visual effect is stunning," a Company publication crowed. "Next year, even the game ball will bear the red and white trademark." Because of Coke's midfield signs at all World Cup venues, it reached twenty-five *billion* viewers during the 1990 playoffs. During the Tour de France, all cyclists carried a water bottle with the Company logo as they whizzed past giant Coke cans and signboards along the route before crossing a Coca-Cola finish line—quite a change from 1950, when French spectators had violently protested Coke support of a bicycle race. Regardless of the sport—field hockey, basketball, volleyball, gymnastics, sumo wrestling, motorcycle races—Coca-Cola sponsored it in almost every country in the world.

The Olympics, of course, furnished the world's most outstanding sports tie-in opportunity. In 1988, the Company paid for the Coca-Cola World Chorus, a hundred-voice choir selected from participating countries. For the opening ceremonies at Calgary and Seoul, the chorus debuted the official song of the event, "Can't You Feel It?" While the lyrics didn't mention Coca-Cola, their resemblance to "Can't Beat the Feeling" conveyed the appropriate message anyway. As a Company publication observed, the Olympics represented "a hot marketing opportunity," and Coke was determined to leverage Olympic symbols to promote sales—through special promotions, contests, and jackets emblazoned with the Coke trademark and the Olympic rings. At the events, the Coke logo was scrawled gaudily in neon, on murals and banners, on huge inflated cans atop buildings, on umbrellas and blimps, while the Company hosted a popular pin-trading center. Altogether, Coke invested about $80 million on its 1988 Olympic promotions.

CREATING SOFT DRINK HEAVEN

By the end of 1988, Coke's international vision had resulted in new joint ventures in Taiwan, China, Indonesia, Belgium, and Holland, while the triple-A program functioned smoothly. For the first time, the Company's after-tax net income topped a billion dollars, with 76 percent of that amount deriving from outside the United States—a dramatic increase of 15 percent in just three years. Highlighting the global business, the 1988 annual report featured Keough and Goizueta smiling in front of a vast world map; breaking precedent, the report touted the international performance before mentioning the United States.

Indeed, the outlook around the world made Coke executives drool. In Norway (annual per capita for Company products: 176), the top three soft drinks were Coca-Cola, Coke light (the international name for Diet Coke), and TaB, with a combined market share of 87 percent. Halfway around the world in China, customers lined up each morning outside the local bottling plant, where supply couldn't keep up with demand. Though the per capita remained minuscule—only 0.4—a new concentrate plant in Shanghai had just opened and three more bottlers would follow within a year. In the Soviet Union, Coke had barely begun. Under Gorbachev, however, the future of free enterprise appeared favorable, and Coke yearned to overtake Pepsi's early lead there. So far, the Company had garnered only an abortive U.S. grand jury investigation into charges that it had bribed its way into the USSR. Neither the bribery accusations nor the lack of hard currency disturbed Coca-Cola particularly. Someday, the Soviet market would bear fruit.

As the chief operating officer of the Company, Don Keough, so charming in public, was proving himself a tough operator who sometimes lost his Coca-Cola patience. Although Keough was immensely likable, immediately establishing contact and rapport—"it is hard not to be knocked over," wrote a *Fortune* reporter, "by his cocked smile, his jet-engine voice, and his touchy-feely nature"—that hands-on management style could turn rough if you didn't produce results. Goizueta found complaints from shell-shocked area managers amusing. "In 1981," he laughed, "everyone thought I was the bad cop and Don the good cop. Now I'm the nice guy and he's the SOB." In planning sessions with Coke men, Keough could be ruthless. When a manager complained of Pepsi's recent inroads, Keough snapped back, "You'll never spend cheaper money than stopping them in their tracks."

In the long run, Keough and Goizueta viewed the Pacific Rim—with two billion people, roughly 40 percent of the world's population—as the ultimate promised land for Coke. Keough's eyes glazed when he talked about Indonesia, a country that, he was quick to point out, sweated squarely on the equator and consisted primarily of

Muslims (median age: eighteen) who didn't touch alcohol. "Now you tell me," Keough beamed, "where else would heaven be for a soft drink?"

BRINGING GRITS TO FRANCE

A better prospect for the early nineties, however, lay in Western Europe, where Coca-Cola already predominated. By the end of 1992, the Company knew, the European Community (EC) planned to remove most of the economic barriers between the nations, effectively unifying a market whose population, one-third larger than the United States, was compressed into a relatively small, accessible area. While other U.S. companies worried about a "Fortress Europe" mentality, Coca-Cola already held the keys to the citadel.

Nonetheless, Keough and Goizueta were dissatisfied with European per capita, just eighty-one drinks a year. To focus on the area, the Company reorganized its three world divisions in the fall of 1988, carving out a fourth EC Group. The central troublemaker of the sector—geographically as well as culturally—was France, with its miserable per capita of thirty-one, despite Coke's presence there since 1920. The Company blamed longtime franchisee Pernod Ricard, too busy selling its Orangina to push Coke properly, and, after a protracted legal battle, Coke finally wrenched the concession away from Pernod early in 1989. In Dunkirk, construction was already under way on a gigantic canning plant to serve all of Europe, while Coke's third-largest concentrate factory opened at Signes. The Winter Olympics would arrive at Albertville in 1992, the same year that Euro Disney was slated to debut just outside Paris, and the Company wanted to prime the French palate. William Hoffman, they decided, was just the man for the job.

Although Hoffman spoke no French—he had never even visited France, having spent most of the eighties developing vigorous Atlanta supermarket promotions—he confidently spearheaded the French renaissance, initiating a program called Let's Think Big, exhorting his newly hired merchandisers to build Europe's largest displays. Hoffman launched his textbook Coca-Cola marketing blitz in Bordeaux, the heart of French wine country, where vending machines and massive soft drink displays were considered gauche. Hoffman and his gang quickly convinced skeptical hypermarket managers that their profits from Coke would spiral if they showcased a solid wall of reduced-price Coke. Beautiful women dressed in red-and-white outfits distributed coupons for free drinks, while Coke men slapped up thirty-five thousand logo stickers, along with 550 illuminated outdoor signs. By the spring of 1989, five hundred vending machines lined Bordeaux sidewalks, where a Company publication proclaimed them "an accepted and welcome part of the landscape."

The Company journalist had mistaken immobilized shock for acceptance, however. Hoffman exerted a bizarre fascination for the natives. "He's so *American!*" they exclaimed, not knowing whether to be charmed or horrified. Stunned by Coca-Cola's "Georgia Week," which included American football, a screening of *Gone with the Wind*, and imported grits, the local café owners watched helplessly as their young consumers abandoned the overpriced $2.50-per-drink Cokes served at their establishments in favor of the ninety-cent variety now available from the street-side vending machines. As the café operators mobilized for a boycott of Coke products, the Company hastily agreed to remove the offending Bordeaux vending machines. Elsewhere in France, however, the flood of coin-operated dispensers only increased. When a right-wing politician accused Coke of subverting French culture and luring youth away from wine, others responded by raising a glass of the bubbly American vintage, proclaiming it "our anti-fascist drink."

The American tactics eventually prevailed, even in France, where volume swelled by 23 percent in 1989.* Meanwhile, in Great Britain, the alliance with Cadbury Schweppes doubled sales in three years, with a huge new bottle/can plant at Wakefield in northern England to supply the increased demand. Throughout Europe, the same dynamic yielded a 10 percent annual volume growth. By the end of 1989, the EC Group contributed 29 percent of the Company's operating profits.

LAPPING UP THE SWEAT AND MUCOS

Unlike the French, the on-the-go Japanese loved vending machines—first introduced by Coke in the early sixties—which now supplied them with ice cream, eggs, beer, whiskey, pornography, toothbrushes, or dating services in addition to beverages, cold or hot—a necessary trait for dispensing Georgia Coffee, Coke's popular non-carbonated, sweetened coffee drink. Because of ferocious competition in the Japanese beverage market, five thousand different flavors vied at any one time. Of the thousand new drinks annually introduced to consumers, only 10 percent survived. To stay in contention, Coca-Cola offered a bewildering array of carbonated, fruit, and coffee beverages, averaging one new flavor per month. The vending manufacturers adapted by proffering up to thirty different choices. Out of the two million machines in Japan selling soft drinks, over seven hundred thousand dispensed Coca-Cola products.

As one Coca-Cola manager observed in 1987, "It's hard to overstate the significance of our business in Japan." That year, the island reaped more profits than any other country, including the United States. By the end of the decade, however, the crucial Japanese trade flashed warning signals. Coke's soft drink market share remained high at 84 percent, but per capita stalled and then slipped, as rumors about illness caused by the bubbly beverages rippled through the entire industry. Japanese health drinks with fiber, calcium, vitamins, and other nutrients gained market share, while carbonated sodas suffered.

Japanese marketers scoured dictionaries for English names, often with disgusting results by American standards. "If you feel your body and skin become dry," one ad suggested, "try to drink Pokka's Mucos please." An isotonic drink similar to Gatorade received the label Pocari Sweat. Coke responded with less nauseating-sounding drinks such as Aquarius (isotonic), FiBi (soluble fiber), and Mone (honey-lemon), but Coca-Cola's product sales still dwindled. Company marketers were frustrated even more when Regain, a non-carbonated caffeine-and-vitamin tonic billed as a pick-me-up, premiered in Japan. The Regain jingle, issued as a CD, hit the top of the pop charts.

---

* In 1991, Coke pulled William Hoffman out of France and back to the corporate womb in Atlanta. He had served his purpose by shaking up the French industry but was considered too abrasive for the long haul. French per capita continued to rise, however.

"Can you fight twenty-four hours, Japanese businessman?" the lyrics inquired, as lightning bolts sizzled from a dark-suited figure clutching a briefcase.

Regain effectively utilized an approach familiar to John Pemberton and Asa Candler, while Coke commercials depicted mindless Japanese teenagers imbibing on sunny summer afternoons—conveying the implicit message that Coke was a drink for indolent youth, not necessarily for industrious students or hardworking adults. Typical Japanese employees commuted up to four hours a day, labored long hours, and returned to cramped apartments in a gray city. They were likely to dismiss the commercials as irresponsible propaganda. Furthermore, Coca-Cola's American image, previously a boon in Japan, had transmuted into a questionable asset. The Japanese no longer looked up to America, with its ailing economy, crime, poverty, and AIDS epidemic. To the Japanese, American workers appeared lazy and self-satisfied, and the "I Feel Coke" commercials only reinforced that view. Despite Coke's frantic marketing efforts—splashing the logo on an entire train and wheeling a "MOBO-TRON" van complete with sixteen-foot video monitor through Tokyo's streets—sales remained flat. As a new decade loomed, frustrated researchers commissioned a sociological study to address the Japanese problem, while dispatching veteran ad man John Bergin to assess the situation.*

BACK TO THE BASICS

As Toyotas and Hondas cruised U.S. highways and Japanese corporations snapped up American real estate and banks, a backlash mentality escalated. Just days after the stock market crash in 1987, the Sony Corporation had outraged Japan-bashers by purchasing CBS Records, along with its cache of classic American song rights. Now, as 1989 drew to a close, Goizueta revealed that Coke was selling Columbia Pictures to Sony for $3.4 billion, by far the largest Japanese buyout of an American enterprise. Suddenly, *Mr. Smith Goes to Washington* belonged to the Nipponese. According to one commentator, the Japanese had "bought a piece of America's soul."

Goizueta ignored the uproar following the sale, which netted $1.2 billion for the Company's 49 percent of the stock. As far as the Coke CEO was concerned, the sale perfectly capped the Hollywood venture, which had been a financial bonanza but a public relations failure. He was still smarting over the David Puttnam affair, in which the outspoken new British head of Columbia, director of *Chariots of Fire* and *The Killing Fields* before coming to work for Coke, had alienated the American movie establishment, loudly complaining about star salaries and runaway budgets, without making a single smash movie. Consequently, Goizueta was delighted to unload Columbia for a healthy profit. As an immense money machine, the entertainment sector had boosted the bottom line while the Company put its beverage house in order. Now, Goizueta intended to pump the cash from the sale into the international business. Just

---

* As a result, the Company launched "The Moment That Refreshes" (*Sawayaka Ni Naru Hitotoki*), a variant on the old "Pause That Refreshes" theme. These ads were aimed at hardworking, stressed adults rather than indolent teens. Coke used the word "moment" because Japanese presumably would resent the idea of "pausing." Nevertheless, the Japanese market would suffer as Japan entered a prolonged period of economic decline in the 1990s.

as he had sought diversification when he took over the Company, he now refocused on soft drinks. "There's a perception in this country that you're better off if you're in two lousy businesses than if you're in one good one—that you're spreading your risk," he complained. He challenged anyone to "tell me something that gives me the return or the growth potential of soft drinks."

Investment guru Warren Buffett agreed with Goizueta. The Sage of Omaha, Buffett, chairman of Berkshire Hathaway Inc., was an old friend and neighbor of Don Keough, who had converted the financier to Cherry Coke back in 1986. Long known as a "white knight" for his long-term equity positions in companies without attempting takeovers, Buffett plunked down a billion dollars for a 6.3 percent stake in The Coca-Cola Company in 1989—an unusual move for the midwestern investor noted for picking undervalued stocks. With its price-to-earnings ratio hovering around thirty, Coke was not cheap, but Buffett shrewdly spotted its limitless potential. Not surprisingly, he joined the board of directors soon afterward.

MURRAY SCHWARTZ: SICK OF COKE?

As the corporate Coca-Cola juggernaut plunged ahead, Emmet Bondurant and Bill Schmidt awaited final decisions from Judge Murray Schwartz. After eight years of bitter litigation, the two trials, which took five months to hear, ended in January of 1989, generating thirteen thousand pages of transcripts. As both sides prepared for possible closing arguments, Schwartz developed another undisclosed illness and could not render judgment on the cases. Bondurant and Schmidt couldn't believe it, since the fifty-eight-year-old Schwartz knew every nuance and angle of the case, for which he had already issued twelve interim opinions. How could he abandon it now?

No one knew the exact nature of the judge's illness, though it was perhaps related to a long history of heart trouble. Nonetheless, rumors also circulated that he had suffered a nervous breakdown, and the Coke cases may have been a contributing factor. Schwartz had lived and breathed the bitter battle for nearly a decade, the theory went, and now that the decision loomed, he apparently couldn't face it.

The case was reassigned to Judge Joseph J. Farnan Jr., a Reagan appointee who signaled his hostility to both sides at the outset, commenting, "Counsel in this case couldn't agree on which door to take to the courtroom." As they prepared their arguments once again, both sides learned that Schwartz had miraculously recovered and climbed back into his judicial seat—but he would not resume the Coke cases. As the retrial commenced, Judge Farnan signaled his complete disdain for the proceedings by openly perusing the L.L. Bean catalog during testimony. Within a few years, the cases would end in a whimper, with The Coca-Cola Company assessed a dollar in damages to each bottler in the suits. The Schmidts sold their bottling company. Big Coke had prevailed.

REVISITING THE HILLTOP

Meanwhile, as the retrial bored Judge Farnan, Coca-Cola decided to reclaim its heritage along with the high ground in cola-ad battles, which had degenerated into a rather confusing star wars. That year, Coke and Diet Coke commercials had showcased twenty-seven different celebrities, along with thirty-one football players, while

Pepsi starred Billy Crystal, Robert Palmer, and Magic Johnson, among others. "I think there can be a real sense of confusion ultimately as to who stands for what," an outside creative director commented. It didn't help when Don Johnson crossed over from Pepsi to Diet Coke, or Ray Charles, a Georgia musician who had sung powerful Coca-Cola odes in the past and presided at New Coke's unveiling, extolled Diet Pepsi in "blind" taste tests. By the end of the eighties, advertising was expensive, imitative, and corporate, with the glorious days of innovation apparently receding into the past. Technically, the gorgeously filmed spots excelled, crammed with special effects, dancing, and music, but they were dead inside. The few genuinely moving commercials often harkened back to classic ads of another era.

In September of 1989, McCann-Erickson temporarily escaped the celebrity onslaught by remaking the 1971 commercial, "I'd Like to Teach the World to Sing." Scheduled to premier during the Super Bowl in January, this time the peaceful celebrants would share Cokes with their children, who would sing "Can't Beat the Real Thing" in counterpoint to their parents' more traditional tune. A detective hunt turned up only twenty-five of the two hundred original cast members, so actors from different countries filled in the balance. It was billed as a twenty-year anniversary, though that was actually two years away.

The four-day shoot did indeed cover the original Italian hillside, but fashioning commercials required more elaborate preparations than eighteen years before. "We had to wake the kids up at 4:30 a.m.," producer Scott Seltzer recalled, "to get there in time for wardrobe, breakfast, make-up, and trundling up the hill. We had tents, food service—it was like a small army on maneuvers." By 9:30 a.m., the hot, tired children were crying for their parents, and production assistants, makeup artists, and wardrobe specialists dropped everything to comfort them. "When I did it last time, it was only half a day. I mean, it was nothing," Linda Neary, the blonde who lip-synched the "Hilltop" introduction, wearily observed. As in the original commercial, it was not Neary's voice that actually sang the song, but Eve Graham, the soloist from the New Seekers. Even in the opening shot of "Reunion," when Neary told her daughter, "You know, it happened right here, twenty years ago," her voice was dubbed to give her an American accent.

A behind-the-scenes video revealed the laborious process behind the seemingly spontaneous final product, as the director drilled the children to enunciate properly, sounding painfully like a first-grade reading lesson: "feeee-ling . . . you . . . get . . . from . . . a . . . Co . . . Ca . . . Co . . . La." Nevertheless, when the children scampered into their parents' arms, the scene elicited a collective gasp, even from the hardened McCann crew. It had an even bigger impact on a forty-year-old American vacationing in Italy. Trudging up the opposite hillside to see what the commotion was, he heard the faint strains of a song from his youth: " . . . and furnish it with love, grow apple trees and honey bees. . . ." He couldn't believe it. Was he in the Twilight Zone? Just as he crested the top, the children dashed up the hill. Caught by the magical moment, the tourist burst into tears.

THE INESCAPABLE PRODUCT

What other product could call forth such strong, spontaneous emotions? None, according to repeated worldwide polls conducted by Landor Associates. "Coca-Cola is so powerful it's practically off the charts," one journalist marveled. Goizueta loved to cite the soft drink's impressive figures. The Company sold over 45 percent of all the world's carbonated soft drinks, more than double Pepsi's record. Coca-Cola stock had appreciated more than 735 percent during the eighties, creating some $30 billion in additional stockholder wealth and more than doubling the performance of the S&P 500 index. In 1989, Goizueta submitted a revised strategy statement, looking toward the millennium. The goal for the 1990s, he wrote, was to "expand our global business system, reaching increasing numbers of consumers who will enjoy our brands and products more and more often."

At the turn of the decade, the Company appeared poised for ten more years of extraordinary expansion. All over the world, Coca-Cola's devoted field force sought every possible niche. In the Amazonian swamps of Brazil, thirteen-year-old Shirley Batista da Silva peddled Coke from a battered canoe. Every day in the Philippines, Valentin Lachica, a proud seventy-three-year-old, refused to leave his stand until he sold fifty cases of Coke, one bottle at a time. In South Africa, where the Company had "disinvested," increasing numbers of lower-class blacks earned their living by hawking the soft drink from tiny outlets called "*spazas*." Around the world, Coca-Cola men— sometimes father/son teams—delivered their product to the most remote locations by burro, gondola, helicopter, and ski lift. The more remote the destination, the more consumers seemed to appreciate Coke. Residents of Ushuaia, Argentina, the world's southernmost city, drank an average of 420 servings per year.

With world momentum going Coke's way, it seemed only a matter of time before the drink was available in every country in the world. The Arab boycott steadily eroded, with Kuwait, Saudi Arabia, and the United Arab Emirates lifting the ban on Coke. In Latin America, rebounding economies followed the Mexican lead by open-ing up to free enterprise, loosening price controls, and finally permitting Coke's profits to match its volume. A gigantic new neon Spectacular lit up Moscow, opposite the huge McDonald's that would serve its first Russian hamburger in January.

One final 1989 event perfectly symbolized Coca-Cola's opportunity and impact. In November, before the world's astonished eyes, the Berlin Wall fell, and as it did Coca-Cola men filled the gap, handing out free drinks. Cars lined up for miles to receive cases as they drove through the West Berlin bottling plant. When a young East German soldier stationed on a watchtower yelled down from his lonely perch, a quick-witted Coca-Cola man tossed him a twelve-pack. Western civilization and its favorite fizzy beverage poured through crumbling walls. The East Germans had watched tantalizing Coke commercials on their TV sets for years; now they could sample the essence of capitalism.

"The Coca-Cola Company is in a stronger position today than it has ever been in its history," Roberto Goizueta observed, and no one could gainsay him. "Frankly," Don Keough added, "we have become the benchmark for companies with global aspirations." If Pemberton and Candler could have seen the worldwide spread of their bubbly pick-me-up, they might have been flabbergasted. On the other hand, Goizu-eta's monomaniacal vision would have seemed comfortingly familiar. "Our success," the Cuban wrote, unconsciously echoing a statement Harrison Jones made nearly seventy years before, "will largely depend on the degree to which we make it impos-sible for the consumer around the globe to escape Coca-Cola."

~ 21 ~

Global Fizz

Coke may have created the closest thing we know of to a perpetual motion machine.
—Financial analyst David Goldman, 1996

If you look in your kitchen sink, there's one spigot that has a C and another spigot that has an H. That spigot that has a C should be used for what God intended.
—Roberto C. Goizueta, CEO, The Coca-Cola Company

Entering the last decade of the twentieth century, the efficient Coca-Cola juggernaut prepared to flood the world, setting the stage for what Roberto Goizueta hoped would be a millennial celebration of unquestioned global dominance. During the penultimate decade of the 1980s, the Coke CEO had revamped and refocused the Company. Now, he saw with perfect clarity that the fall of the Berlin Wall signaled the crowning opportunity of his career. "Every day, every single one of the world's 5.6 billion people will get thirsty," he observed early in 1994. "Only in the last few years have world events allowed us true access to more than half of those people."

Late in 1989, Doug Ivester, the bright accountant who had invented the 49 percent solution that created Coca-Cola Enterprises and allowed Big Coke to invest in bottlers around the world, had been handed his first operational Coke role in Europe, a kind of testing ground for the up-and-coming executive. During the evening of January 8, 1990, Ivester and Heinz Wiezorek, the head of the Company's West German subsidiary, strolled through Alexanderplatz, the main square in East Berlin. Construction cranes towered over them, while newly energized citizens socialized. "We looked around us and said, 'Let's do it,'" Wiezorek recalled. "We decided to start selling Coke for East German marks." When Ivester talked it over with Goizueta, he warned the CEO that he wasn't sure how they would get paid. "I don't care," Goizueta said. "Just ship the product." The gamble paid off nine months later, when East and West Germany united, and the two currencies were given equal weight.

The move into East Germany, with its seventeen million new customers, exemplified Goizueta's new mantra that the soft drink behemoth had to be fast, focused, and flexible. "You need to shorten your reaction time by using your instincts and your experience," Goizueta emphasized. "We are relying more on our gut feelings." It also showed that the Company was determined to continue to strengthen its worldwide bottler system on a country-by-country basis, forming joint ventures with big, aggressive bottlers. In the early 1990s, for instance, Coca-Cola Amatil, the huge Australian bottler half owned by Big Coke, would move into Austria, Hungary, and Czechoslovakia, as well as Indonesia, Papua New Guinea, and New Zealand.

East Germans gulped Coca-Cola as though they had never had a decent soft drink before—mostly because they hadn't. The foamy, foul-smelling Hit Cola, the socialist beverage, sometimes contained bugs and other surprises. Everyone was delighted when Coca-Cola red replaced KGB red, as in Leipzig, where a huge Coke flag hung from the side of the town's once-dreaded secret police headquarters, while hundreds of people lined up at the city's first Coke kiosks. "I get at least 50 letters every day asking how to get Coca-Cola," an amazed East German Coke official told a reporter.

In February 1991, the Company upped the ante, promising to sink $450 million into East Germany alone, to upgrade outmoded government plants and transform 1,500 ex-Communists into devout Coca-Cola men and women. "Coca-Cola is a lucky break for Weimar," one city official observed of the new bottling plant there. "We'll get three to four hundred recession-proof jobs, a steady corporate taxpayer and a major purchaser of goods and services from area companies." Within two years of the fall of the Berlin Wall, sales soared from zero to 1.7 billion drinks. It was, as one industry analyst noted, "the soft drink equivalent of the Marshall Plan."

A GLOBAL BLITZKRIEG

Few marketing gurus were surprised by Coke's swift surge in East Germany, whose citizens had watched Western advertising on their televisions for years while yearning for consumer goods they couldn't get. Eastern Europe and Russia were another matter, however. There, Pepsi had long dominated. Determined to come from behind there, too, Goizueta and his board committed an even $1 billion, to be spent by mid-decade on what they called Project Jumpstart. Previously, Coke products were sold in small amounts for "countertrade," barter for shoddy products. Now, the Company invested directly in Poland and Romania. "Coca-Cola," said a senior Romanian official, "is the symbol of our new life. It brings jobs and color to our streets." Crowds gathered to cheer the arrival of the first Coca-Cola truck in Warsaw, reminiscent of the welcome given the liberating U.S. tanks of World War II. By the end of 1993, Coca-Cola had taken the lead from Pepsi in all of the former Eastern Bloc countries. In Albania, which had no regulatory code for foreign investment, Coke lawyers obligingly helped write laws to ease entry for the soft drink.

As the Soviet Union disintegrated, Coke formed a Ukrainian joint venture, as well as a partnership in Moscow to fund a syrup plant and two thousand kiosks throughout the city. Symbolically, in a kind of modern swords-into-plowshares, the round metal kiosks were produced by the same factory that had made Soviet missiles. The Company announced that it would build another huge bottling plant in St. Petersburg. Because of desperate economic conditions, Coke could hire overeducated new employees. One former physicist, now a soft drink salesman, gratefully pledged all of his energy towards growing the Coca-Cola worldwide business.

Undeterred by the 1989 massacre in Tiananmen Square, Coke continued to expand in China, establishing joint ventures with the Chinese government as well as Hong Kong's Swire Group and the Kerry Group, run by savvy Chinese businessman Robert Kuok. By 1993, there were thirteen bottling plants already in place near the more populous coast, and the Company had received approval to build ten new facilities in the interior, capping a $500 million investment there. "The government now sees Coca-Cola as a symbol of China's 'socialist market' economy," a Coke executive exulted.

The young revolutionaries who once faced tanks eagerly embraced Western culture, including Coca-Cola and disco dancing. They wanted to make money and spend it on consumer goods. In crowded Hong Kong, Swire built the world's tallest bottling plant, fifty-seven stories high, indicating its faith that, when Hong Kong joined China in 1997, nothing would deter the fizzy onslaught. Despite persistent rumors that the soft drink was laced with addictive drugs and caused impotency—familiar historical problems—its market grew swiftly, up 38 percent in 1993, bringing the annual Chinese per capita consumption to two Company drinks a year, and offering an enticing vision of potential future growth in a country with a billion people.

After a sixteen-year enforced absence because it refused to divulge its formula to Indian officials in 1977, Coca-Cola returned to India in late 1993, forming a strategic alliance with Parle Exports, the nation's largest soft drink company, and moving quickly to upgrade existing plants. Goizueta salivated over a virtually untapped market of 840 million people. As in China, the Company paid new entrepreneurs to wheel tricycle Coke carts down alleyways to bring the bubbly drink to new customers. "I used to drink Coke 20 years ago," one fifty-year-old Indian spectator recalled as he hugged a Coke official during the opening ceremonies for the first Coke bottling plant in India. "I will drink it again."

"Just as nature abhors a vacuum," observed one Coke executive in 1992, "so the Coca-Cola system abhors an untapped opportunity." Coke returned to any country where conditions looked a bit more stable. When the war in Afghanistan eased, the soft drink came back. When the repressive Marxist regime in Ethiopia was overthrown, Coca-Cola men turned up in Addis Ababa to do business with the victorious rebels, as they did with the old government. Soon afterwards, the soft drink was available in the newly created splinter nation of Eritrea. After a hiatus caused by civil wars, Coke reappeared in Angola and Sudan. As the U.S. trade embargo on Vietnam looked like it might be lifted, Coke formed a joint venture with a Saigon bottler, ready to jump back in.

Although the Arab boycott officially had ended, bottling rights in Saudi Arabia bogged down in a bitter interfamilial lawsuit, and re-entry into the market there was temporarily delayed, just as Saddam Hussein invaded Kuwait and Operation Desert Storm commenced. Frustrated by Pepsi's Saudi Arabian inside track, Coke dispatched refrigerated semitrailers across the desert from Al-Ain in the United Arab Emirates with twenty thousand cases of free drinks, accompanied by a military escort. Coke hired photographers to snap candid pictures of soldiers enjoying the all-American drink and sponsored USO programs.

Meanwhile, with falling trade barriers and government deregulation to permit higher prices and larger package sizes, Latin America opened wide for more Coke. In 1993, the average Mexican drank 306 servings of a Coca-Cola Company soft drink—3 more per year than Americans. The same year, Chile's consumption rate climbed 16 percent. As the Sandinista regime ended in Nicaragua, Coke moved in again. In Guatemala, there was relative peace at the troubled bottling plant whose union employees had been killed by death squads a decade before, though several Coca-Cola union workers involved in political theater were threatened, beaten, and murdered.

In South Africa, in February 1990, Nelson Mandela, seventy-one, was finally released from his twenty-seven-year incarceration, emerging a heroic symbol of freedom and justice. While on his triumphant 1990 American tour, Mandela snubbed Coke's offers of help, raising the hopes of Tandi Gcabashe and her boycott. "They [Coke representatives] are not the kind of people we do business with," an African National Congress member said. "They are making money off us. Apartheid is good business for Coke." South African black activist Desmond Tutu and Coretta Scott King, widow of the slain civil rights leader, praised Coke, but to no avail. The soft drink was banned from hotels at which Mandela stayed, and he pointedly drank Pepsi during his Atlanta visit.

Soon, however, Carl Ware, Coke's persuasive black executive, befriended Mandela, who pressured the African National Congress to call off the boycott. Behind the scenes, Coca-Cola worked feverishly to help ease what they perceived to be the inevitable end of apartheid.* Ware assured Mandela of the Company's support in a new black-run regime. When Mandela again arrived in Atlanta three years later, in July 1993, he stepped off of a Coca-Cola corporate jet along with Carl Ware, and Coke squired Mandela about the city and hosted a luncheon for him at the Ritz-Carlton. When Mandela received an honorary degree from Clark Atlanta University, Ware— the head of the college's board of trustees—gave a raised fist salute as the choir sang "Lord Bless Africa." At a fund-raising dinner, Mandela explicitly acknowledged his debt to the Coke executive: "Mr. Carl Ware has shown a quiet commitment to the problems that bear on our country," he said. "He has quietly helped the ANC stand on its feet. I want to acknowledge publicly that he has done this."

Despite the global recession of the early 1990s, the soft drink giant grew inexorably around the globe. There were always trouble spots somewhere, of course—Japan and Europe had cold, rainy summers in 1993—but all the factors for continued expansion were in place. It had taken over a hundred years for the Company to make $1 billion in annual net income in 1988, but it took only another five years to break $2 billion a year in 1993.

In 1990, after its shares gained 20 percent (while the S&P 500 declined 7 percent), Coke stock split two-for-one, then jumped an astonishing 73 percent in 1991, allowing *another* stock split early in 1992. For the banner year of 1991, Roberto Goizueta was awarded over $86 million in compensation, much of it quietly buried in a proxy statement in the form of a one-time bonus of one million shares of Coke stock. With excessive salaries of American CEOs under attack during the recession, Goizueta's

---

* One of Nelson Mandela's oldest friends and supporters was Richard Maponya, an elder statesman of the anti-apartheid movement and one of the wealthiest black men in South Africa. Maponya owned a Coca-Cola bottling plant and other businesses. Undoubtedly, Maponya helped persuade Mandela to befriend Coca-Cola. "I think Nelson is coming to see that what is holding us back now is not apartheid but money," Maponya observed.

reward made front-page national headlines, but admirers retorted that he had earned it—if the stock had not gone up, he wouldn't get so much money.

As the recession deepened, however, Coke shares languished for the next two years, even though the soft drink company's steady global growth continued. True, it slowed to a total case volume rise of only 3 percent in 1992, but in 1993 it climbed 5 percent. The thin-skinned Goizueta grew increasingly irritated, eager to convince skeptics that Coca-Cola's fundamentals were sound and that the stock should resume its extraordinary growth.

TROUBLE ON THE HOME FRONT

Although Coke's worldwide momentum appeared unstoppable, the flagship U.S. market was flashing warning lights—one of the primary reasons for Wall Street's nervousness. Seeking to capitalize on Coke Classic's historic image, in 1990 the Company opened a glitzy $15 million museum in downtown Atlanta, followed by a store to sell products emblazoned with the Coke logo on New York's Fifth Avenue. A gigantic new Spectacular in Times Square, lit just before midnight on New Year's Eve, December 31, 1991, featured a forty-two-foot Coke bottle that, aided by sixty miles of fiber-optic tubing, a mile of neon, and thirteen thousand incandescent light bulbs, uncapped itself, offered a straw to a huge invisible mouth—perhaps God's?—and emptied itself in each cycle.

Despite such hoopla over the core brand, however, in 1991 and 1992 the Company's domestic case volume sales grew barely 2 percent. Refusing to admit defeat, Goizueta repositioned the moribund New Coke—its unfortunate nickname aging quickly—as Coke II. Atlanta consumers suggested tongue-in-cheek slogans such as: "Coke II: The Embarrassment Continues." The renamed drink again failed to garner significant sales. A Coke "MagiCan" promotion garnered piles of negative publicity when, instead of cash popping out of "prize" cans, a foul-smelling and tasting liquid—sealed into the bottom to add weight—leaked out and hit some consumer tongues. The $100,000 promotion was scrapped.

On top of such temporary glitches, beverage analysts feared that the market for old-fashioned colas may have reached saturation point. After more than a century of deluging North America with Coke and Pepsi ads, could the marketers hope to squeeze out any more substantial gains? The diet segment, which had grown at 20 percent annual rates during the 1980s, had now slowed to 3 percent yearly growth as consumers switched from obsession with weight to health. Upstart "New Age" drinks such as Snapple and Clearly Canadian were stealing market share. Some experts felt that a decade of Coke/Pepsi domestic price wars may have eroded brand loyalty, turning the drinks from image-rich elixirs into mere commodities bought on sale. Goizueta sniffed at such suggestions, pointing out that Mello Yello—Coke's minor-league response to Pepsi's popular Mountain Dew—sold more than Snapple.

Meanwhile, private-label colas, spurred by aggressive Dave Nichol, the CEO of Canada's Cott, were making inroads into brand-name sales. Cott's high-quality private-label beverage sold as President's Choice Cola in Canada and as Sam's American Choice in U.S. Walmarts. In Great Britain, Cott supplied supermarket giant Sainsbury's cola, as well as entrepreneur Richard Branson's upstart Virgin Cola. "Coke and Pepsi are passé," Nichol boasted. "Cott," Goizueta snarled in response. "We sell more Coke in Nigeria than they sell worldwide." In blind taste tests, *Consumer Reports* noted in an August 1991 cover story, private colas were indistinguishable from Coke or Pepsi. In a funny commercial, RC Cola depicted Coke and Pepsi men baiting fishhooks with their respective soda cans, then pulling humans from the ocean, a can bulging their cheeks. "For years you've been fed the same old line—that there are only two great-tasting colas to choose from," intoned the narrator. "Hey, you don't have to swallow that."

COKE CALLING HOLLYWOOD

But the real problem, as Roberto Goizueta saw it, was his main brand's lackluster advertising. The Interpublic Group, which included McCann-Erickson, Lintas, and others, had produced all Coke product ads for decades. Since the 1985 New Coke debacle, however, the ads had lost fizz and focus. In the fall of 1990, Goizueta complained that "Can't Beat the Real Thing" wasn't working. A Coke marketing executive noted that Pepsi's spots were "hipper" than Coke's. "Then go to a hipper source," Goizueta snapped.

Soon afterwards, Ike Herbert, Coke's veteran head of marketing, called Peter Sealey, who had fallen in love with Hollywood and the relaxed California lifestyle when he oversaw Columbia Pictures. Sealey had left Coke in 1989, staying in California when the Company sold Columbia to Sony. "I had a beautiful place on the ocean, a hot tub, Chardonnay. I was blissing out," Sealey recalled later. "I totally believed I would never return to Coke." But now Coke wanted him back, along with his Hollywood connections. Sealey agreed, though he had to move back to Atlanta and shave his beard because of Goizueta's Castro phobia.

Sealey took over as Coke's first director of global marketing just as Coke stumbled again. During the Superbowl in January 1991, Coke pulled its planned advertising to run a serious rolling text, explaining that frivolous ads were inappropriate because the Gulf War had just begun. Football fans were simply annoyed. One critic called the Coke ads "cheap, phony, patronizing and holier-than-thou." Meanwhile, Diet Pepsi introduced Ray Charles singing, "You've got the right one, baby, uh-huh," surrounded by a chorus of slinky young black women. The Pepsi spots were enormously popular—a particularly bitter blow, since Georgia-born Ray Charles had once sung for Coke. People in offices and schools across the country began to say "uh-huh"—except in the corporate halls of Coca-Cola, where the expression was forbidden.

Pepsi gleefully mocked Coca-Cola's stodgy image. In one ad, after taking a sip of Coke, rap singer M. C. Hammer burst into a smarmy rendition of "Feelings." In another spot, when Pepsi accidentally arrived at a nursing home, the elderly imbibers boogied about and said "Awesome," while frat house boys who received Coke played a sedate game of bingo.

In this tense atmosphere, something had to give. Don Keough, who would retire in two years, didn't want his departing legacy to be a lame campaign. In the summer of 1991, he flew to Manhattan to plead with McCann-Erickson executives to come up with something spectacular. "If you don't pull this off, folks, you are staring at a loss of the business," he told them. In the meantime, Sealey was talking to super-agent

Mike Ovitz, the founder of Creative Artists Agency (CAA), who was eager to do a deal with Coke. In the fall of 1991, Ovitz flew to Atlanta to make his pitch to Goizueta. "Here we've got the greatest star in the world, Coca-Cola," Ovitz told the CEO. "It's instantly recognizable, the most bankable star in the world." Ovitz proposed that CAA use Hollywood actors, directors, and writers to create innovative Coke commercials.

The Coke executives weren't yet willing to go quite that far. Instead, they wanted CAA to work with McCann to create a sure-fire new theme for Coca-Cola. The news of the Coke/CAA partnership terrified the ad industry late in 1991, though no one knew exactly what CAA would do for Coke. Ovitz babbled about bringing "macro-vision" to the task, while Peter Sealey said that CAA's job was "to be in tune with culture. They know what is going to pop a year from now."

With the CAA threat looming, the soft drink ad blitz continued. In a frantic effort to counter the Diet Pepsi "Uh-huh" campaign, Interpublic's Lintas agency went one step further in the celebrity ad wars by exhuming Humphrey Bogart, James Cagney, and Louis Armstrong to appear in Diet Coke commercials. Not only were the dead stars colorized, but they interacted with live actors, while Elton John sang a twist on the long-standing "Just for the Taste of It" theme. Ad critic Bob Garfield was not impressed. "Coca-Cola is obsessed with Pepsi-Cola's youthful image in the U.S., and has been trying desperately, pathetically to approximate it," he wrote. "It speaks to Coca-Cola's notion of the pop-culture vanguard that its lead presenter, in order to seem contemporary, must be surrounded by dead people."

When the Super Bowl rolled around in January 1992, Coke shocked the ad world by opting out of the $1.7 million-per-minute commercials. Instead, Peter Sealey or-chestrated "Helios," the first truly global ad for Coca-Cola, in which McCann-Erickson demonstrated its worldwide capacity. Airing on the same day as the Super Bowl, happy Coke drinkers greeted viewers in twelve languages. The ad, which ran at 6 a.m. Eastern Standard Time on CNN, appeared simultaneously in some 130 countries to kick off the Company's 1992 Olympic coverage.

Meanwhile, Pepsi's much-hyped Super Bowl ads were an inexplicable departure from the venerable "Choice of a New Generation" theme, switching to a blander "Gotta Have It" slogan that was intended to appeal to *all* generations. Instead, as the ever-acerbic Bob Garfield noted, "out of nowhere, Pepsi has decided to be like Coke: to embrace everybody, to be all colas to all people." He objected to the new slogan's "licentious overtones," concluding that "it's the wrong message, to the wrong audi-ence, at the wrong time."

With the traditional feel-good global campaign under way, it appeared that McCann may have found its footing again, at least internationally. But behind the scenes, the infighting continued. From the beginning, the enforced relationship between McCann and CAA was plagued by "suspicion, jealousy, resentment, and one-upmanship," as Goizueta biographer David Greising observed. McCann had recently recruited Gor-don Bowen from Ogilvy & Mather to save the domestic Coke account. But when Bowen suggested "A Spark of Life" as the new theme, Shelly Hochron of CAA blasted him. "That is the worst advertising idea I've ever heard of," she said, and Peter Sealey agreed with her.

Things only got worse for Bowen at a crucial July 1992 presentation in Atlanta. The CAA storyboards weren't particularly impressive, featuring a dog digging up a Coke bottle. Bowen stuck to his "Spark of Life." But veteran McCann ad man John Bergin, an old friend of Keough's, stole the show with a presentation that took Bowen completely by surprise. They were all missing the essence, the majesty of Coca-Cola, Bergin said. "Let the brand be itself." In his talk, he built up to the lyrics of a song he had written: "Always there, Always new, Always real, Always you—Always Coca-Cola." In secret, Bergin had even created a "steal-a-matic," working over an old McDonald's commercial showing a Taiwanese little league team visiting the United States, which he now showed. Bergin staged a coup. Sealey ordered both CAA and McCann to create their own ads, using the "Always" theme.

On October 15, 1992, both teams came to Atlanta for the final shoot-out. This time, Roberto Goizueta would join Don Keough to view sample ads. It was clear from the outset that CAA would win. Sealey had flown to California in order to escort the CAA team back to Atlanta. Ovitz tantalized Goizueta by promising that famous directors like Francis Ford Coppola and Rob Reiner would create Coke spots. Then they rolled the sample CAA spots. As Bergin watched, he was dismayed by their uneven quality and scattershot approach. There was the dog digging up the Coke bottle. In another one, space men identified an alien by asking him trivia questions about Coke. The only appealing ad, Bergin thought, was one in which computer-animated polar bears admired the northern lights and drank Coke.

Bergin was even more dismayed by the reaction of the Coca-Cola executives. Already programmed to like the CAA efforts, they roared with laughter, nudged one another appreciatively, and acted "absolutely giddy," as another McCann man recalled later. Keough bounced happily to the lilting "Always Coca-Cola" tagline sung at the end of each spot. Bergin scribbled a note and passed it to a colleague: "We are dead." CAA had co-opted Bergin's two-word theme, but there was nothing left of his lyrics or core Coke concepts. When the new Coke ads debuted in February 1993, McCann made only two, while CAA produced twenty-four in what Sealey dubbed a "new paradigm" approach to advertising.

The ads signaled the end of the traditional "one sight, one sound, one sell" approach. Instead, each of the disparate spots was supposed to represent a "rifle-shot" directed at one particular market segment. To some critics, they simply appeared uncoordinated. At least, however, they represented new energy and change. Though he called the two dozen commercials "flawed," critic Bob Garfield was basically impressed, calling them "the best Coca-Cola advertising campaign in at least a decade." He loved the polar bears watching the aurora borealis, calling the spots "sweet, unexpected, visually arresting and very nearly majestic." The other efforts were all over the place, but they were at least united by the brilliant new "Always Coca-Cola" theme, along with the red Coca-Cola disk, resurrected from the 1950s.

Most members of the traditional advertising community were underwhelmed by the CAA efforts. "Coke is willing to try anything in its effort to stumble across what made it great," sniffed one ad man. The much-vaunted commercials made by famous movie directors weren't particularly impressive. Indeed, Francis Ford Coppola's was scrapped. "Directing commercials is a whole different world than directing movies," one veteran ad man noted. "You have to think a lot faster on your feet and improvise a lot more." Another advertising executive called the CAA efforts "a creative gang bang with no strategic centrality and not enough gate-keeping to keep the good stuff away from the bad stuff."

Peter Sealey didn't care what the critics said. He was ebullient, pointing out that the twenty-four CAA ads cost less than the seven elaborate commercials McCann made the year before. At the press launch for the commercials, he watched the audience stir and murmur, not sure what to think until the polar bear ad came on. "From then on," he recalled, "it was a love fest. This was an audience on a ride." It appeared that Sealey's California psychobabble would work in Atlanta. "God, you're ringing all the emotional bells there," he burbled about a new ad. "You're talking social facilitation, self-actualization." Years later, he observed, "I have never been more happy in my life than I was in early 1993." Just as he seemed to be on top of the Coca-Cola world, however, Sealey was about to be dethroned.

THE RETURN OF THE AYA-COLA

Although he didn't know it, Sealey's fate was sealed the day Don Keough retired in April 1993. Keough, whom one long-time admirer described as "the heart and soul and probably most of the vascular system of Coca-Cola," would be sorely missed. A master communicator and motivator, Keough could fire up the bottlers, wax poetic about his favorite soft drink, or turn tough task-master when needed. Instead of replacing him, CEO Roberto Goizueta allowed people to speculate whether Doug Ivester or John Hunter would eventually succeed him. Ivester, who had shone in his brief stint in Europe, came back to head the North American Coca-Cola business in July 1990, while gruff Australian John Hunter was made head of international operations.

Most insiders bet on the aggressive Ivester, who, at forty-four, was ten years younger than Hunter. In addition, Goizueta clearly favored him, regarding him as a kind of junior version of himself. Both men were detail oriented, demanding of themselves and others, and came from the technical rather than marketing side of the business. In order to complete his grooming for the top Coke position, for more than a year Ivester met on Saturday mornings with Sergio Zyman—the *enfant terrible* widely perceived as the "fall guy" for New Coke—for lessons in marketing theory. During these sessions, Zyman took the opportunity to criticize Sealey's advertising and marketing programs. Impressed with his tutor's acumen, Ivester briefly tried to get Zyman and Bowen to come up with alternative advertising to CAA.

Now that Ivester was the de facto number two man in the Company, he convinced Goizueta that Sealey was too slow and cautious. Worse, Sealey had failed to rejuvenate Diet Coke advertising or sales. Abandoning the back-from-the-dead colorized-celebrity approach and the ten-year-old "Just for the Taste of It," in January 1993 he had approved a new slogan, "Taste It All," with frenetic lifestyle spots featuring active consumers of all ages. The ads misfired, in part because the product wasn't emphasized enough. "I saw Diet Coke on the screen for maybe one second," a bottler groused. At the end of May, Coke cut Diet Coke's ad budget to the bone, then announced in mid-July that the campaign would be modified or scrapped.

A week later, Ivester marched into Sealey's office at 3 p.m. and told him, "This just isn't working out." Afterward, Coke's personnel director told a stunned Sealey, "You're going to be radioactive now. You'd better leave quickly." Sealey cleaned out his desk. In public, however, Ivester praised Sealey for "taking our advertising to a new level of excellence." The next business day, Sergio Zyman arrived to take his place. Perhaps with some relief, Sealey moved back to California.

The resurrection of Sergio Zyman caused a shudder to run through Coca-Cola and Madison Avenue offices. Known as the "Aya-Cola," the mercurial, arrogant Zyman had antagonized many with whom he had worked back in the 1980s. "Why him?" one secretary asked, bursting into tears. "They used to say they needed one office for Zyman and one for his ego," a long-time Coke watcher said. "I have no desire to work for or with Sergio Zyman ever again," a former Coke brand manager stated bluntly. "Sergio was very much a 'for me' or 'against me' sort of leader. There was no middle ground. He was not subject to logic or numbers or reason." Goizueta defended his new marketing guru, explaining that time had mellowed him. He apparently hadn't changed all that much, however, since Ivester and Goizueta later passed out T-shirts proclaiming "GUTS—Get Used To Sergio."

COKE GOES NEW AGE

Zyman's immediate mission was to create hip products to compete with New Age challengers like Snapple and Clearly Canadian and to meet the private-label cola challenge. Until then, Coke had mounted feeble efforts to reposition Fresca and to introduce Nordic Mist, a Clearly Canadian rip-off, but neither had been given much marketing muscle. In January 1993, Roberto Goizueta called his two top lieutenants, Doug Ivester and John Hunter, into his office to announce a new initiative. Coke wouldn't just sit back and let these products nibble away at market share. Instead, he planned to introduce a flurry of new products, developed and launched in a hurry. The Company already did it in Japan, where new products were continually surfacing, selling, and disappearing. Why not in the United States? "I want it all," Goizueta said. "I don't want them [competitive New Age drinks] to have even these niche products." Nor did it matter, the CEO said, whether they all survived. He envisioned "new products going in, making money, and then you take them out."

It was easy to see why Goizueta was alarmed. In 1984, colas had accounted for nearly 64 percent of the U.S. non-alcoholic beverage market. By 1993, colas slipped below 59 percent, while alternative drinks had grabbed 10 percent of the market. Even before Sealey's ouster, Goizueta hired Sergio Zyman to spearhead the swift creation of Tab Clear, Coke's answer to Crystal Pepsi, a colorless cola intended to appeal to the New Age crowd.* While Zyman created the ad campaign in England, Sealey had remained unconcerned. "I thought it was a stupid product," he recalled later. "I wanted no responsibility for it." The introductory commercial, cast as a faux news program using a real CNN anchor, brought a flood of complaints from viewers who felt it was deceptive. Neither Tab Clear nor Crystal Pepsi dented the market, and they were withdrawn a year later.

---

* While Pepsi could introduce a clear version of its flagship cola without any flack, Coca-Cola knew better than to mess around with a colorless Coke, which would have caused an uproar. Hence, Goizueta opted for Tab Clear, altering the lowly old diet drink.

Goizueta and Ivester didn't care. They wanted brash new products, they wanted them quickly, and they agreed on the man who could deliver them—Sergio Zyman. When he took over as global marketing director in July 1993, Zyman arrived like a whirlwind. Goizueta also gave Zyman a bigger ad budget to boost Coca-Cola Classic, Diet Coke, and its other brands. He was determined to squash the upstart private-label colas in the wake of April 2, 1993, the day Philip Morris had slashed its cigarette prices to halt inroads from generic cigarettes. That day, which came to be known as "Marlboro Friday," supposedly signaled the death knell of brand-name dominance, according to many doomsayers. Goizueta protested angrily when Coke stock took a hit, complaining of "irrational market behavior" and claiming, "We are getting a bum rap."

Goizueta was even more incensed in January 1994, when *Barron's* quoted mutual fund guru John Neff's negative comments on Coke. Neff advised shorting the Company's stock. He called it "the Philip Morris of this year" and observed that Coke managers "tout their stock almost outrageously." Goizueta was incredibly frustrated. Despite a healthy 5 percent worldwide case volume growth in 1993, Coke stock had advanced only $4.50 per share in the last two years, not even breaking $45 as 1994 arrived. Goizueta gave orders on all fronts to move aggressively to increase market share in every conceivable way.

Zyman immediately initiated work on two new drinks, to be called Fruitopia and OK Soda, and stepped up promotions for the newly introduced PowerAde, Coke's counter to Gatorade, the dominant isotonic beverage. In March 1994, Zyman launched non-carbonated Fruitopia in eight fruit flavors with New Age names—Citrus Consciousness, Grape Beyond, Cranberry Lemonade Vision, Lemonade Love & Hope, Pink Lemonade Euphoria, Raspberry Psychic Lemonade, Strawberry Passion Awareness, and—perhaps labeling the reaction of many consumers who thought the names were overly cute—Total Fruit Integration. The bottles were covered with psychedelic, funky icons depicting body, mind, and planet, and offered aphorisms suitable for Fruitopian Life, such as "If you can't judge a fruit by the color of its skin, how can you judge a person that way?" Coca-Cola announced that Fruitopia would go national immediately, supported by a $30 million marketing budget, with plans to go international soon afterwards. Zyman boasted that it was "the first truly global launching of an alternative product."

The quick launch of Fruitopia, without local test marketing, startled beverage veterans, but Zyman claimed that he had invented Presearch, "the study of assumptions and hypotheses developed from current worldwide market information." He was only following the dictates and desires of the marketplace. Consumers, he said, were the real directors of marketing. And what did they order? "We found that consumers want the yin of the new mixed with the yang of the traditional," Zyman explained. Some commentators were not impressed with the Fruitopia strategy, which one called "mind-bogglingly cheesy," asking, "What's the next Fruitopia flavor going to be, Coke? Putrid Peach Paranoia?" There was a chance, he granted, that the Company would succeed. "They've got the ad bucks, the distribution, and probably the same view of 'consumer democracy' as that held by many a prominent politician—that is that the American public is capable of buying anything if you ram it down their throats hard enough."

Though Zyman asserted that Fruitopia would compete with "all alternative beverages," it was clearly positioned to counter Snapple. Even its wide-mouth embossed glass bottles imitated Snapple. Aside from its ultrahip retro-sixties image, however, the Fruitopia line seemed an odd choice. Snapple's biggest sellers were teas, and Fruitopia didn't offer any tea products. Those were left to a new partnership Coke had formed with Nestle, established in Tampa, Florida. In addition Fruitopia's shelf-stable flavors had to be "hot-filled," which meant expensive bottler line alterations. "Bottlers hate this stuff," observed one industry analyst. Zyman merely shrugged. "We will be launching more and more new brands," he said. "We're going to hit home runs, then we're also going to have to hit some profitable singles and even endure some sacrifice bunts."

The month after Fruitopia's debut, Coke introduced another new product. While "Coca-Cola" was the second best-known word on earth, "OK" was the first, so Zyman wanted to co-opt it, too. A typically edgy Zyman enterprise, OK Soda was a brash effort, utterly uncharacteristic of anything The Coca-Cola Company had ever done. Intended to appeal to the cynical, disenfranchised twelve-to-twenty-five-year-old MTV crowd, OK Soda's can was the antithesis of Coca-Cola's bright, upbeat image. Instead, the cans featured the black, grey, and white, bleak postmodern face of a young man who looked utterly blank, with a square saying "OK" slapped part-way over his forehead. The can had no discernible front or back. The flavor, mildly carbonated, was similar to the old "suicide" drink, a mixture of every flavor available at the soda fountain, with a touch of spicy orange. Zyman predicted that OK Soda would be one of his home runs, eventually snaring $1 billion dollars of the market and grabbing 4 percent of the entire U.S. soft drink share.

That seemed an odd prediction for a drink whose bland motto was "Things are going to be OK." The drink was deliberately positioned to be blasé. It wasn't exciting, delicious, or sexy. It was just OK. Nonetheless, beverage analyst Tom Pirko thought it might succeed by appealing directly to seen-it-all teenagers. National Public Radio host Noah Adams was skeptical. "Wouldn't you, if you were 19 years old, . . . feel a bit manipulated that they were coming after you so blatantly?" No. The only problem, Pirko observed, might be that "they're already sort of already truly wasted. I mean, their lethargy probably can't be penetrated by any commercial message." Thus, even though OK was designed to appeal to "their concerns and their angst and their anxiety," it might not be enough.

Teenagers weren't quite as disaffected or stupid as Zyman and Pirko thought. "The better you understand something, the more OK it turns out to be," one can proclaimed. Teenagers surveyed by the Atlanta newspaper simply found it confusing. None of the teens liked the taste. The most positive comment one could summon was: "It's better than water." They didn't like the name, either, which made it sound as if the soda wasn't worth drinking. Consumers were supposed to call 1–800-I-FEEL-OK to report "coincidences" of OKness. Though millions of kids did call, just to see what happened, the calls didn't substantially increase sales. A little more than a year later, OK Soda was quietly pulled from the market.

Supported by a massive ad campaign, Fruitopia did somewhat better than OK Soda, but even with new flavors—Tangerine Wavelength, Apple Raspberry Embrace, and Tropical Consideration—it never really contributed to Coke's bottom line. When Coke decided to imitate Ken Kesey and send psychedelically painted "Magic Buses" across the country to promote Fruitopia, a twenty-year-old sniffed. "It's sort of like they were really looking too hard for something to sell us," she said. "Them pitching it as an out-of-body, out-of-mind experience seems kind of trite to me." The Coke-Nestle partnership didn't work well, either. In 1994, the two companies closed the corporate office in Tampa but agreed to continue joint beverage ventures.

BOOSTING THE CORE BRANDS

While Sergio Zyman was chasing New Age chimeras, he also tried to recharge the Company's major brands—Coca-Cola, Diet Coke, and Sprite. Here, his efforts were apparently more successful. Zyman continued to use CAA as the creator of many ads, including "Hypnosis," which played on the old fears of subliminal messages, with the announcer intoning: "You are getting thirsty, very thirsty. . . . Disregard all other soft drink advertising and drink only Coca-Cola." Others featured the popular polar bears flying off a ski jump and sliding bare-backed down a luge run, to promote Coke's sponsorship of the 1994 Lillehammer Winter Olympics. Critic Bob Garfield, usually a hard sell, loved the new ads, hailing them as superior to Coke's previous efforts of the last thirty years. Since most of them had been under development when Sealey left, however, Zyman couldn't legitimately take much credit.

In fact, Zyman had considered dumping CAA entirely, but Mike Ovitz intervened with Goizueta, who loved the polar bears. Nonetheless, Zyman began to farm out work to other boutique agencies such as Fallon McElligott, Wieden+Kennedy, and Bartle Bogle Hegarty. Eventually, he would hire some twenty-five different agencies to do ads for various company beverages. Zyman, who enjoyed the exercise of power, played one agency off against another. He also hired his own marketing people—most of them without soft drink experience—and placed them around the world, reporting directly to him. "It's very exciting to have all these creative agencies around," one anonymous ad man observed, "but holding them to the same brand values can prove almost impossible." Another critic called the Coke approach "profoundly flawed."

Flawed it may have been, but 1994 produced positive results for Coca-Cola Classic, whose sales drove an impressive 7 percent annual increase in case unit volume in the United States. The increased sales probably had less to do with advertising than with the return of the "contour" bottle in a plastic container with a fatter waist than the old hobbleskirt bottle. Chemist, engineer, and marketer Ray Morgan, who had joined Coke in 1969 right out of college, had already proven that proprietary packaging could make a huge difference—first with Fresca, then with the dimpled green Sprite bottle. In 1990, when Doug Ivester took over the North American sector, Morgan pitched him with the idea of a twenty-ounce contour bottle for Coca-Cola Classic. Ivester enthusiastically approved the project. In March 1994, when the bottles hit Chicago test markets, they outperformed anyone's wildest expectations, boosting sales by 224 percent in a matter of weeks. By the end of the year, the contour bottle was available across three-quarters of the United States, and it went international the following year. Even though Zyman had little to do with the contour bottle, he called it "the best-known package in the world, with the possible exception of the egg."

Zyman could, however, take more credit for the resurgence of Sprite, which had traditionally been sold for its intrinsic qualities as a bubbly lemon-lime drink like 7-Up. Zyman repositioned Sprite as a youth drink with an attitude. While his "anti-hype" approach had flopped with OK Soda, it worked for Sprite. "Image Is Nothing," ads proclaimed. "Thirst Is Everything. Obey Your Thirst." Funky ads showed camels sipping Sprite, and the Company linked the drink to its NBA sponsorship.

Diet Coke remained a problem child, however. Zyman dumped Lintas, the old agency, in favor of Lowe and Partners, which debuted new ads in 1994 with the bland slogan, "This Is Refreshment." Most of the new Diet Coke spots were aimed at "liberated" women, some of whom simply seemed angry and self-absorbed. In one ad, a young woman threw all of her boyfriend's belongings at him, including his cowboy hat, which she stomped on. Then she swigged her Diet Coke. In another spot, the camera panned over a trail of shed clothing, down to the underwear, but instead of leading to a bedroom scene, it ended with a woman enjoying a solitary hot bath with her Diet Coke. While the spots had plenty of attitude, they apparently didn't sell many soft drinks.

The only successful ad relied on good old-fashioned sexism, although of the reverse variety. Women office workers gathered at the window to ogle a sweaty construction worker, a hunk who stripped off his shirt, downed his Diet Coke and smiled at them, as Etta James sang, "I Just Wanna Make Love to You." "They drink in his every ripple," one critic wrote. "When it's over, you almost feel the need for a cigarette ad." The hunk, thirty-three-year-old model Lucky Vanous, quickly became a celebrity, appearing in *People* magazine, doing the talk circuit, and appearing on TV shows. A Lucky Vanous calendar and workout video appeared. Taking advantage of their newly created star, Coke sponsored a radio contest in which thirty women won a lunch with Lucky Vanous by writing the best "Diet Coke fantasy." When he showed up in Atlanta to lunch with the two winners there, Vanous attracted a crowd of three hundred drooling women. Even more converged on him at the New York City lunch. "I mean, look at that!" one woman swooned. "With a body like that, a hunk like that. . . . He's making me hot." Apparently a guileless if not terribly brainy man, Vanous told an interviewer that he didn't indulge in soft drinks. "But if I were to drink one," he added, "I'd drink a Diet Coke."

Despite the hunk phenomenon and other innovative commercials (in one spot, a swimming elephant stole the soft drink from a raft, paying for it with a few peanuts), Diet Coke sales stagnated, along with the rest of the diet drink segment. The baby boomers were no longer quite so obsessed with their weight, it appeared. During the 1980s, Diet Coke had surged to claim a 10 percent share of the total U.S. soft drink market, but now it slipped to 9.7 percent. "Eventually, any category—no matter how hot—will hit its peak," a bottler observed philosophically. Had that happened to diet drinks? He hoped not, but he doubted any advertising would help much.

IVESTER THE WOLF

In July 1994, Roberto Goizueta finally recommended Doug Ivester to the board as president and chief operating officer, officially anointing him as his heir apparent. Outwardly, the round-faced Ivester, forty-seven, appeared to be a quiet, almost introverted accountant. Unlike the aristocratic Cuban-born Goizueta, Ivester was a Georgia boy. A textile factory mechanic's son, Ivester was raised in New Holland, Georgia, as a good, hard-working Southern Baptist. If he got an A, his father commented,

"They give A-pluses, don't they?" Ivester worked as a Kroger bag boy to pay his way through the University of Georgia. After auditing Coke's books for an accounting firm, he joined the Company in 1979. Inside the Company, he was known as a reclusive workaholic. Like Robert Woodruff, he was childless, and some felt that he treated Coca-Cola as his love child. "His hobby is work," observed one acquaintance. After a celebratory dinner with Ivester and the board, Goizueta called him at home at 9 p.m. and got his answering machine. Ivester had gone back to work until 11 p.m.

But Ivester soon proved that he was not such a nerdy introvert. Indeed, his quiet manner hid a fierce competitive spirit. On October 25, 1994, Ivester gave his first speech to "InterBev94" in Atlanta, where the beverage industry held its annual convention that year. As Ivester took the stage, the lights dimmed and the baaing of sheep bleated over the loudspeakers. Videos showed panicked sheep running back and forth, intercut with commercials from Pepsi, Gatorade, and other Coke competitors. In his speech, Ivester lambasted other soft drink firms. "Sheep are only comfortable right up against each other," he said. "They are only capable of looking a few inches past their noses. When troubled, they cry loudly and back into each other." Worst of all, he observed, they panic and engage in price wars that hurt everyone.

But Ivester saved his utter contempt for the private-label soft drinks, which he called "parasites" who relied on the major brands to advertise for them. "The parasites in the soft drink world latch onto normal organisms," he said. "They have never helped build the business, never created new products or packages, and have given nothing back to the community." Their only positive attribute was that, in a Darwinian sense, they helped weed out the weaker sheep. Private-label parasites, Ivester observed, were losing ground in 1994, and he intended to make sure that trend continued, by being neither a sheep nor a parasite, but a wolf—noble, independent yet loyal, turf-oriented, and fond of mutton. "Are there any soft drink wolves?" Ivester asked rhetorically. "I hope you are looking at one now."

The new Coke president told his audience that it would be nice if he could earn their friendship, but that wasn't really his priority. "This is what I really want," he said, leaning forward. "I want your customers, I want your shelf space across the country, your share of customers' stomachs, and I want every single bit of beverage growth potential that exists out there." Ivester ended his dramatic speech with another question. "Will I act like a sheep, parasite, or a wolf? At the Coca-Cola Company, we answer it something like this." Immediately, the auditorium resonated to the eerie sound of howling wolves.

In his first speech inside the Company, Ivester quoted McDonald's founder Ray Kroc. "What do you do when your competitor is drowning? Get a live hose and stick it in his mouth." He pulled a garden hose from beneath his podium. "I've got the hose. I think you know what to do with it." Goizueta observed admiringly, "Doug has the nerve of a night prowler."

True to his word, Ivester instituted a take-no-prisoners marketing blitz that did not rely solely on advertising to drive the business. Coke introduced new packaging for most of its products to complement the return of the contour bottle. Going back to its roots, the Company initiated sampling campaigns in markets worldwide, giving away drinks to get consumers hooked. It also took advantage of its high-profile sponsorships of sporting events as never before. To combat the private-label threat, Coke salesmen offered a detailed analysis of a store's profitability on each beverage and its returns on shelf-space allocation, demonstrating that Coke products added more to their bottom line. The Company concomitantly sponsored the Coca-Cola Foodservice Research Forum to prove its worth to fast food purveyors. Small, independent bottlers struggled to stay in business, while the largest ten bottlers, led by behemoth Coca-Cola Enterprises, accounted for 90 percent of U.S. soft drink sales.

Meanwhile, the New Age threat receded. Snapple sold out to Quaker Oats, which changed the drink's distribution while sales floundered. Coke pounded away at private labels with a commercial showing a man trying to photocopy a Coke. "No matter how hard they try," the announcer intoned, "it always comes out a little flat." By the end of 1994, Coca-Cola had regained its momentum and was named Marketer of the Year by *Brandweek* magazine. Worldwide case volume grew an impressive 10 percent. Coke's stock resumed its upward march, growing 15 percent and reaching $51.50 by year's end, while the S&P 500 declined by 2 percent. In a passage in the annual report clearly directed at John Neff and other nay-sayers, Roberto Goizueta sniffed, "We will never allow ourselves to waste our time listening to those skeptics who claim we can't maintain our historical growth rates, recycling the same cynical reasoning we've heard for several decades now."

INFINITE OPPORTUNITY

The Company was on a roll and appeared unstoppable. In April 1995, Goizueta, Ivester, and Zyman felt comfortable enough to poke fun at themselves as they marked the tenth anniversary of the New Coke fiasco. Imitating television comic David Letterman's lists, Goizueta ticked off his "Top Ten Favorite Blunders" that yielded positive results, such as buying Columbia Pictures or bringing out New Coke. He could afford the levity, pointing out, "Today, we're in the best shape we have been in many decades." Sergio Zyman, widely considered the fall guy for New Coke, basked in the attention. "Anybody who thinks New Coke hurt his career hasn't seen his new house," Doug Ivester quipped.

In the first six months of 1995, Coke captured 85 percent of the growth in the U.S. soft drink business, as the stock jumped past $60. Goizueta wanted increased volume everywhere, including neglected markets in the United States, pointing out that Southern Californians drank less Coke per capita than Hungarians. The Company pushed vending machines into nontraditional outlets such as casinos, churches, nail salons, and post offices. No longer content with mere "availability," Goizueta now talked about "pervasive penetration," a project spearheaded by Ivester. On a trip to Rome, Georgia, which boasted the highest Coke per capita consumption on earth, Ivester still found plenty of places without Coke—a national park, a Ford dealership, a video store, and a karate studio. The videotaped record of the trip, "The Road to Rome," became an internal company hit.

"The ruthless push to sell Coke absolutely everywhere made Mr. Ivester a star at Coca-Cola," noted the *Wall Street Journal*, and the obsession spread throughout the Coke universe. In South Africa, trademarked taxis served chilled Cokes out of coolers, while a Dutch railroad offered cold Coca-Cola from specially designed vending machines. In Moscow, the Company opened "Coca-Cola University" to indoctrinate former communists in the pursuit of stomach share. To show their support, Bill and Hillary Clinton visited the Moscow bottling plant in May 1995, posing for photographers as they chugged Coke. In Japan's Ginza shopping district, the Company installed a ninety-three-foot-wide, forty-nine-foot-high neon sign. At U.S. theme parks, the Company implemented "Coca-Cola Cool Zones," climate-controlled pavilions with cooling fog and rows of vending machines.

Coke had always tried to entice children without overtly advertising to them, but now the campaign to infiltrate schools intensified. "Based on the awareness that it's easier to establish brand preference at a younger age than it is to change consumers' habits later in life," wrote a Coke spokesman in an internal 1995 newsletter, "The Coca-Cola Company is focusing upon the education market with revitalized efforts around the world." With educational funding from governments in decline, Coke recognized an opportunity to offer money in return for access to young consumers. Carlton Curtis, director of the global effort to penetrate schools, said, "This is an investment channel—investing to build brand and consumption preferences for a lifetime." In Uruguay, where forty thousand children a year trooped through the Montevideo Coke bottling plant, the Company even put out a book in Braille to explain the wonders of Coke to blind children. In the United States, Coke paid schools for the exclusive right to install vending machines and signed a licensing agreement to market back-to-school items featuring the cute Coke polar bears.

Alarmed, Vermont Senator Patrick Leahy proposed tougher nutritional requirements for federally funded school lunch programs. Coca-Cola not only lobbied against the bill in Congress but sent a mass mailing to school officials claiming that soft drinks were "USDA-approved." A spokesman for the National Soft Drink Association protested, "Students drink water during the day and water doesn't contain any nutritional value." Testifying at the committee hearing, Leahy lambasted Coke for what he called its "major misinformation campaign," complaining that company officials refused to testify before his committee. "It seems that Coca-Cola would rather work behind the scenes to try and kill my bill than confront me and the public face to face." Eventually, a much-diluted version of the bill passed, obliging the federal government to provide state agencies with "model language" to ban soft drinks in elementary schools. It had little effect, much to the relief of many school superintendents badly in need of soft drink dollars. University administrators also raked in money, as Pepsi paid $15 million for a ten-year exclusive beverage deal at Pennsylvania State, with Coke paying even more to the University of Minnesota, soon to be followed by Rutgers, Texas A&M, and others.

Around the world, Coke pumped money into newly designated "anchor bottlers"—Coca-Cola Enterprises in the United States, Australia's Coca-Cola Amatil, Latin America's FEMSA and Panamco, South Africa's SABCO, and Malaysia's Fraser & Neave—that executed Coke strategy across geographical borders. They had little choice, since Big Coke owned a substantial chunk of all of them. Doug Ivester proved that he was indeed aggressive, pushing the remaining independent bottlers to carry only Coke products on their trucks. When Ivester visited Vietnam, managers there told him that they couldn't keep up with consumer demand. He immediately got on the phone, found a bottling line sitting on a ship in Singapore harbor, and diverted it to Hanoi. Ivester got the reputation for being hard-nosed but fair. "He follows up on absolutely everything," an associate observed. "He is probably the most competent beverage executive that I have ever met," added a beverage analyst.

In a September 1995 issue, *Fortune* magazine named Coke the "New Champ of Wealth Creation," according to a market value-added formula (market value of all equity and debt minus total capital investments). "The most valuable product on this planet," the *Fortune* reporter concluded, "is sugar water, or at least a particular type of it known as Coca-Cola." To help it stay that way, the Company offered $55 million in prizes during its second "Red Hot Summer" under-the-cap promotion and another $1.5 billion in potential retail discounts. The Discovery space shuttle took a special portable soda fountain—dubbed a "fluids generic bioprocessing apparatus"—into space for "research into fountain dispensers in weightless environments," according to NASA. Adding to its arsenal of drinks, Coke bought Barq's, a popular root beer with a hip, offbeat image. In a fit of hubris, Coke USA president Jack Stahl announced that the Company planned to capture 50 percent of the U.S. beverage market by the end of the year 2000—a tall order, since Company products held only 42 percent at the time.

By the end of 1995, Roberto Goizueta was euphoric. Coca-Cola stock had jumped to $74.25, an annual hike of 44 percent. Worldwide unit case volume had grown another eight percent. In the United States, per capita consumption of Company beverages reached 343 drinks—nearly one a day for every man, woman, and child. In the annual report, an infinity symbol signified "our virtually *infinite* opportunity for growth," as Goizueta observed. All of this had been achieved despite economic problems in major markets such as Mexico, Japan, and Argentina. In a new Coke mantra, Goizueta observed that the human body requires at least sixty-four ounces of liquid every day. "Our beverages currently account for not even 2 of those ounces," he lamented. His goal, of course, was to make sure that every human being on earth drank sixty-four ounces of Coca-Cola—or some other Company product.

With 80 percent of Coke's profits coming from sales outside the United States, Goizueta officially recognized the global nature of the business by reorganizing the Company's management structure. Previously, there had been two primary units— North America and International. Now, he simply divided the world into five groups, North America being one of those partitions. "We not only *see* our business as global," he wrote, "but we *manage* it that way. . . . We understand that, as a practical matter, our universe is infinite, and that we, ourselves, are the key variable in just how much of it we can capture."

THE COCA-COLA OLYMPICS

For Goizueta and Coca-Cola, 1996 was to be the year of ultimate triumph, as the world media descended on Atlanta for the centennial celebration of the modern Olympics. Back in 1987, an Atlanta real estate lawyer named Billy Payne had decided that his city deserved to host the summer Olympics and, although initially skeptical, Goizueta eventually threw his support behind the effort. To avoid the appearance of undue influence, Goizueta made sure that the money came from Coca-Cola USA and giant bottler Coca-Cola Enterprises rather than Big Coke itself, however, and the Company also gave money to Olympic Committees for Toronto and Melbourne. Still, Coke donated $350,000 to the Atlanta bid, far more than it gave any other city. It made its corporate jets available free of charge, hosted luncheons for the International Olympic Committee (IOC) members, and fielded hundreds of volunteers.

In 1990, when IOC head Juan Antonio Samaranch announced that Atlanta had won the 1996 Olympic bid, the Athens, Greece, officials cried foul. It seemed obvious that the event should have gone to Greece, where the games originated and where they were restarted in 1896. "Morally, the Games belong to us," complained Greek bid organizer Spyros Metaxa. "The Olympics deserve Atlanta, the capital of Coca-Cola and of American crime," observed another bitter Greek commentator, referring to the city's high homicide rate. "In the long run, it will perhaps prove better that we did not get them."

It is quite unlikely that Coca-Cola officials overtly bribed anyone, although it is now widely acknowledged that IOC officials have accepted all manner of special favors. Peter Ueberroth, who had presided over the first corporate-sponsored Los Angeles Olympics in 1984 and who served on Coca-Cola's board of directors, candidly advised, "Remember there are ninety votes and those people are not all of the highest integrity." There is no question that Coca-Cola, the largest Olympic sponsor, wielded enormous power. "The ones who decide where the Olympics shall take place," wrote one insider in the 1980s, "are big companies like Coca-Cola, ABC-TV, Adidas." Two IOC members, Kenya's Charles Mukora and France's Jean-Claude Killy, were directors of Coca-Cola companies.

In addition, Roberto Goizueta and Juan Antonio Samaranch had become personal friends since they met at the 1984 Sarajevo winter games. They shared Spanish descent, though Goizueta came from a long line of blue-blooded aristocrats, while Samaranch, the son of a textile mill owner, was designated a noble "Marques" in 1991. Apparently it did not bother Goizueta that Samaranch had served dictator Francisco Franco faithfully for many years, routinely giving him the stiff one-armed fascist salute. When Samaranch arrived in Atlanta during the bidding process, he went straight to meet Goizueta at Coke headquarters, then flew to Washington aboard the Coke jet. When Billy Payne offered Samaranch a set of mint julep glasses, he smiled and asked, "Can you drink Coca-Cola out of these?"

Regardless of how the Olympics came to Atlanta in 1996, Goizueta and his executive team were determined to milk the opportunity for all it was worth. "As a marketing property and a volume-driving opportunity, the Games in Atlanta will be like nothing this Company has ever seen," gloated an internal publication. "Really, it's a soft drink marketer's dream: During one of the hottest periods of the entire year, millions of scorched, thirsty visitors from all over the entire world will be packed into a circle 3 miles in diameter [and] the Company's products will be within an arm's reach."

Coke had already established sports as the ideal way to connect with consumers. Doug Ivester continually urged, "We need to activate our sponsorships," while Sergio Zyman, a running enthusiast, wanted to paint the Coke logo on every possible sporting event. Zyman realized that mere advertising was insufficient. Experiential event marketing to "bring the brand alive"—a concept pioneered by former ski racer Mark "Dill" Driscoll in the 1980s—could touch individual consumers most effectively. Driscoll had already promoted Cherry Coke, Sprite, and Coke Classic with wildly painted vans and opportunities for consumers to play games and sample free drinks. Now, the Company called on Driscoll to choreograph the Olympic torch relay.

Although the idea of a torch relay ostensibly hearkened back to ancient Greece, it actually came from the Nazis, who invented the dramatic prelude to the Berlin Games in 1936. At the 1984 Los Angeles Olympics, AT&T sponsored an American torch run, but it made participants pony up $3,000 for the privilege. In 1996, Coke paid $12 million for the right to sponsor the torch as it crossed America on an eighty-four-day, fifteen-thousand-mile journey during which ten thousand runners—none of whom had to pay anything—would carry the flame. Over half of the participants were "Community Heroes" chosen for their good works by local United Way agencies. Coca-Cola chose another 2,500 winners of a contest called "Share the Spirit: Who Would You Choose?" in which consumers could nominate either themselves or a friend—five hundred of them coming from seventy foreign countries. The remainder of the slots were reserved for former Olympic athletes and corporate sponsors.

The event was masterfully planned and executed down to the minute. In addition to foot-power, the torch traveled by bicycle, train, horse, canoe, steamboat, sailboat, and airplane. The circuitous route brought the Olympic flame within two hours of 90 percent of the U.S. population. NBC-TV covered the event every day, while internet junkies could keep abreast of its progress on America Online and the Atlanta Committee on the Olympic Games website. Although the runners did not wear Coke logos, just about everything else did, including the "escorts" who ran alongside. "The torch relay will be one long commercial," lamented Michael Jacobson of the Center for Science in the Public Interest, and Sergio Zyman was delighted to agree. "Three things have been constant at the Olympic since 1928—the athletes, the fans and Coca-Cola."

Dill Driscoll hired enthusiastic, fresh-faced young promoters to stage what he called a "15,000-mile rolling street party." Ahead of the torch runner, his crew arrived with five flatbed trucks, accompanied by motorcycles with Coke-bottle-shaped sidecars. The "Red Army" set up a mobile stage for the welcoming ceremony, with a big screen depicting stirring Olympic moments intercut with stirring Coca-Cola commercials. "I wonder if Coca-Cola has anything to do with this," one onlooker pondered sarcastically. "A few high-spirited spectators have even run with a Coke held high," observed a contemporary reporter, "as if it were the sacred flame from Greece." The crew sold pins, jackets, pennants, mugs, gold Coke bottles, license plates, baseball hats, and key chains with the Coke logo on them, as well as ice-cold Coke, with the proceeds going to a local charity.

"It's almost like hosting the Olympics for one day," Wisconsin Governor Tommy Thompson said at a ceremony en route. Thompson asked high school band members, "Did you all get a bottle of Coke? Next to milk, it's a good drink." They shouted back, "Better!" The feel-good Coke reps had a harder edge, however, towards any Pepsi that dared to appear during the relay. In a small town in Ohio, they refused to allow high school students to escort the torch because the school district sold Pepsi products, and they knocked a Pepsi carton off the wall when a spectator refused to trade it for Coca-Cola. In Senoia, Georgia, Coke officials suggested draping the Pepsi vending machine next to the town hall with a black cloth but eventually settled for putting a Coke machine next to it.

It was indeed a "sea-to-shining-sea Coca-Cola carnival," as a cynical foreign journalist observed. Yet it also provided heart-warming moments. A boy with Down syndrome carried the flame while his mother ran alongside shouting to the crowd, "This is my son! This is my son!" Children with recorders played "America the Beautiful" along the roadside. War veterans from a hospital lined the roadside and waved tiny American flags from their wheelchairs. Parents took their children out of school for this onetime event. In Selma, Alabama, blacks and whites walked together over the Edmund Pettus Bridge where civil rights marchers once were beaten back. "My God, the relay is the biggest thing to happen [here] since the illegals starting coming across," exclaimed a resident of a tiny town near the Mexican border. Even in big cities, even in the ghettos, the torch relay worked. "This is the first time I have seen New York City as a small town," a resident said. As one reporter observed, the torch relay was "crassly commercial and touchingly open-hearted—all at the same time."

Everywhere, people were moved by genuine emotion—including the Coke employees traveling with the torch. One disabled young man took more than an hour to carry the flame a half-mile. "He barely made it," staffer Susan McWhorter remembered, "but the accomplishment on his face was phenomenal." The torch runners themselves were transformed. "The whole thing was like a mountain-top experience," one participant recalled. "I equate it to the birth of my children, graduation, or getting married." Another runner was initially skeptical. "I was cynical because of all the Coke hype, but I was so moved by the reaction of everyday people, crying and waving flags. It was a real revelation. Though I never thought I would do it, I ended up buying the torch."* Coca-Cola bused some forty million people to the relay, where they cheered, cried, and drank Coke. The memory of the event, as one Coke executive observed, was indelibly burned into their brains. On day eighty-four in Atlanta, riding one of the Harleys with a Coke sidecar, Dill Driscoll led the torch parade into the courtyard at Coke headquarters on North Avenue, where a literal red carpet was rolled out as Company employees cheered.

Muhammad Ali, the former boxing great, shambled up to the great Olympic saucer in Atlanta on July 19, 1996, and finally lit the giant caldron for the seventeen-day Olympics. The rolling street party was at an end, but the Coca-Cola Games, as many journalists dubbed them, were just beginning. "Coke Here, There, Everywhere," observed the *Atlanta Journal-Constitution*. "Within the Ring, the Coca-Cola trademark was so omnipresent it seemed an atmospheric condition." Hawkers with Coke-bottle-shaped backpacks dispensed the drink. The red logo flashed on the floors and ceilings of Atlanta rapid transit stations. Collectors traded various Coke-embossed Olympic pins. Visitors crowded the World of Coca-Cola museum.

The centerpiece, however, was Coca-Cola Olympic City, a twelve-acre theme park where Coca-Cola charged adults thirteen dollars for the privilege of gazing at a sixty-five-foot high Coke bottle and buying Company soft drinks from bottle-shaped vending machines that attracted children with a cool spray from underneath giant bottle caps. Ingenious interactive games allowed consumers to "compete" against Olympic athletes, simulating a sprint against Jackie Joyner-Kersey, batting against a video of pitcher John Smoltz, taking part in a wheelchair race, or mountain biking down a

---

* Each runner received a torch, so that it was the flame that was passed rather than the torch. When it was all over, runners could purchase their torch for $275.

virtual reality trail. Meanwhile, for those who couldn't make it to Atlanta, Coke developed Olympic Celebration Zone merchandising areas in supermarkets around the country as part of its Coca-Cola Red Hot Olympic Summer promotional campaign, with $1.6 billion in discounts and prizes.

Coke's designation as the official Atlanta soft drink prevented other brands from being served at city-sponsored events or on city property during the Olympics. "The odds of finding a cold (or a lukewarm, or a hot) Pepsi in Olympic Atlanta were akin to discovering the Holy Grail inside the Georgia Dome," one reporter observed.

During the games, the Company featured Coke as the star in one hundred commercials, each airing only once, in 135 countries, tailoring the approach so that Coke supported appropriate patriotic fervor. In Ukraine, for instance, Coke ads featured pole vaulter Sergey Bubka. Many of the ads were reruns from the previous few years, including the familiar polar bears, but, to lend an international flair, some were imported from other countries, such as a spot showing boys from India playing cricket, using a Coca-Cola crate as a wicket. These were augmented by "just-in-time" ads created from the previous day's Olympic events.*

Roberto Goizueta boasted, "We have gone from simply teaching the world to sing, to teaching the world to drink Coca-Cola." Goizueta and Ivester greeted powerful customers and bottlers from all over the world, each executive shaking at least two thousand hands during the course of the Games. There seems little question that Coke's Olympic efforts, which cost some $250 million, paid off, although the Games themselves were marred by disorganization, a bombing, and complaints about commercial tackiness. "Atlanta's Olympic Games," wrote French newspaper *Le Monde*, "touched on some classic themes of the American myth—immodest ambition, an obsession with gold, the powerful reign of the dollar." Groused another reporter, "Atlanta was every bit as ready for the Olympics as America was for New Coke."

1996: YEAR OF TRIUMPH

Goizueta and Ivester were too busy celebrating to worry about such carping. Ten days after the Olympics ended, Goizueta greeted Oswaldo and Gustavo Cisneros to Coke headquarters in Atlanta, where they signed a contract to form a joint venture with the huge Venezuelan bottling family. For $500 million, Coke grabbed 50 percent ownership in the only country in the free world where Pepsi had always predominated. It was a remarkable coup, administering a stunning blow to Pepsi's pride, particularly since new PepsiCo CEO Roger Enrico had been personal friends with Oswaldo Cisneros. "Ozzie took his 30 pieces of silver and ran," Enrico observed bitterly. The purchase followed years in which Pepsi management had ignored the Venezuelan bottlers. Doug Ivester negotiated the top-secret deal, meeting the Cisneros team in hotels and airplane hangars. Once the bargain was made, a 727 jet carrying thousands of Coke

---

* Most Olympic ads were created by ad agency Wieden+Kennedy. A few months before, Mike Ovitz had left CAA to join Disney as an executive, and Shelly Hochron had also left to form Edge Creative, a kind of independent yet in-house ad agency for Coca-Cola. Edge Creative continued to make non-Olympic Coke advertisements.

bottles flew from Mexico to Caracas, and crews worked overtime repainting 2,500 delivery trucks with the Coca-Cola logo. Overnight, Pepsi virtually disappeared from Venezuela.*

Less than two weeks later, Goizueta declared victory in Russia, another longtime Pepsi stronghold. In 1994, Pepsi still held 60 percent of the Russian market, but now Coke had pulled ahead. After the 1985 New Coke debacle, Roger Enrico had penned *The Other Guy Blinked: How Pepsi Won the Cola Wars.* "If he thinks we blinked," Goizueta said testily a few years later, "we will respond by giving Pepsi two black eyes." Now, he had done just that. *Fortune* crowned the Coke CEO the monarch of soft drinks. A March 1996 *Fortune* cover showed Goizueta, arms folded, sitting atop a giant Coke bottle, as Coca-Cola grabbed top ranking as America's most admired company. "Pepsi's Enrico: Bottled Up by Coke," an October 1996 cover announced, featuring a somber Enrico trapped inside yet another oversized Coke bottle.

By year's end, Coca-Cola Company sales accounted for over half of non-U.S. soft drink consumption. The stock, which had split two-for-one in May, climbed to $53 for a 43 percent total return for the year.† "If you invested in our Company just two years ago," Goizueta wrote in the annual report, "your investment has more than *doubled.*" Worldwide unit case volume for the year was up 8 percent, with 6 percent growth in the United States. Earnings per share grew 19 percent, boosted by company share repurchases and the sale of French, Belgian, and British bottlers to Coca-Cola Enterprises, the huge American anchor bottler that moved into Western Europe during the year.

"It may sound incongruous from one of the world's most valuable companies, about to celebrate its 111th birthday," Goizueta said, "but, truly, *we are just getting started.*" Just turned sixty-five, Goizueta clearly felt that he himself was just getting started, too. "As long as I'm having fun and adding value," he said, he planned to remain CEO. At the annual company meeting, one shareholder rushed up to Goizueta and gushed, "You should be like the Pope and never retire." Delighted, Goizueta repeated the anecdote over the next few months. He intended to be another Robert Woodruff, the grand old man of Coca-Cola, pulling the company strings for years to come. And, like Woodruff, Goizueta was so obsessed with Coca-Cola that he regarded its sales record as the pinnacle of human progress. "A billion hours ago, human life appeared on Earth," Goizueta intoned. "A billion minutes ago, Christianity appeared. A billion seconds ago, the Beatles changed music forever. *A billion Coca-Colas ago was yesterday morning.*" The overwhelmingly important question remained: "What must we do to make a billion Coca-Colas ago be this morning?" As Goizueta himself observed, "Working for The Coca-Cola Company is a calling. It's not a way to make a living. It's a religion."

---

* Eventually, Pepsi found a new bottler, and Coke had to pay a $2 million antimonopoly fine, but Venezuela belonged to Coca-Cola. The following year, Coke sold the Venezuelan bottler to the anchor bottler Panamco, getting its $50 million investment back along with a larger ownership in the anchor bottler.

† Giant anchor bottler Coca-Cola Enterprises, whose stock had languished for years, did even better in 1996, up over 80 percent.

DEATH AT THE PINNACLE

The following year, the Coke juggernaut rolled on, with a January 1997 "Get Caught Red Handed" promotion offering two hundred thousand instant prizes, including T-shirts, cameras, coupons, and Club Med vacations, to Coca-Cola Classic drinkers "caught" imbibing by a roving Red Crew, deployed by Dill Driscoll's experiential marketing outfit, that made flash visits to stores, movie theaters, and residential neighborhoods. The promotion signaled Coke's intention to expand Coke Classic marketing year-round rather than focusing only on summertime. Come summer, the Company offered more than five hundred thousand MasterCard ATM money cards worth twenty to a hundred dollars inside selected twelve-packs and cases of Coke Classic and Cherry Coke.

At the Super Bowl, Coke introduced a Coca-Cola Red Zone where fans could play interactive simulated football games, while Harleys with Coke sidecars passed out drinks for tailgate parties. One lucky fan won Coke-sponsored Super Bowl tickets for life. Like Coca-Cola Olympic City, such interactive marketing was intended to involve fans, going beyond the mere presence of ubiquitous Coke signs. The Company allowed Pepsi to pay exorbitant amounts for exclusive pouring rights for teams such as the Seattle Mariners and Los Angeles Lakers (leaving Coke with twenty-four of twenty-eight major-league baseball teams and similar domination of other sports). Meanwhile, Coke opened Coca-Cola Sky Field, an entertainment park at Turner Field, the home of the Atlanta Braves, and Monster Refreshment, a similar effort featuring three 25-foot Coke bottles, at Fenway Park in Boston. "Five years ago, we were just there," said Steve Koonin, in charge of sports marketing for Coke. "Now, we're a friend of the fan, and we're fun. And we're winning."

In the same spirit, Coke opened a new Everything Coca-Cola store in Las Vegas, where cash registers sat inside giant bottle caps, T-shirts were stacked in huge six-packs, and the fitting rooms were shaped like old fountain glasses. An eight-foot fiberglass Coke polar bear loomed over customers. Coke hired Chris Lanning, a former Gap executive, to oversee its new retail division. "We'll find out what shop concepts best connect with consumers," he said, "with their special Coca-Cola memories."

Coke also forged ahead with new products. With no formal test marketing, Coke introduced Surge, its highly caffeinated citrus counter to Pepsi's Mountain Dew. The first ads—launched during the Super Bowl—featured a teenager placing a can atop a pedestal and screaming "Surge!" A group of crazed adolescents then swarmed up a muddy hill to claim the green-tinted carbohydrate-loaded beverage. The slogan for the "fully loaded" drink was "Feed the Rush." Coke clearly meant business, giving away millions of free drinks to high schoolers and slotting $50 million for marketing. The positioning for Surge aped Pepsi's "Dew Dudes," the hip, daredevil teens who engaged in sky surfing and street luging while fueled by Mountain Dew. Surge's name and positioning were precisely the opposite of Mello Yello, Coke's lackluster previous effort in the category. Soon afterward, Coke introduced Citra, a yellow noncaffeinated grapefruit drink targeted against Squirt, a similar product from Cadbury Schweppes.

In the meantime, Sprite, with its "Obey Your Thirst" campaign and interactive "Sprite Playgrounds" at state and county fairs, pushed past Mountain Dew, Dr Pepper, and Diet Pepsi to claim the number-four U.S. soft drink spot behind Coke Classic,

Pepsi, and Diet Coke. And Coke pushed its Cool Nestea brand past Snapple (sold by Quaker Oats for a loss) to claim second place in the iced tea category behind Pepsi's Lipton. Overseas, Coke sales bounced back in Latin America and Europe after a slow period. In Russia, Coke now outsold Pepsi two to one, and the Company revealed that it would sink another $100 million there by the end of 1997. The Company announced a $360 million capital investment program in South Africa, Zimbabwe, and Tanzania. Big Coke continued to buy and sell bottlers at a furious pace—$7 billion worth announced or completed in the first six months of 1997—building a more powerful anchor bottler system over which the Company exerted ever-growing control.

For the second year in a row, *Fortune* named The Coca-Cola Company the most admired American company. When Coke stock surged to $60 in March, a few financial analysts irritated Roberto Goizueta by declaring the price hyperinflated, with a high price-to-earnings ratio of 37. "Nowhere is it written," sniped Alan Abelson in *Barron's*, "that Coke will continue to grow even at 18 percent a year appreciably into the future," and famed analyst John Bogle agreed. Nonetheless, the stock continued to climb, nudging over $72 in June.

At the pinnacle of success, Goizueta began to sound even more philosophical than usual. "What's it like to be you?" one young admirer asked. "Sometimes I wish I was like you," Goizueta answered. "It isn't easy. You work 24 hours a day. You don't take much vacation." Then he brightened. "But I'm having a great deal of fun, and I'm blessed to be in a position to be paid handsomely to have a lot of fun." Though still absorbed in the Company, he began to reach out more into the community and the world. Fretting over Atlanta's downtown area, he warned that the city should not lapse into a "giant, collective nap" in the wake of the Olympics. "A great city cannot have a hollow center." He seeded a newly formed Goizueta Foundation with $38 million, preparing to become a philanthropist in the Woodruff tradition. He expressed admiration for the late Cardinal Bernardin, a strong voice for social justice.

Yet Goizueta insisted on a fundamental, bottom-line credo: "The mission of any business is to create value for its owners." Churches could minister to spiritual needs, governments to civic needs, and charities to social needs. "While performing its role, business distributes the lifeblood that flows through our economic system, not only in the form of goods and services, but also in the form of taxes, salaries, philanthropy." He said that he got his "psychic income" from the impact he had not only on his company but on society as a whole. "When I was in Eastern Europe," Goizueta explained, "I saw people who for the first time had a real job and were getting paid real money. They thanked me for that, but they really were thanking The Coca-Cola Company." He espoused a strict laissez faire philosophy. "It puzzles me that many Americans want our government to 'fix' our economy or even protect our jobs when much of the rest of the world is thrilled to have government finally playing its appropriate role." He explained that he knew the perils of a socialist system firsthand. "It's the reason I came to this country from Cuba."

Goizueta argued that by boosting the share price, he had done more good than any number of charities, in just one year creating nearly $3 billion dollars in additional wealth for nonprofit organizations holding Coke stock. He emphasized, however, that such gains should not come at the expense of employees. He lamented the downsizing trend in which corporations laid off thousands of loyal employees. "I am against a scorched earth adherence to profits at all costs." Such shortsighted policies would inevitably harm the consuming public upon which businesses relied. "We cannot for the long term exist as a healthy company in a sick society," Goizueta stressed. He praised a recent book by theologian Michael Novak entitled *Business as a Calling*.

As part of that calling, Goizueta was unrepentant about forming alliances with nonprofit organizations that helped promote Company products. In a 1997 speech to the annual meeting of the Boys & Girls Clubs of America, the CEO laid out his vision of "strategic philanthropy," a program through which bottlers would place vending machines and help with retail programs and special events at Boys & Girls Clubs throughout the country. Coke would help the organization raise $60 million over the next decade, he promised. "It's a new world of giving," he said. Of course, while Coke gave nonprofit organizations a piece of the profits, the Company made money, too, while gaining exclusive access to young consumers. In the coming years, Coke would extend such "strategic philanthropy" to financially strapped high schools, installing vending machines in educational institutions that took a percentage of the proceeds.

Goizueta's enthusiasm and dedication to his job were clearly undiminished by time or age. By 1997, he had been CEO for sixteen years, compiling an incredible record. "Hell, considering what he's done for the shareholders," one analyst said, "you should make him CEO of the Century." Yet Goizueta wasn't satisfied. "Success is a journey, not a destination," he said, translating one of his grandfather's aphorisms. Obviously, he wasn't ready for that journey to end, as he jetted around the world on Coca-Cola business. When asked about his successor, Goizueta made a point of *not* naming Doug Ivester. "He or she must have energy, intellectual character, integrity, an inquisitive, innovative mind, determination, a sense of purpose, and an engaging personality," he answered, naming his own qualities—other than the last, a trait he always envied in Don Keough. Over after-dinner drinks in the spring of 1997, Bernard Marcus, chairman of Atlanta-based Home Depot, confided to Goizueta that the two of them were the soul of their companies, and that souls lived on forever. The comment pleased Goizueta, who nonetheless pointed out later that evening that he was two years younger than Marcus.

In August 1997, Goizueta flew to Monte Carlo for a meeting with fifty of Coke's biggest international bottlers, adding a day trip to Spain, his ancestral home. When he returned to Atlanta, he never quite recovered from the jet lag. Lunching with Morgan Stanley analyst Andrew Conway on September 2, Goizueta assured him that case volume growth worldwide would continue at around 7 percent for the next few years. Then, chatting about his recent travels, the CEO admitted, "Andrew, I'm a little fatigued. I haven't quite recouped from the trip." Four days later, Goizueta checked himself into Emory University Hospital, where doctors detected a growth on his lungs. Goizueta, a heavy smoker since his teenage years in Cuba, had lung cancer.

During his two-week stay in the penthouse Woodruff Suite in the hospital—where Robert Woodruff spent his last days—Goizueta frequently checked Coke's stock price, which had declined from its June high, while reviewing financial plans and global strategy with his top executives. Two fax machines in an adjoining room brought reports from around the world.

By the time they detected the cancer, however, it was too late for anything but desperate measures. Doctors administered massive radiation doses in combination with chemotherapy and sent the Coke chief home, where he got a get-well card signed by two thousand employees. "Please let my talented doctors and my terrific family worry about me," he dictated in reply. "You, my Coca-Cola family, just worry about the Company." With characteristic determination, Goizueta faced death calmly. When doctors or nurses asked how he was feeling, he said, "Fantastic."

Goizueta's wife of forty-four years, Olguita, kept vigil by his side, and his three living children visited frequently. Olga lived in Atlanta, but Roberto ("Robby"), a theology professor at Loyola, arrived from Chicago, while Javier, a Procter & Gamble employee, flew from Brazil. Goizueta's attention to detail never wavered. Reading aloud a letter to him, Olguita tried to skip over the pleasantries at the end. "Don't et cetera me," her husband said sternly. "Now start over, from the top."

On October 7, Goizueta returned to the hospital, suffering from a throat infection and fever, probably due to damage to his immune system caused by the aggressive radiation and chemotherapy. On October 16, the board of directors met without Goizueta for the first time in seventeen years. The next night, Goizueta asked to take a final communion with Olguita. Just after midnight, on Saturday, October 18, 1997, Roberto Goizueta died, his head cradled in his wife's arms. He was sixty-five years old, one month shy of his birthday.

At the funeral ceremony, attended by over a thousand mourners—including Jimmy and Rosalyn Carter, Warren Buffett, and other luminaries—former Atlanta mayor and United Nations ambassador Andrew Young delivered the eulogy. "For him," Young said, "business was not a job, it was a mission ordained by God." The black leader praised Coca-Cola as the fourth largest employer in South Africa, asserting, "This is certainly a better community, and indeed this is a better world, because of the love, the dedication and the devotion that he shared through business as his calling." Goizueta was marketing not just a product, Young said, but "a way of life." Eldest son Roberto S. Goizueta also spoke at the funeral. "He died as he had lived," he said, "fully engaged in the Company's affairs." As the service ended, the organ began a solemn recessional. As mourners filed out of the church, they recognized the tune and began to hum along as it swelled and quickened, hearing the familiar words in their heads: "I'd like to teach the world to sing in perfect harmony." Goizueta would have loved it.

The outpouring of tributes and grief was remarkable, similar in many respects to the death of a head of state. Coke offices around the globe closed for the day of his funeral. Flags flew at half-mast not only at Coca-Cola plants around the world, but at twenty-two thousand McDonald's restaurants. The *Atlanta Journal-Constitution* devoted page after page to Goizueta testimonials, including a huge pen-and-ink cartoon of a polar bear gripping a Coke in its paw, a giant tear falling from its eye. "He Was the Real Thing," read a typical headline.

Roberto Goizueta left an astonishing legacy. When he became CEO in 1981, The Coca-Cola Company was a stumbling giant, diversified into a hodgepodge of businesses, many of which weren't terribly profitable. Many of the bottlers were bitter at the Company for forcing them to give up their birthright to cheap syrup. Paul Austin, the former leader, had Alzheimer's. The stock was languishing, and Pepsi was gaining. Under Goizueta's long reign, Coke got rid of ancillary businesses but diversified into the world of entertainment by buying Columbia Pictures, then sold it a few years later for a huge profit. During the 1990s, he had narrowed his vision to only soft drinks. "He was the most focused human being I ever met," Don Keough recalled after his death. Goizueta applied his laser-beam intelligence to the marketing of Coca-Cola. "He didn't play golf or tennis," Keough continued. "All of his hobbies were linked to The Coca-Cola Company. It was his passion." Goizueta made a few blunders—notably New Coke—but no one could argue with the results. Under his direction, the Company's market value exploded from $4.3 billion to $145 billion, and Coke increased its U.S. market share by nearly ten points, up to nearly 44 percent. Worldwide, Coke's soft drink share had grown from 35 to 50 percent.

Yet as a human being Roberto Goizueta remained an enigma. When David Greising published his biography, *I'd Like the World to Buy a Coke*, a few months after Goizueta's death, it proved to be a workmanlike business narrative. "His unique gift as an executive," Greising wrote, "was his ability to change his own formula, to quickly understand his mistakes, adapt, and ultimately triumph." But readers learned little of the leader's inner life. Perhaps, when you knew his devotion to his family and product, you knew Goizueta. For all his aloof grandeur, however, the business giant sometimes showed a softer side. Pictures of the CEO with children at the Varsity showed him grinning as he delighted in passing out Coca-Cola pins. He also loved the Coke polar bears, giving away ties emblazoned with them.

Goizueta rarely spoke about his past, insisting that he preferred to look forward. But he never forgot the day he fled Castro's Cuba in 1960 with forty dollars and one hundred shares of Coke stock. On July 4, 1995, Goizueta addressed a group of immigrants who had just taken the oath of American citizenship. "For me, looking into your eyes this morning is like looking into a mirror," he said, then wondered aloud at his own good fortune, "that a young immigrant could come to this country, be given a chance to work hard and apply his skills, and ultimately earn the opportunity to lead not only a large corporation, but an institution that actually symbolizes the very essence of America and American ideals." He also revealed how he got there. "You must sense the opportunity in your nostrils with every breath, and you must see it in your dreams when you are asleep." Perhaps, as he was laid to his eternal rest, Roberto Goizueta still dreamed of Coca-Cola.

Part VI

Quenching All Thirsts

(1997–2013)

"Neville, please don't do this. What do you think you'll get out of it other than headaches? Coca-Cola is a great company, and I know that it's been your life, but we've been there, done that. We have a good life here in Barbados and a beautiful home in France. We're finding time to relax and enjoy our lives. You've lost ten pounds and look great. It's been like a second honeymoon."

The woman paced the tile floor as she spoke, then paused to look out at the ocean waves breaking on the pure white sand. She spun around just as her husband was about to put his arms around her.

"You know I love you very much, and I'll support whatever decision you make, but I want to be really clear about this. Damn it! Money is certainly not the issue. You've proved that you are a great leader and manager, so it can't be an ego thing—not that they ever appreciated you. They should have made you CEO when Roberto died or when they fired Ivester. Now that the Company is going down the tubes, they want you to come back to save their bacon. Well, the hell with them!"

Neville Isdell smiled and took her in his arms. "Pamela, I know that everything you say is true." He knew that if he went back to the North Avenue tower in Atlanta, once again he would hardly see his wife, would spend most of his life on airplanes, in meetings, arguing with ad men. She was right. At sixty, he was enjoying his well-earned retirement. And yet . . .

"But don't you see that if I don't do this, I don't think I will be able to live with myself? This is the ultimate challenge. I truly believe that I can make a difference, that I am uniquely qualified to help save Coca-Cola. It has been my life's calling, and I simply have to do it."

Pamela sighed, huddling into his chest, and fought back her tears. It's just a stupid soft drink, *she thought.* Why does it always have to come first? *But aloud she said,* "Neville, you will be the best CEO that Coca-Cola has ever had."

~ *22* ~

Ivester Inherits a World of Trouble

One of the virtues of a 113-year-old company is that we've traveled over bumpy roads before. We have seen the movie before.
— M. Douglas Ivester, CEO, The Coca-Cola Company, 1999

Although Goizueta had never specifically anointed Doug Ivester, his ascension to become chairman and CEO of The Coca-Cola Company was a foregone conclusion. "Now that Ivester will be calling the shots," a reporter wrote the day after Goizueta's death, "the only real mystery is whom he will pick as his No 2." The top contenders were Neville Isdell, fifty-five, the Irish "Indiana Jones" who had turned around the Philippines, then led the charge into Eastern Europe and Russia, Jack Stahl, forty-five, former chief financial officer and head of domestic operations, and Sergio Zyman, fifty-two, the volatile marketing head. As the months rolled by, the mystery cleared: Ivester did not intend to appoint a second banana at all. At the age of fifty, he had reached the apex of power, and he had no intention of sharing it. The ambitious, disappointed Zyman soon departed. Neville Isdell, arguably the most competent and charismatic choice for second-in-command, was removed from Big Coke ranks, heading up the new Western European anchor bottler Coca-Cola Beverages, which had been split off from Coca-Cola Amatil.

When an interviewer asked the new Coke CEO point-blank what it would take for him to appoint a president, Ivester coyly replied, "I'm very fortunate right now in that I've got six [presidents]," referring to the heads of his six operating groups. "If I put someone between them and me right now, would there be great advantage to that?" He wanted "short lines of communication." Indeed, Ivester encouraged frequent direct calls and e-mails from his executives, and he deluged them with messages and questions in return. Ivester neither smoked nor drank and, at least on the surface, was always calm and polite, if demanding. Watching a TV show on animals and stress one night at home, he commented to his wife, Kay, "You know, I don't feel stress." She answered, "Of course you don't. You're a carrier."

The transition between Goizueta and Ivester was seamless, but, even as Ivester took command, there were signs of trouble. The stock was down not because of Goizueta's death but because a stronger dollar hurt Coke, which took 80 percent of its profits overseas. In addition, analysts carped at Coke's bottling transactions, complaining that the Company artificially boosted its earnings figures by manipulating the price and timing of sales to captive anchor bottlers. "We question the manner in which these intercompany transactions are reported," wrote two accountants, calling them "nothing more than an exercise in self-dealing" and objecting to the one-sidedness of Big Coke's power. "What is clear is that these affiliates are part of Coke's business model to subsidize Coke's earnings in every way possible."

Just before Ivester took over, *Financial World* put a smashed Coke can on its cover, with the headline, "Why Coke Could Get Crushed." The investment magazine complained that Big Coke took profits from its bottlers and their new stock issues while loading them with debt. "How much longer will Coke be able to use the bottler as a whipping boy?" If gains from bottling sales and stock issuance were excluded, Coke's operating earnings had improved only 11 percent annually over the past five years, nowhere near its lofty goal of 17 to 20 percent.

Nonetheless, Ivester could look back at 1997 with some satisfaction. Just before Christmas, he made his first big move as CEO, announcing the $840 million purchase of Orangina, the fizzy French drink with real orange pulp. Since CCE now owned the Coke bottling system in France, it stood to gain substantially if regulators allowed the deal. Although the "Asian Miracle" was turning into the "Asian Flu"—with the sudden July 1997 devaluation in Thailand spreading across the continent—Ivester and chief financial officer James Chestnut reassured analysts that Coke saw the turmoil as an opportunity to buy Asian bottlers at bargain prices. Ivester compared the situation to the Mexican peso crisis of 1994, during which his company continued to invest, resulting in a 10 percent rise in its Mexican market share.

Coke stock finished strong at $67, up 27 percent for 1997. Worldwide case unit volume grew by 9 percent, and earnings per share 19 percent, just as Coke executives had promised for the past decade. In the annual report, Ivester admitted that 1998 might present "a significant challenge" because of the stronger dollar, but "over time, we manage our currency exposures to mitigate any negative impact from currency fluctuation." He reaffirmed the Company's goals and stated unequivocally, "Never before has this Company been more perfectly poised for pioneering."

He was right, but the world's most far-flung corporate empire was also poised for a world of trouble, rippling out from Asia. In Indonesia, the rupiah went into free fall in January 1998, unemployment soared, and Coke sales plummeted. Doug Ivester urged managers to fight back rather than "to simply hunker down and ride out the storm." He reminded them, "We're investing for the long term and building new capabilities to deal with *any* type of uncertainty." Asian Coke managers tossed out their carefully articulated annual marketing plans and adjusted to new conditions, creating "market impact teams" to work at the street level, getting product to vendors as quickly and cheaply as possible. With more strenuous marketing efforts, promotions, and new cooler placements, sales in the first half of the year steadied. Coke stock rose to $89 a share in mid-July.

Then the bottom dropped out as economic woes hit nearly every country outside the United States in what pundits began to call a global economic crisis. "What started out as a blip on the radar screen in Thailand," said financial guru Paul Volcker, "has somehow turned into something of a financial contagion, particularly in Russia and Brazil." Hedge fund king George Soros spoke darkly of "the disintegration of the global capitalist system." Coke's net income for the third quarter dropped 12 percent. Until then, even with currency exchange problems, Coke had been able to use its expert hedging to minimize the impact, and the volume growth had continued unabated. Now effective hedging became impossible, with most foreign currencies falling, and overall case sales grew only 3 percent for the quarter rather than the usual 7 percent. Indonesia was devastated, with the economy in ruins, riots in Jakarta, and Suharto stepping down.

News of Russian instability caused Merrill Lynch to downgrade Coke stock, but, as the ruble collapsed in August, a Coke executive said, "We are advanced with our [Russian] plans and there is no turning back for us." Indeed, the Company had spent $750 million in Russia since April 1994 to build twelve plants, some of which were running at half capacity or less. Before the devaluation, a British-owned bottler agreed to sell its Russian bottling business to Coke for $187 million, but two months later it was happy to take $87 million and run.

As the world economy deteriorated, Coke projections kept changing. "The numbers keep getting ratcheted down and ratcheted down," complained one analyst. "It's like water torture." In Latin America, Brazilian volume rose only one percent for the third quarter. Japan was flat, and in Germany, where poor weather and bottler reorganization plagued Coke, volume fell 9 percent. Coke had always been considered a safe bet because it was diversified in nearly two hundred countries, but the global malaise of 1998 descended everywhere. Ivester had reassured analysts that, even in bad times, everyone got thirsty. Yet as a *Wall Street Journal* reporter observed, "The economic condition in some countries is so dire that people don't have money to buy bread, let alone sugar water." Coke stock dropped severely then rallied briefly.

Doug Ivester remained outwardly unflappable, just as he had once on the Amazon, when a guide accidentally flipped a crocodile into his narrow boat. Ivester now counseled despondent Coke executives around the world, advising them not to cancel Christmas parties, which would send the wrong message. "Let's capitalize on this," he said, urging managers to look for opportunities in the ruins of the economy. Ivester, whose posture and stride reminded one reporter of the lumbering Coke polar bears, exuded "an almost surreal confidence," she observed. He espoused a mindset in which Coke managers set specific goals as inevitable destinations. "It's not a matter of *if* we're going to get there. It's a matter of *when*."

As 1998 ended, such destinations appeared to be a mirage on the horizon, however. When Ivester abruptly summoned securities analysts for a meeting on December 11, with only a few hours' notice, they wondered whether it was to announce a new disaster. Indeed, Ivester disclosed that the Company's fourth-quarter performance would be even more dismal than he had estimated a few weeks before, because of currency devaluations, higher marketing expenses, and continuing economic turmoil. Yet Ivester underscored his determination to continue Coke's world domination by announcing, at the same meeting, that Coca-Cola would purchase most of Cadbury Schweppes' overseas soft drinks—Dr Pepper, Crush, Schweppes, Canada Dry, and a range of juice drinks and bottled water—for $1.85 billion. The deal excluded Cadbury products in the United States, France, and South Africa. Despite this news, Coke stock immediately tumbled 5 percent to become the day's worst performing Dow stock. Even the imperturbable Ivester admitted during the meeting that Russia was "just a mess." The Cadbury deal was not earth-shattering, and besides, there was no guarantee that regulatory agencies in various countries would allow the sale.

French authorities were, after all, still holding up the Orangina purchase of the previous year.

After some wild ups and downs during the year, Coke's share price ended 1998 precisely where it had started, at $67. Operating income for the year had dropped a percentage point, but net income was off 14 percent. With most of the bottling consolidations completed in 1997, Coke could no longer rely on reselling bottlers to boost earnings per share, which fell 13 percent. Nonetheless, even with an atrocious fourth quarter, Coke grew its case volume by 6 percent worldwide—just slightly below its goal of 7 percent.

PEPSI BOUNCES BACK

To make matters worse for Coke, Roger Enrico was leading a recharged PepsiCo. In October 1997, Enrico spun off Pepsi's restaurants, including Taco Bell, Kentucky Fried Chicken, and Pizza Hut, as Tricon Global Restaurants, allowing Pepsi to focus only on soft drinks and snack foods. Until then, Coke fountain salesmen could stymie Pepsi sales by asking fast food chains, "Why would you want to buy from a competitor?" Pepsi soon struck deals with Pizza Inn, Hard Rock Cafe, Planet Hollywood, and Warner Brothers theaters. Nonetheless, Coke owned 65 percent of the U.S. fountain business, compared with Pepsi's 22 percent. Coke countered by cementing a multiyear contract with Burger King and Wendy's and adding other outlets.

In frustration, Pepsi sued Coke in 1998, alleging that Coca-Cola violated the Sherman Antitrust Act by threatening to cut off supplies to food-service distributors if they carried Pepsi, too.* Coke freely admitted dumping distributors that carried Pepsi. Indeed, its contracts specified that offering Pepsi was a "conflict of interest." But Coke asserted that its archenemy could always sell its soda directly to customers and that its distributors were "an extension of Coca-Cola."

In 1998, as it celebrated its centennial, Pepsi also moved aggressively to offer or acquire new drinks. When acesulfame potassium (Ace-K), a new sugar-free sweetener with a longer shelf-life than aspartame, was approved by the FDA, Pepsi came out with Pepsi One, a new one-calorie diet drink. Pepsi's Mountain Dew continued to grab chunks of market share with teenagers, hardly disturbed by Coke's Surge, which wasn't surging and would sputter out a few years later. To counter Coke's highly successful Sprite, Pepsi now introduced Storm, its own caffeinated lemon-lime effort. Finally, Pepsi bought Tropicana for $3.3 billion, giving it the market-leading premium orange juice to counter Coke's Minute Maid.

The Pepsi Stuff campaign, in which consumers could redeem purchase points for clothing or mountain bikes, fueled a 6 percent sales hike in supermarkets. Still, Pepsi was playing catch-up. In 1997, Pepsi paid $50 million to become the official sponsor of Major League Baseball for five years, even though Coke was sold exclusively in most ballparks. At Shea Stadium, the Pepsi Party Patrol used a shoulder-mounted air cannon to launch Pepsi T-shirts into the upper decks.

---

* The lawsuit, which Pepsi lost two years later, was symptomatic of Enrico's new litigious strategy. Pepsi had already sued Coke in India (where Coke had returned in 1993), accusing its rival of unfairly hiring away Pepsi employees, and in France Pepsi had filed a motion to block Coke's proposed purchase of Orangina. In Italy, Pepsi was delighted when the government began an antitrust probe against Coke.

Overseas, Pepsi sharpened its focus to markets where it had a chance, forming an alliance with Brahma, Brazil's largest brewer, and signing a franchise bottling agreement in Norway. Pepsi built new bottling plants in Venezuela, Russia, Greece, India, China, and elsewhere. From a huge international deficit in 1996, Pepsi International came back the following year with a modest $17 million in positive operating income. As Coke stumbled following its 1993 return to India, Pepsi made inroads there. In Venezuela, in the wake of the Cisneros switch to Coca-Cola, Pepsi came roaring back, teaming up with Polar, a local bottler, and offering deep discounts, heavy advertising, and numerous vending machines. Coke's Venezuelan market share dropped from 81 percent to 70 percent.

On the domestic front, marketing chief Brian Swette resigned amidst complaints from bottlers about ineffective ads and declining Pepsi share. During the 1990s, Pepsi's ad campaigns and slogans had been uncharacteristically lame. "Gotta Have It" implied that people bought the caffeinated beverage only because it was addictive. "Be Young, Have Fun, Drink Pepsi" sounded like a bland fifties' throwback, while "Nothing Else Is a Pepsi" lacked fire. "Generation Next," introduced in 1997, was a wordplay on Generation X, though the ads targeted an even younger cohort (one ad featured a teen with multiple piercings in ears, nose, and eyelids), and they alienated older consumers. In 1999, new marketing chief Dawn Hudson (with input from Pepsi veteran Alan Pottasch) introduced the "Joy of Cola" campaign, in which a cherubic little girl turned nasty when given a Coke instead of a Pepsi, her voice suddenly deepening to a man's. The ads were funny and appealed to a broader audience.

After ignoring the high-margin vending machine market for years, Pepsi threw itself into cooler placement, increasing the number by 240 percent in two years. In the marketplace, Roger Enrico stressed the synergies of Pepsi-Cola, Frito-Lay, and Tropicana, which accounted for $11 billion in annual supermarket sales. Following Coke's lead, Pepsi spun off its company-owned bottlers as the publicly-owned Pepsi Bottling Group, while also arranging other bottler consolidations. The cover of the 1998 PepsiCo annual report featured a line of its products headed by a duckling. "You get your ducks in a row," Enrico wrote in his message to shareholders, "then put some real money behind them." That appeared to be exactly what Pepsi was doing.

HARD EDGE TO A SOFT DRINK

Despite Pepsi's new feistiness, Coke continued to dominate Pepsi outside the United States by a 3.6-to-1 margin. Although it would take a miracle for Coke to reach its goal of 50 percent of the U.S. market share by the year 2001, it had snared 45 percent by 1999, versus Pepsi's 31 percent. The Big Red Machine may have been slowed by global economic woes, but it still appeared unstoppable in the long run. And under Doug Ivester it was indeed more of a machine. As *Fortune* reporter Betsy Morris put it, Ivester seemed the model CEO for the twenty-first century. "He marshals data and manages people in a way no pre–Information Age executive ever did or could." Ivester was the driving force behind Project Infinity, a computerized Coke information network to supply real-time financial and marketing data to the worldwide Coca-Cola system, and he had hired a "chief learning officer" to institutionalize the Coke mantra.

Like Robert Woodruff, who used to root in the trash to ascertain the proportion of Coke bottle caps, Doug Ivester liked to prowl the back alleys of the world to see where Coke was or was not. He spent a third of his time on the road. In a 1998 visit to Shanghai, he was annoyed to find no ice-cold Coke on an impromptu foray. "Why wouldn't you put Coke in here?" he asked a manager as they popped into a tiny cosmetics store. As chief Coke investor Warren Buffett put it, "He looks at any time anyone swigs any beverage other than a Coke as a personal insult."

Like his predecessors, Ivester stressed the need to "do the right thing." Coke employees should always obey the law while helping communities where the Company sold drinks. Even in philanthropy, however, everything had to contribute to the bottom line. "It's the right thing to do, and it's very right for business, too," he stressed. "Use your imagination to leverage community-relations activities against marketing activities," a Coke memo urged. "Make sure the project is measurable." Also, Coke should be assured that it was the "signature" partner that would get public credit for do-gooding.

But many Coke veterans wondered whether a warm heart really beat deep inside Ivester's well-oiled machine. "It is not that Ivester is a brute," wrote *Fortune*'s admiring Betsy Morris, "so much as a relentless force." Tell that to longtime Coke employees such as Ray Morgan, who was forced out of the Company at Christmas 1998 after a thirty-year career that included spearheading innovative vending machines and the return of the Coke contour bottle. While still based in Atlanta, Morgan had been assigned to the Greater European Group and spent most of his time jet-lagged, trying to care for his eighty-seven-year-old mother and seven-year-old daughter. When he asked for a reassignment, he was refused. His story was not unique. "A lot of people have left Coke in the last few years," he said in a 1999 interview.

One former CCE manager commented: "Doug is a very calculating, brilliant guy. He's quietly aggressive. He'll cut your legs off and you won't know it." To his credit, however, Ivester initiated an internal audit of Coke, asking employees to answer the question, "Is The Coca-Cola Company arrogant?" Few people dared to respond, but one anonymous contract worker answered with an emphatic *Yes*. "There is grave cause for concern in a company that has high turnover in any given department and no one bothers to understand why, cause for concern when people are fired because they did not say what others wanted to hear."

Even during Goizueta's last few years as CEO, Doug Ivester's imprint was on Company policy, particularly at giant bottler CCE, where he was chairman. Although Ivester was unfailingly soft-spoken and polite in person, he demanded a no-holds-barred business style, and, in such a fierce competitive environment, unpleasant allegations began to surface. Jeffrey Wright, a former CCE driver, claimed that two managers tried to bribe him in August 1994 in order to defeat a union and he had taped phone conversations to prove it. U.S. Attorney James Deichert portrayed the CCE corporate culture as a "pressure cooker." The government eventually lost the 1997 federal bribery trial, however, despite Wright's testimony, because he had edited the tapes and no longer had the originals. In another case, Coke allegedly advertised a Minute Maid apple juice as containing 100 percent apple juice, when in fact it had added sweeteners from nonapple sources. Coke settled out of court for $1.5 million.

Even as Coke was claiming in the Pepsi lawsuit that its distributors were an extension of the Company, CCE aggressively competed against its own distributors for lucrative vending machine profits. One morning when a California distributor stopped to inspect his coolers on a college campus, he found a CCE machine right next to it, undercutting his price by ten cents a can. "There's just no way I can compete," he complained. Across the country, traditional soft drink distributors found themselves in the same situation. They could buy product cheaper from a Walmart Sam's Club than they could from CCE, but the Coke bottler asked Walmart to limit the amounts it would sell to distributors. Because of the 1980 Soft Drink Interbrand Competition Act, distributors were forbidden to "transship" cheaper product from outside their territories. Ironically, the law had been passed to protect small bottlers, an endangered species twenty years later.* When desperate Maryland distributor B. K. Miller Company sued CCE, accusing it of fraud, wiretapping, and charging discriminatory prices in an effort to drive the distributor out of business, the big bottler countersued, accusing the distributor of transshipment. The case was settled out of court.

Meanwhile, two issues from Coke's past reappeared to haunt Ivester. Coca-Cola had sold its Florida orange groves in 1996, and protesters outside Atlanta's World of Coca-Cola complained that the new Brazilian owners were using child labor.

The orange juice protest fizzled, but in April 1999 four African Americans brought a class action suit against The Coca-Cola Company for discrimination in pay, promotions, and performance evaluations. Cyrus Mehri, the lawyer representing the plaintiffs, had made his name as part of the legal team that won a $176 million discrimination settlement against Texaco in 1998. The complaint alleged that there were "dramatic differences in pay" at Coke's corporate headquarters, such that the average black employee was paid nearly $27,000 less than the average white employee. A "glass ceiling" allegedly prevented most African Americans from advancing upwards, and "glass walls" kept them out of powerful areas such as marketing and finance. If the suit were granted class action status, it would be open to any black employee who had worked at Coca-Cola since April 22, 1995.

The complaint offered juicy hearsay anecdotes, including the allegation that the marketing director for an Alabama Coke bottler introduced himself in 1996 or 1997 as the "Grand Cyclops," a clear reference to the Ku Klux Klan. It also quoted Doug Ivester as saying a few years earlier that it would take fifteen or twenty years before African American employees were well represented at senior management levels. The Company emphatically denied that it practiced any form of racial discrimination, while it hastily created a council on racial diversity.†

MASS HYSTERIA IN BELGIUM

Even as Coke struggled to recover from the global recession, it suffered a catastrophic health scare in Europe. On June 8, 1999, thirty-nine students in Bornem, Belgium, collecting bottle caps for a contest, complained of nausea and headaches and attributed it to their Cokes. They were sent to a health clinic. The media reported it. Two days later, Belgian students in another city reported dizziness and stomachaches after

---

* In 1980, there were 353 Coke bottlers in the United States. By 1999, there were 96.

† Coca-Cola was further embarrassed when an internal report from December 1995 surfaced, recommending that Coke enhance diversity and address "why there are so few African-Americans in certain areas and levels of the business." The report was written by Carl Ware, president of Coke's African unit.

drinking canned Cokes from a vending machine. The media reported it, and concern spread.

Coca-Cola Enterprises, the U.S.-based megabottler partially owned by the Coca-Cola Company, supplied the questionable Coke, although the bottles came from an Antwerp plant and the cans from the mammoth Dunkirk facility. Scrambling to determine the possible cause, Company investigators found that some of the bottled drinks had a faint rotten egg smell because a batch of carbon dioxide had been contaminated with hydrogen sulfide. At the canning plant, some wooden pallets had been disinfected with phenol, another chemical with an unpleasant odor. Although neither problem should have caused any illness, taken together they were embarrassment enough for Coke, which had always prided itself on stringent quality standards.

As fears mounted, Coke officials explained what they had discovered. CCE voluntarily recalled affected bottles and began to seal off its vending machines. Then, on June 14, more students fell ill after buying vended Cokes, and the panicked Belgian government ordered a complete recall while banning all of the Company's products. Word of the purportedly poisoned soft drinks spread rapidly, along with consumers claiming to have imbibed company products that made them ill, too. Eventually, some 250 European imbibers came down with the mysterious Coca-Cola bug. France, the Netherlands, and Luxembourg banned Coke products, too.

Clearly, the Coke brass was caught off guard by how rapidly the crisis escalated. On June 16, two days after the ban, Doug Ivester issued his first public statement, a bland bit of bureaucratese saying that the Company was "taking all necessary steps" to ensure its beverages' quality. But the next day, Ivester flew to Europe to exercise personal damage control. He penned an apology that ran in full-page ads in European newspapers, he appeared in a ninety-second TV spot, and he offered to buy every Belgian—all ten million of them—a free Coke. Even that offer fizzled when the Belgian government called a halt to this "Restore" marketing campaign, claiming it violated anti-trust laws.

Finally, by June 24, both Belgium and France had rescinded their bans, though Coke still had to destroy its surviving stock before it could gear up again. The massive recall cost the company and its major bottler over $100 million, not to mention a severely tarnished image.

Just as the Belgian crisis was finally winding down, the French media publicized rumors that rat poison had somehow contaminated Coke. Then a Polish consumer found some mold in BonAqa, Coke's European bottled water. The mold was not a health problem, but some reusable bottles hadn't been properly cleaned. As a result, Coke spent another $1.8 million to withdraw and destroy the product.

Yet, in all these incidents, Coke probably didn't make anyone sick, as every scientist who studied the Belgian scare concluded. Perhaps there was an off odor (even that much was unclear), but nothing to account for the panic, the nausea, the dizziness. Those are the classic vague symptoms of psychosomatic illness. Coke found itself embroiled in a case of mass hysteria, or what psychiatrists call mass sociogenic illness.*

---

* As this history documents, Coca-Cola had always been subject to slander and rumor. In 1993, it was Pepsi that suffered from what folklorists call an "urban legend"—that the company was somehow putting syringes into its cans. Sure enough, people around the United States came forward to claim that they had found needles in their drinks—all a hoax.

Belgians were already spooked by the recent revelation of dioxin in their meat and poultry, which itself had come in the wake of "mad cow disease." They were ready for another food scare, and what better victim than a gigantic American company that corporation-bashers loved to vilify? It was because of Coke's size, ubiquity, power, and popularity that the rumors spread so quickly. The media reported it, with insufficient explanations and a great deal of sensationalism and credulity. Caught in a catch-22 bind, Coke had no choice but to apologize for something it probably didn't do. Nonetheless, the Company's slow, ambiguous response troubled analysts, and some observers questioned whether Ivester should try to manage such problems single-handedly—wasn't it time to appoint a second in command?

Meanwhile, egged on by Pepsi, the European Union raided Coca-Cola offices in four countries, seizing documents it hoped would prove that Coke illegally tried to force competitors out of the market. Jumping on the Coke-bashing bandwagon, Australian regulators announced an investigation of Coca-Cola Amatil for possible marketing abuses.

GLOBAL IS THE WHOLE POINT, STUPID

As Coke prepared to enter the twenty-first century, then, it was beset with worries. During the first two quarters of 1999, the Company's worldwide volume declined for the first time in a decade, while net income dropped 13 percent in the first quarter, then 21 percent in the second, in the wake of the Belgian health scare. At the Company's annual meeting in Wilmington, Delaware, Ivester admitted that every major market outside the United States was "stagnant or slumping," which had a "gravitational pull on earnings and volume." Even the domestic volume fell one percent in the second quarter because of retail price hikes. During 1999, U.S. soft drink per capita consumption dropped for the first time in decades.

The vaunted anchor bottler program appeared to backfire as well. The huge bottlers, in which Big Coke held substantial shares, were struggling in the difficult economic climate. In Brazil, for instance, cheaper, inferior local soft drinks called "Tubainas" were cutting into Coke's dominant market share. As a result, anchor bottler Panamco—saddled with debt from purchasing the Cisneros bottlers in Venezuela—reported its first loss. Meanwhile, Australian anchor bottler Coca-Cola Amatil suffered in the troubled Asian economy. Former chief executive Norbert Cole, ousted during a restructuring, sued Coke, claiming that it had hurt Amatil by forcing it to give up its European holdings. Big Coke's equity income from its ownership in bottlers dropped from $155 million in 1997 to $32 million in 1998, and it promised to dwindle further in 1999. The anchor bottlers, which were supposed to be Coke's growth engine, now needed cash infusions in the form of increased marketing funds or improved infrastructure. In 1998, for instance, Coke pumped $1.84 billion into its bottlers, of which $1.2 billion went to Coca-Cola Enterprises.

With many bottlers working at partial capacity, Coke hoped to fill the bottling lines with Orangina and Cadbury products, but both deals ran into regulatory roadblocks early in 1999. A French appeals court ruled against the Orangina deal. Australian and Mexican regulators vetoed the Cadbury sale, and the European Union asserted its authority to stop it as well. Although the Company revised its Orangina and Cadbury proposals to attempt to meet regulatory objections, both deals fell through.

While such problems might have given other CEOs sleepless nights, Doug Ivester appeared unfazed, as did his stockholders, who lined up for his autograph at the 1999 annual meeting. "Our long-term growth potential remains unchanged," Ivester said. "Our system has never been better equipped to convert that potential into long-term value."

It appeared that the CEO was correct. Even as the global economy bottomed in early 1999, Coca-Cola continued its implacable world conquest, fueled by a product that cost almost nothing to produce, with one of the highest profit margins on earth. While it promised to pump close to $1 billion into Brazil over the next three years, Coke bought a 20 percent stake in Peru's Inca Kola, a popular yellow bubblegum-flavored drink invented in 1935.

With Big Coke as the midwife, two major Japanese bottlers merged to form Coca-Cola West Japan Company, Coke's eleventh anchor bottler, in which the Company held a 5 percent interest. In Europe, a huge Greek bottler merged with Coca-Cola Beverages PLC to form Hellenic Bottling (Big Coke owning about a quarter share), the second-largest world bottler after CCE. In its Middle East and North African division, Coke forged ahead of Pepsi with a 41 percent market share, opening new bottling plants in Saudi Arabia, Eritrea, and Algeria.

The Company continued its relentless marketing initiative around the world, offering larger sizes and multipacks in Germany, lowering prices in South Africa, promoting a "Win Millions" contest in Thailand where consumers could win a million baht in gold, and enticing Venezuelan consumers with free product and prizes such as houses, salaries for a year, and a free shopping spree. To help restore the faith of Belgian consumers, the Company offered Coke-embossed cell phones for half the going rate if they would only drink one hundred Cokes. In India, the Company sponsored a thirty-city concert tour by singing sensation Daler Mehndi and launched Sprite as "refreshingly honest." In troubled Indonesia, Coke's new ad slogan urged: *Teguk Lagi, Semangat Lagi!*—"Drink Again, Be Spirited Again!"

Even in the disastrous Russian economy, the Company persevered with a "Drink the Legend" campaign, based on an old Russian folktale to appeal to resurgent Russian nationalism. Early in 1999, Ivester flew to Ukraine to open a new $100 million bottling plant, emphasizing that Coke's belief in the future of the former Soviet Union was unshaken. Although its most popular drinks worldwide were Coca-Cola, Fanta, Sprite, and Coca-Cola light, the Company owned more than 160 brands worldwide.

The Company took portions of its memorabilia on the road as the *Traveling World of Coca-Cola*. In Paris, the Louvre even hosted a popular exhibit of sixty original Coca-Cola paintings. The Company launched a range of international fashion and sports clothing, signing up partners for its Coca-Cola Wear label.

Back in the United States, third-generation Coke-bottling man Charles Frenette took over as global marketing director when Sergio Zyman left, with a mandate from Ivester to stress local marketing initiatives around the world. While advertising might be high profile, it had not been the driving force behind Coke's recent market growth. It was the execution on the ground, with the proliferation of vending machines, promotions, and interactive consumer experiences, such as the new NASCAR "Wall of

Speed," in which fans could drive their own cars in a "virtual reality" race. Roberto Goizueta himself had observed, "You let me have the bottling plants and the trucks and the highly efficient systems, and I'll let you have the TV commercials. I'll beat you to a pulp over time." Even with ads, the content wasn't as important as the ubiquity in places such as premovie spots or the burgeoning Internet.

Frenette, who had proven his ability to grow the business in South Africa, was friendly, customer oriented, and maintained a low public profile—the opposite of Zyman. Frenette orchestrated a co-promotion with AT&T, affixing free calling cards to millions of fountain-beverage cups to appeal to teens. The promotion was designed not only to sell more soft drinks but to garner important marketing information as the cards were used. The new marketing head didn't rush to change the agency-du-jour smorgasbord he inherited from Zyman, but he apparently did ask the agencies to modify the quick-cut, disco-beat, techno-hip Coke ads—which old-style Coke adman Bill Backer called "mean-spirited and self-absorbed" and John Bergin termed "bizarre and uncommunicative"—and refocus on the traditional Coke heart tug. In one spot, a solemn little boy, watching a heart-rending performance of *Pagliacci* from the wings, walked onstage to give the suffering opera clown a Coke. It was a subtle tribute to the old Mean Joe Greene ad. Sprite, the fastest-growing U.S. soft drink, continued to thrive with its anti-hype "Image Is Nothing" campaign.

Frenette initially floundered when it came to long-troubled Diet Coke advertising. In 1998, his advertising head, Ian Rowden, ran two-year-old ads while trying to come up with something new. Frenette was never billed as an advertising man, but he excelled as a marketing pro. In 1999, he offered excerpts of six bestselling novels in Diet Coke twelve-packs, spurred by research indicating that diet soft drink consumers tended to be affluent, well-educated, voracious readers. The romance novels—including an excerpt from best-selling Nora Roberts, who admitted to being a Diet Coke addict herself—appealed to Diet Coke's primarily female constituency, though there was also an excerpt from an Elmore Leonard thriller for the men.

Finally, Frenette settled on "Live Your Life" as the diet drink's slogan. Featuring liberated, self-assured, svelte young women, the Wieden+Kennedy ads had a clever edge. In one, a beautiful young woman stopped in the middle of a desert for a Diet Coke. When a good-looking man pulled up and got out, she watched his car roll over a cliff without stopping it, then casually asked, "Do you need a ride?" In another spot, after interviewing a cute young blond, the head of a video dating service observed, "Sounds like you have a pretty good life." Taking a long, ruminative sip from her Diet Coke, the young woman said, "Thank you," in a tone of sudden revelation and left without completing the interview, as the slogan "Live Your Life" appeared. The message? To be fulfilled, you don't need a man: you just need Diet Coke.

Meanwhile, Coca-Cola intensified its drive to penetrate schools to snare youthful consumers early. "Whether it's a morning pick-me-up, a lunchtime refresher or for after class with friends," a Coke internal organ advised, "students want their drinks easily accessible." School officials, eager for soft drink money to supplement their meager budgets, agreed. The Colorado Springs School District signed a ten-year exclusive contract with Coke that guaranteed to bring in $7.5 million—provided, that is, that its 32,500 students bought a sufficient number of soft drinks from the schools' vending machines. A school district official wrote a letter to each of the principals.

"We must sell 70,000 cases of product," he wrote, "at least once during the first three years of the contract." To do so, he urged schools to "allow students to purchase and consume vended products throughout the day" and to add more coolers. "The Coke people surveyed the middle and high schools this summer and have suggestions on where to place additional machines." The school official signed off as "The Coke Dude."

In 1998 and 1999, hundreds of schools became active participants in marketing soft drinks, signing up for exclusive Coke or Pepsi deals in a veritable feeding frenzy.* "This contract is a godsend," a procurement director for a Washington, D.C., public school said as he signed on with Coke, allowing the schools to pay for bus tokens for needy students and to replace textbooks. In yet another Colorado contract, a school district planned to build a new stadium with the Coke cash windfall, as well as to improve computer and video technology and boost literacy programs. "Kids and teachers who spend hour after hour after hour in school get thirsty," a Coke spokesman observed. "Every time they consume a beverage from home, it's a lost revenue opportunity for the school [and Coke]. So it's kind of a 'win win win.' It's good for us, good for people who are thirsty who want our products, good for schools."

Coke soon received an unexpected bonus. Although it was illegal to sell soda as part of the school lunch program, many schools began to give away soft drinks in order to lure students on open campuses into staying for lunch. When Senator Patrick Leahy and several other politicians from milk-producing states proposed legislation to close this loophole, the American School Food Service Association objected, defending the give-away soft drinks as the only way to keep some school lunch programs alive. Ever since John Pemberton, Coca-Cola purveyors had known that "sampling" programs were an excellent way to build business. Now, the schools were doing it for them!

Several new Coke ads made an unabashed appeal to high school students. In one spot, a teenage boy taking an exam reached up and grabbed a Coke that magically appeared overhead. He and a beautiful classmate were lifted up into a fantasy sky of blue. In another ad, a teenager went on and on about philosophical matters until his bored girlfriend suggested, "Do you wanna have a Coke and make out?" In a surreal ad called "Machine Teen Central," active teens swarmed around a Coke vending machine. Fueled by soft drinks, they rode bikes up buildings, glided above the earth on skateboards, and finally tossed schoolbooks into the air to form a stairway to heaven, the book covers changing to a Coke logo.

Unlike Pepsi, with its lip-synching six-year-old consumer, Coke stuck to its seldom-breached rule that it should not show human children under twelve drinking the beverage. But that didn't stop Coke from conveying the appropriate message. In a feel-good polar bear ad, Momma Bear lured a wayward baby cub into swimming to safety by offering a Coke. In another spot, baby robins in a nest fought amongst themselves until Mom flew up with a Coke. "Hey, Mom, you rock," one of her chicks said as he sucked down a Coke.

---

* Schools were not the only ones to grab Coke money in return for exclusive deals. In 1999, the first city in the United States signed a ten-year deal with Coke. Huntington Beach, California, agreed to allow the local bottler to put up Coke signs and to sell beverages on all city property for $300,000 a year in cash and an additional $300,000 in community programs.

Roberto Goizueta had always said that Coke products should be more popular than water. In 1999 Doug Ivester went his old mentor one better, introducing a new bottled water called Dasani—an invented word with an African/Italian ring that supposedly connoted crisp purity. Coke had considered a bottled water product for a long time but could never figure out how to make its customary profits. It hit upon a plan to sell its bottlers a patented mix of minerals, which they would add to regular municipal water and bottle in light blue bottles.

With all of this activity, Ivester didn't appear to be worried. "I have to chuckle sometimes," he said, "when I read that some analyst is fretting about our 'global exposure.' I hate to tell them, but that's the idea."

IVESTER'S SUDDEN DEPARTURE

But time was running out for the unflappable Ivester, though he didn't know it. He remained supremely competent, ruthlessly aggressive, and thoroughly imbued with the Coca-Cola spirit, but no one ever accused him of excessive charm or tact. In September, Ivester created a furor when he revealed that Coke was testing a new vending machine that would automatically charge more in hot weather. "This is a classic situation of supply and demand," the CEO said. "If demand increases, the price tends to increase. . . . In a final summer championship, when people meet at a stadium to have fun, the utility of an ice-Cold Coca-Cola is very high. So it is fair that it should be more expensive." The media jumped all over Ivester's gaffe, with Jay Leno making jokes about it on late-night TV. The Company assured consumers that the machine was merely being tested and had not been installed anywhere, but the damage was done. Ivester remained unconcerned. "It'll blow over in a day or two," he told a colleague. But it didn't. Over a thousand cartoons mocked the greedy hypothetical Coca-Cola vending machine.

As that flap spilled over into October, Ivester appointed three new senior vice presidents in a reorganization that still left him without a number-two chief operating officer. One new VP was Doug Daft, an Australian who had run the Asian Coke division. That realignment prompted a frustrated Carl Ware to resign, since he would now have to report to Daft rather than directly to Ivester. Ware, the Company's highest-ranking black executive, announced his imminent departure just as the racial discrimination lawsuit was heating up.

That same November, Ivester decided to raise the price of Coca-Cola concentrate by seven percent, much more than the rise of general consumer prices, in order to boost earnings and please financial analysts. The bottlers, who had to absorb the price increase, were infuriated. Summerfield "Skey" Johnston Jr., the head of giant bottler Coca-Cola Enterprises, complained to the legendary Don Keough, seventy-two, who had served as a Coca-Cola consultant to the board until 1998, when Ivester had failed to renew his contract.

Keough didn't like Ivester, whom he regarded as a cold fish. "To be a dour, uptight person selling Coca-Cola is a contradiction in terms," he observed in a thinly veiled reference to Ivester. Now Keough talked to Herb Allen and Warren Buffett, the two most powerful members of the Coca-Cola board of directors, who were major shareholders as well.

Allen and Buffett arranged to meet Ivester on Wednesday, December 1, 1999, in Chicago, where the Coke CEO had a meeting with McDonald's executives. That afternoon, the three converged in the airport hangar for private executive jets. The meeting didn't last long. Without sitting down or removing their coats, Allen and Buffett told Ivester that they wanted him to resign.

The following Sunday, at a specially convened board meeting, the board made it official. The following day, Doug Ivester, only fifty-two, announced his premature retirement in a few months. Starting immediately, Australian Coke executive Douglas N. Daft, fifty-six, would step in as president and chief operating officer. He would become the CEO when Ivester departed. Leaders in the business world, even other Coca-Cola executives, were stunned by the news.

Doug Ivester had presided over a disastrous end to the twentieth century, during which Coke's share price fell to a heart-stopping low of $47 in October 1999 before staggering back to drift in the $60s. "The last two years have been a pseudo-trauma for Coke on so many fronts," observed a Merrill Lynch analyst. "When it rains, it pours. But they were in a monsoon." The disastrous Belgian health scare, the failed attempts to buy Orangina and Cadbury Schweppes, the racial discrimination case, the resignation of Carl Ware, the uproar over the price-adjusting vending machines, and the bottlers' fury over the price hike for concentrate—they had all been too much for the board.

In a way, the departing CEO was a scapegoat. Had Goizueta lived, he would have faced the same disasters—a global economic downturn flowing out of Asia, a stronger dollar hurting overseas profits, and the rest. Conceivably, however, the astute, aristocratic Goizueta would have moved more quickly to counter each threat to his beloved company. And Goizueta would have sought help from Don Keough.

Ivester's refusal to appoint a second-in-command may have sealed his fate. Some stockholders faulted him for failing to repurchase huge chunks of stock to stem the share price tumble. All in all, Ivester probably fell, like Caesar, from a "thousand cuts," as one observer put it. And certainly, Ivester's lukewarm personality did not win him many close friends in the company.

Now, of course, the big question was what would happen to Coke.

~ 23 ~

Daft Dilemmas

Optimism, pride and fun have been restored in the system. New leadership is in place.

—CEO Douglas N. Daft letter to shareholders in
The Coca-Cola Company 2000 Annual Report

Doug Daft, fifty-six, was completely unprepared to be thrust to the top of The Coca-Cola Company as its new CEO. *Do I or don't I accept?* he briefly pondered. He said later that he felt like Bilbo Baggins, the middle-aged hobbit who suddenly found himself entrusted with the magic ring of power. "Mr. Daft radiates a kind of shock that it is his turn to run the world's best-known soft-drink company," one observer noted.

A former math teacher and the son of a shoe store owner, Daft had had thirty years of experience with Coca-Cola, primarily in the Middle and Far East, when he was chosen to lead the Company into the new century. Soft-spoken, affable, and direct, he was untested at the highest level, but he had the marketing background that Ivester lacked. He had experience in Japan, with its wild array of beverages, and he had overseen the building of the Chinese business from scratch. Would Daft, the Australian Coke veteran, be able to turn the company around and restore morale? Or would Coke slowly go flat?

The mantle had come to him in part because Don Keough liked him. Daft had reported to him in the 1980s and early 1990s, and Keough considered him an efficient executive who got the job done without fanfare. "The fellow is the right man at the right time," Keough observed. Daft had also befriended board member Herb Allen in Williamstown, Massachusetts, where both men owned summer homes, though Allen was blunter than Keough. "There weren't a lot of choices," he said later. Soon after he became the CEO, Daft brought back Keough as a "senior advisor."

New York Times reporter Constance Hays noted that Daft was regarded as "a kind of eccentric professor," who had once shown up for a meeting wearing mismatched shoes. "His spectacles and tufted hairstyle gave him an owlish appearance," Hays wrote, "but he was also known to be a keen competitor."

A STRATEGICALLY ALIGNED HATCHET JOB

Even while Ivester was still officially the CEO—he was supposed to resign in April 2000 at the Company's annual meeting—Daft moved with unexpected speed to change the Company. Goizueta's mantra had been that Coke should think globally but act locally. Daft pronounced that Coca-Cola must not only act locally, but also *think* locally. Instead of directing the far-flung beverage empire from the North Avenue tower in Atlanta, managers should live in their territories. He promised to reassign hundreds of staffers from headquarters to posts overseas.

At the same time, however, he moved Steve Jones, a top Coke executive in Japan, back to Atlanta to be the company's chief marketing officer, a hint that Coke might intend to offer more diverse beverages, as in Japan. Daft also swiftly convinced Carl Ware to reconsider his resignation, appointing him as the executive vice president in charge of corporate affairs and government relations.

In mid-January 2000, Daft announced that Jack Stahl, then in charge of Coke's North American business, would serve as his president and chief operating officer, the second-in-command spot that Ivester had never filled. An accountant, Stahl had joined the Company in 1979 and had once served as its chief financial officer. Clean-cut and polite, he scribbled daily management lessons down on index cards. His in-depth knowledge of the domestic business would presumably complement Daft's international background. "There is no doubt that Doug Daft is moving lightning quick to get the Coca-Cola Company headed in the right direction again," an impressed Lehman Brothers analyst said.

Then Daft sent a mysterious voicemail asking people to cancel vacations, trips, and meetings so that they could be in their offices on Wednesday, January 26, 2000, for an important announcement. No one knew what to expect. A press release spoke of a "strategic organizational alignment," not unexpected from a new CEO. On that fateful day, they discovered that this was a euphemism for a massive layoff of 6,000 Coca-Cola employees worldwide, 20 percent of the workforce. Nearly *half* of the employees at Atlanta headquarters—2,500 people—would lose their jobs.*

The cuts were necessary, Daft said, in order to "ensure a strong future for The Coca-Cola Company," allowing it to be more nimble and to focus primarily on marketing. Some jobs, such as groundskeeping and payroll management, would be outsourced. But rest assured, the layoffs would all be done "with care and sensitivity."

That was cold comfort to some employees who learned that they were fired when they listened to their answering machines. Many others kept working in a tense limbo, not knowing whether they would be axed. "There was a three-person panel formed to determine my future," one executive recalled. "Then I was sitting on a[nother] three-person panel to assess the grade below me. I hated every single minute of it." Weeks later, he lost his job. The new Coke leader was no longer compared to a kindly absentminded professor. Within the company he was nicknamed Daft the Knife.

That same Wednesday morning of January 26, the Company released its full financial results from the previous year, including write-downs of $813 million for the cost of overbuilt factories and equipment in Russia and Japan, as well as hits for oversold concentrate that burdened its bottlers. The Company estimated that severance packages and other expenses related to the job cuts would cost another $800 million. "It's

---

* The 6,000 figure was an overestimate. In the end, 5,200 people lost their jobs.

not as if they were short a few million dollars," said one stunned analyst. "It's *$1.6 billion*." The day of the announcement, shares of Coca-Cola fell $2.80, tumbling another $3.50 the following day.

The dismissals also created a public furor over the pending racial discrimination lawsuit. Lawyer Cyrus Mehri had asked U.S. District Court Judge Richard Story in Atlanta to sanction a class-action suit that would cover more than 2,000 current and former African American employees, in addition to the eight individuals he represented (four more had joined the original plaintiffs). Yet blacks who were fired were being asked to waive their rights to join the hypothetical class action in order to get their severance packages. Outraged, Mehri complained to the judge and the press that Coke was attempting to "buy the silence of its African-American employees."

Concerned black workers approached Larry Jones, an African American benefits manager in the Coca-Cola human resources department, asking his advice, so he organized a meeting of a hundred and fifty black workers at an Atlanta church. Two days later, Jones met with Jack Stahl to ask his help in changing the policy so that black employees would not be forced to sign the waiver. The next day, Jones learned that *he* was being fired. The Company insisted that his termination had nothing to do with the church meeting or his advocacy, but Jones didn't believe it. Even after the Company finally backed down on the waiver issue, allowing dismissed black employees to receive severance pay and still remain in a class action, Larry Jones became a vocal critic and activist, organizing more meetings and talking about a possible Coca-Cola boycott. When Doug Ivester announced in February that he would resign as CEO immediately rather than wait until April, his $120 million "golden parachute" only added fuel to the fire.

Attempting to salvage the situation, Daft assured the media in March that "diversity is a top priority for me," but *New York Times* reporter Constance Hays noted archly that the Company "has no women among its senior or executive vice presidents" and no blacks other than Carl Ware. "White men control the company."

RIDING FOR BLACK JUSTICE

Doug Daft, the white man at the helm of the Company, did *not* appear to be in control during his first year. Two weeks before the annual meeting, Coke summoned analysts to the Regent Hotel in New York City, where they expected to hear Daft's dynamic plans to turn the Company around. Instead, they were treated to four interminable hours of lectures and videos about Coke's local marketing efforts around the world, ranging from a soccer game in Burkina Faso to a beach party in Chile. Finally, Daft told them that Coca-Cola projected a 5 or 6 percent volume growth for 2000, which few believed. "It's achievable," Daft insisted, "and we've got the programs to do it."*

On April 19, in Wilmington, Delaware, Daft presided over his first annual meeting, usually a brief, businesslike convocation of contented shareholders. This time (a

---

* Daft was wrong. Coke volume grew only 4 percent in 2000.

harbinger of future fractious annual events) it lasted for two and a half hours. Daft was interrupted by protestors who demanded more recycled plastic in Coke containers. A shareholder resolution against using genetically modified corn in high-fructose corn syrup was introduced and defeated. But the meeting was dominated by the racial issue.

Larry Jones arrived with a busload of angry black former and present Coke employees who wore red hats emblazoned with "Justice Ride," a reference to civil-rights-era freedom riders. At a church rally before they departed, they joined hands and, to the tune of *Kumbaya*, sang, "We are riding for justice, Lord, come by here." A little girl held a sign that read "Will the Real Thing Do the Right Thing?"

At the meeting, Jones came to the microphone and complained that Carl Ware was the only high-ranking black executive the Company had ever had. "In 114 years, you only found one of us qualified? How long do we wait? We are *never* going to be anything but black employees." Then, his voice dropping dramatically, he intoned, "Let's stop—buying—Coca-Cola!" This anguished call for a boycott came from a man who, like any loyal Company employee, had always forced his family to drink nothing but Coke.

Jesse Jackson followed Jones to the microphone. He too criticized the Company, pointing to its board of directors, composed mostly of old white men. "*Someone* has not gotten the message." There also were no Hispanics on the board, though they represented 27 percent of Coke consumers. "Law bills are up; share price is down," he complained. "Coke will lose this case in a court of law, but worse, in the court of public opinion." Jackson nonetheless stopped short of endorsing a boycott, probably because Coca-Cola supported his PUSH/Rainbow Coalition group, which also owned Coke shares. Behind the scenes, Jackson had met with Daft, Stahl, and Ware, encouraging them to settle the case quickly.

The boycott never gained momentum, but the discrimination case dragged on in messy fashion, due in part to Jackson's machinations. Jackson was buddies with Willie Gary, a high-rolling African American personal-injury lawyer in Florida. In January, Jackson had introduced his friend to then-CEO Doug Ivester, hoping Gary could be some kind of legal peacemaker. Then in April, Jackson advised one of the plaintiffs, who was looking for a new lawyer, to contact Gary. Smelling big money, the Florida lawyer tried to join the existing suit, but the judge refused.

In mid-June, with lawyer Cyrus Mehri threatening to file a huge class-action brief chock-full of incriminating stories, the Company reached a tentative settlement, though the details remained hazy, and Judge Richard Story would have to approve the final settlement. Minutes after the announcement, Willie Gary and Johnnie Cochran (famous for defending O. J. Simpson) filed a *new* lawsuit representing four black Coke employees, seeking an outrageous $1.5 billion. It didn't faze Gary that he had garnered millions of dollars for Coca-Cola advertising on his MBC Network, a cable channel for black viewers. Gary scoffed at the "phantom settlement."

It wasn't until November 2000 that the Company agreed to a $192.5 million settlement, with an average payout of $40,000 in cash to around 2,000 African American former and current employees, and up to $300,000 to the four remaining original plaintiffs. In addition, an outside watchdog panel would monitor Coca-Cola's treatment of minorities and women for another four years.

In follow-up interviews, some Coke officials just made things worse. They admitted that black employees had frequently been paid inadequately and had been passed over for well-deserved promotions. But hey, they pointed out, that was true for a lot of white employees as well! "We bled [over this lawsuit]; there's no ifs ands or buts about that," said Carl Ware. "Fortunately, that's behind us."

Not quite. Until the following spring, employees still didn't know exactly how much they would receive. Willie Gary urged potential plaintiffs to sign a petition saying that they were "saddened and ashamed" of Mehri's efforts. In the end, only twenty-three opted out of the settlement, and Judge Richard Story finally approved it, but it was a torturous, protracted process.

In April 2001, the Company hired Deval Patrick as Coke's general counsel. A black lawyer raised by a single mother on Chicago's South Side, Patrick had served as assistant U.S. attorney general in the Clinton administration and, most recently, had been general counsel at Texaco, where he had helped settle another racial discrimination lawsuit.

"THIS IS THE BEST THEY CAN DO?"

Meanwhile, Coke's fabled marketing machine appeared to be broken. With the "Always Coca-Cola" theme wearing thin after seven years, early in 2000 the Company switched to "Coca-Cola. Enjoy." The television spots were predictable. In one, a young man dives down a huge waterfall, then swims to the bottom to retrieve a refreshing Coke to share with his friends. Another non-verbal beach scene features loud music over dizzying edits of surfboarding and parasailing, with Coke-swilling at the end. "Rather bland and forgettable," one viewer noted.

Worse, however, was "Best Friends," which begins with a celebratory college graduation. "I'll miss you!" one girl says to another. "Best friends forever!" they chant simultaneously. But when one suggests toasting the occasion with a Coke, the other stammers that she forgot to bring one. "I never liked you," snaps the brunette. "Cause I'm prettier than you?" counters the blonde. This degenerates into a catfight in which one loses her glasses, fumbles on the ground for them, and pulls down another graduate. "Next time," the ad advises as a Coke bottle appears on-screen, "enjoy." Intended to be funny, the ad was not only unbelievable but also associated bad karma with the drink.

The short-lived, ineffective campaign was replaced in April 2001 by "Life Tastes Good," a reference to the old "Coke Adds Life" slogan. Without naming the soft drink, this effort remained diffuse and generic. One spot, using quick jump cuts, depicts hip young blacks and whites (but no mixed-race couples) smooching, dancing, swimming, skateboarding, and drinking Coca-Cola. "I'll drink to that / wherever you're at, / it's understood, /no doubt in my mind / that life tastes good," the rap cover song advises.

Another commercial shows five teenagers in a stifling, airless subway car, riding home from a rock concert. "We were six weeks from graduation," a boy says in a voice-over. "Ears ringing, voices all screamed out." He takes a can of Coca-Cola from his slack-jawed sleeping friend's pack and starts to drink it. "And as I watched them sleep, it hit me: That was the best night of my life. And I kind of wished we could all stay on that train forever." The spot ends with the little ditty and the words *Life Tastes Good.*

Coca-Cola." Teenagers might have identified with the ad, but most viewers would have been horrified at the thought of being trapped forever in that subway car, and the air of lassitude was the opposite of Coke's usual frenetic, joyful pace.

The ads didn't work. "Summer is upon us," one Coke insider said in mid-July 2001, "and the Life Tastes Good ads are having no impact in the marketplace. Panic is setting in." Coca-Cola Classic sales had slumped 6.5 percent for the four weeks ending in mid-June. Then, after the terrorist attacks on the World Trade Center on September 11, 2001, the slogan became almost an insult. Life didn't seem to taste very good after all. The Company dropped the slogan and offered no replacement for over a year.

Nor was Diet Coke doing well. A short-lived, lame slogan, "Live It Up, Drink It Down," was scrapped in 2000 during an actors' strike. The next year it was followed by "That Certain Something," aimed at independent young women. In one spot, a woman falls in the mud and, Diet Coke in hand, laughs it off—again, a negative event associated with the drink. In another, a husband who is folding his pregnant wife's underwear describes his attraction to her. "There's something oddly reassuring about thin, washed-out, cotton underwear," he says. "It's a really strange ad," observed one critic. "For starters, let's just pause to note that Diet Coke apparently wants its brand to be as familiar to you as old underwear." At least the ad evoked a positive, sweet sentiment, except that many obstetricians warned pregnant women against consuming caffeine and NutraSweet. In desperation, the Company delivered steel tubs filled with free Diet Coke cans chilled in blue ice to chic Hollywood salons for five days before the 2001 Academy Awards ceremonies.

Everyone in the industry recognized the consumer trend away from carbonated soft drinks, which were slowly losing market share to juices, water, teas, vitamin-enhanced beverages, and other new entries in the increasingly fragmented marketplace. Doug Daft knew that the Company had to act. "The world in which we operate has changed dramatically," he said, "and we must change to succeed." He recounted the story of his frustrating attempts to push Coca-Cola in Indonesia in the early 1970s. "Then I launched Fanta, and the business just tripled and quadrupled."

The moral, obviously, was to pursue other alternatives. Overseas, Fanta was sold in a hundred and eighty-eight countries, but since 1986 it hadn't even been available in the United States, where it had the image of an old-fashioned orange or grape soda pop. Coke's Minute Maid orange juice lagged far behind Pepsi's premium Tropicana brand, and its Dasani bottled water, introduced in 1999, trailed Pepsi's Aquafina.

Coke did make moves into non-carbonated beverages in the first two years of the new century. It made sense for the Company to purchase established brands that could take advantage of Coke's marketing muscle and ubiquitous distribution system. On November 20, 2000, Doug Daft announced a bold bid to purchase Quaker Oats, owner of Gatorade, the dominant sports drink that held 83 percent of the category, dwarfing Coke's Powerade imitator. Coke agreed to pay $16 billion for Quaker, intent on owning Gatorade, but also acquiring Cap'n Crunch cereal, Quaker Oatmeal, Rice-A-Roni, and Aunt Jemima pancake mixes. Regulations would require Coke to keep these food products for two years, but then analysts expected them to be spun off for $5 billion or so.

The following day, a jubilant Daft posed for pictures with the Quaker CEO, but that evening, during a long meeting of the Coca-Cola board, a unanimous vote vetoed the deal. Warren Buffett, Coke's major shareholder, apparently feared the deal's impact on his holdings. Although the board issued a statement affirming its "enthusiastic support" of Daft, the new CEO was publicly humiliated, and Pepsi subsequently swooped in and bought Quaker. "The collapse of the deal leaves Coke without a clear strategy for pulling ahead in the noncarbonated beverage business," observed the *New York Times*, "the only rapidly growing segment of the soft-drink industry."

Coke did make smaller acquisitions, buying the P. J. Bean Company of Ozone Park, New York, in order to get its Planet Java bottled coffee drinks, hoping to make it a competitor to Frappuccino, the successful Starbucks/PepsiCo joint venture. Then the Company purchased Mad River Traders, a small Connecticut firm that made juices and teas such as Mountain Style Lemonade and ginseng-fortified Forbidden Fruit. In its biggest and most effective grab, Coke bought Odwalla, maker of fruit and vegetable juices, based in Half Moon Bay, California, for $181 million.

The Company created a few beverages from scratch, but they were late imitations of front-runners. KMX, a caffeinated energy drink meant to compete with Red Bull, was a flop. In Brazil, Coke introduced Kuat, a drink made from guarana (an Amazonian fruit with caffeine, reputed to be an aphrodisiac) to compete with the dominant Guarana Antarctica. Most significantly, it created Simply Orange, a not-from-concentrate orange juice, to challenge Tropicana Pure Premium.

Recognizing that the Company was perhaps too big and bureaucratic to be creative, Coke in March 2001 also funded a new subsidiary called Fizzion, which would provide $250,000 seed money to each of fifteen start-up ventures it hoped to recruit for its incubator offices near Coke headquarters. The idea was to promote services and products that could help the Company. But Fizzion soon fizzled.

Reaching out in other directions, Coca-Cola expanded its joint venture for ready-to-drink teas and coffees with Nestle, renaming the effort Beverage Partners Worldwide. The Company also announced a joint marketing effort with Procter & Gamble in which Coke would distribute Pringles potato chips—about the same size as its beverages—in vending machines. In return, P&G would help Coke add nutritional supplements to new drinks. In May 2001, Doug Daft revealed that in Cape Coral, Florida, Coke and P&G were test-marketing Elations, a drink containing glucosamine, supposed to slow cartilage deterioration. Daft called Elations, aimed at the geriatric market, "youth in a bottle," and said that he hoped it would eventually be available "in every gas station, supermarket and convenience store in America."

But his elation was short-lived. The drink disappeared in the midst of a rancorous breakup with Procter & Gamble. Coke belatedly realized that selling P&G's Pringles and Sunny Delight juices would displace its own drinks, and that it could add its own nutritional supplements without P&G's help. Procter responded by suing Coke, claiming that the Company was stealing its trade secrets for calcium fortification.

While Coca-Cola struggled, an aggressive Pepsi surged. It purchased SoBe, the hip purveyor of Zen Blend, Tsunami, Strawberry Carrot Elixir, and other "functional beverages" that promised health benefits by including ingredients such as ginkgo, bee pollen, St. John's wort, and kava kava. Pepsi snagged the Big Boy chain's business from Coke. To reignite interest in the cola wars, Pepsi resumed a version of the venerable Pepsi Challenge campaign, pitting Pepsi One against Diet Coke in blind taste tests.

In March 2001, the iconoclastic Motley Fool's financial advisor Matt Richey compared Coke and PepsiCo, pointing out that, while their sales figures were remarkably similar, Coke carried a market capitalization nearly double that of Pepsi. "There's a myth to dispel here," wrote Richey. "Pepsico is growing sales four times faster than Coke; Pepsico has a better ratio of cash versus debt. . . . There's no doubt which company is running the better operation here."

For the first three months of 2001, Coca-Cola was the worst-performing stock in the Dow Jones Industrial Average, plummeting 25 percent. In a call with analysts and reporters, Doug Daft admitted, "The past year has been incredibly challenging on many levels." Veteran beverage analyst Manny Goldman summed up the general reaction. "Come on, this is *Coca-Cola!* It has the greatest distribution in the world, fabulous brands, a history of great marketing, and this is the best they can do?"

FLAILING AND FAILING

It almost seemed that Doug Daft was jinxed. The bad news just kept coming. In Senegal, the Company suspended production when a "moldlike substance" was found in Sprite and Coca-Cola bottles. In France, Coca-Cola bottles with a "packaging defect" that might cause the glass to splinter were recalled. In Belgium, Fanta Pomelo, a newly developed citrus drink following Daft's "think local" initiative, was withdrawn because it changed color and developed an off-taste when exposed to light. Coming so soon after the huge 1999 Belgian health scare, the recall was particularly unfortunate.

In October 2000, a Coke shareholder sued the Company for having misled investors and artificially boosting the share price by requiring bottlers to buy more concentrate than they needed—a practice known as "channel-stuffing." RC Cola won an anti-trust case against Coca-Cola that provided evidence of the heavy-handed bullying tactics employed during the Ivester era. "Coca-Cola products will occupy a minimum of 100 percent total soft-drink space," read one agreement with an Arkansas drugstore chain. Other restrictions allowed competitive brands to appear only on bottom shelves. Coca-Cola Enterprises offered "clean agreements" to grocery stores in Phoenix, Arizona, giving them extra discounts on wholesale Coke if their weekly newspaper ads didn't include other drinks. "They call it clean," said a local RC Cola and 7-Up bottler. "Clean us out is what they did."

Looking for evidence of similar practices overseas, European Union investigators conducted dawn raids in Coke's British, Belgian, and Spanish offices, while Costa Rica's anti-trust commission began an inquiry into whether Latin America's biggest Coke bottler, Panamerican Beverages, had tried to shut out competitors the same way. As Coke's business declined, its bottlers suffered. Panamerican fired 3,300 employees. Coca-Cola Enterprises, the dominant U.S. bottler, axed 2,000 workers.

Increasingly, The Coca-Cola Company was perceived as offering unhealthy beverages. In 2001, Coke got terrible press for its campaign called H2NO, urging restaurants to discourage customers from drinking tap water rather than soft drinks. Of course, Dasani, which was specially treated tap water, was a different matter. "Coca-Cola now seems eager to promote water," a cynical journalist noted, "just not the free kind." When Coca-Cola signed a $150 million deal to make Coke the only global marketing partner for the film *Harry Potter and the Sorcerer's Stone*, demonstrators protested, even though the Company was supporting literacy programs as part of the promotion. "It's a betrayal of [author J. K. Rowling's] audience to allow Harry Potter imagery to be used to sell junk food to kids," said Michael Jacobson of the Center for Science in the Public Interest, who dismissed soft drinks as "liquid candy."

The public schools of Madison, Wisconsin, had signed a three-year contract with Coke in 1997, giving the schools a $100,000 signing bonus and $515,000 in upfront commissions. But in 2000, loud public opposition led the Madison school board to cancel a renewal of the deal, even though Coke offered another $100,000 bonus, promised to reduce the advertising on its high school vending machines, and agreed to loan the district four vending machines in which they could put whatever nutritious drinks they chose. The following year, a study of Massachusetts children indicated that one extra soft drink a day gave children a 60 percent greater chance of becoming over-weight. Coke announced that it would include its juice, milk, and water products in school vending machines and would end exclusive contracts in a few districts, but the concern over childhood obesity would only build, along with criticism of Coca-Cola.

Coke appeared to be under siege internationally as well. In July 2001, the International Labor Rights Fund, in conjunction with the United Steelworkers union, filed a lawsuit in federal district court in Miami against The Coca-Cola Company and two bottlers for complicity in the murder and intimidation of union employees at Colombian Coke bottling plants.* The most explosive charges involved the Bebidas y Alimentos plant in Carepa, owned by Miami businessman Richard Kirby. Three union organizers had been killed there in the mid-1990s, allegedly with the approval of the plant management. A spokesperson for Coke denied any culpability, insisting, "We adhere to the highest standards of ethical conduct and business practices," but the accusations were destined to plague the Company for years to come.

Meanwhile, in Asia, Coca-Cola served as a convenient symbol for U.S. capitalism and imperialism. In October 2001, the radical People's War Group bombed a Coke plant in southern India in protest of the American invasion of Afghanistan. A month later, Maoist rebels attacked a Coca-Cola factory in Nepal.

In reaction to the problems besieging him from all sides, Doug Daft made a flurry of personnel changes. President and COO Jack Stahl, who was still identified as an Ivester apostle and who had opposed the Quaker/Gatorade purchase, found himself shut out of important meetings. He departed on March 5, 2001, having signed an agreement not to say anything "disparaging" about Coca-Cola. Three days later, Steve Heyer, a hotshot executive at Turner Broadcasting, was hired as an apparent heir to Daft, swiftly moving up the ladder from job to job.

In July, Daft summoned Brian Dyson, sixty-five, out of retirement to serve for a two-year term as a vice chairman and COO, a stopgap measure. Dyson was identified with the New Coke debacle and had had a rough time as head of Coca-Coca Enterprises, but Don Keough liked him and remembered his stirring speech to the disheartened bottlers back in 1989, in which Dyson said, "We are willing to do *whatever is necessary* for as long as is necessary to turn this business around. Together, we must *fix the problem.*" But Coke's twenty-first-century problems wouldn't yield to Dyson. A

---

* The lawyers for the case—Terry Collingsworth of the International Labor Rights Fund and Dan Kovalik of United Steelworkers—brought suit under the Alien Tort Claims Act, an obscure law passed in 1789, arguing that it allowed foreign rights abuses to be tried in U.S. courts.

week after Dyson came aboard, Charlie Frenette, who had served as chief marketing officer, then head of Coke's European and African operations, resigned, signing a gag order similar to Stahl's.

In October 2001, Coke announced a confusing reshuffle of its ad agency assignments, with most assignments going to the Interpublic Group and WPP Group. Most Coca-Cola Classic ads were consolidated at McCann Erickson, part of Interpublic. Sprite, which had been handled by Lowe Lintas for years, was shifted to Ogilvy & Mather, part of WPP, because Steve Heyer was impressed with the agency. At the same time, Diet Coke was snatched from Wieden+Kennedy and given to Lowe Lintas. In the most dramatic shift, Powerade, Dasani, and Minute Maid advertising went to Foote, Cone & Belding, part of Interpublic. Until then, Foote, Cone had created Pepsi's ads for the directly competing drinks, Gatorade, Aquafina, and Tropicana. Pepsi sued to prevent the admen from revealing their marketing strategies. In November, the companies reached a settlement, agreeing that the Foote, Cone creatives who had worked on the Pepsi accounted couldn't make Coke ads until the following summer. "The good news is that it's over," said an ad executive. "I'd like to get back to the business of advertising instead of testifying."

In the welter of confusion plaguing his first two years as Coke's CEO, the desperate Daft reached back to his Asian past and hired a *feng shui* expert to study the *chi* of the Coca-Cola headquarters on North Avenue. The *feng shui* master moved furniture around, repositioned mirrors, and removed a table and potted plants from Daft's office to create a more open space for good energy flow. And he placed a large ceramic rooster near Daft, presumably to add to his power aura. But the changes did little other than to make some insiders conclude that Daft was, indeed, daft.

PLAYING NOT TO LOSE

Over the next two years, Steve Heyer's prominence within the Company became ever more apparent as Daft got quieter. In March 2002, a journalist observed that Heyer was "an aggressive force at Coke and may be gunning for Daft's job." In May, the fifty-year-old Heyer became the head of the company's Latin American division. In December, he was named president and chief operating officer, as Brian Dyson once again retired.

Smart, abrasive, and self-assured, Heyer was expected to shake things up. In the slick 2002 annual report, which came out in the spring of 2003, Daft unaccountably wasn't in a photo of top Coke executives, while Heyer appeared front and center, sitting on a table around which others stood or sat. Amidst swirling speculation that he might stage a coup, Heyer reassured everyone that Daft was "going to stick around for a long time," and that "so far as I'm concerned, my ambitions have been paid in full. If this is my last job at the Coca-Cola Company, that's great." Few believed him. "Clearly he has a strategy that's not yet been revealed to Wall Street," said an investment banker. "I've got to believe that he's going to do something transformative."

The first tangible results of Heyer's handiwork appeared at the onset of 2003. With much fanfare, Coke unveiled ads with a new slogan, "Coca-Cola . . . Real," hearkening back to the venerable Real Thing era. Heyer gave the campaign to a relatively small upstart agency, Berlin Cameron, which previously had handled only Dasani and

Mello Yello. Rhythm-and-blues singer Mya and hip-hop artist Common sang "Real Compared to What?" in a rip-off of a classic jazz song. In one ad, Common (born on Chicago's South Side as Lonnie Rashid Lynn) maintains the common touch by rejecting plans for a toy action figure modeled on him. The idea, of course, was that he remained authentic, like the "real" Coca-Cola.

Actor David Arquette and his wife at the time, Courtney Cox, appeared in a low-key ad in which Cox shares a single bottle of Coke with her husband by loading his glass with ice so that she gets all of the remainder. In another spot, sexy actress Penélope Cruz, dressed in a clinging halter top, walks into a bar and downs an entire bottle of Coke in one gulp, as stunned customers stare. She burps loudly, then smiles demurely. The ads weren't bad, and they were a distinct improvement over the "vertiginous photography . . . kids on street luges [and] grinning ethnic actors trying to look gently urban" that critic Bob Garfield despised.

Yet all the new ads had a slightly negative twist, and the slogan was just about as dull as the failed "Coca-Cola, Enjoy." The ads didn't reverse the shift toward supposedly healthier alternatives. Nor did Coke's sponsorship of *American Idol*, the top-rated TV talent contest, where contestants sipped Coke while sitting on Coca-Cola-red sofas in front of screens with spinning Coke bottles. "There's something a bit sad about how the ground has shifted under Coke," observed one journalist. "At this point when it comes to the flagship brand, Coke is no longer playing to win; it is playing not to lose, clinging to the one magic formula it could always count on." To stem the tide, the company introduced Vanilla Coke and Diet Coke with Lemon. The two line extensions temporarily boosted sales in the cola category, but they had no staying power. Diet Coke ads featured yet another slogan, "Do What Feels Good," showing a young man and woman who end up dancing in a movie theater aisle after lip-synching to *Casablanca* lines. Sweet, but the ads didn't lift sales.

The Company continued its efforts to add non-cola beverages. It tried another line extension, Sprite Remix (to offer a "tropical taste"), which bombed. With more success, the company brought Fanta back to the United States, introducing four sexy multi-ethnic women dubbed the Fantanas, who dressed in color-coded hot pants to represent Strawberry, Grape, Pineapple, and Orange. In television spots the sexy Fantanas magically appeared to offer hydration. "Wanta Fanta? Don't you wanta, wanta Fanta, don't you wanta?" they sang seductively. Coke was clearly appealing to horny teens who would mentally replace "Wanta Fanta?" with another F-word.

The Company introduced BeginIt, a whey-fruit drink, and Swerve, a vitamin-fortified dairy beverage, as healthy alternatives, but few swerved out of their way to buy them. Plain old water seemed the most hopeful "new" drink, so Coke bought Valser, a Swiss bottled-water company, and Neverfail Springwater in Australia. The Company ramped up marketing efforts for Dasani, shifting from the traditional emphasis on purity to show attractive young people cavorting, flirting, dancing, and romancing between slurps of Dasani. In one commercial, a young black couple grope each other in an elevator while a security camera captures the steamy scene, but it turns out they're married. "There are no spas, babbling brooks or yoga," a Dasani brand manager noted. Coke priced Dasani as a mid-range water, below the imported Evian and above the cheaper Dannon, both of which the Company also distributed. Coke announced plans to introduce Dasani to the European market soon.

COKE AND THE PARAMILITARIES

Even as the Company struggled to regain market share in 2002 and 2003, however, accusations against the world's dominant soft drink firm escalated. In April 2002, Coca-Cola held its annual shareholder meeting at Madison Square Garden to show its solidarity with New York City following the terrorist attacks. Inside, talk-show host Charlie Rose hosted celebrity appearances at the Coke event. Outside, the Teamsters union inflated a giant rat sporting a Coca-Cola logo, complaining that the Company ignored the intimidation, torture, and assassination of union workers in Coke bottling plants in Colombia.

But as the Miami judge dithered, the lawyers who brought the Colombian lawsuit feared that the case would wither without public agitation. "It was clear we would be stuck in legal limbo," recalled Terry Collingsworth of International Right Advocates. "We needed to put heat on the company. Otherwise, it would be in their interest to delay." In the fall of 2002, he found Ray Rogers in the ramshackle Manhattan offices of Corporate Campaign, Inc. Rogers had spent his career embarrassing corporate wrong-doers, starting in the 1970s with a campaign against the textile firm J. P. Stevens, which inspired the movie *Norma Rae*. As he read the stories of murdered union leaders in Colombia, Rogers felt that familiar tingle of the call to battle, and the image-conscious Coca-Cola Company would make the ideal target. When Rogers discovered that in the late 1970s Coke union members had been killed by death squads in Guatemala in nearly identical circumstances, his mind was made up. He prepared to take on Coca-Cola.

In March 2003, Jose Martinez, the district court judge in Miami, dismissed the Colombian claims against The Coca-Cola Company, accepting the argument that the Atlanta corporation was not responsible for what happened in Coke bottling plants without even looking at the bottler's agreements or allowing any discovery process. The judge did permit the case to continue against the two Colombian bottlers, however. The frustrated lawyers appealed, but they urged Rogers to begin his campaign.*

Rogers scrambled to prepare for Coke's annual shareholder meeting, held on April 16, 2003, in Houston, Texas, where he initiated the Campaign to Stop Killer Coke. Outside the meeting, along with fifty union supporters, he waved inflammatory protest signs featuring a "Colombian Coke Float," a glass of Coke with bullet-riddled bodies floating in it. "Unthinkable! Undrinkable!" shouted the text below.

Inside the meeting, two Colombians, members of the plaintiff union Sinaltrainal, approached the microphone to tell their stories in Spanish through interpreters. 'I'm one of 65 members who are threatened with death by the paramilitaries," said William Mendoza. "Bodyguards are with me all day, and some nights they stay at my house for increased security. My family has been victimized." The previous summer, Mendoza's four-year-old daughter had nearly been kidnapped. The next day, the union leader

---

* The Company would later portray Ray Rogers as a mercenary propagandist who cynically used Coca-Cola for self-promotion, but Rogers received no money from the lawyers and managed his campaign on a shoestring, relying on donations. A vegetarian bachelor, he lived a semi-monastic life, and his staff consisted of a retired junior high teacher, part-timers, and a homeless man who sometimes lived in the office, along with a cat rescued from a shelter.

said, an anonymous caller threatened to kill his daughter if he continued to interfere with "the alliance we have with Coca-Cola."

A shareholder resolution submitted by an investment fund sought a human rights code of conduct that would apply to the Company's bottlers. It was defeated, but Coke felt the pressure, as the fund manager expressed fear that the protests would hurt the Company's reputation and drive down its stock price. A Coke spokesman categorically denied the allegations. "Labor groups are falsely trying to connect Coke with right-wing paramilitary groups."

Yet no one could deny the carnage in Colombia. Since 1986, nearly 4,000 Colombian union leaders had been murdered, with 184 killed the previous year. The crucial question was whether managers at Coke bottling plants were in collusion with the paramilitary thugs. The most disturbing and damning stories, which Ray Rogers soon helped to spread, occurred in Carepa at the Bebidas plant owned by Miami businessman Richard Kirby.* In 1994, two union members at the Coke plant were killed, followed by a third in 1995, shot on his doorstep as his wife and children looked on. At that point, remaining union leaders fled, but the Coke workers continued to meet secretly, then came out into the open.

On December 6, 1996, union member Isidro Gil, the bottling plant gatekeeper, opened the iron gates to allow a delivery truck to leave. Two men on a motorbike slipped in and shot Gil through the middle of his forehead, followed by several more bullets to make sure, then sped off. That night, the Sinaltrainal union offices were fire-bombed. Two days later, paramilitaries entered the bottling plant and assembled the workers at gunpoint, explaining that they could either resign from the union or leave Carepa to avoid being killed. A plant manager allegedly distributed already-prepared resignation letters, which everyone signed. The Coke bottler then slashed wages.

The Sinaltrainal men called for a worldwide boycott of Coca-Cola, but Ray Rogers knew that unionized Coke workers elsewhere wouldn't support a boycott, since it might threaten their jobs. Instead, he focused on university campuses that had signed lucrative exclusive agreements with Coke. "Young people, especially students, are Coke's highest priority marketing target," Rogers noted in his campaign literature. He figured that idealistic college students would make perfect activists, and he was right. In 2003, Bard College and Lake Forest booted Coke. Both were small schools, but then University College Dublin, with 20,000 students, voted to ban Coca-Cola. "This seems to have come out of nowhere," said a dazed spokeswoman for Coca-Cola Ireland, though she noted that "the problem is thankfully minor at the moment."

Coke was blindsided by the negative coverage. Ray Rogers' website, www.killer coke.org, which conveyed the lurid details of the Colombian murders, was attracting thousands of visitors. The Company bought the www.killercoke.*com* domain, which clicked through to Coke's denial of complicity, but it was an ineffective response.

---

* Richard Kirby, who also owned parts of other Colombian bottling plants, refused to discuss the murders when the union contacted him. "I'm not interested in politics," he told a reporter. His son Richard Kirby Kielland was actively involved in running the plant and allegedly hired a manager with close ties to the paramilitaries. He and his father later said that they had tried to sell the Bebidas plant in 1997 after the killings, but The Coca-Cola Company wouldn't sanction the sale. "Nobody tells the paramilitaries what to do," Richard Kirby said. "They tell you." He said that they had burned four of his trucks and kidnapped his wife's sister.

The Company said that it had a policy to protect its own workers and expected its bottlers to do the same, but Deval Patrick, Coca-Cola's African American general counsel, admitted, "No written code is enough; it's just words on paper, we know that. But we have taken the first steps." That wasn't enough for Ray Rogers. In October 2003, when Equal Justice Works gave Patrick their annual Scales of Justice award as an "advocate for civil rights, equality, and fairness in the workplace," Rogers handed out fliers labeling him the "Killer Coke counsel." When a member of the audience raised the issue during the awards ceremony, Patrick impulsively promised that Coke would send an independent delegation to Colombia to investigate the charges.

In December 2003, *Forbes,* a conservative business magazine, published an article headlined "Coke's Sinful World," pointing out that "the biggest bottlers aren't subsidiaries of Coke, nor are they completely independent. Coke effectively controls them by maintaining big equity stakes and a heavy presence on their boards. . . . Yet it keeps its stakes in the bottlers below 50%, thereby avoiding . . . any unpleasant liabilities." The Company owned about a third of Femsa, which had just bought Panamerican Beverages, owner of one of the accused Colombian bottlers, and many top Coke executives served on the Femsa board. Yet The Coca-Cola Company denied responsibility for "unpleasant liabilities" such as murders of union employees.

WATER PROBLEMS IN INDIA

Meanwhile, Coca-Cola was having trouble halfway around the world in India, where it had returned in 1993 and now owned twenty-six bottling plants, with seventeen franchisee-owned bottlers and sixty distribution centers. But the Company had managed to achieve only 6 drinks per capita yearly consumption, despite sinking nearly $1 billion and hiring Bollywood heartthrob Aamir Khan to tout Coke in TV spots. In August 2002, after Coke and Pepsi defaced a Himalayan mountainside with competing ads, the Indian solicitor general threatened legal action against them. Up until then, the Company had owned all of Hindustan Coca-Cola Holdings, but a few days later it was forced to sell 49 percent to Indian business partners and employees.

Coke was under fire in the village of Plachimada in the state of Kerala in southwestern India, where a Coke bottling plant had gone into operation in March 2000. Within two years, many villagers were convinced that Coke's six bore wells and two open wells were depleting the water table, as nearby local wells ran dry except for a few feet of bitter-tasting liquid. Led by a little old woman named Mailamma, villagers set up a large thatched-roof shelter across from the Coca-Cola plant and began a twenty-four-hour protest vigil in 2002. Within a year, the protests were attracting national attention, with the village becoming an "activist carnival," as one writer put it.

FLOW, a documentary about water, included footage of the Plachimada protestors chanting, "Coca-Cola, Go Away," and holding signs saying, "Water Is Our Birth Right!" Various women complained on camera. "Before this company came, our lives were comfortable and beautiful. . . . After the company came, within six months the taste of the water changed." Another said, "When we bathe, our heads swim. It pains, and we scratch all over."

In April 2003, the Plachimada village council revoked the plant's operating license, but the Kerala state government stayed the decision. The case went to the state's high court for a decision in December. In the meantime, a BBC radio crew showed up in July. When local farmers told the crew that Coke had given them sludge from their water purification process to use as fertilizer, the BBC reporters took a sample. The University of Exeter tested it and found that it contained toxic lead and cadmium; a predictable uproar ensued. Hindustan Coke stopped giving away the "fertilizer."

A month later, the Centre for Science and Environment (CSE) of New Delhi called a press conference to announce that it had found pesticide in Coke and Pepsi, including high levels of DDT, malathion, lindane, and chlorpyrifos. "Each sample had enough poison to cause—in the long term—cancer, damage to the nervous and reproductive systems, birth defects and severe disruption of the immune system," warned the CSE report.

The Indian Parliament promptly banned the soft drinks from its building, as did authorities in West Bengal, Punjab, and Rajasthan. Protestors smashed Coke bottles, and sales plummeted. In desperation, Coke asked the Indian Supreme Court to put an injunction on the bans, since they threatened its right to do business, but the judges refused. The American Embassy lamely defended Coke and Pepsi, saying that it was "their top priority to provide the consumer with safe products."

A week later, the Indian minister of health revealed that new tests in state-run labs found the soft drinks to be "well within the safety limits prescribed for packaged drinking water at present," though it still found minuscule amounts of pesticide. Hindustan Coke promptly distributed fliers assuring consumers that "Coca-Cola re-freshes you with world-class and safe products in India." The CSE director said that she hoped the debate would at least raise awareness of India's lack of water standards or pesticide policy.

For the time being, the pesticide scare subsided, but the protests over Coke bottling plants' alleged depletion of the water table continued and spread. In May 2003, farm-ers in the village of Mehdiganj, near the Ganges River in Uttar Pradesh, staged their first rally near the local bottler. Protests also began at two other Coca-Cola bottling locations elsewhere in India.

MECCA COLA AND THE IRAQ INVASION

The United States invaded Iraq in March 2003, declaring victory a few weeks later, but the ill-conceived war was far from over, and it fanned anti-American sentiment throughout the world, with calls for boycotts of American products such as Coca-Cola. A leaked internal memo from the London office of McCann-Erickson, Coke's major international advertising agency, observed, "The war risks tarnishing the repu-tation of American culture and the mythic 'American dream.'" It advised American multinationals to stress their "strong local roots." In India, radical groups attacked Coke distribution centers and bombed a plant in Andhra Pradesh. "We are primarily Indian, employing Indians," said Sunil Gupta of Hindustan Coca-Cola Holdings, heeding McCann's advice, but he wasn't convincing.

In France, Tawfik Mathlouthi, a Tunisian, had launched Mecca Cola in November 2002 as an ideological alternative to Coke. Its red-and-white label imitated Coca-Cola, as did its flavor, but its slogan differentiated it clearly enough: "Don't drink stupid. Drink committed." Mecca Cola pledged to donate 10 percent of its profits to Palestinian children's funds and another 10 percent to French charities.

Mecca sales in Europe and the Middle East took off after the Iraq invasion, with some shipments also going to areas of California and Michigan. Four competing drinks quickly jumped into the fray in the remainder of 2003—Arab-Cola and Muslim Up in France, Qibla Cola in England, and Cola Turka in Turkey. A Coke spokesman in London dismissed the impact of the new anti-American colas as "minimal" and emphasized that Coke was apolitical and unaffiliated with any religion or ethnic group, but such avowals meant nothing to Mecca Cola adherents.

LAYOFFS AND WHISTLEBLOWERS

On March 27, 2003, a week after the Iraq invasion, Doug Daft authorized another round of layoffs in which 1,000 workers would be fired.* "It's D-Day for a bunch of departments," said one grim Coke executive. Matthew Whitley, an accountant in the Coca-Cola fountain unit, was outraged but not surprised that he was among those who were axed. Two months prior to being fired, Whitley jumped the chain of command, complaining to Steve Heyer about a number of issues that had been bothering him. The most recent was a Planet Java frozen coffee drink in which metal residue had been found, yet it was still being promoted.

Heyer told the fountain unit managers about these allegations, and a week later, Whitley, 37, received a dismal performance review. "I was basically blacked out," he recalled. "No more communication with me." Six weeks later, he was fired, after working for Coca-Cola for 11 years. For 75 years, there had always been at least one person from his family working there. Whitley hired Marc Garber, a Georgia lawyer who specialized in whistleblower cases and whose motto was "It's not the size of the dog in the fight, it's the size of the fight in the dog." In May, Whitley sued, alleging that the fountain division was run as "an illegal racketeering enterprise." The Company released a statement describing Whitley as a "disgruntled former employee" who was trying to squeeze Coke for $44.4 million, but the story broke on CNN, and it soon became apparent that Whitley the whistleblower wasn't just whistling Dixie.

Whitley revealed that in 2000 the Company had convinced Burger King to test-market a frozen Coke slushy in Richmond, Virginia, as part of its "value meal." When the promotion wasn't going well, Coke executives gave a man $10,000 to take hundreds of children to Burger King for value meals. As a result, Burger King invested $65 million to buy equipment to make the slushies and advertise them in a national promotion, which resulted in half the expected sales, and the hamburger chain abandoned the promotion. In June 2003, the Company admitted that the tests had indeed been rigged, and it subsequently paid Burger King $21 million in order to retain the account, while firing Tom Moore, the head of Coke's fountain division.

The Whitley suit also alleged that Coke had used slush funds to hide losses from its iFountain program of computerized drink dispensers. The Company had used

---

* In fact, during 2003 Coke would eliminate 3,700 employees worldwide.

"phantom truck deliveries" to boost sales figures. Prior to the stroke of midnight on the last day of the fiscal quarter, trucks filled with Coke syrup drove a few feet away from the loading dock. To further boost sales figures, Coke had engaged in channel-stuffing, coercing distributors to take more syrup than they needed at the end of each quarter.* Finally, Whitley said that Coca-Cola had given $1 billion in "marketing allowances" to customers, though only a quarter of the funds were actually spent on advertising. The rest amounted to "payola," the lawsuit asserted, to keep customers. In effect, Coke was inflating its net operating revenue by $750 million a year by mis-labeling the payments.

In October 2003, Coke settled with Matthew Whitley for a mere $540,000, with over half going to his attorney. General counsel Deval Patrick admitted that Whitley was "a diligent employee with a solid record" and expressed disappointment that "he felt he needed to file a lawsuit in order to be heard." The damaging revelations con-tinued to reverberate, however, as both the SEC and the FBI launched investigations of channel-stuffing and other improprieties.

A pattern was emerging. In its desperation to boost sales, Coca-Cola was willing to go to extraordinary lengths, sometimes pushing beyond legal limits. In Mexico in mid-2002, a new Peruvian soft drink called Big Cola commissioned anyone with a vehicle to pick up bottles and deliver them to small mom-and-pop stores, where most Mexicans bought their soft drinks. Half the price of Coca-Cola, Big Cola was making inroads into Coke sales. To counter it, Coca-Cola mounted its ABC (Anti–Big Cola) initiative, offering to swap two bottles of Coke for every bottle of Big Cola. And the Company threatened to remove Coke coolers if any of the Peruvian product was found in them.

In the village of Itzapalapa, small shop owner Raquel Chavez balked. "My shop is free," she said. "Even if it is only one customer who wants Big Cola I have to offer him the best service." The Coke salesman offered ten Coke bottles for each Big Cola. Chavez turned him down. Coca-Cola subsequently refused to fill her orders, and her business suffered dramatically. In the summer of 2003, she and five other stores com-plained to the Mexican Federal Competition Commission, which eventually fined the Coca-Cola system $13 million for monopolistic practices.

TRYING TO STEP WITH IT

As concern over the American obesity epidemic mounted, Coke faced more intense criticism. In August 2002, the Los Angeles school board voted to abrogate its contract with Coca-Cola, inspiring similar efforts in several other districts. Soon thereafter, a California bill was introduced that would ban all soda from public schools. Coke mounted an intense lobbying campaign, but a weakened bill that exempted high schools was passed into law. Coca-Cola Enterprises president John Alm produced a video for politicians declaring that the fight against obesity was "a war that's been

---

* The 2000 case filed by a shareholder against Coca-Cola for allegations of channel-stuffing in Japan in the late 1990s was still pending, and now it was amended to include newly revealed information.

declared on our company." In June 2003, CCE made a contribution of an undisclosed sum to the National Parent-Teacher Association, and CCE public relations director John Downs, Jr., joined the PTA board of directors.*

Coke continued to make exclusive contracts with school systems, offering a variety of products, with schools typically receiving a 30 percent commission for soft drinks versus 15 percent for non-carbonated beverages. Thus, when a South Carolina high school banned soda sales, its profit from vending machine sales dropped from $40,000 to $6,000 a year. "We do not believe that having vending machines in schools represents a commercial presence in the classroom," said a Coke health and nutrition spokeswoman, "because the machines aren't in the classroom." They were merely in the hallways.

At the end of the year, Coca-Cola Enterprises announced that it wouldn't sell soft drinks inside elementary schools during school hours and would urge bottlers to limit vending machine hours in middle and high schools. It would also stop giving out book covers splashed with the Coke logo. These were small retreats, token efforts that didn't have much impact on sales.

In December 2003, in a relatively rare appearance, Doug Daft told colleagues that obesity represented the biggest challenge the industry had faced in half a century. But it was "absurd and outrageous" to attempt to solve it through simplistic legislation against soft drinks. Instead, the Coke CEO said beverage companies should provide choices and encourage healthy, active lifestyles. Ultimately, it was parents and teachers who must help children make "sensible choices." Coca-Cola paid for a school program called "Step With It!" distributing red pedometers and encouraging kids to take at least 10,000 steps a day. Increasingly, though, soft drinks seemed out of step with the times. Sales of Coca-Cola Classic fell by 3 percent in 2003, with total profits down by 4 percent.

WORN OUT

As 2004 began, Doug Daft must have felt the weight of the Coca-Cola world on his shoulders. For four years, he had faced seemingly insurmountable problems. As soon as one was settled (the racial discrimination lawsuit), two more popped up (murders in Colombia, water depletion in India), like the hydra-headed monster of Greek myth. And now one of those heads seemed to be coming directly at him.

On January 14, the Securities and Exchange Commission revealed that it was moving beyond a mere probe to a formal investigation of the charges raised by the Matthew Whitley whistleblowing case. FBI agents descended on Atlanta as well, questioning current and former employees about channel-stuffing in international markets such as Japan. According to two ex-Coke men, the agents were particularly interested in the role Daft had played as head of the Asian business at that time. "They're serious about this one," said one former employee. "They're gathering as

---

* In 2001, The Coca-Cola Company gave $200,000 to the Center for Consumer Freedom, a front organization initially funded by tobacco giant Philip Morris. CCF lobbied against controls on soft drinks.

much info as they can, and they're going to turn it over to the U.S. attorney." One subordinate claimed that Daft had angrily dismissed attempts to tell him about the illegal Japanese practices.

Three weeks later, on February 19, 2004, Daft informed the board that he planned to retire at the end of the year. Though some speculated that he was being forced out, the board was apparently taken completely by surprise. Daft was just worn out. He said later that his health had been shattered by the stress and that he "wouldn't have survived" if he had remained as Coke's CEO.

Steve Heyer was the obvious heir apparent. In December, he had forced out Jeff Dunn, the head of Coke's North American business, and taken on his responsibilities. Even though Heyer had been at Coke for only three years, he had more longevity that any other serious contender, since executive ranks had been thinned by massive layoffs and attrition.

Yet the Coca-Cola board didn't immediately anoint Heyer. Instead, it appointed a search committee, headed by Don Keough, seventy-seven, who had just rejoined the board after its age restriction was lifted. Wanting to avoid the sort of hasty choice that had resulted in an ill-prepared Daft taking over in 2000, the board hired a search firm to find potential candidates. As analysts and media pundits second-guessed likely choices, the search process dragged through March, with a hundred possible candidates in consideration.

In the lame duck interim period, more blows hit the Company. On March 9, 2004, as protestors continued their chants, the Coke bottling plant in Plachimada, India, was forced to close down after the High Court of Kerala upheld a government order prohibiting Coke from drawing groundwater from the village wells, at least until the June monsoon season. In defiance of the court, the Plachimada village council once again denied the plant's license renewal.

In England, where Coke introduced Dasani in early March, a furor ensued when newspaper revealed that the bottles merely held municipal water drawn from the River Thames, then filtered and treated at the CCE plant at Sidcup, a London suburb. "It's the real thing," sneered the *London Times*, "Coke's tap-water from Sidcup." The British Food Standards Agency questioned whether the Company could legitimately put "pure" on Dasani labels.

On March 19, only weeks after the product introduction, Coca-Cola ordered a recall of 500,000 Dasani bottles in England after it found excess levels of bromate, a chemical linked to a higher risk of cancer after long-term exposure. It turned out that British regulations required adding calcium to bottled water. Coke's addition of calcium chloride, in conjunction with an ozonation process, inadvertently created the bromate. Dasani was dead in the UK, and the company scrapped plans to introduce it in Germany and France.

Then, just nine days before the annual shareholder meeting, Coke general counsel Deval Patrick, the highest-ranking African American in the Company, announced that he was resigning. The *Wall Street Journal* reported that Patrick was leaving because some unnamed Coke board members were unhappy with the way he was handling the ongoing SEC and FBI investigations into channel-stuffing. A few days later, the Company reversed itself, saying that Patrick would remain at Coke through the end of the year. Daft reaffirmed that "Deval has my and the board's confidence and support." Patrick later revealed that he had quit out of frustration that Daft had reversed his initial approval of an independent investigation into the murders in Colombia.

On Wednesday, April 21, 2004, Daft presided over the annual shareholder meeting at the Hotel du Pont in Wilmington, Delaware. Early in the meeting, activist Ray Rogers of the Killer Coke campaign strode to the microphone. "The Coca-Cola system," he began, "is rife with immorality, corruption, and complicity in gross human rights violations, including murder and torture." He accused Daft of lying about the Colombian situation and recounted the story of Isidro Gil's death and the subsequent disbanding of the union. He revealed that New York City Councilman Hiram Monserrate had recently returned from a fact-finding mission in Colombia and had concluded that plant managers may have been working with paramilitaries.

Rogers went on and on in a kind of Coca-Cola filibuster. After five minutes, Daft told him that his time was up. "Please do not interrupt me, Mr. Daft," he said, and continued, shifting to talk about water issues in India. Daft ordered his microphone turned off. Plainclothes security officers, who turned out to be off-duty Wilmington police hired for the occasion, converged. "I was attacked by Coca-Cola's thugs, their security," Rogers recalled a few days later on television's *Democracy Now!* "First one came up behind me, clothes-lined me, tried to put a choke hold on me. When that didn't work, four then jumped me, pulled my legs out from under me, threw me to the floor."

Roger, sixty, was only 5'7", but he had once held a weight-lifting record for New England, and he still worked out regularly. He had no intention of leaving voluntarily. "Just be gentle, please," Daft begged from the podium. As six security officers now struggled with Rogers, Daft ordered, "Security people, please stand down." But they continued to drag the activist from the meeting. "The fact of the matter is," Rogers told the TV reporter, "I was not involved in disorderly conduct. The Coca-Cola Company was."

Black activist Jesse Jackson then came to the microphone and said that dragging Rogers out was wrong and "beneath the dignity of this company." He went on to complain about the resignation of Deval Patrick, "a man of tremendous integrity."

Doug Daft's final shareholder meeting had devolved into a circus. He said that the claims against Coca-Cola were "false and outrageous," and that the Killer Coke campaign on college campuses was "twisting the facts."

Mercifully, the meeting finally came to an end.

"A CASE STUDY IN BUSINESS DYSFUNCTION"

April passed without any resolution to the search for a new CEO. Many Wall Street analysts and bottlers still wanted inside candidate Steve Heyer, but within the Company he had developed an unsavory reputation as a harsh taskmaster who ran through too many secretaries, fired Jeff Dunn unnecessarily, and was not a team player. He had ditched chief marketing officer Steve Jones and hired Dan Palumbo, but then Heyer basically took over his job.

It may in fact have been one of the new television spots that finally iced Heyer's chances. In the spring of 2004, Berlin Cameron made a new "Real" ad in which two boys play a fierce game of one-on-one basketball on a hot summer day. Drenched in sweat, one of the players finds two cans of Coke in the kitchen refrigerator. He gulps down one of them, then uses the other to cool himself, rubbing it on his face, inside his waistband, and under his armpit—after which he gives it to his friend to drink. The ad had been running for a week when Heyer proudly showed it to the Coca-Cola board of directors. They were appalled, and Heyer frantically called the admen and told them to pull it off the air.

Don Keough, the venerated chair of the search committee, thought the ad represented everything that was wrong with recent Coke ads. It was jarring and negative. Though he had applauded Heyer when he arrived at Coca-Cola, Keough was having second thoughts. He had also heard about Heyer's temper. "Castigating somebody publicly—it's obscene, in my view," Keough told a reporter that April.

On the short list of outside candidates were Robert Eckert, the Mattel CEO; Rick Lenny, head of Hershey Foods; Carlos Gutierrez of Kellogg; Bob Nardelli, a Coke board member and Home Depot CEO; Kerry Clark of Procter & Gamble; and Steve Burke of Comcast. But by late April, the board had settled on Jim Kilts, the head of Gillette, who had previously worked at consumer food firms Kraft and Nabisco. The *Atlanta Journal-Constitution* ran an article full of glowing testimonials to Kilts, calling him "a solid leader" who had "a relentless focus on the business." But when the board offered him the job, Kilts declined. He didn't want to move to Atlanta.

Bob Nardelli and Steve Burke also turned the job down. Then it looked like Jack Welch, the legendary General Electric leader who had retired in 2001, might take the Coca-Cola challenge. At his wedding on April 24, he said he would seriously consider the job. But during his honeymoon, he decided against it.

As the turmoil and indecision continued, observers began to snipe at the Coca-Cola board itself. How could they have allowed Daft to announce his resignation without a clear successor in mind? Maybe the board was too powerful and was scaring off potential candidates. Some shareholders agitated for Warren Buffett, Coke's major stockholder, to get off the board because of conflicts of interest.

In a scathing article in *Fortune*, business writer Betsy Morris called the board an "old-boys club" that was "ineffective to the point of farce." She quoted a P&G executive who mused that the bumbling search for a new CEO was "one of the strangest processes" he'd ever seen. Morris called The Coca-Cola Company "a case study in business dysfunction," featuring "a story of byzantine maneuverings and warring tribes, of spin and counterspin, of old grudges and character assassinations." She then indulged in her own brand of character assassination, labeling Don Keough a Machiavellian "shadow CEO," a meddler acting out of his own "thwarted dreams, outsized ego, and overt, old-fashioned cronyism."

Yet Keough was arguably the keeper of the flame, one of the few left who could remember what Coca-Cola once had meant and might mean again. The first person Keough called after Daft announced his resignation in February was Neville Isdell, a Coke veteran who had lived on five continents in the service of the soft drink. At sixty, he was enjoying his retirement on Barbados, finally finding time to spend with his family. Keough wanted to know if he would throw his hat into the ring for the CEO position. Isdell, whose wife hated the idea, agonized over the decision but finally concluded, "Could I live with myself if I turned down the ultimate challenge?"

After he told Keough he was interested, Isdell waited for over two months, still thinking that he was a leading candidate. On April 28, Coke board member Herb Allen called to ask if he would consider serving as the president under Jack Welch for a year or two. He refused. A few days later, after Welch had backed out, Keough finally called to offer Isdell the job. After the close of the business day on May 4, 2004, the Company announced that dark horse candidate Neville Isdell would be the next Coca-Cola CEO and chair of the board.

~ 24 ~

Turnaround

The best corporate partnerships, in fact the only sustainable ones, are those that are focused on a company's core business. For Coca-Cola, the most important issue is water. . . . When challenged at an analysts' meeting, all I had to do was hold up a can of Coke to illustrate the importance of that key ingredient.

—E. Neville Isdell, *Inside Coca-Cola*

After the prolonged, embarrassing search for a new CEO, in which over a hundred people were considered, some analysts were underwhelmed by the choice of a retired Coke lifer like Neville Isdell. The appointment signaled a yearning to "return to the pre-1998 days," said one skeptic. "We respectfully disagree."

Yet many Coke observers thought that Isdell might just be the savior the Company needed. At 6'5", the red-haired Irishman was smart, charming, and a good listener, but he was also no one's pushover, and in 1981 he had proven his ability to revitalize the ailing business in the Philippines, where he donned army fatigues and hurled a Pepsi bottle against a wall while screaming a Filipino obscenity. The son of an Irish policeman (a ballistics and fingerprint expert), Isdell grew up in Northern Ireland until age ten, when in 1954 his father took a job in Northern Rhodesia (renamed Zambia in 1964).

At Cape Town University, Isdell was a star rugby player and anti-apartheid activist planning to become a social worker, until his former girlfriend's father, a Coke bottler in Zambia, offered him a job as a manager trainee. He subsequently switched to work for The Coca-Cola Company, rising in the ranks, stationed in South Africa, Australia, the Philippines, West Germany, Atlanta headquarters, and England. He had retired in 2001 as vice chair of the Coca-Cola Hellenic Bottling Company.

A hands-on manager, Isdell enjoyed talking about his days of driving Coke delivery trucks on a horrendous African road called the "Hell Run," and though he enjoyed the good life at his part-time home in Provence, sipping fine French wines, he never minded getting his hands dirty in the field. One of his fellow rugby players recalled that Isdell had liked to call the plays. "He was a great strategist."

The day after the announcement that he would be the new CEO, Isdell flew in from his home in Barbados to Atlanta to meet with 2,000 employees on Wednesday afternoon, May 5, 2004, in the courtyard of the North Avenue headquarters, as the old disco hit "We Are Family" played. Isdell told them that this was the third most special day in his life, after his wedding and the birth of his child. He said that his new job was "a mountain I had to climb." Then he flew back to Barbados until June, when he would move to Atlanta to take the reins.

By that time, the mountain he had to climb seemed nearly insurmountable. "Morale is in the dumps," a recruiter noted. "It's a great brand, yes—but lately, people are saying it's become a lousy place to work." The FBI and SEC channel-stuffing and European Union anti-competitive practices investigations were ongoing. So was the Killer Coke campaign. U.S. soft drink sales were flattening in what appeared to be a saturated market, while sodas provided 80 percent of company revenues. Aside from Dasani, Powerade, and Minute Maid, Coke's attempts to branch out into alternative drinks were often flops. Concerns over sugary soft drinks' role in the obesity epidemic were escalating. *Super Size Me,* a documentary in which thirty-two-year-old Morgan Spurlock gained twenty-four pounds in a month by eating only at McDonald's fast food outlets, debuted two days after Isdell's Atlanta employee rally. The film shows Spurlock eating a Super Size meal, washing it down with a forty-two-ounce Coke, then vomiting in the parking lot.

No wonder Doug Daft fled Atlanta to return to his native Australia even before Isdell showed up in June. During his first months on the job, Isdell kept a low profile. Even though a former colleague called Isdell "the best speaker and communicator that I've seen at Coke," the new CEO took a vow of public silence for his first a hundred and twenty days, as he hopped around the globe to assess the state of the far-flung Coca-Cola empire.

What he found was disheartening, "an atmosphere of fear and disaffection," as he later admitted. He found managers who were out of touch or incompetent. Bottlers in Mexico and Brazil were unhappy with the Company's advertising, which Isdell called "atrocious." Isdell inherited C2, a newly introduced mid-calorie cola that was neither a real diet drink nor a full sugar offering. Overpriced and poorly marketed, it failed.

Steve Heyer had championed C2 and the advertising Isdell despised. Worse, Heyer had deeply offended McDonald's, Coke's most important fountain customer, by gloating over a new contract with Subway, inaccurately implying that Subway got better terms. On his first day on the job, Isdell flew to Chicago to assure the McDonald's CEO, "I will fix the problem." Heyer seemed oblivious to his fate, calling Isdell a "terrific guy" and asserting that they would be "great partners." But Heyer was forced to announce his impending departure less than two weeks after Isdell took the reins at Coke.

Isdell began to fill management gaps. He named fellow Irishman Irial Finan, another Coke veteran, as head of Coke's bottling investments, Chuck Fruit as chief marketing officer, and Cynthia McCague as head of human resources. But he didn't name a new president to replace Heyer. "I simply did not believe that there was anyone in the company at the time who was qualified for the job," he recalled, "which illustrates how badly flawed Coca-Cola's succession management had been."

ENDING THE SILENCE

When Neville Isdell became CEO in June 2004, Coca-Cola stock sold for a bit over $51, but it sank below $45 by September 1. Summer soft drink sales had slumped, in part because of bad weather (cool, with lots of hurricanes) and obesity concerns, but mostly because giant bottler Coca-Cola Enterprises kept raising prices as part of its strategy to optimize profits rather than volume. Four analysts downgraded Coke shares. On Wednesday, September 15, Merrill Lynch cut its recommendation from "buy" to "neutral," and the stock fell to $41.

Isdell had sworn not to speak in public until October, but he broke his silence that day. He was amazingly blunt. "We have a lot of good people, but not much depth in talent." There was no silver bullet that would turn things around. The key to restoring a "winning culture" was attending to the nitty-gritty details, "the millions of things that need to be done right every day." Yes, the relationship with CCE was fraught with tension, but the two cousin companies were talking about how to fix it. "We need to anticipate and meet the needs of increasingly health-conscious consumers," he said, but Isdell insisted that "carbonated soft drinks can grow. They're the largest beverage category in the world, and they're the most profitable." Most of that growth would come from outside North America, notably in China, India, Indonesia, Brazil, and Africa. He promised to hold a meeting for stock analysts in two months.

His candor didn't help. On September 17, Coke shares dipped below $40. Isdell later admitted, "There were legitimate concerns that if the share price dropped too low, the Company could be a takeover target," either from a leveraged buyout or a Nestle merger. "We had to grow revenue and improve the bottom line to move our stock price up again, or we risked losing control of the Company."

Behind the scenes, in mid-October Isdell flew to Brussels to meet with the European Commissioner for Competition, Mario Monti, agreeing to a settlement of the five-year-old EU anti-trust investigation. Coke would allow some competitive drinks to be sold in its coolers, along with other concessions and promises that would, Monti announced, "level the playing field." The Company admitted no guilt and paid no fine. The two men hit it off. Later, after Monti left his position, Isdell asked him to join Coca-Cola's international advisory board.*

As expected, third-quarter results for the Company, announced in late October, were dismal. Volume had increased only 1 percent worldwide and had fallen 3 percent in North America. When Isdell met with stock analysts at New York's Plaza Hotel on November 11, he made "no grand pronouncements, no rosy promises." Don't expect 2005 to be much better than 2004, Isdell warned. But over the long haul, he expected sales volume growth of 3 to 4 percent annually. He announced a permanent $400 million annual increase in marketing, boosting the total yearly expense to well over $2 billion. "The opportunities out there are absolutely enormous," Isdell emphasized, but the Company needed better execution around the globe, along with effective advertising and new products. "We want our people to believe they can succeed again."

---

* Asking former adversaries to join ranks would become an Isdell trademark. As part of the settlement of the racial discrimination suit, Coke had agreed to allow an independent task force to monitor its progress towards a diverse workforce. It was due to end soon, but in November 2004 Isdell personally appeared before U.S. District Judge Richard Story to ask him to extend it another year. After the task force was finally dismantled, Isdell invited its chair, former U.S. Labor Secretary Alexis Herman, to join the Coca-Cola board of directors.

THE COCA-COLA MANIFESTO

To re-instill that confidence, in March 2005 Isdell began a four-month process, kicking it off in a London hotel with a three-day meeting with a hundred and fifty top Coke executives, who were shocked to see enlarged quotations from an internal employee survey on the walls. "*We don't trust management,*" read one. "*Our marketing is terrible,*" asserted a second assessment. "*We have no strategy,*" lamented another. Isdell split participants into small groups for the first day of the "catharsis stage," as he put it. The next day, he opened up the floor for discussion. One executive suggested that Coke needed to buy another large company, as Pepsi had long ago purchased Frito-Lay snack foods. "Why would we buy another company when we can't seem to figure out how to run this one?" Isdell asked. "Or do we need to buy another company in order to run ours because we can't?"

Over four hundred Coke employees took part in this intensive self-assessment, which ultimately produced a large-print pamphlet entitled "Our Manifesto for Growth," a kind of capitalist reverse spin of the Marx-Engels *Communist Manifesto.* "In recent years, we've lacked a clear direction and a common understanding of our purpose as a company," it began. "We've dealt with challenges reactively and separately, not as a team. We've been too focused on the short term."

The pamphlet contained no startling innovations, but plenty of hackneyed aphorisms. "Accountability: If it is to be, it's up to me," for instance, or "Innovation: Seek, imagine, create, delight." At its heart were five Ps. Not surprising, the first was Profit, followed by People ("being a great place to work where people are inspired"), Portfolio (a wide range of beverages), Partners ("a winning network" of bottlers and customers), and, finally, Planet ("being a responsible global citizen").

The "Manifesto" was vague on details, but at least it acknowledged that there was a problem and provided a blueprint of sorts. Most importantly, it involved employees, convincing them that management actually cared about them. "It became *their* plan," Isdell said. "They owned it and believed in it. No edict from the mount or sales job was needed."

A YEAR OF TRANSITION

As predicted, 2005 proved to be a wait-and-see year, with the stock bumping along just over $40. In March, Isdell appointed two high-profile managers. Mary Minnick, forty-five, a twenty-two-year Coca-Cola veteran who had been running Coke's Asian operations, moved to Atlanta as the head of marketing, innovation, and strategic growth, a new position. She thus became the most powerful female leader the Company had ever had.* With her tough, demanding personality, she was dubbed Scary Mary and Minnick the Cynic. Some observers speculated that she might become Isdell's heir apparent, though Irial Finan and Don Knauss, head of Coke North America, were also seen as contenders.

At the same time, Isdell brought back Muhtar Kent to run a newly designated division covering North Asia, Eurasia, and the Middle East, which included Japan,

---

* Chief marketing officer Chuck Fruit, in poor health, resigned in July 2005.

China, and Russia. Kent, fifty-two, a Turkish-American, had worked as Isdell's right-hand man in Eastern Europe as Coke moved quickly to build market share after the end of the Cold War in the early 1990s. "We were corporate cowboys," Isdell recalled fondly. But in 1998, Kent had resigned from Australian bottler Coca-Cola Amatil two years after he shorted its stock just before the bottler announced disappointing results, which gave the appearance of illegal insider trading. Kent claimed that his financial advisor had shorted the stock without his input and that the timing was a "bad coincidence." His reputation tarnished, he gave up his $324,000 profit and paid the cost of the investigation.

Since then, Kent had been CEO of Efes Beverage Group, a Turkish Coke bottler and beer brewer. The scandal was "in the past," a Company spokesman said, while Isdell praised Kent for his "deep understanding of building brands and operations in developed and developing markets."

In 2005, the Company began to move new alternative drinks into the pipeline. To compete in the "energy drink" category of high-caffeine drinks, pioneered by Red Bull and now led by drinks called Rockstar and Monster, Coke introduced Full Throttle, marketing it to young blue-collar macho men, "the guy's guy," as a manager put it. Vault, touted as a hybrid citrus-energy drink, was Coke's new attempt to compete with Pepsi's Mountain Dew, following the demise of Coke's ill-fated Surge in 2002. Powerade Option was intended to compete with Pepsi's Propel Fitness Water, a flavored vitamin-enhanced water.

But the biggest gamble was the June introduction of Coca-Cola Zero, a second low-calorie cola. Diet Coke, already a huge success, primarily attracted women. Coke Zero was supposed to appeal to weight-conscious men who didn't want to be seen drinking a "diet" soda. The Company dispensed twenty million free samples, along with a TV spot featuring G. Love (Garrett Dutton) singing a version of the classic 1971 Hilltop commercial, recast as "Chilltop" and capped by the tagline "Everybody Chill." Filmed on a Philadelphia rooftop, the spot was a kind of hip-hop desecration of the original: "I'd like to teach the world to chill, / Take time to stop and smile. / I'd like to buy the world a Coke / And chill with it a while."

The campaign flopped, with lackluster initial sales. In trying to position Coke Zero as a no-calorie alternative to Coke Classic without cannibalizing Diet Coke sales, the vague ads failed to convey the essential message that Coke Zero had zero calories. In September, Isdell directed flavor scientists to use the original Coca-Cola formula for Coke Zero, sweetened in the United States with aspartame and acesulfame potassium. In November, new commercials carried the message "Coca-Cola taste, zero calories. . . . Try to believe it!" Isdell insisted that Coke Zero was meeting expectations, but its future remained uncertain.

Coca-Cola's marketing efforts also remained uncertain. Mary Minnick nixed new Coke Classic ads prepared under Steve Heyer. They were never made public. In July 2005, she held a meeting in Paris with eight advertising agencies, asking them to submit ideas to reassert Coca-Cola's iconic status. Wieden+Kennedy, a Portland, Oregon, agency, won the shootout, stealing most of the Coca-Cola Classic ad assignments from Berlin Cameron, which Heyer had championed. Nonetheless, Berlin Cameron's swan song was a hit, a Christmas ad bringing back the beloved Coke polar bears, along with cute Coke-sipping penguins.

CONFRONTING CONFLAGRATIONS

Neville Isdell spent much of 2005 trying to put out fires. In April, the Company reached a settlement with the Securities and Exchange Commission, agreeing to strengthen its internal accounting controls, and the Justice Department simultaneously closed its two-year investigation. Coke paid no fine and neither admitted nor denied the channel-stuffing allegations.

But the problems caused by the obesity epidemic wouldn't go away. Coke agreed to put clearer calorie content on its labels, but that didn't mollify critics who wanted sugary Coke products out of schools. In June, New Jersey became the first state to ban soft drinks from high schools. In August, the American Beverage Association* announced that Coke, Pepsi, and the rest of the soft drink industry would voluntarily ban sugar sodas in elementary and middle schools but would still allow half of their high school vending machines to carry soft drinks.

With thirty-eight states considering school nutrition legislation, this partial retreat didn't satisfy critics, who also pointed out that Minute Maid orange juice contained more calories than the equivalent amount of Coca-Cola, and that sports drinks contained about half the calories of soda. In November 2005, lawyers who had successfully conducted class-action suits against tobacco took aim at soft drinks. Law professor Richard Daynard said that soft drink coolers were "a little like having a cigarette machine in a school." They planned to sue on the grounds of deceptive advertising, arguing that school vending machines implied that the contents were good for students. Caffeine and sugar were a "toxic cocktail that children cannot easily refuse," another lawyer said.

The tide of public opinion was shifting. Even Coke's hometown paper, the *Atlanta Journal-Constitution,* editorialized that "schools ought to end their unholy alliance with the soft drink industry," arguing that "the lawyers shouldn't stop with soda" and should also tackle junk food.

"I don't think there is anything inherently wrong with carbonated soft drinks," Neville Isdell responded defensively, but "certain consumer perceptions" needed to be addressed. To do so, Coke had established the Beverage Institute for Health and Wellness to support nutritional research, education, and outreach, and to help create healthful drinks. The Step With It! program, begun under Daft, had reached over one million students. Coke now enlisted bicycle racer Lance Armstrong and other sports figures to promote "Live It," a program to encourage sixth-graders to exercise and eat a balanced diet. None of the material featured the Coke logo, but the nutritional advice didn't mention beverages either.

Obesity wasn't just an American problem. According to the World Health Organization, over 1 billion adults were overweight, and "obesity has reached epidemic proportions globally." In response, Coke funded "Active Factor" sports activities in Australia, sponsored bicycling in Denmark, worked in Thailand to promote "Thai Kids on the Move" in schools, and started exercise programs in Korea, Italy, and China.

---

* The National Soft Drink Association had renamed itself in 2004 as non-sodas gained market share.

In the Philippines, Coke piloted Nutribreak, providing juice drinks and protein-rich food supplements to prevent malnutrition.

Yet Coca-Cola also helped to fund the Center for Consumer Freedom, a corporate front group that had originally defended the tobacco industry. In 2005, the CCF took out full-page newspaper ads lambasting the "food police" and trial lawyers who "force-fed a steady diet of obesity myths." A Coke spokesman acknowledged that the Company gave money to CCF to provide "another voice in the debate," though she added that Coke did "take the obesity issue very seriously."

Isdell presided over his first annual shareholder's meeting in April 2005, fielding a variety of hostile comments about the Colombian murders, water depletion in India, childhood obesity, and plastic bottles. "As a former student activist," Isdell said with apparent sincerity, "I came to the Colombia issue with an open mind. But ultimately I came to the conclusion that the allegations are not true." He cited a recently completed investigation by Cal Safety, a California monitoring firm Coke had hired. But when Ray Rogers, head of the Killer Coke campaign, got to the microphone, he lambasted the report as "tantamount to the fox guarding the henhouse," since Coke had paid for the investigation. Cal Safety had looked only at current conditions at Colombian bottlers, not at the murders of the past. Rogers and college student activists called for an independent investigation.

The University of Michigan threatened to ban Coca-Cola products if the Company didn't commission an independent audit. Coke demurred, fearful that the results could be used in the pending lawsuit, and the university threw Coke off campus at the end of 2005, joining eight other U.S. colleges where the soft drinks were no longer allowed.

The previous month, the International Labor Rights Fund brought suit against Coca-Cola and a Turkish bottler for firing employees who had tried to unionize. When they occupied an Istanbul bottling plant, they and their family members were beaten by police. Coke said that the protestors had worked for a third-party contractor, even though their job was to deliver Coca-Cola products.*

Throughout 2005, Coke's water usage in India continued to cause problems. As the Plachimada plant remained closed, Coke noted that local water supplies continued to dwindle anyway. Elsewhere, protests in Mehdiganj escalated. "My crops stopped growing," complained a farmer just outside the bottling plant. "My mango trees are without fruit." Yet the beverage industry accounted for only .02 percent of India's water use, while 81 percent was used for irrigation. "There were two million wells in India 30 years ago," wrote Michael Specter in a *New Yorker* article the following year. "Today, there are 23 million. . . . As sources dry up and wells are abandoned, farmers have turned on each other." Others committed suicide. But Coke was the most popular villain.

"Why would we want to destroy something or drain something that is so critical to our business?" asked Harry Ott, director of Coke's new Global Center for Water Excellence. Coke was using water not only for its beverages but also for washing and

---

* A year later, a U.S. judge would dismiss the case, saying that Turkish courts should adjudicate it.

processing. The Company began rain-harvesting efforts, claiming to return much of the wastewater to aquifers, but in a drought, there was little rain to harvest.

The Global Center for Water Excellence was part of the fifth P, "Planet," in the "Manifesto for Growth." In July 2005 the Company published "Toward Sustainability," in which Isdell wrote, "The issues facing the world are more urgent than ever—and they affect us all. If local communities suffer from water scarcity, so do we. If HIV/AIDS ravages the communities in which we operate, the people impacted are our employees, our customers and our consumers." The Company would focus on *water, AIDS,* and *health and wellness* (obesity) issues. Coke began an effort to use less water in its plants, to improve wastewater treatment, and to promote access to clean, safe drinking water.*

As the largest private-sector employer in Africa, Coca-Cola was directly affected by the massive AIDS pandemic there. Coke offered voluntary testing and anti-retroviral treatment to all its employees, supported public education programs, and used its delivery trucks to distribute condoms along with soft drinks.

"Toward Sustainability" highlighted Coke's school exercise and nutrition programs and its purportedly healthy drinks. "We increasingly provide low- and no-calorie alternatives, juices and juice drinks, water, sports and energy drinks, teas, coffees, soy-based drinks, and fortified beverages with nutritional benefits."

Of course, Coca-Cola profited on such drinks, but it was clear that Neville Isdell was trying to reclaim what former CEO Paul Austin had called the "halo effect." With ever-greater scrutiny of every ingredient, however, that wasn't easy. For instance, Human Rights Watch had recently documented the use of child labor on El Salvador's sugar plantations that provided sweetener for Coke. Children as young as 10 hurt themselves while swinging machetes. Though no children worked in the sugar refineries, "child labor is a problem on family-owned farms and farm cooperatives in El Salvador," Coke acknowledged in "Toward Sustainability."

TURNING POINT

Although challenges remained (and new ones continually surfaced), by early 2006 Isdell's game plan appeared to be working. In February, the Company announced an encouraging 4 percent volume increase in 2005. In April, just before the annual shareholder's meeting, the University of Michigan ended its Coca-Cola ban after Coke arranged for a third-party investigation of bottler labor practices in Colombia, to be conducted by the International Labor Organization (ILO), an agency of the United Nations. Coke had also asked The Energy and Resources Institute (TERI), a respected nonprofit with Asian offices, to look into water depletion allegations in India. And Isdell had hired Ed Potter, a veteran labor lawyer, as director of global labor relations.

As usual, Ray Rogers of Killer Coke was first to the microphone at the annual meeting, calling the planned ILO investigation "a new scam," but the day belonged

---

* Following the devastating Indian Ocean tsunami of December 26, 2004, Coca-Cola gave away 1.2 million bottles of clean drinking water, along with food, medicine, clothing, tents, and $10 million in cash.

to Isdell. "We are well on our way to becoming the company you expect us to be," said the CEO. "My message to you today is that the transition is complete." Coke's first-quarter profits rose 10 percent, with sales volume up 5 percent. Demonstrating faith in its future, Isdell said that the Company planned to buy back over $2 billion of its own shares that year. With less fanfare, he had elevated Muhtar Kent to a new position in charge of all Coke operations outside North America, indicating that Kent might be a candidate to succeed him.

Coca-Cola Blak, a coffee-flavored cola, had just been introduced. Tab Energy, directed at women, would soon debut. As part of its partnership with Nestle, Coke planned to introduce Enviga, a green tea product that claimed to burn calories so that it was in effect a super-diet drink.

"Welcome to the Coke Side of Life," the new advertising campaign, featured "the best Coke advertising in a long, long time," according to *Advertising Age*'s Bob Garfield, highlighting "the fizzing, bubbling sound of a soft-drink pour . . . one of the most fetching, evocative and appetizing sounds on earth." In another cute spot called "Ringtone," a boy sitting on a park bench next to an attractive girl makes odd cell phone noises to attract her attention, then fishes a Coke out of his backpack, holds it to his ear, and says, "Hello?" He hands it to the charmed girl, saying, "It's for you." It was the best-liked TV spot of the month.

To reverse declining sales for Sprite, Coke introduced edgy ads for the lemon-lime drink. One featured two sumo wrestlers, one painted green, the other yellow, smashing into a young man to create the "lymon" flavor in what Coke dubbed "sublymonal" advertising. Viewers could record the commercials, find hidden codes, and plug them into www.sublymonal.com for more content or prizes. The weird ads were aimed at teens.

The Sprite ads were first steps towards interactive online advertising. At the same time, MyCokeRewards.com allowed consumers to open accounts and accumulate points by entering codes found under bottle caps and inside twelve-packs. Within a year, five million people had signed up and claimed prizes such as video rentals, magazine subscriptions, music downloads, or more Coke beverages. Every second, an average of seven codes were entered. The site allowed Coke to compile digital profiles of consumers, collecting "psychographic" information about their interests and tastes. As more TV viewers fast-forwarded past commercials, Coca-Cola Zero sponsored "Gold Rush," an online game in the form of a seven-week reality series in which actors quaffed the diet drink.

ESPIONAGE, PESTICIDES, AND NEGOTIATIONS

On Wednesday, July 5, 2006, Joya Williams, 41, a Coca-Cola administrative assistant, was arrested for trying to sell trade secrets to Pepsi. In May, a letter postmarked from the Bronx had appeared at Pepsi headquarters, offering "very detailed and confidential information." It was signed by "Dirk," purportedly a Coke executive. Pepsi promptly turned the letter over to Coke, which called the FBI. In the subsequent sting operation, "Dirk" (Ibrahim Dimson of the Bronx) demanded $75,000 for an undisclosed new Coke product sample and $1.5 million more for additional items. In June, Coke security cameras caught Joya Williams stuffing documents and a liquid container into her bag. It transpired that Dimson and Edmund Duhaney, who lived in the Atlanta suburb of Decatur, had served prison time together, and that Williams was a friend of Duhaney's.

The two men took a plea bargain, but Williams insisted that she was an innocent dupe. Yes, she testified, she had taken the documents and a sample drink home, but only to catch up on work. Her boss, Javier Sanchez Lamelas, was in charge of marketing soft drinks with the sacred Coke name, and she was under huge pressure. The Coke account was "like a whole city without that company," she said. Lamelas was "very in your face, not patient, no mistakes." Among the documents she had taken were "Red Books," confidential marketing reports covering demographics and consumer trends. Coke's lawyers went berserk when the judge said he planned to allow nearly seven hundred pages of documents to be made public, and he backed down.

To no one's surprise, Williams was found guilty and sentenced to eight years in prison. The conspiracy to sell Coke secret documents was amateurish and naive, and the "trade secrets" probably didn't amount to much, but the incident revealed the pressure-cooker atmosphere inside the North Avenue headquarters.

On the other side of the world, a more serious trade secret was threatened. In August 2006, the ever-volatile situation in India exploded, as the New Delhi–based Center for Science and Environment claimed that it found twenty-four times the allowable pesticide level in Coke and Pepsi products. India's Supreme Court consequently ordered both companies to disclose their ingredients, recalling the time in 1977 when Coke had withdrawn from India rather than reveal its secret formula. Coke managed to avoid that catastrophic outcome, but three states banned soft drink sales in schools and government offices, Kerala banished them completely, and protestors smashed bottles.

Coke denied the allegations, citing its own lab results, but the Company remained vague about the actual pesticide content because there probably *was* a small amount in the drinks. India's groundwater was badly contaminated, and most food products contained pesticide residue. As one Indian defender noted, however, "One can drink a can of Coke every day for two years before taking in as much pesticide as you get from two cups of tea." Coke ran an ad asking, "Is There Anything Safer for You to Drink?" Most effectively, the Company ran a TV ad featuring Aamir Khan, a hugely popular Indian movie star noted for his social responsibility. Khan examined a test tube held by a man in a white lab coat inside a Coca-Cola bottling plant, then grabbed a Coke Classic from the manufacturing line and gulped it down. He invited viewers to visit a bottling plant themselves, and several thousand did. Sales ticked up. The crisis was over.

Coca-Cola simultaneously maneuvered to still the shrill voice of the Killer Coke campaign. Ed Potter, Coke's director of global labor relations, called Terry Collingsworth, the lawyer for the International Labor Rights Fund, whom he had known for years. "Terry, you and I can work on this together," Potter said. "I've got to make my daughter happy!" It turned out that Potter's daughter, a college student, had exclaimed, "Dad, you're not going to work for Killer Coke, are you?" when he told her about his new job. In August 2006, Collingsworth and Potter set up mediation among Coke, the lawyers, and Sinaltrainal, the Colombian union. In October, Miami judge Jose Martinez, after sitting on the case for five years, dismissed the alien tort lawsuit, saying that there was insufficient evidence to link the Coke plant managers with paramilitary executioners. He warned against "unwarranted international fishing expeditions against corporate entities."

Collingsworth agreed to delay filing an appeal, pending the outcome of negotiations. As a sign of good faith, Sinaltrainal was supposed to curtail its public complaints about Coke. The outlines of a settlement were quickly roughed out. Coke would compensate Colombian victims and their families and would agree to a new workers' rights policy. And the lawyers would call off attack dog Ray Rogers's Killer Coke campaign. But agreeing on precise details wasn't so easy. The negotiations, which were supposed to take six weeks, dragged on for a year and a half.

BOTTLER TENSIONS

Back in the United States, tensions between The Coca-Cola Company and its bottlers grew intense during 2006, starting in January when Walmart asked Coke to deliver Powerade to Walmart warehouses. Until then, bottlers had always delivered right to store shelves, making sure products were well displayed. But such service added to costs, and Walmart demanded the new setup. Fearful that Walmart might otherwise create its own sports drink to replace Powerade, the Company agreed, asking its two largest Coke bottlers to begin shipping to Walmart warehouses, allowing the giant discounter to stock the shelves. Fifty-six smaller Coke bottlers sued Big Coke and Coca-Cola Enterprises, its largest bottler, claiming that direct store delivery was "at the core of successful marketing." There hadn't been such internecine strife since the 1970s. "It's like suing your family," said the CEO of Ozarks Coca-Cola Bottling. "I'm not saying our underwear has Coca-Cola on it, but just about everything else does." A year later, the suit was settled. Warehouse delivery for selected products would continue, with the bottlers receiving some of the resulting profits.

Meanwhile, giant bottler CCE thumbed its nose at Big Coke by carrying non-Coke products such as Arizona Tea, since Coca-Cola's Nestea, part of its ailing partnership with Nestle, wasn't selling well, and neither was Coke's new Gold Leaf bottled tea. Neville Isdell thought that CCE execution was "very poor" and pressured for the removal of CCE chief John Alm, who departed at the end of 2005. But the new CCE chief executive, John Brock, annoyed Isdell by launching a series of price increases, which eroded Coke's market share. Big Coke responded by raising concentrate prices. "It was a bitter tit-for-tat exchange," Isdell recalled.

The frustrated Coke CEO launched Project Diesel, an effort to merge the remaining independent bottlers with CCE for cost efficiencies. The CCE board rejected the plan. Isdell asked the Coke board to approve a hostile takeover bid for CCE, but the board feared a bidding war or an outside buyer. Isdell backed down.

SUSPENDED FROM SCHOOL

The simmering controversy over soft drinks in school also came to a head in 2006, as Connecticut voted to bar all sodas from its schools. Coke had been negotiating with the class-action lawyers and the Center for Science in the Public Interest, hoping to stave off a lawsuit. Coke executives held simultaneous discussions with the American Heart Association and former President Bill Clinton's foundation, finally arriving (along with other soft drink firms) at a voluntary solution. Coke, Pepsi, and others would phase out the sale of *all* soft drinks in *all* public and private schools over a three-year period.

Isdell complained that it made no sense to exclude diet sodas while sugar-laden sports drinks and juices were permissible. His advisors told him that the problem was the artificial sweetener aspartame, widely rumored to cause everything from blindness to multiple sclerosis. Annoyed, Isdell correctly observed that "there is absolutely no evidence of any health risk from aspartame." A few days later, after Isdell presented the Fulbright Prize for International Understanding (sponsored by Coke) to Bill Clinton, he commended Clinton for drinking his customary Diet Coke, then lamented, "It's a terrible pity that kids are no longer going to be able to drink it in high schools." Clinton subsequently intervened, and diet sodas were put back on the approved list.

When the agreement was announced in May 2006, Professor of Law Richard Daynard crowed, "This would not have happened but for the threat of litigation." Michael Jacobson, head of the Center for Science in the Public Interest, groused, "I'd like to get rid of the Gatorades and diet soft drinks completely," but his critique was muted, and there would be no class-action lawsuits.

HEIR APPARENT

As 2006 came to an end, Isdell promoted Muhtar Kent as president and chief operating officer, anointing him as the clear heir to the Coke throne. That year, Kent had overseen an impressive 6 percent increase in international sales. Isdell called Kent "a man of the highest integrity and deepest skills." Kent dismissed his short sale of his own company's stock as an "honest mistake 10 years ago that's been fully investigated and fully resolved." Now he planned to focus on re-booting sales of carbonated soft drinks in North America.

By that time, Don Knauss, sensing that Kent would be appointed ahead of him, had departed to become CEO of Clorox. He was replaced as head of Coke's North American business by veteran J. Alexander "Sandy" Douglas. Having been passed over, Mary Minnick left Coke a few weeks later, and Kent then had two other Coke marketing executives reporting directly to him.

It soon became apparent that Isdell and Kent were real business partners, with what Isdell called "an absolute level of trust" in each other. When Coke bought an ailing bottler in the Philippines, which was in Kent's international domain, he asked Isdell, "You go and do the launch, would you? You've got real equity from your days there." Isdell called them "two halves of a whole. Each of us runs half a company." Kent asserted, "We have the same passion for the business, the same priorities."

Those priorities had been to turn around international problem markets in the Philippines, India, Japan, and Nigeria, all now growing again. "But North American is still a market that is leaking in the bucket," Kent said. During the first quarter of 2007, international sales volume rose 9 percent, but North American volume fell by 3 percent. Isdell noted that 95 percent of the world's population lay outside North

America, so that's where most future growth would be. Nonetheless, the home market remained crucial.

Kent admitted that he was "unpleasantly surprised by how deep some of the problems were" in the United States. He recalled that in the 1980s, he used to take groups from Eastern Europe to America to see how Coca-Cola did it right. Yet "the Polish market is today infinitely better looking and better managed," he said. It all came down to the nitty-gritty details. *Coke signs must be everywhere. Packaging has to attract impulse buyers. The price has to be right. So does the marketing.*

GETTING THE TARGET OFF THEIR BACKS

In January 2007, Coke bought a Super Bowl ad for the first time since 1998, even though a thirty-second television spot cost $2.6 million. One of the ads, an animation, imitated the video game Grand Theft Auto, in which a young man in a leather jacket leaps out of a car on a tough city street, grabs a Coke in a store, then yanks a terrified driver out of his convertible. But the protagonist pays the storeowner and gives the driver a free Coke, as he throws cash into the guitar box of a street singer who croons, "Give a little love and it all comes back to you." In the rest of the spot, the hero performs various other Coke good deeds.

It was an effective spot, but the "Happiness Factory" ad would become a classic, eventually providing a whole new Coca-Cola theme. A young man puts his coin into the slot of a vending machine, and the animation shows a Rube Goldberg world inside the machine, where the rolling coin sets off a chain reaction in which little creatures fly with an empty Coke bottle to get it filled, capped, and cooled. A cheering mob escorts the bottle, sending it down a ramp to where the unsuspecting customer grabs it from the machine.*

These two "Coke Side of Life" ads were whimsical and upbeat, but they failed to stop the steady erosion of market share for sugary colas, which were widely perceived as a major cause of the obesity epidemic. As part of the effort to "get the target off our backs," as Isdell put it, Coke executives stopped talking about carbonated soft drinks, referring to them instead as "sparkling beverages." Isdell insisted that Coke Zero, Diet Coke, and other low-calorie drinks should be considered health and wellness beverages. Video games, he said, were as much a problem as soft drinks—*oops*, sparkling beverages. Kids these days needed to get off their butts and get some exercise!

Yet Coke simultaneously sought to glue more young people to their computer terminals watching YouTube, in order to sell more drinks. In March 2007, an ingenious faux documentary helped to boost Coke Zero sales. In the ad, Coca-Cola Classic executives want their lawyers to sue Coke Zero for "taste infringement" because it is indistinguishable from regular Coca-Cola. The Candid Camera approach captured the reaction of a real Coke lawyer, unaware that actors played the Coke execs. "We're playing with the Coke equities in a way that makes you think about Coke Zero

---

* The idea for a Happiness Factory ad originated with the Red Cell agency, inspired by the 2005 Charlie and the Chocolate Factory movie remake. But the Dutch outlet of Wieden+Kennedy executed the spot with its own interpretation.

differently: not as a diet product and more associated with the taste of Coke," said an executive for Crispin Porter + Bogusky, the edgy Miami firm that made the spots. Aimed at young men, the ads were introduced on YouTube and through e-mail rather than television, part of an innovative shift in Coke's marketing strategy.

At first, Coke marketers weren't sure what to make of the wild, unpredictable, democratic world of the Internet. In 2005, Fritz Grobe, a juggler, and his friend Stephen Voltz, a lawyer, discovered that when they dropped candy Mentos into Diet Coke, it caused a fizzy eruption, which they could enhance by restricting the flow with a nozzle. Experimenting in Grobe's backyard in rural Maine, they became impresarios, and in June 2006 they posted a hilarious video of their "Experiment 137" on the Web at www.eepybird.com. Dressed in white lab coats and protective goggles, they choreograph a fantastic, varied geyser display using a hundred and one 2-liter bottles of Diet Coke and five hundred and twenty-three Mentos. At the end of the two-minute video, they toast each other with Diet Coke, then spit-spray it at each other and laugh.

The video went viral, attracting millions of viewers, and Grobe and Voltz appeared on the *Late Show with David Letterman* and the *Today Show*. Coke initially distanced itself from the odd phenomenon but then embraced it, inviting Grobe and Voltz to produce their geysers at North Avenue headquarters and hosting "Experiment 214" on the Coke website for several months.

Packaging also helped sell colas. In Australia, Coke Zero sales took off. Why? Partly because the bottles and cans were a distinctive, macho black. So Coke switched to black in North America, pursuing what Kent called a "red-black-silver strategy"—red for Coke Classic, black for Coke Zero, and silver for Diet Coke. In 2007, Coke also introduced Diet Coke Plus, enhanced with niacin, vitamins B6 and B12, zinc, and magnesium, in an attempt to attract health-conscious women.

In February 2007, Coke paid $250 million for New Jersey–based Fuze Beverage, a six-year-old company that made enhanced juices and teas called Slenderize, Refresh, and Vitalize in flavors such as Banana Colada and Peach Mango. They came in tall bottles with colorful pictures of fruit. Fuze also marketed two energy drinks, NOS and Rehab, a hangover remedy (one of Coca-Cola's original selling points).

Three months later, that purchase was dwarfed by Coke's acquisition of Glaceau, based in Whitestone, New York, for a staggering $4.1 billion. In 1995, founder Darius Bikoff first made Smartwater, a distilled water with added calcium, then added Fruitwater with natural fruit flavoring. One morning in 2000, Bikoff took a vitamin C wafer with Smartwater and was inspired to create Vitaminwater, which jump-started sales. Five years later, he told a reporter that the surge in healthful drinks wasn't a fad. "It isn't going away, and Glaceau is the brand of the revolution."

Muhtar Kent agreed, personally wooing Bikoff and agreeing to the whopping sales price, even though Glaceau had posted only $355 million in sales the previous year. Boosted by Coke's massive distribution and marketing, Kent saw that Vitaminwater and its cohorts could become megabrands not just in the United States, but also overseas. Encouraged by these acquisitions, CCE stopped distributing Arizona Tea and promised to carry only products owned by Coca-Cola.

The target may have gotten smaller on Coke's back, but it was still there. The Company sued an Argentinean blogger who defamed Dasani as "cancer water." The Connecticut attorney general launched an assault on claims that Coke's green tea drink, Enviga, "invigorates your metabolism to burn calories," making it a negative-calorie beverage. This was "voodoo nutrition," he said, and the Center for Science in the Public Interest simultaneously filed a lawsuit. Coke eventually settled out of court, modifying its label to clarify that Enviga alone could not produce weight loss.

The Company also settled another frightening health-related lawsuit. Benzene, a flammable ingredient in solvents, had been found in Vault Zero and Fanta Pineapple, due to a chemical reaction between benzoate salt, an antibacterial agent, and ascorbic acid. Sugar impedes the reaction, so it happens only in artificially sweetened drinks. Coke removed the ascorbic acid.

THE NEW WORLD OF COCA-COLA

Few consumers paid attention to these health flaps, however. Instead, Atlanta tourists could visit the new World of Coca-Cola Museum, which opened in May 2007 across from the huge new Georgia Aquarium at the north end of Centennial Olympic Park. The new building had twice the capacity of its predecessor near the moribund Underground Atlanta. Finally giving the morphine-addicted Coke creator his due, Isdell had commissioned a statue of John Pemberton to greet visitors at Pemberton Place before they shelled out $15 to enter the phantasmagoria of Coke-drenched memorabilia and advertising.

First they had to sit in the Happiness Factory Theater, where a bubbly red-clad "Coke ambassador" gave a pep talk before screening an eight-minute version of the Rube Goldberg commercial inside a vending machine. Then visitors were free to wander through the slow-motion bottling line, get bumped and sprayed in the 4D Theater, view classic commercials in the Perfect Pauses Theater, sample Coke drinks from around the world, grab a free 8-ounce bottle, and exit through the Coca-Cola Store, where they could spend more money on some 5,500 Coke-embossed products. One million people a year would visit the Coke museum.

On an interactive video wall outside the 4D Theater, Coke touted its do-good initiatives, though most people didn't pay much attention to this poorly designed feature. Neville Isdell clearly thought that these initiatives were important, however. In January 2007, he spoke at the World Economic Forum in Davos, Switzerland, emphasizing that Coca-Cola was trying to reduce emissions and conserve water, while working with Greenpeace to deploy energy-efficient refrigeration units that didn't use hydrofluorocarbons (HFCs), which are 1,000 times worse than carbon dioxide in causing global warming. Since Coke owned 10 million coolers and vending machines worldwide, a switch to HFC-free units would help substantially to reduce greenhouse gases. Later, a CARE executive praised Coke for "leading the way in water steward-ship" and helping to fund a CDC/CARE program to provide safe water in rural Kenyan schools.

In June 2007, Isdell spoke at a news conference hosted by the World Wildlife Fund in Beijing. There, he announced that Coke would give the fund $20 million to help conserve seven of the world's most vital river basins, including the Yangtze, Mekong, Rio Grande, and the Danube. Isdell also emphasized the Company's commitment to reduce its water usage and improve water recycling at its bottling plants. In the previous five years, Coke had improved water efficiency by 19 percent. "Far too many people suffer from a lack of access to safe water," Isdell said, so "we at the Coca-Cola Company have placed highest priority on being responsible water users." Critics pointed out that saving water was also saving the Company money.

By the end of the year, shareholders were very happy, regardless. That summer, Coca-Cola had been voted the top brand in the world in the annual Harris Interactive Poll, unseating Sony. Coke Zero and Glaceau became the twelfth and thirteenth Coke brands to hit $1 billion in annual retail sales. Coca-Cola stock had risen steadily from its long-term doldrums around $40 and crested at $60 in December 2007, the same month that Isdell announced that Muhtar Kent would become the next Coca-Cola CEO on July 1, 2008. Isdell would remain as chair of the board for another year to ensure a smooth transition.

The turnaround was complete. "The winning culture is back," Isdell and Kent asserted in a jointly signed letter in the 2007 annual report. "Winning changes everything."

"Big Jim" Farley served as a roving ambassador for Coca-Cola for three decades, routinely consorting with government heads, religious leaders, and welcoming committees, such as these Japanese geishas. Japan would grow to become the Company's largest profit center.

On a 1945 radio set, crooner Morton Downey shares his favorite drink with young Margaret O'Brien. One of Robert Woodruff's closest friends, Downey served as a Coke goodwill ambassador and achieved fabulous wealth from his Coca-Cola stock and bottling plants. Despite his smooth public appearance, however, he regularly beat his children and had his daughter lobotomized.

From the Depression on, Coca-Cola men received rousing messages at Company conventions. By the sixties, the Jam Handy Corporation produced the skits using professional actors and singers.

Coca-Cola photographers loved to snap pictures of presidents and other rulers with the proper soft drink. Here Truman, Eisenhower, Kennedy (next page), and Johnson were caught imbibing, and even Fidel Castro enjoyed the fizzy beverage.

Bill Clinton – shown here chugging Coke with wife Hillary at the Moscow bottling plant – joined a long line of U.S. presidents who appreciated Coca-Cola.(AP WIDE WORLD PHOTOS)

The Beatles didn't mind posing with Cokes, and they nearly signed a deal to sing commercials, but the proposed fee was too stiff for Robert Woodruff.

Clasping their Cokes like talismans of peace, world youth taught the world to sing in perfect harmony while encouraging consumption of the right soft drink in the 1971 "Hilltop" commercial.

By 1973, the company finally appealed to hippies and blacks in this relaxed, integrated magazine spot.

"Mean" Joe Greene chugged eighteen 16-ounce bottles of Coke for his famous 1979 commercial, vomiting after the sixth. After all that, the producers used the first take.

Coke CEO Paul Austin, looking depressed, worried, and lost in his 1979 executive suite, suffered from undiagnosed Alzheimer's disease. (*The Atlanta Journal-Constitution/Louis Favorite*)

CEO Robert Goizueta (below right) and president Don Keough stand outside Atlanta's first World of Coca-Cola museum, which opened in 1990. During the eighties and early nineties, the two executives complemented one another perfectly—at least in public.

The implacable, inscrutable Boss at his desk. (Above)

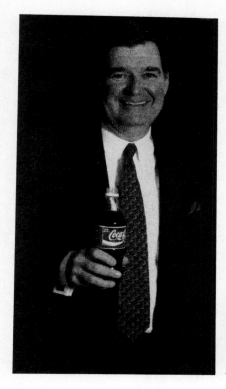

Doug Ivester, who took over as CEO after Roberto Goizueta's death in 1997, looked mild-mannered, but he liked to think of himself as a predatory wolf. After a brief reign, he was ousted in late 1999. (*The Atlanta Journal-Constitution /Renee Hannans*)

Australian Doug Daft was unprepared to assume the CEO mantle after Ivester was forced out. He fired thousands and morale sank as investigations and scandals mounted. He left in 2004. (*Courtesy Coca-Cola Company*)

In the late 1990s Coke and Pepsi offered millions of dollars to American school districts for exclusive vending privileges. (©Jerry Dolezal)

Colombian Coke Float

Unthinkable! Undrinkable!
CAMPAIGN TO STOP *Killer Coke* WWW.KILLERCOKE.ORG

The Campaign to Stop Killer Coke, begun by activist Ray Rogers in 2003, claimed that The Coca-Cola Company was responsible for the murder of union members who worked in Coke bottling plants in Colombia. Right-wing paramilitaries committed the violence, but who ordered it? *(Illustration by Jay Lynch, Corporate Campaign, Inc.)*

Coca-Cola also faced international protests and censure for allegedly depleting the water table in India in the early twenty-first century, though the Company claimed that it added back water through rain harvesting and that the real water problems were caused by drought and poor agricultural practices. *(Illustration by Carlos Latuff, www.KillerCoke.org)*

Irish native Neville Isdell (right) came out of retirement in 2004 to restore morale and turn the Company around. He brought back Muhtar Kent (left), son of a Turkish diplomat, despite an old insider trading scandal. Kent took over as CEO in 2008 and continued the world-wide Coca-Cola conquest. *(Courtesy The Coca-Cola Company)*

In 2012, Coca-Cola returned to Myanmar, leaving Cuba and North Korea as the only countries where Coke does no official business. CEO Muhtar Kent flew to Myanmar to deliver one of the first cases to a shop owner. *(Courtesy The Coca-Cola Company)*

~ 25 ~

Surging Ahead

Our Mission: To refresh the world . . . Inspire moments of optimism and happiness . . . Create value and make a difference.
—"2020 Vision" (The Coca-Cola Company, 2009)

By the time Muhtar Kent became CEO of the Company in the summer of 2008, the U.S. economy was sliding into recession as the housing bubble burst. The entire stock market declined, dragging Coca-Cola stock back down to $50 a share. As gas prices simultaneously rose to $4 a gallon, people cut back on buying drinks at convenience stores after filling up at the pump, and Dasani sales declined as people drank more tap water.

Despite these setbacks, Kent remained upbeat. "The strategy is in place," he said. "What we need to do is execute that strategy better." Coke would continue to snap up alternative beverages—it bought 40 percent of Honest Tea in February 2008—but despite declining cola sales, Kent insisted that "sparkling beverages are the oxygen of our company." Still, he emphasized that he wasn't satisfied, remaining "constructively discontent," an echo of Robert Woodruff's old mantra.

In many ways, Muhtar Kent was the ultimate international Coca-Cola man, associated with the Company since he was 25. The son of a Turkish consul general, Kent was born in December 1952 in New York City, but he was educated in private schools in Turkey, otherwise living in Thailand, India, and Iran as his father served as ambassador to those countries. In British universities, where he obtained an MBA, Kent was not the best student. He loved to party, and with his dark good looks and flashing smile, he was something of a playboy. In the summer of 1977, just after graduation, he toured California with a friend and loved it. "In America," he said, "if it makes sense, people do it." The next year he joined Coca-Cola, working mostly in Europe. He spoke fluent English, Turkish, Italian, and French.

Kent became a hard-charging Coke man who worked long hours. "I call him Bulldozer," said his former boss at Efes Beverage Group in Turkey. "He's very stubborn. He never stops pushing." At 6'1", Kent had a commanding, though nonthreatening presence, with a friendly, gregarious demeanor. He loved fast cars, driving a classic Porsche and following Formula One racing. He and his wife, Defne, had a daughter, Selin, and a son, Cem.

Necdet Kent, his father, had served as a role model. Always immaculately dressed, the elder Kent was an international diplomat with a strong humanitarian bent. During

World War II, as consul general in Marseilles, Kent saved Turkish Jews from the gas chambers. Muhtar Kent, a nonpracticing Muslim, was friends with Ecumenical Patriarch Bartholomew, the head of the Eastern Orthodox Christian Church.

Kent's tolerance for diversity ended with the cola wars, however. Early in his career, a beggar in Morocco asked for spare change to buy a Coke. To encourage his good taste, Kent gave him a $10 bill and said, "Buy a case of Coke."

THE CONTROVERSIAL BEIJING OLYMPICS

The 2008 Summer Olympics, scheduled to open in August in Beijing, would mark the eightieth anniversary of Coca-Cola's Olympic sponsorship. Coke was going all out for this event because China, with its 1.3 billion people, was an extraordinarily important market. There were already 36 Coca-Cola bottling plants in China, with 30,000 employees. Even with the low per capita annual average Chinese consumption of twenty-five servings of eight-ounce Coke products (compared to nearly four hundred in the United States), China was already Coke's fourth biggest market, and Kent expected it to become the Company's top market "in the not-too-distant future." In 2001, the day after the announcement that Beijing would host the Olympics, Coke began distributing 1 million congratulatory cans throughout China. Now the Company splashed signage all over Beijing while funding fifty-eight rural Chinese schools to build goodwill.

Coke would literally roll out the red carpet for the Olympic torchbearers as they ran across China, as shown in Chinese TV ads. Declaring 2008 to be the "Year of Shuang" (according to officials, *Shuang* meant "a physical and emotional state of refreshment"), Coca-Cola prepared to spend some $90 million on the event, including a 40,000-square-foot Shuang Experience Center, a Chinese version of the World of Coca-Cola Museum, featuring a film showcasing Coke's sponsorship of the Olympic torch relay around the world.

Yet the feel-good torch relay was lurching towards catastrophe. On March 10, 2008, when Buddhist monks in Tibet protested the long-term Chinese occupation there, China cracked down hard, resulting in an estimated a hundred and forty deaths. Two weeks later, the torch run began in ancient Olympia in Greece, where pro-Tibet protestors disrupted a speech by a Chinese official. Similar protests plagued the relay in Istanbul, London, and Paris, as it pursued its twenty-one-stop, six-continent itinerary.

The torch, which was supposed to stand for world peace and unity, had become the center of raging controversy. Coke braced for its sole American stop in mid-April in San Francisco, where eighty runners would carry it, accompanied by a blue-clad Chinese paramilitary squad called the Flame Protection Unit. Trained in marksmanship, martial arts, and hand-to-hand combat, its members had roughed up some protestors in England, leading a British Olympics official to call them "thugs."

Activists hanging a "Free Tibet" sign from the Golden Gate Bridge were arrested. Majora Carter, a forty-one-year-old environmental activist who had won a "genius award" from the MacArthur Foundation, was chosen by Coca-Cola as one of the runners (Coke was pushing its "green" initiatives). Surrounded by the blue Chinese guards, she carried the flaming torch aloft in her left hand, but as she jogged, she unfurled a Tibetan flag hidden up her right sleeve. She waved the flag for five seconds before a guard wrested it from her. The San Francisco police relieved her of the torch.

A Coke spokesman said, "It's unfortunate that Ms. Carter used an invitation to participate in the torch relay as a platform to make a personal political statement." Coke issued a carefully worded press release "expressing deep concern for the situation on the ground in Tibet," but saying that it would be "inappropriate . . . to comment on the political situation of individual nations." The Company reaffirmed its belief that "the Olympics are a force for good."

That was just the beginning of the protests. At Coke's annual shareholders meeting, held a week later, Lhadon Tethong, head of Students for a Free Tibet, begged Coke to alter the torch route so that it did not go through Tibet on its way to Beijing. "Coke will be underwriting bloodshed in Tibet." The response: Coke had no control over the torch route.

Because China supplied weapons to Sudan, Dream for Darfur activists wanted Coke to disavow the "Genocide Olympics." Actress Mia Farrow, speaking for Dream for Darfur, complained that Coca-Cola had "more feel-good slogans and songs than any other company" but refused to take a moral stand. Isdell and Kent pointed out that Coca-Cola had already spent $5 million on safe-water initiatives in Sudan and had promised an additional $7 million over the next three years for humanitarian efforts. "For an organization that has not eased the suffering of a single individual on the ground in Darfur to criticize those who are helping thousands every day is more than ironic," a Company press release observed.

In April, a Chinese blogger posted a photograph of a 2003 German Coke advertisement showing three Buddhist monks on a roller coaster, with the slogan "Make It Real." The blogger claimed that these were Tibetan monks, the roller coaster represented freedom, and the slogan meant that Tibet should "realize freedom now." The web posting concluded, "Coke! Okay. I'll remember this and won't drink your crappy product." Hundreds of Chinese called for a boycott as the misinformation spread.

Despite the protests from both sides, Muhtar Kent remained optimistic. "We know that the Olympics are going to be a turning point for China, its people, and a catalyst for our connection to these vibrant consumers," he said. Coke issued Olympic-themed cans and bottles in Ethiopian, Russian, Thai, Mandarin, and other languages. For a set of commemorative bottles, Coke paired Chinese artists with global musicians to create a project dubbed *WE8*, standing for "West Meets East in 2008." Collectors could buy the aluminum bottles and download corresponding tunes such as "Global Harmony." During the Olympics, 10,000 people a day visited the Shuang Experience Center, sampling a perfectly chilled Coca-Cola, as did 26 million Chinese along the Olympic torch route in their country.

LEAN, EFFICIENT, AND AGGRESSIVELY *HAPPY*

As the recession deepened, Muhtar Kent announced plans to save $500 million a year by 2011 by becoming "more efficient, leaner and more adaptive to changing market conditions." Coke would put the savings back into brand-building. Kent clamped a hiring freeze on North America, laid off some employees in information technology, and eliminated merit pay raises. He stressed efficiencies in the supply chain and encouraged green initiatives that got good press and saved money. Coke and its bottlers began a switch to hybrid vehicles. Thinner, lighter bottles reduced plastic and saved on shipping costs.

The fragmented bottler system was obviously in need of streamlining, especially with proliferating brands—Coke now owned over four hundred of them. After the failure of Lehman Brothers on September 15, 2008, the entire stock market fell off a cliff, with Coke shares declining back to $42. The following week, in Boca Raton, Florida, Kent called a meeting of the top forty Coca-Cola bottlers from around the world "to discuss the shared vision for the future." With his extensive bottling-side experience, Kent had credibility and probably made forceful points—the meeting was not open to the media.

A month later, giant bottler Coca-Cola Enterprises axed 1,000 employees. As the recession deepened and sales declined in North America, CCE raised retail prices. Big Coke retaliated by charging CCE more for concentrate and cutting $35 million it had promised CCE for promotions. With tensions mounting, Coke and CCE negotiated, hammering out an agreement to consolidate some common supply chain activities and to negotiate mutually agreeable pricing.

The following year, PepsiCo bought its two largest franchise bottlers, which would eventually save hundreds of millions of dollars and allow Pepsi to respond more nimbly to changing market demands. CCE executive John Brock admitted that it would make Pepsi a "more formidable competitor." Kent reiterated his faith in the bottler franchise system as Coke and CCE pursued "virtual integration" of some operations.

By January 2009, with the recession spreading worldwide, soft drink sales had declined for four consecutive years in the United States, and per capita consumption had been falling since peaking in 1998. Coke responded with a new global marketing campaign, "Open Happiness," created by Wieden+Kennedy, to replace "Coke Side of Life." It was a brilliant evolution from the Happiness Factory ad, and it showed that Joe Tripodi, Coke's new chief marketing officer, had been boning up on Coke history and culture. "Our brand isn't here to solve world peace or fix the economy," he said. "We represent a small moment of pleasure in a sometimes very stressful or difficult day." Just as "The Pause That Refreshes" had worked during the Great Depression, "Open Happiness" fit the global recession of the twenty-first century.

The ads all made the contour Coca-Cola bottle the central focus. In a spot called "Crave," a young man on a sweltering day keeps seeing images of Coke bottles in shadows, building outlines, a park fountain, a bicycle, and the front grill of a car before quenching his thirst with an ice-cold Coke and an "ahhh," which appears in skywriting as he walks outside. In another spot, two teens flirt silently in a library until the boy draws a Coke bottle on his arm, which dispenses into a glass the girl has scribbled on her arm. In "Heist," a popular Super Bowl ad, an army of grasshoppers, yellow jackets, and dragonflies, directed by a ladybug, make off with a Coke bottle during a picnic.

The whimsical ads worked, provoking a smile and reminding viewers that Coke was a coveted beverage, an effervescent, inexpensive way to make them (and insects) happy. The ads also met Muhtar Kent's mandate to economize. None of them used words, so they could be aired globally without modification, other than translating the tagline, "Open Happiness."* Two months later, the Company released a pop song featuring Cee Lo Green and other rock stars singing "Open Happiness," set to the lilting tune from the Coke ads but not referring to Coca-Cola in the lyrics, in imitation of "I'd Like to Teach the World to Sing" from 1971. With puerile feel-good lyrics ("It's a brand new day, / Open up a little happiness today"), it rose to number 37 on the pop charts, nestled between Beyoncé and Pink, and was later released in other languages internationally. It became the most popular song in China.

The Company chose this opportune moment to drop "Classic" from the Coke name. It had been used only in the United States and was an unwelcome reminder of the 1985 New Coke disaster that had made the designation Coca-Cola Classic necessary.

The Company aired a Coke Zero ad during the 2009 Super Bowl, a remake of the classic Mean Joe Greene commercial. In this version, a boy offers wounded football player Troy Polamalu his Coke Zero. But before Polamalu can drink it, two Coke brand managers grab it, saying, "Coke Zero stole our taste; they are *not* stealing our commercial!" The football player tackles the brand man, then guzzles the drink, rips off the brand manager's shirt, and tosses it to the kid. Very funny.

While admitting that 2009 was going to be a challenging year, Muhtar Kent insisted that it was an excellent time to "expand the base of the business," since "the airwaves are less crowded and the media costs are lower." As consumers economized (and obesity critics complained about oversized servings), Coke offered a sixteen-ounce bottle for ninety-nine cents as an alternative to the twenty-ounce top seller, whose $1-plus cost was hurting sales. It also introduced "mini-can" soft drinks containing ninety calories. The marketers hoped that consumers would not notice that Coke cost more per ounce in the smaller servings.

Coke promoted its energy drinks, with Full Throttle sponsoring drag races and NASCAR driver Kyle "Rowdy" Busch touting NOS. But Monster and Red Bull dominated the category, with Rockstar a distant third and Coke's two brands lagging far behind. Coca-Cola consequently made a deal to distribute Monster, terminating its previous deal with Rockstar. Meantime, 5-Hour Energy was making inroads as a small two-ounce "shot" of caffeine and vitamins. Students willingly shelled out $3 for the foul-tasting brew, which cost twenty times more per ounce than Coca-Cola. Coke responded with an NOS-branded energy shot.

To counter Pepsi's bottled Frappuccino success, Coke partnered with Italian espresso-maker illy to create a ready-to-drink coffee, illy Issimo, introducing it in Whole Foods outlets. Coke had bombed with Planet Java and Coca-Cola Blak, however, and was only cautiously promoting this new canned coffee. Trying to jump-start its ailing Nestea sales, the Company sponsored *CTRL*, an Internet "webisode" series produced by NBC Universal Digital Studio in which a downtrodden office worker discovers that, by drinking Nestea and using his computer, he can move back in time, become invisible, and read other people's minds. Nestea, billed as "Liquid Awesomeness," was integral to the plot, but *CTRL* failed to produce awesome new sales.

---

* The Company introduced the internal Coca-Cola Design Machine, allowing bottlers around the world to access and customize print advertising, product photography, and packaging designs.

More promising was Coke's field test of its Freestyle vending machine, which it touted as the "fountain of the future." The cooler, whose sleek exterior was created by an Italian car designer, allowed consumers to create over a hundred custom-made beverages with a touch screen; they could ask, for instance, for a peach Coke, raspberry Coke Zero, lime Powerade, strawberry Sprite, or vanilla Fanta, and it would squirt into a paper cup. The top-secret project, code-named "Jet" in 2005, became public when Coke began to test-market it late in 2008 at Willy's Mexicana Grill in metro Atlanta. Early results were promising, with people lining up to try the Freestyle. On a hidden video camera, one woman was captured kissing the machine. In 2009, Coke tested more Freestyles in Atlanta and Southern California restaurants.

2020 VISION

The annual Coca-Cola shareholders meeting of April 2009 was held at the Gwinnett Center just north of Atlanta so that local investors could celebrate the final transition of power. Neville Isdell retired as chair of the board, handing that mantle to CEO Muhtar Kent, who now ruled alone. Isdell was pleased to leave the Company in good shape. "The car is back on the road and going forward," he said. "Muhtar has to make it go faster." Isdell looked back on his career with satisfaction. "I have visited 145 countries, met and supped with men and women of history, and, just as important, spent time with people of many cultures at every level of economic status. . . . I have truly lived on the Coke side of life—happy, optimistic, and to the degree that it is in any way possible, innocent."

Not everyone agreed. At the Coke shareholders meeting, Ray Rogers popped up as usual to denounce Coke executives as "among the world's worst liars, scam artists, and white-collar criminals," adding assertions that included Chinese workers being overworked and underpaid and accusations of murder and intimidation of Colombian union employees. Outside a protest sign advised, "Don't Drink Killer Coke Zero. Zero Ethics! Zero Justice! Zero Health!"

Kent didn't appear to be rattled. He was more concerned that first-quarter revenue had fallen 3 percent, with a stronger dollar hurting international profits. The North American volume was down 2 percent, but global sales were *up* 2 percent. "This business was built for times like these," Kent said. The Open Happiness campaign was just getting started. *Don't worry, be happy!*

As 2009 progressed, Kent's optimism seemed justified. When the Chinese government nixed an attempted Coca-Cola purchase of Huiyuan Juice Group, Coke instead promoted its Minute Maid brands more heavily with flavors such as grape with aloe, pitched in TV ads by Hong Kong pop singer Eason Chan. Another new drink, Minute Maid Pulpy Super Milky, a dairy-juice combo with coconut bits, was an instant hit. The Company introduced Vitaminwater in China. Coke Zero not only sponsored the Chinese version of the popular Aion Internet fantasy but also embedded a Coke character in the game. Sprite was the top-selling soft drink in China. Kent announced that Coke would invest an additional $2 billion in the Chinese market over the next three years.

Coke launched other drinks tailored for specific countries. In Indonesia, for instance, it promoted Frestea Green My Body, in flavors of aloe vera/orange blossom or ginger/

ginseng, targeting active, hip twenty-somethings. In Japan, I LOHAS bottled-water ads showed a lightweight bottle (*ecoru shiboru*, "environmental squeeze") twisted to reduce size for easy recycling. In Russia, the Company sold Rich, a pureed fruit drink squeezed from a tube like toothpaste, and Krushka & Bochka Kvass, its version of the classic beverage made from fermented rye bread. In western Europe, Coke bought Abbey Well bottled water; took part ownership of Innocent Drinks, a smoothie and juice brand; and introduced 4-ounce Burn Energy Shots. In Mexico, where per capital consumption of Coke products reached an unbelievable six hundred and sixty-five 8-ounce servings, the Company planned to invest another $5 billion over the next five years. Coke's Del Valle juice brands sold throughout Latin America. In Africa, Coke committed $12 billion over the next decade.

In the United States, Coke's premium not-from-concentrate juice brands—Simply Orange, Simply Lemonade, Simply Apple, and others—breached the magic $1 billion annual sales level. Coke Zero continued, for the fourth year, to deliver double-digit volume growth in North America and launched global co-promotional campaigns with the James Bond flick *Quantum of Silence* and with *Avatar*, the epic science fiction film that broke box office records. Coke Zero was now available in 133 markets around the world.

Coke's aggressive marketing hype harvested lawsuits as well as sales. An Australian panel said Coke had misled consumers with ads assuring them that Coke products wouldn't make them fat or rot their teeth. Under the so-called Jelly Bean rule, which held that it wasn't legitimate to fortify junk foods, the FDA asserted that Diet Coke Plus (with vitamins) was mislabeled, and two New Jersey consumers sued, complaining that the drink was not healthy as implied. Coke prevailed. Its Powerade Ion-4 sports drink with additional electrolytes claimed superiority over Gatorade: "Don't settle for an incomplete sports drink." Pepsi sued and lost, but Coke withdrew the ads anyway. Coke's Vitaminwater also squared off against Gatorade, with ads showing football players dumping a bucket of Gatorade, with the caption "Out with the old . . . in with the new."

The Center for Science in the Public Interest filed a class-action lawsuit over Coke's health claims for Vitaminwater, calling it "snake oil" and "sugar water" and pointing out that a twenty-ounce bottle contained eight teaspoons of sugar and a hundred and twenty-five calories. "Vitamins + water = all you need" on the label was deceptive, as was the name itself. It would be more accurate to call it Vitaminsugarwater. Vitaminwater varieties such as Defense, Revive, Endurance, and Focus claimed to boost the immune system, promote healthy joints, reduce the risk of eye disease, or improve mental focus. So did Pepsi's SoBe Lifewater brands, such as B-Strong, Electrify, and Immunity, but CSPI sued only Coca-Cola because it was the segment leader. The lawsuit would remain unresolved for years.

Meanwhile, Coke attracted devoted followers without even trying. In August 2008, Dusty Sorg, a twenty-nine-year-old aspiring Los Angeles actor, created a Facebook page for his favorite drink. Within a month, his Coke page had 750,000 friends, and by the spring of 2009, it had 3.3 million fans, second only to President Barack Obama's Facebook page, with its 6 million followers. As the Sorg-created page grew, Facebook administrators flagged the site for obscenities and asked Coca-Cola to take it over. Not wanting the Company to be seen as a heavy-handed corporate bully, Coke marketing men invited Sorg to Atlanta and made a deal. Sorg would continue to run the site. Coke would monitor for obscenities or nude photos but would not even censor pro-Pepsi comments. The Company would, however, post "new opportunities" for products, promotions, and events on the site.

In 2009, global sales volume increased by 3 percent and for the first time Coca-Cola cleared over $8 billion in cash profit. The Company used $1.5 billion to repurchase its own stock, with shares climbing close to $60 in December. The previous month, Muhtar Kent hosted an elaborate two-day presentation for analysts, journalists, and top investors, capped by a gourmet meal incorporating Coca-Cola as a key ingredient, washed down by a sampling of foreign Coke beverages and Freestyle vending machine choices. Kent and his key executives offered their "2020 Vision," with a key goal of doubling Coca-Cola Company sales volume to over 3 billion servings a day.

"We see a world unfolding over the next decade and beyond that represents ideal conditions for extraordinary, sustainable growth," Kent said, peering over his reading glasses and gesticulating vehemently. World population would swell, particularly in developing economies and the world's largest cities. One billion more people would join the middle class, and per capita wealth would increase by nearly 30 percent. "That will mean more people with more wealth with more intense demand for choice, leading highly mobile, on-the-go urban lifestyles that are conducive to the incidence and the consumption of ready-to-drink beverages," Kent continued. He projected that annual retail sales for the entire non-alcoholic industry would reach $1 trillion. "As we look ahead to the year 2020, I am convinced that these next few years will be defining moments for The Coca-Cola Company and the great Coca-Cola system. In a growing world of refreshment, ladies and gentlemen, the opportunities before us are tremendous."

Gary Fayard, Coke's chief financial officer, put it more succinctly: "We've got the best brands in the world. We've got the greatest system in the world. And we've got an operating model that generates more cash than any other business in the world."

LIVING POSITIVELY . . .

The enormous cash flow also gave Coca-Cola leverage to pursue the halo effect through its "Live Positively" initiatives. "Imagine a better world where all people have access to safe water, where packaging has a life beyond its original use, and where communities are healthy and prosperous," a 2010 Coke sustainability summary urged. Coke created the Replenish Africa Initiative, a $30 million program to provide safe drinking water to 2 million Africans by 2015. In Uganda and Kenya, the Company collaborated with the Bill & Melinda Gates Foundation to help mango and passion fruit farmers increase productivity, promising to buy the produce to make juices.

Coke offered Dasani and a few other beverages in a new PlantBottle containing 30 percent byproducts of sugar production. The entire bottle was still made of PET plastic that could be recycled but was not biodegradable. The main benefit was that it wasn't made from petroleum. Coke announced a goal of making a 100 percent bio-bottle by 2020. Since oil supplies would inevitably dwindle and become more expensive, this move made economic as well as environmental sense. Coke sponsored RecycleMania, a recycling contest on college campuses, and helped build the world's largest PET bottle-to-bottle recycling plant in Spartanburg, South Carolina, though the vast majority of Coke containers ended up clogging landfills anyway.* By 2015, all new Coke coolers would be HFC-free. Coke pledged to continue reducing carbon emissions from manufacturing operations and to use more hybrid diesel-electric vehicles. Its Belgian production facility used geothermal heat. By the end of 2010, Coke planned to treat all of its wastewater sufficiently so that fish could survive in it. (By early 2013 it had not quite reached 100 percent compliance.)

In more than 100 countries, the Company sponsored physical activity programs, including Copa Coca-Cola, a free soccer program that had already involved 600,000 students around the world. Coke promised to have activity programs in all two hundred-plus countries in which it operated by 2015. Most products revealed calorie content per serving. The Company sold 750 low- or no-calorie drinks, including NutriJuice, an orange juice with added iron, zinc, lysine, and vitamins A and C, to help address anemia and malnutrition in Filipino children.

Coke bragged about its charitable activities in several Open Happiness commercials. One featured a high school football game with a Coke scoreboard. "If you've had a Coke in the last 79 years," the narrator says, "you've helped support community support programs yesterday and today." Another showed students opening mailboxes and lockers to find Coke bottles, emblematic of the college scholarships the Company gave out, while a third pushed Coke's "Give It Back" recycling effort.

Coke freely admitted that its do-good activities were ultimately designed to boost the bottom line one way or the other. Muhtar Kent pointed out that in Kenya, where Coke drilled a new well, women who had spent hours fetching polluted water in buckets were now operating a local catering business. Like thousands of others in the developing world, they used bicycles or pushcarts to deliver Coke products. "You bring the water," Kent said, "and you emancipate the women." Coke promised to double the number of women in its global supply chain by 2020.

Coke's "Live Positively" efforts convinced some former skeptics. In a December 2009 *New York Times* editorial headlined "Will Big Business Save the Earth?" Jared Diamond, author of *Guns, Germs, and Steel* and *Collapse,* wrote that he once had thought that "big businesses are environmentally destructive, greedy, evil and driven by short-term profits," but now he wasn't so sure. "Coca-Cola's survival compels it to be deeply concerned with problems of water scarcity, energy, climate change and agriculture," Diamond observed. "Economic reasons furnish the strongest motives for sustainability, because in the long run (and often in the short run as well) it is much more expensive and difficult to try to fix problems, environmental or otherwise, than to avoid them at the outset." He concluded that "we should reward companies that work to keep the planet healthy."

TREATED NEGATIVELY

Diamond's praise didn't quiet a chorus of naysayers. The Energy and Resources Institute report commissioned by Coke did not entirely exonerate the Company's practices in India, though it found no pesticides in Coke's bottling plants or wastewater.

---

* Without fanfare, the Spartanburg plant quietly closed in 2011 when it failed to turn a profit.

Two of six bottling facilities examined were located in areas where groundwater tables were "overexploited," according to TERI. The $16 million Kaladera bottling plant had "significant impacts" on local water supplies. TERI suggested several options for the Kaladera facility: truck in water from elsewhere, store excess water (if any existed), relocate the plant, or shut it down. "Coca-Cola has no business operating a bottling plant in such dire conditions, and we are not sure why they opened the factory in the first place," complained anti-Coke activist Amit Srivastava of the India Resource Center. In Kerala, a government committee recommended that Coke pay $47 million in damages related to its closed Plachimada bottling plant, though the ruling had no teeth.

The negotiations with anti-Coke lawyers and Colombian union leaders had fallen apart in 2008. Coke offered $12 million in victim compensation, including a fund for victims of anti-union violence, but with the stipulations that the union plaintiffs resign from their jobs at Coke bottling plants, that a gag order on any union criticism of Coca-Cola be instituted, and that the Killer Coke campaign be dismantled. "You were involved in those crimes, you have to pay and admit it," insisted the uncompromising Edgar Paez, chief negotiator for the Sinaltrainal union. "The whole truth must come out." By this time, however, Coke wasn't feeling as much heat. "We are in a much better position to deal with this dissipating campaign," Coke's Ed Potter observed. Terry Collingsworth finally filed an appeal of the alien tort claims decision on the Colombian murders, but a three-judge panel rejected it in 2009.

The following year, a Canadian documentary, *The Coca-Cola Case*, raised the Colombian stink all over again. The film mostly follows lawyer Dan Kovalik of United Steelworkers, who took a leading role in the failed negotiations, though Collingsworth, Rogers, and the Colombian union leaders are also featured. Viewers see Kovalik's ebullience—"I think this is an historic deal"—turn to frustration and dejection. The Coca-Cola Company objected to the film as "defamatory" and said that it broke confidentiality agreements covering the negotiations, but that only called attention to the documentary, which had to turn away crowds at some showings.

The International Labor Organization's report on Coke's bottlers in Colombia found no major labor rights violations, but the ILO made no attempt to investigate the old murder allegations. It did raise concerns about job outsourcing, however, which allowed the Coke system to underpay and fire employees with impunity. In *Belching Out the Devil*, a book published in the United States in 2009, British comedian-activist Mark Thomas documented such uses of Colombian *fleteros* ("hired transporters"). Among others, he interviewed Carlos Maldonado Anaya, who for twenty-five years delivered Coke products wearing a Coke uniform yet worked for a subcontractor and received minimum wage. He was told he would be fired if he joined a union. The filmmakers for *The Coca-Cola Case* interviewed two young *fleteros* who made $1 an hour for a fifteen-hour day. It took the Colombians two years to earn what Coca-Cola's CEO made in an hour. Coke executives bragged that nearly a third of Colombian Coke bottling employees were unionized, which was technically true but ignored the *fleteros*, who comprised about 80 percent of the labor force.*

---

* Coca-Cola bottlers around the world out-sourced low-paying, non-union jobs, including in the United States, Canada, the Philippines, China, Pakistan, Turkey, Colombia, and Mexico.

Thomas wrote in a cheeky style but made pointed jabs. "Trying to get The Coca-Cola Company to answer a question directly is like trying to run a quiz night in an Alzheimer's care home." He traveled from Colombia to Turkey, where he found similar complaints about underpaid subcontractors, and he interviewed protestors who had been gassed, clubbed, and kicked by police. Thomas went to El Salvador, where he saw child labor among the sugar cane fields. *They get in enough trouble over their drinks being too sugary for kids,* he thought, *without the public finding out that children are helping to supply the sugar in the first place.* In the town of Nejapa, El Salvador, Thomas heard claims that the local Coca-Cola bottler was polluting the stream, killing its fish, and that kids who swam in it developed rashes. Then he was off to India and protests over Coke's water usage, also featured in *FLOW*, a 2008 documentary about the "domineering world water cartel."

Coke managers told Thomas that the Nejapa wastewater met international environmental standards and that the Company provided two local schools with clean water. The undocumented claims in the Thomas book looked more serious when, in 2009, a Coke-owned subsidiary, AMCAN Beverages, in American Canyon, California, paid $7.59 million to the city for wastewater violations. But it was unlikely that Coke would pay any such fine in remote El Salvador.

The Coke Machine, another book critical of the Company, came out in 2010. In it, journalist Michael Blanding again covered the Colombian murders, Indian water issues, Coke's exclusive school deals, obesity problems, and other controversies.

REPRISE, REPRISAL, AND MURDER IN GUATEMALA

The same year, Terry Collingsworth filed a lawsuit against Coca-Cola in the New York State Supreme Court, accusing Industria de Café S.A. (INCASA), a Guatemalan Coke bottler and instant coffee maker, of collusion in threats, murder, rape, and torture of union employees and their families.* INCASA owned a coffee and Coke syrup plant in Guatemala City and a Coke bottling plant in Retalhuleu, a city to the west.

The case, involving two union employees, was eerily reminiscent of the Guatemalan Coke bottler who had reputedly hired death squads to kill union leaders in the late 1970s.† José Armando Palacios, a twenty-seven-year veteran at the Guatemala City plant, allegedly received death threats from the INCASA personnel manager early in 2004 after he joined the union, followed by an attempt on his life. In April 2005, two men pushed into his home, tied up his son, and pointed a gun at his wife and daughter, threatening to kill them if Palacios did not quit the union. The following month, he was fired. Palacios refused to accept severance pay and continued to fight to get his job back. In June, the U.S. Labor Education in the Americas Project (USLEAP) called attention to Palacios's case in a petition to the U.S. government.

USLEAP originated as a response to the Guatemalan Coke bottling union troubles of the 1970s and 1980s, so it seemed fitting that it would become involved in this case. But as the situation evolved, fractures, turf battles, and ego clashes within the

---

* Collingsworth now works for the Conrad and Scherer law firm and International Rights Advocates. The lawsuit ended up in a New York federal district court.
† See Chapters 17 and 18.

international labor movement affected the outcome for Palacios, a short, uneducated, but determined former Coke security guard. His union, SITINCA, was small
and received only lukewarm support from the International Union of Food Workers
(IUF), whose general secretary, Ron Oswald, worked in Geneva. Only a few months
before Palacios was fired, Oswald had signed a joint statement with Coca-Cola to
work towards a labor agreement. USLEAP executive director Stephen Coats, who
did not speak Spanish, worked in Chicago. The only USLEAP representative on the
ground in Guatemala was Bob Perillo, who desperately worked to help Palacios and
his family.

The Coca-Cola Company became involved in the case, discreetly and indirectly.
Coke's Ed Potter hired Stan Gacek, who served on the USLEAP board of directors,
as a "consultant."* On January 26, 2006, Gacek told Coats and Perillo that he understood that Palacios would give up his fight for reinstatement and that Atlanta-based
Coke would pay for security guards for him. But the next day Palacios told Gacek
during a Skype call that he had *not* agreed to give up his fight for his job. Perillo wrote,
"It's clearly urgent that Potter meet [directly] with these [Guatemalan union] folks."

On January 28, as Palacios approached his home, a man driving a red car (the
same color as Palacios' truck) and who resembled him was shot and killed, only three
feet away. Convinced that the gunman was after him, Palacios panicked. After he
negotiated a severance package, he was approached by Rodrigo Romero, a Coca-Cola
lawyer, who said, "We can arrange a meeting between you and a check," if he signed a
blank piece of paper that would be a settlement with Coke, agreeing to drop all legal
claims and to remain silent. Palacios refused to sign and fled to the United States on
February 6, 2006.

IUF's Ron Oswald e-mailed that he was "talking to Potter relatively regularly
through the night," and that he was in "almost daily contact with CCC Atlanta over
this case." Oswald was deeply concerned, not about Palacios, but about the possibility
that he would contact Terry Collingsworth. Coats steered the Guatemalan towards
another lawyer for prolonged, unproductive negotiations with Coca-Cola. With his
wife and daughter still in Guatemala, Palacios feared to mount a lawsuit, but when
they were finally able to join him late in 2008, he approached Terry Collingsworth. In
the meantime, Perillo became convinced that Coats, Oswald, and Gacek were running
interference for Coca-Cola to prevent a major lawsuit. He resigned from USLEAP and
joined Collingsworth as a field investigator in Guatemala.

The second case erupted early in 2008. Union representative José Alberto Vicente
Chávez, who worked at the Retalhuleu Coke bottling plant, was involved in bitter collective bargaining negotiations with INCASA management in February 2008. After
Vicente complained that the company was violating the agreement, he was summoned
to a meeting in Guatemala City. As his family waited for him at the Retalhuleu bus
station around 1 a.m. on March 1, four armed men killed Vicente's son and nephew
and gang-raped his sixteen-year-old daughter. One of the assailants was killed by
police, and the others were caught and convicted. There was no investigation of possible links to the Coke bottler, although one of the killers had two cousins and an

---

* Gacek was laid off as the assistant director of the AFL-CIO's International Department shortly
before going to work as a consultant for Coca-Cola.

uncle who worked in the plant. Vicente and his family went into hiding, though he continued to work for INCASA.

In his 2010 Complaint, Terry Collingsworth asserted that "Coke has the control to prevent and/or remedy violence against workers and trade union leaders in its foreign bottling plants." He quoted Ed Potter's 2005 statement that "Coca-Cola acknowledges that Coca-Cola workers are allowed to exercise rights to union membership and collective bargaining without pressure or interference. Such rights are exercised without fear of retaliation, repression, or any other form of discrimination." The lawsuit would remain unresolved for years. Collingsworth remained hopeful, though no alien tort claim had yet won in U.S. courts.

BOTTLED WATER WOES AND THE SODA TAX

In Atlanta, Coke executives were more concerned about campaigns against bottled water and soda than human rights issues. Since 2006, Corporate Accountability International (CAI) had been mounting Tap Water Challenges across the United States in imitation of the old Pepsi Challenge. Consumers discovered that in blind taste tests, they couldn't tell the difference among Dasani, Aquafina, or local tap water. In September 2007, when the University of Central Florida inaugurated its new football stadium, the temperature neared 100 degrees Fahrenheit. The stadium had no water fountains, and the $3-a-bottle Dasani sold out. Eighteen attendees were hospitalized from dehydration and heat exhaustion.

The adverse publicity forced the university to install water fountains, but the controversy over bottled water had only begun. CAI's "Think Outside the Bottle" campaign asked people to drink public water whenever possible, and in 2008 the U.S. Conference of Mayors passed a resolution to ban bottled water at municipal buildings and events. By that year, the bottled water industry was selling nearly 9 billion gallons a year in the United States, over 25 times the amount sold three decades before. Americans drank more bottled water than beer or milk.

Water had become a cash cow for Coke, but Dasani sales were declining. Consequently, the Company supported the Competitive Enterprise Institute, which launched an "Enjoy Bottled Water" campaign in 2008, calling tap water unsafe and ridiculing opponents of bottled water. Still, Dasani sales fell 16 percent in 2009. By the following year, forty-four American cities had either banned bottled water or actively encouraged the use of tap water, and Illinois, New York, and Colorado had initiated statewide programs. The Grand Canyon National Park planned to ban bottled water, but the head of the National Park Service cautioned in a 2010 e-mail that "there are going to be consequences, since Coke is a major sponsor of our recycling efforts," and the proposed ban was abandoned.

Bottled water may have had its critics, but as a multi-billion-dollar global industry, it wasn't going away. "All of a sudden public water fountains have vanished and bottled water is everywhere," observed Peter Gleick in his 2011 book, *Bottled and Sold*. It proved difficult to build brand loyalty for the clear, flavorless liquid, though, and with the recession, more people switched to cheaper private labels.

In 2009, a much more serious threat surfaced. The Senate Finance Committee discussed a possible tax on sweetened soft drinks as a way to help pay for health care reform. The Center for Science in the Public Interest proposed a twelve-cent tax on twelve-ounce sodas, estimating that it would generate $160 billion in the next decade. The idea was to raise money for good causes while reducing obesity through lower consumption.

A study conducted in 2008 by the Harvard School of Public Health showed that soft drink purchases at Boston's Brigham and Women's Hospital declined 26 percent when prices on soft drinks were raised by 35 percent. An educational campaign at the hospital by itself had little impact, but combined with price hikes, it further reduced consumption. "A very aggressive response—such as a notable increase in the price of soda—may be needed to steer people toward healthier options," concluded Dr. Jason Block, who conducted the research.

The aggressive response instead came from Coca-Cola, which ramped up its budget to lobby the federal government from around $3 million in 2008 to over $12 million in 2009. Coke also provided funding for the American Beverage Association (ABA), the soft drink trade group, and Americans Against Food Taxes, a corporate front group that ran television ads against the regressive "sin tax" that would hit low-income consumers the hardest.

The federal soda tax went nowhere, as did most state efforts. In 2010, New York Governor David Paterson proposed a penny-per-ounce soda tax, but under pressure he backed off. The New York State Assembly Rules Committee submitted a similar bill. The ABA mounted an ad blitz on radio, television, and newspapers, and the bill was defeated. In June 2010, the Washington state legislature passed a budget-balancing bill that included a two-cent tax on twelve-ounce sweetened beverages. Within three months, the Stop the Food & Beverage Tax Hikes coalition (funded by the ABA) gathered enough signatures to put Initiative 1107, a repeal proposition, on the ballot that November. The ABA spent nearly $17 million pushing for its passage, and the soda tax disappeared. Similar efforts to tax soft drinks in the District of Columbia, Texas, Kansas, Hawaii, Mississippi, Philadelphia, and elsewhere were defeated.

Despite massive lobbying, a two cents-per-bottle tax on soda, water, and beer miraculously passed in June 2010 in Baltimore, Maryland. The ABA spokesman wasn't too upset, observing that the tax would expire in three years, "so you couldn't call it a complete loss." Coke could console itself, however, that the Save the Children organization, which had pushed for a soft drink tax to prevent childhood obesity, reversed itself in October 2010. The non-profit said that the policy change had *nothing* to do with its discussions with Coca-Cola about a major grant. The following year, the Coca-Cola Foundation gave Save the Children $75,000 for safe-water programs.

HAPPINESS AMBASSADORS

As these controversies swirled in 2010, three young people were making a mad dash around the world as "Happiness Ambassadors" for Coca-Cola. The idea behind Expedition 206 was for the three Coke representatives to travel to all two hundred and six countries and territories in which Coke sold products. As part of the Open Happiness campaign, in each locale, armed with laptops, iPhones, Blackberries, and video cameras, they asked natives deeply meaningful questions such as "What makes you happy?" and "What do you like to do for fun?"

From the outset, Coke marketers sought online consumer involvement, with citizens of a hundred and fifty countries voting to pick the winners—Tony Martin, thirty, an American teaching kindergarten in Germany; Kelly Ferris, twenty-three, a university student from Brussels; and Antonio Santiago, twenty-four, a university student from Mexico City. Coke then took online suggestions about where to go and what to do. As they toured the world, the three Happiness Ambassadors posted on Expedition206.com and Coke's Facebook page, which now had over five million fans; sent brief Twitter updates; and uploaded YouTube videos.

While it was difficult to measure the program's impact on sales, it got plenty of attention, both on the ground and in cyberspace, racking up 6.5 million media mentions around the globe. In China, 1 billion online followers traded digital Expedition 206 stamps. The ever-smiling Coke ambassadors were building "brand love," as Coke marketers put it. By the time they arrived back at Atlanta's World of Coca-Cola on December 29, 2010, the three representatives were exhausted but apparently still friends. They had visited a mere 186 countries, bypassing security risks such as Somalia, Iraq, and Afghanistan, and missing others because of weather or logistics. Still, they had covered 275,000 miles. And what did they learn? Family, food, drink, and soccer (not necessarily in that order) were what made people happy.

"We did something we'd never done before," said Clyde Tuggle, Coke's chief PR man. "We basically turned over the public relations for our brand to the consumers." Ha. The trip was, of course, tightly choreographed and planned to garner as much positive publicity for Coca-Cola as possible. Yet Tuggle had a point. Coke was pioneering a new marketing approach. The Happiness Ambassadors were part of many Coke efforts to involve consumers interactively. For instance, in 2010 Sprite launched its first global marketing campaign, allowing online fans to remix and mash up songs and to create their own short animated movies.

The Sprite campaign was aimed at teenagers, who would make up a third of the world's population by 2020. "Our success in growing our sparkling category today depends on our ability to grow and connect with teens, the generation of tomorrow," Muhtar Kent emphasized. The following year, a global Coca-Cola Music teen campaign launched with "24hr Session," in which American pop band Maroon 5 holed up in a London studio and, with input from fans around the world, wrote a song downloadable for free from the Coke website, called "Is Anybody Out There?" Coca-Cola knew that plenty of adolescent listeners *were* out there. "You're exactly what I wanted," sang the band, "and exactly what I need." Coke wanted that sentiment to apply to its products.

For the first 100,000 downloads, Coke made a donation to its African safe-water initiative, linking its marketing to do-good efforts. Similarly, the Happiness Ambassadors had visited the 2010 Winter Olympics in Vancouver, calling attention to Coke's much-touted "zero waste" Olympic presence. All Coke products, sold in PlantBottles, were delivered by hybrid trucks and electric carts to HFC-free coolers. Compactors mashed empties on site for quick delivery to a recycling facility that turned them into clothing donated to a homeless shelter, and all Coke staff wore such recycled-bottle shirts.

The three Happiness Ambassadors showed up that summer in South Africa at the 2010 World Cup, where Coke mounted "the biggest integrated marketing campaign executed by any company in the world," according to Joe Tripodi, Coke's marketing chief. The effort grew out of a song by K'naan, a singer/songwriter born in 1978 in Somalia as Keinan Abdi Warsame. He fled the war-torn country for Canada at age thirteen and later wrote "Wavin' Flag," a bittersweet song about his hopes for his native land: "We struggling, fighting to eat, / And we wondering, when we'll be free. . . . When I get older, I will be stronger, / They'll call me Freedom, Just like a wavin' flag."

Coke's admen loved the song's jaunty beat and refrain, and the "oh-oh-oh-oh-oh" chorus suggested "Open Happiness." They paid K'naan to revise the lyrics to match the upbeat "Celebration" theme they had chosen for the World Cup: "In the streets our heads are liftin', / As we lose our inhibition. / Celebration, it surrounds us, / Every nation all around us. . . . When I get older, I will be stronger, / They'll call me Freedom, Just like a wavin' flag."

The song, which didn't mention Coca-Cola in the lyrics, became a sensation, with Coke producing versions incorporating seventeen different local languages, rock stars, and sexy dancers, though they all began with a Coke-emblazoned soccer ball and K'naan singing. Clearly identified with Coke, the song hit number one in Mexico, Austria, China, Germany, and Switzerland, and was among the top pop songs around the world. Before the competition, K'naan traveled with the solid gold World Cup trophy to eighty-four countries, singing for Coke.

With 26 billion viewers, the World Cup commanded a larger world audience than the Olympics and many times more than the Super Bowl. Soccer, as the Happiness Ambassadors had documented, made people happy, at least when their team won. Coke also recycled footage from the 1990 World Cup, in which Roger Milla of the Cameroons performed a spontaneous celebratory dance. The Company found the now-bald Milla and showed him drinking Coke in the stands in a commercial highlighting celebratory soccer dances. Powerade got its share of World Cup attention, too, with its first global marketing campaign.

"We're not doing this because we love soccer," Joe Tripodi admitted. "We're doing this because we think soccer is the best conduit" for what he called Coke's "visual identity system," combining energy, rhythm, celebration, and happiness—with Coke at the center. "We wanted to make sure we had some kind of sustainability angle," so Coke gave money to the player deemed to have the best goal celebration in each match for him to donate to an African school for a safe-water project. "We have a simple story, compelling and authentic," Tripodi said, "that we've scaled around the world." He called this approach "liquid and linked"—liquid because it could flow in so many directions, and linked because the celebration theme was common to all stories.

FIXING NORTH AMERICA

Although Coke was fizzing internationally, rejuvenating the North American market remained Muhtar Kent's biggest challenge. In 2009, carbonated soft drinks had declined for the fifth straight year in this market. In the first quarter of 2010, Coke's worldwide sales volume was up 3 percent, but it fell 2 percent in North America. "Growing here is not optional," said Kent. "It is essential to the health and future of our entire global system."

As part of the cure, Kent shocked analysts, revealing in late February 2010 that The Coca-Cola Company had negotiated an epochal $12.3 billion dollar deal to purchase

Coca-Cola Enterprises in North America. When Pepsi had bought out its two biggest bottlers the previous year, Kent had emphasized his commitment to the franchise bottling system, but now he seemed to be reversing himself. "We are still ardent believers in our franchise system," he insisted. "The Coca-Cola Company will work closely with its bottling partners to create an evolved franchise structure for the unique needs of the North American market." Perhaps he meant that Big Coke intended to fix the bottling system and spin it off to franchisees again in a few years. By eliminating duplication and streamlining delivery systems, Coke estimated that it would save $350 million over four years. When the deal was completed, CCE's 59,000 employees in North America began working for Big Coke in the newly named Coca-Cola Refreshments division. The merger went remarkably smoothly, with few job losses. The deal allowed CCE to retain its thriving European Coke bottlers, acquiring those in Norway and Sweden from Big Coke, with the right to buy German operations in the future.

With full control over most of its distribution in the United States, Coca-Cola focused on filling not only every nook, but also every appropriate cranny for its products. Sure, Coke and Sprite dominated the beverage aisle in the supermarket, but Dasani might be in the produce section, Vitaminwater on the organic food shelf, Diet Coke in a pharmacy cooler, and Fanta in dollar stores. To facilitate impulse buying, Coke wanted its drinks to be in the deli department or near pre-made dinners. Coke store reps had to fill out a Right Execution Daily (RED) form for scoring by a district manager.

The CCE merger allowed Coke to rush new North American drinks into the market, and Coke's Venturing and Emerging Brands (VEB) team hoped to supply them. Deryck van Rensburg, the South African native who headed the 15-member team, stressed that VEB was trying "to identify the next big thing" by importing other promising Coke products from overseas and by partnering with nimble entrepreneurs outside the Company. One might be the next billion-dollar-a-year brand, but most would remain niche players. With over 3,500 non-alcoholic beverages in the United States alone, and some 300 new brands introduced each year, the choices were mind-boggling. VEB was responsible for illy Issimo canned coffee and for the importation of Russian kvass; Vio, a carbonated skim milk; Cascal, a fermented French soda with cherry and currant flavors; Relentless, a British energy drink aimed at white-collar workers; and Sokenbicha, a Japanese blended no-calorie tea. VEB facilitated the partial purchase of Zico coconut water.

VEB's most successful venture thus far was Coke's stake in Honest Tea, which the Company later bought outright. Aside from helping with distribution, Coke took a hands-off approach to such purchases, retaining founder Seth Goldman as head of Honest Tea. A problem arose, however, over his label's prominent claim, "No High-Fructose Corn Syrup," the sweetener used in Coca-Cola. Big Coke objected to the implied criticism of its sweetener, since HFCS is virtually identical to cane sugar, chemically speaking. Goldman refused to change the label, and Coke backed down.

In his 2006 book, *The Omnivore's Dilemma*, Michael Pollan observed that "productive and protean" corn was processed into various additives to our food, but HFCS was the most valuable, with the average American consuming sixty-five pounds a year. "We subsidize high-fructose corn syrup in this country," he noted, "but not carrots." Though HFCS and sugar were equally culpable for the obesity epidemic, many consumers preferred "natural" sugar to processed corn sweetener. Both Coke and Pepsi were in pursuit of the "holy grail" of a natural low-calorie sweetener, but the best option, stevia, left a bitter aftertaste, so it was used only in select drinks, such as Powerade Play and Vitaminwater Zero.

Even without a more effective sweetener, the North American market finally turned the corner in the second quarter of 2010, posting 2 percent growth. "It's not an aberration," Kent insisted. "We've been working on this for two years. I was totally confident it would come." When the next quarter yielded similar results, the Coke CEO crowed, "People once again believe in our business in North America."

Even when he traveled, Kent always kept a sheet of paper with recent sales trends for Coca-Cola, Sprite, energy drinks, sports drinks, juices, coffees, teas, and other drinks. "For the first time in a long time, there's no red on that sheet," he said in February 2011. For the third quarter, North American sales were up. "Two years ago, when we talked of growth in the U.S., people thought I was trying to go to the moon in a glider," Kent gloated.

WINNING THE COLA WAR

In March 2011, when *Beverage Digest*, a soft drink trade journal, published its annual soda ranking, Diet Coke had surpassed Pepsi to become the number two soft drink in the United States. Even though the sales for Coca-Cola, the leader, had dipped by 0.5 percent in 2010, and Diet Coke by 1 point, sales of Pepsi had declined 4.8 percent. It was a humiliating result for the perennial runner-up. "Pepsi lost the cola war last week," *Advertising Age* announced.

As Coca-Cola prepared to celebrate the one hundred and twenty-fifth anniversary of the first serving of Pemberton's Coca-Cola at Jacobs Pharmacy on May 8, 1886, the resurgent Company once again appeared to be an unstoppable juggernaut. That week, when U.S. Navy Seals killed Osama bin Laden, they discovered that he drank Coca-Cola in his bunker.

To kick off the May 2011 anniversary, Coke sold commemorative bottles along with an ad campaign to celebrate "125 years of sharing happiness," 125 days of free prizes through MyCokeRewards.com, and a celebratory message during the 125th lap of the Coca-Cola 600 NASCAR race. Coke draped its twenty-six-story North Avenue tower in Atlanta in white sheets, then put on a light show, turning the building into a giant cup of ice being filled with Coca-Cola, followed by classic advertisements.

For the rest of 2011, the Company surged on. Polishing its halo, it created a $31 million Coca-Cola Japan Reconstruction Fund after the earthquake/tsunami. In partnership with the World Wildlife Fund, it committed $2 million to help protect polar bear habitat and vowed to match an addition $1 million in consumer donations.*

Two more Coke brands crested the annual billion-dollar-sales mark: Del Valle and Minute Maid Pulpy, the first such huge seller originating in China, an emerging market. Coke launched a global campaign to sell Fanta, already a $12 billion-a-year

---

* For the 2011 Christmas season, Coke distributed white Coke cans as part of the polar bear campaign, but it backfired over concerns that diabetics would mistake the cans for silver Diet Coke, and the Company hastily switched back to red cans.

brand, to teenagers, featuring cartoon multicultural characters and the slogan "More Fanta, Less Serious." The admen stressed that they were basically storytellers, and in this case, the story was playfulness.

During the year, over fifteen hundred futuristic Freestyle vending machines, now offering a hundred and twenty-five flavors, expanded into eighty U.S. markets, sending back daily data about consumer choice. A fifth of those surveyed said that they would switch restaurants or convenience stores to use the Freestyle.

The Coca-Cola Company was no longer merely a soft drink business. In December 2011, when Coke paid nearly $1 billion for half of Aujan Industries, a Saudi Arabian company that made Rani, a line of fruit drinks, such purchases had become almost routine. Around the world, the Company sold thirty-five hundred non-alcoholic beverages with five hundred brands, three times as many as ten years before.

The corporation was moving beyond the cola wars, but the Coke brand remained iconic, and the storyline for the flagship brand was happiness. "If you're able to own that emotion in people's mindspace, that's a very power thing," observed Joe Tripodi. In a brilliant move, at the end of 2011 the Company moved the Coca-Cola formula from the SunTrust bank, where it had resided since 1925, to a vault inside the World of Coca-Cola Museum. That would, as Muhtar Kent put it, "unlock some of that magic" associated with the formula, reinforcing its sacred status. By year's end, Coke's Facebook page had over thirty million fans, a number that would nearly double in the next twelve months.

Coke shareholders were certainly happy, with the stock hitting $70 by the end of 2011, and it neared $80 the following year, splitting 2 for 1. In 2011, the Company earned $46.5 billion in revenues, spending nearly $3 billion of that on advertising. Operating income—cash profit—jumped to $10.2 billion. Kent revealed that Coke planned to sink more than $30 billion into the global business over the next five years.

Coca-Cola had survived management disasters, morale problems, obesity concerns, human rights and environmental allegations, and more. In the midst of the worst economic decline since the Great Depression, Coke was thriving. "We intend to be around another 125 years and more," Muhtar Kent said. Then, without a trace of irony, he asserted, "Coca-Cola is the greatest idea in the world that brings people together."

~ 26 ~

World Without End?

You can run from it, but you can't hide. Sooner or later, no matter how far you think you've ventured from the comforts and conveniences of the modern world, Coke will find you. Go to the foothills of the Himalayas, the hurricane pounded fishing islands off the coast of Nicaragua—go to the birthplace of civilization, if you like. Coca-Cola will be waiting for you.
> —*New York Times* editorial, 1991

Traditionally called "Mecca" by devout employees, the North Avenue complex throbs with the worldwide Coca-Cola heartbeat. But the headquarters represent less than the tip of an ever-expanding iceberg. Nearly 150,000 people work directly for The Coca-Cola Company worldwide, but if you include those who work for Coke bottlers, that number jumps over 700,000. And that doesn't count the drink's twenty million retailers or the countless people who indirectly earn their livelihood from Coke by producing containers, trucks, water purifiers, pallets, computers, and the innumerable give-away promotional items. In 2012, for the thirteenth consecutive year, Coca-Cola claimed the number one spot on the Interbrand list of Best Global Brands.

A personal anecdote illustrates the astonishing range of the soft drink. On May 21, 1991, I was interviewing Doug Ivester—who would succeed Goizueta as CEO a few years later—when we were interrupted by the news that Rajiv Gandhi had been assassinated hours after casting a ballot for himself in the Indian elections. We adjourned to a TV monitor and watched CNN in sorrowful silence. As we walked back, another pragmatic Coke executive said, "Well, that's not too good for us." And it occurred to me that any major world event would have an impact on Coca-Cola but that none would really impede the drink's inexorable advance for long. Though Company men had been working closely with Gandhi, they soon enough struck a deal with the new government, and Coke, which had been forced to depart the country in 1977, re-entered India in 1993. It planned to sink another $3 billion into Coke's Indian operations by 2020.

Similarly, when the U.S. government established tentative diplomatic relations with the repressive regime in Myanmar (formerly Burma) late in 2012, Coca-Cola swiftly moved into the country to establish a market, leaving only two nations in the world—Cuba and North Korea—where Coke could be bought only on the black market.

At the outset of this book, I asserted that Coca-Cola both affected and was affected by its times. Clearly, Company officials have reacted to events more than they have caused them. The Company didn't plot the passage of the Pure Food and Drug Act, for instance, or the Depression or World War II—all moments in which Coca-Cola played an important part. Coke employees themselves have always insisted that the soft drink is just a "small pleasure," one that people could certainly live without if absolutely necessary. "No one thinks the world will shift on its axis if Coca-Cola ceased to exist," one executive told me. And yet. And yet. . . .

There is no question that this fizzy, syrupy beverage means much more than Coca-Cola executives would have us believe. Certainly, it means more to them—it is a way of life, an obsession. The lobby at the North Avenue headquarters used to feature a large medallion with an image of a Coke bottle superscribed on top of the globe, with visions of other galaxies yet to conquer spinning wildly above it. These guys really are missionaries. In their homes, many of them maintained what I privately term "Coca-Cola shrines"—autographed photos of Robert Woodruff, gold replicas of the hobbleskirt bottle, and other personal memorabilia.

Members of the international Coca-Cola Collectors Club are, if anything, more obsessed with their shrines. Germinating in a basement room or garage, their collections often literally pushed them out of their bedrooms and homes. "It's kind of like a drug addiction," one collector told me at a gathering that filled an entire Atlanta hotel. At the silent auction, where bids were placed on items and might be topped by someone else, the tension crackled. "It makes you sick, you're so worried," a Delaware woman moaned. Late into the night at these affairs, club members swapped and dickered, invading one another's rooms.

While these fanatical collectors may simply appear ludicrous, they are not the only ones to take Coca-Cola seriously. Social commentators, political activists, nutritionists, and anthropologists have all attacked Coca-Cola as if it were the distillation of Evil on earth. One angry observer called Coca-Cola's history "the most incredible mobilization of human energy for trivial purposes since the construction of the pyramids." It was, he said, "what went wrong with the American dream." Much of the criticism has focused on advertising, which, according to one distressed clinical psychologist, conveys the notion that "life will never be boring, that you will be sexually popular beyond your wildest dreams, and that you'll always be able to dance well if you drink colas."

Coke officials wouldn't argue with that statement. In fact, it seems rather restrained. Beginning with John Pemberton, Frank Robinson, and Asa Candler, its manufacturers have touted the soft drink/patent medicine as a magical potion, though the message has been modified over time, abandoning overt medicinal claims in favor of uplift, joy, and other image-intense attributes. Nonetheless, it still bears a startling resemblance to the fabled Elixir of Life sought by the alchemists. Indeed, an eighteenth-century reference book defined an "elixir" as a "dark-coloured medicine composed of many ingredients and dissolved in a strong solvent"—a pretty good description of the acidic, caramel-colored soft drink.

A NEW RELIGION

Throughout this book, I have treated Coca-Cola as a tongue-in-cheek religion of sorts, but the notion actually isn't so far-fetched. After all, the world's first coin-operated vending machine, invented in the first century C.E., dispensed holy water. The metaphor continually crept into the interviews I conducted. "Coca-Cola is the holy grail; it's magic," one Coke man told me. "Wherever I go, when people find out I work for Coke, it's like being a representative from the Vatican, like you've touched God. I'm always amazed. There's such a reverence towards the product." Shortly before his death, Roberto Goizueta even made it explicit: "Working for The Coca-Cola Company is a calling. It's not a way to make a living. It's a religion."

What else but a religious impulse could account for the idolatry with which corporate worshipers treat the outsized Coca-Cola bottles the Company produces, such as the thirty-foot tall bottle glowing at night atop the World of Coca-Cola museum? Or the forty-nine-foot bottle looming over Atlanta's Turner Field, with its LED lights producing 16.7 million different colors and fireworks spouting out the top after Braves' home runs? Or the six-story, thirty-ton version in New York's Times Square, with its million-dollar computer system to coordinate the displays, wasting enough power to run ten homes?

Or the insane statistics the Company dispenses to the press? "If all the Coke ever produced were in 8-ounce contour bottles, and these bottles were laid end-to-end, they would reach to the moon and back 2,136 times." Or, "If all the Coke ever produced were to erupt from Old Faithful at its normal rate of 7,525 gallons per hour, this geyser would flow for 7,498 years." Similarly, "if all the Coca-Cola ever produced were poured into a six-foot-deep swimming pool. . . ." But enough. Unless you, too, are a Believer, the idea of a breaststroke through forty-nine miles of dark, sweet, fizzy waters eight miles wide probably doesn't appeal.

Anthropologist Clifford Geertz defined religion as "a system of symbols which acts to establish powerful, pervasive, and long-lasting moods and motivations in men by formulating conceptions of a general order of existence and clothing these conceptions with such an aura of factuality that the moods and motivations seem uniquely realistic." That's quite a mouthful, but it's a fairly accurate description of the world according to Coca-Cola. The "pause that refreshes" surfaced just when organized religion was suffering from the writings of Charles Darwin, Albert Einstein, and other scientists. Coke has achieved the status of a substitute modern religion that promotes a particular, satisfying, all-inclusive worldview espousing perennial values such as love, peace, happiness, and universal brotherhood. It provides a panacea whenever daily life seems too difficult, harried, fragmented, or confused. As a sacred symbol, Coca-Cola induces varying "worshipful" moods, ranging from exaltation to pensive solitude, from near-orgasmic togetherness to playful games of chase.

Most religions have relied on a drug-laced drink of one sort or another. Christianity reveres its communion wine, which Coca-Cola has literally replaced at various times. The Greek gods drank nectar, while Dionysus sported as the lord of wine. Teutonic deities quaffed their mead. Arab Sufi monks drank coffee to keep themselves awake for midnight prayers. In India, the juice of the soma plant placated the gods. Throughout history, shamans have relied on coca, tobacco, caffeine, and other mind-altering drugs to induce trance and contact God. "The widespread use of drugs around the world," asserted a contributor to *Man, Myth & Magic*, "makes it plain that man is a discontented animal beset by psychological and physical troubles, by boredom and spiritual ambitions." As Robert Woodruff and Muhtar Kent observed, the world belongs to the discontented.

The most powerful Coca-Cola appeal has not, ultimately, been sexual or physiological, but communal: if you drink Coke, the ads suggest, you will belong to a warm, loving, accepting family, singing in perfect harmony. If we can't quite succeed in finding that stress-free society today, never mind—we'll find it tomorrow. We'll build a better world for you, and me, and everyone. Just Open Happiness. Two guards patrolling opposite sides of a tense border share a Coke and a brief smile in a 2011 ad that implicitly conveys, *If only everyone drank Coca-Cola, the world would live in peace and harmony*. It's a beautifully seductive message, because it's what we all want. A harsh critic of Coca-Cola once admitted that she found the "Hilltop" commercial "almost irresistible," even though it disturbed her.

For some moralists, this manipulation of basic human desires is evil. In *The Brothers Karamazov*, one of Roberto Goizueta's favorite books, the terrifyingly hypocritical Grand Inquisitor mocks all of us "pitiful creatures" who must find "something that all would believe in and worship; what is essential is that all may be *together* in it. This craving for *community* of worship is the chief misery of every man individually and of all humanity from the beginning of time." For the Grand Inquisitor, we are all pathetic, insecure souls desperately seeking any sort of meaning. We must, therefore, find mystery and miracle—a secret formula for living, a 7X of the soul.

In February 1992, ten Tibetan monks visited the World of Coca-Cola in Atlanta. Standing in front of an endless conveyor belt simulating a bottling operation, the maroon-robed monks smiled and nodded, chatting in their own tongue. A translator explained that they enjoyed finding "modern discoveries," and Coke was one of the great ones. The Buddhists seemed delighted with this temple to the great American soft drink—"this church of consumption," as one snide commentator put it. Perhaps instinctively, they saw the museum as a religious manifestation, a necessary ordering of the universe. According to Buddha, all such order is illusory, part of the world of *maya*, but that rendered phenomena like Coke no less important. "Like all great love affairs," Ike Herbert told a group of fountain salesmen shortly before he retired, "ours depends to a large extent on creating a set of illusions, feelings that we are special. We are who we are because we are all things to all people all the time everywhere." Paul Foley, the longtime head of McCann-Erickson's umbrella agency, summarized it best. "We're selling smoke," he always reminded his creative staff. "They're drinking the image, not the product."

SHADES OF HARVEY WILEY

No wonder my mother wouldn't let me drink Coca-Cola, the opiate of the people. She thought it was bad for me: it would rot my teeth, keep me awake, and spread chemicals throughout my body. There was something mysterious and enticing about the dark, bubbly liquid, though. In high school, when I read the witches' incantation in *Macbeth*, I naturally assumed that they were brewing Coca-Cola in their caldron. Like generations before me, I longed for the forbidden drink. Sometimes, after we finished playing football, Billy Krenson and I would go to his house, where his mother served up Coke with cracked ice. Nothing has ever tasted so sinfully good. As another surreptitious Coke drinker described it, "the effervescence was boldly astringent and as clean as a knife; the flavor suggested the corrupt spices of Araby and a hint, perhaps, of brimstone."

Ever since Harvey Wiley, reformers have identified Coca-Cola as the temptation of the devil, particularly for innocent children. Today, Michael Jacobson, founder and executive director of the Center for Science in the Public Interest, leads the crusade, lamenting that a twelve-ounce Coke can contains the equivalent of ten teaspoons of sugar, supplying "empty" calories—while the twenty-ounce bottle delivers sixteen teaspoons and the 7-Eleven Super Big Gulp doubles that amount. In his 2005 publication, *Liquid Candy*, Jacobson observed that sugar-sweetened beverages provided 9 percent of the calories in the American diet, and 13 percent for teenagers. "In 1977–78," he wrote, "boys consumed more than twice as much milk as soft drinks." Twenty years later, those figures were reversed. Jacobson was particularly concerned about girls, who also consume twice as much soda as milk and who build 92 percent of their bone mass by age eighteen. Though American soft drink per capita consumption peaked in 1998, Americans still drank an average of 714 eight-ounce servings of soft drinks per year in 2011—that's about two drinks per day for every man, woman, and child in the United States.

For former CEO Doug Ivester, that was cause for jubilation rather than concern. "Actually," he observed, "our product is quite healthy. Fluid replenishment is a key to health. . . . Coca-Cola does a great service because it encourages people to take in more and more liquids." At the 2012 annual shareholders meeting, I heard Muhtar Kent proudly observe, "People reach for our beverages 1.8 billion times every day. . . . Every one of our drinks is good, offering a choice of great non-alcoholic beverages for hydration and moments of happiness." Indeed, a fifth of American toddlers drink an average of seven ounces of soft drinks a day.

So what? Why all the concern? Because by relying primarily on the instant energy of glucose, people forego vitamins, minerals, fiber, and other necessary nutrients. While it is possible to get those vital nutrients elsewhere, Jacobson argues that the more Coke you drink, the less room you find for healthy food in a typical 2,500-calorie daily "budget." It is more likely that Coca-Cola fiends, particularly those who use it to wash down junk foods, will ingest too many calories—one of the reasons that by 2012 two-thirds of Americans were overweight, and half of those were obese.

That's why New York City Mayor Michael Bloomberg, unable to get a soda tax passed, got the NYC health board to ban the sale of sugar-sweetened beverages in cups larger than sixteen ounces at the city's restaurants, food carts, fast-food outlets, movie theaters, and sports arenas, which went into effect in March 2013. But it didn't stop the Big Gulps sold in 7-Elevens or oversized soft drinks in grocery stores. Even though the health edict was mild and relatively ineffective—anyone could buy a second sixteen-ouncer—the soft drink industry protested loudly that this was tyranny and a threat to freedom of choice.

The obesity epidemic is real and growing. Since the last edition of my Coca-Cola history, I wrote *Inside the Outbreaks*, a history of the Epidemic Intelligence Service (EIS), the disease detectives of the CDC, another Atlanta institution. Much of that book focused on infectious diseases, but near the end I observed that heart disease and stroke—both associated with obesity, along with diabetes—accounted for a third of all deaths around the world. "Humanity's worst problems are self-inflicted," I wrote.

The year 2012 saw an avalanche of media about the causes and impacts of obesity. Richard Jackson, a public health physician and EIS alum, starred in a documentary, *Designing Healthy Communities*, and published a book with the same title in which he noted, "If we do nothing, about a third of our children will become diabetic [due to obesity], with a reduction in their average life span of fifteen years. . . . We are on a trajectory of declining life expectancy for the first time in our country's history."

Jackson's focus was on the built environment, which often promotes automobile travel, discourages exercise, and provides inadequate access to healthy foods, but *The Weight of the Nation*, a documentary that aired on HBO, specifically attacked soft drinks. Among other commentators, it featured Robert Lustig, a pediatrician at the University of California, San Francisco, who urged adoption of a punitive sugar tax in "The Toxic Truth About Sugar," an article published that same year in the prestigious journal *Nature*. Lustig said the same thing on the TV show *60 Minutes*.

"The single best thing to do for weight loss," *The Weight of the Nation* stated, was to "stop drinking sugar-sweetened beverages." In the HBO film, Kelly Brownell, the director of the Rudd Center for Food Policy at Yale University, asserted, "There is nothing in a soft drink that is good for you. . . . The body doesn't seem to recognize calories very well when they get delivered in liquid. In the war on obesity, they're not the only problem, but they're a darn good place to start."

Brownell might have been more convincing if he weren't himself obese, and he presumably did not drink Coca-Cola. Muhtar Kent looked a lot more fit. "It is, I believe, incorrect and unjust to put the blame on any single ingredient, any single product, any single category of food," Kent complained. "Obesity is a serious and complex global health concern," he acknowledged. "It's costly in monetary and human terms. And it has the power to undermine the well-being of individuals, families and communities." But he defended the Company, pointing out that a quarter of its 3,500 beverages were low or no calorie, and that people could choose *them*. "We offer 23 variations of Coke," he said, "a Coke for every person, every lifestyle and every occasion. Coke, Diet Coke, Coke Zero, caffeine-free versions and flavors like Cherry Coke." Early in 2013, the Company made similar points in "Coming Together," a two-minute video asserting that its beverages and programs were part of the solution to obesity, not the problem.

Nonetheless, Kent was not invited to the June 2012 National Soda Summit, an anti–soft drink conference sponsored by the Center for Science in the Public Interest, where former Coke marketer Todd Putnam was the keynote speaker. "It took me 10 years to figure out that I have a large karmic debt to pay for the number of Cokes I sold across this country," he confessed. When he worked for Coke, he recalled that it was "exciting, intoxicating, even. I felt like the king of the world." His sole thought? *"How can we drive more ounces into more bodies more often?"*

A few months later, renegade ad man Alex Bogusky, who had once created spots for Coke Zero, made a devastating four-minute animation for the Center for Science in the Public Interest. Called "The Real Bears," it shows a family of polar bears drinking Coca-Cola to a lilting Beatles-like tune: "Sugar, sugar, I wanna make you happy. . . . Sugar, sugar, so good, so good." Signage on a polar vending machine requests, "Be happy please." The bears get fat, lose their teeth, develop diabetes, can't enjoy sex because of erectile dysfunction, and Dad has his leg amputated with a chain saw because of advanced diabetes. Near the end, they watch a TV commercial that demands "Be happy, dammit!" Then, led by Dad in his wheelchair, they pour their Cokes into the sea.

Aside from sugar, the other major villain in Coke, according to Michael Jacobson, is caffeine, even though a twelve-ounce can contains only a third the stimulant in a strong cup of coffee. Like Harvey Wiley, Jacobson objected to children ingesting *any* caffeine. Scientists tell us that caffeine promotes stomach-acid secretion, temporarily raises blood pressure, and dilates some blood vessels while constricting others. Caffeine is mildly addictive, and when used excessively it can lead to "caffeinism" and its attendant shaky nerves and insomnia. In 1980 and 1981, caffeine was blamed for everything from pancreatic cancer to miscarriages and birth defects, but none of these findings stood the test of time. Indeed, more recent studies indicate that long-term caffeine consumption can reduce the risk of Parkinson's disease, liver ailments, colon cancer, heart troubles, and suicides. And it seems to lower the risk of type 2 diabetes, perhaps providing a counterbalance to the excess sugar that helps cause the disease.

In general, unless a woman drank ten or more cans of Coke a day, Jacobson didn't think there was any danger from the drug, though pregnant women should cut down or eliminate caffeine intake, since the drug is transmitted to the fetus, as it is to the infant through the breast milk of a nursing mother. Surprisingly, caffeine has not been proven to harm children. Jacobson was concerned, however, about withdrawal symptoms. In some studies, children deprived of caffeine displayed impaired performance and attention.

Besides caffeine and sugar, critics have traditionally complained about the phosphoric acid that gives Coca-Cola much of its fabled bite. Science teachers have dropped extracted teeth into Coke to show how it softens and blackens them, and the soft drink does indeed clean windshields, chrome, and battery terminals quite nicely. Nonetheless, Coke's acidity—equivalent to that of orange juice—does not harm the digestive tract, already an acidic environment. As a matter of fact, some doctors still prescribe flat Coke to soothe upset stomachs. Some studies appear to link soft drinks containing phosphoric acid (but not citric acid) with kidney stones, however.

If the acid does not remain long in the mouth, saliva tends to neutralize it. But for those who down multiple daily Cokes, the front teeth bear the brunt of the acid, which can etch the enamel, and it's even worse for those who savor the drink by swishing it around and pulling it through their teeth. Then bacteria feed on the sugar, creating yet more acid and plaque that causes cavities. In other words, soft drinks can provide a one-two dental punch. They can erode teeth and promote the formation of cavities. Studies on rats have shown that the acidic, sweetened drinks are substantially worse for their teeth than plain sugar water. Consequently, drinking Coke through a straw, taking the beverage deep into the mouth, limits contact with the teeth and is therefore best for dental hygiene.

Other health concerns have also plagued Coca-Cola. Although high-fructose corn syrup and cane sugar offer similar mixtures of fructose and glucose, many people distrust HFCS because it is chemically altered from corn, and the jury is out as to whether corn syrup behaves metabolically exactly the same way as cane sugar does. Both can cause obesity. Until recently, some manufacturers used a mercury-based product to separate corn starch from the kernel. A 2008 study conducted by the

Institute of Agriculture and Trade Policy found a tiny amount of mercury in Coca-Cola Classic, but the HFCS industry claims to have fixed the problem as of 2012. Neither IATP nor the FDA had retested for mercury in Coke, however.

Bisphenol-A (BPA), a chemical widely used to guard against contaminants and extend shelf life, also came under fire as a liner in Coke cans, with several shareholder resolutions (all defeated) concerning its safety. In 2010, the FDA expressed "some concern about the potential effects of BPA on the brain, behavior, and prostate gland in fetuses, infants, and young children" and suggested "taking reasonable steps to reduce human exposure to BPA in the food supply." On its website the Company insisted there was no problem: "The clear scientific consensus is that there is no risk to the public from the minuscule amounts of BPA found in Coca-Cola or other beverage cans."

Coke's caramel coloring posed yet another health concern after mice fed 4-Methylimidazole (4-MEI) developed lung cancer in studies conducted by scientists at the National Toxicology Program of the U.S. National Institutes of Health. The chemical process used to produce the caramel in Coca-Cola also yields 4-MEI as a by-product. Michael Jacobson's Center for Science in the Public Interest called for a ban on the coloring, and in 2012 California would have forced Coca-Cola to put a cancer warning on its bottles if the Company had not quickly reduced the MEI level in its California Coke by using naturally produced caramel. "We intend to expand the use of modified caramel globally," said a Company spokesman.

Ever since Pemberton invented Coca-Cola, people have attacked it because of its purportedly bad health effects. Company officials have usually just dismissed such critics. Don't you think maybe, they inquire, after 125-plus years of massive Coca-Cola consumption, we'd notice toothless, neurotic, cancerous, obese heavy users falling over dead on every street corner? Roberto Goizueta used to joke about the "immutable law of the cynical elite," which holds that "nothing so available, so inexpensive, so much enjoyed by so many . . . can be good for you." As for those who lump Coke with junk food and blame it for the poor nutrition and the obesity epidemic, as well as people abandoning their traditional diet, the Coca-Cola executives reply that they advocate drinking the beverage only as part of a balanced diet. It isn't their fault if people don't eat well and don't exercise. And besides, a quarter of Coke's beverages contain low or no calories, and the Company is working on more nutrient-rich drinks. "The consumer decides," said Muhtar Kent. "We provide them with the right choices and the right marketing for these choices."*

If anecdotal cases proved anything (which they don't), Coca-Cola might be the life extender Pemberton claimed. Look at Robert Woodruff, who died at ninety-five and presumably drank his fair share of Coke. On her ninety-seventh birthday in 1959, an Alabama woman attributed her longevity to drinking a Coke at precisely 10 a.m. every day since 1886. But she was nothing compared with legendary figure Luke Kingsley, a Memphis car salesman who told a reporter in 1954 that he had routinely drunk over twenty-five Cokes a day for the previous fifty years. "I have been to the funerals of five

---

* In 1959, one Coke director told E. J. Kahn Jr., "I sometimes shudder at the thought of all those poor people paying a nickel for a Coke when they probably ought to be spending it on a loaf of bread." If any Company men harbor those reservations today, none of them have shared them with me.

or six doctors who predicted it would kill me," the sixty-five-year-old chortled. At the end of the interview, the parched journalist asked for a drink of water. "Water!" barked Kingsley. "That's something you wash your face in. Have a Coke!"

GLOBAL COCA-COLA CULTURE

Even if Coke can't necessarily be held accountable for all the ills of modern life, most intellectuals express revulsion at its ongoing worldwide conquest. To many commentators, Coca-Cola typifies the worst of Western culture. "Coke is the American's fuel, just as television is his soul," a German sneered in the late 1970s. Twenty years earlier, Adlai Stevenson asked, "With the supermarket as our temple, and the singing commercial as our litany, are we likely to fill the world with an irresistible vision of America's purpose and inspiring way of life?" The current answer appears to be a resounding "YES!" Coca-Cola has indeed taught the world to sing to its harmonics, or it is doing so as quickly as possible.

There are hundreds of films in which Coca-Cola makes a cameo appearance (paid or unpaid), from *King Kong* (1933) to *Casino Royale* (2006) and beyond, making it the most widely placed product in the history of movies. Some filmmakers have used Coke as a convenient symbol of Western civilization—witness *Dr. Strangelove* and *On the Beach*, both films in which a Coke bottle serves as a wry commentary on our shallow values in the midst of Armageddon. At the beginning of *The Gods Must Be Crazy*, the totemic bottle falls out of the sky onto the sands of the Kalahari Desert, where it completely transforms the lives of the innocent Bushmen as surely as Eve's apple in Eden. In *The Coca-Cola Kid*, a similar invasion takes place in Australia. In all of these films, the soft drink is presented as a sinister force, a harbinger of unhealthy values.*

Whether Coke deserves such criticism or not, no one doubts that it is invasive. Many years ago, a Coca-Cola executive told his followers, "You have entered the lives of more people . . . than any other product or ideology, including the Christian religion," and that truth has only grown more profound with the passage of time. Despite the rise of Google, Apple, and other global brands, Coca-Cola may remain the world's most widely distributed single consumer product. Today, at North Avenue, Muhtar Kent and other senior Coke managers can punch their computers and call up the history of per capita consumption growth for any country as easily as *Star Trek*'s commander could summon details of obscure planets.

It is certainly unnerving when Coke marketers talk about the battle for the "share of stomach" or the drink's executives discuss its "mind shelf space," which keeps swelling, crowding out other perhaps more worthy uses of our brain cells. And Coke wants to be in your heart as well, wooing "brand love." Former Communists and Myanmar peasants aren't alone in coveting Coke and other symbols of Western culture. Satellite, cable, cell phones, the Internet, and Facebook are bringing the Real Thing into homes

---

* Without making such overt political statements, artists such as Andy Warhol, Salvador Dalí, and Robert Rauschenberg painted Coca-Cola bottles as evocations of materialistic capitalism, while academic folklorists created a subspecialty of "Cokelore." Cormac McCarthy added to their fodder by featuring Coca-Cola prominently in his postapocalyptic novel, *The Road*.

and lives all over the world. It is Always Coca-Cola in all ways, with a universal appeal to Open Happiness. As Roberto Goizueta once put it, "People around the world are today connected to each other by brand-name consumer products as much as by anything else." That's why Coca-Cola executives must be world citizens. "We increasingly at Coca-Cola look for people who are comfortable living in Mumbai or in Germany or in Nairobi," Muhtar Kent observed.

"From infancy to adulthood," historian Barbara Tuchman wrote in 1980, "advertising is the air Americans breathe, the information we absorb, almost without knowing it. It floods our minds with pictures of perfection and goals of happiness easy to attain." Now, decades later, advertising permeates the air that *everyone* breathes, as well as everything seen on the web. The message that they can Open Happiness by drinking Coke has led Mexicans, for instance, to spend their money—often a substantial part of their daily wages—on Company products, with the world's leading annual per capita consumption of 728 beverages in 2011. Perhaps not coincidentally, Mexico also had the world's highest obesity rate.

Whether harmful or not, the messages bounced from satellites or carried through cable certainly connect. In 1990, one researcher attempting to define the "global teenager" by surveying a representative sampling of young people from Argentina, Brazil, China, Egypt, Britain, Guatemala, India, Israel, Kenya, the Soviet Union, and Thailand discovered that, while only 40 percent could correctly identify the United Nations logo, 82 percent knew Coke's symbol. Today, that figure is probably near 100 percent as Coca-Cola marketers, through campaigns such as "Move to the Beat" for the 2012 London Olympics, exploit what they called "a fusion of two global teen passions—sport and music."

Such trends have alarmed many observers, who fear that the variety and spice of human culture will be destroyed by the Coca-Colonization of the world. In his 1996 book, *Jihad vs. McWorld*, political science professor Benjamin Barber argued that Coke insidiously infiltrates and distorts cultures. During the Vietnam War, U.S. propaganda spoke of winning the hearts and souls of men. "The Cola Wars are *only* about the hearts and souls of men," Barber said. "By persuading people they must have the products you sell, you win a war much more permanently . . . than if you simply occupy a town."

Although Coke unquestionably exerts an influence on cultures and does change drinking habits, local habits (and ethnic groups) are far stronger than many critics recognize. They are horrified, for instance, that in regions such as Chiapas in Mexico, Coke and Pepsi are used in Mayan religious services in lieu of *poch*, the traditional alcoholic drink. The scene certainly is startling, as Indians in traditional Mayan dress pour Coca-Cola as a ritual offering. But the fact remains, they still are in traditional dress, and there still are rituals.

In a chapter entitled, "The Future of Humanity," an anthropology textbook portrayed a black-robed, gray-bearded patriarch reading the paper below a Hebraic Coca-Cola sign. "The worldwide spread of such products as Coca-Cola and Wrangler jeans," the caption read, "is taken by some as a sign that a single, homogeneous world culture is developing." Others refuse to panic, however. Already an accepted part of the landscape and lifestyle in an enormous array of cultures, Coca-Cola doesn't appear to be destroying them. In the picture in the anthropology book, the Jewish patriarch is still wearing his black robes and reading his paper, not boogying in his blue jeans.

In other words, we might regard the current cross-pollination of cultures as a kind of evolution rather than a homogenization. The world may be flat, as author Thomas Friedman argued, but bumps and variations remain, and in some ways, as even Friedman has admitted, the Internet has led to greater individualism and protest. "The differences among races, nations, cultures and their various histories are at least as profound and as durable as the similarities," observed the late Australian essayist Robert Hughes, who predicted that the future belongs to "people who can think and act with informed grace across ethnic, cultural, linguistic lines"—a perfect description of today's top Coca-Cola managers.

The Coca-Cola Company's evolution exemplifies the subtleties of globalization. The Coca-Cola brand remains the "oxygen" of the Company, as Muhtar Kent has said, but soda sales are declining. It isn't yet clear whether we are witnessing a long-term shift away from carbonated soft drinks or a modest decline that will bottom out.* It's too early to tell, but Coke now sells over 3,500 different drinks, carbonated or not, around the world. Many are local beverages that Coke bought out, while others were invented to appeal to a particular taste. In its determination to own world hydration, the Company has been forced to diversify, adapt, and experiment, even though it would undoubtedly prefer everyone to buy Coke. But combined sales of Diet Coke and Coca-Cola Zero are creeping up on regular Coca-Cola, and some day they might pass the much-maligned sugar-sweetened drink. At least they are all called by the sacred name.

What Coca-Cola does—with remarkable success—is identify the commonalities of human experience without necessarily altering cultures fundamentally. "You'll find plenty of social scientists who'll point up the differences," Don Keough once told me, "but wherever I go, boys and girls meet, walk in parks, fall in love, get married, have children, have family gatherings. They celebrate the joys of life just the way you and I do." Consequently, Coca-Cola is able to make its global advertising appeal to virtually all human beings.

Writing about Coke's global availability, one American essayist commented, "Somehow that is very, very comforting. It means we can go into much of the world and find our security blanket waiting." While that may sound like the statement of an Ugly American, other travelers who leave their native lands routinely experience the same feeling. For the German, Greek, Japanese, Argentine, or Nigerian, the sight of a familiar Coca-Cola sign is often reassuring. Coca-Cola is unlikely, however, to homogenize world culture completely, with religious sects, nationalistic fervor, and ethnic group loyalists more powerful than ever.

Roberto Goizueta was correct when he told a group of bright-eyed high school seniors, "Corporations are not as pious as I might be tempted to tell you they are. Nor are they evil as some portray them to be. The truth is somewhere in the middle."

---

* At the same time, Coke faced a small but growing challenge from SodaStream, an Israeli company selling machines that produce cheaper homemade soft drinks. It took its stock public in 2010 and mocked Coke in controversial ads and a "Cage" campaign claiming that an average family uses over 10,000 soda containers in five years that can be replaced by one SodaStream bottle.

COCA-COLA POLITICS

Just as missionaries believe that any human soul is ripe for the True Gospel, Coca-Cola marketers rarely distinguish among nations. "We believe in the future of [all] countries," Don Keough once wrote. "We'll ride through whatever political or economic conditions exist." Consequently, Coke never pulled out of Chile when Pinochet was in power. Indeed, the Company appreciated the booming, stable economy under the South American dictator. Nor did the Company leave Indonesia because of atrocities committed by the Suharto regime. "We *do* have a social conscience," one Coke manager told me, "but we don't enter politics. We've never lost an election, because we never run. Our job is simply to provide a moment of pleasure to consumers around the world without concern for the form or type of government under which they live." He paused and smiled broadly. "We make life a little brighter. We serve humanity." Asa Candler would have applauded.

It seems disingenuous, however, to assert that Coca-Cola does not enter politics. At least since World War II, the soft drink, as highly charged with symbolism as with CO_2, has *been* politics. If, instead of courting the Chinese, Roberto Goizueta had tried to persuade his friend George H. W. Bush to withdraw China's most favored nation status, perhaps that country's leaders would have reconsidered Tiananmen Square or the prolonged Chinese rape of Tibet. After all, those sweet-faced Tibetan monks who visited the World of Coca-Cola Museum cried when asked about their country's plight, and with good reason.

Yet Coke still made the most of the 2008 Beijing Olympics, despite activists' protests, and the annual Chinese per capita consumption of Company products rose to 38 in 2011. Muhtar Kent looked forward to the day China would become Coke's top market. "It's like a well-managed company, China," Kent observed admiringly. "You have a one-stop shop in terms of the Chinese foreign investment agency. . . . In China and other markets around the world, you see the kind of attention to detail about how business works and how business creates employment."

Coca-Cola executives argue that the only way to ensure Coke's influence for good is to maintain their products' ubiquitous presence. Besides, if Coke pulled out, Pepsi would simply move in unimpeded, a thought much worse than any human rights violations. Perhaps the influx of Coca-Cola and Big Macs creates goodwill towards the West and can soften China's dictatorial, repressive policies more effectively than can sanctions.

Coca-Cola's official South African divestiture in 1986 represented an exception to the policy of ignoring political considerations, but public opinion obviously dictated that decision. South Africa is one place where Coke officials clearly did serve humanity. Coca-Cola executives practiced a kind of corporate shuttle diplomacy, meeting with Nelson Mandela and other black leaders to assure them of the Company's support in the struggle against apartheid and to ensure Coke a presence in the new order. In a bloodbath, Coke sales would have gone down. Coca-Cola remained a steadfast friend of Mandela throughout his South African presidency and moved its concentrate plant back into the country.

And therein lies the true beauty of capitalism. The Coca-Cola religion has no real morality, no commandment other than increased consumption of its drinks.

Consequently, over its history it has been perfectly willing to coexist with Hitler, bejeweled Maharajas, impoverished migrant workers, malnourished Africans, Guatemalan death squads, clear-cut Belizean rainforests, or repressive Chinese. Unlike most world governments, however, The Coca-Cola Company eventually acts out of enlightened self-interest. Because it values its squeaky-clean image above all else, it generally reacts more quickly to bad publicity than any potentate.

And bad publicity will undoubtedly keep coming. I met Ray Rogers of the Killer Coke campaign at the April 2012 annual Coca-Cola shareholders meeting in an Atlanta suburb, where he and his cohorts repeatedly interrupted Muhtar Kent with a rehearsed call-and-response of "Point of order—You lie!" Kent fielded hostile questions about discarded beverage bottles, worker intimidation in Mexico, chemical caramel, high-fructose corn syrup, and water depletion in India. The newest flap involved alleged racial discrimination against black and Latino workers at two Coca-Cola plants in New York, involving purportedly unfavorable work assignments, unfair discipline and retaliation, and a work environment where racial slurs went unchallenged by management. In an obviously staged response, Kent called on four supportive black employees from the New York plants to stand up at the meeting, and he suggested that Ray Rogers meet with them afterwards, but they subsequently refused to talk to him.

Consequently, it is arguably up to us, the public, to monitor Coke's corporate behavior. Faced with boycotts of sufficient size, loud enough protests, documentaries of appropriate proportion, or shareholder resolutions representing large enough chunks of stock, the Company will act. Sometimes, it will even act pre-emptively to avoid such trouble. For its own selfish ends, then, Coca-Cola does indeed try to promote the peace and harmony it promises in its commercials.

And the Company's pursuit of the halo effect through do-good activities really *does* good. Neville Isdell coined the phrase "Connected Capitalism" to describe "a true marriage between government, nonprofits, and global corporations to fight disease and poverty, heal the planet, improve education, and, ultimately, boost private-sector profits." Muhtar Kent called it the "Golden Triangle of business, government and civil society." Through partnerships with organizations such as the Gates Foundation and the World Wildlife Fund, Coke helped to supply safe water, vaccines, and insecticide-treated bed nets to the poor; to ameliorate climate change; to protect endangered species; and more. The Company promoted physical activity, recycling, education, and water stewardship. In 2011, primarily through its Coca-Cola Foundation, the Company donated $123.5 million to charitable causes, amounting to 1.2 percent of operating income.

At the annual meeting, Kent repeated one of his favorite anecdotes about Preeti Gupta, who started a small store that thrived in her living room in rural India. Coca-Cola gave her a solar-powered cooler so that she could sell chilled Cokes and charge a lantern so her children could see to study at night. And Coke made a few more sales. The Company touts its 5by20 program, aiming to empower five million women to become successful entrepreneurs—selling Coke products, collecting recyclables, growing mangos—by 2020. Through Kiva.org (which has no connection to Coca-Cola), I have helped fund microcredit loans to needy businesses in the developing world, and I noticed that several businesses run by women in the devastated Democratic Republic of the Congo were requesting money to buy and sell Fanta.

In 2006, when I was researching *Inside the Outbreaks*, I visited rural schools in western Kenya where the drinking water came from polluted streams and ponds that sickened and sometimes killed the children. The simple, innovative Safe Water System got the schools to add diluted bleach to the water, dispensed from special narrow-mouthed jars with spigots, and taught the children to wash their hands. There, in the middle of nowhere, Coca-Cola logos were painted on the washing stations outside the latrines. Coke was helping to pay for the program.

In the perfect world of a Coke executive's dreams, the biggest conflicts will be similar to the fight between Miss World and Miss Universe of 1995—the latter signed up to advertise Coke, while her rival shilled for Pepsi. Or consider that when Barack Obama accepted the 2008 Democratic presidential nomination at Denver's Pepsi Center, Coca-Cola Recycling was there to grab the empties, while Coke products were served at Sports Authority Field at Mile High, where Obama gave his acceptance speech. In this perfect world, global politics will be run, not by small-minded, war-prone, ethnocentric nation-states, but by benign multinationals that want only for you to swallow their beverages. Their local bottlers—Serbs, Albanians, Hutus, Tutsis, Indians, Pakistanis, Chinese, Tibetans, Germans, French, Russians, Americans, Arabs, Jews—will discourage strife in order to boost per capita consumption. All you need to restore tranquility is a good burp.

Unfortunately for Coca-Cola (and perhaps for the rest of us), the world doesn't work that way all the time. In the post–Cold War euphoria of the mid-1990s, it appeared that a global economy based on unrestrained international free enterprise might lead automatically to greater good for all. But a global economic downturn shook confidence in the late 1990s, terrorists flew planes into the World Trade Center towers in 2001, and the world fell headlong into a prolonged recession in 2008. Wars, violence, and upheaval continue.

With such harsh realities in mind, it is difficult to take critics too seriously when they rant against Coca-Cola as the monstrous corporation that is ruining the world. Given the choice between a fizzy soft drink and a suicide bomber, I'll grab the Coke any day.

BORN AGAIN

When I started researching this book over two decades ago, I was surprised to find that officials of an American soft drink company had such ready access to powerful world figures. Now, nothing would startle me. After all, Coca-Cola's annual sales surpass the entire economies of many countries in which the drink is bottled and sold. As the colorful Harrison Jones once put it, "The Coca-Cola Company is like an elephant's ass. You throw a rock in any direction and you're likely to hit it." Or as another more recent commentator has written, "Coca-Cola is more durable, less vulnerable, more self-correcting than the Roman Empire. This product is destined to outlast the USA." And aside from controversies over nutrition, obesity, culture, advertising, politics, water depletion, labor issues, and death squads, The Coca-Cola Company has been a force for good in the world.

Even though Coke's motivations stem primarily from concerns over its image, the firm and its bottlers always supply fresh, clean water (or soft drinks) when natural disasters—earthquake, flood, fire, famine—strike. When Hurricane Georges struck Puerto Rico in 1998, for instance, Coke was there to help homeless victims. "They particularly enjoyed and appreciated the Coca-Cola, Sprite and water we gave them," wrote a Coke employee. "It was a great feeling to help, even in a small way." Similarly, when a terrible tsunami devastated Japan in 2011, Muhtar Kent flew there days later to announce a $30 million reconstruction fund.

Unfortunately, Coke lobbies strenuously against bottle-bill legislation and set up a Civic Action Network, a "non-partisan grassroots" organization, to protest such bills, along with soda taxes. A comparison of the litter along Georgia roadsides to states with a redeemable nickel deposit such as Vermont, where I live, certainly indicates that container bills work. But Coke can legitimately point out that it actively promotes recycling of its products. People end up wearing many of the recycled bottles as clothing or felt-like winter hats.

The Company supports innovative educational programs in the United States and elsewhere, and no one could calculate the amount of philanthropic largesse directly or indirectly attributable to Coca-Cola. Aside from the Company's foundation, gigantic funds devoted to the public good contain Woodruff, Whitehead, Lupton, Thomas, Bradley, and Goizueta money, not to mention innumerable local charities of American and foreign bottlers. Robert Woodruff correctly observed that everyone who touched the magical drink would make money, and, fortunately, a great deal of it has been spent wisely, particularly in the city of Atlanta.

Even in normal times, Coca-Cola has certainly proved a boon to local economies around the world, regardless of what one may think of its impact on local culture and dietary habits. University of South Carolina researchers studied what happened as Coke entered Poland and Romania during the 1991–1994 period. They concluded that for every job in the Coca-Cola bottling system, ten jobs were created in the retail sector. In essence, Coke helped to create an entrepreneurial class where there had been none. This "multiplier effect" has been documented in other countries as well, including a 2012 study in Italy estimating a thirteen-to-one indirect job impact.

One of my best friends from high school days has now retired from The Coca-Cola Company. Call him David. He looks and seems the same as ever, aside from creeping gray, and we've kept in touch over the years. David once showed me family pictures taken during a beach vacation. Smiling into the camera, he wore a Coca-Cola T-shirt. "God," I laughed, "you can't even get away from it on vacation, can you?" He laughed, too, then said simply, "I don't want to." I realized at that moment that a subtle transformation had taken place within my friend. Some would call it a transfusion in which his blood flowed a caramel shade. He had been born again, and though he never tried to convert me, I knew he practiced a religion that I continue to find somewhat amusing, somewhat alarming, and ultimately mystifying. He had become a Coca-Cola man.

Yet I must add a cautionary note. When he learned I was working on a new edition, another former Coke man lamented, "I'm not sure whether the title of your book still makes sense, as it absolutely did 20 years ago. For many reasons, I don't think there are nearly as many 'Coca-Cola men' or women as there were two decades ago."

I fear that he is correct. Working for The Coca-Cola Company is no longer the higher calling that it once was. Many come to work for Coke for a while merely as a stepping-stone in a career. But much of the magic, and of the religion, remains, at least more than with most corporations. For this edition, I interviewed a former Coke marketer whose job was cut in one of the purges of the early twenty-first century. He remained somewhat bitter, but he obviously loved talking about Coca-Cola, and, when I commented on that, he paused for a moment, then said, "It's funny, but it sort of gets in your blood."

APPENDIX I: THE SACRED FORMULA

When I set out to write a comprehensive history of Coca-Cola, I had no idea I would stumble across the original formula, particularly not in the bowels of the Company itself. After all, this was the world's best-kept trade secret, one that the Company had already refused to reveal under two judges' orders. In 1977, the Company departed from India rather than hand the sacred formula to the insistent government. Yet one day during my research, an archivist brought out a file with individual yellowing, tattered papers that had been lovingly restored and laminated inside plastic. He explained that this constituted the remains of John Pemberton's formula book, donated to the Company in the 1940s.

I already knew the story behind this formula book. As a young man, John P. Turner had traveled from his hometown of Columbus, Georgia, to apprentice with John Pemberton in his final few years. After Pemberton's death, Turner took the formula book back to Columbus, where he served as a pharmacist for many years. In 1943, Turner's son showed the book to a member of the Coca-Cola board, opening it to a page containing *the* formula. The board member persuaded the Turner heir to let him have the book. "My God!" Harrison Jones, the board chairman, exclaimed when he saw the formula. "Where did you get that?" And that was the last anyone ever saw of it.

The file I received in the Coca-Cola archives stated that this was the "account and formula book belonging to Dr. J. S. Pemberton while a druggist in Columbus," but that is almost certainly incorrect, since one of the recipes for a celery cola includes Coca-Cola by name as an ingredient, undoubtedly placing it in 1888, since Pemberton was working on the celery drink at the time of his death. My heart raced as I carefully leafed through the preserved pages, but of course I assumed that the Company had hidden one crucial item deep in a vault somewhere. Consequently, I was astonished to find what appeared to be a Coca-Cola recipe, unlabeled except for an "X" at the top of the page:

Citrate Caffein Ext. Vanilla Flavoring	1	oz.
Ext. Vanilla	1	oz.
Flavoring	2 ½	oz.
F. E. Coco	4	oz.
Citric Acid	3	oz.
Lime Juice	1	Qt.
Sugar	30	lbs.
Water	2 ½	Gal.
Caramel sufficient		

Mix Caffeine Acid and Lime Juice in 1 Qt Boiling water add vanilla and flavoring when cool.

Flavoring	
Oil Orange	80
Oil Lemon	120
Oil Nutmeg	40
Oil Cinnamon	40
Oil Coriander	20
Oil Neroli	40
Alcohol	1 Qt.
let stand 24 hours.	

The "flavoring" section is obviously the "7X" portion of the formula, though there are only six ingredients (unless you count the alcohol, which serves as a mixer and does not go into the final product in any meaningful quantity). Perhaps he later added the vanilla to the flavoring section as the seventh component. "F. E. Coco" means fluid extract of coca, but kola nuts are not mentioned, only "Citrate Caffein." Pemberton almost certainly received his caffeine from Merck in Darmstadt, Germany, because he praised that firm as producing a superior form of the stimulant from kola nuts.

I photocopied the document, but I simply couldn't believe that anyone in the Company would hand over the original formula to me. Surely, it must only be a forerunner of the real thing. Then I received an unexpected confirmation that I had stumbled onto something far more valuable than I knew. While interviewing Mladin Zarubica, the technical observer who made "white Coke" for Russian General Zhukov, I mentioned that I had a formula. "Oh, really?" he said. "So do I. The Company gave me one when I had to take the color out for Zhukov. Want to see it?" I did indeed. When the photocopy of his January 4, 1947, correspondence arrived, it contained *exactly the same formula* that I had found in the archives—same amounts, same format, even the same misspelling of "F. E. Coco." The only difference was that Zarubica's formula was incomplete, leaving off the final two ingredients in 7X (coriander and neroli). It appeared that Company officials hadn't wanted to release the complete formula and had taken the precaution of altering it in this fashion.

I was astounded. Not only had I come into possession of Pemberton's original formula, right in the Company archives, but also it had ostensibly survived unchanged for at least sixty years after the inventor wrote it out on that acidified paper. This was truly a mystery, however. It contradicted Howard Candler's assertion that his father, Asa, had substantially altered the way Coca-Cola was made. And why didn't the Zarubica formula mention *decocainized* coca leaf, or the fact that the Company no longer used citric acid, but phosphoric? Or that the amount of caffeine had been reduced? And that wasn't the only formula change. Old Asa supposedly fiddled around with 7X as well. Through the years, the amount and type of sweetener have also varied.

It appears that even when the original ingredients and proportions are revealed, the mystique around the formula continues. My final conclusion: the Company did not, in fact, give Mladin Zarubica the *current* working formula for Coca-Cola in

1947—not even a partial version of it. Instead, Zarubica received a truncated version of the *original* formula, enough for his chemist to figure out how to turn brown Coke to white. The mystery of why the Company handed the formula to me in its own archives remains. I can only assume that there had been another clearly labeled Coca-Cola recipe in the Turner book, which had been hidden away, but no one had examined the rest of the formula closely, and the "X" variety had slipped through.

*   *   *

Beginning with Asa Candler, no one at the Company referred to the ingredients by name. Instead, sugar was Merchandise #1; caramel, Merchandise #2; caffeine, Merchandise #3; phosphoric acid, Merchandise #4; coca leaf and kola nut extract, Merchandise #5; 7X flavoring mixture, Merchandise #7; vanilla, Merchandise #8. This nomenclature stuck, although since the Candler era, numbers 6 and 9—perhaps lime juice and glycerin—fell by the wayside, probably subsumed into 7X or some other ingredient.

I cover the effects of the coca leaf and kola nut at length in the body of this book, but the herbal lore surrounding the other ingredients is fascinating, if inconclusive, given the minuscule amounts of each ingredient and the questionable veracity of ancient sources. Cassia, for instance, has been used as a cure for arthritis, cancer, chills, diabetes, dizziness, goiter, headache, and stomachache. Nutmeg fought infection during the Black Death of the fourteenth century, has served as a psychotropic and narcotic, and is prescribed in India for dysentery, flatulence, malaria, leprosy, rheumatism, sciatica, and stomachache. Vanilla is variously an aphrodisiac, a stimulant, or an antispasmodic; cures hysteria; inhibits cavities; and reduces flatulence. And so it goes for the other ingredients.

Since astonishing amounts of money have flowed from the secret formula, it didn't surprise me when no one at the Company wanted to talk about the drink's ingredients. Finally, I was allowed to interview Harry Waldrop, a "senior psychometrician" (no kidding, that was his title) who once had served as one of the elite corps of taste-testers who sample batches of Coca-Cola Classic.

The panel members know 7X by smell as much as by taste, and they can discern the minute differences that aging causes. Just as some wine tasters can roll a 1945 Mouton-Rothschild around their palates and differentiate it from a 1946, Waldrop could spot a two-month-old batch of Coke syrup. "We all know the taste and aroma of the right stuff," Waldrop said, "but it's hard to put it into words. It's when it's off that we attempt a description." The panel members might break up into small groups, for instance, to discuss a slight bitter note they don't like. Although all of the ingredients were carefully measured and tested by gas chromatography and other scientific gauges, Waldrop didn't think a computer could replace human beings. "An electronic nose couldn't pick up the subtleties, the hedonics," he assured me.

Although scientists can probably detect the different ingredients in Coca-Cola, even estimating the approximate amounts, they cannot, according to Company officials, duplicate the precise mixture. Incredible as it may seem, only two people active with the Company supposedly know how to mix 7X. That would necessitate their flying frequently to several concentrate factories around the world, which supply the building blocks for the world's Coke. No one, of course, would talk about such logistics.

*   *   *

After I published this "X" formula in previous editions of this book, I got a call in 2005 from Laura Robinson Vanwagner, whose great-grandfather, Frank Robinson, was the "unsung hero" who had named Coca-Cola, written out the famous Spencerian script, and brewed and advertised the drink. To my amazement, Laura handed me a color photocopy from her great-grandfather's formula book, written neatly on narrow yellow paper with red lines. There were recipes for French Wine Coca, Gingerine, Indian Queen Hair Dye, and Coca-Cola.

I knew about these recipes. Laura's older brother Frank Robinson II had played cat and mouse with me back in 1991 when I was conducting research for the first edition, giving me glimpses of the recipes but never letting me have them. Then, when Frank was getting divorced in 1996, his wife sued him for the formula, which made splashy headlines in the *Wall Street Journal* and elsewhere. Frank held on to the papers and gave them to his sister when he was dying of prostate cancer five years later. She had given them to The Coca-Cola Company archives, she said, but she decided I should have color photocopies as well. Here is the Robinson Coca-Cola formula, also reproduced as a facsimile here, along with its predecessor, French Wine Coca.

CC FOR 36 GALS .
> 216 # [pounds] Sugar
> 18 gals water
> 29 oz lime juice
> 29 " citric acid
> 18 " caffein
> 29 " flavoring
> 3 quts [quarts] coloring
> 15 " f. e. [fluid extract] coca

COCA-COLA FLAVOR
> 1 ½ Qut [quart] alcohol
> 12 oz f. e. [fluid extract] nutmegs
> 19 " ext vanilla
> 13 d [illegible—"drops?"] oil lemon
> 10 d oil cinnamon
> 12 d " nutmeg
> 15 d " coriander
> 12 d " neroli

This early Coca-Cola formula from Frank Robinson is confusing. Why does it include nutmeg twice, as a fluid extract and an essential oil? Like the "X" version, it

French Wine Cola   Coca-Cola

These are facsimiles of Frank Robinson's formulae for making French Wine Coca and Coca-Cola, which Robinson's great-granddaughter gave to Mark Pendergrast, as described in the text. (*Courtesy Laura Robinson Vanwagner*)

includes vanilla, lime juice, coca leaf extract, caffeine, sugar, caramel coloring, and essential oils of lemon, cinnamon, coriander, and neroli, but it leaves out oil of orange.

*   *   *

To confuse matters even more, *This American Life*, a popular public radio program, featured yet another early Coca-Cola formula on a show aired on February 11, 2011. Ira Glass, the host, interviewed me for the show, asking me to comment on a formula he had found published in a 1979 column by Charles Salter in the *Atlanta Journal-Constitution*. In the old leather-bound recipe book of druggist R. R. Evans, a contemporary and friend of John Pemberton's, Salter had found a formula for "Coco Cola Improved":

F E Coca 3 drams USP
Cit acid: 3 oz
Cit Caff: 1 oz
Sugar: 30# [pounds]
Aqua: 2.5 Gals
Lime juice: 2 Pints
Vanilla: 1 oz

FLAVOR 2 OZ TO 5 GALS SYRUP
Alcohol: 8 oz
Oil Orange: 20 drops
" Lemon: 30 drops
" Nutmeg: 10 drops
" Coriander: 5 drops
" Neroli: 10 drops
" Cinnamon: 10 drops
Use 1 ½ oz Caramel or more to color

On the show, I told Ira Glass that the Salter formula was quite similar to the "X" version I had found in the Coke archives and that I thought it was probably a version of the original formula. Glass had his formula made (presumably without the cocaine) but pronounced it "really mediciny . . . like orange-flavored baby aspirin," not that close to the Coca-Cola he knew. On the theory that modern flavors were purer and stronger, the men at Sovereign Flavors cut the flavoring by a quarter and produced something much closer to Coca-Cola. This seemed like fudging. Yet even Coke archivist Phil Mooney admitted that the Salter version might be a "precursor" of the original formula. I subsequently discovered that the Sovereign Flavors folks had used *drams* instead of *drops* of the essential oils, which accounts for the overly strong result.

Even though I had published the "X" formula in 1993 in the first edition of this book, and the Salter formula had been in print since 1979, the radio show created a sensation, going viral internationally. The response was so overwhelming that it crashed the powerful website of *This American Life* for several days, and I was subsequently interviewed by the *New York Times* and international media.

Perhaps the impact of the radio show reminded Coke executives of the powerful pull the Coke secret formula exerted. A few months later, just before Christmas 2011, the Company moved the formula from the SunTrust Bank to a vault inside a new exhibit at the World of Coca-Cola Museum in Atlanta, where I took a tour a few days later. It's a brilliant marketing ploy. You are led into a dark round room where esoteric mathematical formulae swirl on the floor while eerie music tinkles. It's a kind of Coke Holy of Holies room. "At the heart of Coca-Cola there is a secret, protected for well over a century, known only to a few," a dramatic disembodied male voice says. "Now, you are here. The secret is near. Go ahead, drink it in." On the surrounding walls, you see Coca-Cola being poured over ice so that you feel you're inside a giant glass. This gives way to a kaleidoscopic swirl of old Coke ads. Finally, a wall panel rolls open to reveal a dimly lit vault, with mysterious smoke swirling. "The secret formula for Coca-Cola is here," the voice says. "So share a Coke. Be part of the magic. We'll keep the secret. Because keeping the secret ensures that the magic lives on." If you can't make it to Atlanta, you can view a digital video I took on YouTube—just search "Coca-Cola vault Mark Pendergrast."

*   *   *

Despite all the mystique and paranoia built around the famous formula, one day a Company spokesman let down his guard when I asked what would happen if I published the bona fide formula with explicit directions in this book. He grinned. "Mark," he said, "let's say this is your lucky day. I happen to have a copy of that formula right here in my desk." He opened his drawer and handed me a phantom document. "There you go. Now what are you going to do with it?"

"Well, I'd put it in my book."

"And?"

"Somebody might decide to go into business in competition with The Coca-Cola Company."

"And what are they going to call their product?"

"Well, they couldn't call it Coca-Cola, because you'd sue them. Let's say they call it Yum-Yum, and they strongly imply, without being liable for a lawsuit, that Yum-Yum is actually the original Coca-Cola formula."

"Fine. Now what? What are they going to charge for it? How are they going to distribute it? How are they going to advertise it? See what I'm driving at? We've spent over a hundred years and untold amounts of money building the equity of that brand name. Without our economies of scale and our incredible marketing system, whoever tried to duplicate our product would get nowhere, and they'd have to charge too much. Why would anyone go out of their way to buy Yum-Yum, which is really just like Coca-Cola but costs more, when they can buy the Real Thing anywhere in the world?"

I couldn't think of a thing to say.

APPENDIX 2: COCA-COLA MAGIC: THIRTY-FIVE BUSINESS LESSONS

As I researched The Coca-Cola Company's long history, I was struck by the remarkably consistent vision that has permeated it since Coca-Cola was first invented by that gentle morphine-addicted genius, John Pemberton. He considered his drink an elixir of life, a nerve tonic to cure the ills of man. After Pemberton's death in 1888, Asa Candler carried on that tradition of fanatical belief in the product, as did Robert W. Woodruff, the Boss, and aristocratic Roberto Goizueta. Current CEO Muhtar Kent has shown himself to be of the same missionary stripe.

What, then, can readers glean from my lengthy romp through Coke history, aside from the original formula in the previous appendix? Are there messages for the modern entrepreneur? I have distilled the convoluted history's essential parables into thirty-five commandments. Most are simple and seemingly obvious dicta, such as those dispensed by the Boss, but Coke illustrates them dramatically. They are, unfortunately, not quite so simple to put into practice. Other points were learned less willingly in agonized accidents such as the New Coke debacle. Here, then, are time-tested management lessons from the image masters at Coke:

1. **Sell a good product.** And if it contains a small dose of an addictive drug or two, all the better. The product doesn't have to talk or fly, but it does have to perform some useful, universally appreciated function. Coca-Cola tastes pretty good once you get used to it; it tickles the nostrils, quenches thirst, produces a little caffeine lift. Some people think (following inventor John Pemberton) that it cures headaches, hangovers, and stomachaches. Alas, it no longer contains a smidgeon of cocaine, but it's still a good product. In its early days, Coca-Cola was bottled under less-than-ideal conditions, resulting in a variable product spiced upon occasion with blowflies, worms, or shards of glass. Now, however, it is standardized and sanitary, providing a safe drink in parts of the world where sampling the water can be fatal.

2. **Believe in your product.** And I don't just mean an intellectual exercise here. Make your product an icon and your job a religious vocation. Instill in employees the notion that this is the finest product on earth and that they are working for the best company around. Your salespeople should be missionaries, not mere paid hacks. In the golden years of the Company, new employees reputedly received a transfusion of Coca-Cola syrup rather than blood.

3. **Develop a mystique.** An air of mystery, with a touch of sin, sells. As a company official admitted to me, the secret formula really doesn't make much difference. The real formula for success is in the product's "brand equity," developed over

494

the last century and a quarter. So what if somebody took the formula from this book and made a fake Coke? The formula's mystique has always been an important part of its appeal. Who knows what's *really* in that dark, fizzy potion?

4. **Sell a cheaply produced item.** Coca-Cola has always cost only a fraction of a cent per drink to produce, the sweetener (cane sugar in most places outside the United States, high-fructose corn syrup domestically) constituting most of the expense. Like most patent medicines of its time (1886), Coca-Cola wasn't a capital-intensive product; its manufacture, while highly secretive, was neither difficult nor laborious.

5. **Ensure that everyone who touches your product before it reaches the consumer makes substantial amounts of money.** This rule follows naturally. If your product is cheaply produced, it allows for a substantial mark-up at the retail end. Coca-Cola achieved a kind of Midas quality. For many years, everyone who touched it became wealthy, including bottlers, stockholders, wholesaling jobbers, and those who provided the trucks, bottles, pallets, dispensers, and so on. Of course, such success fostered gratitude and devotion.

6. **Make your product affordable to everyone.** For an unprecedented time, from 1886 until the 1950s, Coca-Cola sold for a nickel a drink, and it remains relatively inexpensive around the world so that a citizen in a developing country can purchase the beverage without going broke. Consequently, as an "affordable luxury," Coke has usually survived and even thrived during hard economic times.

7. **Make your product widely available.** Robert Woodruff always strove to place his drink "within arm's reach of desire," a lovely phrase that translated into an obsession to provide outlets virtually everywhere. As old-time Coke evangelist Harrison Jones put it in 1923, "Let's make it impossible ever to escape Coca-Cola."

8. **Market your product wisely.** That sounds simple, but how, when, and where you market and advertise your product will ultimately determine its success. By 1911, Asa Candler was spending over $1 million a year in creating public demand for his drink, making Coca-Cola the best-advertised single product in the world. Two years later, the Company issued over one hundred million novelty items with the logo prominently displayed, all on items that required repeated visual use—thermometers, calendars, matchbooks, blotters, baseball cards, Japanese fans, and signs. It is no surprise that a Coke salesman of that early period reported that one new consumer, "hounded almost to a state of imbecility with Coca-Cola signs," suffered recurring nightmares in which big white devils with red mantels chased him, screeching "Coca-Cola! Coca-Cola!" It would be even less of a surprise today.

9. **Advertise an image, not a product.** As one Coke advertiser liked to remind his creative staff, "We're selling smoke. They're drinking the image, not the product." It was Archie Lee who established a golden age of Coke advertising in the 1920s and 1930s after watching his four-year-old daughter and her friends fighting over her old stuffed Pooh bear. "It isn't what a product is," Lee concluded, "but what it does." Lee positioned Coca-Cola as a gracious product, "the pause that refreshes," providing a social binder. People who drank Coke

were always happy, energetic, wholesome, and friendly. With variations, other advertising greats later embellished that message.

10. **Welcome an arch-rival.** Although some Coke employees might not like to admit it, Pepsi has been good for Coca-Cola. "If Pepsi-Cola didn't exist, I would try to invent it," Roberto Goizueta once said. "It keeps us, and them, on our toes and keeps us lean. We're magnificent competitors." People love stories from the "cola wars," and wise marketers from both companies recognize that the publicity fostered by fierce competition is good for sales, regardless of which company appears to be winning an individual battle.

11. **Use celebrity endorsements wisely—but sparingly.** From its earliest years, Coca-Cola hired celebrity sponsors, hoping that consumers would identify with baseball great Ty Cobb or actress Hilda Clark. By the 1930s, movie stars from Clark Gable and Cary Grant to Jean Harlow and Joan Crawford were pushing Coke, and in the late 1960s singers ranging from Neil Diamond and Leslie Gore to Ray Charles and Aretha Franklin crooned that things went better with the soft drink. There are dangers, however, in relying too heavily on celebrity endorsements. For one thing, viewers may remember more about the star than the product. Coca-Cola has always remained the *real* star of its commercials.

12. **When you do use celebrities, use some local celebs.** While you make a universal appeal, use selected local musicians and actors to promote your product. During the 2010 World Cup, Coke adapted the "Wavin' Flag" song with K'naan in seventeen different local languages, using appropriate national rock stars and sexy dancers, though they all began with a Coke-emblazoned soccer ball and K'naan singing.

13. **Appeal to universal human desires.** Ever since the 1950s, Coke has created "pattern advertising" that, with little or no modification, can appeal to any culture in the world. Nowadays Coke marketers call the approach being "liquid and linked." The Coke message has universal appeal—by drinking this product, you will be self-assured, happy, popular, sexy, youthful, and well coordinated. To reinforce the message, Coke sponsors every sporting event imaginable, from sumo to soccer, as well as musical extravaganzas around the globe.

14. **Get 'em young.** Of course, the sports and music promotions are meant to engage teenagers, among others. Obviously, if you can achieve loyalty among youthful consumers, you've possibly fostered lifelong consumption. In 1894, Coca-Cola postcards depicted three sailor-suited five-year-old boys proclaiming, "We drink Coca-Cola." After the U.S. government sued the Company in 1911—partly because it provided caffeine, an addictive drug, to children—the Company halted all overt advertising to anyone under twelve. This did not stop bottlers from giving away free tablets and rulers with an engraved logo, nor did it prevent Coca-Cola from co-opting the image of Santa Claus in the 1930s, firmly establishing him as a fat, jolly gentleman clad in Coca-Cola red, with a decided preference for the proper soft drink.

15. **Develop cultural sensitivity.** If you intend to sell your product around the world, do not trap yourself in an "Ugly American" image. In the 1920s when Robert Woodruff authorized the drink's global spread, he attempted to make the drink a German drink in Germany, a French drink in France. The

company signed bottling contracts with prominent natives and encouraged the development of a soft drink infrastructure so that the trucks, bottles, pallets, and signs were all produced by local firms. The only thing the company typically sold, and the only thing that had to be imported, was the Coca-Cola concentrate. Thus, the company could proudly and accurately point out how much it contributed to local economies. Through the years, Coca-Cola has developed a group of savvy, culturally sensitive managers from all parts of the world, transferring them frequently in an attempt to transfuse universal Coke values while at the same time providing a broader background for the managers.

16. **Hire aggressive lawyers.** If you succeed, you will undoubtedly need lawyers to protect your trademark, defend your good name, and scare off potential competitors. Coca-Cola lawyer Harold Hirsch practically invented modern trademark-patent law. Before and after World War II, Coca-Cola hired local attorneys throughout the world in an attempt to stifle imitators and competitors and to defend the company against widespread rumors about its ill effects on health. Coke remains one of the more litigious companies.

17. **Don't break the law.** Although Coca-Cola officials or bottlers have indeed resorted to bribery and kickbacks in the past—and, according to some allegations, bottlers have hired paramilitaries in Latin America to eliminate unionized employees—the company does, by and large, live up to its squeaky-clean image. There is no percentage in illegal activities that could besmirch the company's good name. It simply isn't worth it to risk the reputation of a huge multinational concern.

18. **Become masters of influence.** Just because you don't break the law doesn't mean you must sit back and act like an angel. Robert Woodruff was a master of backroom influence. He practically owned Georgia Senator Walter George and Atlanta Mayor William B. Hartsfield. Woodruff befriended presidents. In fact, he and his cronies arguably *created* President Dwight D. Eisenhower, even helping him decide whether to run as a Republican or a Democrat. Similarly, Coke CEO Paul Austin gave Jimmy Carter a crucial boost into the White House. Do not, however, abuse your influence by asking too much of politicians. Just clarify that your product's spread serves the national interest. You don't even need to ask for specific help. The mere *impression* that Coca-Cola chummed with Carter was, for instance, enough to open doors.

19. **Be patient but implacable.** Plan for the long haul. Coca-Cola managers know that they will ultimately sell their fizzy product in every country in the world. It is only a matter of time. There will be temporary setbacks due to war, famine, or politics, but they will always maintain contacts, always remain civil, always be prepared to take advantage of any situation. Thus, when the Arabs boycotted the company in the 1960s because Coke allowed an Israeli franchise, Coca-Cola immediately began a campaign of re-entry that paid off in Egypt during the Carter administration. Similarly, Coca-Cola is back in India following the 1977 expulsion. Ditto China, the former USSR, Nicaragua, Vietnam, and Myanmar. Some day, Cuba and North Korea. Do not be seduced into pursuing short-term gains at the expense of long-term vision. There will be bumps along the road, but set your goals on the horizon.

20. **Adhere to simple commandments.** None of Robert Woodruff's guiding principles—many enumerated here—were terribly complicated. Woodruff himself was practically illiterate; according to associates, he never finished a book in his life. His genius lay in looking at the big picture and in concentrating on a few elemental truths.

21. **Be flexible enough to change.** You must strike a balance between tradition and change. If Coca-Cola has ever displayed an Achilles' heel, its reluctance to adjust to current conditions is it. Asa Candler almost delayed too long before removing the last trace of cocaine from the drink. Woodruff fought hard against producing the King Size Coke of the 1950s, against bringing out other flavors, against using rock music in ads, against lifting the nickel price barrier—all necessary changes. Roberto Goizueta, determined to shake up the staid company in the 1980s, believed in the necessity of change, and was proved correct when he authorized the introduction of Diet Coke, a heretical product because it assumed the sacred Coke name. When he tampered with the original formula in the 1985 New Coke debacle, however, Goizueta was flexible enough to change back in time to avert disaster. To maintain this valuable flexibility, a certain amount of neurosis helps. "The world belongs to the discontented," Woodruff liked to say.

22. **Don't use defensive, negative advertising.** Maybe for an Avis or a Pepsi, comparative ads make sense. Maybe. You're still giving your opponent free publicity, however. Every time Coke has stooped to such tactics, it has looked silly, including Asa Candler's attempts to justify caffeine's presence in the drink. When Coke mocked the Pepsi Challenge taste tests by showing chimpanzees trying to decide which tennis balls were fuzzier, the Atlanta firm looked like the choice chump, not the chimps.

23. **Diversify only when necessary.** When Roberto Goizueta took over as CEO in 1981, he diversified by purchasing Columbia Pictures, a move that made sense at the time. Before the decade was out, however, he unloaded it on Sony for a healthy profit and refocused solely on beverages. Coca-Cola, whose stock performance has been historically extraordinary, is one of the *least* diversified companies in the world. "There's a perception in this country that you're better off if you're in two lousy businesses than if you're in one good one, that you're spreading your risk," Goizueta used to say. But that's silly when soft drinks offer a better profit margin than any alternatives.

24. **Pay attention to the bottom line.** This seems such an obvious point, yet until Goizueta arrived it wasn't something anybody at Coke thought much about. In the paranoid anti-Pepsi culture, Coke men were more concerned with share-of-market figures than with profits. Goizueta discovered, among other things, that the highly regarded soda fountain sector was actually losing money because of costly capital expenditures on metal five-gallon drums.

25. **Terrify your employees.** Perhaps that's putting it a bit strong, but traditional Coca-Cola CEOs from Asa Candler to the present have encouraged a climate of respect and awe. Austere Paul Austin put it well: "A certain degree of anxiety and tension has to exist for people to function at the highest level of their potential." Certainly, Woodruff the Boss inspired terror and adoration. Neville Isdell and

Muhtar Kent were warmer individuals, and Don Keough was a backslapper, but it was not wise to cross any of them.

26. **Promote from within.** The best Coca-Cola managers, almost without exception, have come up through the ranks, inculcated with the Company mission. They have received the transfusion of Coke syrup. Grooming for management traditionally included a form of Coca-Cola boot camp, inductees emerging from a day on the bottling line with bloody knuckles and aching backs. Don Keough arrived at Coke in the 1960s along with Duncan Foods, but it was twenty years before he achieved high status at the company, by which time he sounded more like a traditional soft drink man than anyone. It was Neville Isdell, a Coke veteran, who came out of retirement in 2004 to turn the company around.

27. **Recognize that all publicity is good publicity**—at least when there is enough residual goodwill. Because Coca-Cola already meant so much to so many, the 1985 flavor change actually helped the Company, even though it blew $4 million in the process. When management bowed to public pressure and brought back Coca-Cola Classic, the encore beverage scored heavily against Pepsi. This was the same drink that had been steadily losing market share for twenty years prior to New Coke. The experience of nearly losing their old friend caused many consumers to renew their loyalty to Coke—so that many observers thought that Goizueta and the Company had stage-managed the whole affair. As Don Keough admitted, they weren't that smart, but they did learn that even negative publicity can ultimately help a well-entrenched product.

28. **Use cash wisely.** Robert Woodruff, scared by the debt he inherited in 1923 when he took over the company, took great pride in accumulating a cash hoard. Consequently, the conservatively run company was never in danger of being over-leveraged. Under Goizueta, however, the company finally took on a reasonable debt load. With bottom-line logic, Goizueta and financial wizard Doug Ivester realized that it made sense to borrow money if it could then be re-invested at a substantially higher rate of return. One simple method: repurchase your own stock, thereby driving the price further up. Under Neville Isdell and Muhtar Kent, Coke used its cash to buy into other thriving beverages.

29. **Form joint ventures.** Another wise use of cash involved breaking a long-standing Company commandment: thou shalt not own bottling plants. Ever since Asa Candler gave away the bottling rights in 1899, the Company had viewed itself primarily as a syrup spigot. The bottlers, whose profit margin was narrower than the Company's, prospered on their own. The Company owned selected plants, but only to serve as training grounds for rotating managers, and these plants never did very well. The conventional wisdom held that bottlers performed better as independent entrepreneurs. In 1981, Goizueta was forced to break this taboo in the Philippines, where Pepsi had chewed off 70 percent of the cola market. By purchasing 30 percent of the franchise, the Company negotiated the right to manage the bottling. Within a few years, Neville Isdell, using traditional, aggressive motivation and marketing tactics, turned the market share numbers on their head. Taking the Philippines as a precedent, Goizueta and Ivester pursued successful joint ventures around the world. In

2010, Muhtar Kent negotiated the Coke purchase of anchor bottler Coca-Cola Enterprises in North America.

30. **Think globally, but act locally.** This catchphrase originated with Goizueta, though other CEOs snapped it up in the trendy 1980s and used it as their own. Regardless of the phrase's provenance, Coca-Cola demonstrated its wisdom, dipping into the Company's own history for guidance. In China and Indonesia, for instance, the first task involved building a strong infrastructure—concentrate factories, glass manufacturers, bottling plants, trucks, point-of-purchase signage—in American terms, time-warping back to 1905. In the former West Germany and Japan, on the other hand, the Company already had a well-established business, but, as in the United States of the 1970s, too many bottlers were vying in small territories. The task there was to consolidate.

31. **Pursue the halo effect.** In the troubled early 1970s, Coke CEO Paul Austin tried to create what he termed "the halo effect" for Coca-Cola. By that, he meant that the firm should appear to be in the vanguard of the environmental movement and progressive in race relations, setting up model programs for its Minute Maid migrant workers and creating nutritional soft drinks. None of Austin's ancillary do-good businesses ever amounted to much, but the Company has continued to promote the halo effect, which makes sense. It also really *does* promote good causes, through philanthropy, educational support, public health efforts such as safe-water programs, recycling and other green environmental programs, and relief aid after natural disasters.

32. **Put the enemy on your team.** A good way to co-opt enemies is to recruit them. Neville Isdell invited former European Union anti-trust official Mario Monti to join Coke's international advisory board and grabbed Alexis Herman, the chair of the task force to monitor the Company's racial diversity, for the Coca-Cola board of directors.

33. **React quickly to crises.** When the media or Internet gossip pick up a negative story about your company, rumors and innuendo can spread like wildfire. When in 1999 schoolchildren in Belgium believed that Coca-Cola made them sick, CEO Doug Ivester thought the problem would blow over and was slow to react. Even though the Coke products probably did not make anyone sick, his apologies were tardy. Roberto Goizueta was almost too late in bringing back Coke Classic after the New Coke disaster.

34. **Understand that there is no saturation point.** This is especially true for a product people imbibe. It is remarkable that Big Coke and its bottlers have managed to continue to increase sales even in the United States, through innovative marketing and product placement and choice. The Company specializes in beverages, but now offers some 500 brands and 3,500 drinks worldwide. The moral? Don't rest on your laurels; set ambitious but attainable goals.

35. **Involve your customers.** Coke marketers now talk about their "liquid and linked" approach, meaning that their message is linked by a common theme and can flow in many directions. The stress is on interactivity, with consumers actually participating. When Coke sent three young "Happiness Ambassadors"

around the world in 2010, for instance, fans could follow them on Facebook and suggest places for them to go. The following year, a global Coca-Cola Music teen campaign launched with "24hr Session," in which American pop band Maroon 5 holed up in a London studio and, with input from fans around the world, wrote a song downloadable for free from the Coke website.

NOTE ON SOURCES

To save space in this third edition, which has already reached biblical proportions, I include this bibliographic essay in lieu of specific citations and a full bibliography. Consult the second edition (2000) for citations and sources up to that time. They are also available at www.markpendergrast.com on the Coca-Cola subpage.

Books Directly Related to Coca-Cola: Frederick Allen, *Secret Formula* (1994), a well-documented history of Coca-Cola. Bill Backer, *The Care and Feeding of Ideas* (1993), by the brilliant ad man who created the Real Thing. Michael Blanding, *The Coke Machine: The Dirty Truth Behind the World's Favorite Soft Drink* (2010), a critical look at the Company. Charles Howard Candler, *Asa Griggs Candler* (1950), a biography by Asa's son. William T. Campbell, *Big Beverage* (1952), a novel by a Coke bottler. Mike Cheatham, *"Your Friendly Neighbor": The Story of Georgia's Coca-Cola Bottling Families* (1999). Ricardo Cortés, *A Secret History of Coffee, Coca & Cola* (2012), a well-researched, short illustrated book. Lawrence Dietz, *Soda Pop* (1973). Charles Elliott, *Mr. Anonymous: Robert W. Woodruff of Coca-Cola* (1982), by a close friend and hunting buddy. *Exclusive Territorial Allocation Legislation*, Hearings Before the Subcommittee on Antitrust and Monopoly (1973). John Paul Freeman, "The Real Thing" (1986), a dissertation about Coke advertising from 1969 to 1976. Henry J. Frundt, *Refreshing Pauses: Coca-Cola and Human Rights in Guatemala* (1987), about death squads and unions. Elizabeth Candler Graham, *The Real Ones* (1992), by a great-great-grandchild of Asa Candler. David Greising, *I'd Like the World to Buy a Coke: The Life and Leadership of Roberto Goizueta* (1998). Constance Hays, *The Real Thing: Truth and Power at Coca-Cola* (2005), by a *New York Times* reporter, focusing on Ivester and Daft. Anne Hoy, *Coca-Cola: The First Hundred Years* (1986), an authorized, richly illustrated coffee table book. James L. Hunt, *Relationship Banker* (2009), about Eugene Stetson, covers 1919 sale of Company; Neville Isdell with David Beasley, *Inside Coca-Cola* (2011), by former Coke CEO. E. J. Kahn Jr., *The Big Drink* (1960), a delightful compilation of the *New Yorker* writer's articles on Coca-Cola, and *Robert Winship Woodruff* (1969), Kahn's revealing book on Woodruff. J. C. Louis and Harvey Yazijian, *The Cola Wars* (1980), well researched and critical. *Migrant and Seasonal Farmworker Powerlessness*, Hearings Before the Subcommittee on Migratory Labor (1971). Thomas Oliver, *The Real Coke, the Real Story* (1986), by an Atlanta newspaper reporter about New Coke. Allan Petretti, *Petretti's Coca-Cola Collectibles Price Guide* (2008), the classic guide. John A. Riley, *A History of the American Soft Drink Industry* (1958). Pat Roddy Jr., *75 Years of Refreshment* (1983), a history of a Tennessee Coke bottler. Rowland Sanders, *Papa Coke: Sixty-Five Years Selling Coca-Cola* (1986), by a Coke veteran. Randy Schaeffer and Bill Bateman, *Coca-Cola: The Collector's Guide* (1995), by two knowledgeable Pennsylvania collectors. Bill and Jan Schmidt, *The Schmidt Museum Collection* *of Coca-Cola Memorabilia* (1983); though the museum no longer exists, the book is a good resource. Transport and General Workers Union, Latin American Bureau, *Soft Drink, Hard Labor: Guatemalan Workers Take on Coca-Cola* (1987), about death squads and unions. Mark Thomas, *Belching Out the Devil: Global Adventures with Coca-Cola* (2008), a critical book by a British comedian-activist. Ross Treseder, *As I Remember* (1973), a Coke veteran's memoirs. Pat Watters, *Coca-Cola: An Illustrated History* (1978), by an Atlanta writer. Della Wager Wells, *George Waldo Woodruff* (1987). Sergio Zyman, *The End of Marketing As We Know It*, by a former Coke marketing man.

Books About Pepsi: Stephanie Capparell, *The Real Pepsi Challenge* (2008). Roger Enrico, *The Other Guy Blinked* (1986). Walter Mack, *No Time Lost* (1982). Milward W. Martin, *Twelve Full Ounces* (1962). John Sculley, *Odyssey: Pepsi to Apple* (1987). Bob Stoddard, *Pepsi-Cola: 100 Years* (1997).

Selected Books for Historical and Cultural Context: Samuel Hopkins Adams, *The Great American Fraud* (1907). Ivan Allen Jr., *Mayor: Notes on the Sixties* (1971). Benjamin Barber, *Jihad Vs. McWorld* (1996). George Beard, *American Nervousness* (1881). John Morton Blum, *V Was for Victory* (1976). Taylor Branch, *Parting the Waters* (1988). Fawn M. Brodie, *Richard Nixon* (1981). Gerald Carson, *One for a Man, Two for a Horse* (1961). William H. Chafe, *The Unfinished Journey* (1986). Frederick Clairmonte, *Merchants of Death* (1988). Eric Clark, *The Want Makers* (1988). Robert M. Crunden, *Ministers of Reform* (1982). N. F. Dixon, *Subliminal Perception* (1971). Eddie Fisher, *Eddie: My Life, My Loves* (1981). Stephen Fox, *The Mirror Makers* (1984). Franklin Garrett, *Atlanta and Environs* (1954). Jack Goodman, ed., *While You Were Gone: A Report on Wartime Life in the United States* (1946). Sally Forman Griffith, *Home Town News: William Allen White* (1989). Duff Hart-Davis, *Hitler's Games* (1986). Adelaide Hechtlinger, *The Great Patent Medicine Era* (1970). Seymour M. Hersh, *The Dark Side of Camelot* (1997). Charles Higham, *Trading with the Enemy* (1983). Floyd Hunter, *Community Power Structure* (1953, 1963). Kenneth T. Jackson, *The Ku Klux Klan in the City* (1967). Michael Jacobson, *Liquid Candy* (2005). Haynes Johnson, *Sleepwalking Through History* (1991). Sam Jones, *The Life and Sayings of Sam P. Jones* (1907). Franz M. Joseph, ed., *As Others See Us* (1959). Richard Kuisel, *Seducing the French* (1993). Tom Lutz, *American Nervousness* (1991). Victor Lasky, *Jimmy Carter* (1979). Angelo Mariani, *Coca and Its Therapeutic Applications* (1886). Alice G. Marquis, *Hopes and Ashes* (1986). J. B. Matthews and R. E. Shallcross, *Partners in Plunder* (1935). Mark Megalli, *Masks of Deception* (1991). Peter Meyer, *James Earl Carter* (1978). Mark Crispin Miller, *Seeing Through Movies* (1990). Sidney Mintz, *Sweetness and Power* (1985). H. Wayne Morgan, *Drugs in America* (1981). W. Golden Mortimer, *Peru: History of Coca* (1901). David Musto, *The American Disease* (1987). American Medical Association, *Nostrums and Quackery* (1911). J. Ronald Oakley, *God's Country: America in the Fifties* (1986). Ray Oldenburg, *The Great Good Place* (1989). Vance Packard, *The Hidden Persuaders* (1957). Richard Pells, *Not Like Us* (1997). Frank Presbrey, *The History and Development of Advertising* (1929). Douglas K. Ramsey, *The Corporate Warriors* (1987). Michael Schudson, *Advertising* (1984). Robert Sherrill, *Gothic Politics in the Deep South* (1968). William L. Shirer, *The Rise and Fall of the Third Reich* (1960). Milton Silverman, *Magic in a Bottle* (1941). Andrew F. Smith,

Drinking History: Fifteen Turning Points in the Making of American Beverages (2013). Antony C. Sutton, *Wall Street and the Rise of Hitler* (1976). Norman Taylor, *Plant Drugs That Changed the World* (1965). Richard S. Tedlow, *New and Improved: The Story of Mass Marketing in America* (1990). E. S. Turner, *The Shocking History of Advertising* (1952). Harvey W. Wiley, *Harvey W. Wiley: An Autobiography* (1930). C. Vann Woodward, *Tom Watson: Agrarian Rebel* (1963). James Harvey Young, *The Toadstool Millionaires* (1961) and *Pure Food* (1989).

Selected Videos: *The Cola Case* (2010), on the legal case about Colombian murders. *The Cola Conquest* (1998), a globe-girdling, prize-winning three-hour documentary about Coca-Cola inspired by this book. *FLOW* (2008), about world water issues.

Selected Websites: Eepybird.com, geysers with Mentos and Diet Coke. Facebook .com/cocacola, Coke Facebook page with millions of fans. KillerCoke.org, anti-Coca-Cola website. TheCoca-ColaCompany.com, the Company website. YouTube.com for Coca-Cola commercials, documentaries, and other goodies.

Manuscript Collections: The Atlanta Historical Society has the Joseph Jacobs Papers. The Baker Library, Harvard Business School, houses the R. G. Dun & Company Collection of credit reports for John Pemberton. The Benwood Foundation in Chattanooga has Benjamin Thomas correspondence. The Center for Jewish History, New York City, has Rabbi Tobias Geffen Papers. The Coca-Cola Company archives and legal library contain valuable resources open to selected scholars. The Eisenhower Library, Abilene, Kansas, has the Eisenhower Papers. Emory University's Manuscript, Archives, and Rare Books Library (MARBL) houses the papers of Asa Candler, Charles Howard Candler, Warren Candler, Coca-Cola Collection, William B. Hartsfield, Floyd Hunter, Mark Pendergrast's research papers for this book, John Sibley, and Robert Woodruff. The Library of Congress Manuscripts Division has the James Farley, Averill Harriman, William Allen White, and Harvey W. Wiley Papers. The National Archives, Washington, DC, has U.S. Army, Federal Bureau of Narcotics, and other collections. The National Museum of American History, Washington, DC, has the Pepsi-Cola Advertising History Collection. The Nebraska State Historical Society has the Harry Hollingsworth Collections. Pennsylvania State University owns Harry J. Anslinger papers. U.S. Food and Drug Administration files contain Harvey Wiley material. The Western Reserve Historical Society, Cleveland, Ohio, has Ralph Hayes and Walter C. White papers.

Selected Court Cases: *The Blood Balm Company v. Cooper, Georgia Supreme Court Records*, vol. 83, Oct. Term, 1889. *The Coca-Cola Co. v. John B. Daniel*, Fulton County Superior Court, Spring Term 1901, #8577. *Henry A. Rucker v. Coca-Cola Company*, U.S. Circuit Court of Appeals, Fifth Circuit, No. 1161, Original Record files May 12, 1902. *Hudgins v. Coca-Cola Bottling Co.*, Supreme Court of Georgia, May 10, 1905, *Southeastern Reporter*. *U.S. v. Forty Barrels and Twenty Kegs of Coca-Cola*, Supreme Court, Oct. Term 1915, No. 562. *The Coca-Cola Bottling Co. v. The Coca-Cola Co.*, District Court, Delaware, Nov. 8, 1920. *The Coca-Cola Company v. The Koke Company of America*, Supreme Court of the United States, Oct. Term, 1920. *My-Coca Co. v. Baltimore Process Co.*, in the Circuit Court of Baltimore, Sept. 2, 1924. *Pepsi-Cola Company v. Coca-Cola Company*, Supreme Court of the State of New York, County of Queens, 1938. *The Coca-Cola Company v. Nehi Corporation*,

Supreme Court of Delaware, No. 4, Sept. Session, 1942 Term. *Shreveport Coca-Cola Bottling Co., Inc. et al. v. The Coca-Cola Co.,* U. S. District Court, Delaware, 1991. *Coca-Cola Bottling Company of Elizabethtown, Inc. et al. v. The Coca-Cola Co.*, U.S. District Court, Delaware, 1991.

Selected Periodicals and Newspapers (some are quite old or hard to find): *Advertising Age, Adweek, American Druggist, American Food Journal, American Heritage, American Journal of Pharmacy, American Journal of Psychology, Americas, Amusement Business, Atlanta Civic, Atlanta Constitution, Atlanta Georgian, Atlanta History, Atlanta Journal, Atlanta Journal-Constitution, Atlanta Magazine, Baltimore Sun, Barron's, Beverage Digest, Beverage Industry, Beverage World, Boston Globe, Bottling Industry, Broadcasting, Business Week, Chain Drug Review, Chattanooga Times, Chicago Sun-Times, Chicago Tribune, Chief Executive, Coca-Cola Bottler, Coca-Cola Collectors News, Coca-Cola Nachrichten, Coca-Cola Overseas, Cola Call, Collier's Weekly, Columbus Enquirer, Consumer Reports, Corporate Money, Denver Rocky Mountain News, Detroit Therapeutic Gazette, Drug Topics, Druggists Circular and Chemical Gazette, Dun's Review, The Economist, Editor and Publisher, Emory University Quarterly, Emporia Gazette, Everybody's Magazine, Financial Times, Financial World, Food & Beverage Marketing, Food Business, Food Processing, Forbes, Fortune, Friendly Hand, Georgia State Bar Journal, Georgia Trend, The Guardian, Harper's Weekly, Indianapolis Star, Jet, Journal of American Folklore, Journal of Southern History, Journal of the American Medical Association, Journey* (Coca-Cola in-house magazine), *Ladies' Home Journal, LatinFinance, Life, Los Angeles Times, Magazine of Wall Street, Marketing and Media Decisions, Marketing News TM, Marketing Week, Mediaweek, Miami Herald, Milwaukee Journal Sentinel, Montreal Gazette, Multinational Monitor, The Nation, National Bottlers Gazette, Nation's Restaurant News, New Republic, New York Daily News, New York Daily Tribune, New York Herald Tribune, New York Times, New Yorker, Newsweek, Packaging Digest, People, Pharmacy in History, Philadelphia Inquirer, Printer's Ink, Red Barrel, The Refresher, Sales Management, San Francisco Chronicle, Saturday Evening Post, Science Digest, Scientific American, Sierra, Sloan Management Review, Southern Carbonator and Bottler, Southern Changes, Southern Exposure, Southpoint Magazine, Star Tribune, Sunday Telegraph, Supermarket News, T. O. Digest, Time, Trademark Reporter, U.S. News & World Report, USA Today, Vital Speeches, Wall Street Journal, Washington Post, Washington Times, Western Folklore.*

Interviews: Mark Pendergrast conducted more than 200 interviews for this book. For a list, see www.markpendergrast.com.

ACKNOWLEDGMENTS

Detailed thanks to everyone who contributed to this book would take up pages. See my website, www.markpendergrast.com, for the Acknowledgments for the first two editions. Suffice it to say here that I am deeply indebted to everyone at The Coca-Cola Company who helped me and whom I interviewed when I was researching the first edition, which was published in 1993, and all those who contributed to the subsequent editions, both on and off the record. Special thanks to John Risse for new insights into Ernest and Robert Woodruff and the 1919 sale of the Company; to Matt Considine for sharing his research on Rabbi Tobias Geffen; to Ricardo Cortés for sharing his research on Harry Anslinger and Coca-Cola's Hawaiian coca cultivation research; to Bob Perillo for documents and insights on USLEAP and José Palacios. And my thanks, too, to fellow writers whose work about Coca-Cola and its relations has inspired and informed me, to Coke collectors who shared insights, and to friends and colleagues who read drafts and suggested improvements. Librarians and archivists in Vermont, Georgia, Washington, DC, and elsewhere were essential to this under-taking. And I must single out Irene Angelico and Abbey Neidik of DLI Productions, whose documentary *The Cola Conquest* was inspired by my first edition and then helped to elucidate my subsequent efforts. Thanks to Hamilton Cain, who edited the first edition, and to Tim Bartlett at Basic Books for his editor's eye, support, and insights for this latest edition.

INDEX

Abbreviations: CC = Coca-Cola

Betty Molnar

Mark Pendergrast, a native of Atlanta, Georgia, grew up on West Paces Ferry Road, once known as "Coca-Cola Row." He developed a forbidden thirst for Coke when his health-conscious mother refused to allow it in the house. This book is his revenge. Pendergrast is also the author of *Uncommon Grounds*; *Inside the Outbreaks*; *Mirror, Mirror*; *Victims of Memory*; *Jack and the Bean Soup*; and *Japan's Tipping Point*. He lives in Colchester, Vermont. To find information on his books or to contact him, see www.markpendergrast.com.